76

CONTENTS

SOUTH AFRICA | CONTENTS

KEY TO SYMBOLS

- ✚ Map reference
- ✉ Address
- ☎ Telephone number
- ◷ Opening times
- ✋ Admission prices
- Ⓜ Underground station
- 🚌 Bus number
- 🚆 Train station
- ⛴ Ferry/boat
- 🚗 Driving directions
- ℹ Tourist office
- Ⓣ Tours
- 📖 Guidebook
- 🍽 Restaurant
- ☕ Café
- 🍷 Bar
- 🏬 Shop
- ① Number of rooms
- ❄ Air conditioning
- ≋ Swimming pool
- 🏋 Gym
- ❓ Other useful information
- ▷ Cross reference
- ★ Walk/drive start point

228

105

252

196

UNDERSTANDING SOUTH AFRICA

Understanding South Africa is an introduction to the country, its geography, economy, history and its people, giving a real insight into the nation. Living South Africa gets under the skin of South Africa today, while the Story of South Africa takes you through the country's past.

South Africa has some of the most varied and extreme environments in the world, from the tropical beaches of KwaZulu-Natal to the rolling red sand dunes of the Kalahari Desert. Roaming through these landscapes, in the great game reserves, are the country's amazing wild animals, charismatic creatures that draw countless visitors. But scratch the surface a little and a further attraction becomes clear—the people. South Africa's population is an incredible mix of races, religions and identities, so that it truly merits the nickname 'Rainbow Nation'.

LANDSCAPE

South Africa is a huge country. The total land area is 1,219,912sq km (471,008sq miles)—1,267,462sq km (489,367sq miles) including Swaziland and Lesotho. These are independent countries; Lesotho is completely surrounded by South Africa, but Swaziland borders both South Africa and Mozambique. Contained within the country are tropical rainforest in the east, the spectacular mountains of the Drakensberg, the rolling grasslands of Kruger, temperate woodlands along the Garden Route, cacti-studded plains in the interior and the endless deserted beaches fringing the entire coast.

CLIMATE

As a country in the southern hemisphere, South Africa's seasons are the reverse of those in the northern hemisphere, which means that summer is from November to March, and the coldest months are June to September. Summer is generally hot and, in certain areas, can be humid, with temperatures often soaring above 30°C (86°F). Winter days are often sunny and mild, but don't be deceived—temperatures can drop below freezing at night in some areas. Much of the interior and the north of the country are dry with sporadic rainfall, while areas such as the Garden Route, the Western Cape, have light rainfall all year round.

LANGUAGE

There are 11 official languages in South Africa, but English is widely understood and spoken. Before the end of apartheid, Afrikaans was the only other official language with English, and it is still very visible on signs—many of the country's road signs, for example, are in English and Afrikaans. Many of the African languages are more or less mutually intelligible. The major distinction is between the Nguni languages (isiXhosa, isiZulu, siSwati and isiNdebele) and those that are closely related to Sesotho and Setswana.

ECONOMY

South Africa has for many years suffered from having both a developed and a developing economy within the same country. It is incredibly rich in natural resources—the economy is dominated by mining—and while a small sector of the population is affluent, the majority suffers from poverty and high levels of unemployment.

The government is doing much to redress the imbalance between rich and poor—which in effect still means between white and black. It has introduced empowerment legislation, which is designed to shift a percentage of ownership and management of businesses into black hands. Certainly, the last 15 years have seen significant progress: The economy is the strongest in Africa and an affluent black middle class has emerged, something that was unthinkable during apartheid. Tourism, meanwhile, has been the country's big success story, with South Africa having one of the fastest growing tourism sectors in the world. Visitor numbers hit more than 10 million in 2010 and are set to grow further following the attention the country received during the World Cup.

DEMOGRAPHY

South Africa's population of just over 50 million consists of numerous races, religions, ethnicities and cultures, which can be bewildering for visitors. While many people today resent being classified in terms of race and ethnicity, it is impossible to discuss modern South Africa without touching on these terms.

Most of the population is black African, which makes up around 79 per cent of the total. About 9 per cent is white, while 9 per cent is referred to as 'coloured' (that is, descendants of slaves, white settlers and Africans), the most contentious classification, but one that is nonetheless still used. Many coloured people are partially descended from the pre-colonial San and Khoi populations of the Cape. Around 80 per cent of the coloured population speaks Afrikaans.

South Africa also has a small Asian population, whose ancestors came from South Asia as indentured labourers. It accounts for around 3 per cent of the population and is found mainly in and around Durban.

The African population is further split into different ethnic groups, also known as tribes. The largest group is the Zulu, the majority of them living in KwaZulu-Natal or in the industrial areas of Gauteng. The second biggest ethnic group is the Xhosa, who live in the Eastern Cape province and in and around Cape Town. Many of the leaders of the ruling African National Congress (ANC), including former president Nelson Mandela (1918–), are Xhosa from Eastern Cape, reflecting the area's long history of resistance politics.

There are three ethnic groups whose members are closely related to the populations of three of South Africa's neighbouring countries: the Tswana (Botswana), the Swazi (Swaziland) and the Southern Sotho (Lesotho). These three, along with four other ethnic groups—the Tsonga, the Ndebele, the Venda and the Northern Sotho—have populations that are dispersed in the old homeland areas, although many have now gravitated to the cities in search of work.

South Africa's white population can be divided into two main groups: English speakers and Afrikaans speakers. The ancestors of English-speaking white South Africans first arrived in the country in 1820, while the Afrikaner population is descended from the original Dutch settlers.

Opposite *Young fans supporting the Springboks rugby team*
Below left *Penguins at Boulder Coastal Park, Cape Peninsula*
Below right *Mother and son in the Venda area of Northern Transvaal*

RELIGION

Most South Africans are Christian, with large groups belonging to the Church of England, the Dutch Reformed Church and countless other denominations. A small proportion of Africans practise indigenous religions. There are also significant numbers of Hindus and Muslims, and a small Jewish population.

POLITICS

South Africa is a constitutional democracy with a three-tier system of government: national, provincial and local. All tiers have legislative and executive authority in their own areas. Parliament sits in Cape Town and national government ministries are in Pretoria. Parliament consists of two houses: the National Assembly and the National Council of Provinces. The National Assembly has 400 members, who are elected for a five-year term. The last general election, held in April 2009, saw the ruling African National Congress (ANC) win with an overwhelming 264 seats. Twelve other parties joined the National Assembly, with the majority of the remaining seats (67) going to the opposition Democratic Alliance. The country's constitution is one of the most progressive in the world, and forbids discrimination on any grounds.

Below *Congregation gathered outside St. John's Church in Maseru, Lesotho; the church dates from 1912 and inside has inscriptions to some of the city's most important past residents*

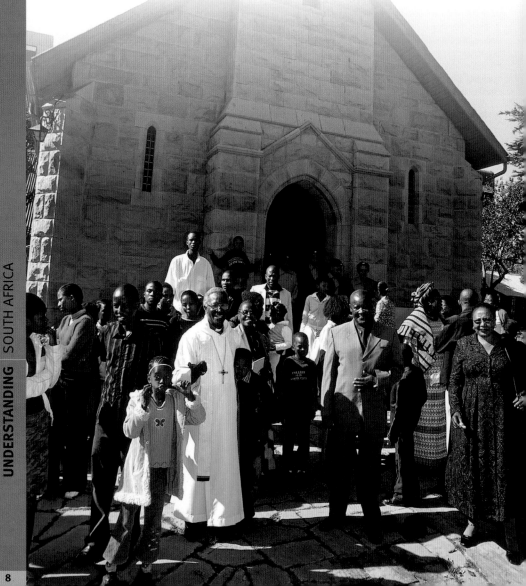

THE CAPE PENINSULA

Sunset The views from the top of Table Mountain (▷ 76–77) are superb at any time of day, but at sunset the panorama of the glittering ocean surrounding the city comes into its own.

History Grand colonial structures grace the wide streets in central Cape Town (▷ 67–71), not far from the brightly painted houses of Bo-Kaap, historically the city's Islamic district (▷ 67).

Beach Cape Town has some of South Africa's finest beaches; laze beneath palm trees on Camps Bay (▷ 63) or swim with penguins on Boulders Beach (▷ 73).

Walk Stroll up to Cape Point (▷ 64), the stark promontory that straddles the Peninsula, with wide-reaching views of the Atlantic and False Bay.

Picnic Join the locals for a concert picnic at the lush Kirstenbosch Botanical Gardens (▷ 74), on the side of Table Mountain.

WESTERN CAPE

Wine On the old estates of the Winelands (▷ 115–119) you can enjoy tasting world-class wines in traditional Cape Dutch homesteads amid rolling landscapes of vineyards and mountains.

Nature The ancient forest giants of Tsitsikamma–Garden Route National Park (▷ 111) lie in beautiful walking territory; or you can take a canopy tour for a bird's-eye view (▷ 132).

Beach Join the family throngs on one of the long, sandy stretches of the Garden Route (▷ 103, 120–121), or watch whales from Hermanus (▷ 113).

Wildlife Oudtshoorn (▷ 108), a quiet town in the Karoo, has 90 per cent of the world's ostrich population. You can see them at one of the many ostrich farms.

Eating The open-air seafood *braais* (barbecues) on the West Coast (▷ 134–135) serve huge portions in a beautiful beach setting.

EASTERN CAPE

Wildlife The Addo Elephant National Park (▷ 144) is the best place in South Africa to see elephants, with enormous herds roving across its grasslands.

Beach Escape the crowds on the endless windswept beaches of the Wild Coast (▷ 151), backed by traditional Xhosa *kraals* (huts).

Wilderness A drive to the viewpoint above the Valley of Desolation (▷ 146) reveals the vast expanse of the Eastern Karoo stretching to all horizons.

Walk The mystical Amatola Mountains (▷ 143) inspired J. R. R. Tolkien's *Lord of the Rings*; they make great walking country.

Surf Jeffreys Bay (▷ 143) is a top site for surfers, where you can learn how to ride the waves.

KWAZULU-NATAL

Wetlands A boat trip across the expansive wetlands of iSimangaliso (▷ 170–171) gives you the chance to see many birds, plus hippos and crocodiles.

Tour Take a guided tour of historic battlefields (▷ 164–165) and let the rolling grasslands come alive with tales of bravery and loss.

Hiking The finest hiking in South Africa is in the magnificent Drakensberg mountain range (▷ 176–179).

Underwater Sodwana Bay (▷ 175) is famed for its scuba diving, and is one of the top places in the country for diving with sharks.

Culture Soak up some traditional Zulu culture in Zululand (▷ 175), from tasting home-brewed beer to watching the time-honoured craft of basket weaving.

LIMPOPO AND MPUMALANGA

Wildlife A tour with a ranger in Kruger National Park (▷ 199–205) is the best way of seeing the 'Big Five'.

Walk Get up close and personal to Kruger's wildlife on a guided walk (▷ 204–205), and enjoy the park's flora.

Overnight Stay in one of the private or public camps in Kruger (▷ 217) and listen out for the roar of lions, or watch hungry hyenas prowling the perimeters at night.

Views Winding for 26km (16 miles) and dropping by as much as 750m (2,460ft), the Blyde River Canyon Nature Reserve (▷ 196) is an impressive sight.

History A stroll among the perfectly preserved gold miners' houses in Pilgrim's Rest (▷ 206) gives an evocative insight into the harsh days of the gold rush.

Above *Young surfer riding the waves off the surfing beach of Umhlanga Rocks, just north of Durban*

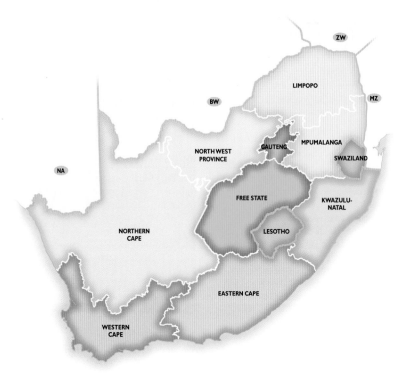

GAUTENG AND FREE STATE

History A harrowing but ultimately inspiring account of the darkest days of apartheid is vividly told at Johannesburg's top visitor attraction, the Apartheid Museum (▷ 225).

Nightlife Taste life in the fast lane with a late-night visit to one of Johannesburg's stylish cutting-edge clubs (▷ 234–236).

Shopping Gauteng has many shopping malls (▷ 234–237), each with hundreds of glitzy shops, restaurants, bars and cinemas.

Drive You'll find the Eastern Highlands in the spectacular Golden Gate Highlands National Park, where you can drive among the bizarre multi-hued rock formations (▷ 232–233).

Township The vast township of Soweto (▷ 231) was a hotbed of political resistance during apartheid and is a fascinating mix of cultures. Visit it on a guided tour and meet local Sowetans.

NORTHERN CAPE AND NORTH WEST PROVINCE

Diamonds Peer down into the Big Hole and learn the story of South Africa's diamond wealth at the Kimberley Diamond Rush (▷ 251).

Views The smoothly shaped rocks and shimmering desert around Augrabies Falls (▷ 246) supply an eerie backdrop to the magnificent waterfalls.

Wildlife Traverse the rolling red sand dunes of the Kgalagadi Transfrontier Park (▷ 248–249) and search for the Kalahari lion.

Adventure The finest way of experiencing the dramatic Gariep (Orange) River is on a thrilling white-water rafting trip (▷ 262).

Flowers An unexpected attraction of the arid Northern Cape is the colourful flowering of the desert in Namakwa every spring (▷ 252–254), when the rains bring a brilliant riot of wild flowers.

LESOTHO AND SWAZILAND

Adventure Lesotho's bleak and beautiful peaks and friendly Sesotho villages should be visited in the traditional way: on the back of a hardy Lesotho pony (▷ 280).

Views You'll find nothing better than the extraordinary and expansive panoramas which unfold from the top of the tortuous Sani Pass (▷ 273), accessible only by horse or 4WD.

Royalty Drive the length of the Ezulwini Valley (▷ 274), browse in its craft shops, and stop off at the royal Swazi household of Lobamba.

Wildlife Swaziland's biggest national park, Hlane Royal National Park (▷ 274), is a superb place to get close to rhino, lion and cheetah.

Nature Wander amid herds of zebra and antelope on a horseback ride across the savannah of Mlilwane Wildlife Sanctuary (▷ 276).

THE PROVINCES OF SOUTH AFRICA

South Africa is divided into nine provinces. In this book, some of them have been grouped together. Chapters about the Cape Peninsula and the independent kingdoms of Lesotho and Swaziland have also been included.

The Cape Peninsula has South Africa's most agreeable city, Cape Town, characterized by Table Mountain and its magnificent bay.

Western Cape has a huge range of environments and sights, including the rolling vineyards of the Winelands, the forests and beaches of the Garden Route and the dry expanse of the Karoo.

Eastern Cape is a less visited area but is nevertheless immensely rewarding for its beautifully preserved Cape Dutch architecture, the deserted beaches of the Wild Coast, and the superb wildlife viewing at the Addo Elephant National Park.

KwaZulu-Natal is a subtropical region with a magnificent stretch of coastline, historic inland battlefield sites dating from the Zulu and Anglo-Boer wars, and the Drakensberg Mountains, a spectacular wilderness area ideal for hiking.

Limpopo and Mpumalanga have South Africa's premier attraction: the Kruger National Park, which has some of the best places to view game in southern Africa.

Gauteng and Free State hold the country's two most important cities—the metropolis of Johannesburg and the administrative capital, Pretoria—as well as the towns and parks of the Eastern Highlands.

Northern Cape and North West Province cover a vast area of the arid north, on the fringes of the Kalahari Desert, and include excellent game parks and the diamond capital, Kimberley.

Lesotho and Swaziland are independent countries that border South Africa, respectively providing a chance to experience traditional Sesotho or Swazi culture. Swaziland has excellent game viewing, while Lesotho is famed for its magnificent mountain scenery.

TOP EXPERIENCES

The 'Big Five' South Africa is famous for its national parks, particularly Kruger. Heading off into the wilderness to spot lion, leopard, rhino, buffalo and elephant (the 'Big Five') is an unforgettable experience.

Adrenaline sports From the world's highest bungee jump to superb white-water rafting or great white shark diving, South Africa has an astounding range of heart-pumping activities.

Majestic landscapes The Drakensberg have some of the most beautiful vistas and best hiking in southern Africa.

The San legacy Get to grips with South Africa's ancient history through the rock art of the San people, going back more than 20,000 years.

The Two Oceans South Africa's shores are washed by the Atlantic on one side and the Indian Ocean on the other, making it an unbeatable scuba-diving destination.

Architecture From traditional Cape Dutch homesteads to Zulu beehive huts, the country has astoundingly rich and varied architecture.

A *braai* Don't miss out on this great South African institution, the traditional Afrikaner barbecue, best enjoyed at sunset with a cold beer.

The nightlife In cities like Johannesburg, Durban and Cape Town, nightlife rivals Europe's clubbing capitals.

Beach life The country's endless coastline is blessed with stunning beaches, from the wind-lashed expanses on the West Coast to the palm-fringed coves of the east.

Traditional culture Take in some traditional African culture—dancing, singing or a festival—such as the remarkable Umhlanga Reed dance in Swaziland.

Tasting wine Visit one of the centuries-old estates in the Western Cape's verdant Winelands area.

Above *Lioness, Kruger National Park*
Left *Table Mountain rising above the mist, seen from Bloubergstrand*

GAME PARKS AND WILDLIFE

GAME PARKS

No trip to South Africa is complete without at least one visit to a major game park. The country has some of the best game viewing in Africa, with an excellent infrastructure that makes going on safari a hassle-free (and relatively affordable) undertaking. The main game parks are extremely well organized with good facilities for game viewing, including well-surfaced roads and excellent accommodation. The actual game-viewing experience is a much more independent one than in other countries in the region, with many visitors choosing to self-drive on the extensive network of roads found in parks such as Kruger National Park.

It is worth considering taking a guided tour, however, as game rangers will be more adept at spotting wildlife and are an excellent source of information on the region's flora and fauna.

WHEN TO GO

The optimum times of the day for game viewing are early in the morning and late in the afternoon. The best time of year is in winter, from July to September, when dry weather forces animals to congregate around waterholes; at this time vegetation is lower and less dense, making it easier to spot wildlife. Summer weather, from November to January, when rainfall is at its highest, also has its advantages as animals will be in good condition after feeding on the new shoots, and there are chances of seeing mating displays and young animals. The landscape is green and lush in summer, but the thicker vegetation and the wide availability of water will also make it likely that wildlife will be more difficult to spot and far more widely dispersed.

FIELD GUIDE

The 'Big Five' are fairly common in South Africa. The term was coined by hunters who wanted to take home trophies of the largest, most charismatic animals. So, in hunting parlance, the Big Five were elephant, rhino, buffalo, lion and leopard. Equally deserving of top status, however, are zebra, hippo, giraffe and cheetah. Whether they are the Big Five, or the Big Nine, these are the animals that most people come to South Africa to see; and with the possible exceptions of the leopard and the black rhino you have an excellent chance of seeing them all.

WHAT TO LOOK FOR

**Common/Masai giraffe *(Giraffa camelopardalis)*
1.** Yellowish with patchwork of brown marks, usually two horns, sometimes three. Their long necks have the same number of vertebrae as in humans. Usually seen browsing around trees.

Buffalo *(Syncerus caffer)* 2. Often found on open plains but also at home in dense forest, they have distinctive curving horns. Buffalo may look docile but can be aggressive.

Cheetah *(Acinonyx jubatus)* 3. The fastest land mammal, they can reach speeds of 90kph (55mph) over short distances. Often seen in family groups walking across the plain or resting in shade. Found in open, semi-arid savannah, rarely in forested country.

Lion *(Panthera leo)* 4. Nearly always seen in a pride (group), lions hunt at night and sleep during the day, but are usually easy to spot.

Leopard *(Panthera pardus)* 5. Found in varied habitats ranging from forest to open savannah. Generally nocturnal, and difficult to spot during the day; look for them resting in trees.

Black rhinoceros *(Diceros bicornis)* 6. Long hooked upper lip. Prefer dry bush and thorn scrub habitat. Males are usually solitary, while females prefer small groups. One of the most endangered animals in Africa because of poaching for its horn.

White rhinoceros *(Ceratotherium simum)*. Square muzzle and bulkier than the black rhino. Found in open grassland, often in groups of five or more. Also endangered but less so than black rhino.

Elephant *(Loxodonta africana)* 7. Often seen in large herds. Can be aggressive when there are young around.

Hippopotamus *(Hippopotamus amphibius)* 8. Prefer shallow water, graze at night and have strong sense of territory, which they protect aggressively. Live in large families, or 'schools'.

Mountain zebra *(Equus zebra zebra)* 9. Smallest of the two zebra sub species, with short mane and broad stripes (mix of dark and paler stripes).

**Common zebra/Burchell's zebra *(Equus burchelli)*
10.** Broad stripes which cross the top of the hind leg in unbroken lines.

Blue wildebeest/gnu *(Connochaetes taurinus)* 11. Often seen grazing in large herds.

Eland *(Traurotragus oryx)*. World's largest species of antelope, can grow to 1.8m (6ft). Grey to light brown; both sexes have spiral horns.

Impala *(Aepyceros melampus)* 12. Very common in the Kruger National Park. Rich light brown with white underbelly, thick black tufts of heels on hind legs, and long horns (males).

Red hartebeest *(Alcelaphus buselaphus)* 13. Colour varies from reddish-brown to fawn. Dark patches on front of shoulders and whitish rump.

Steenbok *(Raphicerus campestris)* 14. An even brown with white underside and white ring around the eyes. Prefer open plains; usually seen alone.

Oribi *(Ourebia ourebi)*. Slender with long neck, oval ears and short straight horns.

Reedbuck *(Redunca arundinum)*. Horns (males only) hook sharply forward. Brown to greyish-brown fawn with white underbelly and short bushy tails.

Springbok *(Antidorcas marsupialis)* 15. Upper part of body is fawn, separated from white underbelly by dark brown lateral stripe. Reddish-brown stripe runs between the base of the horns and the mouth.

Bushbuck *(Tragelaphus scriptus)* 16. Shaggy coat with variable pattern of white spots and stripes. High rump gives characteristic crouch. Often seen in thick bush.

Common duiker *(Sylvicapra grimmia)*. Grey-fawn with darker rump and pale underbelly. Small in stature, found in open grassland.

Warthog *(Phacochoerus aethiopicus)* 17. Almost hairless and grey with very large head and curving tusks. They run with tail sticking straight up in the air. Can often be seen in family groups near water.

African wild dog *(Lycaon pictus)* 18. Large head and slender body; coat has mixed pattern of dark, white and yellow. Rare and is threatened with extinction.

10 11 12
13 14 15
16 17 18

UNDERSTANDING | SOUTH AFRICA

Dassie/rock hyrax *(Procavia Capensis)*. There are three main groups of these brown guinea pig-like mammals, but rock hyrax are most common. Live in colonies among boulders and on hillsides.

Bat-eared fox *(Otocyon megalotis)*. Distinctive large ears and short snout. Greyish-brown coat with bushy tail. Mainly nocturnal.

Civet *(Civettictis civetta)*. Yellow-grey coat with black and white markings and black rings around eyes. Found in woody areas or thick bush. Shy and nocturnal.

Black-backed jackal *(Canis mesomelas)* 19. Fox-like canine with red-fawn coloured coat and black-grey area on its back.

Spotted hyena *(Crocuta crocuta)* 20. High shoulders, powerful neck, and low back with distinctive loping walk. Larger than related brown species, with dark spots and rounded ears.

Brown hyena *(Hyaena brunnea)*. Brown variety is smaller, with pointed ears and shaggy coat. Both species of hyena are nocturnal.

Serval *(Felis serval)* 21. Narrow frame and long legs with small head and large ears. Similar coloration to cheetah but spots are more spread out.

Caracal *(Felis caracal)* 22. Also known as African lynx. Small, reddish-sandy coat with paler belly. Distinctive tufted ears and black stripe from eye to nose. Nocturnal and rarely seen, but are found in hilly terrain.

Baboon *(Papio ursinus)* 23. Live in large troops. Heavily built, with bright-pink buttocks. Males have manes and can be very aggressive. Opportunistic and can become pests in park camps.

Vervet monkey *(Cercopithecus aethiops)* 24. Much smaller than baboon, with grey coat and small black face. Feet, hands and tip of tail are black. Treated as vermin in many locations.

Blue-headed Agama lizard *(Agama atricollis)* 25. Grow to up to 20cm (8in) in length and can often be seen scuttling over walls and rocks near campsites. The orange-headed Agama lizard can also be seen, but is not as common.

Reed frog (*Hyperolius viridflavus*) 26. The male of this species has a distinctive call, sounding like a loud creak. Rests on branches that are overhanging water.

Crocodile (*Crocodylus niloticus*) 27. Found throughout tropical and southern Africa in rivers, mangrove swamps and some lakes. Nile crocodiles can weigh more than 1,000kg (2,200 lb) and grow between 2.5m (8ft) and 5.5m (18ft) in length. Up to 70 per cent of their diet is fish but other prey includes zebra and wildebeest.

Fish eagle (*Haliaeetus vocifer*) 28. Usually seen perched high up in trees, from where they have a good view of their territory. Large, white-breasted eagles have a distinctive call. Diet is mainly of live fish, although they do eat some water birds and their young. They can be found near lakes and rivers south of the Sahara.

Martial eagle (*Polemaetus bellicosus*) 29. This is the largest eagle in Africa, surviving on the open plains and semi-desert areas, down to the Cape. They soar to great heights and distances and swoop down to their prey of mammals such as lyrax and antelope.

Bateleur (*Terathopius ecaudatus*) 30. This striking-looking eagle spends most of its time flying and belongs to the snake eagle group.

Little bee eater (*Merops pusillus*) 31. Vivid yellow and green plumage. Often found near woodland streams. They feed on insects and butterflies and perch in groups at night or in cooler weather.

Marabou stork (*Leptoptilos crumeniferus*) 32. Grow to a height of 1.5m (5ft) with a wing span of 2.6m (8.5ft). Scavengers, they exist on carrion and scraps.

Lilac roller (*Coracias caudata*). So called due to bird's courtship flight (fast dive followed by a rocking and rolling motion). Highly territorial birds, they live in pairs or small groups and make their nests in tree-holes or termite hills.

Cape gannet (*Morus capensis*). Large black and white sea bird with a yellow head that is known for following the 'sardine run' along the KwaZulu-Natal coast in winter. They catch fish by spectacular plunge dives.

African penguin (*Sphenicus demersus*) 33. Small black and white penguin with a pink section of skin above the eyes. They are also known as the jackass penguin because of their donkey-like bray.

Southern right whale (*Eubalaena australis*). Can be spotted along the coast from July to November when the females calve in the bays. They reach lengths of up to 16m (53ft). The name derives from early whalers considering them as the 'right' whale to kill because they float when dead.

Humpback whale (*Megaptera novaeangliae*). About the same size but less common than the southern right, distinguished by its white throat and flippers and dorsal fin. Highly acrobatic, they are often seen breaching out of the water.

Great white shark (*Carcharodon carcharias*). Weighing up to 2,250kg (5,000 lb) and reaching lengths of 6m (20ft), this is the world's largest predatory fish, with a pointed snout, razor-sharp serrated teeth and an appetite for any kind of flesh, living or dead.

Cape fur seal (*Arctocephalus pusillus*). The only seal commonly seen along the southern African coast, breeds in noisy colonies on islands and along the west coast. Males are much bigger than females and can weigh up to 190kg (420 lb).

LIVING SOUTH AFRICA

UNDERSTANDING | LIVING SOUTH AFRICA

In 2004 South Africa took to the streets to celebrate the 10th anniversary of the arrival of democracy. A decade had passed since the majority of South Africans voted for the first time in a general election. Now, almost 20 years later, much has happened since Nelson Mandela's famous inauguration speech in 1994. Racial barriers have been demolished and there is a substantial black middle class, something unthinkable during the darkest days of apartheid. South Africans have learned to revel in being the 'Rainbow Nation'. The term paraphrases that coined by Desmond Tutu, the country's first black Anglican archbishop, during a speech in the last days of apartheid: 'We, the Rainbow People of God...'. This is an easily justifiable title as the country has the most diverse population in Africa, with far more complex distinctions than simply black and white. About 79 per cent of the population is black African, 9 per cent white, 9 per cent 'coloured' (mixed race descendants of slaves, white settlers and Africans), and just 3 per cent Asian. There are also numerous national languages and religions.

LAUGHING AT RACISM
The comedy scene has become a platform for some of the most popular, and controversial, portrayals of modern South Africa. Few have made a bigger career out of it than Mark Lottering. Born in the townships of the Cape Flats outside Cape Town, Lottering defines himself as coloured. Much of his material focuses on how different races interact and the general absurdity of racism. He has been at the forefront of a shift on the comedy circuit; where once only whites stood, black and coloured comedians now talk openly about race issues in front of a mixed audience. Lottering's stand-up shows are both hilarious and shocking—and have landed him a TV show and several international tours.

Clockwise from above *A group of students in Johannesburg that is representative of the ethnic diversity of the country; woman showing off a bright headdress in Shakaland; Muslim man and his son in Bo-Kaap, the Islamic district of Cape Town*

PROUDLY SOUTH AFRICAN

Launched in 2001 and one of many 'nation building' post-apartheid exercises, Proudly South African (www.proudlysa.co.za) is a popular nationwide campaign to promote products and services made in South Africa. The Proudly South African logo appears on many items and is also supported by big companies like South African Airways and Eskom (South Africa's electricity provider). To be part of the programme a business must incur at least 50 per cent of production costs in South Africa, make good-quality items and be environmentally friendly. However, it's the employment element of the campaign that's the most important. It is estimated that for every R1 million spent on local rather than imported products, 20 jobs are created, and the scheme endorses only those products that are made by workers in good conditions.

FESTIVAL OF LIGHTS

One of the highlights of Durban's events calendar is *Diwali* (or Deepavali), the Hindu Festival of Lights. Although the traditionally Zulu province of KwaZulu-Natal doesn't seem an obvious spot for a Hindu celebration, it is in fact home to the majority of South Africa's 1.2 million Indian population. *Diwali*, which occurs in October or November (the date falls according to the lunar calendar), symbolizes the triumph of good over evil. The shops in Durban's Indian district are illuminated by hundreds of tiny oil lamps in the days leading up to *Diwali*, with clothing and food sales taking place around the city. The highlight and culmination of the festival is a vast fireworks display held on the beach. Other places across the country join in too, such as in the Indian township of Lenasia in Johannesburg, which also holds a spectacular fireworks display.

TOP WOMEN

Before South Africa's first democratic elections the country ranked 141st in the world for gender representation. In the space of a few years, the country has risen to third in the world for the number of women in government. In 2010 women comprised 44 per cent of South Africa's MPs, and one of the country's most prestigious positions, Premier of the Western Cape, is held by the popular and outspoken Helen Zille. This is a step in the right direction, and more is being done to encourage women to participate in the political life of the country. Laws on domestic violence and child maintenance are designed to have a positive impact on women's lives — some commentators are saying it won't be long before South Africa has a female president.

BLACK DIAMONDS

As a free South Africa began to breathe, a new black middle class began to emerge. According to an annual study by the University of Cape Town's Unilever Institute, in 2007 the number of black middle income earners had doubled since 2003 and now stands at about 3 million adults, good-naturedly referred to as 'Black Diamonds'. When apartheid fell, educated black South Africans began to move into previously 'whites-only' suburbs. Since then, the number of black middle class families living in the suburbs of South Africa's metropolitan areas has risen from 23 per cent in 2005 to 43 per cent today. This figure represents 47 per cent of South Africa's black population, and while the other 53 per cent still live in townships, it's a massive step towards full integration.

The key to understanding South African music is in realizing where it comes from. Whether it's the adaptation of Dutch instruments in the 17th century by Indonesian slaves or the mutation of 1990s house music into township kwaito, home-grown and foreign influences mingle to produce a singularly South African sound. Like so much of the culture, music is inextricably linked with the political upheavals of the last century. From demonstrations against apartheid in the 1960s to the reflection of disillusioned white youth in the 1980s, music has a history of expressing social currents and it remains a powerful force. Forums for hearing music are as varied as the styles, as diverse as catching a gospel choir in a church, squinting through the dense smoke of a Cape Jazz club while listening to the traditional music of Cape Town, or seeing a rock band at an open-air festival.

GOD'S MUSIC

Vocal harmony has its roots in communal dances accompanied by elaborate call-and-response patterns. This tradition has long been popular in South Africa, but it was the group Ladysmith Black Mambazo that first propelled it onto the international stage. The beginnings for the group were not easy; at their first concert in Soweto in the 1980s, they received R5.28 (£2–£3) each. But the group went on to become a huge hit. When Paul Simon invited them to sing on his *Graceland* (1986) album, they were thrust into the limelight, and they remain the most popular South African group of all time. Made up of 10 male singers, including frontman and founder Joseph Shabalala, the group continues to tour, and has now recorded more than 50 albums.

Clockwise from above *Local dance troupe preparing to perform at Bourke's Luck Potholes on the Blyde River; Mama Africa restaurant in Cape Town is known for its great live music; street musician playing the saxophone in Johannesburg*

GOD BLESS AFRICA

Few songs are as powerful as 'Nkosi Sikelel' iAfrika' ('God Bless Africa'), the national anthem composed by Enoch Sontonga in 1897. It was originally a freedom song, and its history means it still packs an emotional punch. It was once the anti-apartheid anthem, which led to the singers sometimes being dispelled with tear gas. Today, it is sung at most types of gathering. However, the fact that it is now combined with the old apartheid-era anthem, 'Die Stem' ('The Call'), and has verses in Zulu, Xhosa, Sotho, Afrikaans and English, means that much of the population knows only a small part. To combat this, the First National Bank launched an initiative in 2004 to distribute 10 million leaflets to schools across the country. The scheme, entitled 'Your Anthem Needs You!', aims to encourage people to learn all verses, regardless of ethnicity or language.

ALL THAT JAZZ

Jazz has been hugely influential in South Africa since emerging from the Johannesburg slums in the 1920s. There were turbulent times when many of the biggest stars left South Africa due to apartheid, but the jazz scene is once again flourishing, and is particularly strong in the townships. A good place to hear jazz is at the annual Cape Town International Jazz Festival, one of the top jazz festivals in the world. Many of the godfathers of Cape Jazz, such as Abdullah Ibrahim (aka Dollar Brand, 1934–) and Hugh Masekela (1939–), regularly take part, while newcomers, using a range of influences from the harmonica of migrant west African miners to drum 'n' bass, are also making a big impact. Every year top international talents perform and the event is now hosted at the Cape Town International Convention Centre (CTICC), attracting some 40,000 people.

SOUND OF THE CITY

Zola, a young musician from Soweto, encapsulates South Africa's biggest force in music today. He has become a national phenomenon and recognized leader of the latest music movement, kwaito. This mix of dance, hip-hop and rap is the sound of young, black Johannesburg, and has a resolutely urban feel, its deep beat overlaid with chanted *tsotsi* (township gangster) slang. Born and bred in Soweto, Zola raps about guns and crime and his music has a dark, angry edge to it. But he is also a TV presenter and extols the importance of kwaito's responsibility to young people: 'Turn the gun into a microphone' is one of his mottos. Ubiquitous in the clubs of the black community, kwaito is now also popular in designer nightclubs, until recently the preserve of the white and wealthy.

THE WHITE ZULU

No one better sums up the white rebellious musical force that opposed the repressive social laws of apartheid in the 1980s than Johnny Clegg. Born in 1952 in England, Clegg spent nine years in Zimbabwe before moving to South Africa. In the 1970s, Clegg began performing traditional Zulu material with Sipho Mchunu, and later added a mix of Western rock to form the band Juluka. Clegg remains something of a South African legend, and still draws thousands of fans when he performs. Known as the 'White Zulu', Clegg challenged the racial boundaries manifest in music under apartheid, and blazed a crossover trail that survives to this day. Although his popularity in South Africa is mainly among the white population, his tours are sell-outs and he remains a big influence both in South Africa and internationally.

Few people leave South Africa without visiting at least one of its parks. In contrast to many protected areas elsewhere in Africa, however, the parks are shared with residents, many of whom enjoy the outdoors lifestyle. During the school holidays, the parks and reserves become busy with South Africans; there are reductions on entry for citizens of the country, although the majority of those visiting the parks are still from the wealthier sections of society. South Africa's protected parks have a considerable impact on the country, both in terms of revenue—an estimated one million people visit Kruger every year—and in terms of area. Kruger alone is slightly larger than many countries, and that's still considerably smaller than the new Great Limpopo Transfrontier Park, which from 2002 also incorporated Mozambique's Limpopo National Park and Zimbabwe's Gonarezhou park. It forms the largest wildlife reserve in Africa (although at the moment you can only cross between South Africa and Mozambique). South Africa's other national parks are also growing. For instance, the Addo Elephant National Park in the Eastern Cape now encompasses five neighbouring game reserves, stretching from the Indian Ocean to the Little Karoo, and sheltering elephant, rhino, lion, buffalo, leopard, whales and great white sharks.

THE GODFATHER OF CAMPS

Skukuza is the biggest camp in Kruger National Park, and indeed in the whole of South Africa. It can accommodate an astonishing number of people—more than a thousand at full capacity—turning it into something like a small, bustling town. The facilities are impressive, but a sense of isolation and of the wilderness may be hard to come by. Hundreds of huts, *rondavels* (circular African-style thatched huts), campsites and family bungalows stretch through the straggling undergrowth. It has its own airport, a bank and post office, two swimming pools, an auditorium showing nature films, a cafeteria and restaurant, a church and a nursery selling indigenous plants. Finally, for those who can't leave their clubs behind, the camp has its own 18-hole golf course.

Clockwise from above *Elephant strolling along the road in Kruger National Park; gamekeeper feeding a lion at Tshukudo Game Lodge; buffalo spotted on a game drive at Mala Mala*

A CHANGE IN DIRECTION

David Mabunda grew up just outside Nelspruit, close to Kruger, but as a 'non-white' was forbidden from entering the park under the apartheid government. He first experienced the magnificence of South Africa's animals when his parents' employers took his family with them on a visit to the park. Mabunda's passion for the great outdoors was born. Following several years of study abroad and stints in Sri Lanka, Tanzania and Zimbabwe, he returned to South Africa to work in land management. After the collapse of the apartheid regime, he became the first black director of Kruger National Park in the 1990s, and in 2003 was appointed Chief Executive Officer of South African National Parks, presiding over the country's most important natural means. Today he heads a 3,000-strong workforce and manages 20 national parks.

SUPER PARK

In early 2002, South Africa, Zimbabwe and Mozambique agreed to establish the Great Limpopo Transfrontier Park. It is a merger of the world-famous Kruger—with its extraordinary abundance of wildlife and stunning geological splendour—and two other game reserves in Mozambique and Zimbabwe. The park brings together some of the best and most established wildlife areas in southern Africa. The cross-border park, measuring 35,000sq km (13,650sq miles), is managed across an unprecedented three international boundaries. It contains the 'Big Five' animals and a huge variety of other game. It's also the place where tropical, moist, temperate and dry savannah climates all converge. The creation of the park is the first phase of the establishment of a bigger conservation area measuring a staggering 100,000sq km (39,000sq miles).

DISPLACEMENT WITH A HAPPY ENDING

The Makuleke region fell outside the borders of Kruger National Park until 1969, when the people of the clan were forcibly removed by the apartheid government so that the park could be extended. More than 24,000ha (60,000 acres) of land was taken. However, a historic decision by the Land Claims Court reinstated the land to the Makuleke in 1998. The clan chose not to challenge the conservation status of the area and reached an agreement with South Africa National Parks to bring in private sector support to assist with the management of the land. The deal was worth R45 million, and later that year the first luxury lodge was opened. The community is being trained to take over the entire business within 20 years. In the meantime, they earn a percentage of all takings and more than 100 jobs are being created.

TOUGH JUSTICE

By 1980 Swaziland's rhinos were in dire need of protection, with up to 45 being killed every year. The consequence has been the introduction of some of the most stringent anti-poaching laws in the world. The law stipulates that poachers face a minimum sentence of five years in prison, and that they must 'replace' the slain animal by paying to have another introduced to the reserve where it was poached, which can cost the equivalent of hundreds of thousands of South African rands. Anti-poaching game rangers have been armed with shotguns and have the right to shoot to kill if they need to protect themselves, a move which has been criticized outside Swaziland. While two poachers have been killed in the last few years, not a single rhino has been lost since 1993. These laws have almost certainly saved the region's rhino population from extinction.

South Africans take their sport seriously. The entire country is sports mad, and playing and watching sport is part of the national lifestyle, be it watching a soccer match or surfing. Who watches what, however, still largely depends on background and race. While soccer is hugely popular among black South Africans, cricket and rugby union remain largely the preserve of the white population. Rugby and cricket thus enjoyed impressive funding for years, resulting in a number of world-class stadiums dotted around the country. Yet feelings run high no matter what sport is being watched, from the festive rivalry between the Johannesburg soccer teams Kaizer Chiefs and Orlando Pirates, to the emotional roars that accompany every match of the national rugby team, the Springboks, who won the Rugby World Cup in 2007. The biggest growth industry in recent years has been adventure sports — South Africa's good climate and range of environments make it an ideal place to try adrenaline activities. It has the world's highest bungee jump, offers cage diving with great white sharks, and has some of the world's best paragliding in the Kalahari desert. Along with surfing, hiking and mountain biking, a popular activity with visitors is 'kloofing', which involves boulder-hopping (literally, leaping from boulder to boulder), hiking and swimming down *kloofs* (gorges).

PARALYMPIANS LEAD THE WAY

There were some who were disappointed at the performance of the country's Olympic team in the 2008 Beijing games, where it finished 71st, with only one silver medal for the long jump. So it was left to the country's Paralympians to restore national pride. And they did — with an outstanding performance. At the Paralympics the South Africans notched up 30 medals, including 21 golds, to finish an impressive 13th. The top woman competitor was swimmer Natalie du Toit, who won five gold medals for butterfly and freestyle events, while male athletes included Hilton Langenhoven — pentathlon and long jump — and Oscar Pistorius — 100m and 200m — who each won three gold medals.

Clockwise from above *The Two Oceans Marathon takes place around the Cape Peninsula; the annual Cape Argus Pick 'n' Pay Cycle Tour attracts some 35,000 participants; South Africa has many superb surfing beaches, some suitable for world-class surfing championships, and others where novices can learn*

WORLD CUP FEVER

South Africa was jubilant when it was awarded the 2010 FIFA World Cup. Work got underway immediately to ensure everything was in place for a successful championship, including the building of impressive new stadiums around the country — the state of the art Green Point Stadium in Cape Town, the impressive Moses Mabhida Stadium in Durban and the Mbombela Stadium near Kruger National Park to name but three. While there were concerns about crime levels in South Africa in the run up to the tournament, in reality the event was an unmitigated success, fulfilling its aim of bringing the country worldwide attention and boosting tourism. It also introduced to the world the vuvuzela, a long horn adapted from a traditional rural instrument. Its monotone sound echoed round the stands at every match, to the thrill of some and the irritation of others.

GOLF STUDIES

Proof that South Africans really do take their sport seriously can be found at the Tshwane University of Technology in Pretoria. The institute now offers degrees in Golf Studies, a four-year course accredited by the Professional Golf Association of South Africa. The degree prepares students to become professional golfers, coaches and managers, and is proving a huge hit with its 70-plus students. The course was first introduced as an incentive to keep young golfing talent in the country; many young hopefuls are lured to Europe and the US with scholarships. A key proportion of the Golfing Studies course involves practical golf sessions, with students spending much of their days on the greens. Golf has also been added to the curriculum of a handful of the country's high schools, with pupils spending up to two hours a day practising.

SURF'S UP

Jeffreys Bay, or 'J-Bay', as it's known to surfers, is South Africa's top surfing destination — and never more popular than during the annual Billabong Pro championship, one of the stops on the Association of Surfing Professionals World Championship Tour. The six-day competition, held every July, attracts more than 45 of the world's top surfers, who jet into the Eastern Cape town in the hope of winning the US$250,000 prize. J-Bay is said to have the world's most consistent right-hand break, and the aptly named Supertubes break is the venue for the contest. This seaside town comes to life during the festival, when surfers and backpackers from all over the world swarm to the beach to watch the surfing events and take part in the all-night parties that follow.

STAMINA RACES

South Africa has three major annual events that are open to international participants. The Comrades Marathon between Durban and Pietermaritzburg covers 90km (56 miles) of hilly terrain. Athletes have 12 hours to complete the course and are not allowed to be physically assisted. The Two Oceans Marathon follows a beautiful 56km (35-mile) route around the Cape Peninsula. The 109km (68-mile) Cape Argus Pick 'n' Pay Cycle Tour, also around the Peninsula, is the largest individually timed cycling event in the world, attracting 35,000 participants. The present winning time is around 2.5 hours for the professional cyclists, who amuse themselves by doing a second lap and still beating many of the amateurs, some of whom take the day to complete the course.

South Africa is the economic powerhouse of Africa, contributing about one-quarter of the continent's gross domestic product (GDP). The country leads the continent in industrial output (40 per cent of Africa's total output) and mineral production (45 per cent of total mineral production) and generates more than 50 per cent of Africa's electricity. With low inflation, dropping interest rates and booming house prices, some commentators have proclaimed this period South Africa's 'golden era'. The currency, the rand—which is one of the most traded developing-world currencies—has recovered remarkably to become one of the world's top performers. Tourism remains one of the biggest boom industries, with impressive visitor numbers. But the country still faces big challenges. It has a terrible record in terms of unequal distribution of income and an exaggerated divide between rich and poor. Unemployment sits at around 25 per cent, according to official figures. However, things are changing and there is action to redress the balance between rich and poor through 'empowerment'; more specifically, the Black Economic Empowerment (BEE), which means selling stakes in a company to black-owned and controlled companies, thus transferring some equity and control. The government is keen to spread the wealth derived from the country's incredibly rich mineral resources, and is implementing a range of initiatives and industrial charters.

GOLD CHANGING HANDS

South Africa is the world's largest gold producer, with an astonishing 40 per cent of global reserves. Mining—as one of the bedrocks of the economy—has spearheaded the country's Black Economic Empowerment (BEE) initiatives. BEE encourages the redistribution of wealth and opportunities to those who were disadvantaged by apartheid. Each sector of the economy has been drawing up voluntary BEE charters that outline policies and goals for more black participation. An example of this includes a 2003 deal, worth US$1.5 billion, between three corporations that created the country's largest black-owned mining company, African Rainbow Minerals. The company flourished and had more than doubled its production by 2010.

Clockwise from above *A South African Airways 747; mined by De Beers in South Africa in 1988, this gem is the second largest diamond in the world and weighs 599 carats; grape harvesting in the Western Cape*

GRAPE EXPECTATIONS

Wine is one area that seems unstoppable in the world market, and the South African wine industry has grown phenomenally since the lifting of apartheid-era sanctions in 1994. In 2007, South African winemakers exported more than 300 million litres (790 million gallons), or R3.5 billion worth of wine, making the country the world's ninth largest wine exporter. The UK is by far the largest destination for South African wines, accounting for 28 per cent of overseas sales. South African wines represent both excellent value and high quality; they are also in fashion, with producers having benefited considerably from the decline in popularity of wines from traditional wine-producing countries such as France. It remains to be seen whether South African wines can conquer the US market.

DIAMONDS ARE FOREVER

De Beers, the world's biggest diamond-mining group, estimates that at least 11 per cent of its 11,000 South African employees are infected with HIV/AIDS. Following heavy criticism of the government's stance on the disease, the diamond giant announced that it would supply its workers with anti-retroviral drugs, following a similar move by minerals giant Anglo-American (which has a 45 per cent stake in De Beers). The group has since received widespread acclaim for its initiative, launched in 2003, whereby anti-retroviral drugs are supplied free to its infected workers, their spouses or life partners, and former workers who have retired from the company. The scheme also involves a system of education for the entire workforce on the prevention of infection.

TOURISTS FLOCK TO SOUTH AFRICA

Research by a major bank in South Africa showed that tourism had replaced gold as the country's top foreign exchange earner. In 2007, foreign exchange from tourism totalled R159.6 billion, compared to R36.7 billion from gold exports. Since 1994, arrivals have grown tenfold, from 640,000 to 9.1 million in 2007. According to the research, tourism now contributes about 13 per cent to South Africa's gross domestic product. Despite a global slump, the country continued to defy world tourism trends, and in 2007 achieved an 8.3 per cent increase in overseas arrivals over the year before. The 2010 soccer World Cup (▷ 25), which was hosted in major destinations all over South Africa, saw tourism numbers reach 10 million. It is expected that the positive publicity generated during the tournament will encourage the upward trend to continue.

THE MOHAIR ROUTE

For those who want a slightly different itinerary to follow while they are in South Africa, there's the unusual Mohair Route, named after the soft and silky fleece of the angora goat, the economic backbone of the Karoo region. South Africa is in fact the world's largest producer of mohair, with a 60 per cent share of the global market— an impressive statistic given that the industry began with a tiny herd of just 13 animals imported from Turkey during the mid-18th century. The route starts in the historic central Karoo town of Graaff-Reinet (▷ 152–153) and ends in Uitenhage, taking in a number of farms and towns which depend on the hardy goats. In the Karoo, however, you'll find that mohair lacks the luxury connotations that it enjoys in many countries abroad and is simply regarded as a locally produced staple that a large number of livelihoods depend upon.

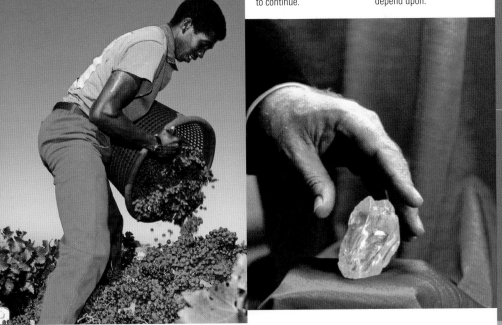

J. M. Coetzee

Booker Prize-winning author of *Disgrace*

WINNER *of the* NOBEL PRIZE *in* LITERATURE

ELIZABETH COSTELLO

South Africa's contemporary art scene is immensely exciting. Following years of neglect, it seems to be finding its feet, as artists respond to the changing cultural scene with imagination and flair. This certainly hasn't always been the case. During apartheid, simply owning a painting that was considered 'subversive' could have led to a jail sentence. Black artists were largely ignored and lacked the funds to promote their work. Since the advent of democracy, funding for the arts has been more equally distributed. This revival has also been driven by private enterprise, with new galleries opening up and showcasing contemporary artworks, including an exciting 'neo-tribal' art movement. Theatre, too, has come alive again; apartheid had been an abundant source for commentary, and now that it has passed, actors and playwrights have had to grapple with new subject matter. The film industry has been less successful, but is now gaining some momentum. Literature, meanwhile, is perhaps South Africa's greatest cultural hotbed.

J. M. COETZEE

South Africa has produced a number of internationally recognized and award-winning novelists, but the most celebrated is John Coetzee. The author of 12 novels, he has won the Man Booker Prize twice. He was first awarded the UK's most prestigious literary prize in 1983 for *The Life and Times of Michael K*, and again in 1999 for *Disgrace*. In 2003, he was awarded the Nobel Prize for Literature, only the second South African with such an honour, after Nadine Gordimer. He is a reclusive figure, never giving interviews, but is regarded as one of South Africa's most brilliant commentators on the effects of apartheid. His fellow countrymen were understandably disappointed when, in 2002, he emigrated to Australia, following further disenchantment with the politics of his birth nation, where the heroine of his novel *Elizabeth Costello* (2003) is based.

THE TOWNSHIP PHOTOGRAPHER

Zwelethu Mthethwa is one of the most successful artists on the contemporary scene, a photographer originally from Durban but now based in Cape Town. In the 1980s, he studied fine art at the University of Cape Town, but his real breakthrough came when he was awarded a Fulbright Scholarship to study at the Rochester Institute of Technology in the US. Here he first experimented with colour photography, and colour became a crucial component of his work. He is famous for his portrayals of township life, using large-format photography, pastels, paint and screen prints. Some of his best-known images focus on township interiors and sugar cane workers. He has exhibited his work throughout the world, including France, the US and Italy, and is celebrated as one of South Africa's success stories.

Above left *Cover of* Elizabeth Costello *by J. M. Coetzee*
Above right *Paintings on display at the Pan African Market, Cape Town*

THE STORY OF SOUTH AFRICA

South Africa is the self-proclaimed Cradle of Humankind, home to some of the oldest fossil human remains in the world. It is believed that our earliest ancestor, *Australopithecus africanus*, made its first tottering, bipedal steps on South African soil nearly three million years ago. Other ancestral species evolved and died out until, within the last 100,000 years, one of them developed still further into *Homo sapiens*, or modern humans. The earliest fossil remains of modern man in southern Africa are thought to be those from the Klasies River mouth in the Eastern Cape and Border Cave on the KwaZulu-Natal border. They are dated as being more than 50,000 years old. The descendants of these Stone-Age people were the San (once known as Bushmen) and Khoi (originally called Hottentots, a disparaging term today, by European settlers), who inhabited the Western Cape when the first Europeans arrived in the 15th century. The San were hunter-gatherers, living in small egalitarian communities. They were nomadic and moved with the seasonally migrating herds of wild game, carrying few personal possessions. They lived mostly in the dry interior. The Khoi, on the other hand, were pastoralists with a concept of ownership of property and a degree of social hierarchy, and occupied the coastal lands. The two groups, although distinct, had a certain level of interaction.

FOOTSTEPS FROM THE PAST

Although it's hard to picture it today, the parched expanse of baked red earth which makes up the Great Karoo in the Western Cape was once a vast lake surrounded by lush swampland. Around 300 million years ago, the lake was inhabited by invertebrates, and the shores were tramped by dinosaurs. Today, the area has revealed an exceptionally rich fossil record, from the aquatic creatures that perished in the lake to the footprints and tail-drag marks left behind by dinosaurs. The Karoo is now recognized as one of the world's most important palaeontological sites, not just for its number of fossils, but for the fact that the layers of rock contain a virtually unbroken record of species stretching back 50 million years.

Clockwise from above *Khoi village on the Gariep (Orange) River; Bushman painting in the Drakensberg; Australopithecus africanus skull discovered in Sterkfontein*

NEW ARRIVALS

The San and Khoi, regarded as the original, indigenous inhabitants of South Africa, were joined from about AD500 by peoples who had gradually migrated south, bringing with them new technologies such as iron smelting and crop cultivation. The ancestors of the vast majority of South Africa's present-day population, the newcomers spoke a number of languages known as the Bantu group. Like the Khoi, they were essentially herders, although it was their crop-raising and iron-smelting skills that brought about extensive trade networks. The large degree of contact between the different groups is reflected in the fact that some of the newer groups incorporated the Khoi-San clicks (characteristic of these tongues) into their language: Today these clicks can be heard in both Xhosa and Zulu. Most of the original Khoisan languages have now died out in South Africa, but they still exist in small pockets in Tanzania and Namibia.

THE LOST CITY OF GOLD

Mapungubwe formed the centre of the largest African civilization and trade hub in the subcontinent between AD1200 and 1300. It was the home of a thriving, complex society that traded in gold and ivory with countries such as China, India and Egypt. Set in what is now South Africa's Limpopo Province, the Iron-Age site is evidence of African civilization before colonization and probably the earliest known site in southern Africa where evidence of a class-based society existed. At its height, the kingdom supported a population of 5,000. Mapungubwe was abandoned in the 14th century when climate changes resulted in the area becoming colder and drier, leading to migrations north to Zimbabwe. The site was discovered in 1932, and was excavated by the University of Pretoria, but their findings were not made public knowledge until 2002, when a room containing a wealth of archaeological artifacts was discovered. Mapungubwe was made a World Heritage Site in 2003.

ENTER MRS PLES

The most famous of all hominid fossils in South Africa is the skull of an *Australopithecus africanus* discovered in 1947 at Sterkfontein Caves, near Krugersdorp. The skull, the most complete example of an Australopithecine skull found by archaeologists, is affectionately known as 'Mrs Ples', a nickname derived from the former species name, 'Plesianthropus', which means 'almost human'. *Australopithecus africanus* is believed to be a distant relative of mankind, and the discovery by Dr. Robert Broom received international publicity. 'Mrs Ples' and her relatives lived in South Africa around 2.5 million years ago, sharing some of our traits such as walking upright. But 'Mrs' Ples is now known to be a 'Mr'—a CAT scan in 2002 revealed that the skull belonged to an adolescent male.

ART OF THE PAST

The sandstone caves of the Drakensberg are some of the best places in the world to see rock art. Here the caves are covered with the intriguing shapes, images and depictions produced by the San, who were once prolific in the area but were driven out by European settlers. Most of the best-preserved paintings are fairly recent, dating back some 200 to 300 years, but they form part of a long-standing tradition; some of the earliest cave paintings in southern Africa date from 28,000 years ago. There have been numerous attempts to interpret the meaning of the images, but the most popular theory maintains that they were a mix of scenes from daily life, such as hunting and tracking, and images used in magic and rituals, one of which was a trance-like dance thought to influence weather and hunting possibilities.

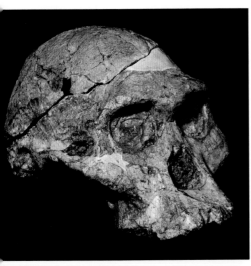

The first European to set foot on South African soil was Portuguese explorer Bartolomeu Dias, who landed at Mossel Bay in 1488 on his way to the spice islands of Asia. Over the next 200 years more Portuguese traders and their Dutch and British competitors made the journey to the east via the Cape of Good Hope. The hostile reception they received from the Khoi discouraged permanent settlers, but the Cape became an important restocking point. It was not until 1652 that the Dutch East India Company (the Vereenigde Oostindische Compagnie, or VOC) built a fort and established a supply station under the command of Jan van Riebeeck. A permanent settlement grew as workers completed their contracts and settled as farmers. As the settlers moved east and north they came into increasing contact with Bantu-speaking Africans, which prompted uneasy trading relations and a state of almost constant warfare. During the 18th century, Dutch power began to wane, and in 1795 the British sailed into False Bay and annexed the Dutch colony. Their sovereignty was finally accepted by other European powers in a peace settlement of 1816. The British set out to fund their expansion and, in 1834, to ban slavery—much to the chagrin of many Dutch settlers.

Clockwise from above *Dutch governor Jan van Riebeeck entertains native Khoi on the claversingel; depiction of the Great Trek—Boer farmers emigrating north to the Transvaal; Shaka Zulu, the famous 19th-century Zulu leader*

EVA OR KROTOA?

In the late 1650s, Jan van Riebeeck took a young local girl into his household. Krotoa, or Eva as she became known by the Dutch, was from a local Khoi tribe but became completely assimilated in the van Riebeeck household. She was educated with his daughters, baptized and formally adopted by the family. Eva became an important link between the Dutch settlers and the local tribal groups, although she struggled with her identity from the start. In 1664, Eva married Pieter van Meerhof, the station's doctor, becoming the first indigenous person to marry a European. Her story has an unhappy ending: Her husband perished during a trip to Madagascar and she ended her years as an alcoholic, shunned by both European and Khoi society.

VOICES FROM THE PAST

In mid-2003, developers in the district of Green Point outside Cape Town unearthed a mass grave, thought to be more than 200 years old. Archaeologists uncovered upwards of a thousand individual bodies. Most were thought to have been slaves, and the findings were a shocking reminder of the city's past. The graves were shallow and disordered, most bodies were buried without coffins, and tests on bones and teeth revealed harsh living conditions, back-breaking work and a poor diet. By the time the slave trade was halted in the British Empire, around 63,000 slaves had been brought to the Cape.

Although slaves were of African descent, many of the later peoples came from the Indian subcontinent and southeast Asia, a legacy that can still be seen in the Cape Malay culture.

THE GREAT TREK

Having had enough of being told what to do by the British, scores of Dutch settlers (Boers) set out with their families and servants in search of new land beyond the British colonial boundaries. Between 1835 and 1840, around 5,000 people left the Cape colony and headed north and east in a movement that became known as the Great Trek. They were called the Voortrekkers, a hardy bunch who overcame harsh obstacles. Their experiences became fertile ground for 20th-century Afrikaner nationalism, and the Voortrekkers were used as a symbol of Afrikaner culture. One thing not often mentioned in the myths that grew up around the Trek is that a large number of Khoi servants and freed slaves also made the journey alongside their masters or patrons.

INTERNATIONAL LANGUAGE

Afrikaans is the language of around 60 per cent of the white population and 90 per cent of the non-white population, but it was recognized as a distinct language only in 1925. Originally spoken by Dutch settlers and the imported workforce of indentured labourers and slaves from Asia and East Africa, it was regarded as a dialect, and remains closely related to 17th-century Dutch. Cape Dutch (as it was known) had a gradually diverging vocabulary, absorbing words from various languages — those of European settlers (German, French and English), of slaves and workers from Indonesia and East Africa, and of the indigenous Khoi and San. Many Afrikaans words clearly indicate their exotic origins. One such is *piesang*, meaning banana, which comes from the Malay word *pisang*.

SHAKA ZULU

The early 19th century heralded an era of radical change among Bantu-speaking Africans in the east. Under the command of the most famous pre-colonial African, Shaka Zulu, the Zulu nation was transformed into an enormously powerful political and military force. He set about raiding and defeating all surrounding chiefdoms using his *impis*, organized regiments of full-time soldiers. During the 1820s the *impis* (who amounted to a 40,000-strong army) became increasingly predatory, while at home Shaka's reign grew ever more autocratic; his punishments of any sign of opposition were notorious. This led to a period of unprecedented disruption, fighting and suffering throughout the region. Shaka's reign of terror eventually came to an end in 1828 when he was assassinated by one of his half brothers, Dingane.

In the mid-1800s, two separate republics, the Orange Free State and the Transvaal, were established by the Boers. The British meanwhile set up the new colony of Natal based around present-day Durban, but this and the Cape remained of little importance to the British Empire. This was all to change in 1867 when alluvial diamonds were discovered near the confluence of the Harts and Vaal rivers. By 1872, tens of thousands of fortune-hunters had converged on the site, which soon revealed itself as the world's richest diamond pipe. In 1886, there was a further mineral discovery: of gold on the Witwatersrand in the Transvaal Republic. Miners from across the world rushed to the new reef, and the main town on the Rand, Johannesburg, grew rapidly. Boer President Paul Kruger (1825–1904) saw a serious threat to Afrikaner independence as huge numbers of newcomers, mostly British, descended on the gold fields. The British demanded that voting rights be given to the 60,000 foreign whites on the Witwatersrand, but Kruger refused, and war broke out in October 1899. The Second Anglo-Boer War lasted until 1902, and included a series of humiliating defeats for the British, although the latter's scorched earth policy finally brought the Boers to surrender.

GANDHI'S ROLE

Mohandas Karamchand Gandhi, who arrived in Natal in 1893 to work as a lawyer, had his first taste of racial discrimination shortly after his arrival. During a train journey, he was thrown from the carriage at Pietermaritzburg station after refusing to move to a third-class carriage (car). During the Second Anglo-Boer War, he observed that the role of South African Indians was confined to bearing stretchers for the wounded—a duty which Gandhi undertook himself during the battle of Spion Kop. He took up the Indian cause and developed his philosophy of non-violent resistance. He led huge protest marches and sparked off strikes by Indian workers. When he returned to India in 1914, he was already being called the 'Great Soul' or Mahatma.

Clockwise from above *The British are defeated by the Zulus at Isandhlwana, 1879; Cecil Rhodes, prime minister of the Cape Colony; the British are defeated by the Boers at Spioenkop, 1890*

THE GRAND IMPERIALIST

Cecil John Rhodes (1853–1902) played a central role in the history of southern Africa. Born in England, he moved to South Africa at the age of 17, and soon went to Kimberley to make his fortune—he slowly bought up shares in diamond-buying concerns. He spent a year at Oxford University, returning to South Africa in 1874, where he gained control of diamond-mining activities—by the late 1880s he had the monopoly. He then set his sights on a career in politics, and by 1890 he was prime minister of the Cape Colony. Rhodes continued to advocate British expansion, including the founding of the colony which took his name—Rhodesia (now Zimbabwe and Zambia). Rhodes remained hugely influential until his death in 1902.

SCORCHED EARTH

During the Second Anglo-Boer War, the infamous scorched earth policy (burning farmhouses and flushing out Boer support) of the British commander Lord Kitchener (1850–1916) left much of the countryside a smouldering wasteland, and tens of thousands of Boer women and children were made homeless. The British decided to introduce 'concentration camps', to which these destitute people were brought. Poor administration meant that food and medical supplies in the camps ran out, leading to 26,000 deaths. Memories of the British scorched earth policy were often revived by Afrikaner politicians during the 20th century. Less widely known was the policy of rounding up African workers and placing them in similar concentration camps; at least 14,000 died.

STARVING OUT THE ENEMY

October 1899 to February 1900 saw the most famous of the Boer War sieges, that of the diamond capital Kimberley. Some 4,000 Boer soldiers marched on the town, hemming in 500 British troops and 50,000 civilians, including Cecil Rhodes. Although the Boers failed to break through the town's defences, they did their best to starve Kimberley into surrender. However, the extensive stores owned by the De Beers Diamond Mining Company meant that food never ran out. The inhabitants did suffer, however, and—inevitably—the African population suffered the most. There were widespread cases of scurvy and high infant mortality. The arrival of fresh British troops at nearby Modder River sparked an attack on the Boers and the town was finally relieved. With that, the whole impetus of the war turned against the Boers.

BRITAIN'S WORST DEFEAT

When Lord Chelmsford (1827–1905) invaded Zululand in January 1879, it was thought that the Zulus, armed only with their shields and spears, would suffer a swift defeat. In reality, the Anglo-Zulu War became one of the most documented wars in southern Africa, and brought about the worst defeat in British colonial history. Isandhlwana was the site of the first—and for Britain, the worst—battle of the war, when thousands of Zulu warriors, under the command of King Cetshwayo, advanced on the poorly prepared British troops. More than 1,300 British soldiers and their African allies were killed. It took another five months of fighting for the British, under the command of Lord Chelmsford, to defeat the Zulus, at the battle at Ulundi. Although Cetshwayo attempted to regain control of part of his former kingdom he was eventually deposed and died in exile in 1884.

Following the Boers' surrender to the British in 1902, the British and Boer territories moved towards union, and a unified South Africa came into being in 1910. The Act of Union and the entrenchment of voting arrangements in the Boer republics, by which Africans were denied any political rights, felt like a powerful slap in the face for many. Most had supported the British during the Anglo-Boer War and had assumed that their loyalty would be recognized in the post-war settlement. Black and coloured (mixed race; ▷ 7) people in the Cape had their voting rights embedded in the Constitution, but they feared that the Cape government's willingness to placate the two northern former republics was a very bad omen. In 1936 these voting rights were removed by law. There was also a rise in opposition movements at this time. Many of these were spurred on by the Land Act of 1913, which prohibited black people from buying or leasing land outside the designated 'native' reserves, effectively restricting black access to just 8 per cent of South Africa's land. Afrikaners, meanwhile, were also dissatisfied. In the early 20th century, many were forced to move to the cities. Caught between the British who dominated the economy, and black workers, who competed with them for jobs, their plight came to be known as the 'poor white problem'.

BIRTH OF THE ANC

The changing laws regarding voting rights began to stir up more opposition to white dominance. In 1911, Pixley ka Isaka Seme (1882–1951), a lawyer, called on Africans to forget the differences of the past and unite as one national organization. On 8 January 1912, more than 100 tribal chiefs and church and community leaders gathered in Bloemfontein and formed the South African Native National Congress, later renamed the African National Congress. Under Seme's leadership, the ANC was politically moderate and its most common form of protest was to make appeals to the Imperial authorities.

A NEW BREED

The year 1944 saw the dawn of a new era in African nationalism, when a fiery idealist named Nelson Mandela (1918–) joined forces with Oliver Tambo (1917–93), Walter Sisulu (1912–2003) and Anton Lembede (1914–47) to form the ANC Youth League. While the traditional ANC had limped ineffectually along, the Youth League injected a fierce Africanist ideology and refused to work with other organizations. These militant young activists revitalized the ANC, led by Lembede and his rejection of moderate opposition. Industrial strikes became a key weapon in the fight against oppression, and in 1946 the African Mineworkers' Union launched a crippling strike with more than 100,000 gold-mine workers laying down their tools.

CHAMPION OF THE WORKERS

The first few decades of the 20th century saw a burst of short-lived but radical opposition movements. The most successful of these was the Industrial and Commercial Union (ICU), led by the charismatic Clements Kadalie (1896–1951). A champion of farmers' and workers' rights, at just 23 he led a prominent dock strike in Cape Town, which forced managers to accede to demands for significant wage increases and better working conditions. By 1926, he had created a membership of more than 150,000 workers. His success did not last, however; internal rifts led to the downfall of the ICU in 1928. Kadalie was arrested for apparently inciting racial tension but later settled in East London and became involved in the ANC.

Clockwise from left *The Great Trek frieze in the Voortrekker Monument, Pretoria; British and South African soldiers capture Cassino, 1944; the Boer Peace Treaty is signed in 1902 by Christiaan De Wet and Kitchener*

SOUTH AFRICA GETS ITS CALL UP

White and black South Africans made contributions to the Allied effort during both World Wars. In 1917, during World War I, the sinking of the SS *Mendi* carrying about 850 South African troops from Cape Town to France bears witness to a remarkable tale of brotherhood and bravery in the face of death. About 805 black privates, five white officers and the ship's crew sang and danced together as the ship sank, with the loss of all still on board and many who leapt into the icy waters. South Africa's political involvement was at the highest level with the then Prime Minister General Jan Smuts serving as a member of British Prime Minister Lloyd George's war cabinet during 1917–18. Smuts was also a very good friend of British Prime Minister Winston Churchill. In fact, Churchill had such a high opinion of his old friend that he even toyed with the idea of leaving Smuts in charge of Britain when he went to the Teheran Conference in 1943.

CELEBRATIONS WITH A STING IN THE TAIL

In 1938, D. F. Malan (1874–1959) and his colleagues at the right-wing Gesuiwerde Nationale Party (GNP, or the Purified National Party) rallied the white Afrikaner population to take part in a commemorative celebration of the Great Trek (▷ 33). A team of ox wagons journeyed from Cape Town to Pretoria in a symbolic re-enactment of the Trek, and by the time the wagons reached Pretoria, more than 200,000 Afrikaners had gathered in the city to join forces with them and take part in the festival. Malan — who was soon to become the first leader of an apartheid government — succeeded in whipping up nationalistic fervour. The foundation stones were laid for the Voortrekker Monument (which today stands more as a monument to skewed interpretations of history) on 16 December. This happened to be the exact date when, a hundred years earlier, the Zulus had been defeated by the Boers at the Battle of Blood River.

Although the first apartheid government was voted in under D. F. Malan in 1948, the full agenda of legislation was not finalized until the mid-1950s. The term 'apartheid' simply means 'apartness', and the ruling Nationalist Party stated that their long-term aim was the total separation of races. In the meantime, they had to be practical and recognize that white industry relied upon African labour. In effect, apartheid became a way of ensuring a continuous supply of cheap labour while denying Africans any political rights. Legislation such as the Group Areas Act tightened previous segregation regulations, and the government launched a massive national campaign to remove Africans from urban areas. Africans living in vibrant urban communities, such as Sophiatown in Johannesburg, were forcibly removed to bleak townships away from central city districts. The 1960s saw a huge upsurge of opposition from the ANC and the new, more militant Pan African Congress (PAC), particularly against the hated pass laws, which dictated that the black population carry identity documents at all times, severely restricting their movements. The government responded brutally: Violent suppression became the norm; both the ANC and PAC were banned; and forced removals increased as the government set about dividing the country into clear racial zones and 'homelands'.

THE SHARPEVILLE MASSACRE

In March 1960, the Pan African Congress called on all Africans to leave their passes at home and present themselves at the nearest police station. They hoped that the prison system would be swamped and the pass laws revoked. On 21 March, large crowds gathered across the country, but were dispersed by police. In the township of Sharpeville, however, the crowd stayed on the streets even when they were buzzed by jets. At 1.15pm there was a scuffle and the police panicked. They later claimed that they had come under attack but this has been denied by almost all eyewitness accounts. What is clear is that the police opened fire on the crowd with sten guns. The terrified people ran for cover but the police continued to fire on them as they fled. Most of the 69 dead and 180 wounded were shot in the back.

Clockwise from above The District Six Museum in Cape Town commemorates a once vibrant mixed area of the city that was destroyed by apartheid; Steve Biko, leading anti-apartheid campaigner in the 1970s; segregation extended right down to the country's shoreline at the height of apartheid

ARCHITECT OF APARTHEID

Hendrik Verwoerd (1901–66), prime minister from 1958 to 1966, did much to push through early segregationist legislation. He set up the system of independent homelands, where Africans were to govern themselves away from the white areas. In 1961, with growing friction between South Africa and Britain, he succeeded in creating the Republic of South Africa. The new republic was expelled from the British Commonwealth. Verwoerd appointed John Vorster as Justice Minister, in which post he passed a string of repressive laws. In 1966, Verwoerd was killed in a fatal stabbing. Ironically, the assassination was not racially motivated: Dimitri Tsafendas said that he had been ordered to assassinate Verwoerd by the tapeworm in his stomach.

THE SOWETO UPRISING

A key turning point in protests against apartheid was the pupil protests of 1976, in which black school children took to the streets to protest against new rules enforcing the Afrikaans language in schools. On 16 June, a school pupils' committee in the black township of Soweto organized a mass march to deliver their grievances to the authorities. This peaceful march was met with a brutal and shocking response. Police opened fire on the crowd, killing 13-year-old Hector Pieterson. After the Soweto Uprising, as the incident became known, rioting erupted around the country and a constant and violent level of unrest spread through the townships. By the following year, more than 500 protestors had been killed in the revolts. The 16 June is now a national holiday — Youth Day.

THE WORLD'S FIRST HEART TRANSPLANT

During the late 1960s, a virtually unknown South African surgeon by the name of Christiaan Barnard performed the world's first human heart transplant at Cape Town's Groote Schuur hospital. The operation turned Barnard into an instant celebrity and put South Africa on the medical map. The brilliant doctor travelled the world giving lectures and was celebrated wherever he went, including being received by the Pope in Rome and President Johnson in the US. Before performing the transplant, Barnard had spent years experimenting with the procedure. Barnard went on to pioneer other heart-related operations and devoted the last part of his career to slowing the aging process. Arthritis forced Barnard to end his career in the 1980s. He died in 2001 of an asthma attack while on holiday in Cyprus at the age of 78.

CRY FREEDOM

One of the best-known names in the struggle against apartheid is Steve Biko (1946–77). He was co-founder and president of the Black Peoples Convention (BPC), the leading black consciousness movement in the 1970s. In 1973, Biko was banned as an individual by the government and suffered numerous arrests and interrogations. On 12 September 1977, he died in police custody. His death was blamed on a hunger strike, but the work of Donald Woods, the editor of the East London *Daily Dispatch*, put pressure on the government to open an inquest (this campaign was the subject of the movie *Cry Freedom*, 1987). The inquest revealed that Biko died of brain damage, but it was not until the 1990s that this was attributed to beatings while in custody. However, the influence of the Truth and Reconciliation Committee meant that no one was ever charged with his murder.

ROAD TO FREEDOM

By the late 1980s, the government had more or less lost control of large portions of the townships. Growing unrest and international sanctions were hitting the economy hard. The government, fearing revolution, was forced to embark on a gradual series of reforms under the presidency of P. W. Botha (1916–2006), who set about dismantling some of the segregationist policies. However, this did nothing to assuage the unrest and was seen as little more than an attempt to hold off further sanctions. Following a stroke, Botha was replaced by F. W. de Klerk (1936–), who was handed the reins of a country in turmoil. He revoked the ban on the ANC and released Nelson Mandela in 1990, launching a new era of reform. De Klerk signed an agreement with Mandela in May 1990 to revoke repressive laws and release political prisoners. Mandela persuaded the ANC to stop armed resistance, and a fragile process of negotiation began. The next four years saw escalating levels of violence and the negotiations repeatedly broke down, but on 27 April 1994 the first democratic elections passed peacefully.

THE BANG-BANG CLUB
As violence rocketed in the townships in the early 1990s, a small team of photojournalists took to the streets to record what was going on. The foursome, made up of Ken Oosterbroek, Kevin Carter, Greg Marinovich and Joao Silva were nicknamed the 'Bang-Bang Club', a reference to the fighting (or the bang-bang of a gun) they witnessed. The name stuck and their images of the horrific violence, murders and gangland executions remain the most compelling record of the 'Hostel Wars'. The horror of their subject matter took its toll: Oosterbroek was killed in crossfire on 18 April 1994, and Kevin Carter committed suicide a few weeks after winning the Pulitzer Prize for a photograph of a starving child in the Sudan. The remaining members published their story, *The Bang-Bang Club*, in 2000.

Clockwise from above *Muhammad Yunus, Mary Robinson, Kofi Annan, Graca Machel (Mandela's wife), Nelson Mandela, Jimmy Carter, Li Zhaoxing and Archbishop Tutu at the launch of a humanitarian campaign in Johannesburg, 2007; aerial view of the all-white community of Orania; black township residents lining up to vote in the first national elections in 1994*

THE FIRST ELECTIONS

On 27 April 1994, Nelson Mandela, at the age of 76, voted for the first time in his country's elections. More than 19 million people, around 91 per cent of registered voters, joined him at the polls, most of them for the first time in their lives. Despite very long waits, voting was peaceful and the ANC won by a landslide. On 10 May, Mandela was inaugurated as South Africa's first black president in front of 60,000 cheering supporters. His inauguration speech was watched by millions and his pledge stirred the nation: 'We shall build a society in which all South Africans, both black and white, will be able to walk tall, without any fear in their hearts, assured of their inalienable right to human dignity — a rainbow nation at peace with itself and the world.' During his five-year presidency Mandela (known affectionately as 'Madiba') was credited for the largely peaceful transition from apartheid to black and white unity in the country.

NAMIBIA LEADS THE WAY

South Africa's history has been intertwined in more ways than one with its northern, desert neighbour. Namibia, or South West Africa as it was then known, was effectively run as a South African province from 1920, when the former German colony was given to South Africa to administer as a mandate after World War I. Unlike other countries that were given mandates, South Africa refused to surrender control of Namibia to the United Nations, ignoring pressure from the world community. The apartheid regime proceeded to pursue its racist policies of homelands and segregation and it was only after decades of continuous pressure from the international community that negotiations in New York led to South Africa eventually granting Namibia independence in 1988. Free elections were held in the early 1990s and a majority government was voted into power.

ONE STREET, TWO PRIZES

South Africa has the distinction of having the only street in the world that produced not one but two Nobel peace prize laureates. The famous Vilakazi Street in Soweto township was home to both former South African president Nelson Mandela and outspoken anti-apartheid cleric Desmond Tutu. Tutu, who was awarded the prize in 1984 after being nominated for the third time, humbly declared at the ceremony that he was merely 'a little focus' of the stalwarts of the struggle for freedom from apartheid. Mandela received his Nobel peace prize in 1993 together with former president F. W. de Klerk as the country headed towards its first democratic election in the following year. The Nobel committee said the award was in recognition of their work on 'the peaceful termination of the apartheid regime, and for laying the foundations for a new democratic South Africa'.

POCKET OF THE PAST

Hidden in the dusty depths of the Northern Cape is the small town of Orania, unexceptional but for one thing: It is inhabited exclusively by whites. Founded in 1991 by Afrikaner professor Carel Boshoff, Orania is dedicated to white separatism and the creation of an Afrikaner Volkstaat, or 'people's state'. What was originally a community of just eight families has grown to more than 1,500 residents, drawn by a fear of crime and a longing for the return of apartheid. The village is guarded by a statue of Hendrik Verwoerd (1901–66), revered as the architect of apartheid, although the town is not closed to black visitors. Over recent years, however, Orania has tried to distance itself from racial implications and instead uphold itself as a model of environmentally-friendly living, with the aim of merely maintaining a traditional Afrikaner culture. In 2010 the country's black president, Jacob Zuma, visited the community.

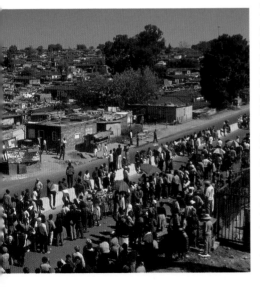

Above *HIV/AIDS activist outside the US consulate in Cape Town, 2004*
Left *Nelson Mandela (centre) with South Africa's current president, Jacob Zuma (left), and former president Thabo Mbeki (right)*

Few envied Nelson Mandela (1918–) the task of dealing with the aftermath of apartheid, but few could imagine any meaningful progress without his leadership. Mandela commanded huge popular support among the African population and won the backing of much of South Africa's white population as well. During his presidency, he managed successful negotiations for a new constitution, launched a reconstruction plan that put housing, health and education at the forefront, and instigated the Truth and Reconciliation Commission (see right). Some areas experienced more success than others: The government failed to build its promised one million new houses by 2000, but it did bring water and electricity to the majority of homes. President Jacob Zuma (1942–), elected in 2009, faces different problems. The divisions of apartheid still affect the country, but poverty, unemployment and HIV/AIDS are the most pressing challenges.

THE HEALING OF OLD WOUNDS

A crucial step in the healing process of post-apartheid South Africa was the creation of the Truth and Reconciliation Commission (TRC), headed by Archbishop Desmond Tutu. The aim of the commission was to uncover the atrocities of apartheid—but not to punish its perpetrators. The commission sat from April 1996 until July 1998, during which time it heard testimonies from more than 20,000 people, revealing harrowing stories of torture, disappearance and murder. Both victims and perpetrators could give their accounts, and those who confessed to their crimes could apply for amnesty from prosecution. The TRC became a vital component in the transition to full and free democracy, and despite some flaws, was lauded as an enormous success.

LOVE LIFE

No issue is more important in South Africa today than that of HIV/AIDS. There are more people living with the disease here than in any other country, and an estimated 900 people die of it every single day. AIDS is the biggest killer in the country. It is also an issue that landed former president Thabo Mbeki in hot water. His famous denial that HIV causes AIDS was followed by uproar, not least because his stance was preventing the free distribution of anti-retroviral drugs. This policy was reversed in 2003, and national campaigns, such as the hugely successful Love Life campaign, aim to educate young people about AIDS. Current president Jacob Zuma, however, fuels controversy by admitting to unsafe sex in his polygamous relationships and by announcing himself to be HIV negative.

ON THE MOVE

On the Move gives you detailed advice and information about the various options for travelling to South Africa before explaining the best ways to get around the country once you are there. Handy tips help you with everything from buying tickets to renting a car.

ARRIVING BY AIR

The three main international airports are in Johannesburg, Cape Town and Durban. Johannesburg's O. R. Tambo International Airport is the regional hub, with many daily flights to Europe, North America, Asia and Australia. Although most flights arrive in Johannesburg, some carriers fly directly to Cape Town. There is a huge choice of routes, but for the lowest fares you need to book at least three months in advance, especially over Christmas.

AIRLINES

South Africa's national carrier is South African Airways (SAA), but most major international carriers fly here, including British Airways, Virgin Atlantic, KLM, Lufthansa, Delta and Qantas (▷ 46).

AIRPORTS

O. R. Tambo International

Airport (ORTIA), formerly known as Johannesburg International, is at Kempton Park on the R24, 24km (15 miles) northeast of central Jo'burg. The airport now ranks as the major hub for air travel in southern Africa, with almost 60 airlines carrying 17 million passengers annually. International flights usually arrive early in the morning and depart in the late afternoon or evening.

There are two terminals, Terminal A and Terminal B. Work that began in 2009 to expand and improve the airport in preparation for the 2010 World Cup is ongoing. Terminal A is for international air traffic; Terminal B is for domestic air traffic. In both terminals departures are on the upper level, while arrivals are handled on the lower level.

There are information kiosks in International Arrivals and Departures, and Domestic Arrivals (tel 011-9216262). Baggage trolleys and porter services are available at designated areas in each terminal and also in the drop-off areas. There are orange-uniformed porters (look

Above *South African Airways jet at Cape Town airport*

for their ACSA permits) in each terminal; expect to pay around R5 per item of luggage.

The VAT Refund desk is in the lounge of International Departures in Terminal A (for information on VAT refunds, ▷ 289). There are elevators in all terminals, suitable for wheelchair users (two are equipped with Braille).

Each terminal has restaurants and snack bars, shops selling a range of newspapers, clothes and gifts, plus banks (▷ 45). International Arrivals has desks for the rental of mobile phones and South African SIM cards (▷ 299), and a post office. There is a duty free shopping mall in International Departures, with an extensive range of shops, including the second biggest duty free gift shop in the world. Internet access is available in International Departures. Left (stored) luggage (tel 011-

3901804), on the upper level of the parking area near International Arrivals, is open 24 hours, and costs R50 per item.

There are ATMs on the public concourse of International Arrivals, Domestic Arrivals, level 1, and the Domestic Departures public concourse and lounge. Foreign currency exchange is available at branches of ABSA Bank, American Express, Rennies/Thomas Cook Foreign Exchange and Master Currency, all on the public concourse of the International Arrivals Hall. ABSA Bank also has an exchange service for foreign nationals in the International Departures lounge

Cape Town International Airport
(CPT), formerly known as D. F. Malan, has a large volume of international and domestic flights passing through every day. It's the second largest airport in South Africa, with an annual turnover of 7.2 million passengers. The airport is 22km (13.5 miles) from central Cape Town, a 20-minute drive on the N2. There is an international

and a domestic terminal, connected via a walkway. Both terminals have undergone substantial refurbishment in recent years.

Long-haul flights arrive in the morning and depart in the late afternoon or evening.

International Departures has a public concourse filled with cafés mall-style duty-free shops and other stores (selling newspapers, luggage and gifts) and cafés. Other facilities include a bank, an ATM and an ABSA bureau de change. International Arrivals has an ATM and a Master Currency bureau de change; a restaurant and bar are on

the upper level. Arrivals also holds all the major car rental desks, as well as desks where you can rent mobile phones and South African SIM cards (▷ 299). There is a tourist office desk in the middle of the hall.

The VAT Refund desk is to the left of the check-in desks in the International Departures hall (for information on VAT Refunds, ▷ 289).

Domestic Arrivals has two ATMs, cafés and a post office. Domestic Departures has a bank, three ATMs and an ABSA bureau de change. Left luggage (tel 021-9362884) is in the Domestic Arrivals Terminal, costing R15 per bag per day.

TRANSFERS FROM AIRPORT TO CITY			
	JOHANNESBURG (JNB)	**CAPE TOWN (CPT)**	**DURBAN (DUR)**
DISTANCE	24km (15 miles)	22km (13.5 miles)	35km (21 miles)
TAXI	Taxi stand outside main terminal building Price: around R350	Taxi stand outside International and Domestic terminals Price: around R200	Taxi stand outside Arrivals Terminal Price: around R150
	Journey time: 20 min	Journey time: 20 min	Journey time: 30 min
	Airport Link Taxis: tel 011-7922017	Touchdown Taxis (official operator): tel 021-9194659	Taxi Izzy Cabs: tel 0833-86254; www.izzycabs.co.za
SHUTTLE BUS	Magic Bus: tel 011-5480822	Magic Bus: tel 021-5056300;	Shuttle Bus: King Shaka Shuttles:
	Airport Link Shuttle: tel 011-7948300;	www.magicbus.co.za	tel 031-3017165;
	www.airportlink.co.za	Way 2 Go: tel 021-6380300;	www.kingshakashuttles.co.za
	Both drop off at the major hotels in	www.way2gotransfers.co.za	Drop off at the major hotels in and
	Johannesburg and Pretoria. Reserve	City Hopper: tel 021-9344440	around Durban.
	seats ahead.	Desks in Arrivals, but it's cheaper to	Price R250
	Price: R250–R335	reserve seats ahead: the bigger the	
	A free shuttle bus connects hotels	group, the lower the fare per person.	
	within the airport's environs.	Price: R120	
	Some backpacker hostels provide free		
	pick-up (arrange ahead).		
CAR RENTAL	Desks are in Parkade Centre, opposite	Desks are in the international	Desks are in the arrivals hall.
	main terminal building across from	arrivals hall.	Avis: tel 032-4367800
	pick-up/drop-off zone.	Avis: tel 021-9278800	Budget: tel 032-4365500
	Avis: tel 011-3945433	Budget: tel 021-3803140	Europcar: tel 032-4359500
	Budget: tel 011-2301200	Europcar: tel 021-9358600	Hertz: tel 032-4360300
	Europcar: tel 011-3903909	Hertz: tel 021-9353000	
	Hertz: tel 011-3909700		

USEFUL TELEPHONE NUMBERS AND WEBSITES

Airports

General: www.acsa.co.za

Johannesburg: tel 011-9216262

Cape Town: tel 021-9371200

Durban: tel 032-4366000

Airlines

British Airways: tel 011-4418400;
www.britishairways.com

Delta: tel 011-4824582; www.delta.com

Emirates: tel 011-3901215;
www.emirates.com

Kenya Airways: tel 082-2345786;
www.kenya-airways.com

KLM: tel 011-8819696; www.klm.com

Lufthansa: tel 0861-842538;
www.lufthansa.com

Qantas: tel 011-4418550; www.qantas.com

Singapore Airlines: tel 011-8808560;
www.singaporeair.com

South African Airways: tel 011-9785313;
www.flysaa.com

Virgin: 011-3403400; www.virgin-atlantic.com

Trains

Shosholoza Meyl: tel 086-000888;
www.shosholozameyl.co.za

The Blue Train: tel 012-3348459;
www.bluetrain.co.za

The Pride of Africa, (operated by Rovos Rail):
tel 012-3158242; www.rovos.co.za

Car rental companies

www.avis.co.za

www.budget.co.za

www.europcar.co.za

www.hertz.co.za

King Shaka International Airport

In 2010 Durban's original international airport was replaced, with this new airport in La Mercy district north of the city and named after a renowned Zulu warrior. While it is still the smallest of the country's international airports it is now able to handle far more air traffic and larger aircraft, and is an important domestic hub as well.

The airport has one terminal, with departures located on the upper level and arrivals on the ground floor. All the usual facilities, such as ATMs and bureaux de change can be found in the arrivals area, as well as a wide range of shops, cafés and restaurants. There's also an outdoor piazza. Also on the ground floor are a tourist information centre, providing advice and literature about the KwaZulu-Natal region, internet facilities, and offices of all the major car rental companies.

The Transfers chart (▷ 45) has more information on getting from the airports to the cities, and lists the telephone numbers of the main car rental companies.

CAR RENTAL

South Africa is best explored by road, and many visitors choose to rent a car on arrival. All the major airports have car rental desks (▷ 45), although it is wise to make an advance reservation, especially during high season.

» You will need a full driver's licence to rent a car, but it will be valid only if it is printed in English and includes your photograph. Otherwise, you should obtain an international driving permit in your home country before departing for South Africa.

» The minimum age for drivers is usually 21; those under 23 may have to pay an additional levy of R50.

» A credit card (or cash) deposit will be needed when you pick up your keys.

» Thoroughly check your rental car before you set off and point out any scratches, dents or other anomalies. These must be marked on the rental form, otherwise you may find you are charged for the damage when you return the vehicle.

» Most rental companies rent out cars with full tanks of petrol (gas). Be sure to remember to fill up just before returning the car, or you risk being charged much more for fuel by the car rental firm than you would pay at a petrol station.

» Given South Africa's size, and the amount of ground you are likely to cover, it is a good idea to opt for an unlimited kilometre package, rather than being limited to a set distance per day.

» Check if there are any limits to taking the car off road. This is

Above *Intercape buses connect a vast number of cities throughout southern Africa* **Opposite** *All the major car rental firms are represented at South Africa's major airports*

particularly important if you plan to drive yourself around one of the national parks, as some roads in the reserves are unsurfaced and could be outside the scope of your rental agreement.

» Let the rental company know in advance if you intend to take a car into neighbouring countries such as Swaziland and Lesotho, as you will require extra paperwork from them to cross borders.

» Particular hazards worth watching out for include stray animals and people walking in the road, especially at night or in the countryside, and hijackers, particularly in and around the big cities and on quiet country roads. Never stop for anyone other than the police, whose vehicles are clearly marked.

» See pages 55–57 for more advice on driving in South Africa, including rules of the road and speed limits.

ARRIVING OVERLAND

There are good roads between South Africa and Namibia, Botswana, Mozambique, Lesotho, Swaziland and Zimbabwe. The Department of Home Affairs in Pretoria (tel 012-8106323) can provide up-to-date details of the opening and closing times of border posts.

Main Entry Points

Botswana The main border crossings into South Africa are at Pioneer Gate, Ramatlabama and Tlokweng Gate. The crossing is usually swift and efficient. The R49 from the Tlokwen border point connects with the N4 at Zeerust, heading towards Johannesburg. From Ramatlabama there is a road leading to Mafikeng, which connects with the R52 to Jo'burg.

Lesotho From Lesotho, the main border crossings are Maseru Bridge, Maputsoe Bridge and Calendonspoort. There are several other crossings, such as Sani Pass, that are open for limited periods and can be crossed only in a 4WD vehicle and, in some cases, on horseback or on foot.

Mozambique The journey by road between South Africa and Maputo has improved due to the completion of the section of toll road between Mbombela (Nelspruit) and Maputo via the border at Komatipoort.

Namibia The main crossing point is Vioolsdrif, with less frequently used border crossings at Ariamsvlei and Rietfontein.

Swaziland Crossings between South Africa and Swaziland are at Ngwenya/Oshoek, Lavumisa and Mahamba. The N17 then the R33 heads from Oshoek to Johannesburg via Carolina.

Zimbabwe The only border crossing between Zimbabwe and South Africa is at Beitbridge. It is a notoriously slow crossing at peak times, with long waits and time-consuming baggage searches.

Arriving by Long-Distance Bus

Three main long-distance bus companies cover routes across South Africa's borders, and some services go as far as Malawi.

» Translux (tel 011-7738056 from overseas or 0861-589282 in South Africa; www.translux.co.za) runs buses from Johannesburg to Blantyre (Malawi), Bulawayo and Harare (Zimbabwe) and Lusaka (Zambia), and from Pretoria to Maputo (Mozambique).

» Intercape (tel 012-3804400 from overseas or 0861-287287 in South Africa; www.intercape.co.za) runs buses from Johannesburg and Pretoria to Gaborone (Botswana), Windhoek (Namibia), Maputo (Mozambique) and Victoria Falls in Zimbabwe (via Namibia).

» Greyhound (tel 011-2768500 from overseas or 083-9159000 in South Africa; www.greyhound.co.za) runs buses from Pretoria to Maputo (Mozambique), Harare and Bulawayo (Zimbabwe).

Arriving by Car

If crossing any international borders in a private car, you must have the vehicle registration document, insurance and a driver's licence printed in English with your photograph. If you've rented a car, it's important to check with the rental company that you are permitted to drive the car into another country.

If you are planning to drive around South Africa, remember that distances are vast and the going can be slow, even though roads are generally good (▷ 48).

GETTING AROUND

South Africa has an efficient transportation network with the best road system and flight network in Africa. Highways (motorways/expressways) are of a very good standard, comparable to those in Europe and the US. A well-developed fleet of private long-distance buses criss-crosses the country, and the train system (although painfully slow) provides another way of getting around, with two companies specializing in luxury train travel. City transportation, on the other hand, is a problem. South Africa's cities lack safe and reliable urban public systems (the exception is Cape Town; ▷ 49), often making private transportation the only option for visitors. Safety is an issue throughout South Africa—see safety tips for each mode of transportation on the following pages.

BY ROAD

South Africans rely on their cars, and the road system is correspondingly excellent. A web of highways, known as N roads, stretches across the country linking the major cities. The N1 links Cape Town with Johannesburg and Pretoria; the N2 links Cape Town with Port Elizabeth and Durban; while the N7 links Cape Town with Namibia. Parts of the N roads are toll roads, although there is always an alternative non-toll route indicated by signposts before you get to the toll plaza (as the toll booths are called). Smaller highways connect towns in between.

The real joy of driving in South Africa, however, is veering away from the major highways and exploring the countryside along the far regional

Above Driving is a great way to see more of the open country

(R) roads. Although these tend to be slower, they are usually quieter and pass through some of the most spectacular scenery in the country. Many people also choose to self-drive through the national parks, such as Kruger, and this can be a great way of going on safari. Here, roads tend to be well maintained and are usually tarred.

The good road system means that South Africa is also easily explored by bus, and there is a wide network of luxurious long-distance buses, although they are not as cheap as you might expect. Three major bus companies cover the country, and there is also a good value backpacker bus (▷ 52).

There is an enormous network of short- and long-distance minibus taxis, but these are best avoided because of high accident rates and security issues.

RAIL AND AIR

In contrast to the excellent roads, the rail system is relatively unreliable and in need of modernization. Although comfortable, trains tend to be slow and inefficient. However, a splendid way of experiencing some colonial style is by taking one of the luxury trains which are becoming increasingly popular with foreign visitors (▷ 54).

Given the huge distances involved in exploring South Africa, domestic flights are perhaps the most practical option for getting about, particularly for those spending only a short time in the country. The national carrier, South African Airways (SAA), has numerous daily flights connecting the major cities and towns (▷ 50). The last few years have also seen several 'no-frills' airlines spring up (▷ 50), offering low-fare flights between the major destinations.

GETTING AROUND IN CAPE TOWN

Although the heart of Cape Town is easily explored on foot, there are also a number of sights and attractions worth visiting along the peninsula. The public transportation system is skeletal, and most visitors to the city either rent a car or rely on taxis or organized tours to get out of town. It is worth noting, however, that Cape Town is the only large city in South Africa with any sort of reliable public transportation system.

BY BUS

Buses run throughout the day, but they tend to be slow and inefficient and on the whole are best avoided. However, there are three exceptions:
» The Waterfront bus covers the short distance from Cape Town City Bowl to the Victoria & Alfred Waterfront. Buses leave from the rail station on Adderley Street every 15 minutes from 6am until 11.15pm, seven days a week. Buses from the Waterfront run from 6.20am until 11.30pm. Tickets are bought on the bus and cost R8 one way.
» Another useful service runs from the City Bowl along the Atlantic seaboard. This route starts from the main bus station on Grand Parade and runs approximately every 15–30 minutes from 5.30am to 6.30pm (Mon–Fri) and from 6 to 6 (Sat); there are no buses on Sundays. The bus stops at Sea Point and Camps Bay and ends in Hout Bay, taking about an hour to cover the whole seaboard. There is a useful information kiosk at the main bus terminal on Grand Parade (freephone 0800-656463; www.gabs.co.za).
» Sightseeing Cape Town is a red double-decker topless hop-on hop-off bus that takes a 135-minute route around the city. There are two routes: buses on the Red Route run every 40 minutes, and on the Blue Route every 60 minutes. Stops include the lower Cableway station, Camps Bay, Kirstenbosch, all the city centre museums, and Hout Bay on the peninsula. A one-day ticket costs R120, children R60, and the wheelchair-friendly buses run between 9.30 and 4.30. The start point is outside the Two Oceans Aquarium at the Victoria & Alfred Waterfront (tel 021-5116000; www.citysightseeing.co.za).

BY METRO

The Metrorail train line serves the Southern Suburbs, running from the main train station on Adderlely Street as far as Worcester (in the Winelands). This is mainly a commuter service, but the ride to Simon's Town on False Bay is a worthwhile visitor excursion, with the train running alongside the crashing waves of False Bay for the last stretch. However, don't take the train any farther: Beyond Simon's Town there's a risk of mugging.
» It is best to use the trains only during the rush hours (7–8am and 4–6pm) or in the middle of the day, as there is a risk of mugging if the train is not busy. It is also a good idea to travel first class; signs indicate where the first-class car will be when the train comes in.
» The first train is around 5am, and they then run approximately every 15 minutes between the central station and Simon's Town, until around 7pm. Train times change seasonally, so check with Metrorail (tel 0800-656463; www.capemetrorail.co.za) in advance.
» Tickets, which can be bought from the kiosks at the main concourse in Cape Town station, cost R12 one-way between Cape Town and Simon's Town.

BY TAXI

Taxis are the safest way of getting around at night and convenient during the day. Cape Town has several different types. Metered taxis are regulated by the Cape Town Municipality and leave from taxi stands around town. You can now pay in some taxis by credit card.
» The most useful taxi stands are: outside the train station at Adderley Street; at the Victoria & Alfred Waterfront; near the Park Inn hotel on Greenmarket Square; halfway along Long Street; and at the lower Cableway station. Expect to pay around R10 per kilometre. If you are outside central Cape Town, you will have to call a taxi in advance.
» Companies include Unicab (tel 021-4481720) and Marine Taxis (tel 021-4340434). Hotels and restaurants are usually happy to call one for you.
» Rikki taxis are an alternative to standard metered taxis. These shared London Hackney cab vehicles, recognizable by their bright advertising, are good value and reliable; they pick up several people on each route, significantly bringing down fares. Rikkis must be called in advance and there are now a number of free Rikki phones around the city in supermarkets, cafés and petrol (gas) stations (tel 0861-745547; www.rikkis.co.za).
» Minibus taxis serve the city on fixed routes, but are best avoided by visitors for security reasons.

BY CAR

Renting a car gives you the freedom to explore the peninsula without having to rely on taxis.
» Parking is generally not a problem. Most of central Cape Town has demarcated areas, costing R6 per hour. There are official parking attendants (in blue uniforms) who patrol the central area—they'll ask how long you want to stay and you hand them the coins. Hotels and guesthouses usually have secure parking, but call ahead to check.
» Fuel prices are reasonable and there are plenty of large petrol (gas) stations around the city. None are self-service and they only accept cash, although most have ATMs.

DOMESTIC FLIGHTS

Because of the vast distances in South Africa, flying can be an excellent way of seeing as much of the country as possible in a short space of time, and thanks to the introduction of budget airlines not necessarily much more expensive than travelling around by bus. The main hub of South Africa's far-reaching and efficient domestic air services is Johannesburg. South African Airways (SAA) links it to just about anywhere in the country, including the Greater Kruger National Park.

SAA has had to deal with an upsurge of competition in recent years, and prices have dropped correspondingly as a result. Several no-frills carriers have started up following the example of Kulula, which launched in June 2001. These carriers are very similar to the plethora of low-cost airlines found in Europe and North America, offering ticket-free no-frills flight at very reasonable cost; in effect, this means you have to pay extra for any snacks and refreshments you have on board, there are no numbered tickets or designated seats, and any extras such as in-flight magazines are limited. These flights can represent excellent value for money, often costing only a little more than a long-distance bus ticket for the same journey — and taking just a fraction of the time.

DOMESTIC AIRLINES
South African Airways (SAA) has the most comprehensive network of flights. It works in conjunction with its subsidiaries SA Airlink and SA Express, making it the largest domestic carrier, with regular daily flights connecting Johannesburg with many towns and cities within South Africa.
» Central reservations: tel 011-978000, freephone 0861-359722; www.flysaa.com.

British Airways Comair
operates several flights each day between Cape Town, Durban, Johannesburg and Port Elizabeth. The company is basically a domestic subsidiary of British Airways, and has been running in South Africa for more than 60 years.
» British Airways Comair: tel 011-9210111; www.comair.co.za

Kulula was the first no-frills airline to launch in South Africa. Like Comair it is also owned by British Airways. It has daily services between Cape Town, Durban, Johannesburg, Port Elizabeth and George. The airline's cheapest fares are available through its website.
» Kulula: tel 0861-585852; www.kulula.com

1 Time is another no-frills airline with services between Johannesburg and Cape Town, Durban, George, Port Elizabeth and East London.
» 1 Time: tel 0861-345345; www.1time.aero

Mango is the newest no-frills airline, with services between Johannesburg, Cape Town, Durban and Bloemfontein.
» Mango: tel 0861-162646; www.flymango.com

PRICES
Return fares from Johannesburg to Cape Town with standard carriers are in the region of R1,100–1,900. No-frills carriers are slightly cheaper, and offer one-way tickets (as opposed to return/round-trip tickets). Expect to pay in the region of R800 for a one-way fare from Cape Town to Johannesburg.

BUYING TICKETS
The method of buying your ticket depends on which airline you choose to fly with. The no-frills domestic airlines offer their cheapest fares online; standard carriers may have online offers, but over-the-phone fares should be similar. Whatever the carrier, it's worth making reservations as far in advance as possible, as prices fluctuate considerably — although you may find good deals on last-minute flights: Check with travel agents, as they often have the best access to the cheapest deals.

FLIGHT INFORMATION	
Johannesburg to Cape Town:	2 hr 10 min
Johannesburg to Durban:	1 hr 10 min
Johannesburg to East London:	1 hr 30 min
Johannesburg to George:	1 hr 50 min
Johannesburg to Kimberley:	1 hr 15 min
Johannesburg to Port Elizabeth:	1 hr 40 min
Baggage allowance for SAA domestic flights	
Hold luggage:	First Class, 40kg (88lb); Business Class, 30kg (66lb); Economy Class 20kg (44lb)
Hand luggage:	7kg (15.5lb) per bag (2 bags per passenger in First and Business classes; 1 bag in Economy Class).

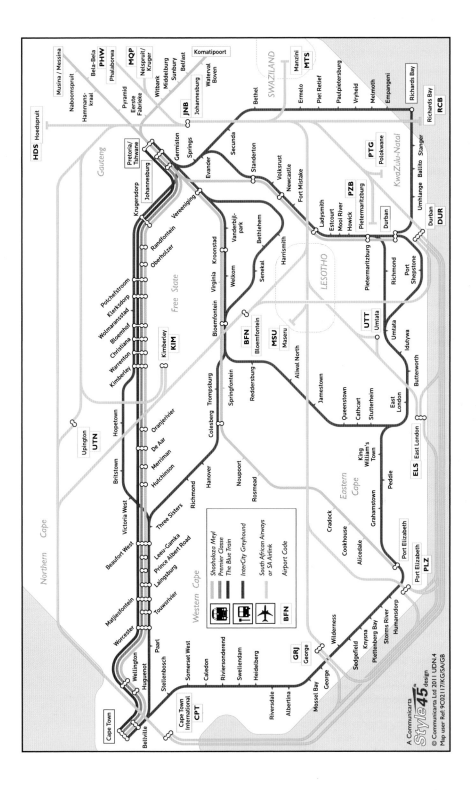

LONG-DISTANCE BUSES

There are three main bus operators running luxury services — known as coaches — and between them they cover just about every visitor hub town and city in South Africa. There is also an excellent company catering for budget travellers and backpackers. After flying, buses tend to be the most popular way of covering long distances: They are well maintained and comfortable, the roads are excellent and it's a safe mode of transportation.

PRICES

Coaches are cheaper than flying, and are far more efficient than trains. If you're on a budget, note that prices for short-distance trips are relatively expensive; they become better value for longer trips. Sample fares include:
» Johannesburg to Durban (6 hours, costing R150).
» Cape Town to Port Elizabeth (13 hours, costing R270).
» Cape Town to Pretoria (21.5 hours, costing R450).

MAIN BUS OPERATORS

Greyhound (tel 083-9159000 in South Africa, 011-2768550 from overseas; www.greyhound.co.za) runs services around much of the country, including popular routes from Cape Town to Port Elizabeth (via the Garden Route) and from Johannesburg to Durban. You can reserve online but tickets must be picked up at a Greyhound office or Computicket outlet (see Tickets) at least four hours before departure. If you're planning to spend some time on the road, Greyhound's passes are good value: seven vouchers to be used over a period of 30 days, R2,376; 15 vouchers to be used over a period of 30 days, R4,224; 30 vouchers to be used over a period of 60 days, R8,580.

Intercape (tel 0861-287287 in South Africa, 012-3804400 from overseas; www.intercape.co.za) covers an extensive network around the country, and has similar luxurious coaches, with air conditioning and reclining seats; some have televisions on board and hostesses handing out snacks and drinks. There are good year-round discounts, including family deals (up to 50 per cent off for children) and a standard 5 per cent discount for students.

Translux (tel 0861-589282 in South Africa, 011-773805 from overseas; www.translux.co.za) has an extensive 24-hour network and comfortable double-decker coaches. Although it does not offer online reservations, its website does have useful timetable information. Translux offers a range of special seasonal offers.

INTERNATIONAL ROUTES

All three of the main bus service providers include some routes across international borders, and between them cover Maputo (Mozambique), Windhoek and Walvis Bay (Namibia), Harare, Victoria Falls and Bulawayo (Zimbabwe), Blantyre (Malawi) and Gaborone (Botswana).

TICKETS

As well as individual companies, Computicket (tel 083-9158000; www.computicket.com) sells tickets for all national bus services. However, for phone and internet reservations it accepts only credit cards issued in South Africa. You can pay in person with foreign-issued credit cards if you visit a Computicket outlet, found in all major shopping malls in the big cities.

BAZ BUS

Baz Bus (tel 021-4225202; www.bazbus.com) is probably the most popular bus service with visitors and is specifically designed for backpackers: It is a good way to see the country on a budget. One of the best aspects of the service is that, with a few exceptions, the bus collects and drops off passengers at their chosen backpacker hostel. When you are moving on, it is important to remember to call the Baz Bus to arrange to be collected; during busy times of the year it is advisable to call as soon as you have decided what your next move will be.

Tickets are priced per segment (see table). You are allowed to hop off and on as many times as you like along the given segment, but must not backtrack (unless you buy a return ticket). This is where the savings are made, since other commercial buses such as Translux and Greyhound charge high prices for short trips. However, for long distances without stops, the mainline buses provide better value.

Baz Bus vehicles are fairly cramped, particularly at busy times, but a trailer at the back has space for large items of luggage such as rucksacks and surfboards.

BAZ BUS	
ROUTE	PRICE
Cape Town to Durban	R2,430
Durban to Cape Town	R2,430
Cape Town to Port Elizabeth, via the Garden Route	R1,250
Port Elizabeth to Cape Town, via the Garden Route	R1,250
Cape Town to Johannesburg, via the Drakensberg	R2,900
Johannesburg to Cape Town, via the Drakensberg	R2,900
Cape Town to Johannesburg, via Swaziland	R3,500
Johannesburg to Cape Town, via Swaziland	R3,500
Johannesburg to Durban, and back to Johannesburg via Swaziland and the Drakensberg	R1,540

TRAINS

A high-speed rail link between O. R. Tambo International Airport and downtown Johannesburg has recently been completed and eventually this will also expand to Pretoria (www.gautrain.com). Otherwise, however, unlike the domestic air and bus network, train travel is relatively inefficient. Although most of the major cities are linked by rail, services are slow and some routes are poorly covered, with only one or two trains a week running along certain stretches. However, many visitors to South Africa make a point of taking one of the luxury trains, such as the Blue Train between Pretoria and Cape Town, and the journey is one of the highlights of their trip.

SHOSHOLOZA MEYL

The most frequent services are run by Shosholoza Meyl (tel 086-0008888; www.shosholozameyl.co.za), part of Passenger Rail Agency of South Africa (PRASA). These trains, with names such as Trans Oranje and the Komati, run most days of the week, and while they are fairly comfortable and inexpensive, the lengthy journey times are off-putting. Reservations must be made at least 24 hours in advance, at most stations, or you can make them through the national reservations telephone number that is given above.

Named trains are split into two classes (no longer officially called first and second, but effectively just that). The 'sitter' class is made up of rows of plastic seats, and the 'four-sleeper' (the most comfortable option) has four fold-down beds in each cabin and shared washing facilities in each carriage (car). 'Coupés' are also available in four-sleeper class,

sleeping two people at a slightly higher price. Accompanied children under the age of five travel free; children between five and 11 pay half price.

All trains have a problem with security: If you leave your compartment, make sure a train official locks it after you. The four-sleeper is the most secure, as you

SHOSHOLOZA MEYL JOURNEY TIMES AND FARES		
ROUTE	**TIME**	**PRICE**
Johannesburg to Durban	14 hours	R350 (tourist class)
		R1,000 (premier class)
Cape Town to Johannesburg	27 hours	R520 (tourist class)
		R350 (six-sleeper)
		R2,210 (premier class)

Above *Cape Town's rail station was refurbished for the 2010 World Cup*

can lock yourself into the cabin during the night.

Refreshments are available on all trains, with either a dining car or a trolley selling snacks.

Shosholoza Meyl also operates a more upmarket service, the Premier Classe (tel 086-0008888 in South Africa, 011-7744555 from overseas; www.shosholozameyl.co.za), between Pretoria and Cape Town once a week. The carriages are a bit nicer than on the regular train, with proper food in a sit-down dining car and extras like toiletries and dressing gowns provided in the coupés.

LUXURY TRAINS

The Blue Train (tel 012-3348459; www.bluetrain.co.za), represents the ultimate in luxury train travel, with regular departures between Pretoria and Cape Town. Passengers travel in beautifully designed compartments with a colonial theme, equipped with either twin or double beds, private bathrooms with shower and bath, air conditioning, TV, and large windows to show off the passing landscapes. Meals, served in an elegant dining car, are accompanied by the best of South African wines. Expect to pay well for the privilege, though: A one-way fare from Pretoria to Cape Town, taking one day and one night, is R21,860 for two people sharing. Other Blue Train specials run from Pretoria to game lodges in KwaZulu-Natal, Limpopo and North West Province.

The Pride of Africa is a similar luxury train experience, operated by Rovos Rail (tel 012-3158242; www.rovos.co.za), which also runs between Pretoria and Cape Town with occasional trips to Victoria Falls. The beautifully restored cars date from 1911.

The chart below gives the journey times (hours in the larger number) between major hubs. As it is not always possible to travel using one single mode of transport, the chart highlights which other modes should be used. The chart assumes that domestic flight is the best travel option. See transport map on page 51 for more details.

Journeys other than by air:
A = Bus
B = Rail
C = Air and bus
D = Air and rail
E = Air, bus and rail
F = Bus and rail
* = Change at Port Shepstone

	Bloemfontein	Cape Town	De Aar	Durban	East London	George	Johannesburg	Kimberley	Knysna	Komatipoort	Kroonstad	Margate (Port Shepstone*)	Mossel Bay	Mthatha	Musina/Messina	Polokwane/Pietersburg	Port Elizabeth	Richards Bay	Rosmead	Sun City
Cape Town	135																			
De Aar	B 723	B 1305																		
Durban	105	210	D 1025																	
East London	300	130	D 1045	120																
George	425	050	D 1035	150	430															
Johannesburg	115	210	B 1231	110	125	155														
Kimberley	425	200	B 347	345	400	430	130													
Knysna	C 1145	A 640	F 2535	C 900	A 825	A 055	C 655	C 1430												
Komatipoort	D 1548	D 1558	D 1548	D 1558	D 1553	B 1618	D 1216	B 1558	E 2728											
Kroonstad	B 240	A 1535	B 957	B 1319	A 1015	C 655	A 300	B 630	F 1752	B 2345										
Margate	415	635	D 2725	A* 145	400	520	135	420	C 1020	E 1805	850									
Mossel Bay	A 930	A 625	F 2350	C 1240	A 1025	A 040	830	C 1230	E 135	C 3220	E 1745	C 1450								
Mthatha	A 435	505	D 2700	505	A 340	705	140	540	A 1205	D 2255	D 720	A* 455	A 1350							
Musina/Messina	D 1810	D 1840	B 3048	D 1734	D 1735	D 1850	B 1411	D 1950	E 3115	B 4020	B 2259	D 2150	E 3250	F 3500						
Polokwane/Pietersburg	D 1121	D 1151	B 2359	D 1105	D 1106	D 1215	B 736	D 1325	E 2426	B 3331	B 1610	D 1401	E 2611	F 2825	B 629					
Port Elizabeth	355	110	D 1155	120	050	420	145	405	A 345	D 1800	1545	A 435	D 530	425	2145	D 1510				
Richards Bay	C 1345	440	D 1333	A 225	425	435	130	405	C 940	D 1720	805	C 535	1000	C 510	D 2050	D 1415	430			
Rosmead	B 642	D 932	D 1017	917	D 942	D 1242	B 1358	B 1427	F 1752	B 3312	B 714	D 1442	F 937	D 1938	B 3242	B 2607	B 602	D 1527		
Sun City	445	200	D 2815	640	455	435	525	2820	C 1110	D 1855	940	2425	D 1130	1850	D 4225	D 3550	445	1820	D 1538	
Upington	415	145	D 2505	405	445	1705	130	2700	C 1100	D 1835	720	C 1120	2030	D 3915	D 3240	435	1600	D 1318	2330	

DRIVING

South Africa's excellent infrastructure makes driving an efficient and straightforward way of getting around the country. Roads are generally well maintained, although the more rural the road, the more likely you are to come across potholes and poor surfaces. South Africans rely heavily on their cars, partly because of the lack of a viable public transportation system. In the cities, there is very little choice of transportation other than driving (the exception being Cape Town), while long-distance trips are facilitated by the excellent system of highways (motorways/expressways). Bear in mind, however, that South Africa is a very large country, so always plan your itinerary carefully, make sure you have water with you, fill up your tank with petrol (gas) before you depart and top it up in the towns that you pass through, and leave plenty of time to get to your destination.

WHAT TO BRING
» You must have either an International Driving Permit, available from your own country, or a foreign driver's licence printed in English, with a photo, and it must be valid for at least six months.
» A credit card is recommended for the deposit on a rental car (cash is usually also accepted, but the amount you are required to leave is usually very high).

Above *Driving through the fertile Venda region, Limpopo*

ROADS
» Main roads are identified by a number. National highways linking the major cities have the prefix 'N' followed by a number.
» The country's main artery, the N1, starts in Cape Town and passes through Johannesburg and Pretoria, ending at the Zimbabwe border.
» The N2 from Cape Town passes along the Garden Route to Port Elizabeth and Durban, and ends at the border with Mozambique.
» The N3 begins at Johannesburg and ends in Durban.

» Regional highways and roads (sometimes two-lane highways) have the prefix 'R'.
» Major urban roads and ring roads carry the prefix 'M'.
» There are a few toll roads in South Africa. These accept cash only, so always keep some coins in the car.

BASIC RULES OF THE ROAD
» Driving is on the left.
» At roundabouts (traffic circles), unless otherwise indicated, traffic coming from the right has the right of way.

AFRIKAANS ROAD SIGNS

doeane	customs
dorp	village
geen ingang	no entry
gevaar!	danger!
grens	border
inligting	information
links	left
lughawe	airport
ompad	detour
pad	road
padwerke voor	road works ahead
poskantoor	post office
regs	right
sentrum	centre
stadig	slow
stad	town/city
stad sentrum	city centre
strand	beach
verbode	forbidden
verkeer	traffic

SPEED LIMITS
» All distances and speed limits are measured in kilometres.
» Urban areas, towns and cities: 60kph (35mph).
» Secondary (rural) roads: 100kph (60mph).
» National highways and urban freeways: 120kph (75mph).

OVERTAKING (PASSING)
» Look out for 'No Overtaking' signs and adhere to them.
» On minor roads, South African drivers will often veer into the hard shoulder to let others overtake, particularly on blind corners. This is not advised.
» If you allow someone to overtake, they may flash their hazard lights as a means of thanking you.
» Rural roads are often straight and flat, but watch for hidden dips, which are particularly well camouflaged in hot conditions.

FOUR-WAY STOPS
South African roads have four-way stops, a crossroad or intersection where each approach road has a stop sign.
» Always come to a complete stop when approaching a four-way stop.
» If you are the only vehicle at the intersection, stop, look left and right and then proceed if the road is clear.
» If another vehicle has already stopped at one of the other stop signs, it has the right of way, so stop and give way.
» If you stop at the intersection at the same time as another vehicle, it is a matter of common courtesy and either vehicle may proceed.

DRIVING IN RURAL AREAS
» Watch for stray animals. Some rural areas have no fences, so cows and goats wander into the road, particularly in the Eastern Cape.
» While the rural roads in areas popular with visitors, such as the Western Cape, are well maintained, farther afield you may find poorly surfaced and potholed roads. Drive slowly and keep a constant lookout for hazards.
» More remote areas like the Northern Cape or the Great Karoo have long, deserted stretches of road between towns or villages, so always make sure you have plenty of fuel and a good map, and carry 2 litres (4 pints) of water per passenger (this is particularly important in the scorching summer).
» There is a small risk of hijacking in South Africa, and visitors can be vulnerable on quiet rural roads. Various scams have been used in the past to lure cars to stop, such as staging accidents and waving at passing drivers for help.
» Never pull over for anyone other than the police (cars are well marked), and never pick up hitchhikers.

ROAD SIGNS AND TERMS
» Traffic lights are called 'robots' in South Africa.
» Street names are often in English and Afrikaans. Those in Afrikaans are usually recognizable, and don't vary significantly from the English.
» Road signs are generally bilingual, but are sometimes in Afrikaans only, particularly in rural Afrikaner areas such as the Winelands. See the box above for some common Afrikaans road signs.

PARKING
» Designated parking areas are indicated with a large white 'P' on a blue background, found in central parts of all cities and towns.
» Payment is usually a system of parking attendants who have hand-held meters, whom you pay on arrival. Expect to pay around R5 per hour.
» Be sure to note the time limit on parking—it is often a maximum of two hours.
» Away from central areas parking is usually free, but unofficial parking attendants will often watch your car for a small fee (R3–R5), which you pay on your return. Expect to find these unofficial attendants also in (free) parking areas belonging to shopping malls, restaurants and visitor sights. Some are employed by local businesses but many are casual opportunists. As they make their living from watching cars, they can usually be trusted to keep an eye on your vehicle.
» Watch for parking restriction signs. Traffic wardens will fine you if you fall foul of restrictions.
» It is illegal to park facing oncoming traffic, that is on the right-hand side of the road.

FUEL
» Petrol (gas) stations are not self-service. You will be assisted by an attendant. Make sure you stipulate what fuel your car takes (unleaded, super, diesel, etc).
» Attendants will expect a small tip (around R3–R5). They may also wash your windscreens and check oil and water (a good idea if you've been driving for a long stretch).
» Petrol stations accept only cash or petrol cards (not an option for visitors), so always carry enough cash with you. However, most petrol stations, especially along the major highways and in cities, have ATMs.
» Large petrol stations are modern and usually have small shops selling magazines, snacks and drinks. Most also have toilets, and some have coffee shops or chain restaurants, such as Wimpy.

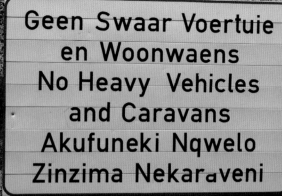

Above *Climbing up the Swartberg Pass*
Right *Road signs are often in a number of languages*

» Petrol stations are usually found in towns and cities not on highways, so it's advisable to fill up the tank if planning a long journey.

SAFETY

» Lock all your doors while you're driving in built-up areas.

» Keep windows rolled up enough to prevent people from reaching into your car.

» Keep valuables out of sight while driving in built-up areas.

» Never leave valuables in your car when leaving it unattended. If you must, store items out of sight.

» Avoid driving at night, particularly along the beachfront area of Durban and in downtown Johannesburg.

» Townships should be avoided if you are driving without a guide, as it is easy to get lost and become vulnerable. Do not go into townships at night.

» Don't stop at remote picnic spots.

» Don't pick up hitchhikers and be very wary of people flagging you down. Stop only for the police.

» Hijacking hotspots include northern KwaZulu-Natal and approach roads to Kruger National Park.

» Some urban areas, mostly in Johannesburg, have 'Hijacking Hotspot' signs. These mean that you can drive over a red traffic light (checking both ways before you do so) if you feel at risk.

» Carry a mobile phone with you at all times in case of emergency (but note that it is illegal to use a hand-held phone while driving).

» If you break down or are involved in an accident, call the emergency services as soon as possible (Police: 10111; Ambulance: 10177).

» Major routes have yellow SOS phones set at 2km (1.2-mile) intervals along the road, or call the South African AA emergency rescue number (freephone 0800 010101).

» Check with your car rental company before you set off, as some provide their own SOS emergency telephone numbers.

» South Africans often drive fast. Don't feel pressured into joining them, but you should be aware of what the traffic around you is doing at all times.

» The maximum allowable alcohol blood content is 0.05 per cent, but you should never drive under the influence of alcohol. Drivers face penalties and may lose their licence if they fail a breath test.

» Be especially wary on the roads over Christmas when the number of road deaths soars dramatically.

TAXIS

» In the major cities, metered taxis are run by the municipality.

» They are found at taxi stands, usually outside airports and train stations and at key visitor sights in central city areas.

» Check that the meter is working and set to the minimum fare when you set off.

» If there is no meter, or it is not working, be sure to agree a fare before setting off.

» You can't usually hail a taxi in the street, although in some towns taxis may stop for you.

» Taxi drivers are usually tipped up to 10 per cent of the fare.

» You can phone for a metered taxi. Ask your hotel or restaurant to call a taxi on your behalf, or ask at the local tourist office for names of reputable companies. Check fares before departing.

VISITORS WITH A DISABILITY

Although the idea of easy access to museums, hotels and restaurants for visitors with a disability only recently began to take hold in South Africa, things are developing quickly, and a number of places to stay advertise facilities with wheelchair access. Some attractions now have amenities specifically for visitors with a disability.

The fact that South Africa is a very car-friendly country should make getting to the major sites relatively easy, and most places have disabled parking near the entrances. Getting around game parks should not prove too difficult, although park accommodation and washing facilities are rarely wheelchair-friendly. However, the situation is gradually improving within the parks.

AIR TRAVEL

The international airports are all well equipped for passengers with a disability, having elevators to all floors and wheelchair access to most toilets. The airport in Johannesburg is particularly user-friendly for visitors with a disability, with wheelchair access to all toilets and a large number of elevators, some equipped with Braille.

Domestic airlines provide assistance and seating for all wheelchair users, but you should notify your carrier before you travel. No-frills carriers have limited space for wheelchair users, so it is essential to telephone ahead.

If you have a visual or hearing impairment and have a guide dog, you are permitted to bring the dog into the cabin with you on SAA flights, provided the airline is given notice in advance. Guide dogs travel free of charge.

TRAINS

Shosholoza Meyl trains are wheelchair accessible, but you must phone ahead to request a ramp to board the trains. Doorways to individual compartments and communal washing facilities are wide enough for wheelchairs, although conditions are cramped and you may find turning a problem.

BUSES

Mainline buses are not easily accessible by wheelchair. The main companies offer assistance from the driver or hostess, which in effect means that passengers with limited mobility will be assisted onto the buses and to their seats.

AROUND TOWN

The wide pavements (sidewalks) and colonial layout of many South African towns make moving around in a wheelchair fairly easy, although many pavements are still not ramped. Some older quarters, such as Bo-Kaap in Cape Town City Bowl, are cobbled and hilly, making access difficult and uncomfortable.

The government has introduced legislation concerning access for people with disabilities, with the result that many museums and other visitor sights are now wheelchair-friendly. You can expect ramps, elevators and suitably equipped toilets in the main cities, but there are often no facilities whatsoever in more rural areas or in the older museums.

HOTELS AND GAME PARKS

Large hotels will have some rooms suitable for guests with disabilities, and some guesthouses may have wheelchair access (usually advertised on their websites).

Game parks are adding to their facilities to make their various types of accommodation more accessible. Many sites have introduced short Braille trails for visitors with a visual impairment. Among these are the Kirstenbosch Botanical Gardens in Cape Town.

Below *Wheelchair access sign*

SOURCES OF TRAVEL INFORMATION

Disabled People South Africa
tel 021-4220357; www.dpsa.org.za
A national body representing people with disabilities; they have contact details about transport and accessibility.

Epic Enabled
tel 021-7857440; www.epic-enabled.com
Its excellent range of tours for people with disabilities use fully modified overland trucks, camp assistants and also wheelchair-friendly accommodation.

Flamingo Tours
tel 021-5574496; www.flamingotours.co.za
Arranges tailor-made tours and fly-drive holidays for visitors with disabilities.

National Council for Persons with Physical Disabilities in South Africa
tel 011-4522774; www.ncppdsa.org.za
Provides advice about how to go about renting wheelchairs in South Africa, as well as other services for people with disabilities.

Rolling SA
tel 033-3304214; www.rollingsa.co.za
Organizes range of South African holidays for wheelchair users.

South African National Parks
tel 012-4265000; www.sanparks.org
Its website includes a section with up-to-date information on accessing the national parks for people with disabilities.

REGIONS

This chapter divides South Africa into eight regions (▷ 11). Chapter names are for the purposes of this book only and places of interest are listed alphabetically in each region.

SIGHTS 62
WALKS AND DRIVE 80
WHAT TO DO 84
EATING 90
STAYING 94

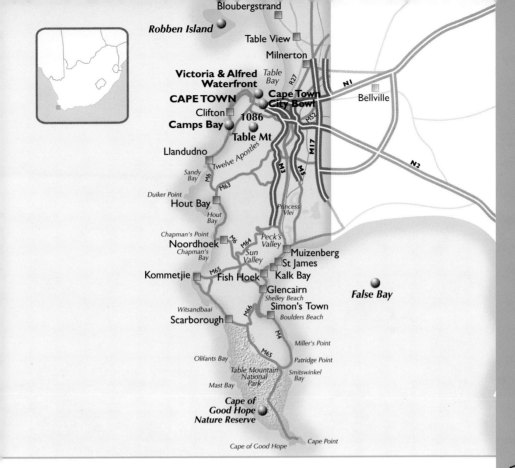

CAPE PENINSULA

The Cape Peninsula is characterized by a mountainous spine lined with a rugged coast and string of beaches, with a mixture of environments and communities, and is an instantly likeable and captivating place. It has a long history from when the first Portuguese seafarers landed in Table Bay and it was Francis Drake who described it in 1580 as 'the most stately thing and the fairest Cape we saw in the whole circumference of the world'. It is also home to Cape Town, South Africa's 'Mother City', which is dominated by the iconic Table Mountain with its distinctive flat top and 'table-cloth' of swirling white cloud. It's often dubbed one of the world's most beautiful cities, and for good reason; it adjoins a national park with dramatic scenery, is lapped by the cool Atlantic Ocean where dolphins and whales frolic, and it is blessed by a sunny climate most of the year. There are a number of interesting things to see and do. The city centre has fine museums and historical buildings, the V & A Waterfront is one of the world's most popular tourist attractions, receiving in excess of 10 million visitors a year, while a visit to Robben Island or a township tour show the effects of South Africa's years of apartheid. Must-do activities include walking up or taking the dizzying trip to the top of Table Mountain in the cable car, and driving down the spectacular Atlantic seaboard to take in the sweeping ocean views at the Cape of Good Hope and Cape Point. Few places in the world can offer such a mix of open spaces, mountain hiking, lazing on the beach and tasting world-class wines all in one day.

CAMPS BAY AND THE ATLANTIC SEABOARD

Just along the coast from Cape Town are the famous beaches of Clifton and Camps Bay—perfect arches of powder-white sand sloping into the chilly turquoise waters. The closest seaside residential areas to Cape Town City Bowl are actually Green Point and Sea Point, but these lack the beaches—as well as the charm and character—of other Atlantic seaboard areas. Both are a mixture of high-rise apartment blocks lining the rocky waterfront and more attractive bungalows creeping up the mountain. Green Point and the brightly painted Victorian bungalows known as De Waterkant Village are the focus of Cape Town's gay scene, with a correspondingly lively nightlife. To explore the Atlantic seaboard, your best means of transport is a rental car or taxi.

CLIFTON

The Cape's best-known beaches stretch along Clifton, and are renowned as the playground of the young and wealthy: This is the place to see and be seen. Clifton's four sheltered beaches are stunning, but the water is very cold—usually only around 12°C (54°F). The beaches, reached by a series of winding footpaths, are divided by rocky outcrops and are imaginatively named First, Second, Third and Fourth. Each has a distinct character. If you're bronzed and beautiful, head for First Beach. Less glamorous visitors may prefer Fourth, which is popular with families. Most of the relatively small-scale development has been behind the beaches, against the cliff face (some grand houses can be glimpsed from the winding steps leading down).

CAMPS BAY

Following the coast south, you soon skirt around a hill and come out above Camps Bay, a long arc of sand backed by the series of hills known as the Twelve Apostles. This has to be one of the most beautiful beaches in the world, but the calm cobalt water belies its chilliness. The sand is also less sheltered than at Clifton, and sunbathing here on a windy day can be quite painful. But there are other distractions to compensate, as the beachfront is lined with a number of excellent seafood restaurants.

INFORMATION

www.tourismcapetown.co.za
⊞ 326 B11 ⓗ The Pinnacle, corner of Burg and Castle streets ☎ 021-4054500 ⓒ Mon–Fri 8–6, Sat 8.30–2, Sun 9–1 ⓘ Selection of restaurants, bars and cafés in Camps Bay, Sea Point and Green Point ⓖ Camps Bay and Sea Point have seaside shops selling towels, swimsuits and sunscreen

TIPS

» If you have the time, carry on past Camps Bay towards Hout Bay. The road is spectacular, clinging between the slopes of the Twelve Apostles and the crashing ocean.
» There is limited parking along the seaboard in high season, but you'll usually find a space before 11am. Parking along the main road is free.
» Although there are no snack bars on the beaches, vendors march up and down selling cold drinks and ice creams.
» There are toilets on Fourth Beach at Clifton.

Above Clifton Beach
Opposite Camps Bay, backed by the Twelve Apostles hills

INFORMATION

www.capepoint.co.za

➕ 326 C11 ☎ 021-7809010

🕐 Oct–Mar daily 6–6; Apr–Sep daily 7–5 ✋ Reserve: adult R80, child (under 12) R20. Funicular (runs 9–5.30): adult round-trip ticket R45, one-way R35, child round-trip R20, one-way R15 🍴 Two Oceans Restaurant and kiosk ❓ Information office can provide hiking maps of the area 🏛 Curio shop 🚻 At bottom of funicular 🅿 Main parking at bottom of funicular

TIPS

» Take a hat and plenty of sunscreen, as the Point is fully exposed to the sun.
» If you have brought a picnic, make sure it is out of sight of the baboons that stalk around the parking area.
» When driving along the approach road to the main parking area near the funicular, stop at the point where the road first joins the coast. A five-minute walk across some smooth rocks brings you to Platboom Bay, one of the least visited and most beautiful beaches in the reserve.

Below *Viewpoint over Diaz Beach at the tip of the Cape Peninsula*

CAPE OF GOOD HOPE NATURE RESERVE

Cape Point's towering cliffs straddle the ground between the Atlantic seaboard and False Bay, giving astonishing ocean views. Beyond the tip are plains and deserted beaches with excellent hiking trails.

CAPE POINT

Cape Point Lighthouse is nothing special in itself, but the climb up from the parking area is worth the effort for the spectacular views of the peninsula: On a clear day, the ocean views stretching as far as the eye can see are incredible—as are the winds, so be sure to hold on to hats and sunglasses. You can take the funicular to the top, but the 20-minute walk gives you better views of the coast. There are a number of viewpoints, linked by a jumble of footpaths. The site proved to be unsuitable for a lighthouse, as it was often shrouded in mist even when everything was clear at sea level. If you have a good head for heights, there is a dramatic walk along the left side of the cliff to the modern lighthouse at Diaz Point. The round trip takes about 30 minutes, but do not attempt the walk if it is windy.

THE NATURE RESERVE

The Cape of Good Hope Nature Reserve, part of the Table Mountain National Park, is one of the area's highlights, and sits astride the tip of the peninsula south of Cape Town. The reserve was established in 1939 to protect the unique flora and fauna of this stretch of coast. It is an integral part of the Cape Floristic Kingdom, the smallest but richest of the world's six floral kingdoms, with as many different plant species within its boundaries as there are in the whole of the British Isles. You may also spot several species of antelope: eland, bontebok, springbok, Cape grysbok, red hartebeest and grey rhebok, as well as the elusive Cape mountain zebra.

The treacherous waters around Cape Point have taken their fair share of ships; five wrecks can be seen offshore when walking in the reserve. There are several marked hiking paths in the area, including the spectacular route along the coast from Rooikrans towards Buffels Bay. The most popular walk leads from the main parking area, down a steep set of steps to Diaz Beach. See page 81 for a recommended walk around the Silvermine Nature Reserve, one of the key places in the Cape Floristic Kingdom.

Left *Groot Constantia wine estate*
Above *Roza Van Gelderen*, by *Irma Stern, painted in 1929*

CAPE FLATS

Cape Flats, an area inland from Table Mountain and close to the airport, is home to Cape Town's exposed high-density townships. The first township in the country was built just outside Cape Town in 1901, but was thought to be too close to the heart of the city (▷ 69). Its people, were moved to Langa, which is still there today. Others include Crossroads, which had very poor living conditions for many years, Guguletu, Mitchells Plain and Khayelitsha, which at one point had more than one million residents. An organized tour is the recommended way to visit the townships (for advice on safety ▷ 57). Contact the tourist office in the City Bowl for more information.
✚ Off 326 C11 🚻 The Pinnacle, corner of Burg and Castle streets ☎ 021-4264260 🕓 Mon–Fri 8–6, Sat 8.30–1, Sun 9–1

CAPE TOWN CITY BOWL

▷ 66–71.

CONSTANTIA

To the south of Table Mountain is Cape Town's most elegant suburb, verdant Constantia with its wine estates. This district was South Africa's first wine-making site, and it provides an attractive introduction both to Cape Dutch architecture and to the country's wines.

There are five estates here, including Groot Constantia (tel 021-7945128; www.groot constantia. co.za) with its own fine Cape Dutch architecture, rolling vineyards and wine tastings. This is a delightful place to spend a few hours, although

it does get swamped with tour buses in high season. The main house was originally home to Cape Governor Simon van der Stel between 1699 and 1712. By the time of his death, he had planted most of the vines, but it was not until 1778 that the estate became famous for its wines. The main house is now a museum full of period furniture. Wine tasting takes place in the sales area close to the main entrance.

The other estates worth visiting are Klein Constantia (tel 021-7945188; www.kleinconstantia. com), a hilly estate that is known for its dessert wine Vin de Constance, allegedly Napoleon's wine of choice; Constantia Uitsig (tel 021-7946500; www.constantia-uitsig.com), which has luxury accommodation and three restaurants; and Steenberg (tel 021-7132222; www.steenberghotel.com), which has a luxury hotel, a good restaurant and a golf course.
✚ 326 C11

FALSE BAY

▷ 72–73.

HOUT BAY

The view of this deep bay is frequently photographed from Chapman's Peak Drive (▷ 80), and deservedly so: Hout Bay, a half-hour drive from the City Bowl, is a perfect cove with a white sandy beach, clear blue waters and a busy fishing port. Activity is focused around the port, at the western end of the bay, and the collection of shops and restaurants at the other end. Next to the port is a commercial complex known as

Mariners Wharf, the first of its kind in South Africa and popular with domestic visitors. It is based on Fisherman's Wharf in San Francisco, with a string of fish 'n' chip kiosks, gift shops, boats for rent and a fish market. Several boat charter companies organize trips from here to nearby Duiker Island. Another reason for coming here is the World of Birds on Valley Road, which has more than 400 bird species on display in a series of walk-through aviaries (tel 021-7902730; www. worldofbirds.org.za; daily 9–5).
✚ 326 B11 🚻 The Barn, Beach Crescent, Hout Bay ☎ 021-7918380 🕓 Mon–Fri 8.30–5.30, Sat–Sun 9–1

IRMA STERN MUSEUM

www.irmastern.co.za
Irma Stern (1894–1966) was one of South Africa's pioneering artists in the mid-20th century. Her handsome house displays a mixture of her own works, a collection of objects from across Africa, and some fine pieces of antique furniture from overseas— 17th-century Spanish chairs, 19th-century German oak furniture—and Swiss Mardi Gras masks. Stern's portraits are particularly poignant and those of her close friends are superb; her religious art is rather more disturbing. The studio, complete with paintbrushes, palettes and easels, has been left exactly as it was when the artist died.
✚ 326 C11 ✉ Cecil Road, Rosebank 7700 ☎ 021-6855686 🕓 Tue–Sat 10–5 🎟 Adult R10, child (2–16) R5 ♿

INFORMATION

www.tourismcapetown.co.za

326 C11 The Pinnacle, corner of Burg and Castle streets ☎ 021-4264260 Mon–Fri 8–6, Sat 8.30–1, Sun 9–1

INTRODUCTION

The area between the sea and the mountainous horseshoe formed by Signal Hill, Table Mountain and Devil's Peak is known as Cape Town City Bowl. Closest to Table Mountain are the residential suburbs of Tamboerskloof, Gardens, Oranjezicht and Vredehoek, attractive and wealthy Victorian suburbs with a good selection of hotels and restaurants. At the heart of the area are the high-rise blocks of the Central Business District (CBD), with Bo-Kaap rolling up the eastern slopes of Signal Hill and Company's Garden cutting a small green swathe in the middle.

Rock art by the San people is evidence that human life in the Cape dates back some 30,000 years. The first move to settle the Cape by Europeans wasn't until 1652. The Dutchman Jan van Riebeeck arrived on 6 April at Table Bay and erected a small fort—the site of which is where Grand Parade now stands. The settlement grew and towards the end on the 17th century the area was developing as an agricultural region. It was around this time that the first vines were planted that would produce Cape Town's famous wines.

Ownership passed from Dutch to British hands at the beginning of the 19th century and the city's growth followed that of the industrializing European cities, changing the face of Cape Town beyond recognition. The city's docks were very busy once gold and diamonds had been discovered in South Africa.

Apartheid urban planning forced many of the descendants of the slave population out from the heart of the city and the poorer African population was allowed to settle only on the outskirts and in surrounding townships, many of which still exist (▷ 65). Today, Cape Town has regained its racial mix and is the most cosmopolitan city in the country.

It is easy to get around on foot as most of the major sights and historic buildings are concentrated within this compact area. The main rail station and long-distance bus station are both on Adderley Street, one of the city's main arteries and home to many examples of the elegant colonial buildings that characterize the city's past. To explore more of the city and to visit Table Mountain, the suburbs or the beaches, it's a good idea to rent a car; otherwise taxis are quite affordable.

Above *Cheerful candy-coloured houses in Bo-Kaap*

WHAT TO SEE

BO-KAAP

Bo-Kaap, to the west of the City Bowl, is Cape Town's old Islamic quarter and one of the city's most individual residential areas. It was developed in the 1760s and today feels a world away from the nearby CBD. Here the cobbled streets form a tight web across the slopes of Signal Hill, the closely packed houses painted in bright greens, pinks and blues. Most visitors come for the Bo-Kaap Museum (tel 021-4813939; www.iziko.org.za/bokaap; Mon–Sat 10–5), in an 18th-century house on Wale Street and dedicated to the Cape's Muslim community. The house itself is one of the oldest in Cape Town to survive in its original form. It was built for artisans in 1763 and it was here that the Turkish scholar Abu Bakr Effendi started the first Arabic school. Effendi originally came to Cape Town as a guest of the British government to try to settle religious differences among the Cape Muslims. Inside the house are furnishings from a wealthy 19th-century Muslim family, and the back room has displays dedicated to the contribution made by slaves to the economy and development of Cape Town. The photographs are the best exhibits, giving a fascinating glimpse of life in Bo-Kaap in the early 20th century.

✚ 68 A1–B1

ADDERLEY STREET

Adderley Street is one of the city's busiest shopping areas, running through the heart of town between Government Avenue and the foreshore. It's an odd mixture of impressive 19th-century bank buildings and more modern but less attractive buildings. Look out for the Standard Bank Building on the corner of Darling Street, a grand structure built in 1880, shortly after the diamond wealth from Kimberley reached Cape Town. Diagonally across from it is the equally impressive Barclays Building (1933), made of sandstone from Ceres to the northwest of Cape Town. At the northern end of Adderley Street is a large roundabout (traffic circle) with a bronze statue of Jan van Riebeeck, the first commander of the Cape settlement, which was given to the city by Cecil Rhodes in 1899.

✚ 68 B1

CITY HALL AND GRAND PARADE

From Adderley Street, a short walk down Darling Street will take you to the City Hall and the Grand Parade. The latter is the largest open space in Cape Town and was used for garrison parades before the Castle (▷ 69) was completed. Twice a week the oak-lined parade is taken over by a market; otherwise it is used for car parking. The neoclassical City Hall, built in 1905, overlooks the parade. Nelson Mandela made his first speech here after his release from prison in 1994 to more than 100,000 people. Sixteen years later, in 2010, the parade was the site of the FIFA World Cup Fan Fest, with a giant TV screen broadcasting the matches. City Hall's clock tower is a half-size replica of Big Ben in London. In 1979, the municipal government moved to a new Civic Centre on the Foreshore and the hall is now the headquarters of the Cape Town Symphony Orchestra and houses the City Library.

✚ 68 C2

COMPANY'S GARDEN

Running alongside Government Avenue is the peaceful Company's Garden, on the site of the original vegetable garden created by Jan van Riebeeck in 1652 to grow produce for settlers and ships bound for the east. It is now a small botanical garden, with lawns, a variety of trees and ponds filled with Japanese koi. The grey squirrels living among the oak trees were introduced from America by Cecil Rhodes (Cape Prime Minister from 1890 to 1896). There is a statue of Rhodes in the gardens, close to the oldest statue in Cape Town, that of Sir

TIPS

» If you want to shop for antiques, walk past the Methodist church on Greenmarket Square onto Church Street. A daily antiques market is held in the area between Burg and Long streets.

» Footsteps to Freedom (tel 083-4521112; www.footstepstofreedom.co.za; Mon–Sat 10.30; R150, child under 18 R80). is a guided historical walk around central Cape Town that starts at the tourist office and lasts three hours. Stops include the Castle, District Six Museum and Company's Garden. Both English and German are spoken.

Below View over the city from the Table Mountain Cableway

REGIONS • CAPE PENINSULA • SIGHTS

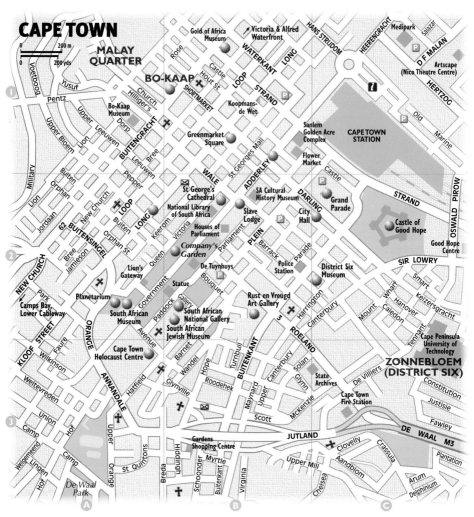

CAPE TOWN

0 ____ 200 m
0 ____ 200 yds

MALAY QUARTER

BO-KAAP

Gold of Africa Museum

Victoria & Alfred Waterfront

Medipark

D F MALAN

Artscape (Nico Theatre Centre)

Bo-Kaap Museum

Koopmans-de Wet

Greenmarket Square

Sanlem Golden Acre Complex

CAPE TOWN STATION

Flower Market

St George's Cathedral

National Library of South Africa

SA Cultural History Museum

Slave Lodge

City Hall

Grand Parade

Castle of Good Hope

Good Hope Centre

Houses of Parliament

Company's Garden

De Tuynhuys

Police Station

District Six Museum

SIR LOWRY

Lion's Gateway

Statue

Bouquet

Rust en Vreügd Art Gallery

Cape Peninsula University of Technology

Planetarium

South African Museum

South African National Gallery

South African Jewish Museum

State Archives

ZONNEBLOEM (DISTRICT SIX)

Camps Bay, Lower Cableway

Cape Town Holocaust Centre

Cape Town Fire Station

Gardens Shopping Centre

JUTLAND

DE WAAL M3

De Waal Park

STREET INDEX

George Grey, Governor of the Cape from 1854 to 1862. At the northern end of the gardens are the gleaming white, colonnaded Houses of Parliament.

✚ 68 B2 ✉ Government Avenue, 8001 🕐 Dawn–dusk ✋ Free 🍴

DISTRICT SIX MUSEUM

www.districtsix.co.za

Housed in an old Methodist church, this is one of Cape Town's most powerful museums, providing a fascinating glimpse of the stupidity and horror of apartheid. District Six was once the vibrant, cosmopolitan heart of Cape Town, an inner city suburb with a population of many races and renowned for its jazz scene. In 1966, P. W. Botha, then Minister of Community Development, proclaimed District Six a white group area. Over the next 15 years, an estimated 60,000 people were given notice to give up their homes and move to the new townships on the Cape Flats (▷ 65). The area was razed, and to this day remains largely undeveloped, although the government has handed over the first pocket of redeveloped land to a small group of ex-residents. The museum contains a fascinating and moving collection of photographs, articles and personal accounts depicting life before and after the removals. Often there are musicians at the back, playing guitars and tin pipes and adding immeasurably to the atmosphere of the place.

Above *Brightly decorated man adding to the colour at Greenmarket Square*

✚ 68 C2 ✉ 25A Buitenkant Street, 8001 ☎ 021-4667200 🕐 Tue–Sat 9–4, Mon 9–2 ✋ Adult R20, child (under 12) R10 🍴 🏛

GREENMARKET SQUARE

Greenmarket Square is the old heart of Cape Town and the second oldest square in the city. For long a meeting place, it became a vegetable market during the 19th century, taking on a more significant role in 1834 as the site where the freeing of all slaves was declared. It is still a popular meeting place today, lined with outdoor cafés and restaurants. A busy daily market sprawls across the cobbles, with stands selling African crafts, accessories and clothes. On one side of the square is the Old Town House, built in 1751 to house the town guard. It was made the first town hall in 1840 when Cape Town became a municipality. Much of the exterior remains unchanged, and with its decorative plaster mouldings and fine curved fanlights it is one of the best preserved Cape baroque exteriors in the city. Inside is the Michaelis Collection of Flemish and Dutch paintings (tel 021-4813933; Mon–Fri 10–5, Sat 10–4; entry by donation).

✚ 68 B1

CASTLE OF GOOD HOPE

www.castleofgoodhope.co.za

This is South Africa's oldest colonial building, finished in 1679. Its original purpose was to defend the Dutch East India Company from rival European powers. Under the British the Castle served as government headquarters, and since 1917 it has been the headquarters of the regional South African Defence Force. The castle is home to three museums. The William Fehr Collection is one of South Africa's finest displays of furnishings reflecting the social and political history of the Cape. There are landscapes by Thomas Baines, an English painter who lived in Cape Town in the mid-19th century, as well as 17th-century Japanese porcelain and 18th-century Indonesian furniture. The Secunde's House recreates the conditions under which an official for the Dutch East India Company would have lived in the 17th, 18th and early 19th centuries. The third museum is the Military Museum, which has absorbing displays of regimental uniforms and medals and a collection illustrating the conflicts of early settlers. The informative free tours take in the torture chambers, cells and the battlements, or there are maps in seven languages for self-guided tours.

Below *Guard at the Castle of Good Hope*

✚ 68 C2 ✉ Grand Parade, Darling Street, 8001 ☎ 021-7871260 🕐 Daily 9–4 ✋ Adult R25, child (2–16) R10 ➤ Free guided tours at 11, 12 and 2 🍴

Above *The South African Museum also houses the Planetarium*

SOUTH AFRICAN MUSEUM AND PLANETARIUM

www.iziko.org.za/sam

This is the city's oldest museum, covering natural history, ethnography and archaeology. There are extensive displays of the flora and fauna of southern Africa, including the 'Whale Well', where you can listen to the sound of whale song, but the highlight is the 'IQe—the Power of Rock Art' exhibition. The exhibits focus on the significance and symbolism of San rock art, with some fascinating examples including the beautifully preserved Linton panel, which depicts the trance experiences of shamans. The exhibition is beautifully arranged and is accompanied by the haunting sound of San singing. Nearby are the ethnographic galleries, with illuminating displays about the San, Khoi and Xhosa peoples, among others, as well as the original sixth-century clay Lydenburg Heads (▷ 197).

Shark World, in the natural history section, is an interactive multimedia area exploring sharks and their environment. At the Planetarium next door, presentations change every few months, but an hourly view of the current night sky is usually on show.

✚ 68 A2 ✉ 25 Queen Victoria Street, 8001 ☎ Museum: 021-4813800; Planetarium: 021-4813900 ⏰ Museum: daily 10–5; planetarium show times: Mon–Fri 2 (also Tue at 8), Sat–Sun 12, 1, 2.30 ✋ Adult R15, child (under 16) free, Sun free to all; planetarium shows: adult R20, child R6 🛒

MORE TO SEE

GOLD OF AFRICA MUSEUM

www.goldofafrica.com

The museum presents the history of gold mining on the continent, outlining the first mining by Egyptians in 2400BC and the subsequent development of trade networks across Africa. There are comprehensive displays of 19th- and 20th-century gold artworks from Mali, Ghana and Senegal, including some exquisite jewellery, masks, staff finials, hair ornaments and statuettes. Downstairs you can watch goldsmiths at work.

✚ 68 B1 ✉ 96 Strand Street, 8001 ☎ 021-4051540 ⏰ Mon–Sat 9.30–5 ✋ Adult R30, child (under 16) R20 🍴 🏛

LONG STREET

Slicing through the middle of town, trendy Long Street is lined with street cafés, fashionable shops, bars, clubs and backpacker lodges. It has a distinctly youthful feel about it, but it also contains some fine old city buildings. Among its more interesting ones is the Slave Church Museum at No. 40 (tel 021-4236755; Mon–Fri 9–4; free). The oldest mission church in South Africa, built between 1802 and 1804 as the mother church for missionary work carried out in rural areas, it was used for religious and literacy instruction of slaves in Cape Town. The building was saved from demolition in 1977 and restored to its present fine form. At No. 117 is one of Cape Town's Victorian gems, now an antiques shop, with an unusual cylindrical turret outside with curved windows; inside is a fine cast-iron spiral staircase leading to a balustraded gallery.

✚ 68 A2–B1

SOUTH AFRICAN JEWISH MUSEUM

www.sajewishmuseum.co.za

The Jewish Museum has a rich and rare collection of items depicting the history of the Cape Town Hebrew Congregation. There are displays of bronze Sabbath oil lamps, Chanukkah lamps, Bessamin spice containers, Torah scrolls, Kiddush cups and candlesticks. Another section of the museum is devoted to the history of Jewish immigration to the Cape, mainly from Lithuania. Displays include photographs, immigration certificates, videos and a full reconstruction of a Lithuanian *shtetl* (village). On the opposite side of the courtyard is the Holocaust

Below *Tribal costume in the South African Museum*

Centre, one of Cape Town's newest museums, comprising an intelligent and shocking examination of the Holocaust.

➕ 68 B2 ✉ 84 Hatfield Street, 8001 ☎ 021-4651546 🕐 Sun–Thu 10–5, Fri 10–2 ✋ Adult R50, child (4–18) R15 🍴 🏛

CAPE TOWN HOLOCAUST CENTRE

www.ctholocaust.co.za

On the opposite side of the courtyard to the Jewish Museum, this moving and at times shocking exhibition documents the rise of anti-Semitism in Europe, the creation of ghettos and death camps, the horrors of the Final Solution, and the liberation at the end of World War II. It also covers racism in general and the similarities of apartheid and Nazi Germany. The hi-tech multimedia equipment really drives the messages home.

➕ 68 A3 ✉ 88 Hatfield Street, 8001 ☎ 021-4625553 🕐 Sun–Thu 10–5, Fri 10–1 ✋ Free

SOUTH AFRICAN NATIONAL GALLERY

www.iziko.org.za/sang

The South African National Gallery houses a mixture of local and international art. There's a collection of 18th- and 19th-century British sporting paintings donated by Sir Abe Bailey, and changing exhibitions of contemporary South African art.

➕ 68 B2 ✉ Government Avenue, 8001 ☎ 021-4674660 🕐 Tue–Sun 10–5 ✋ Adult R15, child (under 16) free, Sat free to all 🍴 🏛

RUST EN VREUGD

www.iziko.org.za/rustvreugd

This 18th-century building, just off Government Avenue and hidden behind a high whitewashed wall, was declared a national monument in 1940. Today it houses six galleries, displaying a collection of watercolours, engravings and lithographs depicting the history of the Cape. Of particular note are watercolours of ascents of Table Mountain by Thomas Baines (a British artist who made journeys throughout South Africa), lithographs showing Khoi and Zulu people, and cartoons by 18th-century British cartoonist George Cruikshank, depicting the first British settlers arriving in the Cape. Commercial exhibitions are held upstairs.

➕ 68 B2 ✉ 78 Buitenkant Street, 8001 ☎ 021-4643280 🕐 Tue–Thu 10–5 ✋ Donation

ST. GEORGE'S CATHEDRAL

www.sgcathedral.co.za

The cathedral is best known as the seat of Archbishop Desmond Tutu's diocese from 1986 until 1996. It is from here that he led more than 30,000 people to City Hall to mark the end of apartheid, and where he first gave voice to the notion of the 'rainbow nation'. The building was designed by Sir Herbert Baker in the early 20th century. Inside, the Great North window is a fine piece of stained glass dedicated to the pioneers of the Anglican Church.

➕ 68 B2 ✉ 5 Wale Street, 8001 ☎ 021-4247360 🕐 Mon–Fri 8.30–4.30, Sunday services ✋ Free 🍴 🏛

SLAVE LODGE

www.iziko.org.za/slavelodge

Slave Lodge is the second oldest building in Cape Town. It has had a varied history, but its most significant role was as a slave lodge for the Dutch East India Company (VOC). Between 1679 and 1811, it housed up to 1,000 slaves at a time; conditions at the lodge were terrible and up to 20 per cent of the slaves died each year. Exhibition galleries display the history of the slaving in southern Africa and conditions aboard a slave ship. Using sound, images and animation, another display shows the grim conditions in which slaves lived in the Slave Lodge.

➕ 68 B2 ✉ Corner of Adderley and Wale streets, 8001 ☎ 021-4608242 🕐 Mon–Sat 10–5 ✋ Adult R15, child (under 16) free

Above *Gold staff finial symbolizing the king's authority, made by the Akan people of Ghana and in the Gold of Africa Museum*

Below *St. George's Anglican cathedral*

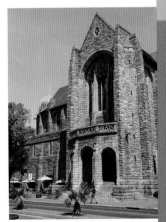

INFORMATION

www.simonstown.com

✚ 326 C11 ℹ Publicity Association, 111 St. George's Street, Simon's Town 7995 ☎ 021-7868440 ⊗ Nov–Mar Mon–Fri 9–5.30, Sat 9.30–1, Sun 10–1; Apr–Oct Mon–Fri 9–5, Sat 9.30–1

INTRODUCTION

False Bay is on the other side of the peninsula from Cape Town, where its warmer waters can be as much as 8°C (14°F) higher than elsewhere on the Atlantic seaboard. The area is sheltered and well developed for visitors with a string of seaside resorts and villages, and some excellent beaches that get busy with domestic visitors in summer. In spring, False Bay is the haunt of calving whales, and there are excellent opportunities for seeing southern right, humpback and Bryde's whales. The bay is easily reached from central Cape Town by the M3, which runs around the mountain and along the coast.

Simon's Town, the chief settlement on False Bay, is named after Governor Simon van der Stel, who decided in 1687 that an alternative, more protected port was needed in winter when Table Bay suffered from northwesterly winds. It was not until 1743 that the Dutch East India Company built a pier and barracks. In 1795, the town transferred to British hands, and following the end of the Napoleonic Wars in Europe, the British turned Simon's Town into a naval base, which it remained until 1957. The area was propelled to the forefront of popularity as a holiday resort when Cecil Rhodes bought a cottage in Muizenberg in 1899. Many other wealthy people followed, including authors Agatha Christie and Rudyard Kipling. Although a significant coloured population lived in False Bay, much of the area was designated 'white' under the Group Areas Act in the 1960s. Today, Kalk Bay has one of the few remaining coloured populations on the coast.

WHAT TO SEE

MUIZENBERG

Muizenberg has long been a popular local swimming spot. Today the town and its waterfront are rather run-down, but the beach itself is still excellent: a vast stretch of powdery white sand sloping gently to the water. The town has a handful of historic buildings, including Het Post Huijs on the main road, thought to be the oldest building in False Bay, dating back to 1673. Farther along is Rhodes Cottage, the summer retreat of Cecil Rhodes, where he died in 1902.

KALK BAY

Kalk Bay is one of the most attractive settlements in False Bay, with a bustling fishing harbour, a number of antiques shops and an appealing bohemian

Above *Jackass (African) penguins sun themselves at the water's edge on Boulders Beach*

character. Watch for the returning fishing boats at the harbour around noon. Their arrival is followed by a daily impromptu waterside auction, where you can buy a variety of fresh fish at the counters. Main Road is an attractive spot for a stroll, lined with antiques and bric-a-brac shops and a handful of arty cafés. Behind Kalk Bay is the beginning of Boyes Drive, a scenic route to Muizenberg. It's a spectacular road with sweeping views of False Bay and the Atlantic, and takes just 10 minutes to complete. Look for the signs from Main Road as you head out of Kalk Bay towards Simon's Town.

SIMON'S TOWN

This is the most popular town on False Bay, with a family-friendly atmosphere and numerous Victorian buildings lining Main Street. There are a few small museums, including Simon's Town Museum (Court Road, tel 021-7863046; Mon–Fri 10–4, Sat 10–1, Sun closed; entry by donation) in the 18th-century Governor's residence, an informative local history museum and the Heritage Museum (King George's Way, tel 021-7862302; Tue–Fri 11–4, Sat 11–1; entry by donation), which charts the history of the Muslim community in Simon's Town and the 7,000 people who were classified as coloured and therefore relocated to the Cape Flats townships (▷ 65). But most people come here for a swim, a stroll along the main road, and a seafood lunch overlooking the harbour. Also take some time to wander up the hill away from the main road—the quiet, bougainvillea-bedecked houses and cobbled streets are a welcome retreat from the bustle below.

The main beach, Seaforth, is a short drive to the south of town, and has changing and toilet facilities, snack bars and a clean stretch of shady lawn bordering the beach, with some picnic spots and bench seats. The swimming is safe here but there is no surf because of offshore rocks that protect the beach.

BOULDERS BEACH

About 2km (1.2 miles) south of Simon's Town is a delightful series of small sandy coves surrounded by huge boulders (hence the name). The beach is safe for swimming and gently sloping, making it good for children, but the main attraction is the colony of African penguins that live and nest between the boulders. The area, part of the Table Mountain National Park (tel 021-7862329; Dec–Jan daily 7am–7.30pm; Oct–Nov, Feb–Mar 8–6.30; Apr–Sep 8–5; R25, child (under 16) R5), has been created to protect the birds, and their numbers have flourished. This is one of only a few colonies on the mainland. The first cove tends to be packed with families on weekends and during school holidays; to find a more peaceful spot, walk along the boardwalk or crawl under the rocks on one side of the beach. Avoid the nesting areas at all times. An information centre tells you all you need to know about penguins.

TIPS

» In high season (mid-December to early February) drivers can avoid the traffic along the coast by taking the M65 from the Atlantic seaboard side, which crosses the mountains from Noordhoek to Fish Hoek.

» If you stop off for a meal in the resort of Fish Hoek, bear in mind that the town prohibits the sale of alcohol.

» Ask at Simon's Town harbour about boat trips to the Cape of Good Hope and Seal Island.

Below left *Bright beach huts, Muizenberg*
Below *Boats in Kalk Bay harbour*

REGIONS | **CAPE PENINSULA • SIGHTS**

73

KIRSTENBOSCH BOTANICAL GARDENS

www.sanbi.org

The biggest attraction in the southern suburbs is Kirstenbosch, South Africa's oldest, largest and most exquisite botanical gardens. It is one of the finest such gardens in the world, and its position and surroundings alone are incomparable. The gardens stretch up the eastern slopes of Table Mountain, merging seamlessly with the fynbos (indigenous woody plants) of the steep slopes above.

Although it is a joy to wander aimlessly in the gardens, it is worth seeking out some of the smaller specialist sections. The Fragrance Garden, for example, is set out so that visitors can fully appreciate the scents of the herbs and flowers. The Dell is one of the most enjoyable sections, following a beautifully shaded path snaking beneath ferns and along a stream.

Indigenous South African herbs can be inspected in the Medicinal Plants Garden, each one identified and used by the Khoi and San peoples in the treatment of a variety of ailments. For a sense of the past, visit Jan van Riebeeck's Hedge, a hedge of wild almond trees planted by the first Governor of the Cape in 1660 as part of a physical boundary to try to prevent cattle rustling. Segments still remain today within the garden. The Skeleton Path can be followed all the way to the summit of Table Mountain.

One of the most enjoyable ways of experiencing the gardens is at a Sunset Concert, held throughout summer. Every Sunday, a lower section of the gardens is transformed into an open-air concert venue, with the slopes above acting as seating. Hundreds of Capetonians spread out blankets on the grass and relax with wine and a picnic, while international artists play classical concerts, jazz, fusion-rock or pop. It's great fun and should not be missed if you're here in summer. Concerts are held every Sunday from from 5pm November to March.

➕ 326 C11 ✉ Rhodes Drive, Newlands 7700 ☎ 021-7998899 🕐 Sep–Mar daily 8–7; Apr–Aug 8–6 💵 Adult R37, child (6–17) R10 🚌 Golden Arrow service from Adderley Street to Kirstenbosch, takes around 50min 📷 'Eco-tours', or tours by motorized golf cart (reserve in advance)

🍴 🖻 🏛 🚻

RHODES MEMORIAL

www.rhodesmemorial.co.za

The Rhodes Memorial towers grandly on the slopes of Devil's Peak. This extravagant granite memorial to Cecil John Rhodes (Cape Prime Minister 1890–96) is made up of eight bronze lions flanking a wide flight of steps, which lead up to a Greek temple. Inside is an immense bronze head of Rhodes, above which is inscribed: 'To the spirit and life work of Cecil John Rhodes who loved and served South Africa'. There is also a magnificent view of the Cape Flats and the Southern Suburbs, and a pretty little restaurant set in a garden of hydrangeas.

➕ 326 C11 ✉ Off Rhodes Drive, Rondebosch 7707 ☎ 021-6870000 🕐 Nov–Apr daily 7–7; May–Oct 6–6 💵 Free 🍴

SOUTHERN SUBURBS

www.tourismcapetown.co.za

Cape Town's affluent suburbs stretch around Table Mountain, starting in the north with Woodstock. Observatory is an appealing area of tightly packed Victorian bungalows and student hangouts. Mowbray, Rosebank and Rondebosch lie just below the University of Cape Town, and are popular with students. Newlands backs right up to the slopes of Table Mountain and is known for its test cricket ground. On Boundary Road is Josephine Mill, the only surviving watermill in Cape Town. In summer, concerts are held in its grounds. The suburb of Claremont has little of interest other than the Cavendish Square shopping mall (▷ 87). To the west lie the prosperous valleys of Constantia (▷ 65) and Tokai.

➕ 326 C11 ℹ The Pinnacle, corner of Burg and Castle streets ☎ 021-4054500 🕐 Mon–Fri 8–6, Sat 8.30–1, Sun 9–1

Left *The grandiloquent Rhodes Memorial was built in 1912 on a spot where Rhodes liked to sit*

ROBBEN ISLAND

Lying 13km (8 miles) offshore from Cape Town's Victoria & Alfred Waterfront (▷ 78), Robben Island is best known as the notorious, isolated prison that held many of the ANC's most prominent members during the years of the struggle against apartheid, including Nelson Mandela (for 18 years) and Walter Sisulu. A visit here gives a fascinating insight into the workings of apartheid, with informative tours led by former political prisoners. It was originally named by the Dutch after the word for seals, 'robben', which used to be found here. The island functioned as a leper colony until 1931 and then a military base until 1960, when it was handed over to the Department of Prisons. It was declared a UNESCO World Heritage Site in 1999.

ISLAND TOURS

The island can be visited only on a tour organized by the Robben Island Museum. They run throughout the day, and passengers are ferried to the island by catamaran. All tours are led by former political prisoners, who paint a vivid picture of prison life. Lasting 2.5 hours, it begins with a drive around the key sites on the island, including the lime quarry where Mandela was forced to work, the leper cemetery and the houses of former warders.

BACKGROUND

Robben Island's effectiveness as a prison did not rest simply with the fact that escape was virtually impossible. The authorities anticipated that the concept of 'out of sight, out of mind' would be particularly applicable here, and to a certain extent they were correct. Its isolation tried to break the spirit of political prisoners, not least that of Robert Sobukwe, leader of the Pan African Congress (▷ 38), who was kept in solitary confinement for nine years. Other political prisoners were spared that at least, but were separated from the common law prisoners in 1971, being deemed a bad influence, and conditions were harsh, with forced hard labour and routine beatings. Black inmates fared worse than coloureds, and were given smaller food rations. Contact with the outside world was virtually non-existent: Newspapers were banned, and letters were limited to one every six months. Yet despite (or perhaps because of) these measures, the B-Section, which housed Mandela and other major political prisoners, became the international focus of the fight against apartheid. The last political prisoners left the island in 1991.

INFORMATION

www.robben-island.org.za
➕ 326 B11 ☎ 021-4134200 (Nelson Mandela Gateway) 🕐 Tours: daily 9, 11, 1, 3 💵 Adult R200, child (under 17) R100 🚌 Golden Arrow bus runs from Adderley Street to the V & A Waterfront 🚢 Boat crossing lasts half an hour 🍴 Restaurant in the Nelson Mandela Gateway 🏪 Small shop on the island selling postcards and books

TIPS

» If you have to wait for the catamaran crossing, check out the small museum upstairs in the Nelson Mandela Gateway, which has good interactive displays.
» Tickets sell out, so make reservations a day in advance (or several days in high season).
» Don't drink any tap water on the island.
» Phone ahead in bad weather to see if the catamaran is running.

Above *The forbidding outer wall of the prison block*

INFORMATION

www.tourismcapetown.co.za
www.tablemountain.net
www.sanparks.org
✚ 326 C11 ℹ The Pinnacle, corner of
Burg and Castle streets ☎ 021-4054500
◷ Mon–Fri 8–6, Sat 8.30–1, Sun 9–1

Above *The unmistakable landmark of
Table Mountain seen from Signal Hill*

INTRODUCTION

Table Mountain started to form around 700 million years ago when mud and
sand deposits were laid on the seabed, and it was still under water until 160
to 300 million years ago. It was pushed further upwards about 70 million years
ago, when exposure to the elements helped shape the mountain. Now, rising
a sheer 1,086m (3,563ft) from the coastal plain, Table Mountain dominates
almost every view of Cape Town. For centuries, it was the first sight afforded to
seafarers, its looming presence visible for hundreds of kilometres. Its size still
astonishes visitors today, but it is the mountain's wilderness, bang in the middle
of a bustling conurbation, that makes the biggest impression. Table Mountain,
managed by Table Mountain National Park, sustains more than 1,400 species of
flora, as well as baboons, dassies (rock hyraxes) and countless birds.

WHAT TO SEE
THE CABLEWAY

The dizzying trip to the top of the mountain in the Aerial Cableway takes just
under 10 minutes. There are two cars, each carrying up to 65 passengers; as you
ride up, the floor rotates allowing a full 360-degree view. At the top, paths criss-
cross the area around the station, with numerous viewpoints giving astounding
panoramas. From here you can also pick out the other formations that flank the
main flat-topped massif: Signal Hill and Lion's Head to the west, Devil's Peak to
the east, and the spine of the Twelve Apostles stretching south. The restaurant

sells cold drinks and beers, which you can take to the nearest viewpoints to enjoy with the sunset—better value than the cocktail bar in the station.

✉ Lower Cableway station, off Kloof Nek Road, 8001 ☎ 021-4248181 🕐 Dec–Jan 8am–8.30pm; Feb 8–7.30; Mar 8–6.30; Apr 8–5.30; May to mid-Sep 8.30–5; mid-Sep to Oct 8–6; Nov 8–7, but times can change according to weather conditions 🖐 Adult round-trip ticket R180, child (4–18) R90 🚌 Infrequent Golden Arrow buses drop off at Kloof Nek on their way to Camps Bay, from where it's a 1.5km (1-mile) walk up to the lower Cableway. Alternatively take a taxi

🍴 🍹 🎁

ROUTES UP THE MOUNTAIN

Much of the area is a nature reserve and a delightful wilderness to hike through. There are an estimated 100 paths to the top of Table Mountain, but the most popular route starts 1.5km (1 mile) beyond the lower Cableway station and follows a course up Platteklip Gorge. There's another path from Kirstenbosch Botanical Gardens (▷ 74). Both routes take about three hours to the top. Even the most used routes should not be taken lightly: Conditions can change alarmingly quickly, and fog (the famous 'Table Cloth' that flows from the top) and rain often descend without warning. The Cableway stops operating in poor weather or high winds, so do not rely on taking a cable car back down after climbing up. Numerous people have been caught off guard and the mountain has claimed its fair share of lives. Be sure to buy a detailed map (from the tourist office or lower Cableway station) and follow the mountain code—ask about it at the tourist office.

TIPS

» Look for dassies (rock hyraxes), rodent-like small mammals which scamper about the rocks. Bizarrely, their closest genetic relative is the elephant.

» From the beginning of November to the end of February, the Cableway is half price after 6pm and the last car down is as late as 9.30—ideal for watching the sunset over Cape Town.

» Signal Hill's summit at 350m (1,150ft) also has spectacular views. You can drive up, and it is a popular spot at sunset. The two-hour hike up Lion's Head is equally popular and provides 360-degree views.

» For Mountain Rescue ☎ 10177; for weather reports ☎ 021-4248181.

.

Below *Ride the Cableway up Table Mountain*

INFORMATION

www.waterfront.co.za

✚ 68 B1 🏢 Foreshore 8001
ℹ️ Clocktower Centre ☎ 021-4087600;
daily 9–9 🚌 Waterfront bus, run
by Golden Arrow, runs every 15 min
between rail station on Adderley Street
and Waterfront, R4 one-way 🍴 Huge
selection of restaurants, cafés and bars
🛍️ Large shopping mall, plus smaller
boutiques and markets

TIPS

» The outdoor amphitheatre in the middle
of the Waterfront is a great place to catch
live jazz at the weekend and during the
annual Cape Town International Jazz
Festival (▷ 89).

» Look for frolicking Cape fur seals as
you cross the swing bridge from the Clock
Tower.

» Behind the main shopping malls are a
couple of indoor markets selling local arts
and crafts.

Opposite *The bright red clock tower is a
useful landmark*

Below *Victoria & Alfred Waterfront at dusk*

VICTORIA & ALFRED WATERFRONT

Cape Town's original Victorian harbour is the city's most popular attraction, for
both visitors and locals, with its numerous shops, restaurants and cinemas. The
whole area was completely restored in the early 1990s, and today it is a lively
district. At the same time, it remains a working harbour, and this provides much
of the area's true charm. Original buildings stand shoulder to shoulder with
mock-Victorian shopping malls, boutiques and alfresco restaurants, all crowding
along a waterside walkway, with Table Mountain looming in the background. The
Nelson Mandela Gateway to Robben Island (▷ 75) has done much to raise the
cultural profile of the area.

THE CLOCK TOWER

At the narrow entrance to the Alfred Basin is the original Clock Tower, a
distinctive red, octagonal Gothic-style tower built in 1882 to house the Port
Captain's office. It stands in front of the Clock Tower Centre, the smartest
collection of shops, offices and restaurants along the Waterfront, with a helpful
tourist office upstairs.

TWO OCEANS AQUARIUM

www.aquarium.co.za

A top attraction along the Waterfront is the aquarium, which focuses on the
Cape marine environment created by the merging of the Atlantic and Indian
oceans. The display begins with a walk through the Indian Ocean, where visitors
follow a route past tanks filled with a multitude of brilliantly hued fish, giant
spider crabs and phosphorescent jellyfish, floating in a mesmerizing circular
current. Children are well served, with touch pools and the Alpha Activity Centre,
where they can enjoy free puppet shows and face painting. The top draw,
however, is the predators exhibit, an enormous tank complete with glass tunnel
that you can walk through, which holds ragged-tooth sharks, eagle rays, turtles,
and some impressively large hunting fish. The penguins are fed daily at 11.30
and 2.30, while the predators are fed daily at 3. Experienced divers can arrange
to dive with the sharks.

✉️ Dock Road ☎ 021-4183823 🕐 Daily 9.30–6 ✋ Adult R96, child (4–13) R46, (14–17) R74

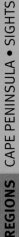

CHAPMAN'S PEAK

The most spectacular route on the Cape Peninsula is the famous Chapman's Peak Drive, which has unrivalled views of Hout Bay, the coastline and the ocean. It starts at Hout Bay (⊞ 326 B11).

THE DRIVE
Distance: 15km (9 miles)
Allow: 30 minutes
Start at: Hout Bay
End at: Noordhoek

★ Begin at Hout Bay. Follow the signs for Chapman's Peak Drive, which will allow you to skirt around the town. On the far side of the bay, the road branches off to the left and begins to climb. Chapman's Peak Drive begins just outside Hout Bay at the toll-booth, where you will have to stop and pay R30 (per car). Keep your ticket. Once past the booth, continue straight up the road (there is only one road, so you can't get lost). It hugs the coast, rising to 600m (2,000ft). There are viewpoints all along this first stretch.

❶ Die Josie Lookout, at around 170m (558ft) above the ocean, is the

Above *Hout Bay seen from Chapman's Peak*
Opposite *Cape sugarbird on a protea flower*

first viewpoint worth a stop—ignore all the earlier ones. It is on the first headland, reached after about 6km (3.5 miles). Park the car on the right and get out to marvel at the views of Hout Bay. Unsurprisingly, this is one of the most photographed views of Cape Town, with the perfect arc of the beach setting off the blue of the sea and the green of the surrounding hills.

The road continues around the headland, clinging to a narrow ledge between the stark, yellow-hued rocks and the thrashing ocean below. Look for the giant nets above the road, which catch falling rocks from above.

❷ Chapman's Point, a further 2.5km (1.5 miles) along, is the next striking lookout point. This headland juts into the ocean, giving you your first glimpse of the expanse of white sand at Noordhoek beach, shelving steeply into big surf.

Continue along the road, which now begins to slope down towards the seaside village of Noordhoek, until you reach the other toll. Show your ticket here and pass through. If you want to visit the beach, take the first road on your right. However, the beach is unsafe for swimming and should be avoided after dark. To get back to Cape Town, pass back through the toll on the same ticket.

WHEN TO GO
This drive is spectacular at any time of the year, particularly at sunset. The road periodically closes in bad weather; check it's open at www.chapmanspeakdrive.co.za.

WHERE TO EAT
RED HERRING
There's a bar upstairs and à la carte restaurant downstairs, serving great steaks, plus grilled fish and calamari. ✉ Red Herring Trading Post, Beach Road, Noordhoek ☎ 021-7891783 🕐 Tue–Sun 12–10, Mon 6.30–10,

WALK

SILVERMINE NATURE RESERVE

More than 2,000ha (5,000 acres) of the Steenberg, the mountain range that straddles the road south from Cape Town, have been set aside as the Silvermine Nature Reserve. As well as being part of the larger Table Mountain National Park, it is also part of the Cape Floristic Kingdom, the smallest but richest of the world's six floral kingdoms. This walk takes in much of the area's indigenous plant life, with the striking backdrop of the peninsula seaboard along the way. It starts and ends at Silvermine Dam (⊞ 326 C11).

THE WALK
Distance: 9.5km (6 miles)
Allow: 4 hours
Start/end at: Silvermine Dam
How to get there: From Cape Town take the M64, better known as Ou Kaapseweg ('Old Cape Road'), which bisects the reserve. The way into the reserve's western section is on your right at the top of the pass. Drive straight up to the parking area near the reservoir (2km/1.2 miles)

★ Set off from the parking area at the reservoir of the Silvermine Reserve.

❶ The Reserve overlooks the narrow 'waist' of the Cape Peninsula, extending from Kalk Bay in the east to Noordhoek in the west. It was given its name in the 1680s by Dutch settlers who believed, all too optimistically, that a fabulous lode of silver lay beneath the high ground.

Cross the dam wall and make your way south to the route intersection. Take the left path, and continue up the hill until you reach the vehicle track, bearing right along the ridge to Noordhoek Peak (754m/ 2,473ft), which is about 2.5km (1.5 miles) from the reservoir. The views en route take in the sweep of the western seaboard from the Noordhoek Valley below to Kommetjie in the hazy distance. The view across to Hout Bay in the north is even better from the top of the peak (the track leads all the way up).

❷ As you head for Noordhoek Peak, don't forget to tear your eyes away

from the views and look at the plants covering the terrain around you. The Cape Peninsula encompasses what is thought to be the world's highest concentration of plant species—nearly 3,000 are crammed into its narrow confines, most belonging to what is known as fynbos ('fine bush'), a heath-like vegetation that includes proteas, ericas, reed-like restios, leucadendrons and various bulbs. Around 200 are indigenous; more than 900 are to be found in the Silvermine area. Many species are rare and endangered, and most bloom briefly and gloriously after the winter rains have passed, before the hot summer winds begin. Of special note are the golden conebush, a winter-flowering plant, the creamy blackbeard sugarbush and the year-round pagoda tree. Fynbos attracts a lively complement of birds, among them ground woodpeckers, sugarbirds and the brilliant orange-breasted sunbirds. You may also spot the rock kestrel and, hunting above the slopes, the imperious black eagle.

Once you've taken in the views of the seaboard, retrace your steps and, after about 300m (330 yards), bear left to the Elephant's Eye cave.

❸ Elephant's Eye cave is a dramatic cleft in the landscape, with a fern-festooned interior and wide-reaching views from its mouth of the wine estates of Constantia and the protected Tokai Forest. In good weather, you can see beyond the Southern Suburbs (▷ 74) out to the

stretches of the townships on the Cape Flats (▷ 65), with the peaks of the Winelands in the hazy distance.

Continue south to rejoin the vehicle track and walk the 2km (1.2 miles) back to the reservoir. Look for the Prins Kasteel waterfall on your way.

WHEN TO GO
The short spring season (usually the end of August to the end of September) is the best time to see the wild flowers blooming on the hillsides. The heat can be intense in summer, so avoid walking in the sun between 11 and 3. Winter days are often wet and chilly.

WHERE TO EAT
There is an attractive picnic spot near the parking area, which is accessible to wheelchair users by a boardwalk.

PLACE TO VISIT
SILVERMINE NATURE RESERVE
☎ 021-7809002 ⏰ Sep–Apr daily 7–6; May–Aug daily 8–5 💰 Adult R20, child (2–12) R10

THE HEART OF CAPE TOWN

This leisurely walk begins at the point where Wale Street meets Adderley Street, Cape Town's busiest thoroughfare, and leads southwards, around and through the spacious Company's Garden. The latter part of the route takes you back into the heart of the city.

THE WALK

Distance: 2.8km (1.7 miles)
Allow: 2.5 hours
Start/end at: St. George's Cathedral

★ Begin in Wale Street at St. George's Cathedral (▷ 71), which in the last years of apartheid served as a forum for protest against injustice, both as a political pulpit for Archbishop Desmond Tutu and as a launch pad for the pivotal peace marches that helped pave the way to full democracy in 1994.

From the Cathedral, turn right and walk a few paces east along Wale Street, then turn first right and make your way south along Government Avenue, a leafy, pedestrian-only road running the length of Company's Garden, where Cape Town began. The tame squirrels that you'll see scurrying among the oak trees here are an exotic species, introduced by the mining tycoon and Cape premier Cecil Rhodes (▷ 35), who imported their ancestors from America a little more than a century ago. The handsome Houses of Parliament are on your left, here seen from the rear of the building.

❶ The Houses of Parliament complex, built of white-trimmed terracotta brick, began life in 1885 and has since been much enlarged—mainly to accommodate the apartheid government's intricate constitutional 'reforms' of the 1980s—into a labyrinthine warren of chambers, offices and corridors. Continue along Government Avenue for 400m (440 yards). The South African National Gallery (▷ 71) is the white building on your left.

❷ In front of the South African National Gallery is a series of fountains fronted by a rather austere but striking statue of South African statesman Jan Smuts (1870–1950). A few metres beyond the Gallery is the Old Synagogue, built in 1863 in Egyptian revival style and now incorporated into the complex of the modern Jewish Museum (▷ 70).

Turn back towards the gardens and turn left, walking along the front of the South African Museum and its Planetarium (▷ 70). From here, walk straight ahead between the rose gardens at the start of Company's Garden. Take a moment to turn around and take in the lovely views of Table Mountain behind you, perfectly framed by the boughs of the trees. Continue into Company's Garden proper.

❸ Company's Garden (▷ 67–69), which the first European colonists planted as a market garden in 1652, was transformed by architect Sir Herbert Baker into an elegant park, with flower beds, trees and shrubs. At the far end is Cape Town's oldest statue, that of a grizzled Sir George Grey, Governor of the Cape from 1854 to 1862. Behind the statue stands the National Library of South Africa, the country's oldest reference repository (it dates from 1822) and among the world's earliest free libraries. The building is based on the Fitzwilliam Museum in Cambridge, England; the entrance lies between Queen Victoria Street and Government Avenue.

Take the right exit from the gardens, turn left onto Government Avenue and walk back to Wale Street. From here, cross the road and head up Adderley Street (▷ 67).

❹ You'll see the old Slave Lodge (▷ 71) on your right, and farther down this busy shopping artery are some handsome old bank buildings interspersed with 1960s shopping malls, such as the Sanlam Golden Acre complex.

Two blocks before the latter—about 300m (330 yards) from Wale Street—turn left into Shortmarket Street, crossing the traffic-free St. George's Mall and leading into Greenmarket Square (▷ 69).

❺ Greenmarket Square was built as early as 1710 as a market place, a function it still fulfils nearly 300 years later through its lively daily market on the cobbles. The tree-fringed square is lined with cafés and is a popular meeting place.

Take a stroll around the market before heading to the top (southern) corner of the square, walking up one

block and turning right into Church Street, the heart of the city's trade in antiques and quirky collectables. A small street market here sells assorted antiques and bric-a-brac. At the top of Church Street, turn left onto Long Street.

❻ On Long Street (▷ 71) you can stroll past the cafés, restaurants and quirky shops

One block on, turn left down Wale Street and you'll see St. George's Cathedral one block down.

WHEN TO GO
You'll get the most out of the walk on a weekday between 9 and 5, when the whole area is bustling. Avoid walking away from Long Street late at night. The summer months are the most pleasant, although it can get intensely hot around midday in December, January and February. Expect lower temperatures and rain in winter.

WHERE TO EAT
CAFÉ MOZART
A great place for lunch amid the antique shops; serves light meals.
✉ 37 Church Street, City Centre 8001
☎ 021-4243774 🕒 Mon–Sat 7–3

Opposite Delville Wood Memorial and South African Museum in Company's Garden
Below The Houses of Parliament

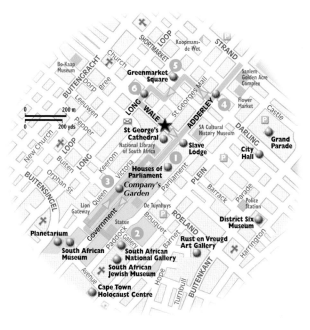

Above *Colourful posters at Greenmarket Square, Cape Town*

CAMPS BAY AND ATLANTIC SEABOARD

THE BRONX
www.bronx.co.za
Cape Town's most popular gay bar and club gets packed out at weekends. The clientele is mostly men, but women are welcome. DJs play techno every night, and there is karaoke on Monday.
✉ 22 Somerset Road, Green Point 8005 ☎ 021-4199216 🕓 Daily 8pm–late ✋ Free

CAFÉ CAPRICE
www.cafecaprice.co.za
This is one of the most popular cafés and bars on the main road along popular Camps Bay Beach. There are outdoor seats overlooking the sand, tasty snacks and delicious fresh-fruit cocktails. The crowd, famously beautiful, congregates from sunset.
✉ 37 Victoria Road, Camps Bay 8005 ☎ 021-4388315 🕓 Daily 9am–late ✋ Free

DIZZY JAZZ CAFÉ
The busy Dizzy Café hosts nightly live jazz and is popular with locals due to its fairly small size, giving it a more intimate feel than other venues. Its friendly crowd gives the place an appealingly down-to-earth atmosphere. Good food is served and the most popular nights are Thursday to Sunday. The music usually starts around 8.30pm.
✉ 41 The Drive, Camps Bay 8005 ☎ 021-4382686 🕓 Wed–Mon 5pm–late ✋ From R30

GREEN POINT MARKET
This large curio market is a good bet for African crafts, usually cheaper here than elsewhere. There are also food stalls, and buskers.
✉ Beside Green Point Stadium, Green Point 8005 🕓 Sun 8–5

KARMA LOUNGE
www.karmalounge.co.za
Minimalist African-style décor, ocean views, a long list of cocktails and a champagne bar and cigar lounge make this an unbeatable spot for an evening of socializing in beautiful Camps Bay. Live DJs start the night in chilled mood, gradually upping the tempo into the early hours.
✉ Penthouse Suite, The Promenade, Victoria Road 8005 ☎ 021-4387773 🕓 Wed–Sun 7pm–late ✋ From R30

LA MED
www.lamed.co.za
La Med is hugely popular, with a busy bar overlooking the sea. There's a good choice of pub food, but the reason to come is its legendary sundowners, though it is hard to find a seat at sunset. The bar turns into a raucous club later in the evening.
✉ Glen Country Club, 2a Victoria Road, Clifton 8005 ☎ 021-4385600 🕓 Daily 9pm–late ✋ From R30

NOORDHOEK BEACH HORSE RIDES
www.horseriding.co.za
Noordhoek Beach is a popular spot for horse rides: the long, hard-packed sand is perfect for galloping, and more sedate sunset rides are also available. Booking is essential.
✉ Noordhoek Beach 9301 ☎ 082-7741191 ✋ From R350

PARA-PAX
www.parapax.com
Paragliding from Lion's Head is very popular, with gliders landing by the sea between Clifton and Camps Bay. Para-Pax can also organize tandem paragliding sessions.
☎ 021-4617070/082-8814724 ✋ Single tandem paragliding session R950

ST. YVES BEACH CLUB
www.styves.co.za
A popular spot with Cape Town's 'beautiful crowd', this is a place to see and be seen as well as to enjoy the wonderful ocean views from the comfortable decking area. Come early to relax with a cocktail while watching the sun go down, or come late in the evening to enjoy the thumping dance floor.

✉ The Promenade, Victoria Road 8005
☎ 021-4300826 ● Mon–Sat 7–late

CAPE TOWN
AFRICAN IMAGE
This bright and interesting curio shop has a far larger selection of goods than most of the craft shops in town. It has a wide range of tribal art and crafts from across Africa, and unusual gifts made from all kinds of recycled items, such as bags made from cola bottle tops and decorative chickens made from plastic bags. There's another branch in the Table Bay Mall at the Victoria & Alfred Waterfront.

✉ 52 Burg Street, City Centre 8001
☎ 021-4238385 ● Mon–Fri 9–5, Sat 9–1

AFRICAN MUSIC STORE
www.africanmusicstore.co.za
This lively little shop sells a comprehensive choice of albums by major southern African artists, as well as compilations and reggae. The staff are knowledgeable and incredibly helpful and will happily let you listen to any number of CDs before making your choice.

✉ 134 Long Street, City Centre 8001
☎ 021-4260857 ● Mon–Fri 9–6, Sat 9–2

ARTSCAPE THEATRE CENTRE
www.artscape.co.za
The Artscape is Cape Town's major arts complex hosting a busy schedule of opera, theatre and classical music concerts. There are three stages—the Main Theatre, the Arena and the Opera House—which show a mix of classical concerts, musicals and dance, as well as new experimental theatre.

✉ 10 D. F. Malan Street, Foreshore 8001
☎ 021-4109800 ✋ From R50

CAPE PHILHARMONIC ORCHESTRA
www.cpo.org.za
Cape Town has a well-respected Philharmonic Orchestra based at the former City Hall. The 80 musicians are under the direction of a resident conductor and visiting guest conductors; they also perform regularly in the Artscape (▷ above) and at Kirstenbosch (▷ 74).

✉ Artscape Theatre, 10 D.F. Malan Street, Foreshore 8001 ☎ 021-4109809
✋ From R110

CAPE TOWN OPERA
www.capetownopera.co.za
The city's opera company stages regular performances, mostly the classics, and has a reputation for developing singers from different racial backgrounds—opera is no longer the reserve of the white and wealthy. Performances are usually held at the Artscape complex (▷ above).

✉ Artscape Theatre Centre, 10 D. F. Malan Street, Foreshore 8001 ☎ 021-4109807
✋ From R100

DOWNHILL ADVENTURES
www.downhilladventures.com
The city's best-known adventure operator organizes a range of mountain biking excursions, including the popular Table Mountain double descent (90 percent downhill) and rides around Cape Point. You can also rent bicycles. The Cape's strong winds have made it a very popular site for kitesurfing. The best spot is Dolphin Beach at Table View, north of the city centre, where winds are strong and waves perfect for jumping. Downhill Adventures offers beginners tuition and recommends three sessions before going alone. They also organize half- and full-day sandboarding trips to dunes about an hour's drive north of the city, and day and multi-day surfing courses.

✉ Overbeek Building, corner of Kloof, Long and Orange streets, City Centre 8001
☎ 021-4220388 ● Cycling tours of Cape Point Winelands R695; kitesurfing R1,350; sandboarding R550; surfing R550 per day

FASHIONTV CAFÉ
www.ftv.co.za
This local branch of an international chain has become a magnet for any celebrities who are in town. It includes a separate club, bar and restaurant, so you can enjoy a chilled drink or quiet dinner if you don't want to dance.

✉ 114 Hout Street, City Centre 8001
☎ 021-4266000 ● Restaurant and bar: Mon–Sat 10am–late; club: Wed, Fri–Sat 9pm–late ✋ Club from R40

FICTION
www.fictionbar.com
Taking its inspiration from graphic novels past and present, this popular bar and club, which stages live DJ nights, is a city centre highlight. Music varies between drum and bass to house to hip hop, and there are also themed nights. It's always loud and always lively.

✉ 226 Long Street, City Centre 8001
☎ 021-4245709 ● Tue, Thu–Sat 9pm–4am ✋ From R70

GREENMARKET SQUARE MARKET
Cape Town's best-known and liveliest market sells a wide variety of arts, crafts and curios from across Africa. The square has a pleasant, bustling atmosphere, helped by the various buskers and entertainers who line the cobbles, and a number of laid-back cafés and restaurants around the edge of the square.

✉ Greenmarket Square, City Centre 8001
● Mon–Fri 8–5, Sat 9–2

JAZZART
www.jazzart.co.za
This is the oldest modern dance company in South Africa, founded in 1975. Jazzart has a long history of cultural involvement and multiracial performances, and the company continues to be actively involved with disadvantaged communities, working as a racially mixed group and creating a fusion of Western and African dance styles.

✉ Artscape Theatre Centre, 10 D.F. Malan Street, Foreshore 8001 ☎ 021-4109848
✋ From R65

JEWEL AFRICA

www.jewelafrica.com

You'll find a wide range of good quality gold, silver, platinum and precious stones here, including diamonds and tanzanite. The shop claims to be Africa's largest jewellery showroom, and specializes in personal designs (which can be completed in 24 hours).

✉ 170 Buitengracht Street, Bo-Kaap 8001 ☎ 021-4245141 🕐 Mon–Fri 9–7.30, Sat 9–5.30, Sun 4–7

JO'BURG

One of the city's most popular and best-established bars is trendy Jo'burg, serving pints and cocktails. Early evenings are relaxed, but the pace picks up from 9pm when DJs play funky house and drum 'n' bass. .

✉ 218 Long Street, City Centre 8001 ☎ 021-4220142 🕐 Daily noon–4am 🖐 Free

LABIA

www.labia.co.za

This is Cape Town's most enjoyable cinema, showing independent international films and hosting the Out in Africa film festival. A café serves good pre-movie snacks, and the whole cinema is licensed to serve alcohol, so you can sip your glass of wine while you watch the movie.

✉ 68 Orange Street, Gardens 8001 ☎ 021-4245927 🕐 Daily noon–11 🖐 From R25

MEMEME

Mememe is one of many tiny boutiques on Long Street. It sells good clothes and accessories, most created by local designers.

✉ 117a Long Street, City Centre 8001 ☎ 021-4240001 🕐 Mon–Fri 9–5.30, Sat 9.30–3.30

MERCURY LIVE AND LOUNGE

www.mercuryl.co.za

For something different and local try this live venue, which features South African rock bands, performing in both English and Afrikaans. There are occasional DJ evenings. Mercury Live and Lounge is especially popular with the under 30 crowd.

✉ 43 De Villiers Street, Zonnebloem 7925 ☎ 021-4652106 🕐 Mon, Wed, Fri, Sat 9pm–late 🖐 From R20

MONKEYBIZ

www.monkeybiz.co.za

Monkeybiz, something of a local sensation, creates employment for Township women, who make beautiful and quirky one-off bead works, including figures, animals and accessories. Their work is also sold at the tourist office.

✉ 43 Rose Street, Bo-Kaap 8001 ☎ 021-4260145 🕐 Mon–Fri 9–5, Sat 9–1

PAN AFRICAN MARKET

www.panafrican.co.za

Occupying a whole building, this 'market' is actually more like a set of shops, each selling arts and crafts from across the continent. It has a range of good-value jewellery, including Zulu beadwork and Masai necklaces, as well as a vast choice of masks, sculptures and gifts. There is also a small restaurant serving traditional African dishes.

✉ Long Street, City Centre 8001 ☎ 021-4264478 🕐 Mon–Sat 8.30–6

PERSEVERANCE TAVERN

www.perseverancetavern.co.za

The Perseverance is famed for being Cape Town's oldest pub, built in 1808. It serves bottled and draught beers and good pub food. There's a beer garden and plenty of little drinking corners. The pub gets full at the weekend, and is especially popular for its Sunday roasts.

✉ 83 Buitenkant Street, City Centre 8001 ☎ 021-4612440 🕐 Mon–Sat 12–12 🖐 Free

SCUBA SHACK

www.scubashack.co.za

The Cape waters are cold but are often very clear and good for wreck and reef diving. Scuba Shack offers a full range of PADI-recognized instruction, as well as organized tours to the best dive sites and great white shark cage dives. There's also an office at Kommetjie on the peninsula (tel 021-7856742).

✉ 289 Long Street, City Centre 8001

☎ 021-4241115 🖐 A single dive R605 (including equipment); a PADI Open Water course from R3,200

STREETWIRES

www.streetwires.co.za

This wire sculpture co-operative is a great place to find interesting Township craftwork without feeling under pressure to buy. Look out for the key rings and sculptures.

✉ 77 Shortmarket Street, City Centre 8001 ☎ 021-4262475 🕐 Mon–Fri 8.30–5

UWE KOETTER

www.uwekoetter.co.za

This shop sells traditional, high-quality, exclusive pieces from one of the country's best-known designers. The emphasis is on diamonds, but there are less expensive options. Tours of the workshop are available.

✉ 4th Floor, Amway House, Dock Road, City Centre 8001 ☎ 021-4257770 🕐 Mon–Fri 9–6.30, Sat 9–3.30

FALSE BAY

THE BRASS BELL

The best-known pub in False Bay, with a spectacular setting right on the waves—a great spot for a cold beer while watching the sunset. Live music at weekends. There's a fish and steak restaurant upstairs.

✉ Next to rail station, Kalk Bay 7975 ☎ 021-7885455 🕐 Daily 11am–late 🖐 Free

INDIA JANE

One of a small Cape Peninsula boutique chain selling high fashion items from South African designers, with some one-off pieces.

✉ Station Building, Main Road, Kalk Bay 7945 ☎ 021-7883020 🕐 Daily 9.30–5.30

HOUT BAY

NAUTICAT

www.nauticatcharters.co.za

Daily 35-minute cruises run from Hout Bay to Duiker Island in a glass-bottomed boat. Duiker Island is a Cape fur seal and bird sanctuary, home to thousands of seals and seabirds. It is illegal to land on the island but the boats circle it and get very close to the seals.

✉ Hout Bay Harbour, Hout Bay 7872
☎ 021-7907278 ⏰ Trips daily 8.45, 9.45, 11, 12.45, 2.45, 3.45 ✋ Adult R60, child (2–14) R30

MILNERTON
MILNERTON GOLF CLUB
www.milnertongolf.co.za
This is a true links course, beautifully located with spectacular views of Table Mountain. It is 6,011m (6,552 yards), par 72, but watch out when the wind blows.
✉ Bridge Road, Milnerton 7741 ☎ 021-5521047 ✋ R395

MTN SCIENCENTRE
www.mtnsciencentre.org.za
This is South Africa's only interactive science museum, aimed at helping children learn about scientific discoveries and technological innovations. There are more than 280 displays, most of them interactive, as well as an auditorium and an exhibition hall.
✉ Century City, Milnerton 7446
☎ 021-4059435 ⏰ Mon–Thu 9.30–6, Fri–Sat 9.30–8, Sun 10–6 ✋ Adult R20, child (3–18) R25, family R78

RATANGA JUNCTION
www.ratanga.co.za
South Africa's largest theme park is a re-creation of a 19th-century mining town, crammed with impressive thrill rides and roller-coasters, as well as more sedate family rides for young children. Tickets allow unlimited number of rides.
✉ Century City, Milnerton 7441 ☎ 0861-200300 ⏰ Wed–Fri, Sun 10–5, Sat 10–6 (extended during school holidays) ✋ Adult R142, child (up to 1.3m/4.2ft tall) R70

SOUTHERN SUBURBS
BAXTER
www.baxter.co.za
This is Cape Town's more alternative theatre complex, with a long-term involvement in black theatre and a good reputation for supporting community theatre. In addition to putting on small, independent plays, it hosts international productions and musicals.
✉ Main Road, Rondebosch 7700 ☎ 021-6857880 ✋ From R55

CAPE TOWN CITY BALLET
www.capetowncityballet.org.za
A small and tightly knit company without state sponsorship, the Cape Town City Ballet maintains a high standard, performing well-known classics as well as more modern works.
✉ UCT School of Dance, Lover's Walk, Rosebank 7700 ☎ 021-6502400 ✋ From R65

CAVENDISH SQUARE
www.cavendish.co.za
Trendy Cavendish Square mall has clothes, household and book stores, as well as a range of restaurants and a cinema complex. It's very popular with the younger generation and the fashion-conscious.
✉ Dreyer Street, Claremont 7708 ☎ 021-6575620 ⏰ Mon–Sat 9–7, Sun 10–5

DAY TRIPPERS
www.daytrippers.co.za
This operator is one of the most popular for arranging all-round active tours and is popular with backpackers. A number of their trips include kloofing (canyoning).
✉ Santos Park Unit 8, Voortrekker Road, Maitland 7405 ☎ 021-5114766 ✋ Full-day Cape Point trip R425, including lunch

INDEPENDENT ARMCHAIR THEATRE
www.armchairtheatre.co.za
The Armchair, as it's known by students, is a great little venue where you can catch some local rock, hip-hop and folk acts. There are live bands on most nights, but the venue also hosts stand-up comedy nights and screens movies.
✉ 135 Lower Main Road, Observatory 7925 ☎ 021-4471514 ⏰ Daily 8pm–late ✋ From R15

KIRSTENBOSCH SUMMER CONCERTS
www.sanbi.org
The summer concerts held in idyllic Kirstenbosch Botanical Gardens are a highlight of the Cape's arts calendar. Music varies from jazz and classical to pop. People spread out on the lawns, unpack picnics and enjoy the music and views.
✉ Kirstenbosch Botanical Gardens, Rhodes Drive, Newlands 7708 ☎ 021-7998899 ⏰ Nov–Mar Sun from 5pm ✋ From R40

MOWBRAY GOLF CLUB
www.mowbraygolfclub.co.za
Mowbray is one of the oldest clubs in Cape Town and hosts the national championships. It's a par 74 course

Left *Popular Jo'burg bar*

with plenty of trees and water holes.
☒ Raapenberg Road, Mowbray 7700
☎ 021-6853018 ✋ R425 for 18 holes,
R240 for 9 holes

NEWLANDS SAHARA PARK CRICKET GROUND

www.cricket.co.za

Despite redevelopment, this famous
test match ground still has a few
of its famous old oak trees, and
you can still watch a game from a
grassy bank with Table Mountain as
a backdrop.
☒ 161 Campground Road, Newlands
7700 ☎ 021-6572003 🕓 Cricket season:
Nov–Mar ✋ From R60

WESTERN PROVINCE RUGBY FOOTBALL UNION GROUND

www.wprugby.com

This is the city's main rugby ground,
and international games are played
here. Wear a hat and bring plenty of
sunscreen as shade is limited around
the ground.
☒ Boundary Road, Newlands 7700
☎ 021-6594600 🕓 Rugby season:
Apr–Oct ✋ From R85

TABLE MOUNTAIN

ABSEIL AFRICA

www.abseilafrica.co.za

Abseil Africa operates what it claims
is the world's highest and longest
commercial abseil (rappell)—a 112m
(367ft) drop down Table Mountain.
☒ Top Cableway station, Table Mountain

☎ 021-4244760 ✋ R595 (excluding
Cableway fee), weather permitting

VICTORIA & ALFRED WATERFRONT

BUENA VISTA SOCIAL CAFÉ

www.buenavista.co.za

This Cuban-themed bar and
restaurant caters to an affluent
crowd. The music is a hot mix of live
Cuban bands and a DJ playing Latin
sounds. The broad balcony is ideal for
drinking cocktails on a hot evening.
☒ 15 Alfred House, Portswood Road,
Victoria & Alfred Waterfront ☎ 021-
4210348 🕓 Daily noon–late ✋ Free

CINEMA NOUVEAU

Cinema Nouveau is the alternative
arm of the mainstream complex—
Nu Metro—upstairs, and screens
a good range of foreign films and
independent American films.
☒ Victoria & Alfred Waterfront 8001
☎ 021-4258223 🕓 Daily 11–9
✋ From R25

QUAY FOUR

www.quay4.co.za

Quay Four's large, shady deck
overlooking the water is the perfect
place for an early evening drink.
Locals and visitors, who come here
for the views and the good-value
meals, draught beer and cocktails.
☒ Victoria & Alfred Waterfront 8001
☎ 021-4192008 🕓 11am–midnight
✋ Free

TABLE BAY DIVING

www.tablebaydiving.com

This operator organizes dive charters
and PADI courses, as well as selling
scuba and snorkelling gear.
☒ Quay 5, Victoria & Alfred Waterfront
8001 ☎ 021-4198822 ✋ From R350
(excluding equipment)

VAUGHAN JOHNSON'S WINE SHOP

Johnson's is one of the best-stocked
wine merchants in the area, selling
an exhaustive range from the
Winelands and across the country.
The staff here are knowledgeable and
can arrange a shipping service.
☒ Victoria & Alfred Waterfront 8001
☎ 021-4192121 🕓 Daily 9.30–9

VICTORIA WHARF

www.waterfront.co.za

The area's best-known shopping
mall is also its most central. Clothes
shops (including international labels
such as Levis and Diesel) sell their
wares at marginally cheaper prices
than back home.
☒ Victoria & Alfred Waterfront 8001
☎ 021-4087600 🕓 Mon–Sat 9–9, Sun
10–6

WATERFRONT BOAT COMPANY

www.waterfrontboats.co.za

The company has several boats,
among them a large catamaran and
stylish yacht, and offers a range of
boat tours including a circular trip
around Robben Island, and sunset
and dinner cruises.
☒ Quay 5, Victoria & Alfred Waterfront
8001 ☎ 021-4185806 ✋ From R190 for
1.5-hour sunset cruise

WORDSWORTH BOOKS

www.wordsworth.co.za

This bookshop and coffee shop
stocks an excellent selection of
travel literature, with a good section
on South Africa, plus a range of
guidebooks and maps.
☒ Victoria Wharf, Victoria & Alfred
Waterfront 8001 ☎ 021-4256880
🕓 Daily 9–9

FESTIVALS AND EVENTS

JANUARY
CAPE TOWN MINSTREL CARNIVAL

Popularly known as the Coon Carnival (despite its derogatory connotations), Karnaval begins in Bo-Kaap and ends at the Green Point Stadium. The procession of competing minstrel bands, complete with straw boaters and bright satin suits, is quite a spectacle.
☎ 021-4264260 ⊕ 2 January

J&B METROPOLITIAN HANDICAP

www.jbmet.co.za
South Africa's equivalent to the UK's Ascot or Australia's Melbourne Cup, this is the country's annual horse-racing meet at Kenilworth Race Course, where everyone is expected to dress up. The parties after the racing continue into the night.
⊕ Last Saturday in January

FEBRUARY
CAPE TOWN PRIDE

www.capetownpride.co.za
Cape Town Pride starts with a gay pride parade touring central Cape Town and culminates in a street party which goes on until the early hours in Green Point.
⊕ Last weekend of February

MARCH/APRIL
CAPE TOWN FESTIVAL

www.capetownfestival.co.za
This week-long arts and cultural festival is held at various venues throughout the city. A music stage is set up in Company's Garden, and children's events are held on one day of the week.
⊕ March

CAPE TOWN INTERNATIONAL JAZZ FESTIVAL

www.capetownjazzfest.com
This is the city's biggest annual jazz event, taking place in the Convention Centre over a weekend in April. Four stages feature local and international jazz artists, from local legends like Hugh Masekela to international acts like Elvis Costello and Jamie Cullum. An open-air pre-festival is usually held at the Grand Parade.
☎ 021-4225653 ⊕ Last weekend of March or first weekend of April

CAPE ARGUS PICK 'N' PAY CYCLE TOUR

www.cycletour.co.za
At 109km (68 miles) long, this is now the largest individually timed cycling event in the world. The gruelling circuit goes around Table Mountain to False Bay, across the mountains and along Chapman's Peak Drive to the Atlantic Seaboard and back into central Cape Town.
⊕ One Sunday in mid-March

TWO OCEANS MARATHON

www.twooceansmarathon.org.za
The popular Two Oceans Marathon covers 56km (35 miles) and follows a similar course to the Cape Argus Cycle Tour. Nearly 10,000 competitors take part, many of them running for charity, so expect to see the usual wacky costumes.
⊕ Late March, early April

MAY
GOOD FOOD AND WINE FESTIVAL

International chefs such as Gordon Ramsay and Giorgio Locatelli bring their culinary skills and love of food to the city with all sorts of demonstrations, tastings and general gourmet fun.
⊕ Last weekend in May

OCTOBER
CAPE TIMES/DISCOVERY HEALTH BIG WALK

www.bigwalk.co.za
This is the world's largest timed walk, with an estimated 20,000 people taking part. Sponsored walkers can choose one of eight routes, the longest passing through the Southern Suburbs and along False Bay.
⊕ One weekend in mid-October

NOVEMBER
OUT IN AFRICA

www.oia.co.za
The South African Gay and Lesbian Film Festival, known as Out in Africa, has been running for more than 10 years. One part of the festival is held at the Victoria & Alfred Waterfront, but there are also satellite events in other cities, such as Johannesburg.
⊕ November

DECEMBER
MOTHER CITY QUEER PROJECT

www.mcqp.co.za
This vast costume party is the biggest gay event in town. There's an annual theme and an upbeat atmosphere. The venue changes every year.
⊕ Saturday night in mid-December

PRICES AND SYMBOLS

The restaurants are listed alphabetically (excluding The) by town or area, then by name. The prices given are the average for a two-course lunch (L) and a three-course dinner (D) for one person, without drinks. The wine price is for the least expensive bottle.

For a key to the symbols, ▷ 2.

CAMPS BAY AND ATLANTIC SEABOARD

AQUA

www.aquacapetown.co.za
Formerly known as Tank, this restaurant and sushi bar was revamped in 2010. An airy, super-fashionable seafood and sushi restaurant with distinctive blue-and-white décor, it has a giant aquarium and attractive tables on the piazza in the Cape Quarter. The inventive sushi is among the best in Cape Town and features caviar and scallops as well as the more usual ingredients, while main dishes include Norwegian salmon, seared tuna, beef fillet with aniseed or venison with red berries. The restaurant is also famous for

its chocolate martinis and you can watch the beautiful people in the lounge area.
✉ Cape Quarter, 72 Waterkant Street, De Waterkant 8001 ☎ 021-4190007 🕐 Daily 12–3, 6–11 ✋ L R150, D R185, Wine R90

BLUES

www.blues.co.za
Blues is one of the most popular restaurants in the Cape, with superb views over Camps Bay and a Californian-style menu. There are meat main dishes, but the main reason to come to Blues is the fantastic seafood—the oyster platters are famous.
✉ Victoria Road, Camps Bay 8005 ☎ 021-4382040 🕐 Daily 12–11.30 ✋ L R240, D R300, Wine R145

CAFÉ SOFIA OYSTER BAR

www.cafesofia.co.za
This is something of an institution for oyster lovers, who indulge in their seafood passion whilst enjoying the wonderful ocean views. There's also a wide range of tapas and salads, and big jugs of sangria, making this

Above *Waterfront dining is a Cape Peninsula pleasure*

a great place for sharing lunch or dinner with friends. It's also a good place to come for breakfast, to gear up for a day's sightseeing.
✉ The Promenade, Victoria Road, Camps Bay 8005 ☎ 021-4383660 🕐 Daily 8am–midnight ✋ L R70, D R120, Wine R55

THE CODFATHER

www.codfather.co.za
This stylish, laid-back place is a breath of fresh air compared to some of the area's more pretentious restaurants. The Codfather offers a great range of superbly fresh seafood; there's no menu—the waiter takes you to a counter where you pick what you fancy from the day's choices. Everything is served grilled and accompanied by vegetables, rice or chips (fries). There's also a revolving sushi bar, serving good fresh sushi and sashimi.
✉ Corner of Geneva Drive and The Drive, Camps Bay 8005 ☎ 021-4380782 🕐 Daily 12pm–late ✋ L R120, D R250, Wine R70

THE NOSE

www.thenose.co.za

This wine bar and restaurant has tables spilling onto the trendy Waterkant piazza. A wide-ranging wine list is accompanied by excellent pub food such as bangers and mash, hotpots and handmade burgers. There's an inviting interior, and if you are not too hungry, there are snack platters to share.

✉ Cape Quarter, Dixon Street, Green Point 8005 ☎ 021-4252200 🕐 Daily 11am–late ✋ L R140, D R180, Wine R80

OCEAN BLUE

You're sure to be made welcome at this friendly seafood restaurant, on the road that overlooks the beach. The seafood is excellent, especially the grilled prawns and butterfish kebabs, and the daily specials are well worth trying.

✉ Victoria Road, Camps Bay 8005 ☎ 021-4389838 🕐 Daily 8.30am–10pm ✋ L R100, D R120, Wine R70

CAPE TOWN

THE AFRICA CAFÉ

www.africacafe.co.za

This trendy and tourist-friendly restaurant offers an excellent introduction to the continent's cuisines. The menu is a set 'feast' and includes 14 dishes that rove around Africa, from Kenyan patties to Cape Malay mango chicken curry and Egyptian dips. You can order more of the dishes you like, as well as coffee and dessert—good value if you're hungry.

✉ Heritage Square, 108 Shortmarket Street, City Centre 8001 ☎ 021-4220221 🕐 Mon–Fri 10–4, 6.30–11, Sat 10–2, 6.30–11, last reservation 9pm ✋ L R90, D R170, Wine R120

ARNOLDS

www.arnolds.co.za

Kloof Street's iconic café is best known for its generous breakfasts, which are served all day until 5pm. The usual eggs and bacon are on offer plus extras like warthog ribs, ostrich *boerwors* (sausage) and giant croissants. The evening menu has a good range of game dishes.

The service is fast and friendly, but you may have to wait for a table on weekend mornings.

✉ 60 Kloof Street, Gardens 8001 ☎ 021-4244344 🕐 Mon–Fri 6.45am–late, Sat–Sun 8am–late; happy hour 4.30–6.30 ✋ Breakfast from R11, L R140, D R170, Wine R60

BIESMIELLAH'S

www.biesmiellah.co.za

Biesmiellah's is one of the better known restaurants specializing in Cape Malay cuisine in Cape Town. This family-run place serves a delicious selection of dishes and is the place to come for sweet lamb and chicken curries and sticky puddings. No alcohol is served.

✉ 2 Wale Street, City Centre 8001 ☎ 021-4230850 🕐 Mon–Sat 10.30am–11pm ✋ L R85, D R100

BOO RADLEYS

www.booradleys.co.za

Caught somewhere between New York gangsterland and a chic part of Paris, this is a great city centre spot for a glass of South African wine or a juicy burger, sitting on one of the comfortable banquettes. There's nothing pretentious here—steaks, pasta, and other standard bistro fare are the order of the day—but it's the lively atmosphere that brings regulars here time and again.

✉ 62 Hout Street, City Centre 8001 ☎ 021-4243040 🕐 Daily 10am–11pm ✋ L R70, D R100, Wine R55

BUKHARA

www.bukhara.com

Expensive but easily Cape Town's best Indian restaurant, Bukara serves a menu of aromatic and flavoursome curries and tandoori dishes. Diners can watch the chefs at work in the glass-walled kitchen, preparing dishes such as creamy black lentils, prawns cooked in coconut milk, butter chicken and lamb rogan josh, accompanied by excellent freshly made naan bread and rotis.

✉ 33 Church Street, City Centre 8001 ☎ 021-4240000 🕐 Mon–Sat 12–3, 6.30–late ✋ L R175, D R215, Wine R85

FIVE FLIES

www.fiveflies.co.za

Despite the unappetizing name, this is a long-standing restaurant that is a popular haunt of lawyers and judges. It has a string of rooms with black-and-white checked floors, high ceilings and crisp white linen on the tables. Serves well-prepared traditional food, such as steak pie or simply grilled fish.

✉ 14 Keerom Street, City Centre 8001 ☎ 021-4244442 🕐 Mon–Fri 12–3, 6–11, Sat–Sun 6–11 ✋ L R185, D R235, Wine R115

FORK

www.fork-restaurants.co.za

An informal yet intimate ambience is created by the hanging lamps, dark wood tables and checkered tea-towel napkins at this restaurant serving imaginative tapas using seasonal and locally sourced ingredients. Enjoy their marinated sardines with rocket (arugula) and crostini, roast pork belly with a mustard and parsley crust, or parcels of puff pastry filled with mushrooms and Parmesan. Also delicious is the chorizo sausage with *galette* (a flat round cake). Expect excellent service and wine list.

✉ 84 Long Street, City Centre 8001 ☎ 021-4246334 🕐 Mon–Sat noon–11pm ✋ L R45, D R100, Wine R130

MAMA AFRICA

www.mamaafricarest.net

This popular restaurant and bar was one of the first in Cape Town to serve 'traditional' African dishes. It's long been a big hit with tourists, and the dishes, most of which focus on exotic game (such as crocodile kebabs, springbok steak and ostrich fillet) are tasty, served with *pap* (maize porridge) and beans. Although it's a little overpriced and the service is often slow, the lively atmosphere and great live music make it a fun place to spend an evening. The focal point of the restaurant is a bright green carved snake-shaped bar. Be sure to make a reservation.

✉ 178 Long Street, City Centre 8001 ☎ 021-4261017 🕐 Mon–Sat 7pm–midnight ✋ D R185, Wine R60

MILLER'S THUMB

Adored by locals (so bookings are essential), this is owned by a husband and wife team—Solly does the cooking while Jane reels off what's on the menu in a mouth-watering way—and serves delicious seafood, plus steaks and some vegetarian choices. There's a Creole twist on some dishes like the blackened fish and New Orleans-inspired seafood jambalaya, or you can opt for a curry with Mozambique prawns and cashew nuts.

✉ 10b Kloof Nek Road, Gardens 8001 ☎ 021-4243838 ⏰ Tue–Fri 12.30–2.30, 6.30–10.30, Mon, Sat 6.30–10.30 ✋ L R120, D R155, Wine R65

PANAMA JACKS

www.panamajacks.net

Set in a rickety boathouse decorated with flags, and not easy to find among Cape Town's docks. A visit is well worthwhile for the excellent seafood and steaks. Specials include abalone and West Coast crayfish, while the hake crusted with Parmesan and the seared tuna are superb. There are some delightful traditional Italian desserts like Italian kisses or banoffee pie. Large groups can pre-order generous seafood platters served in large frying pans.

✉ Quay 500, Cape Town Harbour 8001 ☎ 021-4473992 ⏰ Sun–Fri 12–12 (dinner menu from 4pm), Sat 4–12 ✋ L R150, D R220, Wine R70

PLANET RESTAURANT

www.planetbarandrestaurant.co.za

As one might expect of a restaurant within the Mount Nelson, the city's finest hotel, the Planet is probably the best fine-dining experience in Cape Town. Specialities such as springbok and ostrich feature, the latter cured with rooibos, the South African 'bush tea'. There are two fixed menus referred to as 'journey' menus, for a minimum of two people, presenting a taste of the best the kitchen has to offer, and even a specialist vegan menu.

✉ Mount Nelson Hotel, 76 Orange Street, Gardens 8001 ☎ 021-4831000 ⏰ Daily 6.30–10.30pm ✋ D R300, Wine R100

SAVOY CABBAGE

www.savoycabbage.co.za

Widely regarded as one of the best restaurants in Cape Town, producing its own best-selling cookbook, the Savoy Cabbage serves contemporary South African cuisine. The menu changes daily, and includes dishes such as kudu loin with chestnuts, veal sweetbreads and a soft-centred chocolate pudding. There's a good wine list too, especially for reds. Reserving ahead is essential.

✉ Heritage Square, 101 Hout Street, City Centre 8001 ☎ 021-4242626 ⏰ Mon–Fri 12–2.30, 7–10.30, Sat 7–10.30 ✋ L R200, D R250, Wine R85

YINDEE'S

www.yindees.com

Yindee's is an excellent Thai restaurant serving authentic spicy curries, stir-fries and soups. The setting is appealing, with a string of rooms in a sprawling Victorian house. Diners sit on cushions at traditional low tables. Service can be slow, but it's popular, so reserve in advance.

✉ 22 Camp Street, Tamboerskloof 8001 ☎ 021-4221012 ⏰ Mon–Fri 12.30–2.30, 6.30–11, Sat 6.30–11 ✋ L R130, D R160, Wine R80

CONSTANTIA

THE GREENHOUSE

www.cellars-hohenort.com

One of two highly rated restaurants at the Cellars-Hohenort hotel (▷ 96), the Greenhouse is set in a pretty conservatory with a white-themed décor. The chef produces top-quality food—mostly modern South African, including fresh local fish and game—and divine desserts. There's an excellent wine list to match.

✉ Cellars-Hohenort Hotel, 93 Brommersvlei Road, Constantia 7806 ☎ 021-7942137 ⏰ Tue–Sat 7pm–9.30 ✋ D R400, Wine R200

FALSE BAY

BLACK MARLIN

www.blackmarlin.co.za

Occupying an old whaling station, this is well known for its excellent seafood and is a good place to stop for lunch on the way to or from Cape Point. There are fabulous sea views and diners may spot whales in season. The menu features warming shrimp chowder and lobster bisque, grilled crayfish, a generous seafood platter and pasta options. Book ahead as it's popular with tour buses in summer.

✉ Miller's Point, 2km (3 miles) south of Simon's Town, 7995 ☎ 021-7861621 ⏰ Mon–Fri 12–10, Sat–Sun 8am–10pm ✋ Breakfast R30, L R120, D R160, Wine R75

THE BRASS BELL

www.brassbell.co.za

For a spectacular setting almost in the waves of False Bay, head to this relaxed pub and bistro—the oven-baked pizzas and fish and chips (fries) are the best. Downstairs gets packed with a young crowd, especially on the outside terrace around sunset. The more expensive bistro upstairs serves fresh fish and steak.

✉ By the rail station, Kalk Bay 7975 ☎ 021-7885455 ⏰ Daily 10am–late ✋ L R140, D R180, Wine R60

OLYMPIA CAFÉ & DELI

A Kalk Bay institution, this laid-back café serves some of the freshest bread in the Peninsula, plus light lunches (sandwiches crammed with delicious fillings), salads and quiche, fabulous cakes and fresh daily specials, often seafood. There's a relaxed atmosphere and good service, but expect to wait on weekends. The bakery at the back turns into a tiny theatre at night.

✉ 134 Main Road, Kalk Bay 7975 ☎ 021-7886396 ⏰ Mon–Sat 7am–9pm, Sun 7–3 ✋ L R60, D R120, Wine R50

HOUT BAY

DUNES

www.dunesrestaurant.co.za

This sprawling restaurant overlooks the dunes behind Hout Bay Beach, and is popular with families. The menu is large and the service quick, but it's best to stick to simple dishes, like calamari or fish and chips (fries). Reserve in advance on weekends or you will be seated in the courtyard instead of the balcony.

Beach Road, Hout Bay 7806
☎ 021-7901876 ⏱ Daily 9am–11pm
🖐 L R150, D R180, Wine R90

FISH ON THE ROCKS
www.fishontherocks.co.za
Try the simple and delicious fresh
fish and chips (fries) or deep-fried
calamari and prawns at this no-frills
place, which overlooks the harbour.
✉ Harbour Road, beyond Snoekies
Market ☎ 021-790 0001 ⏱ Daily 9–8.30
🖐 Meals from R16, Wine BYO

SOUTHERN SUBURBS
BARRISTERS GRILL
www.barristersgrill.co.za
Although the mock-Tudor timber
interior of the Barristers Grill is
traditional, this is a steakhouse that
has moved with the times. During the
day it is a trendy café and bistro, with
outdoor tables where you can enjoy
a leisurely breakfast or a quick lunch,
including meat-free options.
✉ Corner of Kildare and Main streets,
Newlands ☎ 021-6717907 ⏱ Daily
8am–late 🖐 L R75, D R175, Wine R85

DON PEDRO'S
www.donpedros.co.za
Something of an institution, Don
Pedro's is an informal, bustling
restaurant, serving huge portions of
steaks, Malay curries, pasta and pizza
at cheap prices. It's the focal point of
the Woodstock community, with a
mixed crowd.
✉ 113 Roodebloem Road, Woodstock
7925 ☎ 021-4476152 ⏱ Daily 8am–late
(often as late as 5am) 🖐 L R100, D R130,
Wine R55

OBZ CAFÉ
www.obzcafe.co.za
Obz Café is a large, breezy deli-cum-
restaurant, with a long bar and tables
dotted around the parquet floor. It
opens all day for light meals, coffee
or cocktails—the tapas, salads and
sandwiches are good—with larger
meals served in the evenings. The
small theatre next door sometimes
hosts live music and comedy.
✉ 115 Lower Main Road, Observatory 7925
☎ 021-4485555 ⏱ Daily 🖐 L R60,
D R90, Wine R50

VICTORIA & ALFRED WATERFRONT
BAIA
www.baiarestaurant.co.za
This fine seafood restaurant is
spread over four terraces with
moody, stylish decoration and
lighting. The venue is very smart
(and the meals relatively expensive)
and it has become a huge Cape
Town success. Expect delicious
seafood dishes following a
Mozambique theme, such as spicy
beer-baked prawns or grilled crayfish.
Some tables have striking views
of Table Mountain. Service can be
erratic, and you need to reserve
in advance.
✉ Top Floor, Victoria Wharf, V & A
Waterfront 8001 ☎ 021-4210935 ⏱ Daily
12–3, 7–11 🖐 L R230, D R290, Wine R95

BALDUCCI'S
www.balduccis.co.za
This Italian restaurant overlooks the
harbour. It serves a good choice of
pasta dishes and main meals ranging
from ostrich steaks and luxury lamb
burgers to *confit de canard* (preserved
duck) and crusted kingklip (eel-like
fish). There is also a sushi bar.
✉ Victoria Wharf, V & A Waterfront 8001
☎ 021-4216002 ⏱ Daily noon–11
🖐 L R200, D R260, Wine R100

QUAY FOUR
www.quay4.co.za
Quay Four is one of the most
enjoyable restaurants on the
Waterfront, on a huge deck
overlooking the bustle of the harbour.
The main deck has a relaxed pub
style, offering simple seafood such as
fish and chips (fries) served in frying
pans, and there's live music nightly.
There are also some great vegetarian
options and platters to share.
Upstairs a smarter bistro specializes
in seafood but has meat dishes too.
It's a WiFi hotspot.
✉ Quay Four, V & A Waterfront 8001
☎ 021-4192008 ⏱ Daily 9am–11.30pm,
bar until 1.30am 🖐 L R140, D R170,
Wine R85

Above *Baia is one of the Victoria & Alfred
Waterfront's smartest restaurants*

PRICES AND SYMBOLS

The hotels below are listed alphabetically (excluding The) by town or area, then by name. Prices are the average for a double room for one night, including breakfast. All the hotels listed accept credit cards unless otherwise stated.

For a key to the symbols, ▷ 2.

CAMPS BAY AND ATLANTIC SEABOARD

THE BAY

www.thebay.co.za

Just across the road from Camps Bay's beautiful beach, the Bay is a member of the Small Luxury Hotels of the World group. The modern and very comfortable rooms have a pleasant contemporary feel, with either mountain or ocean views. Some rooms have a private patio with direct access to the large heated pool and deck. Other facilities include a beach-facing restaurant and a wellness centre, and guests can also use both the Camps Bay Tennis Club and Squash Club, which are very close by.

✉ 69 Victoria Road, Camps Bay 8005
☎ 021-4384444 ❂ R3,900 ❶ 78 ▨ ⬡

BAY ATLANTIC

www.thebayatlantic.com

The family-run Bay Atlantic guesthouse has some of the loveliest views in the Peninsula. The six light and airy double rooms are attractively furnished, with terracotta tiles and fresh white linen, TV and private bathrooms. Some have a private balcony with stunning views of Camps Bay and the Twelve Apostles. The spacious Penthouse Suite leads directly onto a large balcony with sun loungers. There are also two apartments with kitchen next door. The quiet garden has a good-sized pool, and breakfast is served on a balcony overlooking the bay. Parking is available.

✉ 3 Berkley Road, Camps Bay 8005
☎ 021-4384341 ❂ R1,000 ❶ 6 ▨ ⬡

Above Guests at the Bay Atlantic can enjoy the splendid views while relaxing by the pool

BIG BLUE BACKPACKERS

www.bigblue.za.net

This spotless and airy backpackers' hostel is set in a gorgeous mansion dating from 1885, with spacious dorms, single and double rooms (with own bathroom or shared bathrooms), all with polished yellowwood floors, high ceilings and ceiling fans. Some doubles have extras such as complimentary toiletries and coffee-making facilities. The bar leads onto a small pool, and there's internet access, a travel centre, TV room and kitchen.

✉ 7 Vesperdene Road, Green Point 8005
☎ 021-4390807 ❂ Dorm R110, double en suite R450, excluding breakfast (R25) ❶ 70 beds ▨

HUIJS HAERLEM

www.huijshaerlem.co.za

These two beautifully converted adjacent houses have four rooms in each, connected by well-tended gardens. All rooms have private bathrooms and are very comfortable, with solid antique furniture, brass beds (some four-poster), large bathrooms and sea views. There's a solar-heated salt-water pool in the peaceful garden. Both houses have a breakfast room and lounge—one decorated with Dutch furniture, the other in South African style.

✉ 25 Main Drive, Sea Point 8005
☎ 021-4346434 ✋ R1,700 ① 8 ≋
✝ No children under 14

VILLA ROSA
www.villa-rosa.com
The rose-tinted Victorian villa known as the Villa Rosa sits high above Sea Point. It has eight bright, comfortable rooms, with traditional furnishings, and touches such as fresh flowers and original fireplaces. All rooms have stone-tiled, private bathrooms and TV; some have fridges. Excellent breakfasts are served with breads and jams. This friendly, welcoming and relaxed place also has a pleasant balcony overlooking the sea.

✉ 277 High Level Road, Sea Point 8005
☎ 021-4342768 ✋ R840 ① 8

DE WATERKANT VILLAGE
www.dewaterkant.com
This is more of a mini-empire than a guesthouse: Village and Life owns more than 40 historic Bo-Kaap-style houses and apartments in the trendy Waterkant area, each stylishly decorated, sleeping between one and six. It also owns the Waterkant House, a guesthouse with nine chic rooms, a splash pool, lounge and a terrace (R1,350 per room; www. dewaterkanthouse.com). The other main property is the gay-friendly The Charles, which has 10 luxury rooms spread across three renovated Georgian houses with flower-filled courtyards and roof decks with good views (R1,750 per room; www. thecharles.co.za). Other properties in stylish and historic buildings are available across Cape Town.

✉ 1 Loader Street, Green Point 8005
☎ 021-4379706 ✋ From R1,080
① 80 ≋

CAPE TOWN
THE BACKPACK
www.backpackers.co.za
The Backpack was the first Cape Town hostel and today is one of the best run and most comfortable in town. Occupying several houses, the hostel offers a choice of large spotless dorms, single and double rooms, and double rooms with private bathrooms. Polished wood floors and African art make it more attractive than many other hostels. A tiled courtyard leads to a high-ceilinged bar with a TV. Meals and snacks are served throughout the day, and there are linked gardens with a small swimming pool. A well-organized and informative travel office is also on site.

✉ 74 New Church Street, City Centre 8001
☎ 021-4234530 ✋ From R250 per bed
① 105 beds ≋

CAPE HERITAGE
www.capeheritage.co.za
Centrally located in a rambling renovated townhouse dating from the late 1700s, this charming hotel has 15 individually styled rooms decorated in muted colours, some with four-poster beds and original yellowwood floors. All the rooms have soundproofing and newly renovated bathrooms, minibar, WiFi, satellite TV and DVD players. Breakfast is served in the airy black-and-white breakfast room, and there are five good restaurants in the Heritage Square complex.

✉ Heritage Square, 90 Bree Street, City Centre 8001 ☎ 021-4244646 ✋ R2,170 ① 15 ⚙

THE GRAND DADDY
www.granddaddy.co.za
One of the hippest and coolest places to stay in the city centre, the Grand Daddy is perhaps best known for its genuine American Airstream trailer park on the roof of the hotel, which offers possibly one of the most unique hotel experiences in the world. Within the body of the hotel itself are elegant, calming rooms of muted beige and cream shades, some of which have balconies or

patio areas. The Daddy Cool bar is a glitzy affair, occasionally offering live music, and food can be had in the restaurant or on the roof. They even offer complimentary parking for one car per room.

✉ 38 Long Street, City Centre 8001
☎ 021-4247247 ✋ R1,500 ① 25, plus 7 trailers ⚙

KENSINGTON PLACE
www.kensingtonplace.co.za
This stylish boutique hotel in a quiet, leafy area overlooks the City Bowl. It's small, welcoming and well run, with excellent and friendly service. The rooms are a good size, each one individually and attractively styled with a mix of ethnic and ultra-chic furnishings in muted beiges and creams. There's lots of light from the large windows, some of which have wonderful views over the city. Breakfast is served on a leafy veranda overlooking the small swimming pool and tropical gardens. Parking is available.

✉ 38 Kensington Crescent, Higgovale 8001
☎ 021-4244744 ✋ R3,300 ① 8 ⚙ ≋

LONG STREET BACKPACKERS
www.longstreetbackpackers.co.za
One of central Cape Town's most sociable hostels is spread around a leafy courtyard, with small dorms and rather cramped doubles, some with their own bathrooms and balconies overlooking vibrant Long Street. There's a fully equipped kitchen, TV lounge, pool room, internet access, travel office and free pickup from the airport. There's good security with a 24-hour police camera by the entrance. The hostel has a lively atmosphere, with occasional parties organized and weekly *braais* (barbecues).

✉ 209 Long Street, City Centre 8001
☎ 021-4230615 ✋ From R130 per bed, excluding breakfast ① 65 beds

MANDELA RHODES PLACE
www.mandelarhodesplace.co.za
This is an ideal city centre option if you're looking for a bit more independence than standard hotel accommodation provides. The

apartment-style rooms are spacious and allow for either self-catering, using the plush kitchen facilities, or a more conventional staff-assisted service. Parking is an added bonus given the very central location, and communal facilities include a rooftop swimming pool and an on-site gym and spa. For business travellers there are also meeting rooms and conference facilities.

✉ Corner of Burg and Wale streets, Cape Town 8000 ☎ 021-4814000 🖐 R2,600 🛏 20 ⬛ ⬛ ⬛

MOUNT NELSON

www.mountnelson.co.za

Cape Town's famous colonial hotel is set in landscaped parkland, with views of Table Mountain. A grand palm-lined avenue leads to the main building. Rooms are luxurious, with all possible facilities, but the romms may be rather old-fashioned for some tastes (expect lots of floral fabrics and chintz). There's a heated swimming pool, tennis courts, squash court and a beauty salon. The celebrated Planet Restaurant serves Cape specials and contemporary food, and there are Sunday jazz brunches in the Oasis Restaurant. Service is impeccable, and the hotel is well worth visiting just for the sumptuous cream teas on the veranda or in the lounge. Parking is available.

✉ 76 Orange Street, Gardens 8001 ☎ 021-4831000 🖐 R7,300 🛏 201 ⬛ ⬛ ⬛

PARKER COTTAGE

www.parkercottage.co.za

Parker Cottage is a stylish and atmospheric guesthouse formed from two restored Victorian cottages in a quiet City Bowl suburb. The eight bedrooms, all with large private bathrooms containing claw-foot baths, have highly polished wood floors and fireplaces and are filled with tasteful antiques. There are bright flamboyant touches and a Victorian feel to the furnishings. Breakfast is served in the high-ceilinged breakfast room.

✉ 3 Carstens Street, Tamboerskloof 8001 ☎ 021-4246445 🖐 R850 🛏 8

TABLE MOUNTAIN LODGE

www.tablemountainlodge.co.za

Table Mountain Lodge has eight beautifully decorated rooms. They are breezy and comfortable, with fresh white linen, wooden furniture and floors, huge windows and large bathrooms. There's a small garden and a splash pool, a breakfast room and a tiny bar. The owners are very friendly and welcoming.

✉ 10a Tamboerskloof Road, Tamboerskloof 8001 ☎ 021-4230042 🖐 R1,020 🛏 8 ⬛ ⬛

URBAN CHIC

www.urbanchic.co.za

This is an Italian-owned hotel with rooms on several floors, where the room rates rise the higher you go, as the views of Table Mountain improve. The décor is contemporary and sleek, with pale colours, dark mahogany finishes, modern art on the walls and large bathrooms. Each room has WiFi, satellite TV, minibar and a Juliet balcony. The stylish Gallery Café on the first floor overlooks lively Long Street and specializes in fusion and Asian cuisine, with gourmet sandwiches also available.

✉ Corner of Long and Pepper streets, City Centre 8001 ☎ 021-4266119 🖐 R1,590 🛏 20 ⬛

CONSTANTIA
THE CELLARS-HOHENORT

www.cellars-hohenort.com

Set in two converted manor houses on a wine estate, this is one of the most luxurious hotels on the Peninsula. The rooms are individually decorated, with huge beds, antiques and spacious bathrooms. Facilities include two restaurants (▷ 92), a beauty salon, tennis court, golf course and gardens overlooking False Bay.

✉ 93 Brommersvlei Road, Constantia 7806 ☎ 021-7942137 🖐 R4,200 🛏 46 ⬛ ⬛

FALSE BAY
BOULDERS BEACH LODGE

www.bouldersbeachlodge.com

One of the most relaxing places to stay in the area is a stone's throw from the beach. The rooms in this friendly, well-run guesthouse have a simple, refreshing design, with private bathrooms; most are arranged around a paved yard, without sea views. There are also two-catering apartments with kitchens. At night you may see the local penguins exploring the grounds after the day visitors have gone home and it's quiet. Parking is available.

✉ 4 Boulders Place, Boulders Beach, Simon's Town 7975 ☎ 021-7861758 🖐 R900 🛏 12

SOUTHERN RIGHT

www.southernrighthotel.com

This hotel, set back from the sea, is a fashionable place, but family-friendly. The rooms have private bathrooms, high ceilings, dark polished wood floors and four-poster beds. The stylish bar and restaurant serves pub meals, seafood and grills. Parking is available.

✉ 12–14 Glen Road, Glencairn, False Bay 7975 ☎ 021-7820315 🖐 R500 🛏 8

THE WINSTON

www.thewinston.co.za

With stunning ocean views and a relaxing decked area around the pool, The Winston is a great place to unwind in this popular Cape Town suburb. There are five spacious suites, decorated with a nautical theme, with large windows offering panoramic views. In addition, whale watching is possible from your very own patio during the season. Breakfast is served in a bright and convivial dining room.

✉ 15 Erica Road, Simon's Town 7975 ☎ 021-7861700 🖐 R950 🛏 5 ⬛

HOUT BAY
CHAPMANS PEAK HOTEL

www.chapmanspeakhotel.co.za

The original hotel has 10 standard rooms with simple, contemporary décor, beige fabrics and large windows, some with sea views. It also has a popular restaurant. In addition, there are 24 stylish rooms and two suites in the new block, with ocean or mountain views, additional flat-screen TVs, under-floor heating,

baths big enough for two, and minibars. This is a great location, just across from the beach and at the start of the picturesque Chapman's Peak Drive (▷ 80).

✉ Chapman's Peak Drive, Hout Bay 7806 ☎ 021-7901036 💶 From R920 ⓘ 35 🏊

SOUTHERN SUBURBS
KOORNHOOP MANOR HOUSE
www.koornhoop.co.za

This converted Victorian house in a large, peaceful garden has eight rooms with private bathrooms, floral print interiors and TV. There is a communal lounge and a breakfast room. You will also find three huge and extremely good-value three-bedroomed apartments with kitchen and access to a garden. Parking is also available.

✉ 24 London Road, Observatory 7925 ☎ 021-4480595 💶 R720 ⓘ 8, plus 2 apartments

VINEYARD HOTEL AND SPA
www.vineyard.co.za

Centred on an 18th-century house set in attractive landscaped parkland, this hotel has modern rooms with large wraparound windows, wooden floors and attractive flashes of colour such as bright yellow towels and red rugs. Rooms on the ground floor have patios that open on to the gardens and there are fine views of Table Mountain. In addition, there are five cottages with kitchens. Communal facilities include a wellness spa housed in a stunning glass and steel building with state-of-the-art gym and indoor heated pool, and the award-winning The Square and Myoga restaurants.

✉ Colinton Road, off Protea Road, Newlands 7700 ☎ 021-6574500 💶 R2,820 ⓘ 207 🔲 🏊 🍴

VICTORIA & ALFRED WATERFRONT
CAPE GRACE
www.capegrace.com

This luxurious hotel is a large development in a great spot, just a short walk from the main Waterfront shops and restaurants. The large, comfortable rooms are traditionally decorated, with contemporary touches, and with balconies either overlooking the Waterfront or with views of Table Mountain. There's a spa, a stylish bar and the celebrated Signal restaurant, where service and food are excellent. An attractive swimming pool and deck with a bar opens out from the restaurant. Parking is also available.

✉ West Quay Road, Victoria & Alfred Waterfront 8002 ☎ 021-4107100 💶 R5,020 ⓘ 121 🔲 🏊

VICTORIA & ALFRED
www.vahotel.co.za

The Victoria & Alfred is a stylishly converted fishing warehouse set in the middle of the V & A Waterfront, with spacious, cool and comfortable rooms. All have king-size beds and TV with DVD player; some have dramatic mountain views. The large marble and stone bathrooms come with a separate WC. The restaurant has a pleasant outdoor deck, also with views of the mountain and serves seafood and steaks. There's a fashionable, airy bar attached. Service is friendly and efficient. Parking is available.

✉ Pierhead, Victoria & Alfred Waterfront 8001 ☎ 021-4196677 💶 R4,390, excluding breakfast (R100) ⓘ 94 🔲 🏊 🍴

Above *Four-poster beds in the Parker Cottage hotel in the City Bowl*

SIGHTS 100
WALKS AND DRIVES 120
WHAT TO DO 128
EATING 134
STAYING 136

WESTERN CAPE

The Western Cape is arguably the most beautiful and varied of South Africa's nine provinces. It has just about everything the country has to offer, from endless beaches and indigenous forests to the historic wine estates in the Cape Winelands and the scorched semi-desert of the Karoo. After Cape Town it's also the most popular region for visitors and the easiest way to explore is by car. Highlights include the Whale Coast, where from July to November you have one of the best vantage points in the world for land-based whale watching, and the patchwork of pretty wine estates around Stellenbosch, Paarl and Franschhoek, which offer wine tasting and gourmet alfresco lunches among vines and ancient oak trees. The famous Garden Route follows an outstanding section of verdant coastline, sweeping beaches and a series of picturesque inland lakes and offers a vast choice of accommodation, restaurants, shopping and activities from bungee jumping to walking with an elephant. In this region the Tsitsikamma—Garden Route National Park is a lush ancient coastal forest, the fashionable town of Knysna sits on a spectacular lagoon and is surrounded by nature reserves, and Plettenberg Bay is blessed with wide, white sandy beaches. Inland there are attractive country villages nestled in deep valleys and surrounded by olive orchards and vineyards, many with fine examples of historic Cape Dutch gabled architecture, and the mountains are criss-crossed by the Western Cape's many dramatic mountain passes. North of Cape Town the less visited West Coast offers a picturesque string of fishing villages with whitewashed cottages, and inland is a region of high valleys where fruit is grown—and this is one of the few places in South Africa that gets snow in winter.

BREDASDORP

www.tourismcapeagulhas.co.za

This old Overberg (▷ 110) town is South Africa's first *dorp* (town). It was founded in 1837 by local farmer Michiel van Breda, who built a church around which the village grew. The small Shipwreck Museum (Mon–Fri 9–4.45, Sat–Sun 11–4) on Independent Street houses a collection of oddments salvaged from along the coast. The display is enhanced by sound effects: for example in the Shipwreck Hall you hear the distinct shrieks of seagulls and the thunderous sound of waves on a stormy night.

✚ 327 D11 ℹ Cape Agulhas Tourism Bureau, Long Street, Bredasdorp 7280 ☎ 028-4242584 ⓒ Mon–Fri 8–5, Sat 9–1

BREEDE RIVER VALLEY

www.tourismcapewinelands.co.za

A mere 310km (192 miles) long, the Breede River (also known as the Breë, meaning 'broad') is one of the most important rivers in the Cape. Leaving the mountains behind at Swellendam (▷ 110), the river flows across an undulating coastal terrace, meandering through the wheat fields of the Overberg (▷ 110) before entering the Indian Ocean at St. Sebastian Bay. Worcester (▷ 112) is the main town in the region, but along the broad valley are important agricultural market towns such as Prince Alfred Hamlet, Ashton and Bonnievale, as well as the attractive villages of Tulbagh (▷ 112), McGregor and Montagu (▷ 106).

These old towns and villages are surrounded by vineyards and fruit farms that display wonderful variations in colours through the seasons. Mountains rise to 2,000m (6,560ft) behind the farmsteads and their peaks are capped with snow in the winter. They also offer challenging hiking trails and beautiful hidden valleys. The Brede River valley acts as the dividing line between two contrasting regions. To the southwest are the verdant Winelands and the city of Cape Town. To the northeast is the start of the Karoo, a vast expanse of semi-desert.

✚ 327 D11 ℹ Cape Winelands Regional Tourism, 29 Du Toit Street, Stellenbosch 7600 ☎ 0861-265263 ⓒ Mon–Fri 8–4.30

CALEDON

www.tourismcaledon.co.za

The regional capital of the Overberg lies just off the N2 at the foot of the Swartberg Mountains and is known for its naturally occurring hot springs (▷ 128). Caledon is a typical rural town—small and quiet, with a couple of sights. If you are planning an overnight stay, you should carry on to Swellendam. The House Museum (Mon–Fri 8.30–4) can be found at 11 Constitution Street, in a Victorian building, originally the Freemasons' Lodge. It has displays about local history, domestic items and crafts, and there is a working kitchen where bread is baked every Friday and then sold in the museum shop, along with a variety of home-baked goods, dried flowers and arts and crafts. Mill Street has a collection of historical buildings that have been declared national monuments, and Holy Trinity Church (ask for key at the House Museum) on Prince Alfred Drive is a small, neat church dating from 1855.

✚ 326 C11 ℹ Caledon Tourist Bureau, 22 Plein Street, Caledon 7230 ☎ 028-2123282 ⓒ Mon–Fri 9–4

CAPE AGULHAS

www.tourismcapeagulhas.co.za

Cape Agulhas is the southernmost point in Africa and forms part of the Agulhas National Park, one of South Africa's newest parks. This is where the warm waters of the Indian Ocean meet the cooler waters of the Atlantic Ocean, and while the beach is rocky this is a good area for fishing. The Cape's scenery lacks the grandeur you might expect of such a significant spot, but the top of the attractive Victorian lighthouse has good views of the ocean, which has claimed many ships and lives. There are limited visitor facilities in the park (a couple of toilets), but there are ongoing plans to build accommodation, lay out nature trails along the coastline and build a tarred road. For now, the closest accommodation is in the village of L'Agulas or Struisbaai.

✚ 327 D12 ℹ Cape Agulhas Tourism Bureau, Long Street, Bredasdorp 7280 ☎ 028-4242584 ⓒ Mon–Fri 8–5, Sat 9–1

THE CEDERBERG

▷ 102.

CERES

www.ceres.org.za

Ceres is famous for its fruit and, more specifically, its fruit juice—namely the Liquifruit and Ceres brands, both of which are packed here. Surrounded by the harsh and rugged Skurweberg Mountains (which see snowfall in the winter), this attractive farming town was founded in 1854 and aptly named after the Roman goddess of agriculture. In the heart of town shady trees line the winding Dwars River. The Togryers' (Transport Riders') Museum (tel 023-3122045; Mon–Fri 9–1, 2–5, also Sat 9–12 in summer only), at 8 Oranje Street, is worth a quick visit for its collection of horse-drawn vehicles.

✚ 326 C10 ℹ Ceres Tourism, in the library on Owen Street, Ceres 6835 ☎ 023-3161287 ⓒ Mon–Fri 9–5, Sat 9–12

Opposite *Vineyards in the Breede River Valley*
Below *Cape Agulhas lighthouse*

TIP

» The region is known for its excellent
Goue Valley wines; sales and tastings
take place at the Goue Valley shop on
Voortrekker Street in Citrusdal, near the
tourist office.

Opposite *The dramatic sand dunes in
De Hoop Nature Reserve*
Below *The rocky terrain typical of the
Cederberg Wilderness Area*

THE CEDERBERG

The Cederberg, the mountain range north of the Cape Peninsula, is celebrated
for its rugged scenery, stunning rock formations and centuries-old rock paintings
produced by the native San people of the region. There are more than 250km
(155 miles) of hiking trails in the mountains, passing bizarre sandstone features
like the Wolfberg Arch and the Maltese Cross. The highest peaks are Snow Peak
at 2,028m (6,652ft) and Table Peak at 1,969m (6,458ft). Other trails focus on San
rock art, usually found in caves or under overhangs (▷ 122–123 for details of a
rock art walk). The main administrative focus for the wilderness is the Forestry
Station at Algeria.

The roads into the Cederberg are gravel, with steep and twisting sections;
some of the steepest stretches have been covered with tarmac. There are two
roads from which you can access the main trails. The most popular runs south
from Clanwilliam along the Rondegat River Valley to Algeria, and then on to the
small towns of Cederberg and Uitsig. The second road is the route serving the
remote mission station at Wuppertal, in parts requiring a 4WD vehicle.

CLANWILLIAM

Clanwilliam, on the northern edge of the Cederberg, is a peaceful agricultural
town that makes a good base for exploring the mountains. During spring,
the profusion of wild flowers that blankets the area attracts a large number of
visitors. There is a handful of sights in town, including the Old Gaol (Mon–Fri
8–12.30) built in 1808, a stocky, white, fortress-like building overlooking the
main street, with a small collection of local history items, including an incredible
giant threshing machine that was shipped out to South Africa in parts from
Ipswich, England. On the outskirts of town the Clanwilliam Dam is popular with
powerboat enthusiasts.

CITRUSDAL

Another good base, if a less picturesque one than Clanwilliam, is Citrusdal. As
the name implies, it is the focus for the local citrus industry, nestling in a valley
filled with lush citrus orchards. During spring, the air is heavy with the scent
of orange blossom. Even more impressive is the town's striking setting at the
southern edge of the Cederberg. There are some intriguing San paintings on the
Hex River farm, 20km (12 miles) north of Citrusdal, as well as the oldest orange
tree in South Africa, a national monument that still bears fruit.

DE HOOP NATURE RESERVE

www.capenature.co.za

This important coastal reserve extends 5km (3 miles) out to sea, protecting the shoreline and marine life. It is divided into two sectors: The western region is for hiking, game viewing and birdwatching, while the eastern section is for mountain biking (▷ 128). The reserve covers an exceptionally varied and rich environment within its 34,000ha (84,000 acres). There is a large freshwater *vlei* (a hollow where water collects in the wet season) surrounded by marshlands; the coastline is made up of sandy beaches and rocky headlands; and inland are giant sand dunes backed by the Potberg Mountains.

With such a variety of terrain crammed into a relatively small area, the region supports a great range of wildlife. More than 250 bird species have been recorded here, while elusive leopard, bontebok (a large antelope) and Cape mountain zebra share the land with the more common eland, baboon and two more—smaller—antelopes, the grey rhebok and klipspringer. There is also a chance of seeing southern right whales, which calve in the shallow waters between July and December.

➕ 327 D11 ☎ 028-5421253 🕐 Office and gate: daily 7–6 🚍 From Bredasdorp, follow the R319 towards Swellendam. After 8km (5 miles) take a signposted right turn onto a gravel road. After 40km (25 miles) you reach Ouplaas—take a right for the western sector

of the reserve or continue straight on for another 10km (6 miles) for the eastern sector. The office and parking are at Potberg

GANSBAAI

www.tourismgansbaai.co.za

This small, modern town is a prosperous fishing port with a deepwater wharf and several fish canning factories. Like Hermanus at the other end of Walker Bay, it has some excellent vantage points for whale watching, but most visitors come to Gansbaai to see Dyer Island or go cage diving with great white sharks. Dyer Island is an important breeding place for African penguins, and nearby Geyser Island has a breeding seal population. The area between the two islands is known as Shark Alley, as great white sharks prey on the breeding seals (▷ 129 for details of shark viewing).

➕ 326 C12 🖅 Gansbaai Tourism Bureau, corner of Kapokblom and Main streets, Gansbaai 7220 ☎ 028-3841439 🕐 Mon–Fri 8.30–5.30, Sat 9–4, Sun 9–2

GARDEN ROUTE

www.gardenroute.co.za

The Garden Route is a 200km (125-mile) stretch of the south coast extending from Mossel Bay in the west to Plettenberg Bay in the east. The high levels of publicity it has attracted has made it hugely popular, and few visitors to the Cape miss it. Though some people maintain that its attractions are overstated, few can deny the beauty of the rugged coast backed by lush mountains. The region is separated from the interior by the Tsitsikamma and Outeniqua mountain ranges. In contrast to the dry area of the Karoo, which lies on the other side of the mountains, rain falls all year round on the Garden Route and as a result the ocean-facing mountain slopes are covered with luxuriant forests.

The most popular stretch of the route follows the coast from Mossel Bay to Storms River in Tsitsikamma—Garden Route National Park. The larger towns, such as George (below) and Knysna (▷ 105), are highly developed, while in other areas you

can experience untouched wilderness and wonderful hikes, including one of the most famous in the country, the Otter Trail. This runs along the coast in Tsitsikamma—Garden Route National Park (▷ 111), one of the most popular parks in South Africa. A second national park, Wilderness—Garden Route (▷ 112), is also very popular. If your preference is for the beach life, there's a choice of seaside villages or livelier surf spots.

➕ 328 F11

GEORGE

www.tourismgeorge.co.za

Often referred to as the gateway to the Garden Route, George lies in the shadow of the Outeniqua Mountains, but unlike most of the towns along the Garden Route, it is not on the sea. It owes its status to the fact that it has an airport, and it is also an important intersection between the N2 coastal highway and the N9 running through the Outeniqua Pass into the Karoo.

The main reason overseas visitors come to George is to play golf on one of its four excellent courses (▷ 129), but the town itself—a modern grid of streets interspersed with some attractive old buildings—repays a short visit. St. Mark's Cathedral (daily 9.30–4.30), on the corner of Cathedral and York streets, is unusual for its large number of stained-glass windows. The George Museum (Mon–Fri 9–4.30, Sat 9–12.30), on Courtenay Street, has displays about the local timber industry, as well as musical instruments and a collection of old printing presses.

The exhibition at the Transport Museum (Mon–Sat 8–5) celebrates the history of steam train travel in South Africa, and is well worth a visit. It has 13 steam locomotives, a 1947 Royal Mail coach and a room dedicated to model railways, in addition to a collection of vintage cars and flight memorabilia. You'll find the museum on Mission Street, just off Knysna Road.

➕ 327 E11 🖅 124 York Street, George 6529 ☎ 044-8019292 🕐 Mon–Fri 8–5, Sat 9–1

GREAT KAROO

www.centralkaroo.co.za

The Great Karoo is a vast, ancient plateau making up nearly a third of the total area of the country. Endless plains stretch between stark mountain ranges, with little but characteristic steel windmills peppering the horizons. The landscape is a parched expanse of baked red earth inhabited by tough merino sheep. The sheer scale of the Great Karoo is remarkable — the average farm covers more than 20,000ha (50,000 acres). Hundreds of millions of years ago this whole area was an enormous swamp inhabited by dinosaurs, making it a key palaeontological site.

The area gained historic significance during the 19th century, when the Voortrekkers — Boer farmers escaping British domination — penetrated the interior with their ox wagons. The southern districts of the Great Karoo are traversed today by the N1 highway between Cape Town and Johannesburg, and along it are a few regional supply towns such as Beaufort West.

♦ 327 D–E9 ♦ Beaufort West Tourism Bureau, 57 Donkin Street ☎ 023-4151488 ⊕ Mon–Fri 9–5, Sat 9–12

GROOTBOS PRIVATE NATURE RESERVE

www.grootbos.com

This nature reserve and luxury camp covers more than 1,000ha (2,500 acres) of fynbos-clad hills. Almost all of the fynbos (or woody plants) can be spotted by their small leaves, which are hard and leathery. The reserve, which has won several conservation and eco-tourism awards, lies inland from Gansbaai, with stunning views of Walker Bay and the surrounding countryside. This semi-wilderness is an ideal place to gain an impression of the variety and brilliance of the native Cape flora — fynbos. There are also milkwood forests and a collection of ponds that attract a variety of bird life. Activities include horseback riding and game drives through the hills, boat trips to Dyer Island and trips to the De Kelders caves.

♦ 326 C11 ☎ 028-3848000 ⊕ Open to overnight guests only ➡ From Hermanus, follow the R43 through Stanford and continue for 13km (8 miles). Grootbos is clearly signposted on the left

HEX RIVER VALLEY

www.hexrivervalley.co.za

Approaching from the arid landscapes of the east, this is the first glimpse you get of the fertility and glory of the Cape. The soils of the Hex River Valley are naturally productive and this has long been an important grape-growing region. More than 60 of the table wines produced in South Africa for export originate from here, and there are an estimated eight million vines growing in the valley and on the mountain slopes. This multitude of vines provides a vibrant backdrop: bright greens in summer; rich bronzes and reds in autumn; and snow-capped peaks setting off the leafless plants in winter.

To complement the natural beauty of the valley, the long history of farming here has left many handsome examples of early Cape Dutch homesteads, built between 1768 and 1815. Some of these fine buildings have been restored and converted to superior guesthouses. A one-time coach house known as Die Monitor has been turned into De Vlei Country Inn, a popular overnight or lunch stop.

♦ 326 C10 ♦ Hex River Valley Tourism Bureau, corner of the N1 and Voortrekker Road, De Doorns ☎ 023-3562041 ⊕ Mon–Fri 8–5, Sat 8–12

KAROO NATIONAL PARK

www.sanparks.org

This National Park was created to conserve a representative area of the unique Karoo environment. The current boundaries of the park encompass an area of Karoo plains that merge into mountain slopes and a high-lying plateau. The park is accessible via one of its hiking trails, by 4WD vehicle or on a guided tour arranged at the office.

There is a diverse range of game and smaller wildlife in the park, mostly small mammals, birds and reptiles — including five different species of tortoise (this is the largest number in a conservation area in the world). In particular, look for the tent tortoise: Well camouflaged, it looks like an inverted egg carton. The reserve is also home to two endangered species: the black rhino and the riverine rabbit. While the statistics are impressive, actually spotting any of these animals requires a high degree of patience, effort — and luck.

♦ 327 E9 ☎ 023-4152828 ⊕ Gates: 5am–10pm; park office: 7–7 ✋ Adult R100, child (under 12) R50 ❓ Trail and park maps available at park office ➡ Main entrance is signposted off the N1, 5km (3 miles) southwest of Beaufort West

Left *Steel windmill, Great Karoo*

KNYSNA

Knysna is the hub of the Garden Route, with a stunning lagoon, noble forests and plenty of restaurants and hotels. Many artists and craftspeople have gravitated to Knysna (the 'K' is silent) and it is a pleasant spot to spend a day or two. The lagoon-side town is fully geared up for visitors—its restaurants serve Knysna's famous seafood, especially its oysters, which are cultivated in the lagoon. Development is booming, with a waterfront complex known as the Knysna Quays (▷ 130) setting the pace. The heart of town is a grid of leafy streets lined with Victorian bungalows, bed-and-breakfasts, craft shops and coffee shops. Don't come here for the beaches. For that you should travel 20km (12 miles) to Brenton-on-Sea.

THE LAGOON

Much of Knysna's life revolves around the lagoon. The Heads, the rocky promontories that lead from the lagoon to the open sea, are dramatic, and there's some good scuba diving. The Knysna National Lakes, more than 15,000ha (37,000 acres) of protected area, are also wonderful to explore, especially by kayak. Featherbed Nature Reserve is the unspoilt western side of The Heads. This is a private nature reserve that can be reached only by taking the Featherbed Co. Ferry (tel 044-3821693; www.knysnafeatherbed.com), which runs from the John Benn Jetty, 400m (440 yards) west of the rail station. It's home to South Africa's largest breeding herd of blue duiker *(Cephalophus monticola),* an endangered species of antelope. There's also a cave once inhabited by the Khoi (original inhabitants of the region), which has been declared a National Heritage Site.

KNYSNA FOREST

On the southern slopes of the Outeniqua Mountains, behind Knysna, are the remnants of the grand forests that first attracted white settlers to the region. Although much of the game that once thrived here has vanished, magnificent trees (including yellowwood and assegai) remain, and there is an impressive variety of bird life, including the vivid Knysna lourie with its red wing feathers. Various short walks have been laid out in the forests, focusing on magnificent trees. East of here and of Knysna is Diepwalle Forest, which has an elephant walk. However, don't expect to see any—the Knysna elephants are extremely rare and only six are on record at present.

INFORMATION

www.tourismknysna.co.za
✚ 327 F11 🛈 Knysna Tourism, 40 Main Street, Knysna 6570 ☎ 044-3825510
🕓 Mon–Fri 8–5, Sat 8.30–1

TIPS

>> Fully equipped houseboats with kitchens are available on the lagoon. No nautical experience is needed; they are easy to operate and allow you to explore the lagoon at leisure (Lightleys Holiday Houseboats, tel 044-3860007; www.houseboats.co.za).
>> Be prepared for crowds and/or long waits at restaurants during busy times, as the area is very popular.

Above *The peaceful waterways of the Knysna lagoon are best explored by boat*

LAMBERT'S BAY

www.tourismlambertsbay.co.za

Once just a small fishing village, Lambert's Bay on the west coast has become a popular holiday town and gets busy in summer. The famous Muisbosskerm restaurant has played a role in drawing visitors to the region, but the bay first appeared on maps many centuries ago—this was the last point at which Portuguese explorer Bartolomeu Dias went ashore, before sailing around the Cape for the first time in 1487. Today, this modern town has one absorbing, if pungent, attraction: Bird Island. This rock outcrop of just 3ha (7.5 acres) is now joined to the land by a concrete jetty. It is an important breeding ground for Cape gannets and cormorants, and also attracts Cape fur seals. Early morning and evening are the best times to see the birds, but be warned: You may find the screeching and overpowering smell of the birds leaves a longer-lasting impression than the extraordinary sight of them.

🛉 326 B9 🛈 5 Medical Centre, Main Road ☎ 027-4321000 🕒 Mon–Fri 9–5, Sat 9–12.30 🎫 Bird Island: adult R30, child (under 18) R15

LITTLE KAROO

▷ 108–109.

MATJIESFONTEIN

www.matjiesfontein.com

In 1975, the entire village of Matjiesfontein was declared a national monument—little surprise considering its beautiful Victorian houses. The town itself consists of not much more than a couple of dusty streets, but these are lined with perfectly preserved period houses. The highlight is the Lord Milner Hotel, resplendent with turrets and adorned balconies. It was built by a Scot, Jimmy Logan, an official working for the Cape Government Railways in the 1890s, who originally came here hoping that the dry air would cure a chest complaint. He settled in the area where he made a fortune, and the history of the town is a reflection of his life. His hotel became fashionable, attracting many rich and influential guests who, like him, suffered from lung complaints. These included Cecil Rhodes and the Sultan of Zanzibar.

Another famous resident of Matjiesfontein was the writer and feminist Olive Schreiner, whose first novel, *The Story of an African Farm* (1883), was set in the Karoo. Today the town is a popular stopover on the journey between Johannesburg and the Cape.

🛉 327 D10 🛈 Lord Milner Hotel, Matjiesfontein 6901 ☎ 023-5613011

MONTAGU

www.tourismmontagu.co.za

The long, oak-lined streets of this delightful Karoo town are full of whitewashed Cape Dutch houses sitting beneath jagged mountain peaks. Founded in 1851, the settlement was named after John Montagu who, as the colonial secretary from 1843 to 1853, had been responsible for the first major road-building scheme in the Cape. Long Street alone has 14 national monuments along its length, and with so many well-preserved buildings, it is easy to get a vivid impression of how the settlement would have looked in its early days. Joubert House (Mon–Fri 9–5, Sat–Sun 10.30–12), the oldest building in the town, built in 1853, is now part of the museum (the main museum building is farther along Long Street). It has a collection of late 19th-century furnishings and ornaments, and part of the garden is devoted to a collection of indigenous medicinal plants.

🛉 327 D11 🛈 Montagu Tourism Bureau, 24 Bath Street, Montagu 6720 ☎ 023-6142471 🕒 Mon–Sat 9–5, Sun 9.30–12.30, 3–5

MOSSEL BAY

www.visitmosselbay.co.za

Built along a rocky peninsula providing sheltered swimming and mooring in the bay, the town of Mossel Bay is one of the larger seaside communities along the Garden Route. During school

Above *Attractive painted house in Montagu*
Opposite *Gannets on appropriately named Bird Island, Lambert's Bay*

vacations the town is packed—it receives some one million domestic visitors in December alone. For the rest of the year, however, it is just another coastal town, its appeal not enhanced by the fact that, since the discovery of offshore oil deposits, Mossel Bay is also the home of the Mossgas natural gas refinery and a multitude of oil storage tanks. These unattractive additions to the landscape are visible from any approach into town.

You may also notice a number of Portuguese flags and names around the town. These relate to the first European to anchor in the bay—Bartolomeu Dias, who landed in February 1488. All the museums in town are on one site, known as the Bartolomeu Dias Museum Complex. Here you'll find the Culture Museum, the Shell Museum, the Aquarium and the Maritime Museum (all are open Mon–Fri 9–4.45, Sat–Sun 9–3.45).

In the middle of the bay is Seal Island, which can be visited by cruises departing from the harbour in Mossel Bay. The island is inhabited by African penguins and Cape fur seals (the best month to see seal pups is November). It's also possible to see great white sharks and small hammerhead sharks, which prey upon the seals.

🛉 327 E11 🛈 Mossel Bay Tourism Bureau, corner of Church and Market streets, Mossel Bay 6500 ☎ 044-6912202 🕒 Mon–Fri 8–6, Sat–Sun 9–4

INFORMATION

www.tourismgeorge.co.za

327 E11 George Tourism Bureau (regional office), 124 York Street, George 6529 044-8019292 Mon–Fri 8–5.30, Sat 9–1

INTRODUCTION

Unlike the stark Great Karoo to the north, the Little (or Klein) Karoo is made up of a series of parallel fertile valleys enclosed by the Swartberg Mountains to the north and the Langeberg and Outeniqua mountains to the south. In addition to the Cango Caves and the ostrich farms of Oudtshoorn, farther afield lies spectacular and peaceful countryside, dotted with attractive villages. Here too are some of South Africa's most dramatic *kloofs* (gorges) and passes—14 in all. Another incentive is Route 62, a fine stretch of road following the R62 and marketed as the 'longest wine route in the world'.

The Karoo was for centuries impassable thanks to its series of peaks and valleys. However, in the 19th century, dozens of passes were built across the Cape's mountains, effectively opening up the area. The history of the largest town in the Karoo, Oudtshoorn, goes back to around this time.

WHAT TO SEE
OUDTSHOORN

www.oudtshoorninfo.com

By far the largest town in the Little Karoo, the regional capital is a major visitor attraction, thanks to the nearby Cango Caves and the countless ostrich farms surrounding it—dating back to the two fashion booms for ostrich feathers (1865–70 and 1900–14) that truly established the town. At the peak of its fortunes, ostrich feathers were selling for more than their weight in gold. While ostrich farming no longer brings in as much wealth, it remains an important business and visitor attraction. The town itself is appealing, with broad streets, smart sandstone Victorian houses and a good choice of restaurants. There are several 'ostrich palaces' built by the town's 'feather barons' in the 19th century, which, although not open to the public, are still worth a look since their ornate exteriors were an important part of their design. Most examples of these are in the old part of town along the west bank of the Grobbelaars River. In the heart of town, next to the old Queen's Hotel on Baron van Rheede Street, the C. P. Nel Museum (tel 044-2727306; Mon–Sat 9–5) contains displays about the ostrich feather boom.

327 E11 Oudtshoorn Tourist Bureau, Baron van Reede Street, Oudtshoorn 6625 044-2720041 Mon–Fri 8–5, Sat–Sun 9–1

Above and opposite top Oudtshoorn is known for its ostriches; at some farms you can have a ride to make your visit memorable

OSTRICH AND WILDLIFE FARMS

Visiting an ostrich farm in the area can be great fun, although the appeal of all things ostrichey can fade quickly. To keep visitors interested, some farms have introduced different species. Opinions vary as to which farm is the least commercialized, but Highgate Ostrich Farm (tel 044-2727115; www.highgate. co.za; daily 8–5), 10km (6 miles) from Oudtshoorn off the R328 towards Mossel Bay, is perhaps the best organized. It's a very popular show farm and has won prizes for its high standards.

CANGO CAVES

www.cango-caves.co.za

Tucked away in the foothills of the Swartberg Mountains are the Cango Caves, a magnificent network of calcite caverns, recognized as among the world's finest dripstone cave systems. The only access is on a guided tour, the most popular of which takes in six caves and gives you a good overview. The caves contain an extraordinary series of bizarre formations, including incredible stalagmites, stalactites and flowstone (thin layers of rock deposited by the flow of water). The timescale of some of the formations is hard to comprehend; many of the pillars took hundreds of thousands of years to form, while the oldest flowstone is more than a million years old.

✚ 327 E10 ☎ 044-2727410 🕒 By guided tour only: daily and hourly 9–4 and lasting 1 hour or 90 min 🖐 Adult R64–R80, child (5–15) R32–R52, depending on tour 🍴 🏛 ❓ Child day care and money exchange available 🚌 28km (17 miles) north of Oudtshoorn along the R328, signposted from town

TIPS

» Tours of the Cango Caves take limited numbers, so you may have to wait more than an hour to get in. Try to arrive early to avoid this.
» Wear shoes with a good grip when visiting the caves as the ground can be slippery.
» There are no tour companies that organize daily trips to the ostrich farms or the caves. The best way to get there is to rent a car for the day.

SWARTBERG PASS

One of the most spectacular passes in South Africa, the Swartberg Pass is a national monument in recognition of the engineering genius of Thomas Bain, who built it in the 1880s. It is 24km (15 miles) long and rises to 1,585m (5,200ft) with a number of perilously sharp, blind hairpins. As you descend towards Prince Albert, there are plenty of shaded picnic sites at which to pause and enjoy the stunning views.

✚ 327 E10

CALITZDORP

www.tourismcalitzdorp.co.za

This attractive Victorian village is a successful agricultural hub and an important area for port wine production in South Africa—and there are quite a lot of similarities between the climate of Calitzdorp and the Douro valley in Portugal. It is possible to visit five port farms (ask at the tourist office), and a port festival is held here in July every other (odd) year. At harvest time, fresh fruit is sold along the wide roads of the village.

✚ 327 E11 ℹ Voortrekker Street, Calitzdorp 6660 ☎ 044-2133775 🕒 Mon–Sat 9–5, Sat 9–12

MORE TO SEE
PRINCE ALBERT

www.patourism.co.za

This village on the edge of the Swartberg Mountains, just 2km (1.2 miles) from the Swartberg Pass, feels remote and rural. Canals from these hills bring water to the gardens, helping to give an oasis feel to the settlement. As you walk about the old streets between houses of the Victorian era, you quickly gain an impression of Karoo life at the end of the 1800s.

There's an excellent Saturday morning market on Church Street selling home-made cheese, pickles, olives, dried fruit, bread and cakes, and the Olive Food and Wine Festival is held on the last weekend of April.

✚ 327 E10 ℹ Church Street, Prince Albert 6930 ☎ 023-5411366 🕒 Mon–Fri 9–5, Sat 9–1

Below Proteas—South Africa's national flower—bloom around the Swartberg Pass

THE OVERBERG

www.tourismcapeoverberg.co.za
The Overberg, roughly the area to the east of the Hottentots Holland Mountains, extends as far as Mossel Bay on the Garden Route. To the north are the Langeberg Mountains and to the south the ocean. In the early days of settlement, people would refer to the area as 'over the berg'. It was not until the construction of Sir Lowry's Pass that the region began to be cultivated. Most visitors pass through on their way to the Garden Route and it has a handful of interesting stop-off points. Swellendam (▷ below), Caledon and Bredasdorp (▷ 101) all have fine examples of early Cape Dutch buildings. But the big draw is the Whale Coast and the whale-watching hotspot of Hermanus (▷ 113).
✚ 327 D11 🚹 Cape Overberg Tourism Association, 22 Plein Street, Caledon 7230 ☎ 028-4251157 🕓 Mon–Fri 8.30–4, Sat 8.30–12.30

PLETTENBERG BAY

www.tourismplettenbergbay.co.za
'Plett', as it is commonly known, is one of the most appealing resorts along the Garden Route and has particularly fine beaches. It has become fashionable in recent years, and during the busy Christmas season the town is transformed. For the rest of the year the place is more sedate. There are three beaches—Robberg, Central and Lookout—all good for swimming, but Lookout is the most attractive. There is also excellent deep-sea fishing and, in season, good whale and dolphin spotting. The nearby Keurbooms River lagoon is a safe area for swimming and watersports.
✚ 328 F11 🚹 Plettenberg Bay Tourism, Melville's Corner, Main Street, Plettenberg Bay 6600 ☎ 044-5334065 🕓 Mon–Fri 9–5, Sat 9–1

ROBERTSON

www.tourismrobertson.co.za
This small, prosperous town, with its tidy jacaranda-lined streets, orderly church squares and neat rose gardens, could be in a time warp.

Stop off to explore its attractive centre and the nearby vineyards, one of which is the Robertson Valley Wine Route (tel 023-6263167; www.robertsonwinevalley.com) that follows the Breede River Valley (▷ 101).

One of the most welcoming estates is Van Loveren (Mon–Fri 8.30–5, Sat 9.30–1). Tastings are conducted in a restored *rondavel* (round hut with a conical roof) in the middle of a garden. Robertson Winery (Mon–Thu 8–5, Fri 8–6, Sat 9–3), on Constitution Road, is the oldest winery in the area and has tastings and cellar tours (by prior arrangement). Nearby, the village of McGregor is made up of a collection of perfectly preserved, whitewashed thatched cottages radiating out from the Dutch Reformed Church (not open to the public).
✚ 327 D11 🚹 Robertson Tourism Bureau, corner of Voortrekker and Reitz streets, Robertson 6705 ☎ 023-6264437 🕓 Mon–Fri 9–4

SWARTLAND

www.tourismswartland.co.za
North of Cape Town, following the N7 towards the Northern Cape, the landscape is made up of rolling wheat country known as the Swartland, or 'Black Country', after the dark rhinoceros bush which once covered the area. Most of the towns in the region are small, prosperous farming communities; the main towns of the wheat industry are Malmesbury and Moorreesburg. The area contains the Olifants River valley, the eastern boundary of

which is made up of the spectacular Cederberg Mountains (▷ 102). The Olifants River is named after the elephants that were spotted here by the first European explorers more than 300 years ago.
✚ 326 C10 🚹 1 Church Street, Malmesbury ☎ 022-4872989 🕓 Mon–Fri 8–5, Sat 8.30–12

SWELLENDAM

www.tourismswellendam.co.za
Founded in 1745, Swellendam is the third oldest European town in South Africa, and one of the most attractive. The heart of town bears testament to its age with its mature oak trees and whitewashed Cape Dutch homesteads. Many of the original houses were destroyed in a fire in 1865, and more were pulled down in 1974 when the main street was widened. Despite all this, Swellendam has retained its appeal and it makes a pleasant base for exploring the region—the Breede River Valley (▷ 101) and the Little Karoo (▷ 108–109) are all within easy reach.

The Drostdy Museum (Mon–Fri 9–4.45, Sat–Sun 10–3.45) on Swellengrebel Street is often described as one of the country's great architectural treasures. The main H-shaped building dates from 1747, when it was built as the official residence and seat for the local magistrate, the *landdrost*. Inside, the displays concentrate on local history.
✚ 327 D11 🚹 Swellendam Tourism, Oefeningshuis, Voortrek Street, Swellendam 6740 ☎ 028-514858 🕓 Mon–Fri 8–5, Sat–Sun 9–12

TSITSIKAMMA—GARDEN ROUTE NATIONAL PARK

This is one of the most popular national parks in the country, second only to Kruger. It consists of a stretch of lush, coastal rainforest extending for 80km (50 miles), and protects an area of 5km (3 miles) out to sea. The Tsitsikamma rainforest is the last remnant of what once covered this coast, the narrow strip of towering hardwoods combining with a haze of climbing vegetation to create an unforgettable forest scene. The coast is rocky and wild, and the deep river gorges and spectacular Storms River Mouth make this area the Garden Route's most entrancing section.

THE PARK

The park is split into two sections, both accessible only from the N2: There is no access by road between one section and the other. In the west is De Vasselot, including the resort of Nature's Valley, with a number of short walks through the forest and across rivers, as well as a lovely stretch of sandy beach. In the east is Storms River Mouth, where the wild Storms River surges into the frothy sea through a deep gorge. Again, walking is the main pastime here, with a number of enjoyable hikes across the forested cliffs. There is a huge variety of birdlife in the park, the brightest of which is the Knysna lourie that can be spotted by the flash of red in its wings when it takes flight. You might also spot the rare African black oystercatcher, with black plumage and red eyes, beak and legs. Animals that you might see include the blue duiker, the smallest antelope in the country—the adult male stands less than 30cm (12in) high.

HIKING

There are a number of short hikes from both Storms River and Nature's Valley; detailed maps are available at both camps. The unidirectional 42.5km (26.5-mile) five-day Otter Trail between Storms River and Nature's Valley is one of South Africa's best-known treks (reservations must be made up to a year in advance, tel 044-5316700; www.sanparks.org), which follows the coastline, crossing rivers, traversing forests and passing waterfalls. The Tsitsikamma Trail is a 60km (37.5-mile) six-day inland trail run by South African Forestry (tel 042-2811712; www.mtoecotourism.co.za), while the Dolphin Trail (tel 042-2803588; www.dolphintrail.co.za) is a three-day professionally guided trail to the east of Storms River, on which luggage is transported, accommodation is in luxurious lodges and all meals are included.

INFORMATION

www.sanparks.org

✛ 328 F11 ☎ 042-2811607 ⏱ Storms River Mouth Gate: daily 6am–10pm; reception: daily 7.30–6 💰 Adult R100, child (under 12) R50 🍴 Tiger's Eye Restaurant open for breakfast, lunch and dinner 🛒 Shop stocks groceries, wine and beer ❓ Range of accommodation in two main camps 🚗 Off the N2, 4km (2.5 miles) after the Storms River Bridge

TIPS

» Don't miss the short boardwalk stroll from the restaurant at Storms River Mouth camp to the suspension bridge over the gorge, as the views are incredible.
» The best time to visit is between November and February, but bear in mind that it rains year round.

Opposite *Central Beach, Plettenberg Bay*
Below *Lush forest drops into the sea along the coast in Tsitsikamma—Garden Route National Park*

TULBAGH

www.tourismtulbagh.co.za
Tucked away in the Tulbagh Valley and surrounded by mountains is this prosperous and peaceful village, the centre for several small wine estates and fruit farms. At its heart is a fine collection of traditional Cape buildings, making it one of the best examples of a rural Victorian settlement in South Africa.

However, the apparent preservation of the buildings is somewhat artificial. Much of Tulbagh was destroyed by a sudden earthquake in 1969, after which the buildings underwent heavy restoration, giving the village its present-day pristine appearance. The main attraction is delightful, tree-lined Church Street. The majority of the buildings are in private ownership, but three are part of the Town Museum (Mon–Fri 9–5, Sat 10–4, Sun 11–4). At No. 4 there is an excellent photographic display tracing the history of Tulbagh's houses. Number 22 has been furnished with 19th-century items and No. 14 is now a guesthouse, restaurant and shop.

Below *Aloes and other succulents flourish in the Karoo Desert National Botanical Garden, Worcester*

🕂 326 C10 🛈 4 Church Street, Tulbagh 6820 ☎ 023-2301348 🕐 Mon–Fri 9–5, Sat 10–4, Sun 11–4

WEST COAST NATIONAL PARK

www.sanparks.org
Although it may not seem remarkable at first sight, West Coast National Park, stretching from the southern side of the natural harbour formed by Saldanha Bay, remains unmatched in South Africa. Covering some 30,000ha (75,000 acres), it protects the rich marine life in Langebaan lagoon and the rare coastal wetlands surrounding it. The attraction is the varied and impressive birdlife, and there are several hides allowing good viewing. Almost 250 bird species have been recorded here and the variety is quite remarkable, from flamingos and black oystercatchers to swift terns and Cape gannets.

Apart from the prolific birdlife, wild flowers are a big draw when they bloom after the first spring rains (Aug, Sep). Postberg Nature Reserve (open Aug, Sep only), within the park, holds the majority of blooms. The main towns near the national park are Langebaan, a modern holiday resort on the lagoon, and the industrial town of Saldanha.

🕂 326 B10 🛈 Off R27, north of Cape Town ☎ 022-7722144 🕐 Oct–Mar daily 6am–7.30pm; Apr–Sep 7–6.30 💷 Adult and child R40; in flower season (Aug–Sep) adult R80, child R40 🖭 ❓ There are two entrances: if approaching from the south on the R27, look out for signs on the left. The main entrance is accessed from the main road leading south from Langebaan town; it also houses the information office

WHALE COAST
▷ 113.

WILDERNESS—GARDEN ROUTE NATIONAL PARK

www.sanparks.org
This is one of the most relaxing places to stay along the Garden Route. The park covers 2,612ha (6,450 acres) and incorporates five rivers and four lakes as well as a length of coastline stretching 28km (17 miles). The series of freshwater lakes is between the Outeniqua foothills and sand dunes at the back of a fine, long, sandy beach.

You can explore the park either on foot or by kayak, the latter being ideal for spotting birds. The main camp has canoes and boats for rent—a small fee is payable at reception, where you can also pick up a map of the park and useful information about the countryside. Accommodation in the park is good value, but the nearby holiday resort of Wilderness has a wider choice of places to stay as well as a selection of restaurants.

🕂 327 F11 🛈 4km (2.5 miles) east of Wilderness off N2 ☎ 044-8770046 🕐 Reception open 24 hours 🗓 Adult R80, child (under 12) R40 🖭

WINELANDS
▷ 115–119.

WORCESTER

www.worcestertourism.com
Worcester, the capital of the Breede River Valley (▷ 101), has a number of interesting buildings and some good museums. Worcester's most famous son is artist Hugo Naudé (1868–1941), and Hugo Naudé House, a gallery filled with his and other South African artists' work, is at 115 Russell Street (Mon–Fri 8.30–4.30, Sat 9–12). The giant KWV brandy cellar on Church Street is the largest in the world, with 120 copper pot stills producing 10- and 20-year-old brandies (Mon–Fri 8–4.30, tours at 10am and 2pm). The excellent Kleinplasie Museum (Mon–Sat 9–4.30), on Robertson Road, is an open-air museum depicting the lifestyle of the early pioneer farmers of the area.

The Karoo Desert National Botanical Garden (daily dawn–dusk), off Roux Street, combines semi-desert plants with landscaped gardens filled with plants from arid regions. The area bursts into bloom after the spring rains, and there are several short trails in the gardens.

🕂 326 C11 🛈 Worcester Wine and Tourism, 25 Baring Street, Worcester 6850 ☎ 023-3482795 🕐 Mon–Fri 8–5, Sat 8.30–12.30

WHALE COAST

The evocatively named Whale Coast lives up to its title from July to November, when large numbers of southern right whales visit the sheltered bays along the coast of Walker Bay to breed, escaping the heavy winter storms in the oceans around Antarctica. They can be seen close to the shore from Cape Town's False Bay all the way east to Mossel Bay on the Garden Route. The best months for whale watching are September and October (calving season) when daily sightings are almost guaranteed.

The most exhilarating stretch of the coast is along the R44 between Gordon's Bay and Hermanus (far more enjoyable than the faster R45), where the mountains plunge straight into the ocean, forming a coastline of steep cliffs, sandy coves, dangerous headlands and natural harbours. There is a string of small seaside resorts along here, starting with Gordon's Bay and passing through Betty's Bay (known for its botanical gardens and colony of African penguins), Kleinmond, Onrus and Vermont. But most visitors go straight to Hermanus—and with good reason.

HERMANUS

Hermanus has grown from a rustic fishing village to a much-loved visitor resort. It is the self-proclaimed world's best land-based whale-watching site, and indeed its waters are host to impressive numbers of southern right whales during calving season. But don't expect any private viewings—Hermanus is popular and has a steady flow of visitors throughout the season. While this means it can get very busy, there is also a good selection of accommodation and restaurants.

The best months to see whales are September and October, when you're virtually guaranteed to see them breaching and lobtailing (the action of a whale's tail slapping the surface of the water) close to the shore. For the best sites, head along the Cliff Path that starts at the new harbour in Westcliff and follows the shore all the way round Walker Bay to Grotto Beach, a distance of slightly more than 15km (9 miles). Grotto Beach, with fine white sand, is the largest of a number of good beaches just a short distance in either direction from central Hermanus.

The Old Harbour in the heart of town is a national monument and a focal point of visitor activities. A ramp leads down the cliff to the attractive old jetty and a group of restored fishermen's cottages, including a tiny local history museum (Mon–Sat 9–4.30, Sun 12–4).

INFORMATION

www.hermanus.co.za

✚ 326 C12 🛈 Greater Hermanus Tourism Bureau, Old Station Building, Mitchell Street, Hermanus 7200
☎ 028-3122629 🕙 Mon–Fri 8–6, Sat 9–5, Sun 9–3

TIPS

» Watch for the town's Whale Crier, who wanders along the coast blowing a kelp horn to alert visitors to where the whales are.

» Stanford, a sleepy Victorian village, is a pleasant trip from Hermanus and has the popular Birkenhead Brewery (tel 028-3410183; www.birkenhead.co.za; Wed–Sun 11–5; brewery tours Wed–Fri 11 and 3) just outside it, which offers brewery tours, pub lunches, beer and wine tasting.

Above *At Hermanus you can see whales close up without having to go on a boat*

INTRODUCTION

This series of fertile valleys is quite different from the rest of the Western Cape and was among the first areas to be settled after Cape Town. The Cape's wine industry was started by Governor Simon van der Stel in 1679. Previously, vines had been grown in Company's Garden (▷ 67–68) and in the area known today as the Cape Town suburb of Wynberg. The first wine was produced in 1652, and there was soon a great demand from the crews of ships when they arrived in Table Bay—red wine kept better than water on ships and helped fight off scurvy. As the early settlers moved inland and farms were opened up, more vines were planted. Stellenbosch became the first settlement to be established outside Cape Town in 1680. It flourished rapidly as a market town, and by chance the soils and climate proved to be ideal for grape growing.

The industry received its first real boost between 1688 and 1720 with the influx of Huguenot settlers from France, who brought their wine-making skills with them. A further boost came in 1806 when the English, at war with France, started to import South African wines. In the 20th century, under apartheid, sanctions hindered exports. Farm workers, mostly 'coloureds' (people of mixed race), suffered under the 'tot' system, when part of their wages was paid in wine. The inequality in the wine industry is slowly changing, and some farms are now partially owned by black empowerment consortiums.

While the wine industry flourished during the 18th and 19th centuries, the farmers built grand homesteads with cool wine cellars next to their vines; most of these have been lovingly restored and today can be visited as part of a Winelands tour. Some have even been converted into luxury hotels. The best itinerary would involve a night in either Stellenbosch or Franschhoek, with a day to explore the towns and some of the surroundings, followed by a night on a wine estate. Alternatively, any one of the towns makes an easy day trip from Cape Town when combined with a couple of wine estates, although it's worth staying longer to appreciate the area fully.

WHAT TO SEE

STELLENBOSCH

www.tourismstellenbosch.co.za

The hub of the Winelands, Stellenbosch is the oldest and most attractive town in the region, with a handful of good museums and a large university, giving it a lively atmosphere and a fun nightlife. It's a fairly large place and makes a perfect base for visiting the wine estates. The old town has a pleasing mix of architectural styles: Cape Dutch, Georgian, Regency and Victorian. No other town in South Africa has such an impressive concentration of early Cape buildings. However, as in Swellendam (▷ 110) many of the earliest buildings were lost to fires in the 18th and 19th centuries; what you see today is a collection of well-restored buildings. Houses line broad streets, dappled with shade from avenues of centuries-old oak trees, and ditches still carry running water to the town gardens. With its carefully restored white-walled buildings, Dorp Street, which runs east–west in the southern part of town, is one of the finest of these classic Stellenbosch streets.

The most engaging museum in town is the Village Museum (tel 021-8872948; Mon–Sat 9.30–5, Sun 2–5) at 18 Ryneveld Street, a fascinating tour through four houses, each representing a different period of the town's history. West of here is the Braak, at the western end of Church Street, the original village green and a one-time military parade ground.

✚ 326 C11 ⓘ 36 Market Street, Stellenbosch 7600 ☎ 021-8833584 ⓘ Mon–Fri 8–6, Sat 9–5, Sun 10–4

Opposite Simonsig vineyard, one of the large wine estates around Stellenbosch

» If you are in the car, make sure one of the drivers stays off the wine. You should never drive under the influence of alcohol and South Africa's drink-driving laws are stringent. Alternatively take a guided day tour from Cape Town.

» The wine estates have some of the best restaurants in the Western Cape, so be sure to stop off for lunch.

STELLENBOSCH WINE ROUTE

www.wineroute.co.za

When it opened in April 1971, this was South Africa's first wine route. It has been hugely successful, attracting tens of thousands of visitors every year, and today the membership is made up of around 200 private cellars. It's possible to taste and buy wines at all of them, and the cellars can arrange for your purchases to be delivered internationally. Many of the estates have developed excellent restaurants as well as providing popular picnic lunches. The estates listed below are just a tiny selection of the total.

STELLENBOSCH WINE ESTATES

Delheim (tel 021-8884600; www.delheim.com; daily 9–5, cellar tours daily 10.30–2.30) is a large estate with a garden restaurant providing good views towards Cape Town and Table Mountain. Tastings are conducted in a cool downstairs cellar.

Hartenberg (tel 021-8652541; www.hartenbergestate.com; sales and tastings: Mon–Fri 9–5.15, Sat 9–3), a privately owned estate founded in 1692, is off the Bottelary Road, 10km (6 miles) north of Stellenbosch. In summer, lunches are served in the shady peaceful gardens; in winter, the tasting room doubles as a restaurant with warming log fires. A variety of red and white wines are produced, but reds seem the most successful: Winners of national awards include their 2003 Shiraz and Pinotage.

The long pine-lined avenue and cluster of Cape Dutch buildings of Neethlingshof (tel 021-8838988; www.neethlingshof.co.za; sales and tastings: Mon–Fri 9–5, Sat–Sun 10–4) make this a pleasant estate to visit, and there are two fine restaurants on site. The first vines were planted here in 1692 by a German, Barend Lubbe, and the manor house was built in 1814 in traditional Cape Dutch H-style. Today this has been converted into the Lord Neethling restaurant. Not only has Neethlingshof won a clutch of awards—the Lord Neethling Pinotage is a consistent trophy winner.

Spier estate (tel 021-8091100; www.spier.co.za; sales and tastings: daily 10–4.30) is the Winelands' most commercial wine estate with a vast array of activities in addition to tastings of their own wines and those of other Stellenbosch estates. Spier wines are well regarded, and their Private Collection Chenin Blanc '01 is especially good. Other attractions are several restaurants, a cheetah park, a birds of prey area, horseback riding, fishing, golf and a spa. An annual open-air music and arts festival is held in the amphitheatre during summer, and the acclaimed restaurant Moyo is located in the grounds.

The large Simonsig estate (tel 021-8884900; www.simonsig.co.za; sales and tastings: Mon–Fri 8.30–5, Sat 8.30–4; cellar tours Mon–Fri 10 and 3, Sat 10) has been in the Malan family for 10 generations, and in recent years has produced some exceptionally fine wines. The estate has an attractive outdoor tasting area with grand views of the mountains, and a restaurant featuring local produce. One wine worth looking out for is Kaapse Vonkel, a sparkling white considered the best of its kind in South Africa, while the Chardonnay is consistently excellent and reasonably priced.

FRANSCHHOEK

www.franschhoek.org.za

With its Victorian whitewashed houses backed by rolling vineyards and the soaring slopes of the Franschhoek Mountains, this is the most pleasant of the Wineland villages. Franschhoek is famed for its cuisine and is often dubbed the gourmet capital of South Africa, so a visit here should guarantee an excellent meal. On the culture front, the Huguenot Memorial Museum (Mon–Sat 9–5, Sun 2–5) is housed in two buildings either side of Lambrecht Street, with displays tracing the history of the Huguenots in South Africa. Huguenots—Protestants fleeing persecution in France—arrived in the Franschhoek Valley in 1688

Below *The 1938 Huguenot Memorial in Franschhoek recognizes the Huguenot contribution to the wine industry*

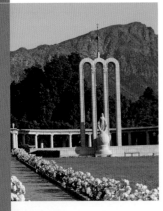

REGIONS • WESTERN CAPE • SIGHTS

(Franschhoek means 'French corner'). Next to the museum is the stark Huguenot Monument dating from 1938.

➕ 326 C11 ❶ Franschhoek 7690 ☎ 021-8763603 🕙 Mon–Fri 9–6, Sat 10–5, Sun 10–4

FRANSCHHOEK WINE ROUTE

www.franschhoek-cellar.co.za

All the vineyards lie along the Franschhoek Valley, so this is one of the most compact wine routes in the region. What makes it such a rewarding route is that many estates have opened their own excellent restaurants and several also provide luxury accommodation. Note that there are now 42 wine estates along the Franschhoek route, with more being added every year; below is a selection of some of these. If you don't want to estate-hop, all the valley's wines can be tasted at the Franschhoek Vineyards Co-operative (www.franschhoek-vineyards. co.za; Mon–Fri 9.30–5, Sat 10–4, Sun 11–3), on the right just before you enter the village when approaching from Stellenbosch.

FRANSCHHOEK WINE ESTATES

Boschendal estate (tel 021-8724272; www.boschendal.com; sales and tastings: daily 8.30–6.30) has been growing vines for 300 years; today a third of the estate is owned by a black empowerment consortium (▷ 26, 27). It is one of the most popular estates in the region, not least for its excellent food and agreeable wine-tasting area beneath a giant oak. Much of the wine produced on the estate is white; their sparkling wines are highly regarded. The main manor house (1812) is open to the public as a museum.

Mont Rochelle (tel 021-8762770; www.montrochelle.co.za; sales and tastings: daily 10–7; cellar tours Mon–Fri 11, 12.30 and 3) has one of the most attractive settings in the region, with splendid views of the valley. Owner Miko Rwayitare has doubled the area under vines in the last few years and completely redeveloped the estate, now offering two white and three red wines. Tastings are informal and friendly.

The original manor house and cellars of La Motte estate (tel 021-8763119; www.la-motte.com; sales and tastings: Mon–Sat 9–5) were built in 1752, and the grand old cellars (worth a visit in themselves) are now used as a classical concert venue in the evenings. Wine tasting takes place in an area overlooking the cellars.

PAARL

www.tourismpaarl.co.za

Paarl runs along the eastern base of Paarl Mountain, a giant granite massif that is part of the Paarl Mountain Nature Reserve (daily 7–7), which has a network of footpaths, a circular drive and a couple of dams. Like much of the Winelands, Paarl has a strong Afrikaner identity, encapsulated by the Taal Monument (Oct–Mar daily 8–8; Apr–Sep 8–5), which celebrates the Afrikaans language. This controversial but striking monument, inaugurated in October 1975, stands outside the town on the slopes of Paarl Mountain. It is made up of three concrete columns linked by a low curved wall, with each column representing different influences felt in the language. The relative heights of each column and the negative connotations associated with them have been the subject of fierce debate. Several old buildings survive in the town, but they are spread out rather than concentrated in a few blocks, as at Stellenbosch.

➕ 326 C11 ❶ 216 Main Street, Paarl 7646 ☎ 021-8724842 🕙 Mon–Fri 8–5, Sat–Sun 10–1

PAARL WINE ROUTE

www.paarlwine.co.za

The Paarl Wine Route has 30 members, including two of South Africa's better known wine estates, KWV and Nederburg. However, only the largest estates conduct regular cellar tours.

Below *The Taal Monument in Paarl*

PAARL WINE ESTATES

Fairview Estate (tel 021-8632450; www.fairview.co.za; wine and cheese sales and tastings: daily 9–5, last vouchers 4pm) has the rather unusual attraction of a goat tower—a spiral structure that is home to two pairs of goats. In addition to a variety of good wines (look for the popular Goats do Roam and Bored Doe blends—a humorous dig at French wines), visitors can taste delicious goat's and Jersey milk cheeses.

The Laborie vineyard (tel 021-8073390; www.laboriewines.co.za; sales and tastings: Nov–Apr Mon–Fri 9–5, Sat 10–5, Sun 11–3; May–Oct closed Sun), part of KWV (see below), is a carefully restored Cape Dutch homestead, and has been developed with tourism firmly in mind. It's an attractive spot, with a tasting area overlooking rolling lawns and vineyards, and a highly rated restaurant.

A short distance from the Laborie estate is the KWV Cellar Complex (tel 021-8073007; www.kwvwineemporium.co.za; sales and tastings: Mon–Sat 9–4, Sun 11–4; cellar tours Mon–Sat 10, 10.15 (in German), 10.30, 2.15), which contains the five largest vats in the world. The Kooperatieve Wijnbouwers Vereniging van Zuid-Afrika (Co-operative Wine Growers' Association) was established in Paarl in 1918 and is responsible for exporting many of South Africa's best-known wines. They are also known for their brandy (Worcester, ▷ 112).

The annual production at the Nederburg estate (tel 021-8623104; www.nederburg.co.za; Nov–Mar Mon–Fri 8–5, Sat 10–4, Sun 11–4; Apr–Oct Mon–Fri 8–5, Sat 10–2) exceeds 650,000 cases. Every April the Nederburg Auction attracts international buyers and is considered one of the top five wine auctions in the world. Nederburg wines win countless annual awards—the 2005 Manor House Shiraz and the 2010 Sauvignon Blanc included.

MORE TO SEE

THE BRANDY ROUTE

The Brandy Route (South African Brandy Foundation, tel 021-8097618; www. sabrandy.co.za) has been running for some years and incorporates 13 cellars around Stellenbosch, Wellington and Worcester, including KWV Brandy Cellar (▷ 112), the largest brandy cellar in the world. There are several cellars to the east of Worcester on and around the R62, known as the R62 Brandy Route.

VERGELEGEN ESTATE

www.vergelegen.co.za

This is one of the Cape's finest estates, with a superb manor house stocked with antiques and historical paintings. It has formal gardens, and the surrounding parkland is open for exploration. The modern cellars are buried on Rondekop Hill, overlooking the estate—there are good views of the mountains and False Bay from here. The Lady Phillips Restaurant and Rose Terrace are open for lunch and there's also a picnic hamper service.

☎ 021-8471334 ⊙ Daily 9.30–4 💷 R20, fee includes wine tasting and a cellar tour at 10.30, 11.30 and 3 ⑪ 🚗 Turn off N2 at exit 43, signposted Somerset West, and then turn left onto R44. Turn right at traffic lights and after 1km (0.6 miles) turn left into Lourensford Road. After 4km (2.5 miles) look for estate signpost on the right side of the road

AFRIKAANS LANGUAGE MUSEUM

www.taalmuseum.co.za

This small museum in Paarl gives a detailed chronicle of the development of the Afrikaans language and the people involved.

✉ Gideon Malherbe House, 11 Pastorie Avenue, Paarl 7625 ☎ 021-8723441 ⊙ Oct–Mar daily 8–8; Apr–Sep 8–5 💷 Adult R12, child (under 12) R2

BUTTERFLY WORLD

If you have children in tow, and are looking for something to please them, a good place to visit is Butterfly World at Paarl. It's the largest such park in South Africa,

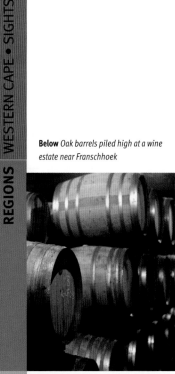

Below *Oak barrels piled high at a wine estate near Franschhoek*

where butterflies fly freely in flower-filled landscaped gardens. There is also a craft shop and the Jungle Leaf café.

✉ Klapmuts, Paarl 7625 ☎ 021-8755628 🕐 Daily 9–5 ✋ Adult R43, child (3–18) R25 💾 🏛

WELLINGTON

www.tourismwellington.co.za

Wellington, like the other Winelands towns, stands amid pleasing countryside and has a number of fine old buildings, with the added bonus of far fewer visitors thronging the streets. There are several wine estates in the environs, but the town is best known for its dried fruit.

✚ 326 C11 🚩 Old Market Building, Main Street, Wellington 7655 ☎ 021-8734604 🕐 Mon–Fri 8–5, Sat–Sun 10–1

JONKERSHOEK NATURE RESERVE

www.capenature.org.za

Some 12km (7 miles) out of Stellenbosch, beyond the Lanzerac Hotel, is this forestry plantation, open to the public for hiking, fishing and mountain biking, with a choice of five self-guided trails. If you prefer the view from a car, you can follow a circular gravel road through the forest for 12km (7 miles).

☎ 021-8661560 🕐 Daily 7.30–5 ✋ Adult R30, child (3–18) R15

BOTANICAL GARDENS

The Botanical Gardens are part of the University of Stellenbosch, with a fine collection of ferns, orchids and bonsai trees. One of the more unusual plants to look for is the welwitschia from the Namib Desert. Its single pair of broad leaves grow from a woody stem.

✉ Neethling Street, Stellenbosch 7600 ☎ 021-8083054 🕐 Daily 9–5 ✋ Free 🍴

Above *Spiky specimens in Stellenbosch Botanical Gardens*

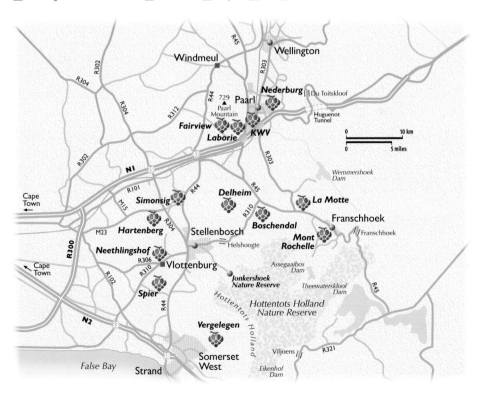

THE GARDEN ROUTE

Rated among the country's most scenic routes, this drive takes you along the southern maritime terrace from the seaside town of Mossel Bay eastwards to the Tsitsikamma—Garden Route National Park. On your right is the Indian Ocean shoreline; on your left stretches the evergreen grandeur of the Outeniqua and Tsitsikamma mountain ranges.

THE DRIVE

Distance: 210km (130 miles)
Allow: 2 days
Start at: Mossel Bay
End at: Storms River Mouth

★ Start in Mossel Bay (▷ 106) where you pick up the N2. Turn left (northwest) onto the N9 for the last 5km (3 miles) of the run into George (66km/41 miles), the gateway to the Garden Route. The seaboard stretch of this part of the drive skirts the resort villages of Hartenbos, Klein-Brakrivier (look out for winter-flowering aloes in the surrounding hills) and Groot-Brakrivier, before the route veers inland.

❶ George (▷ 103), the largest of the region's towns, lies beneath the handsome Outeniqua Mountains, surrounded by fertile countryside. It was named after George III of England, who was king when George became a town in 1811. Among its various museums the Transport Museum includes 13 steam locomotives and a room devoted to model railways.

Return towards the intersection of the N9 and N2. The inland—and arguably the more rewarding—route is the old Passes Road, which starts 3km (2 miles) outside George and takes you through the well-wooded, rugged foothills of the Outeniqua range for 58km (36 miles): Dense forests, tangled patches of fern, wild flowers and dangling creepers all flourish beneath the mountains. The shorter (40km/25-mile), more conventional route follows the N2, initially southeast to the town of Wilderness, from where there are magnificent views across the sand and sea.

❷ Wilderness is an appealingly relaxed seaside village. To access it, take the first left (signposted 'Wilderness'). The town is rather strung out, but most of it clusters around the lagoon at the mouth of the Touws River. It is said to date back to 1877, when George Bennett bought land in the area to start a farm; inspired by the surroundings, he called it Wilderness.

Back on the N2, the road hugs the coast, passing through a forested area, which opens up onto the limpid lagoon stretching for 17km (10.5 miles). Before reaching Knysna,

Oudtshoorn

N9

Robinson   Outeniqua

Blanco

George

Groot-
Brakrivier

Brandwag   N2   Pacaltsdorp

Klein-Brakrivier   Herolds Bay

Hartenbos

★ **Mossel Bay**

the N2 crosses the northwestern reaches of the lagoon via a long, low road bridge. Take a quick detour for a dip in the sea: Just before the bridge, you'll see a minor road to your right, which leads along the lagoon's western bank to the little Norman-style Holy Trinity Church at Belvidere. Continue up the slope and then down to the stylish resort village of Brenton-on-Sea and its fine beach. Retrace the route to the N2 which then passes along the lagoon before plunging into town.

❸ Knysna (▷ 105) acts as the capital of the Garden Route and makes for a pleasant overnight stop. The town is fully geared up for tourists, which means a lot of choice in accommodation and restaurants. It is also quite an arty place with lots of craft shops and galleries.

Forests line the next 25km (15.5 miles) of the drive to Plettenberg Bay. A detour into the town (off the N2 to the right) leads to a couple of superb sandy beaches.

❹ Plettenberg Bay (▷ 110) is possibly the Western Cape's most fashionable resort town. Its glorious position on a mountain-backed bay gave it its original name of Baia Formosa (Beautiful Bay). Its present name is more prosaic, immortalizing an 18th-century governor of the Cape, Joachim van Plettenberg. If you're not visiting Plettenberg Bay continue along the N2, which passes

Keurbooms Lagoon on the right, and the strikingly blue Tsitsikamma Mountains on the left. The N2 crosses over the northern tip of the Keurbooms estuary, climbing and veering to the north. A number of stopping places en route enable you to look back over the bay, lagoon and sea.

For the final part of the drive you follow the N2 for 65km (40 miles) from Plettenberg Bay along the northern edge of the strip-like Tsitsikamma—Garden Route National Park to Storms River. After 19km (12 miles), a loop road (the R102) takes you down to the sea at enchanting Nature's Valley.

❺ Nature's Valley is entered over the high Groot River Pass. There are stupendous views of the sea and surrounding forest from the top of the pass. The R102 drops 223m (731ft) to sea level via a narrow gorge, twisting through coastal forest. From the sea, the road turns back up out of the Groot Valley.

At the top of Groot River Pass, the road crosses the N2 highway and then dips back down along the narrow, forest-fringed road to the Bloukrans River Pass. From the bottom of the pass, look up to the elegantly arched road bridge that spans the immense river gorge—this is the alternative route if you stay on the N2 (and is a popular spot for bungee jumping, ▷ 130). The R102 rejoins the N2 shortly after

Coldstream, the next village along this stretch.

A little less than 7km (4 miles) after you reach the intersection of the two routes, turn right for Storms River Mouth and the Tsitsikamma—Garden Route National Park (▷ 111). The road ends at a restaurant near the entrance to the park.

WHEN TO GO
The Garden Route is pleasant at any time of the year, but while it rains year round here, there is more rain in winter. Plettenberg Bay has an annual average of 320 days of sunshine. It's best to avoid high season, from December to February, when the area is at its busiest.

WHERE TO EAT
THE LOOKOUT
This is a great lunch spot, overlooking the beach, serving seafood and grills.
✉ Lookout Beach, Plettenberg Bay 6600
☎ 044-5331379 ☺ Daily 9am–11pm

QUAY FOUR KNYSNA
www.quay4knysna.co.za
A sister restaurant to Quay Four on the Victoria & Alfred Waterfront in Cape Town (▷ 93), this lively place on Thesen Island is known for its oysters and barbecues of fresh fish. Sit on the deck outside and enjoy wonderful views of the lagoon.
✉ Long Street, Thesen Island
☎ 044-382420 ☺ Daily 7.30–late

Opposite *Plettenberg Bay's sweeping Lookout Beach*

THE SEVILLA TRAIL IN THE CEDERBERG

This is a fairly easy walk along a valley in the Cederberg region. It follows a rocky trail in a deserted valley past 10 beautifully preserved San rock art sites. The walk is waymarked with painted white footprints on the ground. It starts and ends at Traveller's Rest farm (⊞ 326 C9), 34km (21 miles) from Clanwilliam.

THE WALK

Distance: 4km (2.5 miles)

Allow: 2–3 hours

Start/end at: Traveller's Rest farm

How to get there: Traveller's Rest farm is on the Wuppertal Road, 34km (21 miles) from Clanwilliam

Parking: At the farm

★ Start at the Traveller's Rest farm, where you can park and pick up a map of the trail. Cross the road from the farm and enter through the small gate. The trail winds along a stark, rock-strewn landscape alongside a (usually) dry riverbed. Continue straight ahead and follow the waymarkers veering to the left. You will be walking over weathered rock, with a more or less continuous stretch of rocky overhangs and walls to your left. Look for dassies (rock hyraxes), small, rodent-like mammals

that look like overgrown guinea pigs, which inhabit these rocks.

❶ The first rock art site you come to, on your left after 1km (0.6 miles), has a black image of a group of people standing in a circle. This is superimposed over older, more weathered images. Be careful not to touch the paintings as they are extremely fragile.

Follow the rock face around to your left for a few paces, and you will come to the second site.

❷ Site 2 has one of the most intriguing paintings, as it shows what looks like long-necked monsters running side by side. The images probably once had a mystical, symbolic significance. One hundred metres (110 yards)

farther on is site 3, again on your left, on top of a rocky ledge over the riverbed. Look for a huge rounded boulder balanced on a couple of other rocks, with a gap underneath: Behind, under and surrounding it are various examples of rock art.

❸ The finest of these is under the boulder (you'll have to lie underneath it to see it properly), and depicts what looks like the hindquarters of antelope—the front parts of the animals may have been painted in a different shade that has faded with age. A short scramble off the ledge is site 4 (look for the waymarkers), which has clear images of quagga (an extinct species of zebra) and other zebra.

Above *San rock art*
Right *The Cederberg Mountains*

The next part of the trail leads you, after 500m (550 yards), to a rocky shelf above the river, below which you'll see a pretty patch of indigenous forest including wild olive and almond trees. During August and September look for the wild flowers on the surrounding hills and valley.

4 Site 5 is one of the best. It has a fine depiction of a walking archer, and one of a zebra foal that perfectly captures the young creature's first faltering steps. Just a few steps farther on is site 6, with a number of images, including a bright group of dancing women.

Continue around to the left and then straight on down a gully for about 300m (330 yards) until you reach site 7.

5 Sites 7, 8 and 9 are fairly close together. The images at site 7 are quite faded, but include a couple of faint yellow elephants and two shadowy figures whose faces have eerily faded away. About 250m (273 yards) farther along is site 8, a low cave filled with numerous handprints in various shades. After another 50m (55 yards), site 9 has a multitude of images including some groups of running antelope.

If the riverbed is dry, turn right at this point (look for the waymarkers) and cross the riverbed, before turning left at the rough road. If the river is flooded, you have no choice but to retrace your steps from here back to Traveller's Rest farm.

6 Site 10 is just past three cottages, up a gorge, and depicts several processions of people carrying sticks or weapons.

From here, retrace your steps back along the trail to Traveller's Rest farm. For a longer walk you can take the Sevilla Olive Tree Walk, which loops around on the other side of the river and back to the main road.

WHEN TO GO
Summer can be oppressively hot. The best months are May and June, when the weather is cooler and fairly dry, and August and September, when the wild flowers are in bloom in the Cederberg.

WHERE TO EAT
Traveller's Rest serves meals at the Khoisan Kitchen, but you must phone several days ahead to arrange to eat here (☎ 027-4821824; www.travellersrest.co.za) as it usually opens only if large groups are visiting. Otherwise bring your own picnic, as there are no other restaurants on this route.

WHERE TO STAY
There are 12 cottages and a guesthouse and a restaurant at Traveller's Rest (☎ 027-4821824; www.travellersrest.co.za; R380 for two sharing). There are 20 horses on the farm and guided horse trails are available, including some to see the San rock art.

ROUTE 62: ROBERTSON TO THE KAROO

This drive takes you from the lush countryside of the Cape's Winelands to the dry plains of the Little Karoo, a region hugged by two great mountain ranges. Route 62 is a pleasant, scenic alternative to the usual highway route from the Cape to the Little Karoo. The drive can comfortably be completed in a day, but if you want to take in some of the wine estates along the route, allow two days, perhaps spending a night in Calitzdorp.

THE DRIVE

Distance: 266km (165 miles)
Allow: 1 day
Start at: Robertson
End at: Oudtshoorn

★ Begin the drive just outside the town of Robertson (▷ 110), heading east on the R60.

The lime-rich soils, mild climate and good pasturage around Robertson make this one of the country's top horse-breeding areas; you'll see some fine thoroughbreds grazing in the fields as you drive past.

This area is the Breede River Valley (▷ 101), flanked here by the high Langeberg range, which you negotiate via the Kogmanskloof Pass on your way east to Montagu, a distance of 30km (18.5 miles). The pass starts at Ashton; turn left out of the town, off the R60 and onto the R62.

① Kogmanskloof (once known as Cogman's Kloof) is a spectacular pass built by the celebrated road engineer John Thomas Bain in the 1870s. It winds for 6km (4 miles) beneath stark rock walls and soaring peaks, passing through a rock tunnel on top of which stand the ruins of a fort from the Second Anglo-Boer War (1899–1902). If you feel like a break at this point, stop at the pleasant Keurkloof picnic spot on the Montagu side of the tunnel, where you'll find drinking water and toilets.

The road goes on to the attractive town of Montagu (▷ 106), which lies on the edge of the Little Karoo (▷ 108–109), a broad, flat-bottomed basin wedged between mountains to the north and south. The basin is bisected by the R62, which meanders all the way from the Cape Town area to Port Elizabeth, and which takes its inspiration from the famous American Route 66, linking Chicago with Los Angeles. Head out of

Montagu on Long Street, which leads onto the R62. The next stretch takes you the 60km (37 miles) to Barrydale.

② Barrydale is the hub of a prosperous farming district producing apples, peaches, wine and brandy. You can visit the Barrydale Co-operative Cellars, which lay on wine tastings. The landscapes along the way are magnificent. Look out for the wild flowers, especially Livingstone daisies or *mesembryanthemums* (known in South Africa as vygies). The heights of the Langeberg are on your right.

After Barrydale the R62 runs northeast for 80km (50 miles) until it reaches Ladismith.

③ Ladismith is a laid-back little town that nestles beneath the Swartberg's lofty twin Towerkop peaks (2,203m/ 7,225ft). Like its more famous near-namesake, Ladysmith in KwaZulu-

Natal, it is named after the Spanish wife of Sir Harry Smith, soldier and controversial governor of the Cape Colony in the 19th century. You're now entering ostrich country, though the land here is mainly given over to sheep and fruit.

At the mission station of Amalienstein, 36km (22 miles) beyond Ladismith on the 28km (17-mile) stretch of the R62 leading to Calitzdorp, it's worth taking a diversion onto the little side road leading north into the Swartberg mountains via Seweweekspoort.

❹ The scenic river pass of Seweweekspoort is said to have got its name either from the fynbos that decorate the hillsides (one species blooms for seven weeks) or from the period needed by the brandy smugglers to complete their route through the uplands.

Back on the R62, continue to Calitzdorp.

❺ Calitzdorp, with its Victorian buildings, has a rather restful charm. As you get near the town, you'll begin to notice ostriches roaming the fields on both sides of the road, although the area is better known as the port wine capital of South Africa. The three local wineries, all well signposted from the middle of town, produce some of the country's finest port wines. The most appealing estate perhaps is Die Krans Estate, where there's also a pleasant half-hour vineyard walk. The other two are Boplaas Estate and Calitzdorp Wine Cellars. Calitzdorp holds a Port Festival in July every other (odd) year.

From here, the route continues straight to the ostrich capital, Oudtshoorn.

❻ Oudtshoorn lives and breathes ostriches. The approach to the town passes a number of farms and you'll see ostriches wandering around the fields. You can visit a couple of local farms (▷ 130) to see how ostriches are bred and to buy ostrich products (anything from eggs to feather dusters). The wider area's other notable attraction is the remarkable Cango Cave complex (▷ 109), 26km (17 miles) north of town.

WHEN TO GO
Any time of the year is good for this drive. Route 62 runs through the transition zone between the relatively lush and well-watered Winelands and the drier, invariably clear-skied Little Karoo. However, spring (October and November) and autumn (February and March) are probably the best months to tour the area. See www.route62.co.za.

WHERE TO EAT
PRESTON'S AND THOMAS BAIN PUB
Traditional food served in the à la carte restaurant and pub next door, with an attractive open-air terrace.
✉ 17 Bath Street, Montagu 6720 ☎ 023-6143013 🕐 Daily 10.30–2.30, 5.30–late

PLACES TO VISIT
BARRYDALE WINE CELLAR
www.barrydalewines.co.za
✉ Route 62 Wine Route, Barrydale
☎ 028-5721572 🕐 Mon–Thu 8–5, Fri 8–4, Sat 8–noon

CALITZDORP WINE ESTATES
Die Krans Estate (☎ 044-2133314; Mon–Fri 8–5, Sat 9–3); Boplaas Estate (☎ 044-213 3326; Mon–Fri 8–5, Sat 9–3); and Calitzdorp Wine Cellars (☎ 044-213 3301; 🕐 Mon–Fri 8–5, Sat 9–1)

WHERE TO STAY
PORT WINE GUEST HOUSE
www.portwine.net
A pleasant guesthouse dating back to 1830; the eight double rooms have four-poster beds and fireplaces.
✉ 7 Queen Street, Calitzdorp
☎ 044-2133131

Opposite *Ostrich farm, Oudtshoorn*

FOUR PASSES ROUTE:
THE WINELANDS TO THE OVERBERG

One of the popular day drives from Cape Town is known as the Four Passes route. This takes you through the heart of the Winelands region to the Overberg in the Western Cape and, as the name suggests, over four mountain passes. The drive can be completed in around three hours, but it's best to take your time and stop off to take in the views en route.

THE DRIVE
Distance: 115km (71 miles)
Allow: 3–4 hours
Start/end at: Stellenbosch

★ Begin your drive from Stellenbosch, the heart of the Winelands. From here, take the R310 north towards Franschhoek. Driving up out of Stellenbosch, you cross the first pass.

❶ Helshoogte Pass, despite its unpromising name (it means 'Hell's Heights'), has glorious views of the mountains rolling down to neat rows of vineyards.

From here, the road continues straight and you pass several well-known wine estates, including Boschendal. After 17km (10 miles) you reach an intersection with the R45; a left turn would take you to Paarl (12km/7 miles), but the route continues to the right.

This is a pleasant drive up into the Franschhoek Valley, passing several wine estates. The road follows a rail track and part of the Berg River before reaching Franschhoek. Continue straight on through the town until you reach the Huguenot Monument at the end of the main

road. Take a left turn here, and follow the road climbing up out of the valley to Franschhoek Pass.

❷ Franschhoek Pass was built along the tracks formed by migrating herds of game centuries ago, and was originally known as the Olifantspad (elephant's path). Pause at the top and look back over the wide views of the valley, with the little town nestling beneath the rugged peaks and surrounded by vineyards.

One of the more surprising aspects of this drive is the change in vegetation once you cross the lip of the pass, 520m (1,700ft) above

Franschhoek. As the road winds down towards Theewaterskloof Dam glittering in the distance, you pass through a dry valley of scrub vegetation and fynbos (the low-lying indigenous vegetation found in the Cape); the fertile fruit farms and vineyards of the earlier part of the drive are no longer to be seen. During spring, watch for flowering fynbos, when it produces bright-hued (and strange-smelling) blooms.

At the bottom of the valley the road reaches the dam and its large expanse of water.

❸ Theewaterskloof Dam is a popular spot for watersports and fishing. The views of the surrounding mountains and the tree plantations stretching up the slopes are particularly striking from here.

Take a right turn across the dam. The road crosses the narrowest part of the dam, and is a good place to look for birdlife. Continue on the R321, which passes across the valley towards Grabouw and Elgin, before climbing up to Viljoens Pass, the third of the four passes.

❹ The Hottentots Holland Nature Reserve, a popular area for hiking, lies to the right of the road. Much of the countryside here is given over to orchards. The area is an important apple-growing region, and after the apple harvest you'll see people standing at the side of the road selling their produce.

The road continues straight on, passing Eikenhof Dam on the right before reaching the undistinguished twin towns of Elgin and Grabouw. Just after the towns, you'll come to the intersection with the N2 highway. Turn right here and continue straight on. Here the road crosses the edge of the Steenbras Dam before climbing up to the fourth and most spectacular pass, Sir Lowry's Pass.

❺ Sir Lowry's Pass cuts over the Hottentots Holland Mountains and, as you come to the top of the road, you are met with astounding views of the entire plain between the Winelands and Cape Town. There is a signposted viewing site at the highest point of the pass from which you can see the vast stretch of coast curving to your left, with Table Mountain

looming in the background and the Cape Flats in between.

The N2 winds down the slope of the mountain before reaching the plain. From here, continue straight until you reach the turn off to Stellenbosch (intersection 38) and turn right onto the R44, leading back to town.

WHEN TO GO

This drive can be completed all year round, but spring is a particularly good time to visit, as the fruit trees and fynbos will be in bloom. Late summer is also an attractive time, as the vineyards are busy with workers harvesting the grapes. Expect strong winds in winter.

WHERE TO EAT
LA PETITE FERME

www.lapetiteferme.co.za
This smart restaurant is well known for its wholesome country cooking and modern fusion dishes such as rabbit with honey and mustard and kudu fillets with couscous. It has spectacular views over the Franschhoek valley.

✉ Franschhoek Pass ☎ 021-8763016
🕐 Daily 12–4

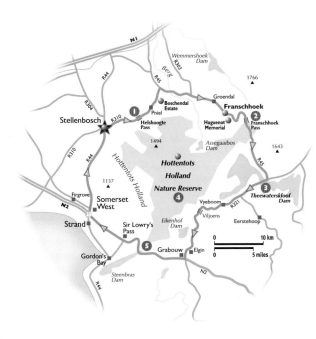

Opposite *Looking back along the Franschhoek Pass towards Franschhoek*
Above *Grapes ripening in the sun*

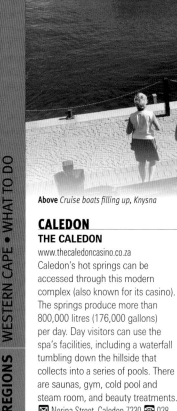

Above *Cruise boats filling up, Knysna*

CALEDON
THE CALEDON
www.thecaledoncasino.co.za
Caledon's hot springs can be accessed through this modern complex (also known for its casino). The springs produce more than 800,000 litres (176,000 gallons) per day. Day visitors can use the spa's facilities, including a waterfall tumbling down the hillside that collects into a series of pools. There are saunas, gym, cold pool and steam room, and beauty treatments.
✉ Nerina Street, Caledon 7230 ☎ 028-2145100 🖐 Full body aromatherapy massage from R350, facials from R220, manicures and pedicures from R250
🚗 1km (0.6 miles) out of town, just off N2

CITRUSDAL
THE BATHS
www.thebaths.co.za
Citrusdal is a popular and long-established natural hot-water spring, surrounded by citrus groves. The first resort was founded here in 1739 and the main Victorian stone buildings survive. There are individual spa baths and Jacuzzis (guests keep the keys overnight if staying here), all set in woodland.
✉ Citrusdal 7140 ☎ 022-9218026
🖐 Mon–Fri adult R35, child R20, Sat–Sun adult R70, child (under 12) R35 🚗 18km (11 miles) south of Citrusdal

DARLING
EVITA SE PERRON
www.evita.co.za
Drag-queen Evita is a South African institution, hosting lively cabaret events at this venue, which is just under an hour's drive from Cape Town. It includes Bambi's Berlin Bar, a shop, restaurant and gallery.
✉ Darling Station, Darling 7345
☎ 022-4922831 🕐 Restaurant and bar: Tue–Sun 10–4; shows usually on Fri 7pm, Sat 2pm and 7pm, Sun 2pm and 4.30pm but check website for dates 🖐 Shows: adult R96, child (under 11) free

DE HOOP NATURE RESERVE
MOUNTAIN BIKING
www.capenature.co.za
Cyclists can use the management roads in the western sector of the reserve. As you ride look for the proteas and ericas forming part of the rare lowland fynbos (fine bush) conserved here. You may also spot bontebok or Cape mountain zebra.
✉ The Reservation Office, De Hoop Nature Reserve, PO Box 66, Bredasdorp 7280
☎ 028-5421678 🖐 Adult R30, child (3–18) R15 per day

FRANSCHHOEK
MANIC CYCLES
www.maniccycles.co.za
Mountain bike hire for self tours of the village and wine farms. Couples may be interested in hiring a tandem bike, and there are also children's bikes and baby seats available.
✉ Franschhoek Centre, Main Road, Franschhoek 7690 ☎ 021-8764956
🖐 Half day R120, full day R200

PARADISE STABLES

www.paradisestables.co.za

These stables offer a range of guided trails through the wine-growing area around Franschhoek. The most popular excursions include stops at wine estates, with wine tasting and lunch included.

✉ 12 Robertsvlei Road, Franschhoek 7690 ☎ 021-8762160 🖐 From R200 per hour; 4-hour rides with wine tasting at two estates R550 (no children under 12)

GANSBAAI

WHITE SHARK ADVENTURES

www.whitesharkadventures.com

One of the most popular activities along the coast is cage diving to view great white sharks. Those with a diving certificate can view them from an underwater cage; non-divers can also do it, but they have to spend the day before the cage dive doing a resort course. Trips last between four and five hours.

✉ 3 Van Dyk Street, Kleinbaai, Gansbaai 7220 ☎ 82-9282000 🖐 Around R1,100, including use of all diving equipment

GEORGE

FANCOURT HOTEL AND COUNTRY CLUB

www.fancourt.com

The Fancourt Hotel has a health and beauty spa with Roman-style baths, where you can enjoy a stress-reducing back treatment or a detoxifying seaweed wrap, among other options. It also has four outstanding 18-hole golf courses, two of which were designed by Gary Player, which are for members or guests of the hotel (▷ 137).

✉ George 6529 ☎ 044-8040010 🖐 From R350

GARDEN ROUTE MALL

www.gardenroutemall.co.za

This is a fairly new 125-store mall with all the usual South African chain stores, restaurants, multi-screen cinema and supermarkets. A good place to stock up with supplies if you are heading on to the Garden Route.

✉ Out of town on the junction with the N2 ☎ 044-8870044 🕐 Mon–Fri 9–6, Sat 9–5, Sun 9–3

MARKLAAN CENTRE

The Marklaan Centre is a set of converted store rooms arranged around an open square, with several art galleries and curio shops to browse. A farmers' market is held here on Fridays from 7am to 10am.

✉ Between Market and Meade streets, George 6529 🕐 Mon–Sat 7–7

GRABOUW

NATURE DISCOVERY

www.naturediscovery.co.za

Budding 'easy riders' will relish the chance to take in the Cape countryside atop a Suzuki saddle, but the less adrenalin-inspired can also enjoy the same routes on more comfortable quad bikes. Tours vary from a couple of hours to full three-day adventures and many are suitable for children. It's a great way to take in the landscape.

✉ Elgin Country Club, Grabouw 7160 ☎ 021-8591989 🕐 Daily 🖐 From R785 for 2-hour trail.

HERMANUS

CURIO MARKET

Market Square, in the middle of town, holds a craft, curio and clothes market, selling souvenirs and practical lightweight clothing.

✉ Market Square, Hermanus 7200 🕐 Daily 8–5

SCUBA AFRICA

www.scubaafrica.com

This scuba company has equipment rental, runs dive courses (NAUI) and organizes daily dive trips. In addition to coral reef and kelp forest dives, there are three good wreck dives between here and Arniston, which is 50km (31 miles) east of Hermanus.

✉ New Harbour, Hermanus 7200 ☎ 028-3162362 🖐 Scuba Diver 6-day course R2,500

SOUTHERN RIGHT CHARTERS

www.southernrightcharters.co.za

For a water-based view of the southern right whales around Hermanus, take a boat trip, which are run daily by this company. The boats are prevented from getting too close to the whales, but views of

them are exhilarating nevertheless. A hydrophone on board allows you to listen to the whales too.

✉ Whale Shack, New Harbour, Hermanus 7200 ☎ 082-3530550 🕐 Daily whale-watching cruises in season (Jun–Dec) 🖐 Adult R500, child (under 12) R200

WINE VILLAGE

www.wine-village.co.za

Advertising itself as the biggest wine shop in South Africa, the Wine Village sells wine from over 600 estates. It can also arrange to ship your purchases overseas.

✉ Corner of the R43 and the R320 on the way into Hermanus ☎ 028-3163988 🕐 Mon–Fri 9–6, Sat 9–5, Sun 10–3

KNYSNA

AFRICAN MARKET

There is an excellent African craft market set up on the side of the road as you enter Knysna on the N2 from George. It has an extensive range of carvings, baskets, drums, curios and other items.

🕐 Daily 8–5 🚗 On N2, entrance to Knysna from west

FEATHERBED NATURE RESERVE

www.knysnafeatherbed.com

This private nature reserve can only be reached by the Featherbed Co. ferry, which runs from the John Benn Jetty at Knysna Quays (▷ 130). The four-hour excursion includes round ferry trip, 4WD vehicle ride up the western promontory of the Knysna Heads, a nature walk and a buffet lunch. The company also operates cruises around the lagoon on a paddle cruiser.

✉ The Heads ☎ 044-3821693 🕐 Daily 10, 11.15, 12.30 🖐 Adult R420, child (4–10) R198, including lunch

KNYSNA FOREST TOURS

www.knysnaforesttours.co.za

Guided hikes around Knysna offer the chance to get out of town and learn more about the wildlife and flora. Half-day, full-day and overnight options are available.

✉ Knysna Railway Station, Remembrance Avenue, Waterfront Drive ☎ 044-3826130 🖐 Half-day tours from R450

KNYSNA MOVIE HOUSE
www.knysnamoviehouse.co.za
This modern cinema has daily shows of new international and South African releases, in comfortable air-conditioned theatres. There are also art house and subtitled releases.
✉ Pledge Square, Main Street, Knysna 6571 ☎ 044-3827813 ◷ Mon–Sat 11.30am–10.30pm, Sun 2–10 ✋ From R30

KNYSNA QUAYS
This modern waterfront development is a mini version of the V & A Waterfront in Cape Town, with a range of shops and outdoor stalls.
✉ Knysna 6571 ☎ 044-3820955 ◷ Mon–Sat 8am–7pm

MOUNTAIN BIKING AFRICA
www.mountainbikingafrica.co.za
Guided mountain bike trails take you around the remaining tracts of indigenous forest in the area. The rides are quite easy, with lots of downhill sections. Bike rental and refreshments are included.
☎ 082-7838392 ✋ Half day rental from R120, full day from R190

WOODMILL LANE CENTRE
www.woodmillane.co.za
An open-air shopping centre built around a restored Victorian timber mill from 1919, with 75 shops, fountains and trees, performing artists, arts and crafts stores and a branch of Pick 'n' Pay supermarket.
✉ Corner of Main and Long streets, Knysna 6571 ◷ Mon–Fri 8–5, Sat 8.30–2, Sun 9–1

LANGEBAAN
CAPE SPORTS CENTRE
www.capesport.co.za
Langebaan lagoon is known for its excellent watersports. Cape Sports organizes windsurfing, kitesurfing and other watersports, with full instruction, by the hour or the day.
✉ On the northern beach, Langebaan 7357 ☎ 022-7721114 ✋ Three-hour lesson R695 (including equipment)

LITTLE KAROO
The ostrich farms around Oudtshoorn are good places to pick up ostrich-related items, from egg shells

to ostrich leather bags. They include the Wilgewandel Holiday Farm, in the Shoemanshoek Valley 2km (1.2 miles) before the Cango Caves (tel 044-2720878; www.wilgewandel.co.za; daily 8–5); Highgate Ostrich Farm, 10km (6 miles) from Oudtshoorn, off the R328 towards Mossel Bay (tel 044-2727115; www.highgate.co.za; daily 8–5); and Safari Ostrich Farm, 6km (4 miles) from Oudtshoorn, on the R328 to Mossel Bay (tel 044-2727311; www.safariostrich.co.za; daily 8–5).

MONTAGU
AVALON SPRINGS
www.avalonsprings.co.za
The hot springs here have been used for more than 200 years. The waters are radioactive and have a steady temperature of 43°C (109°F). There are two indoor pools and five outdoor pools, all at different temperatures, and a 60m (200ft) waterslide.
✉ Uitvlucht Street, Montagu 6720 ☎ 023-6141150 ✋ Day visitors: adult R40–R60, child (under 12) R30–R40, Indian head massage R190, manicure R180 🚗 3km (2 miles) from central Montagu

MOSSEL BAY
DEEPSEA ADVENUTRES
www.deepseadventures.co.za
Keen anglers, adults and children alike will love the chance to take to the ocean and dip their line into the water. Of course, everyone wants to land a shark, but salmon, cob and santer are more likely catches.
✉ Quay 4, Commercial Slipway ☎ 044-4542988 ◷ Tours daily 6am, 1pm summer, 8am, 1pm winter ✋ R550, child (under 12) R450

ELECTRO DIVE
www.electrodive.co.za
The best time for diving is between December and May, when the sea is at its calmest and conditions in the bay are clear and safe. Close to Santos Beach are four recognized dive sites, but none are spectacular. For experienced divers, the Windvogel Reef, 800m (0.5 miles) off Cape St. Blaize (13.5km/8 miles

from Mossel Bay), is recommended, with drop-offs, a few caves, interesting soft corals and sponges.
☎ 044-6903402 ✋ Single boat dive from R250

THE GOODS SHED INDOOR FLEAMARKET
Here there is an interesting collection of stalls selling a variety of items, including clothes, jewellery, arts and crafts, home-made food and hand-crafted furniture in an interesting historical railway goods shed built in 1902.
✉ 68 Bland Street, Mossel Bay ☎ 044-6912104 ✋ Mon–Fri 9–5, Sat 9–3, Sun in high season 10–4

WHITE SHARK AFRICA
www.whitesharkafrica.com
This company offers cage diving and snorkelling to view great white sharks on a 15m (50ft) catamaran aptly named *Shark*. You do not have to be a qualified diver and this trip is open to anyone. It lasts four to five hours and includes lunch and drinks.
✉ Quay 4, Commercial Slipway ☎ 044-6913796 ✋ R1,500

PAARL
BUTTERFLY WORLD
Those with kids in tow should visit Butterfly World, the largest park of its kind in South Africa, with a huge variety of butterflies flying freely in beautiful landscaped gardens. There is also a craft shop and tea garden on site.
✉ Klapmuts, Paarl 7625 ☎ 021-8755628 ◷ Daily 9–5 ✋ Adult R43, child R25 🚗 On the R44, just off the N1 by Klapmuts

PLETTENBERG BAY
BLOUKRANS BUNGEE JUMP
www.faceadrenalin.com
At 216m (708ft), this claims to be the highest commercial bungee in the world. The first rebound is longer than the previous holder of the record, the 111m (364ft) bungee jump at Victoria Falls. The new event at Bloukrans is the Flying Fox, a 200m (655ft) cable slide that lands on the centre of a bridge arch. If you don't fancy either of these,

you can go on a guided bridge walk—definitely not for anyone who suffers from vertigo. Reservations are not necessary.

✉ Bloukrans River Bridge ☎ 042-2811458 🕓 Daily 9–5 ✋ Bungee jump R690 (minimum age 14); Flying Fox R200 (minimum age 6); bridge walk R100 🚗 40km (25 miles) from Plettenberg Bay

KEURBOOMS RIVER FERRIES
www.ferry.co.za
This is a relaxing 2.5-hour ferry trip up the Keurbooms River in the deeply forested Keurbooms Nature Reserve. Guides point out and identify the rich diversity of birdlife, 'nursery' areas for many fish species, and plant and tree species in the indigenous forest. There are stops so you can swim from one of the beaches, breakfast, lunch or picnic baskets can be organized in advance, and there's a cash bar.

✉ Off the N2 6km (4 miles) east of Plettenberg Bay ☎ 044-5327876 🕓 Daily 11, 2 and sunset ✋ Adult R120, child (under 12) R60

OLD NICK'S VILLAGE
www.oldnickvillage.co.za
A group of galleries, craft workshops and studios with a weaving museum, shops and a restaurant cluster around a restored general dealer's store built in the 1880s. There are hands-on activities, a lush indigenous garden and a children's playground.

✉ On the N2, 3km (1.2 miles) east of Plettenberg Bay ☎ 044-5331395 🕓 Daily 9–5

PLETT MARK
Consistently popular with locals, these food markets offer a wide range of dishes that epitomize the multiculturalism of the Cape region. From Asian noodles and Cape Malay curries, to fresh seafood and traditional Sunday roast—if you're hungry in Plett Bay this is the place to come. BYO wine or beer.

✉ Main Street, Plettenberg Bay ☎ 044-5331630 🕓 Wed–Thu 6pm–8pm, Fri 6pm–10pm, Sun 8–3

PRO DIVE
www.prodive.co.za
This scuba diving operator runs daily dives in the area, and offers a full range of PADI courses. One of the more exciting dive sites here is Groot Bank, about 12km (7.5 miles) northeast of Hobie Beach, which has a number of interesting rock formations to explore, including tunnels and caves.

✉ Beacon Island, Plettenberg Bay 6600 ☎ 044-5331158 ✋ PADI courses from R2,000

ROBERTSON
VILJOENSDRIFT
www.viljoensdrift.co.za
This wine estate on the banks of the Breede River offers wine tasting, cellar visits and relaxed one-hour cruises on a river boat. You can pick up a picnic basket made up of deli items and a bottle of wine to take on the boat from the attached shop.

✉ 12km (7.5 miles) from Robertson on the R317 towards Bonnievale Road ☎ 023-6151901 🕓 Daily 10–4, closed Sun in winter; boat trips depart at 12 ✋ Adult R40, child (3–16) R15

STELLENBOSCH
ADVENTURE CENTRE
www.adventureshop.co.za
Adventure Centre can arrange tours and rents out bicycles, along with helmets and maps of the area around Stellenbosch.

✉ Tourist Office, 36 Market Street, Stellenbosch 7600 ☎ 021-8828112 ✋ R120 for a day, R30 per hour

BOHEMIA PUB
www.bohemia.co.za
One of the main student haunts in Stellenbosch with an eccentric, vibrant interior and attractive wraparound veranda. This is one of the busiest bars in town, always lively with a young clientele who come for the cold beers and relaxed atmosphere.

✉ 1 Victoria Street, Stellenbosch 7600 ☎ 021-8828375 🕓 Daily 10am–late ✋ Free

EASY RIDER WINE TOURS
www.winetour.co.za
Unusually, Easy Rider's hugely popular day-long wine tours are aimed at backpackers. These well-

Right *Coming in from a dive*

Above *Tsitsikamma canopy tour*

organized tours take in five estates, with five tastings in each, including lunch and cheese tasting.
✉ Stumble Inn Backpackers, 12 Market Street, Stellenbosch 7600 ☎ 021-8864651 ✋ Adult R400

FANDANGO
www.fandango.co.za
This central venue is a crowded bar and café with tables outside on the square. There's a very long all-day menu with everything from breakfast to tapas, plus internet access, and it livens up in the evenings as a popular venue for after-work cocktails.
✉ Shop 11, Drostdy Centre, Stellenbosch ☎ 021-8877506 ◷ Daily 9am–2am ✋ Free

LANZERAC SPA AND WELLNESS CENTRE
www.stay-lanzerac.co.za
This 300-year-old traditional Cape Dutch wine estate and luxury hotel has a spa overlooking the vineyards, wih saunas, steam rooms and wet rooms, a gazebo for outdoor treatments and a deck area on the roof for relaxing in the sunshine. Some products are made from the by-products of grapes and the wine-making process.
✉ Lanzerac Estate, off Jonkershoek Road, Stellenbosch 7599 ☎ 021-8839444 ✋ Full-day packages from R1,500

OOM SAMIE SE WINKEL
This famous shop has been trading since 1791, and today sells a wide range of goods, such as home-made jams, locally produced baskets and hardware items. It has retained its pre-war character and has all the makings of a tourist trap, but unlike many others it is genuine.
☎ 021-8870797 ✉ 84 Dorp Street, Stellenbosch 7600 ◷ Mon–Fri 8.30–5.30, Sat 8.30–5

SPIER AMPHITHEATRE
www.spier.co.za
This is perhaps the area's most appealing venue—an open-air amphitheatre hosting a summer festival (▷ 133), with classical concerts, jazz events, plays and comedy.
✉ Spier Wine Estate, Stellenbosch ☎ 021-8091100 ◷ Mon–Sat evenings ✋ From R40 🚌 South of Stellenbosch on the R44

SPIER WINE ESTATE
www.spier.co.za
The large, modern Spier wine estate has a state-of-the-art spa in its grounds, open to hotel guests and day visitors. Treatments include facials, wraps and massage.
☎ 021-8091100 ✋ From R275 🚌 South of Stellenbosch on the R44

VINE HOPPER
www.vinehopper.co.za
This is a useful hop-on hop-off bus that runs on two routes through the Stellenbosch Wine Route, stopping at six wine estates on each, and the Stellenbosch tourist office in town.
✉ Adventure Centre, Tourist Office, 36 Market Street, Stellenbosch 7600 ☎ 021-8828112 ✋ R190

TSITSIKAMMA—GARDEN ROUTE NATIONAL PARK
TSITSIKAMMA CANOPY TOUR
www.tsitsikammacanopytour.co.za
The canopy tour involves climbing up to a platform in the trees from where you are attached to a steel rope (there's plenty of safety equipment to prevent falls). From here you glide between different platforms,

enjoying extraordinary views from high above the ground. For the less active, three-hour 4WD tours of the forest are available, known as the Woodcutter's Journey, which include either lunch or morning or afternoon tea. Reservation is essential.
✉ Darnelle Street, Storms River 6308 ☎ 042-2811836 ◷ 3-hour canopy tour: Sep–May 7–4; Jun–Aug 8–3.30; Woodcutter's Journey: daily 8.30, 11.30, 2.30 ✋ Canopy tour R450 (no children under 7); Woodcutter's Journey morning or tea trip R140, lunch trip R200

WILDERNESS
EDEN ADVENTURES
www.eden.co.za
This good-value adventure tour operator organizes daily trips to Wilderness—Garden Route National Park. Activities include kayaking, kloofing (canyoning), mountain biking, abseiling (rappelling), canoe rental and walking tours. The guides are very knowledgeable about the environment and are happy to answer questions.
☎ 044-8770179 ✋ Canoe rental from R300 for 2 people, half-day tours from R475 per person

WORCESTER
WORCESTER AIRFIELD
www.cgc.org.za
Local conditions around Worcester are ideal for gliding and it is not uncommon to record flights of up to 6 hours. This is the most stunning way to appreciate the mountains and valleys surrounding Cape Town. The Cape Gliding Club, based at the airfield, offers 30-minute flights.
☎ 021-6504018 ✋ From R700

WORCESTER MUSEUM
www.worcestertourism.co.za
All manner of colonial history in the Cape region is explored in this excellent museum, with regular demonstrations on traditional ways of bread-making, blacksmithing, tobacco farming, and other activities taking place.
✉ Robertson Road, Worcester 6849 ☎ 023-3422225 ◷ Mon–Sat 8–4.30, Sun 10–3 ✋ Adult R12, child R5

APRIL

CRAYFISH FESTIVAL

www.kreeffees.com

Lambert's Bay celebrates its famous crayfish and lobsters every April, when all the restaurants are given over to a feast of crayfish.

✉ Lambert's Bay Tourist Office, Main Road ☎ 027-4321000 ⊕ Late Mar–early Apr

MAY

PINK LOERIE MARDI GRAS

www.pinkloerie.com

A gay festival with parade and four days of non-stop entertainment for anyone who enjoys a party.

✉ Knysna ⊕ First weekend in May

PRINCE ALBERT OLIVE, FOOD AND WINE FESTIVAL

www.patourism.co.za

A two-day festival with an art exhibition, beer tents, live music, wine and olive tastings, a cycle race, and an olive pip-spitting contest.

✉ Prince Albert ☎ 023-5411366 ⊕ First weekend in May

JULY

KNYSNA OYSTER FESTIVAL

www.oysterfestival.co.za

A 10-day festival that has been going strong for 25 years and features oyster *braais*, oyster tasting, oyster eating and shucking competitions, live entertainment and lots of sporting events, including cycling, running and sailing.

✉ Knysna ⊕ First week in July

STELLENBSOCH WINE FESTIVAL

www.wineroute.co.za

This annual event promotes local award-winning wines, along with traditional rural cuisine.

✉ Stellenbosch ⊕ Last week in July

SEPTEMBER

WILD FLOWER FESTIVAL CALEDON

www.tourismcapeoverberg.co.za

To coincide with the springtime bloom of wild flowers in the Cape, Caledon holds a festival that celebrates the diversity of the flowers and promotes further research and conservation. It is an excellent opportunity to see many of the plants that make up the Cape flora.

✉ Hope Street, Caledon 7230 ☎ 028-2141016 ⊕ Second weekend of September

HERMANUS WHALE FESTIVAL

www.whalefestival.co.za

This festival marks the beginning of the calving season of southern right whales. In essence it is a community festival, but it attracts visitors from all around the Cape. The festivities kick off with an open-air concert at the Old Harbour, and continue with theatre, comedy, live music and various sporting events (including a mini-marathon).

☎ 028-3130928 ⊕ Last week of September

TULBAGH AGRICULTURAL SHOW

www.tulbaghtourism.org.za

The local agricultural show is held on the banks of the Kliprivier and is the oldest of its kind in South Africa. Tulbagh also celebrates Christmas in Winter over the last weekend of June, when the village is decorated with lights and Christmas trees and the restaurants offer traditional Christmas dinners.

✉ 4 Church Street ☎ 023-2301348

OCTOBER

SIMON VAN DER STEL FESTIVAL STELLENBOSCH

This festival commemorates the establishment of Stellenbosch by Simon van der Stel at the end of the 17th century—14 October was his birthday. Horsemen parade in traditional dress and other activities depicting the era are acted out.

☎ 021-8833584 ⊕ Fri and Sat nearest to 14 October

DECEMBER–APRIL

SPIER MUSIC FESTIVAL

www.spier.co.za

The Spier wine estate's excellent summer music festival includes a wide range of performances, from opera to rock concerts. It also includes stand-up comedy.

✉ Spier Wine Estate ☎ 021-8091100 🚗 South of Stellenbosch on the R44

Below *Whale breaching off the coast at Hermanus, which holds a whale festival*

PRICES AND SYMBOLS

The restaurants are listed alphabetically (excluding The) by town or area, then by name. The prices given are the average for a two-course lunch (L) and a three-course dinner (D) for one person, without drinks. The wine price is for the least expensive bottle.

For a key to the symbols, ▷ 2.

KNYSNA
O'PESCADOR

The chef from Mozambique prepares special dishes from his home country. Among them is *caldo verde* (potato and kale soup with chorizo sausage), *bacalhau* (grilled salt cod) and chicken *peri-peri* (a chilli seasoning). More traditional palates can choose the steaks in wine sauce. The atmosphere is relaxed, and while the food isn't cheap, the quality makes up for it. Reserve in advance during holiday season.

✉ Brenton Road, Belvidere, Knysna 6571 ☎ 044-3860036 ⏱ Mon–Sat 6.30–11 ✋ L R140, D R180, Wine R70

QUAY FOUR KNYSNA

www.quay4knysna.co.za
A sister restaurant to Quay Four on the Victoria & Alfred Waterfront in Cape Town (▷ 93), this lively place

on Thesen Island is known for its fish barbecues and oysters, which can be enjoyed over wonderful waterfront views. In the evenings there is often live music.

✉ Long Street, Thesen Island ☎ 044-3824204 ⏱ Daily 7.30–late ✋ L R105, D R150, Wine R70

LANGEBAAN
STRANDLOPER

www.strandloper.com
The Strandloper has acquired near-legendary status, the romantic surroundings of the beach enhanced by the rickety wooden tables and light guitar music. The food is cooked on a mammoth *braai* (barbecue), beginning with mussels, for the shells then serve as handy cutlery for the next courses, which are accompanied in the West Coast tradition by home-made bread and apricot jam. There are some 10 fish courses in all, culminating in half a crayfish. Children get a discount according to their height. Credit cards are not accepted.

✉ On the beach to the north of town ☎ 022-7722490 ⏱ May–Aug daily, lunch starts at 12, dinner at 6; Sep–Apr Sat–Sun lunch only ✋ R190 (set price), Wine R40 🚗 Follow signs for Club Mykonos

MONTAGU
PRESTON'S AND THOMAS BAIN PUB

Diners can choose from the smoking section in the pub, the non-smoking main dining room or the small outside courtyard at this à la carte restaurant. Popular choices include the 'Prestons Platter'—a mix of local dishes—or the Karoo lamb, both served with excellent salads. The pub has an intimate wood bar, and stays open after the kitchen closes— perfect for an after-dinner drink on the terrace.

✉ 17 Bath Street, Montagu 6720 ☎ 023-6143013 ⏱ Daily 10.30–2.30, 5.30–9.45 ✋ L R60, D R120, Wine R45

OUDTSHOORN
COLONY RESTAURANT

www.queenshotel.co.za
This excellent formal restaurant is set in a historic hotel from 1880 with good atmosphere and sevice, crisp white linen on the tables and African-inspired décor. The menu has a very wide range of local dishes such as Karoo lamb grilled with rosemary and served with mint sauce, pan-fried ostrich with port wine sauce, or loin of springbok with Cape gooseberries.

Left *Oysters are a Knysna specialty*

✉ Queen's Hotel, 5 Baron van Rheede Street, Oudtshoorn 6625 ☎ 044-2722101 🕐 Daily 6–11pm 🖐 D R230, Wine R80

PLETTENBERG BAY
THE LOOKOUT
www.lookout.co.za
Surfers and families share the long wooden tables at this beachside bar and restaurant. The shady deck, with stunning views of the sand and surf, is popular for its seafood, with traditional dishes such as lemon-grilled calamari or shellfish platters, as well as light lunches, including big salads and wholesome soups. You can watch surfers share a wave with a dolphin from the terrace.
✉ Lookout Beach, Plettenberg Bay 6600 ☎ 044-5331379 🕐 Daily 9–9 🖐 L R85, D R120, Wine R60

TULBAGH
PADDAGANG
www.paddagangrestaurant.com
Classic South African dishes such as *bobotie*, lamb stew and snoek are served in this original 19th-century colonial house, with outside dining available in summer and beside roaring log fires in winter. The atmosphere is friendly and informal and the place is perennially popular with locals and families (there's a children's menu). Its name comes from the local frogs that inhabit the nearby river.
✉ 23 Church Street, Tulbagh 6820 ☎ 023-2300242 🕐 Mon, Wed–Sat 9am–10pm, Tue 9–5, Sun 9–4 🖐 L R70, D R200, Wine R75

WHALE COAST
BIENTANG'S CAVE
www.bientangscave.com
The name doesn't lie—the venue is an actual cave with an extended deck overlooking the waves of Walker Bay in a prime whale-watching location. Bientang's Cave is known for its excellent seafood buffets, served at simple wood benches and long tables on the rocks overlooking the sea. It's very popular, so reserve in advance on weekends. Access

is via steps from the parking area on Marine Drive, left from the Old Harbour; look out for the Bientang Seaworld sign.
✉ Left of the Old Harbour, Hermanus 7200 ☎ 028-3123454 🕐 Mon–Thu 11.30–4, Fri–Sat 11.30–4, 7–9; open most evenings during the whale season 🖐 L R120, D R200, Wine R75

THE BURGUNDY
www.burgundyrestaurant.co.za
The Burgundy has an attractive setting in a restored rural cottage set back from the Old Harbour. The paved courtyard is the most appealing lunch spot, with tables grouped around a small fountain. This is one of the top restaurants in town, but has a surprisingly relaxed feel, serving good value seafood; the grilled crayfish is especially good.
✉ 16 Harbour Road, Hermanus 7200 ☎ 028-3122800 🕐 Daily 7am–11pm 🖐 L R90, D R150, Wine R60

WINELANDS
LE BON VIVANT
www.lebonvivant.co.za
This well-kept secret is a real find: a small garden set back from Franschhoek's main tourist drag. Tables are laid out in dappled shade during the day, and dinner is served by candlelight. Light, delicious lunches include smoked trout sandwiches, and there's an excellent value five-course dinner covering a range of local dishes.
✉ 22 Dirkie Uys Street, Franschhoek 7690 ☎ 021-8762717 🕐 Thu–Tue 12–3, 6.30–10 🖐 L R120, D R130, Wine R70

BOSCHENDAL
www.boschendal.com
The main restaurant on this popular wine estate, set in the old Cape Dutch manor house, offers a chance to sample a wide range of typical Cape cuisine. The rustic interior is characterized by its sturdy wooden tables. It's only open for lunch, which is a large, set-price buffet affair, starting with butternut soup and a range of pâtés, then a selection of main courses—the most popular is traditional roast

beef—followed by a choice of local cheeses.
✉ Boschendal Wine Estate, Pniel Road, Groot Drakenstein 7680 ☎ 021-8704274 🕐 Daily 12.30–3 🖐 L R250, Wine R65
🚗 From Stellenbosch, follow Adam Tas Road (R310) to Idas Valley and Franschhoek. Cross the traffic lights at the bottom of the Helshoogte pass. Continue over the pass, and through Kylemore, Johannesdal and Pniel villages. The main entrance is approximately 1km (0.6 miles) past Pniel on the right-hand side

MARC'S MEDITERRANEAN CUISINE & GARDEN RESTAURANT
www.marcsrestaurant.co.za
The ambience at Marc's in Paarl is traditional Cape Dutch, with solid wooden floors inside and paved courtyard outdoors, but the food is contemporary and Mediterranean. Diners can enjoy meze or a classic paella. Also strongly recommended are the Greek fish soup with a dash of ouzo, and the grilled steaks accompanied by a choice of different sauces. The wine list is comprehensive, offering an education in the history of wine-making in the Western Cape.
✉ 129 Main Street, Paarl 7646 ☎ 021-8633980 🕐 Tue–Sat 12–2.30, 6.30–9.30, Sun 12–2.30, Mon 6.30pm–9pm 🖐 L R110, D R160, Wine R65

LE QUARTIER FRANÇAIS
www.lqf.co.za
Le Quartier Français in Franschhoek is consistently rated as one of the best restaurants in the region. It has an attractive setting in the fashionable hotel of the same name (▷ 139), with some tables set beneath the trees in the garden courtyard in summer. The menu includes carefully prepared contemporary South African and French dishes, such as salmon with a tapenade crust, but some may find it a little too fussy. Nevertheless, this is the place to come for a special occasion or treat.
✉ 16 Huguenot Road, Franschhoek 7690 ☎ 021-8762151 🕐 Daily 8am–10pm 🖐 L R150, D R220, Wine R70

PRICES AND SYMBOLS

The hotels below are listed alphabetically (excluding The) by town or area, then by name. Prices are the average for a double room for one night, including breakfast. All the hotels listed accept credit cards unless otherwise stated.

For a key to the symbols, ▷ 2.

BEAUFORT WEST
MATOPPO INN

www.matoppoinn.co.za

Set in a quiet residential street, this was originally the 1834 Drostdy, or magistrate's house, now converted into a comfortable guesthouse, with high ceilings and beautiful wood floors. The comfortable rooms are furnished with antiques and brass bed-heads, and all have a private entrance. Traditional Karoo dinners are served in the dining room by candlelight, and there's a neat garden complete with a swimming pool. South African statesman Cecil Rhodes spent many a night here on the way to what was then Rhodesia (present-day Zimbabwe and Zambia).

✉ 7 Bird Street, Beaufort West 6970 ☎ 023-4151055 🖐 R530, excluding breakfast (R50) 🛈 12 🗹 🌊

THE CEDERBERG
BUSHMAN'S KLOOF

www.bushmanskloof.co.za

This private reserve claims to have the world's largest open-air art gallery—it has one of the best San art sites in South Africa. There are more than 130 sites, dating back 10,000 years. Accommodation is in luxurious cottages or in the main building. All rooms have air conditioning, private bathrooms, four-poster beds, log fires and wooden decks overlooking a lake. There are four swimming pools, as well as a sauna and a beauty spa where treatments are given outdoors in the shadow of the rocks. The restaurant serves excellent South African fare in an outdoor *boma*

Above *Bedrooms at the Wayside Inn in Knysna are pleasantly furnished*

(enclosure). Prices are high but include all meals, game drives and tours.

✉ On the Wupperthal Road, over the Pakhuis Pass ☎ 027-4828200 🖐 R5,800 (full board) 🛈 16 🗹 🌊

CLANWILLIAM DAM
PUBLIC RESORT

The only budget option is in this huge resort, set beside the Clanwilliam dam. It has 180 caravan (trailer) and tent pitches (stands) on tiers up the hillside, plus simple, modern, chalets with kitchens. There are plenty of trees offering shade, electric and gas points, and cooking and washing blocks. The resort gets very busy in season, but it's a peaceful area out of the school holidays. There is no restaurant, bar or shop.

✉ Clanwilliam ☎ 027-4828012 🖐 From R50 per person 🛈 180 pitches (stands) 🚏 1km (0.6 miles) out of town

GEKKO BACKPACKERS

This excellent backpacker lodge, set amid orange trees on a citrus farm, is usually a very peaceful spot. There are two dorms and two double rooms, and there's plenty of space for camping. The bathrooms are brightly painted, the large kitchen is fully equipped and there's an honesty bar, a table-tennis room and a small lounge. The surrounding gardens have hammocks strung underneath trees, and guests are free to wander among the orange groves. The farm owner is happy to take guests to swimming holes and San rock art sites.

✉ On Arbeidsgenot Farm ☎ 022-9213721 ✋ From R75 ① 20 beds ⛱ 🚗 Drive along the N7 north from Citrusdal; signpost to left after 20km (12.5 miles)

GEORGE
FANCOURT HOTEL AND COUNTRY CLUB

www.fancourt.com

The neatly furnished rooms are either in the main house or in relaxing garden cottages overlooking the golf courses, which are the main draw here (▷ 129). Other facilities include a spa, gym, tennis courts and swimming pools.

✉ Montagu Street, George 6529 ☎ 044-8040010 ✋ R3,200 ① 150 🔆 ⛱

KNYSNA
BELVIDERE MANOR

www.belvidere.co.za

There are four cottages for guests in the grounds of this beautiful 19th-century manor house on the Knysna lagoon. They offer an element of privacy while also benefiting from the experience and expertise of the staff. There's a bistro for lunch or dinner and even a tiny on-site pub. In winter there's an open fireplace in the communal area.

✉ Duthie Drive, Knysna 6570 ☎ 044-3871055 ✋ R1,400 ① 4 ⛱

PHANTOM FOREST ECO-RESERVE

www.phantomforest.com

This superb collection of luxurious tree houses, set in a magnificent forest, offers ultra-stylish accommodation high above the Knysna lagoon. The tree houses are eco-friendly and equipped with huge beds, sisal carpets and African art, and have private terraces, while the Moroccan suites have a distinctly North African feel. The bathrooms are sumptuous, with views out over the forest. Individual houses are connected by walkway to the excellent restaurant and bar where guests are served sundowner drinks overlooking the lagoon before dining on South African cuisine. There's also a Moroccan-themed restaurant, a beauty spa and pool, and the staff can arrange activities in the area. No children under 12.

✉ Phantom Forest Eco-Reserve ☎ 044-3860046 ✋ R3,750 ① 14 ⛱ 🚗 Signposted from Phantom Pass road, on western edge of lagoon

WAYSIDE INN

www.waysideinn.co.za

The smart Wayside Inn with a Victorian theme is in central Knysna. The bedrooms are stylish, with wrought-iron beds and sisal carpets, ceiling fans (and heating in winter), and a selection of African art, giving them a colonial feel. Each room has a private balcony, and although there's no breakfast room (breakfast is served in your room) or lounge, the veranda is used in fine weather. Hampers can be made to order. Parking is available.

✉ 48 Main Street, Knysna 6571 ☎ 044-3826011 ✋ R780 ① 15

MOSSEL BAY
PROTEA HOTEL

www.proteahotels.com

The rooms of this hotel are in and around a smart manor house, which is the third oldest building in Mossel Bay. Accommodation is a mix of comfortable, well-styled double rooms, with private bathrooms and beautiful views of the ocean, and larger self-catering suites set around the old manor house. Facilities include a restaurant with an outdoor dining area and fine bay views, a swimming pool, curio shop and cocktail bar. It's a popular place, so reserve ahead in high season. Parking is available.

✉ Corner of Church and Market streets, Mossel Bay 6506 ☎ 044-6913738 ✋ R950 ① 31 🔆 ⛱

OUDTSHOORN
QUEEN'S

www.queenshotel.co.za

Queen's, set in tidy gardens, is Oudtshoorn's best-known hotel. It's comfortable and friendly, although the guest rooms lack the charm of the public areas, which are stylish and play up to the building's colonial history, with antiques, animal prints and art deco touches. The Colony restaurant serves South African dishes and a buffet lunch on Sundays. The gardens have a swimming pool and tennis courts, and there's a curio shop and secure parking.

✉ Baron van Rheede Street, Oudtshoorn 6625 ☎ 044-2722101 ✋ R1,300 ① 40 🔆 ⛱

PLETTENBERG BAY
HUNTER'S COUNTRY HOUSE

www.hunterhotels.com

This is one of South Africa's top country hotels and part of the Relais & Chateaux group, which has won several awards for its food and service. Accommodation comprises luxury, individually decorated thatched suites complete with fireplace, antique furnishings, ceiling fan and private patio, and facilities include two swimming pools, a conservatory, antique shop, forest chapel for weddings and a childcare service. Excellent cuisine is served in the candlelit dining room.

✉ Off the N2 10km (6 miles) west of Plettenberg Bay towards Knysna ☎ 044-5011111 ✋ R3,620 ① 21 ⛱

STONE COTTAGE

www.stonecottage.co.za

Stone Cottage is actually two cottages split into four apartments, just five minutes from the main beach and the shops and restaurants in town. The main cottage is a beautifully restored 19th-century building, decorated in neutral tones, with high ceilings and gleaming wooden floors, and furnished with antiques and old photographs. The other cottage has two suites and sleeps from two to six people. Both have views over the bay and have private decks overlooking the beach.

✉ Corner of Harker and Odland streets, Plettenberg Bay 6600 ☎ 044-5331310

✋ From R750 (depending on number of people and which cottage) ⓘ 4 apartments

SWELLENDAM
THE HIDEAWAY
www.hideawaybb.co.za
The best place to stay in Swellendam is this B&B in the middle of town. The hosts have put a lot of thought into decorating their six spacious suites, two of which have large four-poster beds, and all have cool terracotta floors, and hand-crafted wooden furniture mixed with antiques. The rooms are set in a neat, shady garden filled with rose bushes. There's a small splash pool and a lounge, and excellent breakfasts are served, including home-made bread and preserves.

✉ 10 Hermanus Steyn Street, Swellendam 6740 ☎ 028-5143316 ✋ R800 ⓘ 6
🔆 🏊

SWELLENDAM BACKPACKERS
www.swellendambackpackers.co.za
This excellent backpackers' hostel has succeeded in introducing much of the Overberg region to budget visitors. The main house has one small dorm, and the large gardens are dotted with small, individual wooden houses tucked away in secluded corners. These have double or twin beds but no electricity—the manager will supply you with a gas lamp instead. There's lots of camping space, a well-organized kitchen, email access, and substantial home-cooked breakfasts and dinners are available. The Baz Bus (▷ 52) calls twice a day.

✉ 5 Lichtenstein Street, Swellendam 6740 ☎ 028-5142648 ✋ From R120 per bed ⓘ 30 beds

WHALE COAST
LIVESEY LODGE
www.liveseylodge.co.za
This well-run, friendly guesthouse on the outskirts of town has six double rooms set around a leafy garden with a good-sized pool. All rooms have their own entrance and private bathroom, big beds, a TV and mini-bar. There are other nice touches such as books in the rooms. Parking is available.

✉ 13 Main Road, Hermanus 7200 ☎ 028-3130026 ✋ From R700 ⓘ 6 🏊

THE MARINE
www.marine-hermanus.co.za
The historic Marine, part of the Relais & Chateaux group, is one of the finest hotels in the country. The bright white building dominates the cliffs on Marine Drive and offers stunning ocean views. Bedrooms are luxurious with fine furnishings, including silk curtains, plush carpets, pale suede armchairs and marble bathrooms. There are also thoughtful touches like freshly cut flowers in the bedrooms, and some rooms have four-poster beds and his 'n' her bathrooms. A small spa offers facials and massages, and there are two restaurants; the seafood restaurant has an excellent reputation. Parking is available.

✉ Marine Drive, Hermanus 7200 ☎ 028-3131000 ✋ R4,250 ⓘ 42
🔆 🏊

WILDERNESS
MOONTIDE GUEST LODGE
www.moontide.co.za
Moontide has a wonderful setting right on the edge of Wilderness lagoon, with a deck overlooking the water. Accommodation is in thatched cottages with private bathrooms, set under milkwood trees in a beautiful garden. Each cottage has been decorated with fine furniture, and the rough stone walls give them a rustic feel. There is easy access to the hiking trails in the national park and it's just a short walk from the beach.

✉ Southside Road, Wilderness 6560 ☎ 044-8770361 ✋ R1,200 ⓘ 7

WINELANDS
AVENUES
www.theavenues.co.za
Avenues is a relaxed, family-run guesthouse, just a short walk from the middle of town. All rooms have private bathrooms; some have wooden floors and bright, simple furnishings, others are just as comfortable, but with carpets. The garden-facing room (No. 5) is the nicest, with original fittings in the bathroom. Parking is available.

✉ 32 The Avenue, Stellenbosch 7600 ☎ 021-8871843 ✋ R640 ⓘ 8 🏊

LA FONTAINE
www.lafontainefranschhoek.co.za
La Fontaine is one of the finest guesthouses in Franschhoek. Set in a central Victorian house, its stylish understated decoration includes a mix of antiques, African art and fine polished wooden floors. All bedrooms have large Victorian-style bathrooms; some are set in the garden around a pool and have more of an ethnic-chic feel. Breakfast is served on the vine-shaded courtyard. No children under 12.

✉ 21 Dirkie Uys Street, Franschhoek 7690 ☎ 021-8762112 ✋ R1,100 ⓘ 14 🏊

FRANSCHHOEK COUNTRY HOUSE
www.fch.co.za
This historic manor house in the heart of the Franschhoek valley has French-style décor, complete with sweeping drapes, gilt mirrors and candelabras. Facilities include a spa, two swimming pools and manicured gardens with lovely fountains.

✉ Main Road, Franschhoek 7690, 1km (0.5 miles) from town towards Stellenbosch ☎ 021-8763386 ✋ R2,100 ⓘ 26
🔆 🏊

LANZERAC MANOR
www.lanzerac.co.za
This is a very expensive but fittingly luxurious hotel set around an 18th-century Cape Dutch manor house near Stellenbosch. Bedrooms are decorated with checked fabrics and mellow reds, yellows and blues. Each has a private patio overlooking either

the surrounding vineyards or the hotel's gardens, and the bathrooms have a separate shower. Some rooms open onto the pool. The hotel has two restaurants and parking.

✉ 2km (1.2 miles) from Stellenbosch
☎ 021-8871132 ✋ R3,100 🕐 48
💳 🏊 🚗 Towards Jonkershoek Reserve, Jonkershoek Road

DE OUDE PAARL
www.deoudepaarl.com
De Oude Paarl is a smart boutique hotel occupying national monument buildings on the main road, just before central Paarl. It has a dark and moody (but seriously stylish) feel to it, with its individually designed rooms decorated in muted greys and dark reds, and fine stone bathrooms. The building is also home to the Butcher's Steakhouse, the Maroc, a good Moroccan restaurant, and the Cuba Café, a cigar and tapas bar.

✉ 132 Main Street, Paarl 7646 ☎ 021-8721002 ✋ R1,180 🕐 26 🏊 💳

PLUMWOOD INN
www.plumwoodinn.com
This small guesthouse is in a quiet residential street in Franschhoek. The bedrooms are individually styled, with their own private entrance and bathroom, TV, country-style furniture and brightly painted walls. The guest lounge has high ceilings, a cool tiled floor and huge leather sofas. Breakfast is served in the well-kept garden and dinner is available on request. Parking is available.

✉ 11 Cabriere Street, Franschhoek 7690
☎ 021-8763883 ✋ R1,100 🕐 7 💳 🏊

LE QUARTIER FRANÇAIS
www.lqf.co.za
Le Quartier Français is an elegant hotel in the middle of Franschhoek, with enormous rooms set around a central courtyard, as well as some suites and a delightful two-bedroom cottage. There is a small pool and peaceful paths wind around the property. The bedrooms have fireplaces and beautiful stone private bathrooms, plush furnishings in bright colours and views over the gardens. The attached restaurant of the same name (▷ 135) is considered to be one of the best in the Western Cape. Check the website for special deals.

✉ 16 Hugenot Road, Franschhoek 7690
☎ 021-8762151 ✋ R3,750 🕐 22
💳 🏊

RIVER MANOR BOUTIQUE HOTEL
www.rivermanor.co.za
The husband and wife team that runs this beautiful riverside B&B in Stellenbosch are passionate about both the Winelands area and about making their guests as welcome as possible. The rooms are elegantly and traditionally decorated with plush furnishings and roll-top baths in the bathrooms. A small pool is overlooked by a patio area with wicker sofas, and breakfast is served in the garden in good weather. There is also a small spa area offering facials, massage and other pampering treatments.

✉ 6–8 The Avenue, Stellenbosch 7600
☎ 021-8879944 ✋ R1,800 🕐 18 🏊

STUMBLE INN
www.stumbleinnstellenbosch.hostel.com
The Stumble Inn in Stellenbosch is set in two Victorian bungalows. There are spacious double rooms and slightly smaller dorms. The original house has an attractive rambling garden with shady cushion banks and hammocks, a small bar, TV room and a kitchen. The other house has a small pool and kitchen. It's all very relaxed and friendly. Guests can also rent bicycles.

✉ 12 Market Street, Stellenbosch 7600
☎ 021-8874049 ✋ From R200 per double room, excluding breakfast
🕐 60 beds 🏊

THE VILLAGE AT SPIER
www.spier.co.za
Probably the Winelands' most commercial wine estate, but a thoroughly enjoyable place to stay. The Village is a series of condo-style buildings arranged around courtyards, with private pools for each section. Rooms are enormous with stylish decoration, polished concrete floors and large windows which let in plenty of light. All have satellite TV, mini-bar, and beautiful bathrooms. There is a restaurant and bar, a spa and a cheetah park. Parking is available.

✉ Spier Wine Estate, South of Stellenbosch on the R44 ☎ 021-8091100 ✋ R1,800
🕐 155 💳 🏊

WORCESTER
CHURCH STREET LODGE
www.churchst.co.za
The Lodge has pleasant rooms with a country feel, antique wood furniture contrasting with the bright patchwork quilts on the beds. All have little extras such as coffee-making facilities and mini-fridge. The building is modern, with a breakfast room and a Roman-style pool set in peaceful grounds, with fountains and quiet patios.

✉ 36 Church Street, Worcester 6850
☎ 023-3425194 ✋ R550, excluding breakfast (R60) 🕐 21 🏊

Left *The Marine hotel in Hermanus has a wonderful location*

EASTERN CAPE

The Eastern Cape, although far less visited than many parts of South Africa, is a fascinating region of historical towns, wild empty beaches, forested mountains and the sun-baked plains of the Karoo. The province's springboard city of Port Elizabeth (Nelson Mandela Bay) is characterized by its long hours of sunshine and a string of good beaches and warm water around Algoa Bay. To the southwest the resort of Jeffreys Bay is on the international surfing circuit, and as such has a laid-back, youthful atmosphere.

The province's biggest attraction is the recently expanded Addo Elephant National Park, which is the only place in South Africa where you can see the 'Big Seven'—elephant, rhino, lion, buffalo, leopard (the 'Big Five'), plus southern right whale and great white shark. Nearby are a number of private game reserves that have been declared conservation successes for reintroducing animals that were for a long time extinct in this region; they can all be visited.

Inland, the Amatola Mountains offer good hiking, while the Eastern Cape Karoo has vast open spaces and some dramatic rocky scenery, best appreciated at the aptly named Valley of Desolation in the Camdeboo National Park. Historical Grahamstown has some fine 19th-century architecture, interesting museums, and hosts South Africa's largest and most popular arts festival in July.

To the west of the province, beyond the industrial city of East London, and formerly known as the Transkei, the homeland under apartheid for the Xhosa people, is the long and beautiful Wild Coast. As the name suggests, it features a jagged coastline dotted with shipwrecks and deserted beaches pounded by surf.

ADDO ELEPHANT NATIONAL PARK
▷ 144.

AMATOLA MOUNTAINS
The Amatola Mountain region, between Stutterheim and Fort Beaufort has rolling hills, lush indigenous forests and waterfalls. Some areas have been replaced with pine plantations, but there remains an abundance of untouched forest, criss-crossed with trails that are perfect for hiking. Hogsback (see below) is the main hub.
🔢 328–329 J10 ℹ️ Fort Beaufort Museum, Durban Street, Fort Beaufort 5720 ☎ 046-3431555 🕐 Mon–Fri 8–5, Sat 8.30–12.30

EASTERN CAPE KAROO
▷ 146–147.

EAST LONDON
www.tourismbuffalocity.co.za
East London is South Africa's only river port and it is a major industrial city, with an economy based on motor assembly plants and textile and electronics industries. This may seem unpromising for visitors, but the central part of the city has a certain energetic appeal, as well as a handful of attractive period buildings. There are also fine beaches, which teem with visitors over Christmas.

The Ann Bryant Art Gallery (tel 043-7224044; Mon–Fri 9–5, Sat 9.30–12), on St. Marks Road, contains many good contemporary South African works, while the East London Museum (Mon–Fri 9.30–5, Sat 2–5, Sun 11–4), on Oxford Street, focuses on natural history. The highlights of the museum include the world's only dodo egg and a coelacanth, which was netted by a trawler off the coast near East London in 1938. The coelacanth, known as the 'fossil fish', was thought to have been extinct for 80 million years until it was rediscovered

in the 20th century. Outside on Oxford Street is a monument to Steve Bantu Biko, the anti-apartheid activist who died in police custody in 1977 (▷ 39).
🔢 329 K10 ℹ️ 91 Western Avenue, Vincent, East London 5200 ☎ 043-7211346 🕐 Mon–Fri 8.15–4.30, Sat 9–2, Sun 9–1

GRAHAMSTOWN
▷ 145.

HOGSBACK
www.hogsbackinfo.co.za
The quiet village of Hogsback lies in the heart of the Amatola Mountains, surrounded by rolling hills covered in forest reserves. The village is made up of a string of cottages, hotels, tea gardens and craft shops dotted along several kilometres of gravel road. Tucked away down the side lanes are some glorious gardens, more reminiscent of rural England than inland Africa. The beauty of the surroundings and the slow pace of life in Hogsback make this a perfect spot to relax for a few days. The Hogsback Spring Festival is held over two weekends in September, when there's a craft market and many residents open their gardens to visitors.
🔢 329 J10 ℹ️ Next door to Nina's Deli, Main Road, Hogsback 5721 ☎ 045-9621245 🕐 Mon–Sat 9–3, Sun 9–12

JEFFREYS BAY
www.jeffreysbaytourism.org
Surf is king at Jeffreys Bay, or J-Bay as it's known locally. Home to the perfect wave, this is an internationally acclaimed surfing spot and a major

playground for self-respecting surfers. In the evenings, the local bars buzz with talk of 'supertubes' and 'perfect breaks'. Waves can be big—sometimes as high as 3m (10ft)—but J-Bay is renowned for its safety. There are numerous surf shops as well as Billabong and Quiksilver factory outlets, but when surf's up don't be surprised to find many of the local businesses closed. See page 154 for details on where to take surfing lessons.
🔢 328 G11 ℹ️ Jeffreys Bay Tourism, corner Da Gama and Drommedaris roads, Jeffreys Bay 6330 ☎ 042-2932923 🕐 Mon–Fri 8.30–5, Sat 9–12

THE LANGKLOOF
Three mountain ranges lie to the north of the N2 and Jeffreys Bay: the Kougaberge, the Baviaanskloofberge and the Grootwinterhoekberge, known collectively as the Langkloof. The valleys of the Langkloof, referred to as 'the Kouga', are where modern man is thought to have first emerged sometime in the last 100,000 years. The region became the meeting point of San hunter-gatherers and Khoi pastoralists (▷ 30), known collectively as the Khoisan, and their rock art adorns overhangs and caves throughout this area. One of the most scenic routes through the Langkloof is the gravel road along the Baviaanskloof River valley between Patensie and Willowmore. The road meanders through a landscape dominated by red sandstone hills on either side. Take care, however, as it can be steep and narrow in places.
🔢 328 G11

Opposite *Valley of Desolation, Camdeboo National Park, Eastern Cape Karoo*
Right *The Amatola Mountains*

INFORMATION

➕ 328 H10 ☎ 042-2338600 ⊗ Gates and office: daily 7–7 💧 Adult R140, child (under 12) R70 🍴 Restaurant serves breakfast, lunch and dinner 🏪 Shop sells a selection of groceries, meat, bread and wines; fuel (no diesel), laundry, telephone and mail services also available ❓ Range of SANParks chalet and camping accommodation (reservations: ☎ 012-4289111, www.sanparks.org), plus luxury private camp (▷ 158) 🚌 The main park entrance is 72km (45 miles) from Port Elizabeth, along R335

TIPS

» Visitors are prohibited from bringing citrus fruits into the reserve, as the older elephants have a taste for them following a shortsighted feeding schedule in the 1970s. They were fed citrus fruits, which resulted in all the animals feeding in one place, resulting in overgrazing and aggressive behaviour.
» It is illegal to leave your vehicle anywhere other than at signposted climb-out points.
» The speed limit is 40kph (25mph).

Above *Addo is the best place in South Africa to see elephants*

ADDO ELEPHANT NATIONAL PARK

The original elephant park at Addo covered 12,000ha (30,000 acres) and was proclaimed in 1931, when only 11 elephants remained in the area. Today, it is the third largest conservation area in South Africa, encompassing five contiguous game reserves and stretching from the Indian Ocean to the Little Karoo. It is a hugely rewarding park, thanks to the large herds of elephant and the relative ease of seeing them. With the reintroduction of lions in October 2003 and the expansion to include a marine reserve, it is now possible to see the 'Big Seven' at Addo—the original 'Big Five' of elephant, rhino, lion, buffalo and leopard, plus whales and great white sharks. At the opposite end of the scale, the park is also home to the unique flightless dung beetle, which is found wherever there's elephant dung.

WATERHOLES

The relative flatness of the low-lying indigenous bush and the large number of elephants present—around 450—means that the great animals are easily seen. The best places are the waterholes, which are accessible by car. There are lookout points above them, from where you can often see several herds drinking at one time. This can mean watching more than 100 elephants splashing about in the water, a truly awe-inspiring experience. Although you'll see them at any time of the year, one of the best times to visit is January or February, when many of the female elephants will have recently calved.

GETTING AROUND

A network of gravel roads is open to the public from sunrise to sunset for game viewing, although some become impassable in a standard car if there's a lot of rain. Convenient as it is to explore in your own car, it's worth taking a tour in one of the park's 4WD vehicles, as the guides are highly knowledgeable about where the animals are best found.

There are two hides, one of which overlooks a floodlit water hole and can be reserved for the night. The other hide tends to be busier as it is near the main camp's restaurant, but it is good for birdwatching. Night drives, game walks and horseback rides can all be reserved through reception.

GRAHAMSTOWN

Grahamstown is, first and foremost, a student town, home to one of the country's most important places of learning, Rhodes University, which has more than 3,000 students. During term time the town is lively, its pubs and bars packed with students. Grahamstown was founded as a military headquarters in 1812, named after Colonel Graham, but within two years it was a busy border settlement. It evolved into the second largest town in the whole of southern Africa by 1836, although today it feels more like a small country town—pleasant to wander around, with a distinctly English atmosphere.

MUSEUMS

The Albany Museum (tel 046-6222312) comprises several town museums including the Observatory Museum, Natural Science Museum and History Museum, along with Fort Selwyn and the Provost. The highlight of the Observatory Museum (Mon–Fri 9.30–1, 2–5, Sat 9.30–1) is the camera obscura. This rare specimen, which claims to be the only Victorian camera obscura in the southern hemisphere, projects an image of Grahamstown onto a screen. Visitors are led up a tiny spiral staircase to a small room on the roof, where a guide pivots the camera to show a 360-degree view of the town.

In the Natural Science Museum (Mon–Fri 9–1, 2–5, Sat 9–1) most of the displays are aimed at children. Among the more intriguing exhibits are a large iron meteorite that came down in a meteorite shower over Namibia, a Foucault Pendulum (which demonstrates the rotation of the earth), and some dinosaur fossils. The History Museum (Mon–Fri 9–1, 2–5, Sat 9–1) has a collection outlining the area's history, including beadwork displays from the Eastern Cape and traditional Xhosa dress. Off Somerset Street is the Provost (open by appointment only), built in 1837 by the Royal Engineers as a military prison. Fort Selwyn (open by appointment only), on Fort Selwyn Drive, dates from the sixth Frontier War in 1834.

TOWNSHIP

Grahamstown's large township, to the east of the town across the river, is known as Rhini or Grahamstown East. It's a good idea to choose a walking tour, rather than one in a minibus, as this allows a greater degree of interaction with people. Tours can be booked through the tourist office.

INFORMATION

www.makanatourism.co.za
✚ 328 J10 🏠 Makana Tourism, 63 High Street, Grahamstown 6139 ☎ 046-6223241 🕐 Mon–Fri 8.30–5, Sat 9–1

TIPS

» The Grahamstown Festival in July is the largest arts festival in Africa.
» The ugly 1820 Settlers Monument is worth visiting only for the panoramic views of the area.

Below *Pastel store fronts along High Street, Grahamstown*

Above *Zebras roam the grasslands of Mountain Zebra National Park*

INTRODUCTION

The surreal Karoo landscape, clear air and desert sunsets are evocative of the very heart of South Africa. The landscape, created from sedimentary rock around 250 million years ago, is rich in fossils and San paintings and studded with scrub and cacti. The climate is one of extremes: In summer, temperatures are blindingly hot and towns uncomfortably dusty, while in winter the night-time temperatures drop below 0°C (32°F), so come in the spring or autumn if you can. However, if you are here in summer, make sure you have a jacket or sweater for the evenings, when temperatures drop considerably.

WHAT TO SEE

GRAAFF-REINET

www.graaffreinet.co.za

Founded in 1786, Graaff-Reinet is the oldest town of the Eastern Cape, lying between the Sneeuberg Mountains and the Sundays River. Years of prosperity derived from farming are reflected in the excellent local architecture—more than 220 of the town's old buildings have been declared national monuments. Today, Graaff-Reinet is a smart town, with row upon row of perfectly restored houses, leafy streets and a quiet, yet bustling atmosphere. For details of a walk past the sights and museums in Graaff-Reinet, ▷ 152–153.

🕂 328 G9 🛈 Graaff-Reinet Publicity Association, 13a Church Street, Graaff-Reinet 6280 ☎ 049-8924248 🕒 Mon–Fri 8–5, Sat 9–12, Sun 10–12

Below *View over the Valley of Desolation, Camdeboo National Park*

CAMDEBOO NATIONAL PARK AND THE VALLEY OF DESOLATION

www.sanparks.org

Formerly the Karoo Nature Reserve, the Camdeboo National Park is now run by SANParks. It surrounds Graaff-Reinet, and the Valley of Desolation is the best place to appreciate the vastness of the Karoo. The stark rock formations and precariously balanced dolerite columns tower 120m (390ft) above the valley floor, giving stunning views stretching to the horizon. If you just drive up to the first viewpoint you'll see fine views, but continue for another few kilometres and you come to a parking area from where there's a short walk to even better vistas. Elsewhere in the park there are walking trails and 4WD routes.

🕂 328 G9 ☎ 049-8923453 🕒 Daily 6am–8pm ✋ Adult R60, child (under 12) R30

CRADOCK

www.cradocktourism.co.za

This small Karoo town is made up of an attractive grid of wide roads lined with Victorian bungalows and a clutch of churches. It's a pleasant, sleepy place to wander around. The town is known for its connections with the author Olive Schreiner, who wrote *The Story of an African Farm* (published 1883). The Olive

Schreiner House at 9 Cross Street illustrates aspects of her life (tel 048-8815251, Mon–Fri 8–12.45, 2–4.30). The Great Fish River Museum behind the town hall (Mon–Fri 8–4) is in a restored parsonage built in 1849, and depicts early pioneer history. The nearby Fish River is one of the top white water rivers in the world.

➕ 328 H9 ℹ️ Cradock Tourism, J. A. Calata Street, Cradock 5880 ☎ 048-8015000
🕐 Mon–Fri 8.30–12.30, 2–4

MOUNTAIN ZEBRA NATIONAL PARK
www.sanparks.org
The plains and mountains of this Karoo park support more than 280 mountain zebras, the largest group in the world. Other mammals include black wildebeest, kudu, springbok, buffalo and black rhino. The park is also the home of the giant earthworm. Game viewing is by car—there are 37km (23 miles) of rough roads crossing the reserve.

➕ 328 H9 ☎ Reservations: 012-4289111; park: 048-8812427 🕐 Gates: Oct–Mar 7–7; Apr–Sep 7–6 💷 Adult R100, child (under 12) R50 🍴 🏨 🚌 25km (15.5 miles) west of Cradock, signposted from the town

NIEU-BETHESDA
www.nieubethesda.co.za
This small village has become famous through the work of artist Helen Martins (1897–1976). Helen lived a hermit-like existence, devoting her time to her art and the study of Eastern philosophies. Her legacy is the Owl House, the home she decorated with motifs in finely ground glass of every colour, so that the whole interior glitters. It is now a museum (tel 049-8411603; daily 9–5), crammed with her art and ideas. There are several other artists' galleries and a few little shops in the village, but not much else.

➕ 328 G9

PORT ELIZABETH
▷ 149.

MORE TO SEE
KALKKOP IMPACT CRATER
This giant crater was created by a meteorite more than 200,000 years ago. Research has shown that it was originally hundreds of metres deep. Over time the crater has filled, but the ridge, 640m (2,100ft) in diameter, is still visible.

➕ 328 G10 🚌 Follow N9 in the direction of Aberdeen for about 30km (19 miles); at Aberdeen, turn left onto R338 and continue to a right turn marked as Aberdeen Road. From here a dirt road leads to the crater—it should be signposted

MIDDELBURG
www.middelburgec.co.za
Middelburg is a good base for a hike on the Compassberg, the highest peak in the Sneeuberg range. The main route is a three-day circular trail of 48km (30 miles) around the Kompasberg foothills. For reservations, tel 049-8422418.

➕ 328 G9 ℹ️ Middelburg Karoo Tourism, 8 Meintjies Street, Middelburg 5900 ☎ 049-8422188
🕐 Mon–Fri 8–1, 2–4.30

SOMERSET EAST
www.somerseteast.co.za
This neat agricultural town is home to the Somerset museum (Mon–Fri 8–5), which recreates a Victorian parsonage set among rose gardens. The Walter Battiss Art Museum (Mon–Fri 10–4) has the world's largest collection of work by this South African artist (1906–82), who was a friend of Picasso.

➕ 328 H10 ℹ️ Blue Crane Tourism, 88 Njoli Street, Somerset East 5850 ☎ 042-2431333
🕐 Mon–Fri 8.30–4.30

TIP
» Make sure your rental car has air conditioning: You'll be covered in dust if you keep your windows open for long.

Below *House front in Cradock Street, Graaff-Reinet*

MTHATHA

www.mthatha.co.za

Mthatha (formerly known as Umtata) is a sprawling modern town with a small grid of early buildings at its core. Founded in 1871, it was the capital of Transkei from 1976 to 1994 and has grown into a busy administrative city. The main reason for coming here is the illuminating Nelson Mandela Museum (Owen Street, tel 047-5325110; www. nelsonmandelamuseum.org.za; daily 9–4), officially opened by Mandela himself in 2000. The Museum is split across three sites with branches here, at Mvezo, where Mandela was born, and at Qunu, the village where he grew up. All three are dedicated to South Africa's first post-apartheid president, and provide a moving and insightful look at Mandela's life and his struggles. The displays at Mthatha focus on his autobiography, *Long Walk to Freedom* (1994), with extracts complemented by photographs, personal items, letters, artefacts and video footage, including a short excerpt from an interview that he gave in 1961. Although the displays are rather confusing from a chronological point of view, they give a good overview of his life.

Another component of the museum is Mandela's primary school in the tiny village of Qunu (30km/19 miles west of Mthatha), where he lived in his youth. Here, too, are the graves of some of his relatives, as well as his mansion, which can be photographed but not visited. The final element is Mandela's birthplace in the former Transkei village of Mvezo (to the west of Mthatha).

✚ 329 K9 ℹ 64 Owen Street, Mthatha 5099 ☎ 047-5315290 ◷ Mon–Thu 8–4.30, Fri 8–4

PORT ALFRED

www.portalfred.co.za

Port Alfred, east of Port Elizabeth, consists almost entirely of summer homes and bungalows nestling among dunes. One of the largest holiday resorts along this stretch of coastline, it overlooks large expanses of water in all directions—the Kowie River estuary, the lagoon and the chic Royal Alfred Marina. The town's history is closely linked to the settlers of 1820, some 4,000 white British colonists who settled in the Cape area between April and June of that year. There is a small Methodist church 1km (0.6 miles) out of town. Many of the names on the gravestones in its cemetery are those of these early settlers.

The weather on this coast is mild all year round, making it a popular spot with South Africans, who are drawn by the good watersports facilities. Surfing, canoeing, scuba diving and fishing are big business along the Kowie River and West Beach, which is also good for swimming. There are some interesting trails through the nearby dune forests. Occasionally there are return trips from Post Alfred Station on the Kowie Chu Chu, a short, three-carriage brightly coloured mini-train, to Bathurst, a distance of 16km (10 miles (enquire at the tourist office for dates and times).

✚ 329 J11 ℹ Port Alfred Tourism, Info Centre, Causeway Street, Port Alfred 6170 ☎ 046-6241235 ◷ Mon–Fri 8.30–4.30, Sat 8.30–12

SHAMWARI GAME RESERVE

www.shamwari.com

This privately owned reserve, the winner of many international conservation awards, provides the best game viewing in this part of the country. In many respects it resembles the reserves of Mpumalanga along the boundary of Kruger National Park (▷ 199–205). The park covers an area of 20,000ha (50,000 acres) and has been well stocked with game from all over the region, including black rhino, elephant, buffalo, leopard, lion and antelope of all sizes. Wild dogs have also been reintroduced to Shamwari; they were last seen in the area more than 200 years ago. The reserve has seven lodges within its boundaries, all of them expensive. Day visitors are not permitted, but overnight packages include all meals and game viewing, and you can also go on a walking safari.

After long days spent wildlife spotting you can relax in one of Shamwari's four 'retreats' offering pampering spa treatments. The reserve also places a great deal of emphasis on keeping younger guests entertained (children under four years of age are not permitted on safari), with a children's coordinator to hand and organized children's activities that are both educational and entertaining.

✚ 328 H10 ☎ 041-4071010 ◷ Overnight visitors only 🚗 From Port Elizabeth, follow the signs for the N2, Grahamstown. After 65km (40 miles), the park is signposted off to the left

WILD COAST

▷ 151.

WITTEBERGE

The Witteberge Mountains form part of the southernmost limits of the Drakensberg (▷ 176–179) and are the heart of South Africa's skiing industry. The road heading into the Witteberge passes through the small towns of Elliot, Lady Grey and Rhodes, the last being a peaceful mountain village with a scattering of Victorian buildings. If you visit the mountains during winter bring plenty of warm clothes: electricity did arrive a few years ago, but there is still no central heating.

✚ 329 J8

PORT ELIZABETH

PE, as it's often called, is a major port and industrial town, the biggest coastal city between Cape Town and Durban, and a convenient stopping point for visitors to the Garden Route. The heart of town, known as Central, is a grid of Victorian houses and green spaces, and is the most pleasant part of the city. Port Elizabeth is celebrated for its long hours of sunshine and for the warm waters of Algoa Bay, whose long, sandy beaches form the main attraction for visitors. The city also has a large student population, lending the city a lively edge, with a vibrant bar and clubbing scene. It is currently going through a name change transition to Nelson Mandela Bay.

MARKET SQUARE AND AROUND

Market Square, in Central, is PE's most attractive corner, with a couple of fine buildings. City Hall was built between 1858 and 1862; the clock tower was added in 1883. The Main Public Library, shipped out from the UK, dates from 1837 and started life as a courthouse, only becoming a library in 1902. Outside is a fine marble statue of Queen Victoria, erected in 1903. Inside, visitors can see some beautiful early books.

BAYWORLD

Southeast of Central, off Marine Drive in Humewood, Bayworld (tel 041-5840650; www.bayworld.co.za; daily 9–4.30), comprises three attractions: the Main Museum, the Oceanarium and the Snake Park. The Main Museum offers an interesting mix of natural and cultural history; the Oceanarium has displays of more than 40 species of fish, with seal and dolphin shows daily at 11 and 3; the Snake Park houses a collection of exotic reptiles, including some rare and endangered species.

BEACHES

Algoa Bay is one of the most visited stretches of coast in South Africa. The water is warm and calm for most of the year, making it ideal for watersports. The two main northern beaches are New Brighton, good for swimming and fishing, and Bluewater Bay, a long stretch of white sand. King's Beach, the closest to the city, between the harbour and quieter Humewood, is heavily developed. Hobie Beach is popular in the evenings thanks to the nearby Boardwalk entertainment area, filled with bars, clubs and restaurants. Sardinia Bay is a marine reserve with good snorkelling and scuba diving.

INFORMATION

www.nmbt.co.za
✚ 328 H11 ℹ Nelson Mandela Bay, Donkin Lighthouse Building, Belmont Terrace, Port Elizabeth 6001
☎ 041-5822575 🕐 Mon–Fri, 8–4.30, Sat–Sun 9.30–3.30 ℹ Eastern Cape Tourist Board, Boardwalk, Port Elizabeth 6001 ☎ 041-5857761 🕐 Daily 8–4.30

TIPS

» The Donkin Heritage Trail is an enjoyable self-guided tour around Central. An excellent guidebook available from the tourist office describes 47 places of historical interest.
» The Algoa Bus Company runs a service between downtown PE and the beaches.
» Look for the pyramid near the tourist office, a memorial erected by Sir Rufane Donkin in memory of his wife Elizabeth, after whom the city was named. Local folklore claims that Elizabeth's heart is buried under the pyramid.

Opposite *Observing elephants in Shamwari Game Reserve*
Above *Port Elizabeth's 19th-century City Hall is now used as a concert hall*

WILD COAST

The Wild Coast stretches for about 280km (175 miles) from East London north to the Umtamvuna Nature Reserve next to Port Edward in KwaZulu-Natal. Its inland borders are the Drakensberg and Stormberg mountain ranges, and dotted between are small villages, brightly painted *kraals* (a traditional village of huts, often enclosed by a fence), and endless pastureland. It remains a traditional area, with most people speaking only Xhosa, and there is widespread poverty here. During apartheid the Great Kei River was the border between South Africa and the so-called independent homeland of Transkei. Even today, the difference in the standard of living between these two areas is striking. Nevertheless, the Wild Coast has some of the finest and least developed beaches in South Africa as well as a handful of small nature reserves. The main resorts are close to East London, but laid-back Chintsa is much quieter. The best surf on the Wild Coast is at Coffee Bay.

CHINTSA

The combined villages of Chintsa East and Chintsa West nestle among lush hills rolling down to a lagoon and a wide stretch of deserted beach. Although popular during the Christmas holidays with South Africans, the resort is blessedly isolated for the rest of the year and has relaxing outdoor activities such as canoeing, horseback riding and surfing, but the main appeal here is the lazy exploration of the shell-strewn beach, forests and tranquil lagoon. Nearby is the Inkwenkwezi Game Reserve (tel 043-7343234; www.inkwenkwezi.com), a private coastal game reserve with a combination of forest dunes and bushveld, and home to a range of imported game including rhino, elephant, lion, wildebeest and giraffe. Visitors leave their cars at the entrance and are transported around the reserve by safari vehicle.

✚ 329 K10

PORT ST. JOHNS

www.portstjohns.org.za

This small, peaceful town along the banks of the Mzimvubu River has a laid-back atmosphere. Its bohemian air has attracted many artists and, more recently, backpackers, drawn by the stunning beaches. Second Beach is the most attractive, a stretch of soft sand, backed by forested hills. There is a nature reserve within easy reach of town—Silaka (daily 6–6), with great walks through tropical forest—and there is a beautiful stretch of rugged coastline, with a breeding colony for sea birds, Bird Island, just off the beach. The warm, sulphurous springs at Isinuka are just outside town.

✚ 329 L9 🛈 Town Entrance Square ☎ 047-5641187

INFORMATION

www.ectourism.co.za

✚ 329 L9 🛈 Palm Square Business Park, Iron Wood House, Bonza Bay Road, Beacon Bay 5247 ☎ 043-7019600 🕐 Mon–Fri 8–4.30

TIPS

» Many of the roads in the area are not surfaced, but they are usually passable by car.

» Always give yourself plenty of time to arrive at your accommodation before dark, as road safety is a serious issue after nightfall. Cattle straying onto roads and large potholes are two common problems.

» Learn a few words of Xhosa, as many people here speak nothing else.

» The popular Strandloper Trail (*strand* means 'beach' and *loper* means 'walker' in Afrikaans) is a five-day 55km (34-5-mile) hike along the coast from Kei Mouth to Gonubie, overnighting in huts. Hikers are issued with a tide table to assist in crossing the numerous rivers (for reservations, tel 043-8411046; www.strandlopertrails.org.za).

Opposite *Beach at Haga-Haga*
Below *Trekking on horseback is a popular activity along the Wild Coast*

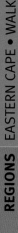
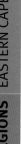

GRAAFF-REINET

Graaff-Reinet survived rebellion and rugged frontier life in the northern wilderness and is now the neatest and most graceful of the Karoo's towns. While the rest of urban South Africa grew haphazardly, Graaff-Reinet was carefully planned and is full of fine architecture. This walk takes in the best of the historic buildings.

THE WALK
Distance: 1.2 km (0.75 miles)
Allow: 1.5 hours
Sart/end at: Drostdy Hotel

★ Begin your stroll at the Drostdy Hotel on Church Street, Graaff-Reinet's main thoroughfare. From Church Street, smaller roads branch east and west, and it is among these that you'll find most of the town's historic buildings, museums and restaurants.

❶ The Drostdy hotel itself is a fine building, designed as the court and residence of the local magistrate (*landdrost*) by French architect Louis Thibault and completed in 1806. Take a moment to position yourself at the hotel's handsome front door and

gaze down the length of Parsonage Street, with its attractive houses framing the pleasing facade of Reinet House (▷ below) at the far (eastern) end of the road.

Cross Church Street and walk straight along Parsonage Street, which runs for about 280m (300 yards).

❷ On Parsonage Street you pass a number of interesting buildings, including the John Rupert Little Theatre on your right (after 100m/109 yards), originally the church of the London Missionary Society but now a small theatre. Also on the right is a row of charming houses built for private occupation but eventually converted for the aged. Perhaps the most appealing of them is No. 17,

Williams House, which has some especially fine woodwork.

At the end of Parsonage Street on the right, at its intersection with Murray Street, is the iron-roofed, gabled, Cape Dutch-style Old Residency, which started life as a townhouse in the early 19th century and now functions as a small military museum. Cross Murray Street at this point to visit Reinet House.

❸ Reinet House was built in 1812 as the Dutch Reformed Church parsonage. It suffered radical alteration over the years but was carefully restored in the 1950s to its original six-gabled, H-plan elegance. It suffered fire damage in the 1980s but was restored again and is now a museum with period furniture and a collection of antique dolls. Apart from its historical distinctions, the museum has two unusual claims to fame: It owns the world's largest vine, a monster which, before it was pruned back in 1983, had a girth of 3m (10ft) and covered an area of 123sq m (1,323sq ft); and it is the only place in the country permitted to distil a powerful home-made brew known as Withond (white dog).

Retrace your steps for 100m (110 yards) along the north side of Parsonage Street, which is lined by small 19th-century houses—No. 18 has an interesting stand-alone gable and little windows of very impure glass. Turn right onto Cross Street.

④ St. James' Anglican church at the corner of Cross and Somerset streets is worth a look. It has some lovely woodwork inside, and the next-door rectory has an eye-catching doll's-house quality about it.

Turn left, then right (north) into cottage-fringed Te Water Street. Look for the imposing Graaff-Reinet Club (1881) on your right. Te Water, which is only 100m (110 yards) long, ends at Church Square, a pleasant area fronted by the Mayor's Garden.

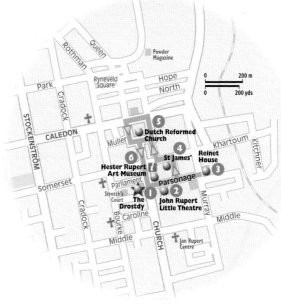

⑤ The Dutch Reformed Church in the square is itself a fine building: Dating from 1887 and built in Gothic Revival style, it was modelled on England's Salisbury Cathedral and contains a splendid collection of ecclesiastical silver.

To return to the Drostdy Hotel, exit the square onto Church Street, where notable buildings include Te Water House from 1818, the Old Library Museum, which dates from 1847, and the Hester Rupert Art Museum, with its collection of contemporary South African art.

⑥ The Hester Rupert Art Museum is in the Dutch Reformed Mission church, dating from 1821. Inside is an excellent collection of works by Irma Stern among other modern South African art. Stern (1894–1966) ranks among the country's most innovative painters, although her canvases were dismissed as 'immoral' and 'revolutionary' by the apartheid government; at one point they were actually the subject of police investigation.

From here, continue back to the Drostdy Hotel for a well-deserved cold drink or meal.

WHEN TO GO

Any time of the year is good for the walk, but bear in mind that early winter mornings and evenings can be bitterly cold in the Great Karoo. By contrast, the hours in the middle of high summer days are often too hot for walking, and can be uncomfortably dusty.

WHERE TO EAT
DROSTDY HOTEL

www.drostdy.co.za
Two excellent and elegant restaurants occupy this historic hotel on Church Street. Karoo lamb is the house speciality and a more casual menu is available in the garden.
✉ 28 Church Street ☎ 049-8922161
🕐 Daily 11–9.30

PLACES TO VISIT
REINET HOUSE
(GRAAFF-REINET MUSEUM)
✉ Murray Street ☎ 049-8923801
🕐 Mon–Fri 8–5, Sat 9–3, Sun 9–4

HESTER RUPERT ART MUSEUM
✉ Church Street ☎ 049-8922121 (ask to be put through to museum) 🕐 Mon–Fri 9–12.30, 2–5, Sat–Sun 9–12

Opposite *Old Library Museum, Church Street*
Left *Reinet House has been lovingly restored*

Above *Beach life in Port Elizabeth*

ADDO ELEPHANT NATIONAL PARK
ADDO ELEPHANT BACK SAFARIS
www.addoelephantbacksafaris.co.za
Take a walk with tame elephants through the bush and forest. The walk is not strenuous, and the pace allows visitors to observe the elephants close up in their natural surroundings. Afterwards, you can take a short ride on one to a waterhole, to watch the elephants swim. Refreshments are included.
✉ 1.5km (1 mile) before Addo's main gate. Turn left at the Zuurburg sign—the farm is 34km (21 miles) from this turn-off ☎ 042-2351400 🕐 Daily 8, 11, 3 👋 R875 per person

EAST LONDON
BUCCANEERS
www.buccaneers.co.za
Buccaneers is a popular pub and grill house that gets very busy at night, when it stages live music.
✉ Eastern Beach, Esplanade 5201 ☎ 043-7435171 🕐 Daily 11.30am–late 👋 Free

EAST LONDON AQUARIUM
www.elaquarium.co.za
The wide variety of wildlife that inhabits the waters of the Eastern Cape can be enjoyed here—pelicans, African penguins, seals and a wonderful array of tropical fish.
✉ Esplanade, East London 5200 ☎ 043-7052637 🕐 Daily 9–5 👋 Adult R20, child R13.

SUGAR SHACK
www.sugarshack.co.za
This friendly backpacker hostel is the best source of local information on surfing in East London. It can organize surfing lessons and has surfboards for rent. Easterns, in front of the Sugar Shack, is the most consistent beach break in the area.
✉ Esplanade Road, Eastern Beach 5201 ☎ 043-7228240 👋 Surf lessons from R180

GRAHAMSTOWN
RAT & PARROT
A popular bar with students, which gets quite rowdy late at night, the Rat & Parrot has a wide choice of beers and other drinks, and good *potjies* (stews in three-legged cast-iron pots).
✉ 59 New Street, Grahamstown 6139 ☎ 046-6225002 🕐 Mon–Sat 12–late 👋 Free

HOGSBACK
Main Road is lined with little craft shops selling gifts and locally made jams (the area is famous for its berries). Look out for Storm Haven and Arminel Crafts. At the entrance to the village you will also see local people selling their crafts, in particular clay animals such as kudu, horses and hogs; these figures are rarely seen elsewhere.

JEFFREYS BAY
JEFFREYS BAY SURF SCHOOL
www.islandvibe.co.za
Most people come to Jeffreys Bay to surf, and this is one of the best places for beginners. Lessons run daily, year round, and include wetsuits, beginners' boards and tuition. There are also seven-day learn-to-surf packages.
✉ Island Vibe Backpackers, 10 Dageraad Street, Jeffreys Bay 6300 ☎ 042-2931625 👋 2-hour lesson R200

PORT ELIZABETH
THE BOARDWALK CASINO AND ENTERTAINMENT WORLD
www.suninternational.com
This modern complex is set around a series of man-made lakes and beautiful gardens. There are numerous entertainment options in

the centre, including the Supersport Arena, which has big TV screens for watching sport. The casino offers 800 slot machines and 20 gaming tables, and there's a selection of restaurants, bars and clubs, specialist shops, a cinema, an information desk and craft market.

✉ Marine Drive, opposite Shark Rock Pier ☎ 031-5661802 ⏰ Casino: 24 hours; shops: daily 9–6

COCO DE MER
www.cocodemer.co.za
Sleek and stylish, with monochrome decor, this 'restrobar' has a tapas restaurant, a cocktail bar where tables are moved back later for dancing and a deck overlooking the beach. Entertainment is provided by house DJs and jazz bands.

✉ Dolphin's Leap Centre, Beach Road, Humewood ☎ 041-5850507 ⏰ Daily 11am–late 🖐 Free

THE FEATHER MARKET HALL
This renovated Victorian market hosts recitals, performances and concerts. The tourist office (Donkin Lighthouse Building, Belmont Terrace, tel 041-5858884; www.nmbt.co.za) has listings and tickets.

✉ 1 Baakens Street, Central 6001 ☎ 041-5855514 🖐 Adult R8, child (2–11) R5

MCARTHUR BATHS
Away from the large hotels there are a couple of excellent municipal swimming pools, including the McArthur Baths, which has a tidal pool, freshwater pool, children's water chute and restaurants.

✉ King's Beach Promenade, Humewood 6001 ☎ 041-5822282 ⏰ Nov–Mar daily 8.30–6; Apr, Sep, Oct 9.30–4.30. Closed May–Aug 🖐 R20

OCEANARIUM
www.bayworld.co.za
Port Elizabeth's aquarium has more than 40 species of fish, as well as a ragged-tooth shark tank, African penguins and turtles. There are seal and dolphin presentations daily at 11 and 3. There's also a Snake Park on the same site.

✉ Bayworld, Marine Drive, Humewood

FEBRUARY
PRICKLY PEAR FESTIVAL
www.nmbt.co.za
With more than 250 products derived from this fruit on sale, crowds of over 25,000 people turn up each year to enjoy traditional food such as pancakes, ginger beer, jam, fish barbecues and local beer.

✉ Cuyler Hofstede farm museum, Uitenhage ☎ 041-5858884 ⏰ Last Saturday in February 🚍 34km (21 miles) northwest of Port Elizabeth

JULY
NATIONAL ARTS FESTIVAL
www.nafest.co.za
Grahamstown hosts this famous 11-day festival, South Africa's premier arts festival and one of the top cultural events in the

6001 ☎ 041-5840650 ⏰ Daily 9–4.30 🖐 Adult R40, child (under 13) R25; ticket covers entry to Oceanarium and Snake Park

OCEAN DIVERS INTERNATIONAL
www.odipe.co.za
.There are a number of good dive sites around Port Elizabeth and the best time for diving is in winter, when average visibility is between 8m and 15m (25ft and 50ft). The best diving is around the protected St. Croix Islands. Ocean Divers runs daily dives to the area's major sites and offers a full set of courses.

✉ 10 Albert Raod, Walmer 6070 ☎ 041-5815121 🖐 Courses from R1,600

OPERA HOUSE
www.peoperahouse.co.za
The delightful historic Opera House was built in 1891 on the site of some old gallows, which has led to many sightings of ghosts and spooks in the building. It's now a venue for a variety of performances from Shakespeare and piano recitals to musicals and comedy.

✉ Whites Road, Central 6001 ☎ 041-5862256 🖐 From R50

country. More than 50,000 visitors pour into town to watch a huge variety of performances, including theatre, dance, fine art, films, music, opera and an increasing variety of traditional crafts and art, plus a huge range of fringe shows.

✉ Grahamstown ☎ 046-6031103 ⏰ Late June, early July

BILLABONG PRO SURF COMPETITION
www.billabongpro.com
In winter (from April to September), when the waves are at their best, Jeffreys Bay comes to life and in July it holds this professional surfing competition. This draws surfers from across the globe and the town gets packed out.

✉ Jeffreys Bay

SAHARA OVAL ST. GEORGE'S PARK
www.epcricket.co.za
Set in the middle of town, in the city park, this is South Africa's oldest cricket ground and was the site of the first test match to be played in Africa, in 1889. St. George's is a pleasant old stadium and an enjoyable venue to watch cricket.

✉ St. George's Park, Central 6001 ☎ 041-5851646 (ticket enquiries) ⏰ Cricket season: Dec–Mar 🖐 From R30

WILD COAST
AMADIBA ADVENTURES
www.amadibaadventures.co.za
A community-based tourism initiative offering one- to six-day trails on foot or horseback through the rural areas and isolated coastline of the Wild Coast. Accommodation is in mobile camps. You will meet the local Xhosa people, and all proceeds from the tours are channelled back into the local community.

✉ Trails start at Mzamba Craft Village, 6km (4 miles) south of Port Edward opposite the Wild Coast Sun Resort ☎ 039-3056455 🖐 4-day horse or hiking trail from R2,240

REGIONS   EASTERN CAPE • WHAT TO DO

Above The Eastern Cape restaurants cater to a wide range of gastronomic preferences

PRICES AND SYMBOLS

The restaurants are listed alphabetically (excluding The) by town or area, then by name. The prices given are the average for a two-course lunch (L) and a three-course dinner (D) for one person, without drinks. The wine price is for the least expensive bottle.

For a key to the symbols, ▷ 2.

EAST LONDON
AL MARE

This relaxed restaurant has the added bonus of outdoor seating and ocean views. There's a wide variety of food and more than 80 wines to choose from. Lunches include inexpensive pizzas, filled bagels and wraps and pasta that children will also like, while evening options include fillet steaks and stuffed chicken breasts. Many items are 'skinny', meaning they are low in fat—butternut soup without the cream, for example.

✉ Aquarium Complex, Esplanade Road, East London 5201 ☎ 043-7220287 🕐 Mon–Fri 12–3, 6–late, Sat 6–late 🖐 L R45, D R105, Wine R45

OCEAN BASKET

www.oceanbasket.co.za
The East London branch of this popular South African chain restaurant specializing in seafood serves a superb choice of fish and shellfish, with prawn platters and large combo plates ideal for sharing. For a light meal, there's also sushi. All of it is as fresh as can be.

✉ Vincent Park Centre, Devereux Avenue, East London ☎ 043-7268809 🕐 Mon–Thu 11.30–9.30, Fri 11.30–10, Sat 12–10, closed Sun 🖐 L R70, D R140, Wine R45

ZHONG HUA

An unpretentious Chinese restaurant, Zhong Hua has typical red-lantern décor, snug booths and round tables that are ideal for sharing dishes—and a chef who comes from Shanghai. The menu has all the popular staples like chicken in oyster sauce and sweet and sour pork, plenty of options for vegetarians and a choice of good-value set menus. The sushi is ideal for a starter.

✉ 48 Beach Road, Nahoon, East London 5241 ☎ 043-7353442 🕐 Thu–Tue 11.30am–late, Wed 3pm–late 🖐 L R45, D R65, Wine R35

GRAAFF-REINET
DE CAMDEBOO

www.drostdy.co.za
The à la carte restaurant in the Drostdy Hotel (▷ 158) is a popular choice for a romantic dinner. The high-ceilinged dining room is furnished with antiques, and the elegantly presented meals are served by candlelight. There are occasional evening buffets, and the menu has a fine selection of Karoo dishes, including roast Karoo lamb served with vegetables and home-baked bread. The wine list focuses on the Cape region.

✉ Drostdy Hotel, 30 Church Street, Graaff-Reinet 6280 ☎ 049-8922161 🕐 Mon–Sat 6.30–10 🖐 D R180, Wine R65

GRAHAMSTOWN
137 HIGH STREET

www.137highstreet.co.za
If you are passing through town, this relaxed café and restaurant is ideal for a snack, a cappuccino, or a cool glass of wine in the attractive courtyard. There are also freshly baked cakes and scones for afternoon tea. There's a simple guesthouse attached.

✉ 137 High Street, Grahamstown 6139 ☎ 046-6223242 🕐 Mon–Fri 7.30am–9.30pm, Sat–Sun 8–2 🖐 L R100, D R150, Wine R60

REGIONS EASTERN CAPE • EATING

NORDEN'S AT THE COCK HOUSE

www.cockhouse.co.za

This excellent restaurant is part of a smart town guesthouse (▷ 158–159), built in the 1820s, which retains many of its original features. Plenty of attention is given to presentation and the quality of the country cuisine, which makes use of local seasonal produce. Try the ostrich carpaccio followed by the Thai poached fish or fillet steak with mushroom risotto. Light snacks are available in the snug yellowwood bar next to the fire.

✉ The Cock House Guest House, 10 Market Street, Grahamstown 6139 ☎ 046-6361287 🕐 Tue–Sun 12.30–2.30, 7–9.30, Mon 12.30–2.30 🖐 L R100, D R150, Wine R60

JEFFREYS BAY
SUNFLOWER CAFÉ

Vegetarians will appreciate the Sunflower Café, with its meat-free pastas, quiches and bakes. During the day it serves light meals, delicious milkshakes and home-made cakes on a small veranda overlooking the street. There are also simple evening meals, including fresh local seafood such as lemon-grilled calamari with rice. The walls are hung with local art.

✉ 20 Da Gama Road, Jeffreys Bay 6330 ☎ 042-2931682 🕐 Tue–Fri 9am–11pm, Sat 9–5, Sun 9–4 🖐 L R35, D R70, Wine R35

DIE WALSKIPPER

www.walskipper.co.za

Set in a commanding position right on the beach, with outside tables overlooking the crashing waves, this is an informal J-Bay favourite. It specializes in seafood and hearty meat dishes like oxtail in red wine and lamb shanks. All main courses are served with rice and, in the West Coast tradition, home-made bread with pâté and jam. Specials include oysters and quail's eggs, and sometimes there's more exotic game on the menu, such as crocodile or ostrich.

✉ Clapton's Beach, Jeffreys Bay 6630 ☎ 042-2920005 🕐 Tue–Sat 12–10, Mon 9–3.30, Sun 12–3 🖐 L R90, D R125, Wine R55

PORT ELIZABETH
34° SOUTH

www.34-south.com

This is the anchor tenant of the Boardwalk complex and occupies a wonderfully cavernous steel and glass structure. Foodies should head here not only for the delicious meals but for the extensive deli and shop, where there's an excellent selection of cheeses, hams and olives for sale, as well as wine, chocolates, fresh bread and fish. The long menu is varied and includes plenty of seafood, including tasty mussel pots, as well as light lunches, crunchy salads and decadent cakes. There's a sister restaurant in Knysna, and both sit on the 34th parallel (hence the name).

✉ Boardwalk Casino and Entertainment Complex, Marine Drive, opposite Shark Rock Pier, Port Elizabeth 6001 ☎ 041-5831085 🕐 Daily 9am–10pm 🖐 L R80, D R120, Wine R75

BLUE WATERS CAFÉ

www.bluewaterscafe.com

Breakfast, lunch or dinner—whatever the time of day diners can't fail to appreciate the panoramic ocean views. Burgers and pancakes are among the lunchtime offerings; for dinner try the blackened kingclip or the biltong fillet.

✉ 7 Shark Rock Pier, Marine Drive, Port Elizabeth, 6001 ☎ 041-5834110 🕐 Daily 8am–11pm 🖐 L R60, D R150, Wine R60

THE BUTCHER'S BLOCK

The Butcher's Block is aptly named. This is an unashamedly old-school, carnivorous eating place (though it also has an extensive seafood menu). Choices that will have meat-lovers drooling include properly aged Karoo lamb, lots of game, and fine steaks. Real connoisseurs can have their cuts of choice prepared by the restaurant's in-house butcher. You can eat indoors in a classically clubby dining room, or al fresco on the sheltered, year-round terrace.

✉ 44 Newton Street, Newton Park, Port Elizabeth 6045 ☎ 041-3653740 🕐 Mon–Fri 12–1am, Sat 6pm–1am, closed Sun 🖐 L or D R145, Wine R100

GINGER

www.ginger-restaurant.co.za

This is a very grown up kind of place, on the beachfront, with upholstered furniture and linen tablecloths and napkins. There's a definite French influence on the menu, with an emphasis on steak and seafood, but there are some Asian influences too. The lunch menu includes a selection of designer sandwiches, gourmet burgers and great salads. It's a little on the pretentious side, but the service is friendly.

✉ Marine Drive, Port Elizabeth 6001 ☎ 041-5831229 🕐 Mon–Sat 12–3, 6.30–10.30 🖐 L R80, D R160, Wine R65

DE KELDER

This is a well-established, old-fashioned, formal restaurant with a welcoming Cape Dutch interior offering delicious food and excellent service. It's best known for its Châteaubriand prepared before your eyes at your table, slow-roasted duck, generous seafood platters, creamy crayfish thermidor, and to-die-for Lindt chocolate brownies to finish off. There's a long wine list and the staff are very knowledgeable.

✉ Marine Protea Hotel, Marine Drive, Port Elizabeth 6001 ☎ 041-5832750 🕐 Mon–Fri 12–2.30, 6–11, Sat 6–11 🖐 L R80, D R120, Wine R85

WILD COAST
MICHAELA'S OF CHINTSA

www.michaelas.co.za

The remarkable thing about this scenic restaurant is that it is perched on top of a dune and accessed by 134 steps or a funicular (call ahead to check that it is operating), so half the fun is actually getting here. The broad outdoor wooden decks overlook the waves. Main course options include a delicately fragrant Thai chicken and prawn curry, superb ostrich fillet medallions and a good selection of seafood. Vegetarians will be impressed by the vegetarian platter, and the Sunday buffet is very good value.

✉ Steenbras Drive, Chintsa East 5275 ☎ 043-7385139 🕐 Wed–Sun 11–9.30, Mon 6–9.30 🖐 L R45, D R85, Wine R60

PRICES AND SYMBOLS

The hotels below are listed alphabetically (excluding The) by town or area, then by name. Prices are the average for a double room for one night, including breakfast. All the hotels listed accept credit cards unless otherwise stated.

For a key to the symbols, ▷ 2.

ADDO ELEPHANT NATIONAL PARK
GORAH ELEPHANT CAMP

www.hunterhotels.com/gorahelephantcamp
This camp has a private concession covering 4,500ha (11,120 acres), but gives access to the rest of the park. Accommodation is in luxurious tents with a colonial theme, complete with four-poster beds, private bathrooms and terraces. A relaxing *boma* (enclosed outdoor area) has a rock swimming pool. Meals are served in a renovated coach house, overlooking a waterhole frequented by elephant, buffalo and antelope. The price includes all meals, guided game drives and night drives. The camp offers a similar experience to the luxury camps around Kruger (▷ 217); the only drawback is that the service is rather over-attentive.

✉ PO Box 454, Plettenberg Bay 6600
☎ 044-5327818 (central reservations)
🖐 R11,980 ❶ 11 ⛱ 🚗 Drive east on N2 from Port Elizabeth, through Colchester, then take N10 (north) onto Addo Heights Road (gravel). After 9km (5.5 miles), Gorah is on your right

CRADOCK
DIE TUISHUISE

www.tuishuise.co.za
It is worth visiting Cradock for Die Tuishuise alone. This guesthouse occupies a series of historical buildings on Market Street, each restored and decorated to reflect the British and Dutch settlers' lifestyles more than a century ago. The bedrooms have beautiful antiques, four-poster beds, private bathrooms and original features such as Victorian fireplaces and polished hardwood floors. Every house has a fully equipped kitchen and lounge and is ideal for families or two couples. Huge breakfasts are served in the Victorian dining room, and dinner is in the Manor House on the corner of the street. The staff are very friendly and helpful.

✉ 36 Market Street, Cradock 5880
☎ 048-8811322 🖐 R880 ❶ 25

Above *Historic Drostdy Hotel in Graaff-Reinet*

GRAAFF-REINET
DROSTDY

www.drostdy.co.za
The Drostdy was designed by acclaimed architect Louis Thibault in 1804, and today is a beautifully restored hotel and a national monument. The bedrooms are at the back of the main house in an appealing complex of 19th-century cottages known as Stretch's Court, originally the homes of emancipated slaves. The bedrooms have a slightly outdated feel (expect a surplus of ruffles and floral fabrics), but the public areas are appealing, with antiques and historical paintings. There's a good restaurant (▷ 156) and a lovely secluded garden, where you can have pre-dinner drinks, a pool and secure off-street parking.

✉ 30 Church Street, Graaff-Reinet 6280
☎ 049-8922161 🖐 R950, excluding breakfast (R90) ❶ 51 ⛱ ⛱

GRAHAMSTOWN
THE COCK HOUSE

www.cockhouse.co.za
This beautifully restored 1820s national monument has nine double

rooms with private bathrooms, each individually decorated with fine fabrics, antiques and original wood floors. A lovely first-floor veranda overlooks the street, and there's a comfortable lounge and library where author Andre Brink penned four of his novels. Attached is a highly rated à la carte restaurant. Past guests at the Cock House include former South African presidents Nelson Mandela and Thabo Mbeki.

✉ 10 Market Street, Grahamstown 6139 ☎ 046-6361287 🖐 R870 ⓘ 9

HOGSBACK
AWAY WITH THE FAIRIES
www.awaywiththefairies.co.za
Away with the Fairies is one of the best backpacker establishments in the country—friendly, relaxed and well run. There are brightly painted dorms and double rooms, plus one cottage with kitchen. There is a well equipped kitchen, clean bathrooms and a comfortable lounge with a fireplace. The surrounding gardens are beautiful, with plenty of camping space and a gate that leads to forest trails. A lively bar serves big breakfasts and evening meals, and staff can organize daily guided walks and sundowner trips.

✉ Signposted from Main Road, Hogsback 5721 ☎ 045-9621031 🖐 R90 per bed, R275 per double room ⓘ 40 beds

JEFFREYS BAY
ISLAND VIBE
www.islandvibe.co.za
Island Vibe hostel is in an excellent position at the top end of Jeffreys Bay, perched high on a promontory with views of, and access to, two beaches. There are large dorms, doubles and camping space, with a kitchen, and a popular bar serving good breakfasts and set evening meals. The place has a big surfer scene, so it can get noisy. Visitors who prefer a quieter atmosphere will appreciate the beach house, which has double rooms with private bathrooms, great sea views and a more peaceful atmosphere. The hostel rents out bicycles, canoes, fishing rods and surf boards.

✉ 10 Dageraad Street, Jeffreys Bay 6330 ☎ 042-2931625 🖐 From R120 per bed, or R250 per double room ⓘ Around 90 beds

PORT ELIZABETH
HACKLEWOOD HILL COUNTRY HOUSE
www.hacklewood.co.za
In a late-Victorian manor house, this luxurious place has enormous bathrooms. The bedrooms, some with striking red walls, are filled with attractive antiques and original paintings. There are also beautiful mature gardens with a tennis court. The elegant dining room has some special touches—for example, guests are encouraged to select their wine from the impressive cellar. Advanced reservations are essential during the high season. Parking is available. No children under eight.

✉ 152 Prospect Road, Walmer, Port Elizabeth 6070 ☎ 041-5811300 🖐 R3,000 ⓘ 8 🏊

MILLBROOK HOUSE
www.millbrookhouse.co.za
The delightful Millbrook House bed-and-breakfast, with five units with kitchens, is in a leafy square in the centre of Port Elizabeth. The early 20th-century house has attractive wrought-iron balconies and a low-key, peaceful atmosphere. It's a good-value, family-run place, with four bright and airy rooms with private bathrooms, pretty furnishings, ceiling fans and satellite TV. There's a small garden with a splash pool and a comfortable lounge.

✉ 2 Havelock Square, Central, Port Elizabeth 6001 ☎ 041-5823774 🖐 R700 ⓘ 4, plus five units with kitchen 🏊

SHAMWARI GAME RESERVE
LONG LEE MANOR
www.shamwari.com
Long Lee Manor is the largest of seven luxury camps within this private reserve. It feels like a smart country hotel that has been dropped in the middle of the African bush. All the rooms are very chic, with plush fabrics and four-poster beds, under-floor heating and satellite

TV. Other facilities include a curio shop, an excellent restaurant and a floodlit tennis court. At the nearby Bushman's River is an outdoor eating area where guests can watch the animals drink while they enjoy a meal. Prices include all meals and game drives.

☎ 041-4071000 (central reservations) 🖐 From R8,500 ⓘ 20 🏊 🏊 🚌 From Port Elizabeth, follow signs for the N2, Grahamstown. After 65km (40 miles), the park is signposted off to the left

WILD COAST
BUCCANEER'S
www.cintsa.com
This superb lodge, set in forests overlooking Cintsa lagoon and the beach, has a wide choice of accommodation. A 2km (1.2-mile) dirt track leads to the secluded site, with a choice of backpacker dorms, double rooms, fully equipped cottages with kitchens and camping. A lively bar serves evening meals and snacks, and there are verandas with ocean views. The lodge stretches down towards the beach, and has a path leading straight to the lagoon. Other facilities include free canoes and surfboards, and a range of free daily organized activities such as guided walks. The Baz Bus (▷ 52) stops here.

✉ Chintsa 5273 ☎ 043-7343012 🖐 From R120 a bed; from R250 for a double ⓘ 84 beds 🏊

THE KRAAL
www.thekraalbackpackers.co.za
The Kraal is situated on a hill above a beach and lagoon. It is made up of traditional thatched Xhosa *rondavels* (thatched huts) with dormitory beds, no electricity, 'eco-loos' and hot showers. This is a simple set-up in an isolated corner of the Wild Coast. You can buy food and basic supplies at the kitchen, but the owners also prepare superb meals.

✉ Port St. Johns 5121 ☎ 082-8714964 🖐 R100 per bed ⓘ 12 beds 🚗 Off the R61; 80km (52 miles) from Mthatha and 40km (25 miles) from Port St. Johns; follow the signs to Mpande/Isilimela Hospital

KWAZULU-NATAL

KwaZulu-Natal is one of South Africa's most popular destinations to visit and its game reserves are among the country's finest. The province extends from the Drakensberg Mountains in the southwest to the humid, sultry subtropical coast in the northeast on the border with Mozambique. The uKhahlamba-Drakensberg Park rises to the border with the mountain kingdom of Lesotho and is South Africa's most dramatic mountain range, with lofty, craggy peaks, sheer cliffs, waterfalls and rolling pastures, and it also harbours the country's most important San rock art.

The landscape of the central region has seen some bloody conflicts between the Zulus, Boers and British during the epic battles that took place at the end of the 19th century and in the early 20th century. Here there are many battlefield sites, museums and monuments to visit and the history is brought to life on evocative guided tours.

On the coast both north and south of Durban, Africa's largest port and a popular surfing and holiday destination, you'll find resorts and nature reserves, as well as a line of high-rise hotels and apartments along its famous Golden Mile of beach. The city is also a melting pot of cultures as a result of its Indian and Zulu heritage. To the north sugar plantations and white sandy beaches lead to the iSimangaliso Wetland Park, a terrain of rolling vegetated sand dunes and lakes dotted with islands and reedbeds that are home to hippo and crocodile. Beyond are a clutch of remote tropical coastline parks of thick dune forest where giant turtles hatch on the deserted beaches.

Inland the Hluhluwe-Imfolozi Game Reserve is Southern Africa's most successful sanctuary for white rhino; it is credited with bringing this species back from the brink of extinction.

THE BATTLEFIELDS ROUTE
▷ 164–165.

DOLPHIN COAST
www.thedolphincoast.co.za
The area north of Durban, between Umhlanga and Tugela Mouth, is known as the Dolphin Coast. It's famous for its stunning beaches, stylish resorts and the bottlenose dolphins that give it its name. The N2 highway bypasses most of the towns, so stick instead to the original main road, which runs through the resorts. After Umhlanga Rocks (▷ 175) come Ballito, Shaka's Rock (where Zulu warriors once leaped into the sea as a test of their manhood), Umhlali, Salt Rock and Sheffield Beach, forming a more or less continuous stretch. All the beaches are excellent, but bear in mind that there are sharks along the coast: Always ask whether the beach is protected by shark nets.
🚹 331 N7 🚹 Sangweni Tourism Centre, corner of Ballito Drive and Link Road, Ballito ☎ 032-9461997 🕐 Mon–Fri 8–5, Sat 9–1

DURBAN
▷ 166–168.

HIBISCUS COAST
www.hibiscuscoast.kzn.org.za
The overall impression of the coast south of Durban—the Hibiscus Coast—is of a long line of holiday homes set in a lush subtropical strip of forest. But it is the sea that deserves your attention. During the winter months millions of sardines travel close to the beaches, attracting dolphins, sharks and birds, and the ocean teems with life.

Port Shepstone is the largest town on the south coast, but is more geared to industry than the holiday trade. The other main town on the coast is Margate, a developed family Blue Flag beach resort with palm-fringed white-sand beaches, which tend to get very crowded during school holidays.
🚹 331 M8 🚹 Hibiscus Coast Tourism, 16 Bisset Road, Port Shepstone 4240 ☎ 039-6827944 🕐 Mon–Fri 8–4.30, Sat 9–12

Above *Bottlenose dolphins off the coast at Margate*
Opposite *White rhino cooling off in the Ithala Game Reserve*

HLUHLUWE-IMFOLOZI GAME RESERVE
▷ 169.

ISIMANGALISO WETLAND PARK
▷ 170–171.

ITHALA GAME RESERVE
www.kznwildlife.com
Ithala, although small and not very well known, is one of KwaZulu-Natal's most spectacular reserves, and game viewing feels much less crowded and more relaxed than in many other reserves. Ithala's landscapes are stunning, with large areas of low-lying grassland, steep-sided forested valleys and granite cliffs reaching 1,450m (4,756ft). The steeply rising terrain has created several different ecosystems with an interesting diversity of wildlife. Twenty species have been reintroduced into the reserve, including a herd of young elephants and the only herd of tsessebi (a large antelope) in Natal. You can see three of the Big Five—elephant, leopard and black rhino—as well as cheetah, eland, giraffe, kudu, white rhino, blue wildebeest and zebra. Birdwatching is another important attraction, and some 320 species have been recorded in the reserve, including black eagle, martial eagle and bald ibis. In June and July the flowering aloe trees come into bloom; their unmistakable large orange flowers are an important source of nectar at this time of year.
🚹 331 M5 ☎ 034-9832540 🕐 Nov–Feb daily 5am–7pm; Mar–Oct 6–6 🚻 Adult R40, child (under 12) R20, car R30 🚶 Guided day hikes can be reserved at reception 🍴 At Ntshondwe Camp 🏕 Camp shop. Petrol (gas) is on sale next to the main gates 🚗 Along R66 from Pongola, then R69 for 73km (45 miles); entrance near the village of Louwsburg

KOSI BAY
www.kznwildlife.com
Kosi Bay, north of Sodwana Bay, is one of South Africa's most popular wilderness destinations. The protected area is more than 25km (15 miles) long and consists of four lakes separated from the sea by a long strip of forest-covered dunes. The lakes are part of a fascinating tropical wetland environment, their shores bordered with reedbeds, ferns, swamp figs and umdoni trees. Five species of mangrove thrive in the estuary, where local fishermen have built traditional fishing traps.

There are also pristine beaches fringed with a stunning coral reef, perfect for snorkelling. The Kosi Bay Hiking Trail, 34km (21 miles) long, is popular; places can get fully reserved six months in advance.
🚹 331 P5 ☎ 035-5920236 🕐 Daily 6–6 🚻 Adult R20, child (3–15) R10, plus R15 per vehicle 🚗 Turn off the N2 at the Jozini turning

INFORMATION

www.tourdundee.co.za

🚩 331 M6 🛈 Tourism Dundee,
Civic Gardens, Victoria Street, Dundee
☎ 034-2122121 ext 2262 ⏰ Mon–Fri
9–4.45, Sat 9–12

Above *War memorial at Spioenkop, the site of a humiliating British defeat to the Boers in 1890*

INTRODUCTION

This area of vast open landscape in northern KwaZulu-Natal is the stage on which major wars between the Boers, British and Zulus were fought. The route covers 11 towns and more than 50 evocative battle sites, all of which can be visited. To the uninitiated there is often little to see other than landscape, so taking an organized tour is the best way of experiencing the sites. The tourist information offices in Dundee and Ladysmith have advice on how best to view the battlefields and can arrange tours. If you decide to tour them yourself, the major sites are signposted and can be reached from Dundee or Ulundi.

The wars fought in the latter half of the 19th century and at the start of the 20th century were mostly about land and who owned it. Tension was further increased by the discovery of diamonds at Kimberley and gold on the Witwatersrand in the Transvaal (▷ 34–35), with everyone wanting a share of the new riches.

WHAT TO SEE

ISANDHLWANA

Early in 1879 British troops entered Zululand to destroy the strongest independent African state in southern Africa. The Zulu king Cetshwayo immediately rallied his troops, stopping south of Isandhlwana. The British, confident of their superiority, had not constructed any defensive positions to protect their camp. On 22 January, a small British cavalry unit was scouring the land to the south of their camp when they spotted some cattle being herded by Zulus and gave chase. Within moments, they reached the lip of a valley to see the entire Zulu army, 25,000 strong, seated in complete silence. The Zulu force advanced: The 1,700 British were outnumbered, suffering a humiliating defeat, three quarters of them killed within two hours. Today it is an atmospheric spot, with white-painted cairns marking the places where British soldiers were buried, and a memorial to the Zulu dead, represented by a giant bronze replica of a Zulu victory necklace.

➕ 331 M6 ☎ Museum: 034-2718165 🕐 Mon–Fri 8–4, Sat–Sun 9–4 ✋ Adult R20, child (under 12) R10 ✋ 80km (50 miles) from Dundee, west along R68, signposted south of Nqutu

RORKE'S DRIFT

Rorke's Drift is across the Buffalo River from Isandhlwana. It was the site of a Swedish mission that had been commandeered by British forces and converted into a hospital and a supply depot. Only 110 men were stationed there when two survivors of Isandhlwana arrived to warn of an imminent attack. Four thousand Zulus appeared 90 minutes later. The ferocious attack was resisted for 12 hours from behind a makeshift barricade of grain bags and biscuit boxes before the Zulu soldiers withdrew, having lost some 400 men; 17 officers were among the British dead. The defence of Rorke's Drift is one of the epic tales of British military history and was immortalized in the 1964 movie *Zulu,* starring Michael Caine. The mission station has been converted into a small museum, which illustrates scenes from the battle and outlines the lives of the men involved, 11 of whom were awarded the Victoria Cross—the most ever awarded at a single battle. Just beyond the museum there is a cemetery and a memorial to those who died.

➕ 331 M6 ☎ Museum: 034-6421687 🕐 Mon–Fri 8–4, Sat–Sun 9–4 ✋ Adult R20, child (under 12) R10 🖼 🚌 42km (26 miles) from Dundee, off R68 between Dundee and Nqutu

NCOME-BLOOD RIVER

www.ncomemuseum.co.za

Blood River is the site of the crushing defeat suffered by Zulus defending their territory against advancing Boers on 16 December 1838. Their short spears were no match for the Boers' rifles, and more than 3,000 Zulus were killed. So many were shot trying to flee back across the Ncome River that it ran red with blood— hence the name. The Boers, led by Andries Pretorius, did not lose a single man and only three were injured, including Pretorius himself, who was stabbed in the hand. The battle is commemorated on the site by a circle of 64 full-sized wagons and the small Ncome Museum.

➕ 331 M6 ☎ Museum: 034-2718121 🕐 Daily 8–4.30 ✋ By donation 🖼 🚌 43 km (26 miles) from Dundee, along R33 towards Dejagersdrif

SIEGE MUSEUM

www.ladysmith.kzn.org.za

This fascinating museum in Ladysmith reconstructs scenes from the Siege of Ladysmith, which lasted 118 days from October 1899, early in the Second Anglo-Boer War, until February 1900. There are displays of weapons and uniforms that were used during the siege.

➕ 331 L6 ℹ️ Ladysmith Tourism, Murchison Street, Ladysmith 3370 ☎ 036-6372992 🕐 Mon–Fri 9–4, Sat 9–1 ✋ Adult R20, child (under 16) R10

TALANA MUSEUM

www.talana.co.za

The Battle of Talana Hill near Dundee took place on 20 October 1899 and was the first major battle of the Second Anglo-Boer War. Talana Museum has been built on the site of the battle, with a self-guided trail that visits the remains of two British forts. The main building has good displays on the Zulu War and the Anglo-Boer Wars, while Talana House has historical displays on the lifestyles of the Zulus and the early settlers in Dundee. Both these buildings were used as dressing stations during the battle.

➕ 331 M6 ✉ Vryheid Road ☎ 034-2122654 🕐 Mon–Fri 8–4.30, Sat–Sun 9–4.30 ✋ Adult R20, child (under 16) R10 🍴 🎁 🚌 1km (0.6 miles) north of Dundee

TIP

» If you drive yourself, note that access to the sites is along dirt roads. Allow enough time to return in daylight, as the bad roads and wandering cattle are dangerous at night.

Above *Military uniforms on display at the Talana Museum*
Below *One of the 64 wagons marking the site of the Battle of Blood River in 1838*

REGIONS KWAZULU-NATAL • SIGHTS

DURBAN

INFORMATION

www.durban.kzn.org.za

✚ 331 M7 ℹ Station Building, 160 Pine Street, Durban 4001 ☎ 031-3044934

🕐 Mon–Fri 8–5, Sat–Sun 9–2

INTRODUCTION

The sprawling conurbation of Durban is Africa's largest port, and although its appeal is not immediately apparent — few original buildings survive and it can feel hectic and overcrowded — it possesses wide beaches, an extensive beachfront and a steamy tropical climate.

The earliest inhabitants of the area were members of the Lala tribe, who fished in the estuary and hunted and grew crops in the fertile tropical forests along the coast. The first Europeans to land here were Portuguese explorers led by Vasco da Gama in 1497, en route to the east, but it was nearly 200 years before any Europeans settled. The first British traders arrived in 1823, spurred on by news of Shaka, the powerful chief of the Zulus, and his empire. The trader Henry Fynn made initial contact with Shaka. He ingratiated himself with the royal household and Shaka eventually granted him a tract of land covering more than 9,000sq km (3,500sq miles). Fynn and his colleague Nathaniel Isaacs ran this area as their own personal fiefdom, taking many Zulu wives and fathering dozens of children. Fynn even declared himself King of Natal.

With the establishment of the Voortrekker republic of Natalia in 1838, the British saw their interests coming under threat. An expeditionary force was sent to Durban from the Cape in 1842; they were besieged by Voortrekkers on arrival, but by June the parliament in Pietermaritzburg had accepted British rule. The development of the sugarcane industry in the 1860s encouraged the growth of Durban as a port and gave the city one of its most distinctive characteristics when the planters imported a large number of indentured workers from India, many of whom remained in Natal. With the development of the Golden Mile in the 1970s, Durban was promoted as a seaside resort for white holidaymakers. Blacks were permitted to walk the length of the whole beach but, on the whites-only Addington Beach, were not allowed to sit down or enter the sea.

Today the city has South Africa's largest Indian population, giving it a mix of English, African and Indian cultures. As with all South African cities, the best way of getting about is by car, and there is a good system of highways and plenty of paying parking places. Durban also has a good, frequent local bus service called Mynah that runs between the city centre, the beachfront and Berea and Morningside suburbs (information office on corner of Aliwal Street and Pine

Above *Durban by night, with the floodlit City Hall in the foreground*

Street, Durban 4001, tel 031-3073503; average fare is R4). For daily guided walking tours of the city, contact the tourist office (▷ Information, left), which offer the Oriental Walkabout and the Historical Walkabout tours; both cost R100 per person and must be booked a day in advance. Minibus tours of the city and its surrounds are run by Strelitzia Tours (tel 031-5795681; www.strelitziatours.com), with a comprehensive range of daily city tours as well as excursions out to the townships.

WHAT TO SEE

CENTRAL DURBAN

Palm-lined Francis Farewell Square is the hub of the colonial heart of Durban, with a bustling street market and commemorative statues, including the art deco Cenotaph monument. City Hall, on Smith Street, is one of Durban's grandest buildings. Built in 1910, it was lauded as one of the British Empire's finest colonial town halls. The nearby Natural Science Museum (tel 031-3112256, Mon–Sat 8.30–4, Sun 11–4) has a grand colonial entrance adorned with palm trees. Inside is a large collection of stuffed African mammals; more interestingly, the museum also houses an extremely rare dodo skeleton and South Africa's only Egyptian mummy. The KwaZuzulwazi Science Centre here has an excellent series of displays dedicated to the Zulu culture.

The Durban Art Gallery (tel 031-3112265; Mon–Sat 8.30–4, Sun 11–4) was one of the first galleries in South Africa to collect black South African art, and today has a mix of collections of work by local artists and superb displays of indigenous arts and crafts. Other buildings worth noting include the old Post Office; Tourist Junction, housed in the 19th-century train station; and the KwaMuhle Museum (Mon–Fri 8.30–4, Sat–Sun 9–4), a fascinating and moving exhibition of life as an African under the old regime—a must if you've missed the Apartheid Museum in Johannesburg (▷ 225) or the District Six Museum in Cape Town (▷ 69). The collection includes waxworks of figures in hostels, a series of photographs of protests and riots, and displays of the Indian merchants of Grey Street and the Grey Street mosque. The Warrior's Gate Moth Museum (Tue–Fri, Sun 11–3, Sat 10–noon) has a large collection of military memorabilia from World Wars I and II and battlefield relics from the Anglo-Boer and Zulu wars.

THE INDIAN DISTRICT

The area around Victoria, Queen and Grey streets is one of the oldest parts of Durban. The distinctive shopping arcades painted in pastel shades were built during the 1920s by Indian traders, although their residents were evicted in the 1970s. Thankfully, the shops remained and today still sell spices, saris and other Indian goods.

Visitors come for the Victoria Street Market (Mon–Sat 6–6, Sun 10–4) on the corner of Queen and Victoria streets, where curios, fabrics and spices are sold from the stands. Upstairs, don't miss trying a local *bunny chow* curry, a Durban speciality, where a small loaf of bread is hollowed out and filled with spicy curry. Look too for the Jumma Musjid Mosque (Mon–Fri 9–4 but not during prayer times) on Queen and Grey streets. It was built in 1927 and is the largest mosque in the southern hemisphere. If you visit, make sure you are wearing either a long skirt or trousers.

VICTORIA EMBANKMENT

The Victoria Embankment was originally built in 1897 as a grand and desirable residential area facing a stretch of splendid beach. Little of this grandeur remains today, although the high-rise blocks are still interspersed with a few sights of interest. At the eastern end is the ornate late Victorian Da Gama Clock. Nearby, at the intersection of Gardiner Street and the Victoria Embankment, the Dick King Statue commemorates the 1842 epic 10-day ride of local hero Dick King to Grahamstown, to alert British troops there to the plight of Durban,

TIPS
» Do not walk around downtown Durban or along the waterfront after dark, as there is a serious risk of mugging.
» Avoid the area around Point Road and Gillespie Street at any time of the day.
» KwaZulu-Natal Tourism operates a Telitourist cellphone service (☎ 082-2392400) with themed recorded visitor information.

Above *A rickshaw driver at the Waterfront, reflecting the city's Indian influences*
Below *The City Hall rises above its attractive palm-lined setting on Francis Farewell Square*

REGIONS KWAZULU-NATAL • SIGHTS

Above *Fruit stall at Victoria Street Market, opposite the Madressa Arcade*
Above right *Gift items for sale on Durban beachfront*

under siege by Voortrekkers opposing British ambitions. The Durban Club, on the opposite side of the embankment, was built in 1904 and is one of the few original buildings surviving. Coming up to date, the restaurant and shopping development of Wilson's Wharf overlooks the harbour, with shops, restaurants, a theatre and a fish market. The Natal Maritime Museum (Mon–Sat 8.30–4, Sun 11–4), on the docks opposite the junction of Aliwal Street and the Victoria Embankment, offers access to a minesweeper, the SAS *Durban*, and two tugs, the *Ulundi* and the *J. R. More*. Beyond the Maritime Museum is BAT (Bartle Arts Trust) Centre (▷ 182).

THE GOLDEN MILE
Traditionally known as the Golden Mile, the waterfront stretching along Marine Drive feels like a seaside resort, with high-rise hotels lining the promenade. The flea market at the northern end of Lower Marine Parade bustles with stalls selling all kinds of Indian snacks and curios, while extravagantly dressed rickshaw drivers wait to pick up visitors. The beaches here are divided into areas designated for surfing, body boarding and swimming; all are protected with shark nets.

BEREA
This residential district, to the west of the City Centre, is one of Durban's oldest and most prosperous. On Sydenham Road, in Upper Berea, are the Botanic Gardens (tel 031-3224000; www.durbanbotanicgardens.org.za; daily 7.30–5.15), founded in 1849, supposedly the oldest botanical gardens in Africa. They cover almost 15ha (37 acres) and are a classic example of a Victorian botanical garden. There are some impressive avenues of palms crossing the park, an ornamental lake, and good displays of orchids and cycads. The tea garden (Tue–Sun 9–4, Mon 10–4) is a pleasant place to relax. The KwaZulu-Natal Philharmonic Orchestra performs by the lake on Sundays during the summer.

USHAKA MARINE WORLD
www.ushakamarineworld.co.za
Opened in 2004, this enormous water park has a wide selection of exhibits and rides. The park is split into three areas: uShaka Sea World is an impressive underground aquarium; uShaka Wet 'n' Wild World has waterslides and rides; and uShaka Village walk is a retail village filled with shops and restaurants. The highlight is the Phantom Ship, where visitors walk through glass tunnels surrounded by ragged-tooth sharks and game fish. Each corridor has a different theme, and there are various presentations throughout the day in pools surrounding the ship.
✉ 1 Bell Street, Point 4001 ☎ 031-3288000 🕒 Daily 9–5; Wet 'n' Wild closed Apr–Oct Mon–Tue 🖐 Sea World and Wet 'n' Wild: adult R99, child (under 16) R75 (combined ticket adult R130, child R99)

HLUHLUWE-IMFOLOZI GAME RESERVE

This is one of Africa's oldest game reserves. The landscapes encompass thick forests, dry bushveld and open savannah. What is unusual about the park is its hilly terrain, which provides great vantage points for game viewing. An extensive network of dirt roads can easily be negotiated in a standard rented car. There are hides at Mphafa and Thiyeni waterholes, but much of the best game viewing is from the road. Good areas are the Sontuli Loop, the corridor connecting Imfolozi to Hluhluwe and the areas around the Hluhluwe River. There are several camps within the park, with a mix of accommodation.

WILDLIFE

The wide range of habitats supports numbers of big game, with large populations of both white and black rhino and nyala (a large antelope). Hluhluwe is the northern sector of the reserve, with a hilly and wooded landscape where elephants are often seen around the dam. There are some areas of savanna in this sector where white rhino and giraffe may be spotted feeding. The park was the birthplace of 'Operation Rhino' in the 1960s, set up to save the endangered white rhino. There has been a growth in the population from around 500 in the 1950s to 6,000 today. Imfolozi, in the south, is characterized by thornveld, savannah areas of thorny bush and acacia trees, and semi-desert, and the grasslands here support impala, kudu, waterbuck, giraffe, blue wildebeest and zebra. Predators are much less easily seen but cheetah, lion, leopard and wild dog are all present.

HIKING IN THE RESERVE

One of the most exciting ways to see wildlife here is on foot. Although it can be less spectacular than viewing from a car, the experience is somehow more intense—little can compare with the excitement of tracking a rhino through the wilderness. Places on guided walks can be reserved at the camp offices; there are two daily walks with a game guard from Hilltop and Mpila camps lasting two to three hours; children under 13 are not allowed. There are also two self-guided walks, and six overnight wilderness trails (in the company of guides) in the southern section of the park.

INFORMATION

www.kznwildlife.com

⊞ 331 N6 ☎ 033-8451000

🕐 Nov–Feb daily 5am–7pm; Mar–Oct 6–6 ✋ Adult R120, child (3–12) R45

🎫 Souvenir shops selling gifts and books about natural history at Masinda and Mpila Camps; small supermarket near Hluhluwe gates 🍴 Restaurant in Hluhluwe section 🚙 Game drives R250; guided game walks R200 🚌 Turning off N2, at Mtubatuba leading west on the R618 (50km/30 miles) to the Imfolozi entrance, or turning opposite the exit to Hluhluwe village, which leads (14km/8.5 miles) to the northern Memorial Gate entrance

TIPS

» The best time to see the reserve is between March and November, when the climate is cool and dry and it's easier to spot game around waterholes and rivers.

» The park makes an easy day trip from Maputaland (▷ 172) or the St. Lucia region.

» There are two entrances, one at Imfolozi and the other at Hluhluwe.

Below *A white rhino with her calf*

REGIONS KWAZULU-NATAL • SIGHTS

ISIMANGALISO WETLAND PARK

INFORMATION

www.isimangaliso.com
www.kznwildlife.com

✚ 331 N6 ℹ St. Lucia office of KZN
Wildlife, Mckenzie Street, St. Lucia
☎ 035 5901676 🕒 Daily 8–4.30

INTRODUCTION

The protected area of the iSimangaliso Wetland Park (formerly the Greater St. Lucia Wetland Park) is the largest estuarine lake system in Africa, with a great variety of flora and fauna. It covers a number of formerly separate nature reserves and state forests, still referred to locally under a collection of old and new names. The entire reserve, covering 3,280sq km (1,280sq miles), starts south of the St. Lucia Estuary and stretches north to the border with Mozambique, and includes ecosystems ranging from vegetated sand dunes and papyrus wetlands to sandy beaches and dry savannah. Most people come here specifically to see the hippos and Nile crocodiles, and the best base for doing this is the town of St. Lucia itself.

St. Lucia was named by the Portuguese explorer Manuel Perestrello in 1575, although European influence in the area was minimal until the 1850s. Up to that time the area was inhabited by a relatively large population of Thongas and Zulus who herded cattle and cultivated the land. Professional hunters began visiting the lake in the 1850s in search of ivory, hides and horns. So successful were they that within 50 years the last elephant in this region had been shot. However, Lake St. Lucia, along with Hluhluwe and Imfolozi was one of the first game reserves to be established in Africa, in 1895. In 1975, the Greater St. Lucia Wetland region was declared, and many conservation initiatives were introduced when St. Lucia won World Heritage status in 1999. In spite of ongoing measures to protect the area, the survival of the lake system has been under constant threat, both from agriculture and the planting of pine forests. The latter are slowly being removed to allow indigenous trees to regrow, and the lake is regularly dredged to prevent it from silting up.

A great way of taking in the reserve and spotting wildlife is actually on the waters of the estuary, aboard a launch (▷ 171). Cape Vidal, 32km (20 miles) north of St. Lucia town, is a particularly rewarding area (note that there is a daily limit on the number of cars allowed on Cape Vidal). It is possible to overnight at

Above *White pelicans are a common sight here*

a number of camps with kitchens throughout the park, including Cape Vidal and False Bay, but reservations must be made in advance. There are also plenty of accommodation options in the town of St. Lucia.

WHAT TO SEE
BIRDS GALORE
A staggering 420 bird species have been recorded in the reserve. In addition to the species found year round in the dune forests and grasslands, there are also many unusual migrant birds. The most commonly seen include pink-backed and white pelicans, greater and lesser flamingos, ducks, spoonbills and ibises. The pelicans arrive every autumn to feed on migrating mullet in the Narrows, north of St. Lucia. At any one time, you might see 6,000 pelicans nesting at the northern end of the lake.

ST. LUCIA RESORT AND ESTUARY NATIONAL PARKS
St. Lucia Estuary, next to the town of St. Lucia, is the gateway to the eastern shores of Lake St. Lucia, with extensive wetland systems and coastal grasslands. There are 12km (7 miles) of self-guided trails, a network extending from the Indian Ocean to the estuary and crossing various habitats—dune forest, grasslands, mangrove swamps. The trail leading from the Crocodile Centre to the estuary takes in some good hippo-viewing spots. The Crocodile Centre (tel 035-5901386; Mon–Fri 8–4, Sat 8.30–5, Sun 9–4) is next to the entrance gate to Cape Vidal; it has displays highlighting the important role that crocodiles play in the ecosystem.

LAUNCH TOURS
You can spot wildlife in comfort aboard the *Santa Lucia,* an 80-seater launch which departs from next to the bridge on the west side of the St. Lucia Estuary. The tours last for 90 minutes and travel up the estuary past thick banks of vegetation as far as the Narrows, allowing plenty of chances to see hippos and crocodiles as well as birdlife.

☎ 035-5901340 🕐 Daily tours at 8.30, 10.30, 2.30 ✋ Adult R130, child (under 15) R65

CAPE VIDAL
Cape Vidal, 33km (20 miles) north of St. Lucia town, is the most striking zone in the reserve. It is an area of vegetated dunes along what must be one of the most spectacular beaches in KwaZulu-Natal, with pure white sand lapped by the warm Indian Ocean. The rocks just off the beach teem with tropical fish and the shallow water is safe to snorkel in. In winter, look for humpback whales, which breed to the north. Thanks to the daily limit on cars that can enter Cape Vidal, the beach is never crowded, and although the area is popular with anglers, this too is restricted, with many fish on a tag and release system. There are a couple of self-guided trails you can follow across the dunes.

☎ 035-5909012 🕐 Gates open Oct–Mar 5am–7pm, Apr–Sep 6–6; office hours 7–6 ✋ Adult and child R20 🏧

MORE TO SEE
FALSE BAY
Lying on the western shores of the estuary, this reserve is less visited than St. Lucia but is a good place to see flamingo and pink-backed pelican during the breeding season from December to April. The surrounding sand forests are similar to Mkhuze Game Reserve (▷ 172) and are inhabited by the rare suni and nyala antelopes, while the banks and marshlands along the Hluhluwe River are rich in birdlife.

✚ 331 N6 ☎ 035-5620425 🕐 Oct–Mar daily 5am–8pm; Apr–Sep 6am–8pm ✋ Adult R25, child (3–12) R13 🚌 From the N2, take the turning to Hluhluwe village, then continue for 15km (9 miles) to the park

TIPS
» The turtle season runs from November to March. Tours to see the protected loggerhead and leatherback turtles laying their eggs are run by Shaka Barker Tours (☎ 035-5901162; www.shakabarker. co.za).
» Keep an eye out for smaller mammals like duiker, warthog, and dassies (rock hyraxes), which are easily missed.
» While hiking around the lake watch out for hippos, snakes and crocodiles.
» When swimming stay away from the estuary, which is inhabited by crocodiles and Zambezi sharks. Look out for for no-swimming signs.
» St. Lucia is a low-risk malarial area and preventive medication must be taken.

Below A preening spoonbill at the edge of the lake

LAKE SIBAYA

Lake Sibaya is the largest freshwater lake in South Africa and was previously connected to the sea. A long strip of thickly forested dunes now runs between the lake and the Indian Ocean. The tropical birdlife is Lake Sibaya's main attraction, with swampy reedbeds and patches of forest providing varied habitats for the many species. Kingfishers, cormorants and fish eagles hunt in the lake, and hippos and crocodiles can also be seen.

✚ 331 N5

LALA NECK

In the northern reaches of the KwaZulu-Natal coast, these secluded beaches are only accessible by 4WD vehicles. They are renowned for being the ultimate game-fishing destinations, but also have clear waters that offer spectacular snorkelling and diving, with good chances of seeing turtles and sharks as well as hundreds of tropical fish. There are no facilities and the only viable way of visiting is by staying at the lodge here.

✚ 331 P5 🛈 Rocktail Bay Lodge, 12km (7.5 miles) north of Manzengwenya along a dirt track running parallel with the beach ☎ 011-2575111 🖐 R20 per vehicle plus R15 per person

MAPUTALAND

www.elephantcoast.kzn.org.za
The region of Maputaland, named after the Maputa River, which flows through southern Mozambique, covers an area of 9,000sq km (3,500sq miles) stretching from Lake St. Lucia to the Mozambique border, and west from the Indian Ocean to the Lebombo Mountains. One of South Africa's least developed regions, Maputaland still seems traditionally African. The land is unsuitable for intensive modern agriculture and the small farmsteads dotting the landscape are connected by a rough network of roads.

The region is part of the huge St. Lucia-Maputaland Biosphere that encompasses iSimangaliso Wetland Park (▷ 170–171) and a number of

smaller regional game reserves up to and including Hluhluwe-Imfolozi (▷ 169). The climate varies from tropical in the north to subtropical in the south and this has created a diverse range of ecosystems. Maputaland's features include South Africa's largest freshwater lake (▷ Lake Sibaya, above), mangrove swamps, coral reefs, dune forest, riverine forest and savannah.

The Ndumo Game Reserve (▷ 173) and Tembe Elephant Park (▷ 175) in the far north of the region are now part of the Ndumo-Tembe-Futi Transfrontier Conservation Area (known as the Futi Corridor). Taking down fences between the reserves has greatly increased the extent of elephant habitat in the region and linked the two parks with Maputo Special Reserve, across the border in Mozambique.

✚ 331 N5 🛈 Hluhluwe Tourism Association, Engen Garage, Hluhluwe 3960 ☎ 035-5620353 🕐 Mon–Fri 8.30–5, Sat–Sun 9–1

MKHUZE GAME RESERVE

www.kznwildlife.com
This reserve, covering 36,000ha (89,000 acres), has landscapes of open grasslands, dense forests, coastal dunes and pans. The area to the north is tropical, whereas the southern part is temperate. Not visited as often as Hluhluwe-Imfolozi because it has fewer rhinos,

Mkhuze has the advantage of being less crowded, and there are good opportunities to see some of Maputaland's more unusual animals, such as the shy nyala antelope. It is also an ideal place to see big game—elephant, giraffe, blue wildebeest, eland, kudu, both black and white rhino, cheetah, leopard and hyena are all present. As part of the Mozambique coastal plain, Mkhuze attracts many tropical birds that are usually only seen farther north: More than 450 species have been recorded here.

A network of roads totalling about 100km (60 miles) crosses the reserve. The best game-viewing areas are the Loop Road, the Nsumo Pan and the airstrip. The Fig Forest Trail (3km/5 miles long, and next to Nsumo Pan) is a self-guided trail traversing one of the last surviving areas of fig tree forest in South Africa. The atmosphere of the forest is magical, as you pass between fig trees reaching 25m (82ft) in height, with girths of 12m (40ft). There is a luxury lodge as well as several camps within the reserve.

✚ 331 N6 ☎ 035-5739001 🕐 Oct–Mar daily 5am–7pm; Apr–Sep 6–6 🖐 Adult R40, child (under 12) R20, plus R30 per vehicle 🚌 🚗 20km (12 miles) along a dirt road from Mkhuze, or off N2 (clearly signposted)

Below Nyala antelope, with their distinctive white stripes, grazing in Mkhuze Reserve

on five different guided walks with a game ranger and there is a KZN camp within the reserve.

✚ 331 N5 ☎ 035-5910058 🕐 Gates: Oct–Mar daily 5am–7pm; Apr–Sep 6–6; office: daily 8–12, 2–4 💷 Adult R60, child (under 12) R30; guided walks: adult R100, child; R50; game drives: adult R200, child R100 🚌 14km (8.5 miles) beyond the village of Ndumo on a rough dirt road

ORIBI GORGE NATURE RESERVE
www.kznwildlife.com
This reserve was established in 1950 to protect an area of thick woodland and towering cliffs where the Umzimkulu and Umzimkulweni rivers meet. It's a popular spot for forest walks, and the ravines and waterfalls are good places for adrenaline-pumping sports activities such as abseiling or white-water rafting (▷ 183). The most spectacular waterfalls within the park are the Samango Falls, Hoopoe Falls and Lehr's Falls.

There are impressive views from the top of the sandstone cliffs, some of which are as much as 280m (920ft) high, and they provide nesting sites for birds of prey. The forest is home to the African python. The vegetation is so dense that although leopards are thought to live here they are never seen, but you can sometimes glimpse small groups of one of the animals on which the leopards prey, the Samango monkey. Birdlife is prolific and this is a good place to see forest species such as the Knysna lourie, grass owl and five different species of kingfisher.

There are a number of clearly marked hikes and paths lead to impressive viewpoints above the gorge. Do not be tempted to swim in the river as there is bilharzia (▷ 290) in the water.

✚ 331 L8 ☎ 039-6791644 🕐 Reserve: daily 6.30am–7.30pm 💷 Adult R10, child (under 12) R5 🏪 Camp shop sells wildlife books, souvenirs, charcoal, firewood and a limited range of food 🚌 21km (13.5 miles) west of Port Shepstone via N2

THE NATAL MIDLANDS
In the region encompassing the towns of Greytown, Richmond, Pietermaritzburg (▷ 174) and Estcourt, the many rivers flowing off the Drakensberg escarpment have created a well-watered fertile landscape. It originally supported a large population of Zulu cattle herders and farmers in the lowlands. San migrated between here and the Drakensberg, following the herds of eland according to the changes of the seasons.

Later the fertile territory attracted first the Voortrekkers and then British immigrants in the 1850s, who all fought for control of the land. It is still predominantly a rural, agricultural area; there are farms cultivating wattle for tanning and paper pulp, cattle and sheep ranches, and studs for horse breeding.

The N3 bisects the Midlands and the majority of traffic simply passes through on its way between Gauteng and Durban. However, by taking the alternative R103, the Midlands towns and countryside can be explored at leisure. This is the Midlands Meander route, a visitor initiative reminiscent of a Sunday afternoon drive through English countryside, highlighting the multitude of craft outlets, country restaurants and rural retreats in the region. For information about the

Meander, tel 033-3308195 or visit www.midlandsmeander.co.za.
✚ 331 L7

NDUMO GAME RESERVE
www.kznwildlife.com
Ndumo, hugging the Usutu River along the Mozambique border, is a low-lying, humid, tropical floodplain renowned for its magnificent birdlife and large numbers of crocodiles and hippos. It is one of the wildest reserves in South Africa and its verdant wetlands have been compared with the Okavango Delta in Botswana.

The pans at Nyamithi and Banzi are ideal areas for experiencing an African tropical swamp. Thousands of birds congregate here in the evenings and it is possible to see flocks of flamingos, geese, pelicans and storks. Buffalo are also occasionally seen in the swampy areas of the reserve, but nyala, hippos and crocodiles are present in large numbers. Black and white rhino, leopard and suni antelope thrive in these thickets, but you would be lucky to see them.

The reserve's roads are in good condition and you can drive around in your own car, or travel by 4WD with a guide. One of the best ways to see Ndumo is on one of the tours organized by the reserve. You can go

INFORMATION

www.pmbtourism.co.za

🚉 331 M7 🛈 Pietermaritzburg Tourism, 177 Commercial Road, Pietermaritzburg 3201 ☎ 033-3451348 🕐 Mon–Fri 8–5, Sat 8–1

TIPS

» Cricket fans and Anglophiles may want to visit Alexandra Park for its splendid Victorian cricket pavilion dating from 1898.

» The warm, dry climate is more pleasant than Durban's humidity, but note that there is heavy rainfall from December to February.

PIETERMARITZBURG

Pietermaritzburg is the joint capital, with Ulundi, of KwaZulu-Natal. This attractive city dates from the late 19th century when it was the capital of the Colony of Natal (Natalia) and was named after the Voortrekker leaders Piet Retief and Gert Maritz. Today, Pietermaritzburg's red-brick buildings and town parks evoke many an English provincial city and it's a pleasant place to stroll around. It is an important trading hub for the local farming industry and is home to a campus of the University of KwaZulu-Natal and many other technical colleges. The city is an intriguing mix of Zulu, Indian, British influences, and during the school term has a bustling, youthful feel with a lively nightlife.

COLONIAL PIETERMARITZBURG

In the heart of the city are its finest Victorian buildings, civic gardens and war memorials. The City Hall, on the corner of Chief Albert Luthuli Road and Church Street, was built in 1900 and is said to be the largest all-brick building in the southern hemisphere and is decorated with stained-glass windows. Opposite is the Tatham Art Gallery (tel 033-3922801; Tue–Sun 10–6), which has exhibitions of French and British 19th-century art as well as an innovative collection of contemporary art. On the same block are the Supreme Court Gardens, filled with war memorials. The old Colonial Building, 100m (110 yards) farther on, was built in 1899; in front of it is a statue of Mahatma Gandhi, commemorating his arrival in South Africa in 1893. The Presbyterian Church (1852), opposite the Colonial Building, was the first British church in Pietermaritzburg. The Lanes, a network of alleyways between Langalibalele Street and Church Street, are lined with small shops and cafés.

THE MUSEUMS

The Voortrekker Museum (tel 033-3946834; www.voortrekkermuseum.co.za; Mon–Fri 9–4, Sat 9–1) on Langalibalele Street, has a collection of period farm machinery, furniture and other everyday objects. There are also newer and more culturally significant exhibitions about Zulu heritage. The Natal Museum (tel 033-3451404; www.nmsa.org.za; Mon–Fri 8.15–4.30, Sat 9–4, Sun 10–3) in Jabu Ndlova Street has a natural history gallery that includes the last wild elephant shot in Natal, in 1911. Also in Jabu Ndlova Street, at No. 11, is the Macrorie House Museum (tel 033-3942161; Mon 11–4, Tue–Sat 9–1), with period furniture and a collection of Victorian costumes.

Above *A statue of Gandhi commemorates his arrival in South Africa in 1893*

SODWANA BAY

www.kznwildlife.com

Sodwana Bay is South Africa's premier scuba-diving destination. It has the world's southernmost tropical reefs, and around 80 per cent of South Africa's 1,200 species of fish can be found here. There are numerous dive sites to explore and anemones, triggerfish, sponges and fan-shaped gorgoniums can be seen in this area of overhangs and caves. Ragged-tooth and whale sharks, humpback whales, dolphins and turtles are other major attractions. Although Sodwana is popular with visitors throughout the year, divers prefer April to September, while fishermen come here in November and December. Sodwana is extremely busy during the school holidays (December and January), and it's preferable to avoid visiting during these times if you can.

✚ 331 P5 ☎ 035-5710051 ⏰ Gates open 24 hours 👤 Adult R20, child (3–15) R10 🅿 🚗 On N2 from the south, take Ngwenya/Sodwana Bay exit. From the north, take the turning to Jozini and Mbazana. Follow the tarred road to Sodwana Bay (120km/75 miles)

TEMBE ELEPHANT PARK

www.tembe.co.za

Tembe was established in 1983 to protect the area's elephants. The present herd of around 500 is thought to be the only indigenous elephant herd in KwaZulu-Natal. Other species in the park include lion, giraffe, black rhino, white rhino and buffalo. In addition to those who stay overnight in the luxury lodge in the park a further five groups of day visitors in 4WD vehicles are allowed in daily. All groups must be accompanied by a ranger, but there is a self-guided walk within the Ngobazane enclosure area.

✚ 331 N5 ☎ 031-2670144 ⏰ Oct–Mar daily 5am–7pm; Apr–Sep 6–6 👤 Adult R35, child (under 12) R18, plus R35 per vehicle 🚗 72km (45 miles) from Jozini, off N2. If you are staying at the luxury lodge (the only accommodation within the park), you can leave your car at the gate and arrange for a 4WD transfer (tel 031-2670144)

UKHAHLAMBA-DRAKENSBERG PARK

▷ 176–179.

UMHLANGA ROCKS

www.umhlanga-rocks.com

This classy resort lies a short drive north of Durban and is now virtually a suburb. There is a good beach, and Umhlanga Rocks' main attraction is the beach's relative safety compared to Durban's waterfront. Also worth a visit is the Sharks Board (tel 031-5660400; www.shark.co.za; Mon–Fri 8–4), on Herrwood Drive, which studies the life cycles of local sharks and investigates how best to protect both them and swimmers. Umhlanga Rocks became the first beach in South Africa to have shark nets erected in 1962 following a series of attacks along the coast. Today the Board is responsible for looking after more than 400 nets, protecting nearly 50 beaches. Tours begin with a 25-minute video followed by a shark dissection (held on Tue, Wed, Thu at 9 and 2, Sun at 2).

✚ 331 M7 ℹ Sugar Coast Tourism, Chartwell Drive, Umhlanga Rocks 4319 ☎ 031-5614257 ⏰ Mon–Fri 8–4.30, Sat 9–12

UMTAMVUNA NATURE RESERVE

This is the southernmost and one of the less visited reserves in KwaZulu-Natal, but it is worth visiting for the fantastic day-long hikes down into a sandstone gorge. The sheer walls of lichen-covered rock, dropping down into thick rainforest, are the focal point of this dramatic landscape. There is no big game here: The reserve is known best for its wild flowers in spring and is regarded as one of the world's top plant spots. One particular shrub, *Raspalia trigyna*, is extremely rare and unique to Umtamvuna. Look out, too, for the colony of Cape vultures that inhabit the area.

✚ 329 L8 ☎ 039-3112383 ⏰ Daily 6.30–5.30 👤 R15 per person 🚗 8km (5 miles) north of Port Edward towards Izingolweni ❓ Map, bird checklist and information leaflets available at the entrance

ZULULAND

www.zululand.kzn.org.za

For many visitors, Zululand—homeland of King Shaka early in the 19th century—is South Africa's most evocative area. Extending from the northern bank of the Tugela River up to Mkhuze and Maputaland, it holds some of the country's most popular reserves, including the iSimangaliso Wetland Park (▷ 170–171) and Hluhluwe-Imfolozi (▷ 169).

The gateway to Zululand is the town of Eshowe, which originally surrounded the *kraals* (huts) of the Zulu king Cetshwayo. Look for the Zululand Historical Museum on Fort Nongqai Road (tel 035-4741147; Mon–Fri 7.30–4), and the Vukani Collection Museum (tel 035-4745274; daily 7–4), one of the largest collections of Zulu art in existence. The rather touristy Shakaland theme park (▷ 185) is 14km (9 miles) north of here, providing a glimpse (perhaps not authentic) of Zulu culture. To the west lies the Battlefields Route (▷ 164–165). On the coast is Mtunzini, a pleasant resort, once home to John Dunn who, in the 19th century, became a Zulu chief—he had 49 wives and fathered 117 children. The second largest town in the state is Richard's Bay, an industrial port. To its north is St. Lucia.

✚ 331 N6

Below *The gateway to Shakaland theme park in Zululand*

INFORMATION

www.drakensberg.za.org
www.kznwildlife.com
www.cdic.co.za

⊞ 330 L7 🚹 Drakensberg Tourism
Association, library building on Thatham
Road, Bergville ☎ 036-4481244
🕐 Mon–Fri 7.30–4, Sat 9–12 🚹 Central
Drakensberg Information Centre, on the
R600, 13km (8 miles) west of Winterton
☎ 036-4881988 🕐 Daily 9–5

Above *Riders in the Giant's Castle game
reserve are dwarfed by the bulk of
Champagne Castle*

INTRODUCTION

The Drakensberg Mountains rise to more than 3,000m (10,000ft) and extend
180km (112 miles) along the western edge of KwaZulu-Natal, forming the
backbone of what is today known as the uKhahlamba-Drakensberg Park (and
also part of South Africa's border with Lesotho). The main reason for coming to
the Drakensberg is for its superb walking. Almost the entire range falls within
protected reserves managed by the conservation body KZN Wildlife (www.
kznwildlife.com). They have a series of comprehensive maps, available from
KZN Wildlife offices. Overnight hikers should read their brochure, *It's Tough at
the Top—Hiking Safely in the Drakensberg*. The Maloti-Drakensberg Transfrontier
Conservation Area initiative is presently being established, which will link the
park with the Sehlaba-Thebe National Park in Lesotho.

The earliest human inhabitants of the Drakensberg were the hunter-gatherers,
the San. They left their imprint on the landscape in numerous rock shelters
and paintings of hunting scenes—and this is the best part of the country to
see San rock art—but came under increasing pressure towards the end of the
18th century as new settlers established themselves. Their numbers declined
dramatically, and the last records of San being seen in the Drakensberg date
from 1878. The Drakensberg's natural resources were exploited by the settlers,
which had terrible long-term effects on the ecosystem. This gave the impetus
for the creation of the National Park, and in 2001 it became a UNESCO World
Heritage Site in recognition of its universal environmental value to mankind.

If you are visiting the Central Drakensberg (the Cathedral Peak or Monk's
Cowl areas), the village of Winterton is your last chance to pick up supplies for

your trip. The small market town of Underberg is the main service point for the southern Drakensberg, and visitors will find it an ideal springboard for trips into the mountains.

May to September is the best time to visit, as the weather is dry and still fairly warm (although there is still snow on the highest peaks). Summers are wet and hot. There is no proper public transport network, so you will need to rent a car to get the most out of the area. For those on a budget, the Baz Bus (▷ 52) runs through the Drakensberg three times a week.

WHAT TO SEE

ROYAL NATAL NATIONAL PARK
www.kznwildlife.com

The Royal Natal National Park is the most popular of all the resorts in the Drakensberg, and is famous for its magnificent scenery: You'll remember your first view of the massive rock walls that form the Amphitheatre, a cliff face arching northwards for 4km (2.5 miles) from the Eastern Buttress (3,047m/9,997ft) towards the Sentinel (3,165m/10,381ft). On the plateau behind the Amphitheatre is Mont-aux-Sources (3,282m/10,768ft). This mountain is the source of five rivers, the most impressive of which is the Tugela, which plunges over the edge of the Amphitheatre wall, dropping about 800m (2,500ft) through a series of five falls. The gorge created by the falls is a steep-sided tangle of boulders and trees; at one point it bores straight through the sandstone to form a long tunnel.

There are more than 130km (80 miles) of walking trails around the park, many of which are half-day strolls that can easily be combined with a drive. Hikes are either climbs to the top of the escarpment or gentle meanders through a countryside of grassland dotted with yellowwood forests, set against the stunning backdrop of the Amphitheatre. Among the most popular hikes are the climb to Mont-aux-Sources (20km/12 miles), a round-trip in Tugela Gorge and a hike to Cannibal Cave (8km/5 miles). There's one camp with huts and two campsites within the park (▷ 191).

🞤 330 K6 ☎ 036-4386310 🕔 Oct–Mar daily 5am–7pm; Apr–Sep 6–6; office and Visitor Centre daily 8–12.30, 2–4 🖐 Adult R25, child (3–13) R13, or adult R50, child R25 with a visit to the San Rock Art Centre; vehicles to Mike's Pass R50 🔲 KZN Visitor Centre sells hiking maps and a leaflet describing walks around the park 🚻 🚌 Access via N2

CATHEDRAL PEAK

Cathedral Peak is the main point of access to some of the wildest areas of the Central Drakensberg. It's a peaceful yet dramatic spot, with views of soaring peaks. The sheltered valleys, one of the last refuges of the San in the Drakensberg, have large numbers of cave painting sites (guided tours only, arranged through the San Rock Art Centre at Didima Camp, just past the entrance to the park; tel 036-4888025; daily 8–1, 2–4). This thatched building also holds displays interpreting the rock art. Leopards Cave and Poachers Cave in the Ndedema Gorge have especially fine paintings.

There is a network of paths heading up the Mlambonja Valley to the escarpment, from where there are trails south to Monk's Cowl (▷ 178) and Injasuti or north to Royal Natal National Park. The hike of 10km (6 miles) to the top of Cathedral Peak (3,004m/9,853ft) is one of the most exciting and strenuous in the area—the views of the Drakensberg to the north and south are unforgettable. The campsite at Mike's Pass, or the two hotels there, are good bases for exploring the area. An alternative to hiking is to drive up Mike's Pass, from where there are views of the Little Berg.

🞤 330 L7 ☎ 036-4888000 🕔 Reception office at Mike's Pass: 7–7 🖐 Adult R20, child (under 15) R10; vehicles to Mike's Pass: adult R50, child R25 to include visit to San Rock Art Centre at Didima Camp 🚻 🚌 Signposted from Bergville and Winterton; some parts of the road are unsurfaced

Above *Sterkspruit Falls at Monk's Cowl in the Drakensberg*
Below *Looking up at the bare rock face of the Devil's Tooth in Royal Natal National Park*

REGIONS KWAZULU-NATAL • SIGHTS

TIPS

» Carry your passport with you at all times; in the High Berg it is easy to stray into Lesotho and guards patrol the border area.

» Entry fees are included in the cost of accommodation within the parks; only day visitors will have to pay fees at the gate.

» The Drakensberg peaks are becoming a top draw for mountain climbers. For information about climbing here, contact the Mountain Club of South Africa (tel 021-4653412; www.mcsa.org.za).

» Although there are some shops within camps, supplies are limited and expensive: It's best to stock up beforehand in one of the surrounding towns.

Below *The landscapes of the Drakensberg acquire a dreamy quality at sunset*

MONK'S COWL

www.kznwildlife.com

The road to Monk's Cowl, in the Central Berg, passes through one of the most developed areas in the region just outside the Drakensberg. Peppered with luxury hotels, golf courses and timeshare developments, it has been dubbed 'Champagne Valley' by locals. Champagne Castle, Monk's Cowl and Cathkin Peak are impressive features in the landscape, and several superb long-distance hikes begin from the valley (including the two-day hike up to Champagne Castle). The short hikes, ranging from one to six hours, get relatively busy, as they attract many day-trippers, especially at weekends. All the routes can be easily accessed: A map of the area is available from the park office and the paths are clear and well signposted.

➕ 330 L7 ☎ 036-4681103 🧭 Park gates: Oct–Mar daily 5am–7pm; Apr–Sep 6–6; office: daily 8–12.30, 2–4.30 ✋ Adult R35, child (3–15) R18 🚌 End of R600 from Winterton

GIANT'S CASTLE

The reserve was established in 1903, when there were a mere 200 eland left in the whole of KwaZulu-Natal, and its formation was successful in helping the eland population to recover. The main camp has one of the most spectacular settings in the region, with the Drakensberg escarpment towering magnificently above it. A wall of basalt cliffs rises higher than 3,000m (10,000ft), and the peaks of Giant's Castle (3,314m/10,870ft), Champagne Castle (3,248m/10,653ft) and Cathkin Peak (3,149m/10,329ft) can be seen on the skyline. The grasslands beneath the cliffs roll out in a series of massive undulating hills, which give rise to the Bushman's River and the Little Tugela River.

The area around the camp has a network of short, easily accessed footpaths through riverine forest, but for more ambitious hikers, who want to get off the beaten track, there are also numerous interconnected hikes of up to three days duration crossing the reserve.

➕ 330 L7 ☎ 036-3533718 🕐 Park gates: Oct–Mar 5am–7pm, Apr–Sep 6–6; camp office: daily 8–4 ✋ Adult R25, child (under 3–13) R13 📖 Hiking trail details available from camp office 🏢 🚌 Signposted from Estcourt (65km/40 miles) on N3

SANI PASS

The road from Himeville to Sani Pass rises steadily through rolling hills until it passes the Sani Top Chalet hotel (▷ 280), when the towering peaks on the escarpment come into view. This is the only road leading into Lesotho on its eastern border with South Africa, and a 4WD vehicle is needed to make the ascent (a project to tar the road is ongoing; ▷ 185). The road is one of the most dramatic in Africa, and the top of the pass is so high that it has a distinct alpine climate. The most rewarding hike in this area is the one-day climb up to the top of Sani Pass at 2,874m (9,427ft), but there are also shorter hikes. There are full border formalities when you cross into Lesotho, so bring your passport with you.

➕ 330 L7 🕐 South African border post: daily 8–4; Lesotho border post: daily 8–4

SAN ROCK PAINTINGS AT KAMBERG

www.kznwildlife.com

The sandstone caves and rock shelters of the Drakensberg are among the best places to see San rock art. Hundreds of individual sites have been identified, but Kamberg and Giant's Castle have the most accessible caves. Although the majority of surviving paintings are fairly recent—some 200 to 300 years old— they form part of an ancient tradition and some of the earliest cave paintings in southern Africa date from 28,000 years ago. Kamberg's San Rock Art Centre gives visitors an insight into the lifestyle of the San. There's a guided walk of two to three hours to the Game Pass Shelter and its impressive array of paintings. Tours must be reserved in advance (tel 033-2637251).

➕ 330 L7 🕐 Park gates: Oct–Mar 5am–7pm; Apr–Sep 6–6; office: daily 8–11.30, 2–3.30 ✋ Adult R28, child (under 12) R15 🚶 Guided tours to Game Pass shelter cost R50 per person and depart at 8, 11, 12.30 and 1.30 🚌 Turn off the N3 highway towards Nottingham Road and follow signposts to Kamberg (48km/30 miles along the Loteni road). The last 19km (12 miles) are on a gravel road

SPIOENKOP DAM NATURE RESERVE

www.kznwildlife.com

This game park focuses on the site of the Spioenkop battlefield, where the British were defeated by the Boers on 23 January 1890. The battlefield overlooks the dam and there is a self-guided trail to the site. You will have a good chance of seeing white rhino, buffalo, giraffe, kudu, impala and zebra.

➕ 330 L6 ☎ 036-4881578 🕐 Oct–Mar 6am–7pm; Apr–Sep 6–6 ✋ Adult R20, child (under 12) R10 🚌 14km (8.5 miles) north of Winterton on R600

MORE TO SEE

DRAKENSBERG BOYS' CHOIR

The Drakensberg Boys' Choir, based at a school on the R600 towards Monk's Cowl, is Africa's best-known choir. It has sung all over the world in the last three decades, including in front of 25,000 people at the Vatican City. It is possible to see the Choir perform during term time on Wednesdays at 3.30 in the school auditorium. Reservations are essential (tel 036-4681012; www.dbchoir.info).

HIMEVILLE

Himeville, north of Underberg, is a small, prosperous village with an English air to it. Arbuckle Street runs through its heart, and there's a small museum in the old fort and prison (Tue–Sun 8.30–12.30).

➕ 330 L7

HIKING

Hiking in the High Berg, which contains all the great peaks, requires a high degree of fitness; exploring the equally remote and empty Little Berg requires only average levels of fitness. For longer hikes, it is essential to plan ahead, as you have to be completely self-sufficient, and places in overnight caves (a popular accommodation choice) and mountain huts must be reserved in advance. Guided hikes are a good idea for the less experienced. Permits are necessary on all but the shortest walks and are available from camp offices for a small fee.

Below *On horseback is a good way to explore the Drakensberg*

THE TUGELA RIVER

The Royal Natal National Park (▷ 177; ✚ 330 K6) has some of South Africa's most spectacular scenery—with mountain slopes, thickly forested valleys and rolling grasslands—all watched over by the massive grandeur of the Amphitheatre, one of the best-known features of the northern Drakensberg. This walk, which follows the course of the upper Tugela River is one of the most rewarding hikes in the park.

THE WALK
Distance: 14km (8.7 miles)
Allow: 6 hours
Start/end at: Thendele Camp

★ Start the hike at the Thendele Camp parking area. The walk heads southwest, directly towards the Amphitheatre and its falls, following the river (or riverbed, if the rains have been poor). There are clear signs along the path to the gorge. The path follows the contours of the slope above the river, meandering through protea grassland and patches of yellowwood forest, which provide welcome respite from the sun.

❶ You'll have views of a number of notable Drakensberg peaks along the walk. The main peak, Mont-aux-Sources, rises to 3,282m (10,768ft). Others are the Sentinel (3,165m/10,812ft), the Eastern Buttress (3,047m/ 9,997ft) and the detached peak of Devil's Tooth, one of the region's hardest ascents, which wasn't climbed until 1950.

The path has a few minor ascents and descents and in due course opens up at the river itself, following its course until you enter the gorge.

❷ The Tugela is the region's largest and, in its upper reaches,

most spectacular river. It rises at the western end of the Mont-aux-Sources plateau, finding its way to, and then plunging over, the Amphitheatre's rim in just under 2km (1.2 miles) of cascades, one of which drops a sheer 614m (2,014ft).

As you enter the gorge you have to cross on large stepping stones made of natural boulders—it's a good idea to have some shoes with extra good grip with you, as the rocks can be slippery.

❸ The Tugela Gorge is a scenic and botanic delight. The walk along it takes you to the base of the crescent-shaped Amphitheatre, part of the Mont-aux-Sources ('mountain of springs') massif, which was named for the number of rivers born on its plateau, among them the Tugela (or Thukela).

The path continues on the other side, and at the 6km (3.7-mile) mark the gorge narrows to form the Tugela Tunnel.

❹ The Tugela Tunnel's sandstone walls are moulded into striking shapes, but to pass through here and see them you have to be willing to get wet: There's a certain amount of boulder-hopping, and after rain you have to wade along the bottom.

Alternatively, you can climb up the sturdy ladder which is attached to the rock face on your left. The ladder follows the contours of the face, and at the top you follow the path with

Opposite *A granite outcrop looms ahead*
Below *The Tugela Gorge dwarfs its visitors*

the assistance of steel pegs buried in the rock face. At the footpath, turn left and descend again; you'll find yourself at the other end of the Tugela Tunnel.

❺ It's from the end of the Tugela Tunnel that you'll have the best views of the waterfall, a spectacular sight and well worth the walk. In midwinter the fall's uppermost cascade freezes to a jagged sheet of ice. You can stop for a picnic here and a quick dip in the shallows.

To return to your car, you have to retrace your steps, so make sure you give yourself plenty of time to get back. Look for the Policeman's Helmet—a large freestanding rock formation—on the return walk.

❻ Although the route is one of the most popular in the region, you may spot the occasional large mammal such as grey rhebok or baboon along the way. You'll certainly see some uncommon birds (more

Above *Sunbird feasting on lion's-ear flowers*

than 230 species have been recorded within the park).

WHEN TO GO
The warmer months from October to March are best for the walk, but bear in mind that the sun will be very strong in December and January. There is little shade along the way, so wear a hat and sunscreen, and carry plenty of drinking water with you. You should also be prepared for sudden summer thunderstorms, in which case you should turn back because of the risk of flash flooding. In spring, the area is carpeted with wild flowers, making it particularly attractive. Winters can be extremely cold (though the days are often crisp and sunny), and the peaks and higher slopes are often covered in snow. The number of day visitors is controlled to prevent overcrowding in the park, but this is likely to be a problem only on weekends and during holiday periods.

PLACE TO VISIT
ROYAL NATAL VISITOR CENTRE
www.kznwildlife.com
The Visitor Centre stocks detailed maps of the area.
✉ Royal Natal Visitor Centre ☎ 036-4386310 🕐 Daily 8–12.30, 2–4 💷 Adult R25, child (3–15) R15 🚗 Well signposted from the N3; 60km (37 miles) from Harrismith, 40km (25 miles) from Bergville

BATTLEFIELDS ROUTE

BATTLEFIELD TOURS
www.fugitivesdrift.com
The top expert on the region, the late David Rattray, used to lead stirring and unforgettable tours of the battlefields. Equally competent guides have now succeeded him. Advance reservations for the tours are essential.

✉ Fugitives' Drift Lodge ☎ 034-6421843
🚌 Approx 50km (31 miles) south of Dundee towards Greytown on the R33

DURBAN

AFRICAN ART CENTRE
www.afriart.org.za
This is one of the best places in Durban to buy beautiful Zulu beadwork, baskets and ceramics. The shop is a non-profit-making outlet for rural craftspeople—the choice is broad and the items on sale are good value.

✉ 94 Florida Road, Durban 4001
☎ 031-3123804 🕐 Mon–Fri 8.30–5, Sat 9–3, Sun by appointment only

BARTLE ARTS TRUST (BAT) CENTRE
www.batcentre.co.za
A popular arts centre on the harbour, BAT has a concert hall, a bar and a restaurant overlooking the water. Has live jazz most evenings.

✉ 45 Maritime Place, Small Craft Harbour, Durban 4001 ☎ 031-3320451 🖐 Free; special events from R20

BEAN BAG BOHEMIA
www.beanbagbohemia.co.za
A vibrant bar on the ground floor of an old converted Durban townhouse, Bean Bag Bohemia is a fun place and is popular in the evenings, when it attracts a well-to-do crowd. There are good snacks with a strong Mediterranean influence—the shared meze platters go well with the drinks.

✉ 18 Windermere Road, Greyville 4001
☎ 031-3096019 🕐 Daily 11am–late
🖐 Free

CAFÉ VACCA MATTA
www.vaccamatta.co.za
This super-sleek bar and club has enormous interiors, lounge areas and bar-dancers. The age limit is 18 during the day for the restaurant, but then it's over-25s only and smart dress code after 7pm, when it becomes a club with varied music including house, hip hop and R&B.

✉ Suncoast Casino and Entertainment World ☎ 031-3686535 🕐 Daily 11am–late

Above *Durban's Victoria Street Market is filled with Indian stores*

THE CATALINA THEATRE
www.catalinatheatre.co.za
The Catalina, a relative newcomer to the city, is an enjoyable little theatre based at trendy New Wilson's Wharf. It seats 175 people and puts on contemporary performances, from flamenco guitar recitals to Indian plays.

✉ 18 Boatman's Road, New Wilson's Wharf, Maydon Wharf, Durban 4001
☎ 031-3056889 🖐 From R40

JOE COOLS
www.joecools.co.za
This hugely popular bar and restaurant is right on the beach, opposite one of the more popular surf sites. The outside terraces have great beach views, and are a good place for an early evening cocktail while watching the sun go down and the beach thin out. Later on, they are lit with strobe lights, as the surfing fraternity puts down its boards and takes over.

✉ North Beach, Durban 4001 ☎ 031-3329697 🕐 Daily 9–late (restaurant 9–9)
🖐 R10–40 after 6pm, entry increasing as it gets later

KINGSMEAD
www.dolphinscricket.co.za
Kingsmead cricket ground, home to the KwaZulu-Natal provincial cricket team, is a modern stadium with large grandstands. All of Durban's big matches are played at this popular venue, and it was host to several matches during the 2003 Cricket World Cup, held in South Africa, Zimbabwe and Kenya. The weather is generally good, but as it's close to the sea there is always a chance of rain or poor visibility.
☎ 031-3354200 ⊘ Cricket season: Dec–Mar ✋ From R60

MUSGRAVE CENTRE
www.musgravecentre.co.za
The Musgrave Centre has 110 shops, with a mix of chic boutiques and national chain stores. There are also restaurants, a food court and a cinema complex. On Sunday an interesting craft and curio market is held on level five of the parking area.
✉ 115 Musgrave Road, Berea 4001 ☎ 031-2015129 ⊘ Mon–Sat 9–5, Sun 10–4

THE PAVILION
www.thepav.co.za
www.numetro.co.za
Based in the suburb of Westville, the Pavilion, with some 320 shops and restaurants, ten pin bowling and other entertainment, is always busy—an estimated 1.7 million people visit this mall each month. The Nu Metro multiscreen cinema shows the latest international releases in plush, air-conditioned surroundings.
✉ Westville 3629 ☎ 031-2759800 ⊘ Daily 9–7 (until 8 Fri–Sat); cinema 9am–11.45pm ✋ Cinema: from R42

THE PLAYHOUSE
www.playhousecompany.com
This theatre complex shows regular performances in five auditoria: the Opera, Loft, Drama, Studio and Cellar Supper Theatre. The eclectic selection of shows ranges from Shakespeare to contemporary political satire and modern dance.
✉ 231 Smith Street, Durban 4001 ☎ 031-3699555 ✋ From R40

SUNCOAST CASINO AND ENTERTAINMENT WORLD
www.suncoastcasino.co.za
This large complex is housed in mock art deco buildings surrounded by palms, and facilities include a casino with 50 gaming tables and more than 1,000 slot machines, an eight-screen cinema, a wide selection of bars (including Café Vacca Matta, ▷ 182), takeaway joints, themed restaurants and a nightclub. There's a boardwalk linking the complex to the beach, where you can sunbathe or rollerblade on the sundeck.
✉ Suncoast Boulevard, Marine Parade ☎ 031-3283000 ⊘ Daily 8am–11pm; casino 24 hours

SURFERS KITE & SURF CENTRE
www.kitesurfers.co.za
You can rent or buy boards at this shop, which also offers training in surfing and kitesurfing at their main training beach at La Mercy.
✉ Shop 23, Lifestyle Centre, Douglas Crowe Drive, Ballito 4420 ☎ 032-9460018

USHAKA SURF LESSONS
www.surfandadventures.co.za
Individuals or groups can learn to surf on the gentle, well-shaped waves of uShaka beach. Board rental, wetsuit and lifejacket are included in the fee. Boogie boards may also be rented.
✉ uShaka Marine World, 1 Bell Street, Point 4001 ☎ 084-8239470 ⊘ Daily 8–4 ✋ Surf lessons, R150 per hour; boogie board hire R50 for 1 hour

VICTORIA STREET MARKET
Durban's ornate Victoria Street Market (▷ 167) is crammed with more than 170 stalls selling African curios, leather goods, fabrics, saris and copperware. The main attraction, however, are the many different spices and pulses imported from India. Upstairs are food stalls serving up delicious and interesting snacks such as *bunny chow* (a half-loaf of bread with the middle scooped out and filled with curry), samosas and tasty Durban curries.
✉ Corner of Queen and Victoria streets, Durban 4001 ☎ 031-3064021 ⊘ Mon–Sat 6–6, Sun 10–4

WINDSOR PARK MUNICIPAL GOLF COURSE
This 18-hole course is next to the Umgeni River, just north of Durban. Equipment can be rented here by the day or by the week.
✉ Windsor Park 4001 ☎ 031-3122245 ✋ From R40

HLUHLUWE-IMFOLOZI
DINIZULU SAFARIS
www.dinizulu.co.za
This established family outfit has an excellent knowledge of Zululand and its parks. Game drives using 4WD open vehicles are organized in both Hluhluwe-Imfolozi and Mhkuze game reserves, along with day trips to other places of interest in the area.
✉ 89 Zebra Street, Hluhluwe 3960 ☎ 035-5620025 ✋ Four-hour trip from R250

MARGATE
AFRICAN DIVE ADVENTURES
www.africandiveadventures.co.za
As well as offering a wide range of NAUI diving courses, this reputable operator specializes in shark dives at the Protea Banks, where schools of hammerhead and Zambezi sharks are regularly seen.
✉ Shelly Beach Harbour, Shelly Beach 4265 ☎ 039-3171483 ✋ Courses from R1,800

ORIBI GORGE
WILD 5 ADVENTURES
www.oribigorge.co.za
In addition to its hiking trails, Oribi Gorge is the ideal spot for a number of adventure sports. Wild 5, based at the Oribi Gorge Hotel, just outside the reserve on the way to Port Shepstone, offers white-water rafting trips in conventional rafts or large inner tubes on the Umzimkulu River, abseiling (rappelling) from Lehr's Waterfall, the last 66m (217ft) being a free abseil where you can feel the spray of the falls on your back, and an exhilarating 75m (245ft) freefall gorge swing for the brave.
✉ Oribi Gorge Hotel, Oribi Gorge ☎ 039–6870253 ✋ Freefall gorge swing from R350

PIETERMARITZBURG
CROWDED HOUSE
www.crowdedhouse.co.za
Pietermaritzburg's main club
is popular with the city's many
students. It plays kwaito, R&B,
alternative and dance music, and
puts on some live bands. Tuesday
is the big night, known as 'Pig
Night'—when you pay your entrance
you are given a glass for the night,
which is then refilled as often as you
like up until midnight.
✉ Chief Albert Luthuli Road,
Pietermaritzburg 3201 ☎ 033-3455977
🕐 Mon–Fri 8am–5pm, Tue, Thu–Sat
8pm–late 🖐 R25; 'Pig Night' R30

RORKE'S DRIFT
ELC CRAFT CENTRE
This shop by Rorke's Drift sells
locally produced Zulu arts and crafts:
baskets, ceramics, dyed cloth and
handmade carpets.
✉ Rorke's Drift 3016 ☎ 034-6421627
🕐 Mon–Fri 8–5.30, Sat–Sun 10–4

Below *Surfing in Durban*

ST. LUCIA
ADVANTAGE CHARTERS
www.advantagetours.co.za
Explore Lake St. Lucia on a two-hour
boat ride or try whale watching
in season; trips run from June to
November, when humpback, minke
and occasional southern right whales
travel along the coast on their way
to the warmer breeding waters of
Mozambique. Other tours available
from Advantage include day-trips
to Cape Vidal as well as deep-sea
fishing trips.
✉ Corner of McKenzie Street and Katonkel
Avenue, St. Lucia 3936 ☎ 035-5901259
🖐 Day tour to Cape Vidal R425; 2-hour
hippo and croc tour R140

SODWANA BAY
CORAL DIVERS
www.coraldivers.co.za
A good value place to learn to dive in
Sodwana is at this live-in dive centre,
which has PADI courses suitable
for all levels from beginners to dive
masters. The package includes dorm
accommodation and equipment.
Some of the best sites for diving off

Sodwana are Two Mile Reef and
Five Mile Reef. The closest
snorkelling site to Sodwana is on
Quarter Mile Reef, 500m (1,640ft) off
Jesser Point.
☎ 033-3456531 🖐 Open water diver
course R3,995

SODWANA BAY LODGE
www.sodwanadiving.co.za
A similar but more trendy set-up to
Coral Divers (see above) is available
at Sodwana Bay Lodge, which offers
a number of all-inclusive diving
packages, with courses including
transport to and from Durban.
☎ 035-5710117 🖐 Open water diver
course from R3,100

UKHAHLAMBA-
DRAKENSBERG
CATHEDRAL PEAK HOTEL
GOLF COURSE
www.cathedralpeak.co.za
Keen golfers will be pleased to
know that the northern and central
Drakensberg has four golf courses.
Cathedral Peak Hotel (▷ 191) has a
nine-hole course; in good weather

the mountain backdrop takes some beating.

✉ Cathedral Peak ☎ 036-4881888
🖐 From R90 for 9-hole round 🚗 From the N3 (heading north), turn off at the Winterton/Colenso exit and turn left onto the R74 Winterton/Bergville, followed by a left onto the R600 in Winterton (at the Engen garage). Follow signs for Cathedral Peak until you see signs for the hotel

KZN WILDLIFE

www.kznwildlife.com

Trout were introduced into the rivers of the Drakensberg around the turn of the 20th century and over the years fly-fishing for trout has become a popular pastime. Fishing licences are available from KZN Wildlife.

✉ uKhahlamba-Drakensberg
☎ 033-8451000 (central booking)
🖐 Trout fishing R35–R80 per day

SANI PASS TOURS

www.sanitours.co.za

Tours go to the top of Sani Pass by 4WD, stopping off at a Basotho village on the way. The road is terrifyingly steep and winding, but the views are outstanding. A picnic lunch in the Black Mountains or lunch at the Sani Top Chalet (▷ 280) is included.

✉ Underberg 3257 ☎ 033-7011064
🖐 Adult R500, child (under 14) R300

THOKOZISA

www.cdic.co.za

A one-stop tourist centre, the home of the Central Drakensberg Information Centre has several shops selling arts and crafts, organic health products, clothing and some hiking gear. There's also a deli where you can pick up final snack items to take hiking, as well as a restaurant and coffee shop.

✉ On the R600 towards Monk's Cowl, 13km (8 miles) from Winterton ☎ 036-4881207 🕓 Daily 9–5

UMHLANGA ROCKS

GATEWAY THEATRE OF SHOPPING

www.gatewayworld.co.za

North of Durban is the grandiloquently named Gateway

FEBRUARY

KAVADI FESTIVAL OF PENANCE

This Hindu festival is celebrated all over South Africa, but especially in Durban. Ritual piercing is performed by the penitents and you will see processions and floats decorated with flowers.

✉ Shri Siva Subramanium Temple, 122 Sidar Road, Durban ☎ 031-3047144

APRIL

SPLASHY FEN

www.splashyfen.co.za

This music festival, held on the Splashy Fen farm 19km (12 miles) from Underberg, has developed into one of the country's leading

Theatre of Shopping, said to be the largest shopping mall in the southern hemisphere, and you could easily spend a day here. As well as the usual host of shops and restaurants, there are plenty of other activities and attractions, from an IMAX cinema and an impressive abseiling (rappelling) and climbing wall, to the world's largest artificial surf wave and a popular championship skateboarding park.

✉ 1 Palm Boulevard, Umhlanga Ridge, New Town Centre 4320 ☎ 031-5140500
🕓 Mon–Thu 9–7, Fri–Sat 9–9, Sun 9–6

ZULULAND

SHAKALAND

www.shakaland.com

This popular Zulu theme park has daily cultural shows, which include Zulu dancing and tours of a 'traditional' village where tribal customs such as spear-making, the beer ceremony and Sangoma rituals are explained. Although not intended to be representative of how the Zulu live today, the food and dancing here are very good.

☎ 035-4600912 🕓 3-hour tours at 11 and 12 🖐 Adult R285, child (6–11) R150
🚗 14km (8.5 miles) north of Eshowe on the R66

alternative music festivals. The focus is on folk, rock and guitar music. It has been running since 1990 and now attracts more than 12,000 revellers.

☎ 033-5630824 🕓 Five days, second week in April

DECEMBER

DURBAN SUMMER SPLASH

www.durban.gov.za

This week-long beach festival includes a variety of events, concerts and competitions along Durban's Golden Mile, from the Bay of Plenty Pier to the Snake Park Beach.

🕓 Second week of December

SIMUNYE ZULU LODGE

www.simunyelodge.co.za

This lodge is a far more authentic and enjoyable introduction to Zulu culture than Shakaland, offering traditional accommodation, trips to local kraals (traditional African villages of huts, usually enclosed by a fence) and a chance to meet some local Zulu people. In the evenings guests are treated to Zulu food, dancing and singing out beneath the stars.

☎ 035-4500101 🖐 Fom R1,030 per person sharing per night 🚗 On the D256, off the R66 north of Eshowe

ZULULAND ECO-ADVENTURES

www.eshowe.com

The ex-mayor of Eshowe, Graham Chennells, is now a registered guide involved in community projects. He runs cultural tours of the surrounding countryside, taking in contemporary Zulu life and visiting innovative projects such as the Eshowe Skills Centre, a paper-making project, and the Rotary Classroom Project (the building of 2,000 classrooms in the region).

✉ Zululand Backpackers, 38 Main Street, Eshowe 3815 ☎ 035-4742298
🖐 Tours from R340

REGIONS KWAZULU-NATAL • WHAT TO DO

PRICES AND SYMBOLS

The restaurants are listed alphabetically (excluding The) by town or area, then by name. The prices given are the average for a two-course lunch (L) and a three-course dinner (D) for one person, without drinks. The wine price is for the least expensive bottle.

For a key to the symbols, ▷ 2.

DOLPHIN COAST
MO-ZAM-BIK

www.mozambikrestaurant.co.za

As the name suggests, this eatery specializes in the spicy peri-peri Mozambique/Portuguese style of cooking and is famous for its grilled prawns. Other good bets are the beef *espetada,* flame-grilled chorizo sausage, chicken livers with garlic and lime, or the peri-peri calamari with olives. Some imported Portuguese wines and beers are on offer. The décor is fashioned to suggest a colourful Mozambique beach hut.

✉ Boulevard Centre, Compensation Road, Ballito 4420 ☎ 032-9460979 ⏰ Fri–Sun 12–3, 6.30–late, Mon–Thu 6.30–late (lunch daily during holiday season) ✋ L R130, D R170, Wine R70

THE HOPS

www.thehops.co.za

This lively family pub and restaurant is on the beach in Ballito and has a large terrace that's good for whale and dolphin spotting and a long bar with a range of beers on tap. There's good pub fare such as bangers and mash, liver and onions and the Hops pie of the day, and given its location, plenty of seafood. You can also build your own basket of snacks such as spring rolls and chicken wings.

✉ 14 Edward Place, Ballito 4420 ☎ 032-9462896 ⏰ Daily 11am–late ✋ L R120, D R160, Wine R55

DURBAN
9TH AVENUE BISTRO & BAR

www.9thavenuebistro.co.za

This simple but stylish restaurant has a classic bistro atmosphere, minimalist décor and attracts plenty of regulars. The small menu changes frequently depending on what's in season and the whim of the chef, but expect the likes of pepper-seared tuna, crispy roasted duck served with sweet potato and butternut mash, or a gorgonzola, pear and pecan nut salad. To finish, there are chocolatey

Above *Traditional and more adventurous fare is served in this region*

choices, sorbets, one or two traditional options or cheese. There is a good wine list too.

✉ Shop 2, Avonmore Centre, 9th Avenue, Morningside, Durban 4001 ☎ 031-3129134 ⏰ Tue–Fri 12–2.30, 6–10, Sat, Mon 6–10 ✋ L R160, D195, Wine R80

BAANTHAI

Well placed in a trendy strip of restaurants and bars, Baanthai is a popular local restaurant serving good Thai food. Starters include paper prawns or spicy tom yam soups. There is a large selection of main dishes, mostly stir-fries and Thai curries, but the house specials are worth trying—Sam's crispy blackened chilli fish or the honeyed barbecue spare ribs. The walls are decorated with delicate murals and there's an outdoor balcony. The restaurant serves no alcohol but they are happy for customers to bring their own wine or beer.

✉ 138 Florida Road, Morningside 4001 ☎ 031-3034270 ⏰ Mon–Sat 12–10.30 ✋ L R85, D R110, Wine R40

CARGO HOLD @ USHAKA MARINE WORLD

www.ushakamarineworld.co.za

The Cargo Hold, the most sophisticated of the three restaurants at Marine World, enjoys a great location and is particularly popular with families. Spread over three floors in the phantom ship at the marine park, it has a glass wall looking directly into the shark tank, where ragged-tooth sharks sidle by while you eat. The impressive menu includes good seafood, steaks, warm salads and Mediterranean starters. Reservations are essential.

✉ The Phantom Ship, uShaka Marine World, 1 King Shaka Avenue, Durban 4001 ☎ 031-3288107 ⏰ Daily 12–3, 6–10 ✋ L R140, D R180, Wine R65

DARUMA

www.daruma.co.za

One of the best Japanese restaurants in the country with another branch in Pretoria, Daruma has booth-style seating and large tepanyaki bars which are great for sociable eating for groups and is popular with Durban's Japanese community. There's a full range of sushi, tepanyaki, tempura, and rice and noodle dishes, and for the daring diner, extras include eel, oysters and sea vegetables imported from Japan.

✉ Southern Sun Elangeni, 63 Snell Parade, Beachfront, Durban 4001 ☎ 031-3370423 ⏰ Daily 12–2.45, 6.30–10.30 ✋ L R115, D R 145, Wine R65

INDIAN CONNECTION

www.indian-connection.co.za

North Indian cuisine is the specialty of this restaurant situated in what was once a rambling family home. Curries come in chicken, lamb, seafood and vegetarian versions,and there is a variety of tandooris to choose from. Highlights of the menu are the excellent fish tikka tandoori, the prawn curry, and the butter chicken. Bring the kids: there is small children's menu. The wine list is brief but adequate.

✉ 485 Windermere Road, Morningside 4001 ☎ 031-3121440 ⏰ Daily 11–3, 5.30–10.30 ✋ L R80, D R100, Wine R45

JEWEL OF INDIA

Worth visiting for its exotic side room, with cushions and low tables where you can kick off your shoes, this is one of Durban's finest Indian restaurants, set in the modern five-star Southern Sun hotel. It specializes in north Indian cuisine, with a full range of rich, spicy curries served with fresh tandoor breads. There is an extensive selection for vegetarians, and Indian musicians provide nightly live music.

✉ Southern Sun Elangeni, 63 Snell Parade, Durban 4001 ☎ 031-3621300 ⏰ Daily 12–3, 5–10.30 ✋ L R100, D R135, Wine R65

JOE COOLS

For superb views of North Beach while you lunch, head to Joe Cools, a large restaurant and pub with decks overlooking the sand. During the day it's popular with families, and in the evenings it becomes a surfers' hang-out. The food is standard pub fare, with burgers, pizza, pasta, seafood and club sandwiches. It's always a lively spot, and a great place for watching people catching the waves from the beach.

✉ 137 Lower Marine Parade, North Beach, Durban 4001 ☎ 031-3329697 ⏰ Kitchen is open daily 9–9; pub open longer hours ✋ L R70, D R115, Wine R45

NEW CAFÉ FISH

Set right on the water with yachts moored within arm's reach, and where fish is delivered directly to the kitchen door by boat, the upstairs bar, with its floor to ceiling windows, is great for a sundowner overlooking Durban's harbour. Downstairs, the formal restaurant, as the name suggests, specializes in seafood—try the crusted kingklip, sweet potato line fish or crayfish thermidor—though meat-eaters won't be disappointed as there are good steaks with interesting sauces. The menu is light on vegetarian options, however.

✉ 31 Yacht Mole, Victoria Embankment, Durban 4001 ☎ 031-3055062 ⏰ Daily 12–3, 6.30–10, bar open all day ✋ L R140, D R165, Wine R65

ROMA REVOLVING

www.roma.co.za

Arrive early for pre-dinner drinks and enjoy the 360-degree view of Durban from this 32nd-floor revolving restaurant. In addition to the good value three-course set meals, with six or seven choices per couse, there's a strong emphasis on seafood and pasta, though there is steak, lamb and veal too. The heavily laden dessert cart includes something tempting for everyone.

✉ John Ross House, Victoria Embankment ☎ 031-3682275 ⏰ Mon–Sat 12–2.30, 6–10.30 ✋ L and D set menus from R159, Wine R60

SAGE AT CHRISTINA'S

www.christinamartin.co.za

This is a training restaurant, but that shouldn't put you off. It's still very popular and manages to maintain a good standard of international cuisine. Menus are as varied as the students' curricula, and presentation is a strong point. The breakfast menu is pure luxury, while the regular Saturday lunchtime themed buffet is always popular. The prices are very reasonable given the exceptional quality of the food. Reservations are essential.

✉ 124 Jan Hofmeyer, Westville, Durban 3629 ☎ 031-3032111 ⏰ Tue–Sat 6.30–10.30, 12.30–3, 6.30–9.30 ✋ L R80, D R150, Wine R55

ULUNDI

www.theroyal.co.za

The Ulundi is one of Durban's best and oldest curry restaurants, located in the five-star Royal Hotel, which dates from the 1840s. It's recently been refurbished, and contemporary monochrome furnishings are set off by the original mahogany walls and bars. It specializes in serving tiny bowls of Indian dishes on large brass platters to share. Starters include chicken satay, samosas and paneer, followed by biryani, excellent curries, and vindaloo lamb cutlets for something a bit different.

✉ Royal Hotel, 267 Smith Street, Durban 4000 ☎ 031-3336000 ⏰ Daily noon–3pm, 6pm–midnight ✋ L R90, D R110, Wine R55

HIBISCUS COAST

LYNTON HALL

www.lyntonhall.co.za

If you're serious about gourmet food, it's worth making a special visit to this restaurant, in a five-star hotel, as it has one of the best reputations in the country. It's famous for its presentation, and flavoured mousses and froths are much in evidence. Examples are venison with teriyaki truffle butter and banana ice cream, or galantine of chicken with mushrooms, carrot purée and lemon air. Reservations required.

✉ Umdoni Park, Old South Coast Main Road, Pennington 4184 ☎ 039-9753122 🕐 Daily 12–3, 7–9 ✋ L R195, D R245, Wine R110

LADYSMITH

THE ROYAL HOTEL

www.royalhotel.co.za

The main dining room at The Royal Hotel has a choice of steaks and pub-style lunches, as well as a daily buffet in the form of a carvery. But don't expect much for vegetarians other than salads. The attached pub serves bar snacks and is popular with locals in the early evening.

✉ 140 Murchison Street, Ladysmith 3379 ☎ 036-6372176 🕐 Daily 12–2.30, 6–9 ✋ L R90, D R100, Wine R40

PIETERMARITZBURG

LITTLE POLAND

www.littlepoland.co.za

The Polish-born husband and wife owners of this small restaurant are passionate about bringing their native cuisine to southern Africa. Dishes include traditional roasted pork with prunes, and *pierogi* (pasta dumplings) and spicy goulash. It's slightly lacking in sophistication but has a warm and friendly atmosphere that brings locals back time and again.

✉ Hilton Jacaranda Centre, Pietermaritzburg 3245 ☎ 033-3434289 🕐 Wed–Sat noon–2.30, 6–9, Tue 6–9 ✋ L R60, D R130, Wine R50

PESTO DELI AND TRATTORIA

www.pestopmb.co.za

This bustling trattoria has a typical décor of red-and-white checked tablecloths and bottles of wine lining the walls. It offers no-frills north Italian food. Begin with a selection of antipasti followed by steak, seafood or veal or one of the delicious pastas such as peppadew pesto and pasta or sun-dried tomato and feta ravioli. There's a wide range of wood-fired pizzas, including some unusual toppings—lamb and mint jelly or brie and cranberry.

✉ 101 Roberts Road, Pietermaritzburg 3201 ☎ 033-3425239 🕐 Daily 12–late ✋ L R50, D R120, Wine R45

ST. LUCIA

QUARTERDECK

Set at the entrance to the little town of St. Lucia, this friendly local restaurant specializes in seafood. Dishes include simply prepared butter fish, a rich white fish grilled and served with chips (fries), and a platter with a variety of local grilled seafood. You can also get burgers with a range of toppings. It's a good value, laid-back place, but the best feature is the open deck, perfect for watching the world go by while you eat.

✉ McKenzie Street, St. Lucia 3936 ☎ 035-5901116 🕐 Daily 10.30–2, 5–10 ✋ L R70, D R100, Wine R50

UKHAHLAMBA-DRAKENSBERG PARK

CATERPILLAR & CATFISH

www.cookhouse.co.za

This guesthouse (▷ 190–191) just outside the Ukhahlamba-Drakensberg Park is home to one of the best restaurants in the region. A popular Sunday lunch destination for people from Gauteng, it serves imaginative dishes using excellent local produce. The house special is Drakensberg trout, but there is also an emphasis on Cajun-style cuisine, including, on the dinner menu, jambalaya, jerk chicken and spicy vegetable etouffee. For lunch, choose from a range of imaginative salads, filled baked potatoes, tasty soups or the po-boy sandwiches.

✉ Top of the Oliviershoek Pass ☎ 087-9406860 🕐 Daily 10–3, 6–9 ✋ L R120, D R150, Wine R55

UMHLANGA ROCKS

BUTCHER BOYS

www.butcherboysgrill.co.za

Butcher Boys is an upmarket chain steak house, with other branches around Durban, specializing in steaks cut to your specification in the butchery, grilled to your liking and served with one of the delicious sauces. There's also chicken and seafood dishes as well as lamb shanks and ostrich medallions. The set menus are good value and there's a 'little butchers' menu for kids under 13. There's also a good wine list.

✉ Lighthouse Mall, Chartwell Drive, Umhlanga Rocks 4319 ☎ 031-5614106 🕐 Sun–Fri 12–3, 6–10.30, Sat 12–3 ✋ L R170, D R200, Wine R65

RAZZMATAZZ

The Cabana Beach Hotel is home to the resort's best restaurant. The outside terrace has brilliant views over the crashing waves below, making it the best spot for lunch or summertime supper; the interior is decorated in simple terracotta and blues. The menu is dominated by seafood and game dishes—try the crocodile kebabs, venison with red wine and blueberry sauce, or ostrich fillet with Cape gooseberries. It's also well known for its crème brûlée, and offers good-value set meals.

✉ Cabana Beach Hotel, 10 Lagoon Drive, Umhlanga Rocks 4319 ☎ 031-5615847 🕐 Daily 12.30–3.30, 6.30–10 ✋ L R125 (set menus R100), D R160 (3-course menus), Wine R50

THE SUGAR CLUB

www.southernsun.com

Enjoy the ocean views from this pricey but lovely colonial theme restaurant in a large Southern Sun chain hotel. The menu is varied, but best known for its seafood including oysters with chilli and lime sorbet and Mozambique langoustines. Traditional desserts include *crêpe suzette,* lemon tart and poached pears and the long wine list includes French champagne.

✉ Beverly Hills Hotel, Lighthouse Road, Umhlanga Rocks 4319 ☎ 031-5612211 🕐 Daily 7am–11pm ✋ L R185, D R235, Wine R105

PRICES AND SYMBOLS

The hotels below are listed alphabetically (excluding The) by town or area, then by name. Prices are the average for a double room for one night, including breakfast. All the hotels listed accept credit cards unless otherwise stated.

For a key to the symbols, ▷ 2.

BATTLEFIELDS ROUTE
FUGITIVES' DRIFT LODGE

www.fugitivesdrift.com

The family home of the late David Rattray, for many years the battlefields' most famous and best tour guide, this is the leading lodge in the region (▷ 164–165). A night's stay includes a trip to Rorke's Drift in the afternoon, followed by a tour to Isandhlwana the following morning. Bedrooms are smart and modern, with huge beds and well-appointed bathrooms with free-standing baths, and all have private verandas. There are also rooms in an annexe cottage. The lounge and dining room—which serves excellent traditional food—is

filled with Battlefields memorabilia. Staying here is a highlight for anyone with any interest in history: Before his death in 2007, David Rattray trained a number of guides, who evoke the past in a compelling way.
☎ 034-6421843 🖐 R5,180 (full board)
🛏 8; cottage sleeps 6 🚗 50km (31 miles) south of Dundee, towards Greytown on the R33

ISANDLWANA LODGE

www.isandlwana.co.za

This luxury lodge opened in 1999 beneath the rock upon which the Zulu commander stood at the start of the Isandhlwana battle (▷ 164). A stunning wood, thatch and stone building, it blends well with its surroundings. The rooms have private bathrooms and a mix of modern and rustic furnishings, but the highlight is the private balconies with views over the valley and battle site. The swimming pool, also with valley views, is carved out of the rock. Well-prepared South African fare is served in the stone restaurant, and guests

Above Traditional guesthouse on the Battlefields Route

can take guided historical tours of the area.
✉ Isandhlwana ☎ 034-2718301
🖐 R3,800 (full board) 🛏 12 🚗 Off the R68, between Babanango and Melmoth

DURBAN
BALI ON THE RIDGE

www.baliridge.co.za

A beautifully restored house on the Berea ridge overlooking the city of Durban is home to this small, elegant bed-and-breakfast with high-ceilinged rooms and wooden floors. The owner is an importer of Indonesian furniture, which she has used to decorate her establishment. There's a comfortable lounge, or sun lounge in cooler weather, private bathrooms and satellite TV in each room, and secure off-street parking.
✉ 268 South Ridge Road, Glenwood, Durban 4001 ☎ 031-2619574 🖐 R800
🛏 8

QUARTERS HOTEL

www.quarters.co.za

Four historic homes in the suburb of Berea have been converted to create this boutique hotel. There's a refreshingly modern feel to it: The bedrooms have simple white walls and dark fabrics, with black-and-white photographs on the walls. Other facilities include a popular on-site brasserie serving meals throughout the day, a shaded courtyard and a modern bar. Most of the rooms have a small veranda overlooking palm-shaded gardens. Parking is available.

✉ 101 Florida Road, Berea 4001 ☎ 031-3035246 ♨ R2,640 🕙 23 ♿

HIBISCUS COAST

TREETOPS LODGE

www.treetopslodge.co.za

A feature of this establishment is its fine wooden sun deck onto which five of the six rooms open. The rooms, all with en-suite bathroom, are decorated in pleasant pinks and blues. The lodge is set in a lush subtropical garden with wonderful birdlife and offers a swimming pool, guest lounge and bar. The town centre and main beach are 10 minutes' walk away.

✉ 3 Poplar Road , Margate 4275 ☎ 039-3172060 ♨ R680 🕙 3, plus 3 units with kitchen ♒

HLUHLUWE-IMFOLOZI GAME RESERVE

HILLTOP CAMP

www.kznwildlife.com

Hilltop is the largest of the camps in the park, with the most spectacular location and sweeping views over much of the park and parts of Swaziland. There are various types of accommodation, covering a wide price range. At the top end are comfortable four-bed chalets with fully equipped kitchens. At the budget end are two-bed rest-huts with a communal kitchen and shower block. Although this doesn't have the exclusivity of the smaller bush camps, the central lounge, restaurant, bar, pool and veranda make for a relaxing end to the day.

Game drives and guided walks can be arranged from here.

✉ Hilltop Camp ☎ 035-5620848 ♨ From R300 (per person for rest-hut); from R600 (per person for chalet) 🕙 60 ♒ 🚗 Turning at Mtubatuba leads west on the R618 (50km/31 miles) to Hluhluwe village, which leads (14km/8.5 miles) to the northern Memorial Gate entrance

ISIMANGALISO WETLAND PARK

KOSI FOREST LODGE

www.isibindi.co.za

This is the only private lodge within Kosi Bay, part of the iSimangaliso Wetland Park. Its thatched bush suites are hidden in the sand forest, shaded by the forest canopy. There is a restaurant and bar on a wooden terrace surrounding a giant forest tree. The bedrooms have low wooden walls with mosquito netting and roll-up canvas blinds. All have private bathrooms, with open-air baths and showers enclosed by reed screens. In season (November–January) you may see see giant turtles nesting on the beach.

☎ 035-4741473 ♨ R3,800 (including all meals) 🕙 16 🚗 From the N2 head north, passing Richard's Bay, Empangeni and Mkuze. About 10km (6 miles) after Mkhuze turn right at signs for Jozini and follow signs to the lodge. Arrange transfers by 4WD to the accommodation before you arrive

ORIBI GORGE

ORIBI GORGE

www.oribigorge.co.za

This small family hotel is in an 1870s colonial building circled by a veranda and feels like an African country house. There are spectacular views of the gorge from various points around the grounds. The rooms are bright and airy, with fresh white walls and green-and-cream fabrics, light wooden furniture and wooden floors. The attached restaurant serves burgers, steaks and light meals; there is also a country pub, a pool, gym, pool table and curio shop. Activities (including white-water rafting and horseback riding) can be arranged with Wild 5 Adventures (▷ 183), as can tours to the local coffee estates.

✉ Oribi Gorge Hotel ☎ 039-6870253 ♨ R950 🕙 18 ♒ 🍴 🚗 Follow the scenic route through the gorge; on leaving the reserve head towards Port Shepstone. The hotel is on the northern side of the gorge, clearly signposted. An alternative route from the N2 is to take the turning on the road signposted to Oribi Flats; continue along this road and the turning to the hotel is signposted down a dirt road next to a coffee estate

PIETERMARITZBURG

CITY ROYAL

www.cityroyalhotel.co.za

The City Royal is a typical small South African town hotel, with newly refurbished, comfortable and spacious double rooms. All are air-conditioned with private bathrooms, floral fabrics, TV, tea and coffee-making facilities, and there's a restaurant on-site and two bars. It's just a couple of minutes' walk from the middle of town, and the staff are friendly and welcoming. Parking is available.

✉ 301 Burger Street, Pietermaritzburg 3201 ☎ 033-3947072 ♨ R725, excluding breakfast 🕙 44 ♿

ST. LUCIA

SEASANDS LODGE

www.seasands.co.za

These attractive tropical-style lodges just outside central St. Lucia are a peaceful place to stay. They have double rooms with a cool white theme and wicker furniture, large beds with mosquito nets and a private balcony; those at the front have sweeping views of the wetlands. The lodges are surrounded by tropical gardens, with a pool. There is a restaurant and bar, and all rooms have air conditioning, satellite TV and French windows.

✉ 135 Hornbill Street, St. Lucia 3936 ☎ 035-5901082 ♨ R960 (excluding breakfast) 🕙 28 ♿ ♒

UKHAHLAMBA-DRAKENSBERG PARK

CATERPILLAR CATFISH COOKHOUSE

www.cookhouse.co.za

The quirky Caterpillar & Catfish

guesthouse is a great place to stay on the Oliviershoek Pass. It's a pine-panelled mountain lodge set in a restored trading post, tucked under large pine trees. The bedrooms are brightly decorated with African artwork, stripped pine and handmade furniture. The huge buffet breakfasts will set you up for a day's walking, and the massage room is ideal for weary hikers. Guided hikes to fascinating local rock art sites are available, and fishing is possible in the well-stocked trout dam nearby. In the evenings, guests congregate in the beautifully decorated piano bar and restaurant (▷ 188), which has live music on some Sundays.

✉ At the top of Oliviershoek Pass, outside the park ☎ 087-9406860 ✋ R396 ⓘ 7 bedrooms, 8 units with kitchen ⌂ From the N3 (heading north) turn off at the Winterton/Colenso exit and turn left on to the R74 Winterton/Bergville. Follow the road, past Winterton and Bergville, for around 80km (50 miles). The lodge is just before Sterkfontein dam on the left

CATHEDRAL PEAK HOTEL
www.cathedralpeak.co.za
The Cathedral Peak Hotel has always been popular with hikers and climbers because of its stunning location close to the high peaks of the Drakensberg (and for weddings, in its stone chapel). These days it has expanded and offers a wide range of activities, attracting large numbers of visitors, so always reserve in advance. It's a big place, with 90 luxurious double rooms, several restaurants and bars and three swimming pools. Other facilities include a nine-hole floodlit golf course, horseback riding, squash, a mountain bike trail, a 10m (33ft) climbing tower, gym, beauty spa and tennis courts.

✉ Cathedral Peak ☎ 036-4881888 ✋ R2,100 (including bed and breakfast, afternoon tea and dinner) ⓘ 96 🏊 🍴 ⌂ From the N3 (heading north) turn off at the Winterton/Colenso exit and turn left on to the R74 Winterton/Bergville, followed by a left on to the R600 in Winterton (at the Engen garage). Follow signs for Cathedral Peak until you see signs for the hotel

Above *Balcony at Quarters Hotel, a boutique hotel in Durban, where you can enjoy views of the city over a cup of coffee*

DIDIMA CAMP
www.kznwildlife.com
The theme of this KZN Wildlife resort, close to the Cathedral Peak Hotel, is the art of the San people, and the chalets are designed to look like caves. Each is thatched and very comfortable, with rustic interiors, satellite TV and fireplaces. The self-catering accommodation sleeps two people; as these sit back to back with each other, they can be converted into four-bed family units. Communal amenities include a central restaurant, a bar and curio shop, and there are guided tours to local sites.

✉ Cathedral Peak ☎ 036-4888000 ✋ R920 (R980 for self-catering) ⓘ 65 ⌂ From the N3 (heading north) turn off at the Winterton/Colenso exit and turn left on to the R74 Winterton/Bergville, followed by a left on to the R600 in Winterton (at the Engen garage). Follow signs for Cathedral Peak until you see signs for the camp

ZULULAND
KWABHEKITHUNGA/ STEWARTS FARM
www.zulu.org.za
This is recommended to get a real feel of Zulu life. The village is the home of Chief Mbhangucuza Fakude, his four brothers and their extended families. They make traditional Zulu beads, baskets and shields, and have now branched out into hospitality. Accommodation is purpose-built and very comfortable, in 12 Zulu beehive-shaped huts, all with private bathrooms and bright interiors. There is also a bar and a swimming pool. For an extra R195 per person visitors are treated to a demonstration of Zulu dancing and singing, and a taste of Zulu food and home-brewed beer.

☎ 086-1276237 ✋ R1,010, including dinner, bed and breakfast ⓘ 23 🏊 ⌂ 36km (22 miles) from Eshowe on the R34 towards Empangeni

LIMPOPO AND MPUMALANGA

The Limpopo and Mpumalanga region is home to the Kruger National Park, which gives visitors some truly spectacular game-viewing experiences and the opportunity to spot the 'Big Five' (lion, leopard, buffalo, rhino and elephant). It's an exceptionally well-organized park with a good infrastructure and at least a couple of days are needed to explore and to stay at the park's rest camps. Alternatively, the adjoining private game reserves combine game viewing with luxury accommodation, excellent food and personalized service and give guests the added benefit of getting more out of wildlife watching by being with an experienced guide. Kruger lies in the dry, flat Lowveld; above are the cool and lush Eastern Drakensberg Mountains, where you'll find the dramatic Blyde River Canyon Nature Reserve, one of Africa's largest canyons, impressive waterfalls and indigenous forests. There are many viewpoints overlooking the canyon with evocative names like God's Window and Wonder View. The country towns like Graskop, Hazyview and Sabie are well used to visitors and the main streets are full of gift shops and restaurants. Pilgrim's Rest is an old gold-mining town and has been perfectly preserved as a living museum where you can even try your hand at gold panning.

Farther north the Afrikaner Limpopo towns are fairly featureless, though there are a number of interesting things to see around Hoedspruit, such as wildlife rehabilitation centres and the Magoebaskloof Mountains (which are particularly beautiful in spring, when the flowering plants and cherry blossoms bloom).

The capital of Mpumalanga is Mbombela (Nelspruit), which is a useful stop for services en route to Kruger, while the regional centre of Limpopo is Polokwane, which straddles the main north road that links South Africa with Zimbabwe.

BARBERTON

www.barberton.co.za

There is a surprising amount to do in this quiet colonial town, much of it connected to the town's gold-mining past. Barberton is famous for being the site of one of South Africa's first large-scale gold rushes. Pioneer Reef was discovered in 1883 and by 1886 more than 4,000 claims were being worked, turning it into a wild frontier town of shacks, gambling dens and whisky bars. Wealth quickly followed, and South Africa's first gold stock exchange opened here in 1887. The gold rush lasted only a few years, and by the outbreak of the Boer War Barberton had been virtually abandoned. However, in recent years the industry has been revived and four gold mines now operate within the area.

🚹 325 M4 🚹 Market Square, Barberton 1300 ☎ 013-7122880 🕐 Daily 8–4.30

BELA-BELA/WARMBATHS

www.belabelatourism.co.za

Warmbaths is one of a number of towns in Limpopo that is undergoing a name change. The resort exists because of the natural hot springs 'discovered' in the 1860s by Jan Grobler and Carl van Heerden while hunting in the region; Bela-Bela, 'he who boils his own', was the name used by the local Tswana people. The springs bubble out of the earth at a temperature of 50°C (122°F), producing about 22,000 litres (4,840 gallons) per hour. The principal springs now lie within the massive Forever Resorts where visitors can enrol in a whole variety of health treatments at the spa (▷ 212). Bela-Bela is less than one hour's drive from Pretoria and the mild climate in winter ensures an average of 286 sunny days a year. All this leads to a staggering 2 million visitors to the town annually.

🚹 324 K3 🚹 Corner of Old Pretoria and Voortrekker streets in the Waterfront development, 0480 ☎ 014-7363694 🕐 Mon–Fri 8–5, Sat 9–4

BLYDE RIVER CANYON NATURE RESERVE ▷ 196.

GRASKOP

www.graskop.co.za

The small mountain resort of Graskop in Mpumalanga is just south of the Blyde River Canyon Nature Reserve (▷ 196), and is the most convenient base for exploring the canyon. Graskop is known in South Africa as the home of the pancake. The legendary Harrie's restaurant (▷ 214) started it all, and now the sweet and savoury pancakes are renowned throughout the land.

There are several hikes from Graskop, including the circular trail of 8km (5 miles) known as Jock of the Bushveld Trail. Other attractions include the Big Swing, which is similar to a bungee jump, and the hair-raising Zipliner (▷ 212).

The road to Hazyview goes over Kowyn's Pass a few kilometres from Graskop. Before descending towards the Lowveld it passes Graskop Gorge and waterfall and there are views looking up to God's Window viewpoint (▷ 196).

🚹 325 M3 🚹 Graskop Tourist Information, Louis Trichardt Street, Graskop 1270 ☎ 013-7671886 🕐 Daily 8–5

HAZYVIEW

Hazyview lies on the banks of the Sabie River on the southwestern edge of the Kruger National Park, surrounded by a large area of banana plantations. Because of its convenient position, facilities for visitors have been expanding since the 1920s, and there is now a wide range of accommodation in the town. Five kilometres (3 miles) from Hazyview is the Shangana Cultural Village, home of a Shangana family descended from Chief Shoshangana, an important tribal leader at the end of the 19th century. Tours of the village include a lesson in traditional medicine, historical explanations and a traditional meal. Tours by arrangement only (tel 013-7377000; www.shangana.co.za).

🚹 325 M3 🚹 Rendezvous Tourism Centre, Main Street, Hazyview 1242 ☎ 013-7377414 🕐 Mon–Sat 8–5

HOEDSPRUIT

www.1africasafaris.com

Hoedspruit is a busy little town at the extreme south of the Limpopo Province, surrounded by game-rich country and views of the Drakensberg escarpment. Its main attractions are outside the town, along the R531 towards Blyde River Canyon Nature Reserve. These include the Bombyx Mori Silk Farm (tel 015-79556; www.silkcollections.com; daily 9–3; tours every hour), the only such farm in South Africa, and a series of wildlife rehabilitation establishments. One of these is Moholoholo, 31km (19 miles) from Hoedspruit (tel 015-7955236; www.moholoholo.co.za; Mon–Sat, guided tours at 9.30 and 3), where orphaned, injured and poisoned animals are cared for.

Just west of Hoedspruit, Khamai Reptile Park (tel 015-7955203; www.khamai.co.za; daily 8–5) has a large enclosure housing many different kinds of reptiles.

🚹 325 M3 🚹 1 Africa Safaris, Kamogelo Tourism Centre, Ferret Street, Hoedspruit 180 ☎ 015-7931110 🕐 Mon–Fri 9–5, Sat 9–2

Opposite *Man riding the Zipliner, the wire rope slide across Graskop Gorge*
Below *Swimmers enjoying the outdoor pool at the Bela-Bela spa complex*

INFORMATION

www.graskop.co.za

⊞ 325 M3 ℹ️ Graskop Tourist Information, Louis Trichardt Street, Graskop 1270 ☎ 013-7671886 ⏰ Daily 8–5 🗔 Kiosk at Bourke's Luck Potholes 🎫 Craft stalls around God's Window ❓ Visitor centre at Bourke's Luck Potholes

TIPS

» There is a good visitor centre at Bourke's Luck Potholes (tel 013-7616019; daily 7–5, ▷ 209) with displays about the canyon.

» For accommodation, the canyon is close to Graskop, Sabie and Pilgrim's Rest.

» North on the R532 takes you to the R36 and the nearby Echo Caves (▷ 209).

BLYDE RIVER CANYON NATURE RESERVE

Some 60 million years ago this deep gash in the landscape was created by the forces of the meandering Blyde River. It was in 1844 that a group of Voortrekkers named the river Blyde (meaning 'joy') after returning safely from Delagoa Bay (Mozambique). Today it tumbles down from the Drakensberg escarpment over a series of waterfalls and cascades that spill into the Blydepoort Dam at the bottom. The canyon is the third largest in the world after the Grand Canyon in the USA and the Fish River Canyon in Namibia, and winds along for 26km (16 miles); it's joined by the similarly spectacular 11km (7-mile) Ohrigstad Canyon near Swadini. The Blyde River Canyon Nature Reserve extends for 27,000ha (66,500 acres) from God's Window viewpoint down to the far side of the Blyde River dam. The canyon drops down 750m (2,460ft) and for most of its length is inaccessible. There are no roads crossing the reserve, but there are a number of viewpoints along the R532, which passes along the lip of the canyon. There is also a drive to the base of the canyon (▷ 208–209).

VIEWPOINTS

The most famous of the canyon's viewpoints is God's Window, right on the edge of the escarpment, overlooking an almost sheer drop of 300m (1,000ft) into the tangle of forest below. The views through the heat haze stretch as far as Kruger. At 1,730m (5,675ft), Wonder View is the highest viewpoint accessible from the road, and Pinnacle Rock is a high quartzite 'needle' that rises dramatically 30m (100ft) out of the fern-clad ravine. From here it is possible to see the tops of the eight waterfalls that take the Blyde River down 450m (1,500ft) in a series of falls and cascades to the bottom.

The viewpoint at the Three Rondavels is by far the most dramatic, with the canyon opening up before you and the Blydepoort Dam shimmering intensely blue at the bottom. These circular rocky peaks capped with grass and vegetation look distinctly like traditional *rondavels* (huts with thatched roofs).

BOURKE'S LUCK POTHOLES

At the confluence of the Treur and Blyde rivers are these unusual rock formations, resembling Swiss cheese and formed by the swirling action of whirlpools. The smooth cylindrical holes are some 15 million years old and are carved out of quartzite. The deepest part of the ravine created by the holes is 30m (100ft).

Above *The distinctive rounded outlines of the Three Rondavels*
Opposite *Tea plantation in the Magoebaskloof*

KOMATIPOORT

This is the last town in South Africa before the main road enters Mozambique at Lebombo. Being so close to the border, it has expanded over the years with the increase in trade. Not far from here, on the Komati Flats, is the Marehall Memorial, a national monument marking the site where Mozambique's President Samora Machel tragically died in a plane crash in 1986 (his widow Graça Machel went on to marry Nelson Mandela in 1998). These days the town is a popular place to pick up supplies for visitors to Kruger National Park—Crocodile Gate is only 9km (6 miles) away. There are supermarkets along Rissik Street.
✚ 325 N4

KRUGER NATIONAL PARK
▷ 199–205.

LOUIS TRICHARDT/MAKHADO
www.soutpansberg-tourism.co.za
Briefly named Makhado, after a famous VhaVenda chief, this town has reverted to its former name of Louis Trichardt following a legal dispute. Louis Trichardt was a Voortrekker leader who set up his camp near here in May 1836. The town is the hub of an agricultural area producing tea, coffee, timber and subtropical fruits. It's a sleepy backwater, disturbed only by the trucks rumbling through on the N1. The Indigenous Tree Sanctuary at the intersection of the N1 and Old Trichardt Street has 145 species of indigenous trees and some Voortrekker graves. The town also has a small Swiss community, which was established through the Swiss Elim missionary hospital.
✚ 325 M1 🛈 Soutpansberg Tourism, corner of Songozwi Street and the N1, Louis Trichardt 0920 ☎ 015-5160040 🕐 Mon–Fri 8–4.30, Sat 8–1

MAGOEBASKLOOF
www.magoebaskloof tourism.co.za
This beautiful mountainous area is good both for walking and exploring by car. The helpful tourist office has

information about these excellent hikes, including the Magoebaskloof Hiking Trail and the easier one-day Rooikat Hiking Trail. One of the best times of the year to visit is in the spring (although many country hotels will be fully reserved), when the area becomes vivid with wild flowers and cherry blossoms. During December and January you can expect to see bright pink and mauve 'pride of India' trees. More than 200 species of orchid have been identified, and there are several yearly flower festivals. The lower slopes are verdant with banana plantations and gum tree forests, resembling a rolling, green patchwork quilt.
✚ 325 M2 🛈 Rissik Street, behind the Elms Gift Shop, Haenertsburg 0730 ☎ 015-2764880 🕐 Mon–Fri 8–5, Sat 9–12

MALA MALA GAME RESERVE
www.malamala.com
Mala Mala, part of Greater Kruger National Park, was established as a safari lodge more than 40 years ago. It was one of the first private reserves to cater to the luxury market and has one of the most luxurious private lodges (with an excellent reputation). Guests have exclusive access to more than 50km (30 miles) of riverfront on the Sand River, as well as lands within the Sabie Sands Game Reserve. The game and

vegetation along the river are superb. Seeing the 'Big Five' is a central part of the Mala Mala experience and guests are given a special certificate to document their sightings.
✚ 325 N3 ☎ 013-7359200 🚗 Approach from the R536, the Hazyview to Skukuza road

MASHISHING/LYDENBURG
www.lydenburgmuseum.org.za
www.lydenburg.org
The descent from Long Tom Pass west to Mashishing, formerly Lydenburg, a quiet agricultural town, opens up vistas of rolling grasslands, cattle ranches and wheat-growing country. The town is famous for the discovery of the so-called Lydenburg Heads—seven clay heads that were found on a farm near the town in 1957. The heads date from AD590 and are some of the earliest southern African depictions of the human form. The Lydenburg Museum (Mon–Fri 8–1, 2–4, Sat–Sun 8–5) is fascinating, with well-presented displays about the history of the Lydenburg region. It was the first home of the heads; today they are in the South African Museum in Cape Town (▷ 70).
✚ 325 M3 🛈 Lydenburg Museum and Information Centre, Voortrekker Street (2km/1.25 miles out of town on the R37) ☎ 013-2352213 🕐 Mon–Fri 8–1, 2–4, Sat–Sun 8–5

LIMPOPO AND MPUMALANGA • SIGHTS

INTRODUCTION

Kruger's figures speak for themselves: 500 species of bird, 114 of reptile, 49 of fish, 33 amphibians, 146 mammals and more than 23,000 plant species have been recorded here. The park measures 60km (37 miles) wide and more than 350km (217 miles) long, conserving 21,497sq km (8,384sq miles), an area the size of Israel. It certainly fulfils most visitors' fantasies of seeing magnificent herds of game roaming across acacia-studded stretches of savannah, and it's home to the 'Big Five' (elephant, leopard, lion, black rhino and buffalo).

The first section of what was to become the National Park was officially formed in 1898 by Paul Kruger. Major James Stevenson-Hamilton, during his 44 years in charge, worked tirelessly to protect and extend the area, until it reached almost its current size. It was also under his care that the area was declared the Kruger National Park in 1926. The next phase in the park's life is for it to become part of the Great Limpopo Transfrontier Park (GLTP). This is a joint initiative between South Africa and the countries that border the Kruger. The GLTP links the Kruger with the Limpopo National Park in Mozambique, plus a number of parks in Zimbabwe. The first step was taken in 2002, when heads of state signed an agreement to establish the GLTP and part of the fence between the Kruger and the Limpopo was symbolically removed. The Mozambique section of the park can now be accessed from the Giriyondo border post, 45km (29 miles) northeast of Letaba, but only by 4WD vehicles, as the roads on the Mozambique side are still under construction.

Despite its size, the park is well developed, with a good network of roads and numerous camps. There is no local public transport. Most people arrive in Kruger on a tour or in their own vehicle. If you are driving yourself and break down, Kruger Emergency Road Services (tel 013-7354325) will tow you to the nearest garage outside the park (the service is not equipped to do any major repairs). While much of the park is designed for self-driving and renting simple

INFORMATION

www.sanparks.org
www.greatlimpopopark.com

✚ 325 N2 ⓘ SANParks reservations ☎ 012-4289111 ⓘ Reception and gate: Nov–Feb 5.30am–6.30pm; Mar, Oct 5.30am–6pm; Apr, Aug–Sep 6–6; May–Jul 6–5.30 ✋ Daily conservation fee: adult R180, child (under 12) R90 🚗 Most camps have guided day drives and night drives (reservations essential) 🍴 Most camps have restaurants open for breakfast, lunch and dinner. Some also have a bar 🏪 All larger camps have shops selling foodstuffs, firewood, petrol (gas) and field guides 📖 Many identification guides for wildlife. Kruger map, travel guide and comprehensive 'Find it' guide

Opposite *Giraffes are easily spotted*
Above *A family group of elephants*

TIPS

» Kruger is a malarial area so be sure to take anti-malaria tablets and cover up after dark.

» Never leave your car unless it is clearly indicated that this is permitted. The animals in Kruger are extremely dangerous and have killed their fair share of foolish visitors.

» Do not under any circumstances feed the animals.

» Most of the camps are at least an hour from the gates, so when you are ready to leave, be sure to give yourself plenty of time to get there. You may be fined if you arrive after the gates close.

» Although isolated dirt roads may seem better for seeing game, viewing is actually more successful on tarred roads as cars are quieter and the animals living near them are more used to traffic.

» If you are unable to make an advance reservation for your preferred camp, it's worth calling once you arrive, as there are often cancellations.

» All reservations should be made through the central offices (Pretoria and Cape Town), but if you're planning on arriving within 48 hours, call the camps direct. Contact numbers are listed in the Staying section (▷ 217).

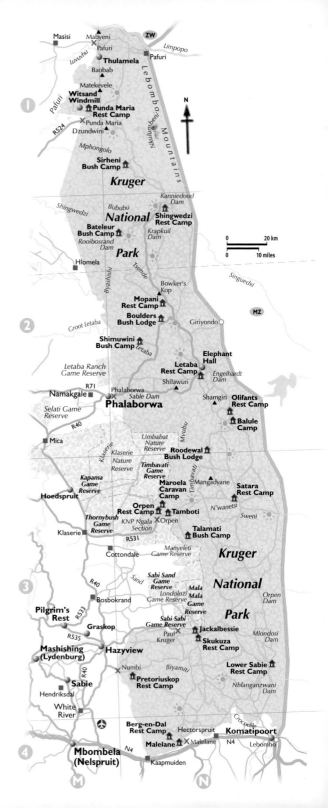

accommodation with no meals provided, it is also possible to stay in a clutch of top-end private reserves in the park. These are often more popular with first-time visitors to Kruger as all game drives are led by rangers, leaving the animal spotting to the experts.

Don't expect to have Kruger to yourself. The park receives 1.5 million visitors a year and the camps cater to up to 5,000 visitors a day. Still, despite the huge number of people passing through, Kruger has managed to keep its magic. Only 5 per cent of the park is affected by the activities of the visitors and few areas in the south come close to the overcrowding seen in East Africa's game parks.

WHEN TO VISIT

The park looks its best after the summer rains when the new shoots and lush vegetation provide a surplus of food for the grazers. As the animals put on fat and become healthier, the females give birth to their young. Migratory birds are attracted to the area at this time of year and display their vivid breeding plumage. On the downside, the thick foliage and tall grasses make it harder to spot animals. In winter the dry weather forces them to congregate around waterholes and the thinner foliage means you can spot more animals. However, they tend not to be in the best condition.

From the point of view of comfort, summer daytime temperatures can rise to a sweltering 40°C (104°F), and afternoon rains are common. The winter months of June, July and August are more comfortable, with daytime temperatures of around 30°C (86°F). Nights can be surprisingly cold at this time of year and temperatures drop to 0°C (32°F). Kruger is at its most crowded during the South African school holidays (June, July, December and January). Accommodation within the park will be completely full and the heavy traffic on the roads can spoil the 'wilderness' experience.

GAME VIEWING

The highest concentrations and variety of game are around Lower Sabie, Satara and Skukuza. The best times for viewing are after dawn and just before dusk, as animals tend to rest during the heat of the day. The network of roads linking the camps outlined overleaf is open to the public only during daylight hours, and the roads are subject to speed limits (monitored by radar). Game viewing requires considerable patience, so do not travel faster than 20kph (12mph) or the chances are you'll have passed the animals before you've spotted them. Hours spent driving around Kruger in a car can be exhausting, so break your journey by stopping at one of the get-out points where you can watch the comings and goings at a waterhole.

PRIVATE GAME RESERVES

There are a number of private game reserves along the western border of Kruger, with some of the most exclusive game viewing opportunities in the world. Here you have the chance to see the 'Big Five' in their natural environment and at the end of the day enjoy five-star luxury and cuisine. These include Kapama, Timbavati, Thornybush, Mala Mala, Sabi Sabi and Sabi Sands.

Below left *Cheetah can be seen in the central and southern Kruger*
Below *Tropic of Capricorn marker stone, on the road to Shingwedzi*

Tropic of Capricorn
To view the rock
you may alight from your
vehicle, at your own risk

Above *Greater kudu, the second largest antelope to be found in the Kruger*
Right *Setting out on a night drive*

WHAT TO SEE
SOUTHERN KRUGER

The greatest concentrations of wildlife are in southern Kruger and many visitors only see this section. The landscape is more varied than elsewhere and supports a wider range of animals. The black and white rhinos, wild dogs and lions, as well as large numbers of giraffe, impala, wildebeest and zebra attract the greatest interest, and most of Kruger's large camps are here. Near the entrance at Malelane Gate is Berg-en-Dal, a large, modern camp with a rather austere institutional feel to it. It is set in a hilly landscape overlooking the Matjulu Dam. Game seen here includes giraffe, kudu, white rhino, zebra and wild dog. Malelane, a luxury private camp that is set in a rugged area of mountain bushveld (open bush country) along the banks of the Crocodile River, is also reached from Berg-en-Dal.

There is a hippo pool close to Crocodile Bridge camp, a small camp in acacia woodland next to the park's southern gate. The area from here to Lower Sabie is good for seeing large herds of buffalo, kudu, impala, wildebeest and zebra. Lion and cheetah can sometimes be spotted tracking the large herds.

The region around Lower Sabie forms part of a classic African savannah landscape, with grasslands, umbrella thorn and round-leaf teak stretching off into the distance. This is regarded as a good area for spotting rhino and is generally one of the best regions for seeing game, which is attracted by water at the Mlondozi and Nhlanganzwane dams. The camp overlooks the Sabie River; accommodation is impersonal but the camp itself is fairly peaceful. The oldest camp in Kruger—and the third largest—is Pretoriuskop, near Numbi Gate. The game drives around here pass through woodland and tall grassland, with good game-viewing areas to the north along the Sabie River and to the south along the Voortrekker Road.

Kruger's largest camp is Skukuza, on the south bank of the Sabie River, from where the park is controlled and administered. The camp has expanded to such an extent that it's possible to forget where you are—it can accommodate more than 1,000 people—but it is still a prime game-viewing area and a good base for game drives.

The road heading northeast towards Satara has a lot of game and is said to have one of the densest concentrations of lion in Africa (leading to the densest population of cars in Kruger). Some 8km (5 miles) from here is Jackalbessie, the largest of Kruger's private camps. It is on the Sabie River and has excellent game-viewing opportunities, with impressive numbers of animals passing through the thorn thickets to the river.

CENTRAL KRUGER

The central area of Kruger is quieter than the south, with smaller camps and fewer cars. There are large areas of flat mopane woodland inhabited by herds of buffalo, elephant, wildebeest and zebra. In the east, Olifants camp has one of Kruger's most spectacular settings, high on a hill overlooking the fever trees and wild figs lining the banks of the Olifants River. The thatched veranda perched on the edge of the camp looks down into the river valley and is a superb place for viewing game. Balule, also on the banks of the Olifants River, is one of Kruger's wildest camps. It is little more than a patch of cleared bush surrounded by an electrified chain-link fence; you can watch animals wandering past just a few metres away. It's a thrill to see hyenas patrol the fence at night, drawn by the smell of *braais* (the traditional Afrikaner barbecues).

In the northern area of the central section, Boulders is an unfenced private camp in an area of woodland. The camp blends in beautifully with its environment and is set among massive granite boulders, hence the name. One of Kruger's largest camps is Mopani, on a rocky hill overlooking the Pioneer Dam just a few kilometres south of the Tropic of Capricorn. The chalets at Mopani have been made from natural materials and it is more pleasant than some of the older camps. Shimuwini ('the place of the baobab'), farther west, has less game than you will see in the south of Kruger, but the private access road leading to the camp follows the Letaba River, where elephants can sometimes be seen bathing. The riverine forest around the camp is a good place for birdwatching.

Letaba, one of the larger public camps in Central Kruger, is a pleasant, neatly laid-out camp on the banks of the Letaba River. Animals to be seen here include, most notably, the large herds of elephant, but the list also contains cheetah, lion, ostrich, sable, steenbok and tsessebe antelopes. There is good game viewing to the east of Letaba along the river and at Engelhardt Dam.

Roodewal is a private bush lodge on the Timbavati River, 29km (18 miles) from Olifants and 42km (26 miles) from Satara. Its unusual feature is a platform built around a nyala tree that overlooks a waterhole. Kruger's second largest camp is Satara, rather too developed for most people's liking, although the functional character is softened by trees and lawns. Satara is set in the flat grasslands of

Below *Olifants is one of Kruger's most attractive camps, blending into the surrounding woodland*

Above *Chameleon*
Below *Yellow-billed hornbill*

the eastern region, which attract large herds of wildebeest, buffalo, kudu, impala, zebra and elephant. There is good game viewing on the road to Orpen.

Maroela and Tamboti are both campsites close to Orpen Gate on the south bank of the Timbavati River; the latter is smaller and you do not need to bring any equipment. Orpen, also nearby, is a small camp just past the entrance gate. The area around the camp is known for its leopard, lion and cheetah. A little to the south is Talamati, set on the banks of the N'waswitsontso River, which is normally dry. The grassland and acacia woodland along the western boundary attract kudu, giraffe, sable and white rhino.

NORTHERN KRUGER

The northern sector of Kruger is a relatively little visited, dry and remote region. As there is no year-round water supply, there isn't the same density of animals as in the south, but the area does support rare antelopes like Sharpe's grysbok, tsessebe, sable and nyala, as well as leopard. The Luvuvhu River, lined with ironwood and ebony, has some of the best wildlife viewing. Huge pythons thrive in the thick forests and some of the largest crocodiles in Kruger can be seen here. The bridge crossing is an excellent spot for birdwatchers after heavy rains—in particular, look out for the cape parrot, Basra reedwarbler, tropical boubou and yellowbellied sunbird. The picnic site at Mooiplaas, between Letaba and Shingwedzi, overlooks a waterhole on the Tsende River where game can often be seen.

The most southerly camp in the northern section of the park is Bateleur, an isolated bushveld camp surrounded by a vast area of woodland. Visitors have exclusive access to the two nearby dams, both of which are good areas for game watching. Further east is Shingwedzi, a large chalet camp. The best game viewing in this area is around Kanniedood Dam and the riverine forest along the banks of the Shingwedzi. In the middle of the northern section is Sirheni, a bushveld camp overlooking a dam. Although game is present here, the area is known for its birdwatching.

Punda Maria, a peaceful rest camp hidden by dense woodland, is the northernmost large public camp in Kruger. It is in a unique area of sandveld (sandy grasslands) dotted with baobabs (a tree with a thick trunk), white lilacs and pod mahogany. There are spectacular views of the surrounding landscapes from the top of the hill called Dzundwini, and good game viewing near the camp on the Mahonie Loop and up near the Witsand windmill. The bridge over the Luvuvhu River is a top place for birdwatchers.

WILDERNESS TRAILS

Seeing the park on foot is the most exciting and rewarding way to experience Kruger's wilderness. However, places on the organized trails are limited and usually reserved months in advance. There are seven trails from which to choose, with a maximum of eight people on each, and each trail is accompanied by an armed ranger. Hikers spend each night at the same bush camp and go out on day walks. The trails are up to 15km (9 miles) long, giving hikers plenty of opportunity for game viewing. Food, water bottles, sleeping bags, rucksacks and cutlery are all provided. Children under 12 are not allowed.

The wilderness trails are run twice a week on Sunday and Wednesday and last for two days and three nights (tel 012-4265117; R3,430 per person). The best time of year for hiking is from March to July when the weather is dry and daytime temperatures are cooler.

The Bushman Trail is good for seeing white rhino and wild dogs; the hikes also take you to nearby San rock paintings. The camp is in a region of mountain bushveld in the southwest of the park, in an isolated valley surrounded by *koppies* (small hills). You check in at Berg-en-Dal near Malelane Gate, from where it's an hour's drive by Land Rover to the trail camp. Accommodation is in thatched bush huts.

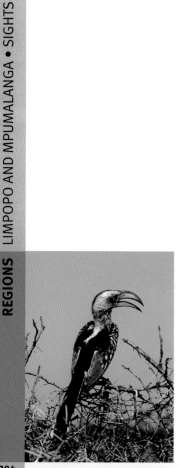

The Napi Trail passes through a variety of habitats following the banks of the Biyamiti River through thick riverine bush and crossing mixed woodlands. Here you should be able to see both black and white rhino, duiker, jackal, kudu and giraffe. Check in at Pretoriuskop.

The Metsi-Metsi Trail camp is in an area of mountain bushveld near the N'waswitsontso River. The trail also visits areas of marula savannah where there are many plains animals. Check in at Skukuza.

The Nyalaland Trail passes through a vast expanse of mopane scrub, dotted with baobabs, aloes and *koppies*. The wildlife here is unique to this sector of the park and nyala are often seen. The birdlife is particularly spectacular. The hutted camp is shaded by kuduberry trees next to the Madzaringwe Stream. Check in at Punda Maria.

The Olifants Trail crosses through classic African plain. There are excellent chances of seeing large herds of buffalo, wildebeest and zebra. The hutted camp overlooks the Olifants River and is 90 minutes by Land Rover from Letaba, where you check in.

The Sweni Trail is southeast of Satara overlooking the Sweni River and crosses through knobthorn and marula savannah where large herds of buffalo, wildebeest and zebra can be seen. Other species to spot include cheetah, lion, sable and steenbok. Check in at Satara.

The Wolhuter Trail passes through lowveld savannah where you might see lion, cheetah, black and white rhino, roan, sable and wild dog. The trail is named after the park ranger Harry Wolhuter, who killed a lion with his knife in 1903. The bush camp has wooden huts and is located near the Mlambane River. Check in at Berg-en-Dal.

Above left *Leopards are shy and largely nocturnal but during the day you may see one in the trees*
Above *Baobab trees are a quintessential part of the Kruger landscape*

MORE TO SEE

ELEPHANT HALL
The air-conditioned museum at Letaba has an excellent display about elephants. There is a small cinema showing wildlife videos and a large hall dedicated to the life cycle of the elephant.
✚ 200 N2 (Letaba) ✉ Letaba Camp ☎ 013-7356664 🕐 Mon–Sat 8–8, Sun 8–6 ✋ Free

THULAMELA
Thulamela, in the northern corner of Kruger Park close to the Levuvhu River, is an important late Iron Age site. Guided walking tours to Thulamela leave from the Pafuri picnic spot twice a day, and you can reserve a place at the Sirheni, Shingwedzi, Punda Maria and Pafuri gates.
✚ 200 N1

Amarula Cream liqueur, made from the fruit of the marula tree and distilled here. It is a young town, established in 1958, when mining for minerals and copper began. With a width of 2km (1.2 miles), the open-cast mine is thought to be the widest man-made hole in Africa. At only 2km (1.2 miles) from Kruger's Phalaborwa Gate (for central and northern Kruger), the town is a convenient base for visiting the National Park and the luxury private game reserves. The airport has daily flights to Johannesburg and there are good facilities for visitors, including accommodation, restaurants and car rental outlets. But as the red triangle signs in town will warn you, watch out for the hippos.

✚ 325 M2 🛈 Phalaborwa Tourism Centre, Hendrick van Eck Street, near the Spar, Phalaborwa 1395 ☎ 015-7813620 ⊕ Mon–Fri 7.30–6, Sat–Sun 8–1

PILGRIM'S REST

www.pilgrims-rest.co.za
Since the last gold mines of Pilgrim's Rest closed in 1972, the town has been completely reconstructed as a living museum to preserve a fascinating part of South Africa's cultural heritage. The restored miners' cottages, with their corrugated iron roofs and wooden walls, are evocative of gold-rush days, although today they are filled with gift shops. Although most of the buildings are strung out along one long street, the town has a clear division between the smart and prosperous Uppertown and the plainer Downtown.

✚ 325 M3 🛈 Main Street, Upper Town, Pilgrim's Rest 1290 ☎ 013-7681060 ⊕ Daily 9–12.45, 1.45–4

POLOKWANE

www.polokwane.org.za
The capital of Limpopo Province is a large modern city that has changed its name from Pietersburg to Polokwane, meaning 'place of safety'. As well as being a good

MAPUNGUBWE NATIONAL PARK

www.sanparks.org
Mapungubwe is the country's youngest national park, on the South African side of the confluence of the Shashe and Limpopo rivers. It forms part of the Greater Mapungubwe Transfrontier Conservation Area. A picnic site overlooks the point in the rivers where South Africa, Zimbabwe and Botswana meet. The park protects important San rock art sites as well as the Mapungubwe Hill, believed to be the site of the first capital of the ancient kingdom of Great Zimbabwe between AD900 and 1300. The park was awarded World Heritage status in 2003. It covers 28,000ha (69,000 acres) of arid bush dotted with acacia thorn and giant baobab trees, and its wildlife includes rhino, elephant, kudu, zebra, eland, waterbuck, gemsbok, giraffe and baboon. The four camps are accessible by ordinary car.

✚ 325 L1 ☎ 015-5342014 ⊕ Gates and office: Sep–Mar 6am–6.30pm; Apr–Aug 6.30am–6pm 🎟 Adult R100, child (under 12) R50 🚌 68km (42 miles) due west from Musina on the R572. It can also be reached from the east via the R521, an alternative route from Polokwane

MBOMBELA/NELSPRUIT

www.lowveldinfo.com
Mbombela, formerly Nelspruit, is above all a town for shoppers. It's a good place to stock up with supplies if you are going to the Kruger National Park, the Eastern Drakensberg, or over the border to Swaziland or Mozambique. Just north of town on R40 are the small but important Lowveld National Botanical Gardens (Sep–Mar 9–6, Apr–Aug 9–5), and the Croc River Reptile Park (▷ 213), which is a good attraction for children.

✚ 325 M4 🛈 Lowveld Tourism Association, Crossing Centre, Nelspruit 1201 ☎ 013-7551988 ⊕ Mon–Fri 8–4.30, Sat 8–1

MUSINA

Musina is the northernmost town in South Africa, close to the border with Zimbabwe. It was originally a mining camp set up around copper mines, but today the local workforce is employed in the Venetia Mine, which is owned by De Beers and is South Africa's biggest producer of diamonds. The main street is lined with shops, banks, petrol stations and fast-food outlets, all catering to the steady stream of traffic to and from the border. It's not an especially attractive town, and is increasingly being dwarfed by large, hastily built townships that are home to Zimbabwean refugees.

✚ 325 M1

PHALABORWA

www.phalaborwa.co.za
This quiet Afrikaner town is known for being the home of South Africa's

base for exploring the relatively undiscovered Limpopo region, it has a few sights of its own. Irish House, on the corner of Thabo Mbeki and Market streets, is home to the Polokwane Museum (tel 015-2902183 for details), which traces the history of the region from the Stone Age to modern times. On the other side of Thabo Mbeki Street is the fascinating Hugh Exton Photographic Museum (Mon–Fri 9–4, Sun 3–5). This is a superb and unusual collection of prints and negatives that trace the first 50 years of the city. The Diggings Site Museum has gold panning demonstrations, and lets visitors have a go themselves. The Polokwane Art Museum (tel 015-2902177; Mon–Fri 9–4, Sat 9–12) has a fine collection of South African paintings and sculptures.

The Polokwane Bird Sanctuary, 4km (2.5 miles) north of the town along Market Street on the R521 (daily 7–5) is set around a couple of lakes in the acacia bush, and there are numerous hides for spotting the 280 or more bird species that have been recorded here.

🚹 325 L2 🛈 Limpopo Tourism Board, corner of Grobler and Kerk streets, Polokwane 0699 ☎ 015-2907300 🕐 Mon–Fri 8–4.30

SABIE
www.sabie.co.za
Sabie, in a valley ringed by mountains and dominated by eucalyptus plantations and pine, lies within one of the largest man-made forests in the world. A late 19th-century gold mining town, it has little left to show of the gold-rush era and is now a prosaic timber-processing town. However, it is one of the more attractive towns in the region, its main road lined with pleasant craft and coffee shops, making it a good place for a stop.

The Forestry Museum on Ford Street (tel 013-7641058; Mon–Fri 8–4.30, Sat 8–12) has displays on the development of South Africa's timber industry. The museum's buildings also contain a satellite office of SAFCOL (the Forestry

Department), which has information about hiking and mountain bike trails in the surrounding region, both very popular activities.

🚹 325 M3 🛈 Sabie Information, in the Sabie Market Mall, Main Street, Sabie 1260 ☎ 013-7671177 🕐 Mon–Fri 8–4.30, Sat 9–1

SOUTPANSBERG MOUNTAINS
www.soutpansberg-tourism.co.za
The Soutpansberg mountain range extends for 130km (80 miles) and reaches 1,753m (5,750ft). Along the high plateau are a number of villages of the VhaVenda people (see below). Some of the valleys and lakes are considered to be sacred sights, including Phiphidi Falls, Lwamomdo Hill and the Thathe Vondo Forest. Many of these are difficult to find and you should enlist the services of a registered guide if you wish to visit them. This will also help ensure that you treat the sights sensitively. You can pick up the Soutpansberg Mountain Meander map, a self-drive guide to day trips in the area, at the tourist office.

The Hangklip Forest Reserve lies 3km (2 miles) west of Louis Trichardt/Makhado and is signposted off the N1. This is an area of indigenous forest around the base of the Hangklip, 1,719m (5,638ft), a wall of rock rising over the forest. The tops of the cliffs are among the highest points of the Soutpansberg. There are a number of one-day hikes through spectacular mountain scenery. From the picnic site there is also an easier 20-minute circular trail that is especially good for birdwatching in the forest.

🚹 325 L1 🛈 Soutpansberg Tourism, corner of Old Trichardt Street and the N1, Louis Trichardt 0920 ☎ 015-5160040 🕐 Mon–Fri 8–4.30, Sat 8–1

TZANEEN
www.tzaneeninfo.com
Tzaneen lies on the eastern side of the Magoebaskloof Mountains, at the heart of a prosperous agricultural region which is the biggest producer of avocados, mangoes, tea and tomatoes in South Africa. Much of

the countryside looks considerably greener than many other parts of South Africa, and the palm trees and banana plantations add to a sense of tropical lushness. Don't miss the Tzaneen Museum on Agatha Street (Mon–Fri 9–4, Sat 9–12), one of the best museums in the region. The private collection of ethnological objects is crammed into three small rooms, forming an amazing display of pottery, pole carvings, drums, books, beadwork and other domestic items. The enthusiastic staff provide a fascinating overview of this priceless muddle of a collection.

🚹 325 M2 🛈 Shop 13, Oasis Mall, Aqua Park, Tzaneen 0850 ☎ 083-3096901 🕐 Mon–Fri 8–5, Sat 9–12

VENDA
Most visitors pass through this former tribal homeland region without stopping. This is a pity, as the Venda region looks and feels more like the 'real' Africa than any other part of South Africa. The lush, green land produces tea, bananas and mangoes, but despite this and the efforts towards improvement made by the ANC government, Venda's infrastructure and housing are still poor, the roads are badly maintained, and most people here rely on subsistence farming.

This is the land of the VhaVenda people, whose culture is steeped in the spirit world; there are many important sacred sites in the region. Originally from Zimbabwe, the VhaVenda are thought to have migrated here at the beginning of the 18th century. They are regarded as some of the finest artists in South Africa, and are particularly renowned for their pottery and drum-making. Thoyoyandou is the former capital of the independent homeland and is the commercial and administrative hub of the district. Its name means 'head of the elephant' in the tshiVenda language. The town has a vibrant African atmosphere, with much of life carried on outdoors—local produce is sold from roadside stands and the people are extraordinarily friendly.

🚹 325 M1

THE PANORAMA ROUTE:
THE MPUMALANGA DRAKENSBERG

This trip along the eastern escarpment, or Mpumalanga Drakensberg, takes you through striking mountain scenery—a landscape of dense evergreen forests, streams and waterfalls—and past the Blyde River Canyon, the world's third largest gorge.

THE DRIVE
Distance: 180km (112 miles) with digressions
Allow: 1 day
Start/end at: Sabie

★ Begin the drive in Sabie (▷ 207). This appealing little upland town began life in 1895 when gold was accidentally discovered in the area. A party of picnickers were amusing themselves by shooting at targets when one of their bullets struck gold-bearing rock. A gold rush ensued, but the seam eventually dried up, and Sabie turned its energies to the planting and harvesting of pines. The town is now the focus of the country's biggest single block of man-made forest.

Drive north along Main Street, which becomes the R532, and out of town. Cross the Sabie River after 1km (0.6 miles), continue for 200m (220 yards), and turn right on the short road to the Sabie Falls, a cataract falling a dramatic 73m (240ft) into a chasm, spanned by a bridge that serves as a viewing platform for the falls. Return to the R532 and proceed for 10km (6 miles) north along the R532, turning right at the signpost to Mac-Mac Pools, which are a little more than 1km (0.6 miles) from the main road.

❶ At Mac-Mac Pools there are picnic spots, superb scenery, and the chance to swim in the clear mountain water (changing-rooms on site). The equally attractive Mac-Mac Falls—magnificent twin cascades that plunge into a ravine lined by trees and ferns—are 2km (1.2 miles) farther along the road. The rather odd name for the pools and waterfall relates to the number of Scotsmen who flocked to the early gold diggings in the area.

Follow the signs to Graskop (▷ 195), another, even more attractive forest village, which is 23km (14 miles) from Sabie. From Graskop follow the signs to God's Window, which is on the scenic R534 loop road that starts on your right a couple of kilometres from the village. There are several viewing points along the 2.7km (1.7 miles) of the loop.

❷ God's Window, on the extreme edge of the escarpment, is one of the most spectacular viewpoints on the route. From this dramatic cleft in the mountains memorable vistas unfold—of the Blyde River gorge, the backing mountains and the hot and hazy lowveld plain that stretches away to the east, across the Kruger National Park (▷ 199–205). The R534 also takes you to Wonder View, 1.3km (0.8 miles) farther on.

Return to the R532. A short distance to the west you'll find two of the escarpment's most beautiful waterfalls: Lisbon Falls, another twin cascade and, 3km (2 miles) to the north, Berlin Falls. Access to both is on gravel. The next, longish stretch of the R532 takes you to a crossing of two small watercourses known as the Treur and Blyde rivers and to nearby Bourke's Luck Potholes, 37km (23 miles) from Graskop.

❸ Bourke's Luck Potholes (1km/0.6 miles beyond the Blyde) are a water-eroded fantasia of rock shapes carved by the river over thousands of years. The potholes are named after early prospector Tom Bourke, who never did make his fortune from the golden lode (although he predicted its presence). Bourke's Luck Potholes are at one end of the Blyde River Canyon Nature Reserve (▷ 196), the immediate area's main attraction. Carved from red sandstone, the canyon's cliff faces plunge 1km (0.6 miles) to the waters below. Strategically sited viewing spots include World's End and Lowveld Lookout, easily reached from the road and revealing panoramas that take in the immensity of the low-lying country to the east, the hump-like peaks known as the Three Rondavels and the Mariepskop massif.

Return to the R532 and swing round to the northwest, past the Blydepoort Dam on your right, to the intersection with the R36, 39km (24 miles) from Bourke's Luck. Close to the intersection (follow the signs) are the Echo Caves.

❹ Echo Caves are a system of caverns and tunnels extending 1.3km (0.8 miles) into the mountain. They are named for the echoes produced when the stalactites are tapped. Evidence of Stone Age human habitation has been found in the caves. Present-day inhabitants of the caves are a huge colony of bats.

Back on the R36, drive south for 22km (13.5 miles) to Ohrigstad.

❺ Ohrigstad was founded as Andries-Ohrigstad by the eastern Voortrekkers in 1845 and abandoned after malaria devastated the settlement (the settlers moved to a healthier spot, which they named Lydenburg). The ruins of the Voortrekker fortifications are signposted to your right, just before you reach town.

Continue south for 23km (14 miles) to the intersection with the R533, which leads you east for 27km (16.5 miles), over Robber's Pass, to Pilgrim's Rest.

❻ The splendidly scenic road known as Robber's Pass was named after a highwayman called Tommy Dennison who, in 1912, held up the Lydenburg coach; he used carved wooden pistols and put on an American accent, and he spent the money in Pilgrim's Rest the next day.

Drive through Pilgrim's Rest (▷ 206) towards Graskop and then turn south on the R532 for Sabie.

WHEN TO GO
February and March, at the end of the rains, are probably the best months for touring: the air is mild and the countryside lush.

WHERE TO EAT
WILD FIG TREE
This is a pleasant and relaxed place to stop off for coffee and cake or a light meal.
✉ Corner of Main Road and Louis Trichardt Street, Sabie ☎ 013-7642239 🕐 Daily 8am–9pm

PLACE TO VISIT
ECHO CAVES
www.echocaves.co.za
☎ 013-2380015 🕐 Daily 8.30–4; tours are 45 mins ✋ Adult R40, child (under 12) R15

Opposite *The spectacular view from God's Window*

PILGRIM'S REST

This is an interesting walk in the old mining village of Pilgrim's Rest (▷ 206; ✚ 325 M3), an evocative (and much visited) living museum high among the hills of the eastern escarpment.

THE WALK

Distance: The various venues are within a few steps of each other

Allow: 3 hours

Start at: Diggings Museum

End at: Joubert Bridge

★ Begin your wander at the open-air Diggings Museum at the top end of what is known as the village's Uppertown, on the right of the R533. You'll get an insight into the working and social lives of the early diggers. Tours, conducted five times a day (at 10, 11, 12, 2 and 3), take in the diggers' huts and include gold-panning demonstrations.

❶ Gold was discovered in the creek of the local stream in 1873, and within days a bustling concourse of hopeful diggers had gathered around the site, their tents and wattle-and-

daub huts soon to be replaced by solid little cottages with iron roofs. Traders and canteen owners set up shop; a church, school and newspaper soon appeared, and the Royal Hotel opened its hospitable doors. When alluvial gold grew scarce, syndicates and companies were formed to dig deeper. Plenty of gold was extracted, but the deposits eventually ran out and the last of the mines, the Theta, closed in the 1970s, by which time Pilgrim's Rest had turned its attention to forestry. The then Transvaal provincial government bought the village, in its entirety, in the 1970s, and its buildings were meticulously restored to the condition they were in during the period between 1880 and 1915.

Turn right out of the museum and cross over onto the first road on the

left, where you'll see the Anglican Church of St. Mary, built by miners from the English county of Cornwall in 1884 and the oldest of Pilgrim's Rest's surviving brick structures. It's an attractive little building, festooned with bougainvillea. Two doors down from the church is the grand-sounding but modest Town Hall, once the hub of village social life, and farther along on your left is Leadley's building, which served as the first hostelry (1885).

The next three venues are also to your left. The Old Print Shop (now a gift shop) and the *Pilgrim's & Sabie News* building tell you something about the turn-of-the-20th-century printing and newspaper-publishing scene. The oddly named European Hotel, the third in the trio, has a charming veranda, today part of a restaurant. A few steps farther along the street (again, on your left) is the Royal Hotel, an evocative place that is still used as a hotel.

❷ The Royal's furnishings and fittings haven't changed much in the past 100 years. Apparently the pub's bar graced a chapel in far-off Lourenço Marques (now Maputo, the capital of Mozambique) until 1893, when an enterprising trader bought the bar and hauled it all the way across the lowveld plain and up the escarpment to serve an entirely different kind of congregation.

Set back from the street on your right (east) stands a cottage once owned by the village hairdresser, stationer and tobacconist. Walk a few paces along and you'll come to the Royal Hotel's old stables, followed by the Tourist Information Centre and the Miner's House, originally built in 1913 for the local doctor but since recreated as a mine-worker's home complete with period furniture and other bits and pieces.

Adjacent buildings include the old Bank House and the Victorian Cottage. Last of the Uppertown venues are the Methodist Church and the cemetery (access via the gravel road to your left) and, back on the main street, the general dealer's store once run by Dredzen & Company and now a house museum.

The Downtown part of the village, separated from Uppertown by a stretch of open space, is less generously endowed with relics of the past (and consequently a lot less crowded with visitors). To explore this part of the village, continue past the Dredzen & Company museum, past the Roman Catholic church of the Sacred Heart and the Dutch Reformed church, and on to the end of the road, where you'll see the arched, stone-built Joubert Bridge, built (over the Blyde River) in 1896. From here, turn back and retrace your steps to the parking area at the Diggings Museum.

WHEN TO GO

Pilgrim's Rest is a pleasant spot at any time of the year, but if you want to miss the biggest crowds of visitors, avoid high season from November to January. Winter nights and mornings can be very cold, and mornings are often misty at any time of year.

WHERE TO EAT
THE VINE

Old-fashioned pub and restaurant with breezy veranda.

✉ Main Street, Downtown, Pilgrim's Rest
☎ 013-7681080 🕐 Daily 12–late
✋ L R60, D R95, Wine R45

TIPS

» Tickets to the village museums (adult R10, child under 12 R5) and sights are not available from individual attractions, and must be bought in advance from the Tourist Information Centre, Main Street, Uppertown (tel 013-7681060; www.pilgrims-rest-co.za; daily 9–12.45, 1.45–4).

» As well as providing rooms in the hotel, the Royal can also organize accommodation in various restored cottages around the village.

Opposite *The general store now sells postcards and other memorabilia*
Below *Panning for gold at the open-air Diggings Museum*

BELA-BELA
FOREVER RESORTS
www.foreversa.co.za

This resort contains the main springs of Bela-Bela (formerly Warmbaths) and is so vast guests are required to wear plastic identity bracelets at all times. The 50°C (122°F) springs are rich in sodium chloride, calcium carbonate and are also slightly radio-active. There are mineral pools, a spa with hydrotherapy and a full range of beauty treatments, plus other activities. Day visitors are allowed until 5pm.

☎ 014-7368500 ✋ 1-hour full-body massage R300

GRASKOP
BIG SWING AND ZIPLINER
The newest activities in the region, the Big Swing and the Zipliner, are just north of town, on the lip of the Graskop Gorge. The Big Swing is similar to a bungee jump but with an outward swing on the descent. After jumping the free fall is 68m (223ft), equivalent to a 19-floor building, and lasts around three seconds. The Zipliner is a zip wire that runs 130m (425ft) across to the other side of the gorge—you slide across in an attached harness.

☎ 013-7671886 🕓 Daily 9–5, weather permitting ✋ Big Swing: R300; tandem, with complimentary Zipliner: R450; Zipliner only: R60

HAZYVIEW
INDUNA ADVENTURES
www.indunaadventures.com

This operator organizes white-water rafting and tubing trips on the Olifants and Sabie rivers—half-day trips in winter and full-day trips in summer.

☎ 015-7378308 ✋ Half day R245, full day R340 🚍 On the R536 9km (6 miles) east of Hazyview

HOEDSPRUIT
BOMBYX MORI SILK FARM
www.silkcollections.com

The excellent farm shop on South Africa's only silk farm sells a wide range of products: silk scarves, blankets, silk-filled duvets and cushions. There is also a tea garden.

☎ 015-7955564 🕓 Daily 9–3, tours on the hour 🚍 23km (14 miles) south of Hoedspruit, on the R531

MONSOON GALLERY
Next door to the famous Mad Dogz Café (▷ 214), this shop stocks a good range of quality arts

Above *White-water rafting gets wild on the Olifants River*

and crafts—the owner has been collecting fine African arts and antiques for decades.

☎ 015-7955114 🕓 Daily 8.30–4.30 🚍 On R527, east of the junction of the R527 and R36

LOUIS TRICHARDT/ MAKHADO
KUVONA CULTURAL TOURS
www.kuvona.com

This operator specializes in tours to see the VhaVenda people, taking in tribal sacred sites, traditional ceremonies and villages in the Soutpansberg and Venda. The company is active in community development through tourism.

✉ Louis Trichardt ☎ 015-5563512

SADDLES HORSE TRAILS
Horseback riding trails, suitable for novices and advanced riders, can be organized in the Soutpansberg Mountains. Longer trips include overnight stays at bush camps, meals and guides.

✉ Lalapanzi Hotel ☎ 015-5165455 ✋ 2-hour ride R280 🚍 28km (18 miles) south of Louis Trichardt on the N1

MBOMBELA/NELSPRUIT
CROC RIVER REPTILE PARK
Like many other crocodile parks in southern Africa, this one claims to be the largest of its type in the country. A lot of effort and expense has gone into creating an exciting attraction, especially aimed at children. The reptiles are on show in a variety of houses, each with a different environment. The turtle pond, crocodile pool and fish pond are linked by a cascading waterway, and there is a tropical house and reptile gallery.

✉ Enviro Park, River Road, Mbombela
☎ 013-7525511 🕙 Daily 8–5;
Sat–Sun handling demonstrations at 11 and 3 👤 Adult R45, child R25 🚗 North of Nelspruit, off the R40 towards White River

O'HAGAN'S
This branch of the South African Irish themed pub chain has a wide selection of imported beers, plus filling pub meals served on an open-air terrace. There is usually some live music at weekends.

✉ Sonpark Centre, corner Barberton and Daan Pienaar Road, Mbombela 1201
☎ 013-7413580 🕙 Daily 11.30am–late
👤 Free

RIVERSIDE MALL
www.riversidecentre.co.za
www.numetro.co.za
This mall proudly claims to be the largest shopping mall in Mpumalanga. It contains the usual mix of shops, restaurants, banks and department stores, and is a good place to stock up on supplies. It's also home to an eight-screen Nu Metro cinema, showing all the latest international releases.

✉ White River Road, Mbombela 1200
☎ 013-7570080; cinema 013-7570300
🕙 Mon–Sat 9–6, Sun 9–3; cinema: daily 12–11 🚗 5km (3 miles) out of town, on the White River Road

PHALABORWA
HANS MERENSKY COUNTRY CLUB
www.hansmerensky.com
This club is based around an 18-hole PGA championship golf course and is

---

SEPTEMBER
SPRING CHERRY AND AZALEA BLOSSOM FESTIVAL
www.magoebaskloftourism.co.za
Around Haenertsburg, the Spring Cherry and Azalea Blossom Festival Craft Fair and Orchid Exhibition takes place—this is when the entire valley is transformed into a bank of vibrant colour.

✉ Magoebaskloof ☎ 015-2764972

---

a must for golfers who want to enjoy the experience of negotiating wildlife on the greens while they are playing. Your caddie's local knowledge will be particularly welcome: elephants do tend to put people off their game. And watch out for the hippos on the 17th hole.

✉ Club Road, Phalaborwa 1390
☎ 015-7813931 👤 Green fees R370

SABIE
THE BIKE DOC
Mountain biking is becoming an increasingly popular activitiy in the forests around Sabie. The Bike Doc rents bicycles and can provide details of local self-guided mountain bike trails, some of which have been used for the national Mountain Bike Championships in recent years.

✉ Corner of Louis Trichardt and Main streets, Sabie 1260 ☎ 013-7642123
👤 From R100

THE BOOKCASE
This second-hand bookshop is full of interesting volumes and collectors' items. The African section is particularly good, with many books from the late 1800s on the great explorers, titles from the 1950s and 1960s on the rise of apartheid, and atlases from the days when most African countries were still colonies. A number of books banned in South Africa during the apartheid years have appeared in this shop.

✉ Main Street, Sabie 1260
☎ 013-7642014 🕙 Daily 8–5

NATIONAL GOLD PANNING CHAMPIONSHIPS
www.sagoldpanning.co.za
Pilgrim's Rest hosts a festival lasting four to five days. Anyone can enter, including small children, and there's also a parade, a wheelbarrow race and a pub crawl.

✉ South African Gold Panning Association, Pilgrim's Rest 1290 ☎ 013-7681471
🕙 End of September

TZANEEN
COACH HOUSE HOTEL AND SPA
www.coachhouse.co.za
The Coach House Hotel is hidden away in the forests. Its Agatha Spa offers health and beauty therapies, from massages and facials to aromatherapy, mud and seaweed wraps, and reflexology.

☎ 015-3068000 👤 Facial R320; full-body massage R380 🚗 15km (9 miles) south of Tzaneen, near to Agatha Forest Reserve

WHITE RIVER
CASTERBRIDGE FARM
www.casterbridge.co.za
Occupying these converted farm buildings is a group of smart boutiques, selling everything from railway sleeper furniture to candles and ceramics. There are also a couple of restaurants and a deli, and a farmyard petting zoo.

☎ 013-7511540 🕙 Mon–Sat 9–4.30, Sun 9–4 🚗 2km (1.2 miles) from White River on the R40 to Hazyview

CYBELE FOREST LODGE
www.cybele.co.za
The lovely spa at this lodge surrounds a tranquil outdoor garden with fountain and fish pond. It has sunken hydrotherapy baths, a steam room and sauna, and a full range of scrubs, polishes, massages and beauty treatments.

☎ 013-7649500 👤 Day packages including lunch from R1,090 🚗 5km (3 miles) off the R40, 28km (18 miles) north of White River towards Hazyview

REGIONS LIMPOPO AND MPUMALANGA • WHAT TO DO

EATING

PRICES AND SYMBOLS

The restaurants are listed alphabetically (excluding The) by town or area, then by name. The prices given are the average for a two-course lunch (L) and a three-course dinner (D) for one person, without drinks. The wine price is for the least expensive bottle.

For a key to the symbols, ▷ 2.

BELA-BELA
O'HAGANS

www.ohagans.co.za

This outlet of the successful chain has an attractive setting on the Waterfront, with outdoor tables. The interior is filled with mock Irish touches, and the menu includes steaks and schnitzels, along with more traditional Irish dishes such as steak-and-ale pie. There's also a good range of beers.

✉ Waterfront development, Pretoria Road, Bela-Bela 0480 ☎ 014-7365068 ◷ Daily 10–late ✋ L R120, D R140, Wine R60

GRASKOP
HARRIE'S

Graskop is famous nationwide for its pancakes, and Harrie's started the craze. There's a wide selection of delicious sweet and savoury pancakes—try one packed with black cherries and rich vanilla ice cream. The veranda is a pleasant spot in summer, and there's a fire indoors in the winter.

✉ Louis Trichardt Street, Graskop 1270 ☎ 013-7671273 ◷ Daily 8–5 ✋ Pancakes from R20

HAZYVIEW
ANT & ELEPHANT

www.antandelephant.co.za

This country restaurant in a lovely tropical garden and mango orchard is a focal meeting point for locals. The long menu offers some interesting starters like home-made French onion soup with a pastry topping or giant mushrooms stuffed with bacon and cheese, followed by a good choice of meat dishes and some seafood. The local trout is excellent—try it baked with creamed spinach and mozzarella.

✉ 6km (4 miles) from Hazyview on the R536 to Sabie ☎ 013-7378172 ◷ Mon–Sat 9am–9.30pm ✋ L R100, D R125, Wine R40

RISSINGTON INN

www.rissington.co.za

The Rissington is best known for its à la carte restaurant, serving delicious food on a terrace overlooking the gardens. The dinner menu has a fine selection of meat dishes, such as venison stew or stir-fried ostrich. Vegetarian dishes include a nut rissole with mushrooms. For dessert, try the chocolate mousse. The wine list has a well chosen South African selection. Reservations essential.

✉ White River Road (the R40) ☎ 013-7377700 ◷ Daily 12–3, 6–10 ✋ L R115, D R190, Wine R80 🚗 2km (1.2 miles) from Hazyview

HOEDSPRUIT
MAD DOGZ CAFÉ

www.countryhouse.co.za

The food here is some of the best in the region, and this makes for a great lunchtime stop-off en route to Kruger National Park. They serve big, wholesome breakfasts, but the lunches are the best, with a range of fusion meals—using tastes from Asia, Europe and Africa. Dishes include spicy Thai beef salad, Creole chicken and Cape Malay *bobotie* (spiced, minced beef). The setting is lovely, with brightly painted tables clustered under thatched roofs.

☎ 015-7955114 ◷ Daily 7.30–4.30 ✋ L R80, Wine R65 🚗 On the R527, east of junction of the R527 and R36

Left *Rissington Inn, Hazyview*

LOUIS TRICHARDT/ MAKHADO
WOOD OWL
www.shiluvari.com

This hotel restaurant, which enjoys an excellent local reputation, has a smart à la carte menu, using local produce such as Venda maize bread and local beef. There are delicious specials, such as beef fillet with buttery sweet potatoes or butternut pumpkin soup, and a good choice of desserts. Local crafts are for sale in the attached shop.

✉ Shiluvari Lakeside Lodge, off the R578 to Elim ☎ 015-5563406 ⏰ Daily 12–3, 6.30–8.30 ✋ L and D set 3-course menu from R120, Wine R65

MAGOEBASKLOOF
TLOU RESTAURANT
www.magoebaskloof.co.za

Set in immaculate grounds full of indigenous trees where you may spot the rare samango monkey, this hotel restaurant offers both a set menu and an extensive à la carte menu. The house special is the Magoebaskloof Pot—tournedos of beef cooked with mushrooms and crumbed fried fruit and presented in a miniature three-legged cast iron pot. The smoked local trout in filo pastry can also be recommended.

✉ Magoebaskloof Hotel, on the R71 between Polokwane and Tzaneen ☎ 015-2765400 ⏰ Daily 7am–9.30pm ✋ L R125, D R165, Wine R65

MBOMBELA/NELSPRUIT
BRAZEN HEAD
www.brazenhead.co.za

An Irish-themed pub decorated with dark wood and leather and copper pots with Guinness and Kilkenny on tap and a good selection of Irish whiskey. Food is good hearty fare like bangers and mashed potatoes, liver and onions and Irish hotpot, and the establishment is well known for its trio of pies on one plate—Guinness and beef, chicken, and ham and minted pea. There's a traditional British Sunday lunch with roast beef and Yorkshire puddings.

✉ Village Shopping Mall, corner of Ehmke and Murray streets, Mbombela 1201 ☎ 013-7553636 ⏰ Mon–Thu 11–11, Fri–Sat 12–11 ✋ L R130, D R160, Wine R68

COSTA DO SOL
www.costadosol.co.za

This well-established restaurant specializes in seafood from Mozambique, brought in fresh from the coast daily. Dishes are a mix of Italian and Portuguese, including good pizza, pasta and veal. It is renowned for its delicious giant Mozambican prawns, simply prepared—grilled with lemon or spicy chilli sauce. The wine list includes some expensive Italian wines.

✉ ABSA Square, Paul Kruger Street, Mbombela 1201 ☎ 013-7526382 ⏰ Mon–Fri 12–2.30, 6.30–9.30, Sat 6.30–9.30 ✋ L100, D R130, Wine R60

PILGRIM'S REST
THE VINE

An 'Olde Worlde'-style pub and restaurant, The Vine is a typical small-town establishment serving wholesome meals and beer on tap. It's a popular place, with a small ladies' bar which gets very busy in the early evenings. There's a breezy veranda outside if you'd prefer a quiet meal. The food veers away from the predictable steaks and grills, and offers some well-prepared traditional South African dishes, including a rich Cape Malay *bobotie* (a sweet and spicy minced beef dish, cooked with raisins and a savoury custard topping), ostrich neck cooked slowly in a *potjie* (a three-legged cast-iron pot), and braised oxtail and *samp* (mashed maize).

✉ Main Street, Downtown, Pilgrim's Rest 1290 ☎ 013-7681080 ⏰ Daily 8am–11pm ✋ L R75, D R100, Wine R40

SABIE
THE WILD FIG TREE

One of Sabie's best restaurants, The Wild Fig Tree serves light lunches (baked potatoes, salads and toasted and open sandwiches) and rather more ambitious meals in the evening. You can choose to dine in the cool interior or on the shaded veranda.

The menu is fairly extensive, with delicious local trout, and a wide choice of game such as guinea fowl, crocodile and warthog, usually grilled or served as sausages. This is one of the few places where you'll see impala and gemsbok on the menu. Vegetarians are also provided for, although this is essentially a place for meat eaters. The home-made desserts and pies are very popular, and there's a small curio shop attached to the restaurant.

✉ Main Street, Sabie 1260 ☎ 013-7642239 ⏰ Daily 8am–9pm ✋ L R95, D R120, Wine R65

THE WINDMILL WINE SHOP
www.thewindmill.co.za

As the name suggests, this is a wine shop (which also sells locally brewed beer) where you can also put together your lunch on a rustic wooden board from deli items like cheeses, cold cuts, olives, marinated mushrooms, chicken liver pâté, pickled fish, smoked trout and home-baked farm breads. You can eat these at a handmade table on the deck or inside next to a roaring fire. Desserts include gooey chocolate brownies, traditional malva pudding or home-made ice cream.

✉ On the R536 between Sabie and Hazyview ☎ 013-7378175 ⏰ Shop Mon–Sat 9–5, lunch Mon–Sat 11–4 ✋ L R55, Wine R45

WHITE RIVER
TAVERNA PORTUGUESA

For a pleasant lunch stop, head to this converted farm building. Daily specials are chalked up on the blackboard, with a mix of light lunches, seafood, steaks and sandwiches. Try the chef's mixed starter combo of calamari, liver and beef strips all done with Portuguese flavours. The outside terrace is popular, and gets very busy during the day. The farm complex also has a number of curio shops.

✉ Casterbridge Farm ☎ 013-7502302 ⏰ Mon–Sat 8.30am–9pm, Sun 8.30–3 ✋ L R90, D R125, Wine R60 🚌 2km (1.2 miles) out of town, between White River and Hazyview

PRICES AND SYMBOLS

The hotels below are listed alphabetically (excluding The) by town or area, then by name. Prices are the average for a double room for one night, including breakfast. All the hotels listed accept credit cards unless otherwise stated.

For a key to the symbols, ▷ 2.

BARBERTON
KLOOFHUIS
www.kloofhuis.co.za

Step out of your bedroom onto an airy veranda in this historic building. The house, built in 1890, served as a mess for the British troops during the Anglo-Boer War (1899–1902). Located on mountain slopes, yet within walking distance of the town centre, the guesthouse is ideally placed for exploring Barberton.

✉ 1 Kloof Street, Barberton 1300 ☎ 013-7124268 🖐 R500 🕐 4

BLYDE RIVER CANYON NATURE RESERVE
BLYDE RIVER CANYON LODGE
www.blyderivercanyonlodge.com

This intimate and individual lodge comprises seven double-thatched rooms with verandas. The whole building is constructed from natural materials and set in beautiful grounds—the owners have gone to great lengths to keep the wildlife totally indigenous, and zebras, warthogs and blue wildebeest often wander across the lawns and through the parking area. There's a bar and a swimming pool, and meals are available on request. You can arrange activities such as mountain biking, kayaking and hiking.

✉ At the foot of the Canyon ☎ 015-7955305 🖐 R1,120 🕐 7 🔄 🏊 🚌 Turn off the R531 on to the road signposted to the bottom of the Blyde River Canyon Nature Reserve and Forever Resorts Swadini

FOREVER RESORTS SWADINI
www.foreversa.co.za

In the middle of a nature reserve on the banks of the Blyde River, this resort is an outdoor-lover's delight. The Orpen Gate of Kruger National Park is only 80km (50 miles) away. The resort itself has hiking trails and boat trips on the adjacent dam where you can view a spectacular waterfall and hippo and crocodile. Accommodation is in chalets, or in the caravan and camping park.

✉ At the foot of the Blyde River Canyon ☎ 015-7955141 🖐 R1,070 for 1–4 people, excluding breakfast 🕐 78 chalets

Above *Wildlife spotting at Mopani Camp*

🔄 🏊 🚌 Turn off the R531 on to the road signposted to the bottom of the Blyde River Canyon Nature Reserve and Forever Resorts Swadini

GRASKOP
THE GRASKOP HOTEL
www.graskophotel.co.za

This is one of the best places to stay in the region, and an ideal base from which to explore the Blyde River Canyon. The Graskop has beautiful public spaces that combine sleek art deco furniture with modern African art and traditional Zulu baskets and weavings. Large Swazi ceramic bowls stand on tables along the corridors, and the bedrooms have dark wood furniture and prints on the walls. There is an à la carte restaurant with an excellent reputation.

✉ Corner of Louis Trichardt Street and Main Road, Graskop 1270 ☎ 013-7671244 🖐 R840 🕐 34 🏊

HAZYVIEW
BIG 5 BACKPACKERS@KRUGER PARK
www.big5backpackers.co.za

The accommodation here is in beehive-shaped huts (with private bathrooms), decorated with bright tribal designs. The lodge has a lounge and a bar with a pool table. Nightly meals use home-grown organic produce. Tours can be organized from here, as well as trips to Kruger National Park. The Baz Bus (▷ 52) stops here.

✉ Impala Street, Numbi Park, Hazyview 1242 ☎ 013-7378000 ⎁ R120 (dorm bed), R350 (hut) 🛏 52 beds 🏊 🚗 Follow R40 to Hazyview, 3km (2 miles) after Protea hotel look for pink sign

KRUGER NATIONAL PARK

SANParks central reservations is on 012-4289111, or at www.sanparks. org. Reservations need to be made 48 hours in advance. There's an additional daily conservation fee of R140 per adult, R70 per child. Prices are per unit, sleeping between one and six people.

CENTRAL KRUGER PUBLIC CAMPS
MOPANI

Mopani is one of Kruger's largest and newest public camps, on a rocky hill overlooking the Pioneer Dam. The chalets have been made from natural materials and are more spacious than in some of the older camps. Facilities include a swimming pool, nature trail, petrol (gas) station, shop, restaurant, bar and launderette. Day walks and night drives can be arranged at reception.

☎ 013-7356536 ⎁ R575 (bungalow), R765 (cottage), R1,330 (guesthouse) 🏊 🚗 74km (46 miles) to Phalaborwa Gate

SATARA

Satara is the second largest camp in Kruger. Facilities include Kruger Emergency Road Service, a car wash, a petrol (gas) station, camp shop, cafeteria and restaurant. Day walks and night drives can be arranged at reception. It's a little on the functional side but made more pleasant by lawns and trees.

☎ 013-7356306 ⎁ R150 (camping), R735–825 (bungalow), R1,425 (cottage), R2,610–2,870 (guesthouse) 🚗 48km (30 miles) from Orpen Gate; 104km (65 miles) from Paul Kruger Gate

NORTHERN KRUGER PUBLIC CAMPS
PUNDA MARIA

This peaceful rest camp is hidden by dense woodland. Facilities include a restaurant, bar, shop and petrol (gas) station. Meals must be ordered in advance. The short Paradise Flycatcher nature trail wanders around the camp.

☎ 013-7356873 ⎁ R160–R180 (camping), R615–R725 (bungalow), R1,400 (cottage) 🚗 8km (5 miles) from the Punda Maria Gate

SOUTHERN KRUGER PUBLIC CAMPS
SKUKUZA

Kruger's largest camp has room for more than 1,000 people, and has a vast range of facilities, including a golf course, supermarket, library, restaurant, bank, post office and doctor. There is also an open-air cinema showing wildlife videos in the evenings. Day walks and night drives can be arranged at reception.

☎ 013-7354152 ⎁ R165 (camping), R365 (safari tent with shared facilities), R735–R1,405 (bungalow) 🚗 49km (30 miles) from Pretoriuskop

KRUGER PRIVATE RESERVES
EARTH LODGE

www.sabisabi.com
The innovative Earth Lodge feels like an ultra-trendy boutique hotel set deep in the African bush. The building has been set deep into the earth, which means that the lodge is virtually invisible, with smooth stone and grass-covered roofs blending into the surroundings. Suites are super-stylish, with muted tones, natural materials and huge beds. The enormous bathrooms have open-air showers and carved stone baths, and all suites have a private plunge pool. The bar area is made out of the roots of trees, and meals are served in an open-air enclosure. Game drives and walks are conducted with a ranger and tracker.

✉ Sabi Sands Private Game Reserve ☎ 013-7355261 ⎁ R8,100 🛏 13 🚗 Accessed by following the R536 from Hazyview to Skukuza; turn off at Glano

KWA MBILI GAME LODGE

www.kwambili.com
The game viewing and service at this small lodge are as good as at other, more expensive ones. You can stay in thatched chalets or safari tents (all with private bathrooms), decorated with African art. Meals are served around a camp fire or on the open veranda. There is also a bar, lounge, curio shop and a pool for a refreshing dip at the end of the day. Game drives, bush walks and all meals are included in the price.

✉ Thornybush Game Reserve ☎ 015-7932773 ⎁ R3,500 🛏 5 🏊 🚗 The main entrance to Thornybush is 9km (5.5 miles) north of Klaserie off the R40; look for signs for Kapama and the Hoedspruit Cheetah project

NGALA

www.ccafrica.com
www.ngala.co.za
Ngala is one of the most opulent of the private lodges in Timbavati and is a member of the Small Luxury Hotels of the World. The lodge is on the Timbavati Flood Plain, a region known for its elephants and lions, and guests have exclusive access to the 14,780ha (36,520-acre) reserve. There's a choice of air-conditioned cottages furnished with antiques, or luxuriously fully furnished safari tents in a satellite camp. Prices include all meals and two game drives a day.

✉ Timbavati Game Reserve ☎ 011-8094314 ⎁ R4,420 (tent) R6,820 (lodge) 🛏 20 cottages, 6 tents ❄ 🏊 🚗 Off the R40, 9km (5.5 miles) north of Klaserie at Kapama

MBOMBELA/NELSPRUIT
PILGRIM'S REST

As an alternative to the Royal Hotel (▷ 211), these miners' cottages from the 1920s, on the hill above the town, are decorated in a style that recalls the village's gold rush days, with brass bedheads and period furniture. Each cottage has a kitchen and a private veranda with valley and mountain views.

✉ District Six Miners' Cottages, Pilgrim's Rest 1290 ☎ 013-7681113 ⎁ R480 (1–4 people, excluding breakfast) 🛏 6

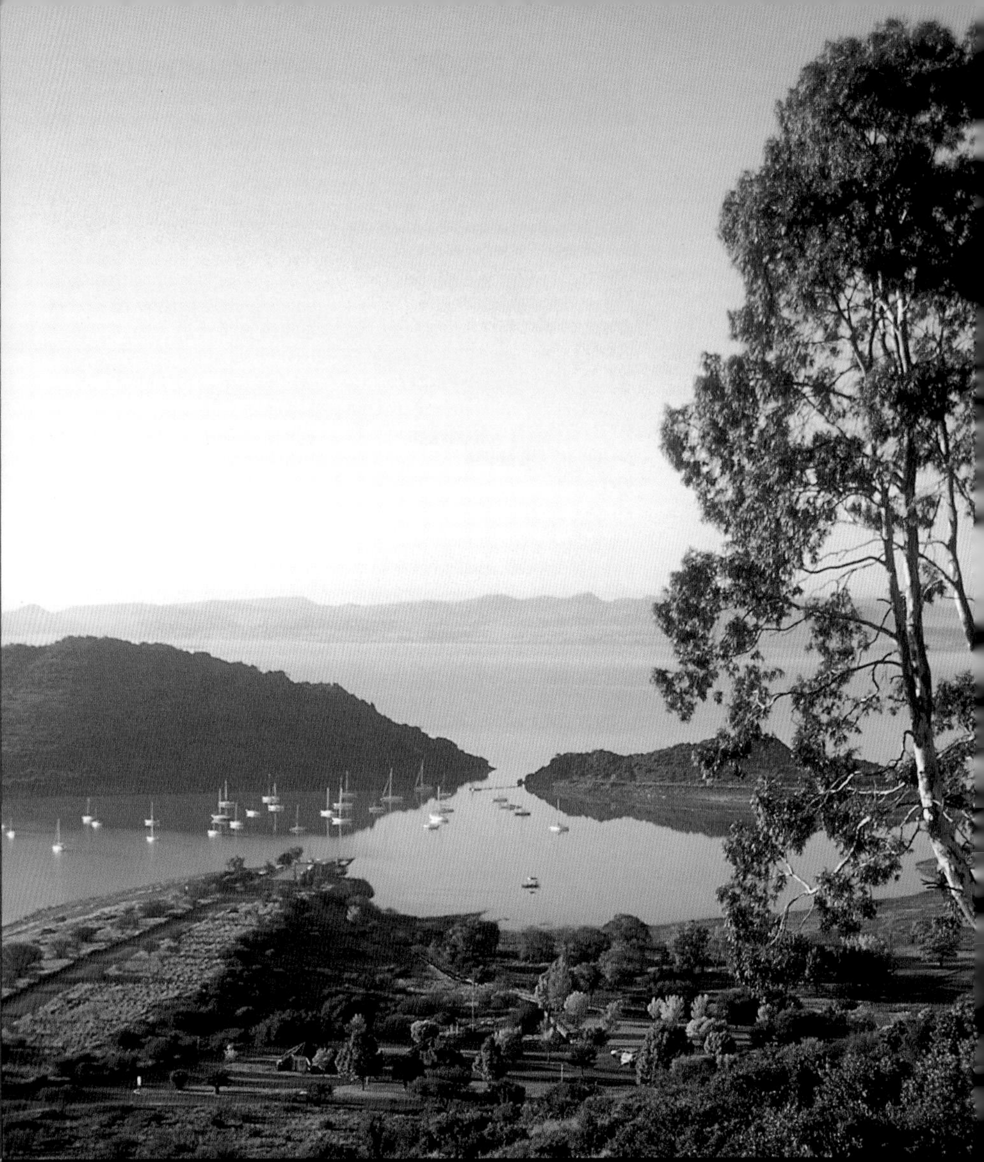

GAUTENG AND FREE STATE

Gauteng, seSotho for 'place of gold', and its two principal cities of Johannesburg and Pretoria have undergone a change of identity since the end of apartheid and now have a distinctive cultural feel. The cities are only 50km (32 miles) apart and linked by an expanding ribbon of development and the new Gautrain; and it won't be too long before they are completely joined up, becoming one of the largest urban spaces in Africa.

Affectionately known as Jozi, Johannesburg is the most important commercial and financial city in southern Africa and has the busiest airport in the southern hemisphere. In addition to excellent shopping malls, restaurants and nightlife, it now has a wealth of contemporary attractions such as cutting-edge museums like the Apartheid Museum, Constitution Hill and the Hector Pieterson Museum in Soweto, all of which look at South Africa's turbulent past under apartheid. There are also museums dedicated to gold, on which Johannesburg was founded, and the emergence of mankind in the region.

Pretoria is a little more staid but has some interesting places covering Afrikaner history, such as the impressive Voortrekker Monument. As the seat of government in South Africa, Pretoria is also home to the Herbert Baker-designed Union Buildings.

To the southwest of Gauteng, the scenery of Free State is of sparsely populated prairie, scattered with dams and mountain rivers, and connected by pretty rural villages. The Eastern Highlands on the border of Lesotho are particularly attractive and perfect hiking or horseback riding country where the Golden Gate Highlands National Park is so named for its beautiful sandstone cliffs that turn golden as the sun sets.

BETHLEHEM

Bethlehem is the principal town of the eastern Free State, an important wheat growing area and one of South Africa's biggest exporters of roses. F. P. Naude, a local church minister, named the settlement Bethlehem ('house of bread'), inspired by the wheat that flourished in the valley. It is a large town with a good range of restaurants and some fine examples of Victorian sandstone buildings. The best way to explore these is to follow the Sandstone Walking Tour; there's a map tracing the walk, which takes about 90 minutes. The most interesting buildings are the Methodist Church (1911), the Strapp Building (1894), the Wooden Spoon (late 1870s), one of the oldest buildings still standing, and the Baartman Coach House (1894). The museum (Mon–Fri 10–12.30), at the top end of Muller Street, has a collection covering the region's local history, and has an early steam locomotive in the grounds.

✚ 330 K6 ❗ Dihlabeng Municipality, 9 Muller Street, Bethlehem 9701 ☎ 058-3035732 ⓒ Mon–Sat 8.30–1, 2–4

BETHULIE

Bethulie is a typically pleasant rural Free State town with a history that is closely related to the development of South Africa. The original settlement, called Heidelberg, consisted of a mission station founded in 1829 by the London Missionary Society. It was taken over by the French Missionary Society in 1833 and renamed Bethulia—'chosen by God'. A few of the original mission buildings are still standing and are thought to be some of the oldest European-built houses in the Free State. The local museum is housed in Pellissier House.

Just outside the town is a spectacular concrete viaduct spanning the Gariep (Orange) River (the railway forms part of the main line to the port of East London). At 1,150m (1,260 yards), the road-rail bridge is the longest of its kind in South Africa.

✚ 328 H8

BLOEMFONTEIN

www.mangaung.co.za

The provincial capital of the Free State is the sixth biggest city in the country and also the judicial capital of South Africa. Central Bloemfontein is a mix of modern tower blocks built during the 1960s and 1970s and handsome sandstone buildings dating from the late 19th century, when Bloemfontein was the capital of the small independent Orange Free State Republic.

Its central position in South Africa makes it an important transport hub and a popular overnight stop for motorists driving between Gauteng and the Cape. Few people actually spend time here, however, and like much of the Free State it has yet to figure on the tourist map (although fans of The Lord of the Rings should note that J. R. R. Tolkien was born here in 1892, moving to England when he was four years old). The city feels friendly, and a large youthful contingent has led to the appearance of a growing number of trendy bars and nightclubs.

The Tourist Office produces a useful self-guided walking map, known as the Rose Walk, which takes in all the best sandstone buildings in town. Most of note are within easy walking distance of each other along President Brand Street.

✚ 323 H7 ❗ Tourist Office, 60 Park Road, Bloemfontein 9301 ☎ 051-4058490/8489 ⓒ Mon–Fri 8–4.15, Sat 8–12

CLARENS

www.goclarens.co.za

Clarens was established in 1912 and named after the Swiss resort along the shore of Lake Geneva where President Paul Kruger died in 1904. This attractive small village is an ideal spot to make your base while exploring the Eastern Highlands. A number of galleries, craft shops and tea rooms surround a grassy square with a few sandstone buildings and shady trees.

There is white-water rafting on the Ash River, and five reasonably preserved cave paintings can be seen on a farm called Schaapplaats, a 15-minute drive from the village (call in at the Clarens Tourist Office and they will phone to let the farm owners know you are coming). If you are heading for Golden Gate Highlands National Park (▷ 222), the Basotho Cultural Village (Mon–Fri 9–4, Sat–Sun 9–5) is 44km (27 miles) beyond the park gate. It provides an insight into the lives of the Basotho people of the region, whose traditions are similar to those over the border in Lesotho. Guided tours take visitors around a scattering of bomas (covered outdoor eating areas) and huts where traditional crafts are demonstrated, local beer can be sampled, and a lively band provides entertainment.

✚ 330 K6 ❗ Clarens Information, Market Street, Clarens 9707 ☎ 058-2561189 ⓒ Mon–Fri 9–5, Sat 9–1

Opposite The mountainous landscape around Clarens, near the Lesotho border
Below Bloemfontein old and new—the sandstone City Hall backed by modern skyscrapers

EASTERN HIGHLANDS

www.goclarens.co.za

The countryside neighbouring the Lesotho border, dominated by sandstone outcrops and eroded river valleys, is the most dramatic scenery in the Free State. The hills once provided shelter for the early San hunters and there are some fine examples of cave paintings. The best way to appreciate the countryside is on horseback or on foot. The highlands are perfect hiking country, and there is some great accommodation out of town on farms and in secluded valleys. Running parallel to the Lesotho border, the R26 passes through all the main towns in this region.

✚ 330 J7 🛈 Clarens Information, Market Street, Clarens 9707 ☎ 058-2561189 🕒 Mon–Fri 9–5, Sat 9–1

FICKSBURG

Named after General Johan Fick, a hero of the Basotho Wars between the Boers and the Basotho people, Ficksburg was founded in 1867 to occupy what was then known as the Conquered Territory. Its role was to prevent cattle rustlers coming over from Lesotho and to strengthen the Boers' general control over the area. Curiously, even today cattle rustling still occasionally occurs in this region. A Cherry Festival is held here during the third week of November each year, when you can indulge in maraschino, schnapps and brandied cherries in syrup.

These days the small town has important trade links with Lesotho, but there is little to interest casual visitors unless they are looking to buy basic supplies.

✚ 330 K6 🛈 In the Highlands Hotel, 37 Vootrekker Street, next to the town hall, Ficksburg 9730 ☎ 051-9332214 🕒 Daily 8–5

GARIEP DAM

www.gariepdam.com

The mighty Gariep Dam on the Gariep (Orange) and Caledon rivers, in the Trans Gariep southwest of Bloemfontein, is the largest dam in South Africa. At the lake's western end is the town also known as Gariep Dam, which has evolved since the completion of the dam wall in 1971 and is now a quiet little Afrikaner town. It's worth going up to the top of town for commanding views of the lake and the surrounding farmlands. The dam hosts an annual International Gliding Championship in December, which has quickly gained a reputation for being the place to try to break world records. At the eastern end of the lake is the Gariep Dam Nature Reserve (tel 051-7540045; daily 7–6), which offers excellent sailing and fishing.

✚ 328 H8

GOLDEN GATE HIGHLANDS NATIONAL PARK

www.sanparks.org

A small (11,600ha/28,600 acres) national park on the edge of the Drakensberg and Maluti mountains, the Golden Gate National Park is in an area of massive cliffs and rocky outcrops. The eroded valleys have produced spectacular golden sandstone rock formations, caves and cliffs set against a backdrop of green grasslands. This is an extraordinary place at sunset when the tones of the rocks are at their most intense. Its proximity to Johannesburg (three hours by car) makes it a popular escape and many day visitors come to hike, rock climb or go horseback riding.

The grasslands that dominate the sandstone slopes are known for their wide variety of wild flowers in summer. You are unlikely to see much wildlife from your car, but once you get up into the wooded valleys and the quiet hills you may see black wildebeest, Burchell's zebra, mountain reedbuck, blesbok, eland and grey rhebok. The larger raptors inhabit the high rocky cliff faces; look for bearded vultures, jackal buzzards and black eagles. The most popular hike here is the two-day Rhebok Hiking Trail (places must be reserved in advance).

✚ 330 K6 ☎ 058-2551000 🕒 24 hours; office: 7–5.30 ✋ Free 🏠 Glen Reenen Shop, selling limited groceries, fuel, beer and wine, firewood, maps 🚗 15km (9 miles) along a tarred road from Clarens

Below *The blue waters of the Gariep Dam, edged by flat-top sandstone hills, are perfect for watersports*

HARRISMITH

Founded in 1849 and named after Sir Harry Smith, Cape Colony's belligerent governor, Harrismith lies on the N3 and is a popular stop en route between Gauteng and Durban. The Platberg, a long, flat mountain of 2,377m (7,798ft), dominates the town, and a challenging race is held along the 5km (3-mile) top every year in October.

✠ 330 L6 ℹ Harrismith Tourist Information, Montrose Country Cell Complex, Harrismith ☎ 058-6223525 🕐 Mon–Fri 8–5, Sat 9.30–12.30

JACOBSDAL

This small town is known for the Landzicht Wine Cellar, where the first wine grapes to be grown outside the Cape Province were cultivated in 1969. Tastings are on offer, and tours are available on request (tel 053-5910164; www.landzicht.co.za; Mon–Fri 8–5). The town's Dutch Reformed Church, consecrated in 1879, enlarged in 1930 and now a national monument, was used as a hospital during the Anglo-Boer War—look for the bullet holes in the front door.

There are two well-known Anglo-Boer battle sites just outside Jacobsdal: Magersfontein (▷ 255) and Paardeberg. The Battle of Paardeberg took place between 18 and 27 February 1900. Although it ended with the surrender of the Boers, and more than 4,000 prisoners of war were taken, the losses on the first day proved to be the greatest suffered by the British for any day during the whole war. More than 300 British troops were killed and around 900 wounded.

✠ 323 G7 ℹ 1 Voortrekker Street, Jacobsdal ☎ 053-5910164

JOHANNESBURG

▷ 224–227.

LADYBRAND

The pleasant country town of Ladybrand is only 15km (9 miles) from Lesotho's capital, Maseru. Along with Ficksburg, the town was founded in 1867, following the war

Above *Jagged rocks near Ladybrand are the site of San rock paintings*

between the Boers and the Basotho people, to help guarantee peace in the so-called Conquered Territory. Ladybrand was named after Lady Catharina Brand, the mother of President Brand of the Orange Free State Republic.

The small Catharina Brand Museum (Tue–Fri 9–12, 2–4, Sat 9–12) on Kerk Street has an exhibit about the huge and influential Lesotho Highlands Water Project (▷ 272), as well as some exhibits on bushmen and early administration of the Lesotho border.

There are two major San rock painting sites nearby, with paintings ranging in age from 5,000 to 250 years old; you can visit them with a guide from the tourist office. It is thought that these sites have the highest concentration of San paintings in South Africa.

✠ 330 J7 ℹ Maloti Tourism, 22 Kerk Street, Ladybrand 9745 ☎ 051-9240377 🕐 Mon–Fri 8–5

LESEDI CULTURAL VILLAGE

www.lesedi.com

The Lesedi Cultural Village includes four African villages representing Xhosa, Zulu, Pedi and Sotho peoples, with three-hour tours taking in all four. The tours include an audio-visual presentation covering aspects of tribal life of the 11 ethnic groups that live in South Africa. There's also music, singing and traditional dancing by more than 60 performers around a large fire in an amphitheatre. The morning tour includes lunch; afternoon visitors are given a dinner of game meat such as impala or crocodile. The Village makes an easy day trip from Johannesburg or Pretoria. If you want to stay longer, the Protea Hotel Lesedi is part of the cultural village.

✠ 324 K4 ☎ 012-2051394 🎫 Tours at 11.30 and 4.30 🎟 Adult R295, child (under 12) R150; the price includes a meal 🚌 On R512, 12km (7.5 miles) north of Lanseria Airport

INFORMATION

www.joburgtourism.co.za

✚ 324 K4 🛈 Johannesburg Tourism, 195 Jan Smuts Avenue, Johannesburg 2001 ☎ 011-2140700 🕓 Mon–Fri 8–5

www.visitgauteng.net

🛈 Gauteng Tourism Authority, 1 Central Place, corner of Jeppe and Henry Nxumalo streets, Newtown
☎ 011-6391600 🕓 Mon–Fri 8–5

Above *The Newtown district of Johannesburg has been extensively revitalized*

INTRODUCTION

The high plateau on which Johannesburg was built was formerly an arid place sparsely inhabited by Boer farmers grazing cattle and cultivating maize and wheat. In little over 100 years, Johannesburg has grown into the wealthiest city in Africa. Settlers from all over the world poured in from the first weeks of the gold rush in the 1880s, producing a vibrant and cosmopolitan town. Apartheid changed all that, creating deep divisions in society that remain evident today. Under apartheid, the African population was evicted to new townships, such as Soweto (▷ 231), 20km (12 miles) to the southwest of the city. However, since the mid-1980s the movement of Africans from the city to the townships has been reversed and this trend has continued and been bolstered by the arrival of new immigrants.

Despite apartheid's demise, Johannesburg is still on the whole a segregated city with its heart and neighbouring suburbs, such as Hillbrow, largely home to a black urban population, which inhabits a condensed area of overcrowded high-rise apartments where poverty and crime are rife. The city's thriving suburbs are clustered around the main highway to Pretoria, the M1. The hills to the north of downtown Johannesburg are where you'll find large residential areas with rows of mansions, well-tended gardens and shopping malls. What is unusual is the amount of protection around the properties—razor wire, guard dogs and armed response warnings are the norm. These suburbs are in fact far safer than central Johannesburg and have a good choice of visitor accommodation, particularly in Rosebank and Sandton. Many of the sights, shopping malls and entertainment complexes are in the suburbs, so there is little reason to venture into the city to find facilities. To the east of Rosebank are the trendy suburbs of Melville, Parkhurst and Parktown, where Johannesburg's more popular restaurants and nightlife are to be found.

WHAT TO SEE

APARTHEID MUSEUM

www.apartheidmuseum.org

One of the finest museums in the country, the Apartheid Museum provides an excellent insight into what South Africa—past and present—is all about. This extraordinarily powerful museum was officially opened by Nelson Mandela in April 2002 and it has since become the city's leading visitor attraction. It is divided into 'spaces', which highlight aspects of South Africa's recent history. When paying your entry fee you are issued randomly with a white or non-white ticket that takes you through one of two different entry points to symbolize the segregation of apartheid. The building itself has an innovative design to reflect the museum's chilling theme, using harsh concrete, raw brick, steel bars and barbed wire.

The museum begins with a 15-minute video, taking you briefly through Voortrekker history to the Afrikaner government of 1948, which implemented apartheid. The 'spaces' are dedicated to the rise of nationalism in 1948, pass laws, segregation, the first response from townships such as Sharpeville and Langa, the forced removals and the implementation of the Group Areas Act. From here, exhibits cover the rise of Black Consciousness, the student uprisings in Soweto in 1976, and political prisoners and executions.

The reforms during the 1980s and 1990s are well documented, including President F. W. de Klerk's unbanning of political parties, Mandela's release, the first democratic elections in 1994, the lifting of sanctions and the new constitution. The exhibitions effectively use multimedia, such as television screens, recorded interviews and news footage, all providing a startlingly clear picture of the harshness and tragedy of the apartheid years.

✉ Next to Gold Reef City, Northern Parkway and Gold Reef Road, Ormonde 2091
☎ 011-3094700 🕐 Tue–Sun 10–5 🎟 Adult R50, child (under 12) R30

CONSTITUTION HILL

www.constitutionhill.org.za

Opened in 2004 on the site of Johannesburg's notorious Old Fort Prison complex, this is one of the city's modern tourist attractions that, like the

Below left *Tempting pastries for sale at a local bakery*
Below *Street artist at work*

Above *Statue of the great man himself in Nelson Mandela Square, Sandton*
Right *The Apartheid Museum, Johannesburg*

Apartheid Museum, uses multimedia tools to enhance its displays. Known as Number Four, the old prison, which closed only in the 1980s, was known for holding hundreds of blacks in appalling, overcrowded conditions; most had been arrested for not carrying their passbooks. Well-known inmates include Nelson Mandela, Mahatma Gandhi and many of the leading anti-apartheid activists. You can wander around the complex by yourself or there are regular tours, which include a video about Mandela's time here, a tour of the women's gaol and a photo exhibition of ex-inmates and wardens. You can still see graffiti on the backs of the cell doors and the giant pots out of which prisoners were given porridge. South Africa's new Constitutional Court has been built here and some of the bricks from the prison were used in the new court as a symbol of the injustice of the past being used to build justice in the future. You can visit the foyer of the court to see the unusual modern architecture, which also has some interesting artwork.
✉ 1 Kotze Street, Braamfontein ☎ 011-3813100 🕐 Mon–Fri 9–5, Sat 10–3
✋ Adult R35, child (5–12) R20

MUSEUM AFRICA

This museum is housed in the city's former fruit and vegetable market. It focuses on the black experience of living in Johannesburg, with displays about the struggle for democracy and about life in the gold mines and the townships; there are mock-ups of both a mine shaft and an informal settlement. Other sections include a gallery dedicated to San rock art and a display about the life of Mahatma Gandhi. The photographic gallery on the fourth floor has a collection of early photographs of Soweto. Most Johannesburg city tours allow at least a couple of hours in this rewarding museum.
✉ 121 Bree Street, Newtown 2001 ☎ 011-8335624 🕐 Tue–Sun 9–5 ✋ Free

KWAZULU MUTI SHOP (MUSEUM OF MAN AND SCIENCE)

This is actually a shop, rather than a museum. It has been here since 1897 selling products used in 'muti', traditional medicines used by indigenous healers to treat physical ailments — as well as for rather more sinister undertakings. While largely misunderstood by white South Africans, their mystical powers are highly revered among much of the African community. The ingredients on sale include leaves, seeds and bark, as well as the rather more specialized items, such as ostrich feet. City tours usually stop here.
✉ 14 Diagonal Street, Newtown 2001 ☎ 011-8364470 🕐 Mon–Fri 7.30–5, Sat 7.30–1
✋ Free

GOLD REEF CITY

www.goldreefcity.co.za

Gold Reef City is built on the site of one of Johannesburg's gold mining areas, but today has developed into a garish theme park with rides, amusement arcades and a gaudy casino. Of greater interest is the Jozi Story of Gold, which includes a visit to the original miners' cottages and the tour of the gold mine, which drops to a depth of about 220m (720ft), taking you down No. 14 Shaft, one of the richest deposits of gold in its day.

✉ Northern Parkway and Gold Reef Road, Ormonde 2091 ☎ 011-2486800
🕐 Tue–Sun 9.30–5 ✋ Jozi Story of Gold: adult R170, childer (under 16) R70; theme park: R150, child (under 1.3m/4ft tall) R100, family R470

JOHANNESBURG ZOO

www.jhbzoo.org.za

The city zoo was established in 1904. It has around 400 different species housed in an area of parkland and gardens covering 54ha (133 acres). The ponds attract free-ranging aquatic birds, which come here to breed. All the enclosures have been upgraded, and the night tours to see the nocturnal animals are a lot of fun, particularly for children, ending with toasted marshmallows and a hot chocolate around a bonfire.

✉ Jan Smuts Avenue, Parktown 2193 ☎ 011-6462000 🕐 Daily 8.30–5.30, last ticket 4
✋ Adult R50, child (3–12) R30 🍴

MORE TO SEE

NEWTOWN CULTURAL PRECINCT AND MARKET THEATRE COMPLEX

After years of deterioration, Newtown is being developed as the cultural heart of Johannesburg, and a huge regeneration project has seen the introduction of closed-circuit TV cameras, a police presence and the revamping of Mary Fitzgerald Square into a smart cobbled plaza surrounded by shops and restaurants. Unlike the rest of the city centre, it is safe to wander around the square and the facilities lining it, including the Market Theatre Complex (▷ 236), Museum Africa (▷ 226) and Newtown Park. There is safe parking on the eastern part of Mary Fitzgerald Square and behind at the back of the Market Theatre. Newtown can now be accessed from Braamfontein in the north by the impressive gleaming white Nelson Mandela Bridge, which spans more than 40 railway tracks.

✉ Bree Street, Newtown 2001

WORLD OF BEER

www.worldofbeer.co.za

Lovers of the amber nectar will appreciate the South African Breweries (SAB) World of Beer. SAB dominate the African beer industry, and their Castle Lager is probably the most popular beer between Cape Town and Cairo. The 90-minute tour covers the brewing process and a variety of mock-up bars, with opportunities to sample the product at the end.

✉ 15 President Street, Newtown 2001 ☎ 011-8364900 🕐 Tue–Sat 10–6 ✋ R30 including two complimentary beers

SOUTH AFRICAN NATIONAL MUSEUM OF MILITARY HISTORY

This museum has exhibits about the role South African forces played in World War II including artillery pieces, aircraft and tanks. There is a more up-to-date section illustrating the war in Angola, with displays of modern armaments, such as captured Soviet tanks and French Mirage fighter planes. Casspirs, the armoured personnel carriers used by security forces in the townships during black uprisings against apartheid are also on display.

✉ 20 Erlswold Way, Saxonwold 2196 ☎ 011-6465513 🕐 Daily 9–4.30 ✋ Adult R50, child (under 16) R20

TIP

» Despite (very successful) efforts in recent years to make downtown Jo'burg safer, it is still not wise to go anywhere on foot; visit this part of the city on an organized tour only. Outlying sights such as the Apartheid Museum can easily be visited by car.

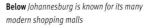

Below *Johannesburg is known for its many modern shopping malls*

INFORMATION

www.sanparks.org
www.tshwane.gov.za
🞢 324 K4 ℹ Tshwane Tourism
Information Bureau, in The Old
Netherlands Bank, Church Square,
City Centre 0002 ☎ 012-3581430
🕓 Mon–Fri 8–5 ❓ The main office of
South African National Parks (SANParks)
is at 643 Leyds Street, Muckleneuk 0002
☎ 012-4289111 (open for telephone
reservations Mon-Fri 7.30–5, Sat 8–1)

INTRODUCTION

Pretoria, also known as Tshwane, is the administrative capital of South Africa
and the third largest city in the country. Despite almost merging into
Johannesburg, 56km (35 miles) to the south, the two cities couldn't be more
different in atmosphere. Like most major cities in South Africa, Pretoria has gone
through a transformation in recent years. With the demise of apartheid, black
South Africans are again permitted to live and work freely in central Pretoria, with
the result that it feels much livelier and more African than before.

Most of the historic and interesting sights are outside the city, dotted around
the surrounding hills, as the heart of the city was designed with corporate and
governmental bodies in mind. Although Pretoria has a fairly good local bus
service (in contrast to many South African cities), it does not cover all the main
sights, so it is best to rent a car or take a half-day tour with a guide.

WHAT TO SEE

VOORTREKKER MONUMENT

www.voortrekkermon.org.za
Set on a hillside to the south of the city, the sombre-looking Voortrekker
Monument was completed in 1949 to commemorate the Great Trek of the
1830s (▷ 33), when the Voortrekkers headed north from the Cape with their
ox-wagons. It's a 40sq m (430sq ft) windowless sandstone block. Inside are 27
marble friezes depicting the trek and scenes from the Zulu wars, while outside
on the walls are 64 ox-wagons. Guides are available to take visitors through what
is essentially the history of the Afrikaner people . There's an elevator and stairs
to take you up to the roof, from where there are far-reaching views over the
surrounding countryside.
✉ Eeufees Road, Groenkloof 0027 ☎ 021-3266770 🕓 Sep–Apr daily 8–6; May–Aug 8–5
💲 Adult R35, child (under 18) R15

CHURCH SQUARE

The oldest buildings in Pretoria are in Church Square, which was once a
Voortrekker marketplace. Today it is the focus of the city and a popular meeting
spot for locals. A rather unattractive statue of Afrikaner political hero Paul Kruger
(▷ 34) stands in the middle of the square, surrounded by fluttering flocks of
pigeons and flanked by late 19th-century banks and government offices. The
most interesting of these is the Palace of Justice, where Nelson Mandela and

Above *Pretoria's jacaranda trees in full
bloom in spring*

other leaders of the ANC were tried during the Treason Trials of 1963–64. On the southwest side is the Raadsaal, or Parliament; the Old Netherlands Bank building now houses the tourist office.

PRESIDENT KRUGER HOUSE
The unpretentious house where President Kruger lived between 1884 and 1900 is now a museum, with a collection of his possessions, as well as objects relating to the Anglo-Boer War. At the back of the house is the state coach and his private rail carriage (car).
✉ 60 Church Street, 0002 ☎ 012-3269172 ⏱ Daily 8.30–5 ✋ Adult R35, child (under 18) R15

MELROSE HOUSE
www.melrosehouse.co.za
The Treaty of Vereeniging, ending the Anglo-Boer War (1899–1902), was signed in Melrose House on 31 May. The house was originally built in 1886 and is regarded as one of the finest examples of Victorian domestic architecture in South Africa. The marble columns, stained-glass windows and mosaic floors all help to create a feeling of serene style and wealth. The house was restored after it was bombed by right-wingers in 1990. Today you might be lucky to catch the occasional classical concerts in the grounds.
✉ 275 Jacob Maré Street, 0002 ☎ 012-3222805 ⏱ Tue–Sun 10–5 ✋ Adult R8, child (2–12) R5 💻

BURGERS PARK
Pretoria's most central city park is a popular meeting place where visitors relax in the shade of rubber trees, palms and jacarandas. The 'florarium' houses a collection of exotic plants shown in contrasting environments, ranging from subtropical flowers to succulents from the arid Karoo and Kalahari regions. Elsewhere in the garden is a memorial to the officers and men of the South African Scottish Regiment who were killed during World War I.
✉ Van der Walt and Andries streets ⏱ Summer 6am–10pm; winter 6–6

MORE TO SEE
TRANSVAAL MUSEUM
This natural history museum is famous for holding the original hominid *Australopithecus africanus* fossil, known as 'Mrs Ples' (▷ 31), even though it's a Mr, but you must get special permission to view it.
✉ Paul Kruger Street, 0002 ☎ 012-3227632 ⏱ Daily 8–4 ✋ Adult R20, child (under 18) R10 🏛

UNION BUILDINGS
The magnificent red sandstone complex of the Union Buildings, designed in grand imperial style by the British architect Herbert Baker and completed in 1913, overlooks the heart of the city. Today it is the administrative headquarters of the South African Presidency and was famously the site of Nelson Mandela's inauguration as first black president on 10 May 1994. Note that the interior is not open to the public, but a good reason for coming here is the city view.
✉ Arcadia 0083 ☎ 012-3005200

PRETORIA ART MUSEUM
www.tshwane.gov.za
The city's main art museum houses a fine collection of South African art and 17th-century paintings, including works by Pierneef, Frans Oerder and Anton van Wou.
✉ Arcadia Park, Arcadia 0083 ☎ 012-3441807 ⏱ Tue–Sun 10–5 ✋ Adult R6, child (under 18) R4 💻

TIPS
» The best time to visit is in spring, when the city is transformed by 60,000 purple-flowering jacaranda trees.
» It is safe to walk around central Pretoria and the suburbs during the day, but avoid walking there at night.

Below *The elegant Victorian facade of Melrose House*

LION PARK

www.lion-park.com

If your ambition is to photograph lions, you are unlikely to get any closer to them than here, a short drive from Johannesburg: There are more than 80 lions in the park, including many cubs (with which you can have close encounters) and a rare male white lion. Although the animals are bred in captivity, they are well cared for and have ample space in the drive-through enclosures. The lions are accustomed to vehicles and don't think twice about strolling right up to a car, so keep windows closed and adhere to any safety notices. Other animals kept here include hyena, cheetah and a variety of antelope.

🞩 324 K4 ☎ 011-6919905 🕓 Mon–Fri 8.30–5, Sat–Sun 8.30–6 🎫 Adult R115, child (4–12) R80 🍴 🏧 🚌 30-min drive from Johannesburg on the Old Pretoria–Krugersdorp road

MAROPENG

www.maropeng.co.za

Maropeng means 'returning to the place of origin' in the Setswana language and this modern, award-winning interactive museum relates the story of the creation of our world and the evolution of man over a four-billion-year period. Opened by Thabo Mbeki in 2005, it makes good use of computer wizardry and multimedia displays. The entrance has been built as a grassy burial mound, while the exit is a sleek structure of modern glass and concrete; the journey from one to the other begins with a boat ride through a tunnel of erupting volcanoes, icebergs, the eye of a storm and swirling gases that made up the planet. There are also displays on how man has changed the environment, population, use of the earth's resources and global appetite. Allow at least two to three hours for the experience.

🞩 324 K4 ☎ 014-5779000 🕓 Daily 9–5, last boat ride at 4 🎫 Adult R105, child (4–14) R60; combination tickets with Sterkfontein Caves available 🍴 🚌 On the D400 off the R24, 15km (9.5 miles) southeast of Magaliesburg

PHILIPPOLIS

The town of Philippolis is the oldest in the Free State, founded in 1823 as a station of the London Missionary Society. It has a number of attractive old buildings along the one main street. Look out for the Dutch Reformed Church, which has a pulpit carved from olive wood, and examples of Karoo-style houses. The tiny Transgariep Museum (Mon–Fri 10–12), in a typical Griqua cottage, tells you about the history of the region. The Griqua—a people of mixed race, former slaves—settled in the area seeking independence. The ashes of author Sir Laurens van der Post are kept in the memorial gardens named in his memory.

🞩 328 H8 🛈 Municipality Building, 25 Kok Street, Philippolis 9970 ☎ 051-7730006 🕓 Mon–Fri 8–5

PRETORIA

▷ 228–229.

SOWETO

▷ 231.

STERKFONTEIN CAVES

www.maropeng.co.za

Dubbed the Cradle of Humankind, the area around the Sterkfontein Caves holds some of the world's most important archaeological sites, where more than 40 per cent of all hominid fossils have been discovered. In 1936 the most important find was made, the first adult skull of the ape-man *Australopithecus africanus*—nicknamed 'Mrs Ples'. The skull, found by Dr. Robert Broom, is estimated to be more than 2.6 million years old (▷ 31).

The caves have six chambers, which are connected by passages. Tours begin in the impressive multimedia visitor's centre, then pass through the six caves, taking in the archaeological sites.

🞩 324 K4 ☎ 014-5779000 🕓 Daily 9–5, last tour at 4 🎫 Adult R110, child (4–14) R65; combination tickets with Maropeng available 🚌 Tours every hour, departing on the half-hour 🍴 🏧 🚌 Off N14 from Randburg towards Hartbeetspoort Dam

XHARIEP

Xhariep is the region to the southwest of Bloemfontein, seldom-visited ranching country with a handful of towns, including Philippolis (see above). During the 19th century this was big game country—in 1848, mail could not be despatched after 4pm because of the danger posed by wild animals. In 1860, a hunt that was organized for Prince Alfred, the second son of Queen Victoria, killed nearly 5,000 animals on a single day. Little wildlife remains today.

🞩 328 H7

Below *Karoo-style houses in Philippolis*

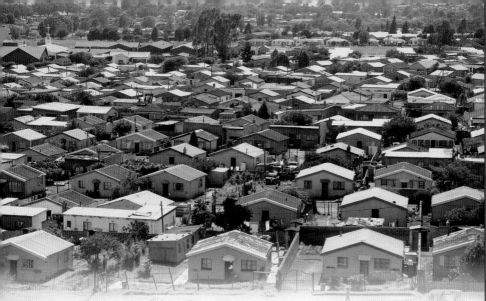

SOWETO

One of the country's highlights, Soweto (short for South Western Townships) is famous as a hotbed of political struggle, the powerhouse of the country's black urban culture. The township grew dramatically in the 1950s and 1960s when black people were forced to relocate from central Johannesburg. Today, Soweto is South Africa's largest urban living space, with an estimated population of at least one million.

MANDELA FAMILY MUSEUM

The most popular sight in Soweto is the house in Vilakazi Street where Nelson and Winnie Mandela lived before he was imprisoned in 1962. The tiny three-room house was rebuilt after being bombed several times by the South African security forces. On his release from prison, Mandela insisted on moving back into this house, but its small size and problems of security put too much of a strain on him and he moved out of Soweto. On the same road is the former home of Mandela's fellow Nobel Prize winner, Archbishop Desmond Tutu.

WALTER SISULU SQUARE

Formerly known as Freedom Square, this is where the Freedom Charter was presented by the ANC to a mass gathering of people in 1955. One of the delegates was Walter Sisulu, after whom the square was renamed in honour of his death in 2003. The authorities broke up the illegal gathering, but the charter, which called for equality for all, remained the cornerstone of ANC policy. The square is attractively paved and has a number of monuments, including the Ten Pillars of Freedom, which represent the 10 clauses of the Freedom Charter.

HECTOR PIETERSON MUSEUM AND MEMORIAL

Hector Pieterson was a 13-year-old shot dead on 16 June 1976 by riot police during a school demonstration, known as the Soweto Uprising (▷ 39). The iconic photograph of Hector's body being carried by a friend with Hector's wailing 17-year-old sister running alongside flashed around the world and sparked the final 10-year battle against apartheid, with townships across the country rising up in revolt. The museum is similar to the Apartheid Museum (▷ 225), with powerful multimedia exhibits.

✉ Khumalo and Pela streets, Orlando West ☎ 011-5360611 🕓 Mon–Sat 10–5, Sun 10–4 🖐 Adult R15, child (13–16) R5 📅

INFORMATION

✚ 324 K4 ℹ Soweto Tourism Information, Walter Sisulu Square of Independence, Kliptown ☎ 011-9453111 🕓 Mon–Fri 8–5

TIPS

» It is not safe to visit Soweto on your own, but there are a number of excellent tours run by reputable operators.
» Choose a tour that includes a walk: Chatting to local Sowetans can be the most enjoyable part of the experience.
» Don't expect many 'sights'—Soweto's main appeal is its atmosphere
» The largest football stadium in Africa, FNB Stadium, also known as Soccer City, is located in Soweto.

Above *Massed painted tin roofs in Soweto, 13km (8 miles) outside Johannesburg and home to millions*

THE EASTERN HIGHLANDS

This trip through the eastern Free State takes in enormous eroded sandstone formations, golden fields of wheat and sunflowers, and fruit orchards (flowering or heavy with fruit, depending on the season), with the lofty Maluti Mountains of Lesotho serving as a backdrop.

THE DRIVE

Distance: 350km (220 miles)
Allow: 2 days
Start at: Harrismith
End at: Ladybrand

★ Begin the drive at Harrismith. Drive along the R712 for 11km (7 miles) then turn left on the R74 towards the Olviviershoek Pass; the entrance to Sterkfontein Dam Nature Reserve is 20km (12.5 miles) on the left.

❶ Lying in the foothills of the Drakensberg, the Sterkfontein Dam Nature Reserve covers an area of more than 180sq km (70sq miles), and the lake formed by the dam has a 104km (65-mile) shoreline, one of the largest in South Africa. It offers excellent watersports and fishing and

you can go hiking—there are good opportunities for viewing raptors, and an interesting vulture 'restaurant' attracts Cape and bearded vultures. The dam forms part of the Tugela Vaal water transfer scheme, which supplies drinking water to the major part of Gauteng.

Retrace your route back to the R712 and follow signs to the Golden Gate Highlands National Park, which is 69km (43 miles) from Sterkfontein.

❷ The Golden Gate Highlands National Park (▷ 222) is famous for its huge, dramatically sculpted rock formations that vary markedly in coloration: Sandstone and iron oxides have combined to create an eye-catching array of reds, oranges, yellows and golden browns. The

Golden Gate itself is the narrow, cliff-flanked valley you drive through on your way to the reception and information office. The park is worth exploring at leisure, and it has two pleasant rest camps (▷ 240). Otherwise, the main road passes right through the middle of the park, and from it you have excellent views of the rock formations.

Continue west towards Clarens, passing on your left the turning for the Basotho Cultural Village (▷ 221).

❸ Clarens (▷ 221) is an attractive village, especially in autumn when the Lombardy poplars turn a deep gold. A willow-fringed stream runs through the village, and it is overlooked by a massive rock feature known as the Titanic.

Above and opposite *The splendid escarpments of the Golden Gate Highlands National Park*

particularly associated with cherries. It hosts an annual Cherry Festival in November, when the town's streets and surrounding countryside are awash with frothy oceans of cherry blossoms. There are parades, a ball and the crowning of a Cherry Queen).

The final run (73km/45 miles) takes you to Ladybrand via Clocolan, a tiny town almost overwhelmed by enormous grain silos. You may pass weavers working the local sheep's wool and angora into tapestries.

6 Your final port of call is Ladybrand (▷ 223). The town is the last on the main road east into Lesotho, and it has benefited from the massive investment in the Lesotho Highlands Water Project (▷ 272).

WHEN TO GO
The countryside is especially attractive in the short spring (usually late October) and in autumn (February and March), when the fruit trees and fields are either in blossom or about to be harvested. Golden Gate Park gets large numbers of visitors and is best avoided during local school holidays. Winters can be uncomfortably cold.

WHERE TO EAT
ARTIST'S CAFÉ
The café serves milkshakes, pies, cakes, waffles, pastries, light meals and sandwiches, and there's a jungle gym for kids.
Windmill Centre, Main Road, Clarens
☎ 058-2561404 ⏰ Daily 8–5

Drive on along the valley of the Little Caledon River on the R711, following the signs to Fouriesburg (36km/22 miles).

4 Fouriesburg is a small town 12km (7.5 miles) from the border with Lesotho. Founded in 1892, it was named after Christoffel Fourie, the local farmer who originally owned the land. In Fouriesburg, turn east into Steyn Street, and drive until the end of the tar road, then turn left onto a gravel road for 1.7km (1 mile) until you reach the Meiringskloof Nature

Park, where among the cliffs is a large open cave, called *holkrans*, once a hideout during the Anglo-Boer War. For visitors with a head for heights there is a chain ladder which goes up a steep cliff face to a dam supplying water to Fouriesburg.

Continue on the R26 west to Ficksburg (55km/34 miles). On the way to Ficksburg, you'll see signs off the R26 to Rustler's Valley.

5 Ficksburg (▷ 222) sits amid lush farmlands. The town is

BLOEMFONTEIN
GOODYEAR PARK
www.cricket.co.za
International cricket matches are played at the Goodyear Park stadium, to the west of central Bloemfontein. The ground is a small stadium where fans can relax and enjoy themselves on grass banks.

✉ Bloemfontein 9301 ☎ 051-4306365 ⊙ Cricket season: Dec–Mar ✋ From R60

JAZZ TIME CAFÉ
www.jazztimecafe.co.za
This is a great place for an evening out with Bloemfontein's young and fashionable. It's a huge cocktail bar with an outside terrace and a mix of live music—jazz, blues and big-band. There's a Middle Eastern theme to the food, with interesting snacks like *zivas* (Yemeni pancakes).

✉ Loch Logan Waterfront 9301 ☎ 824-447730 ⊙ Daily 8pm–12 ✋ Free

LOCH LOGAN WATERFRONT
www.lochlogan.co.za
The attractive Loch Logan outdoor shopping mall sits next to a lake and dam in Kings Park. Some of Bloemfontein's trendiest restaurants and bars are scattered along the boardwalk on the water's edge. In addition to boutiques and galleries, there is an arts and crafts market that stocks good gifts from the region. It's currently being expanded to a four-storey mall to incorporate most of South Africa's chain stores.

✉ First Avenue, Bloemfontein 9301 ☎ 051-4483607 ⊙ Mon–Fri 9–6, Sat 9–5, Sun 9–2

CLARENS
BOKPOORT
www.bokpoort.co.za
The stables at Bokpoort offer the most exciting horseback riding trails in the region. Their standard route lasts for two days, spending a night at a campsite in the Maluti Mountains. There are also shorter trails lasting up to six hours on the surrounding farmland, during which you can see antelope and zebra.

☎ 058-2561181 ✋ From R225
🚗 Signposted 5km (3 miles) out of Clarens, on the road to Golden Gate

JOHAN SMITH ART GALLERY
www.johansmith.co.za
This is one of a clutch of art galleries and shops in Clarens. It sells vibrant oil paintings of South African rural life by celebrated artist Johan Smith, and stocks fine glass, ceramics and paintings by other local artists.

✉ Clarens Square, Clarens 9707 ☎ 058-2561620 ⊙ Mon–Thu 8–4.30, Fri–Sat 8–5, Sun 8–3

JOHANNESBURG
AFRICAN CRAFT MARKET OF ROSEBANK
www.craft.co.za
The former street traders of this area have now been housed in one ethnic-inspired building in the middle of the popular Mall of Rosebank. Curios from all over Africa are for sale at more than 140 stalls. Credit cards are accepted and shipping can be arranged. It's a lively spot, with street performers and musicians, and on Thursday evenings there's African food and a cabaret show.

✉ Cradock Avenue, Rosebank 2196 ☎ 011-8802906 ⊙ Daily 9–6

BASSLINE
www.bassline.co.za
Johannesburg's best jazz venue has moved from Melville into Newtown's old red-brick Music Hall and now has a capacity of 1,000. It regularly hosts South Africa's top jazz, hip-hop

Above *Nelson Mandela Square, Johannesburg*

and kwaito artists. Outside is a lovely statue of a soulful barefoot singer leaning into a microphone.

✉ 10 Henry Nxumalo Street, Newtown 2001 ☎ 011-8389145 🖐 R50

BLUES ROOM

www.bluesroom.co.za

One of the best jazz and blues venues in Gauteng, the Blues Room is a stylish basement bar and restaurant catering to music lovers who are also after a decent meal. There's live music every night and the pace picks up later in the evening when diners take to the floor for a dance. The American-style dishes on the menu are named after blues legends.

✉ Village Walk Mall, Sandton 2146 ☎ 011-7845527 🕐 Tue–Sat 7pm–late 🖐 R60

CATZ PYJAMAS

www.catzpyjamas.co.za

Jo'burg's original 24-hour bistro and cocktail bar has a funky atmosphere, famous nachos and potent sangria. Although it's open all day, it really only picks up late in the evening, carrying on until the early hours.

✉ Corner of 3rd and Main streets, Melville 2092 ☎ 011-7268596 🕐 Open 24 hours 🖐 Free

CINEMA NOUVEAU ROSEBANK

The main art-house cinema shows international (mostly European) and South African independent films, many with subtitles.

✉ Rosebank Mall, corner of Cradock and Baker streets, Rosebank 2196 ☎ 082-16789 (central reservations) 🕐 9.45–8.30 🖐 From R25

ELLIS PARK

www.ellispark.co.za

Ellis Park is the home of the Lions rugby team, and matches are played here regularly during the season (Feb–May). The stadium seats 50,000 spectators and it can be a lively day out, with fans bringing their *braais* (barbecues) and beers with them. It's also home to the city's Kaizer Chiefs soccer club.

✉ Staib Street, Doornfontein 2094 ☎ 011-4028644 🖐 From R40

FASHIONTV CAFÉ

www.ftv.co.za

At this stylish, contemporary venue, where the décor is all wood and glass, you can enjoy a meal, have a quiet drink at the bar, or dance the night away to mainstream commercial music.

✉ Shop L09, Michelangelo Towers, Maude Street, Sandton 2146 ☎ 011-7831866 🕐 Tue–Sat 12pm–2am 🖐 After 10pm: men R150, ladies R50

FNB STADIUM

The country's greatest soccer teams are in Johannesburg, and the FNB Stadium, on the outskirts of Soweto, is the best place to see a match. More popularly called Soccer City, it is the largest of Jo'burg's stadiums and the home of the South African Football Association. This stadium was the venue for the opening and final matches of the 2010 Soccer World Cup.

✉ Nasrec Road, Ormonde 2091 ☎ 011-494 3522 🕐 Football season: Feb–Sep

GOLD REEF CITY

www.goldreefcity.co.za

This large theme park, created around the idea of a 19th-century gold mine, is a big hit with locals and visitors alike. It has a large number of thrilling rides and there's a huge Ferris wheel. Many attractions are aimed specifically at children, with a circus in December.

✉ Northern Parkway and Gold Reef Road, Ormonde 2091 ☎ 011-2486800 🕐 Tue–Sun 9.30–5 🖐 Adult R150, child (under 1.3m/4ft tall) R100, family R470

HYDE PARK MALL

www.hydeparkshopping.co.za

For a taste of Johannesburg's luxurious side, head to Hyde Park Mall, which has long been popular with the ladies-who-lunch set. There are a number of stylish (and expensive) boutiques, cafés and smart restaurants, and an outlet of the Exclusive Books chain, which often hosts book signings.

✉ Jan Smuts Avenue, Hyde Park 2196 ☎ 011-3254340 🕐 Mon–Sat 9–6, Sun 10–1

THE JOBURG THEATRE COMPLEX

www.joburgtheatre.com

This modern theatre is an impressive set-up with four auditoria and frequent performances of South African plays. There is also a schedule of visiting international musicals, ballets and classical orchestras, with a mix of traditional performances and large-scale productions.

✉ Loveday Street, Braamfontein 2001 ☎ 011-8776800 🖐 From R110

JOHANNESBURG ZOO

www.jhbzoo.org.za

Covering 54ha (133 acres) of spacious enclosures surrounded by moats and trees, the zoo is home to more than 2,000 animals from just under 400 species, and has a number of child-orientated displays. The night tours to see the nocturnal animals are particularly fun, ending with marshmallows and hot chocolate around a bonfire. There's a small restaurant on site serving light meals.

✉ Jan Smuts Avenue, Parktown 2193 ☎ 011-6462000 🕐 Daily 8.30–5.30, last ticket 4 🖐 Adult R50, child (3–12) R30

KIM SACKS GALLERY

A selection of quality ethnic art from all over Africa is for sale in this gallery, occupying a lovely old house and regarded as one of the top galleries in the city. There is a good range of contemporary South African pieces, including sculptures, prints, beadwork and ceramics.

✉ 153 Jan Smuts Avenue, Parkwood 2193 ☎ 011-4475804 🕐 Mon–Sat 8–5

THE MALL OF ROSEBANK

www.themallofrosebank.co.za

This mall has one of the most pleasant eating areas, a large open-air piazza lined with cafés, making it ideal for sitting in the sun and watching people go by. The mall's layout incorporates the new line and station for the Gautrain. It has much more of a village feel than the average indoor shopping mall, with a good selection of clothes shops and a busy flea market held on the roof every Sunday (9–5). Just outside, on Cradock Avenue, is the popular African Craft Market, a bustling building housing dozens of stalls selling arts and crafts from across the continent (▷ 234).

✉ Corner of Cradock and Baker streets, Rosebank 2196 ☎ 011-7885530
🕐 Mon–Fri 9–6, Sat 9–5, Sun 9–4

MARKET THEATRE
www.markettheatre.co.za

The Market Theatre was famous for staging community theatre and controversial political plays during the 1980s, but the decline of the central city area made the theatre less popular. The Newtown Cultural Precinct is now once more the hub of Johannesburg's arts scene and the theatre has been revitalized into one of the best in Gauteng.

✉ 56 Margaret Mcingana Street, 2001
☎ 011-8321641 ✋ From R40

MONSOON LAGOON
www.monsoonlagoon.co.za

Johannesburg's biggest and brightest nightclub is this huge special events venue, which regularly hosts TV and fashion parties. It's a trendy, mainstream club (over 21s only) spreading over several levels with a number of dance floors, bars and lounges. Very lavish and totally over the top, it makes for a great night out.

✉ In Emperor's Palace Casino, Jones Road, next to the airport ☎ 011-9281000
🕐 Wed–Sat 9pm–late ✋ From R50–R70

Below *Traditional dancing at Gold Reef City*

MONTECASINO
www.montecasino.co.za

There are two theatres in this casino and entertainment complex. The 1,900-seat Teatro Theatre was built in 2007 specifically to stage South Africa's version of *The Lion King* musical, while the smaller 320-seat Pieter Toerien Theatre showcases new plays by local writers, revues and comedy.

✉ Corner of William Nicol Drive and Witkoppen Road, Sandton 2021
☎ 011-5107000 ✋ From R125

MONTECASINO BIRD GARDENS
www.montecasino.co.za

This is a good family attraction with a wide range of birds, mammals and reptiles. Children will be enthralled by the massed flight of birds that takes place during the presentations at 11am and 3pm (also 1pm Sat–Sun). Various other shows take place during school holidays.

✉ Fourways junction of William Nicol Drive and Witkoppen Road, Sandton 2021
☎ 011-5111864 🕐 Daily 8.30–5
✋ Adult R38, child (3–10) R22.50

ROXY'S RHYTHM BAR

This lively club attracts a student crowd who come for the dance music—deep house, garage, hip hop and drum 'n' bass. There are live acts on some nights, and the theme of a particular evening changes according to the DJ.

✉ 20 Main Road, Melville 2092
☎ 011-726 6019 🕐 Mon–Sat 8pm–late
✋ R30–R60

ROYAL JOHANNESBURG AND KENSINGTON GOLF CLUB
www.royaljk.za.com

There are more than 40 golf courses within the vicinity of Johannesburg. Established in 1890, this is one of the oldest, with two courses. The East Course is of championship standard and is where the South African Open is held, while the West Course is slightly shorter but provides golfers with a fairly stern test of their ability.

✉ Fairway Avenue, Linksfield North 2192
☎ 011-6403021 🕐 No visitors on Sat
✋ Green fees from R380

SANDTON CITY AND NELSON MANDELA SQUARE
www.sandton-city.co.za

The biggest of the city's malls, Sandton City has undergone two major redevelopments in recent years. It has a huge range of chain stores selling clothes, books, music, art and curios, as well as a multiscreen cinema (see Ster Kinekor below), supermarkets, hotels, restaurants, cafés and bars. Across a walkway is Nelson Mandela Square, with boutiques and a number of smart restaurants, and a large statue of a smiling Nelson Mandela looking over the outside tables.

✉ Corner of Sandton Drive and Rivonia Road, Sandton 2196 ☎ 011-2176000
🕐 Shops: Mon–Sat 9–6, Sun 10–4

STER KINEKOR
www.sterkinekor.com

The Sandton City branch of this multiscreen cinema chain shows all the major international releases throughout the day and evening.

✉ Sandton City, corner of Sandton Drive and Rivonia Road ☎ 082-16789 🕐 Daily 11–11 ✋ From R25

WANDERERS' STADIUM
www.wanderers.co.za

The Wanderers' Stadium is one of South Africa's premier cricket grounds and regular international matches are played here in season. This was a major venue for the 2003 Cricket World Cup.

✉ Corlett Drive, Illovo 2196 ☎ 011-3401500 ✋ From R25 (weekend test match), from R100 (one-day international)

PRETORIA
DROP ZONE
www.clubdropzone.co.za

This is a stylish late-night cocktail bar where music has a chilled vibe. It's more popular with young professionals than the usual student crowd, and it's strictly over-21s only. There are promotional nights, top DJs, VIP lounges and a daily happy hour (8–9pm).

✉ 141 Burnett Street, Hatfield 0083
☎ 012-3626528 🕐 Daily 8pm–4am
✋ From R50

HATFIELD PLAZA

www.hatfieldplaza.co.za

This relatively small shopping mall in the lively suburb of Hatfield has a good choice of accommodation and restaurants. The upper levels of the car park are transformed into a lively flea market on Sundays (10–5), selling anything from African crafts to CDs and clothes.

✉ 1122 Burnett Street, Hatfield 0083
☎ 012-3625842 🕐 Shops: Mon–Fri 9–5.30, Sat 9–3, Sun 9–1

LOFTUS VERSVELD RUGBY STADIUM

www.thebulls.co.za

Pretoria is the home of the Blue Bulls Rugby Union, and all their matches are played at this stadium in Sunnyside, close to the middle of town. It is also the venue for occasional soccer matches. It was specially upgraded for the 2010 FIFA World Cup.

✉ Kirkness Street, Sunnyside 0002
☎ 012-4200700

MENLYN PARK

www.menlynpark.co.za

Pretoria's premier new mall for 'shoppertainment' is Menlyn Park, which has some 300 shops and restaurants, a 15-screen cinema, an IMAX cinema, a bowling alley, an unsual drive-in cinema, go-karting and other family entertainments. Its architectural focal point is its large tent-like roof that can be seen from some distance away.

✉ Atterbury Road, Menlo Park 0181
☎ 012-3488766 🕐 Shops: Mon–Thu 9–7, Fri 9–9, Sat 9–7, Sun 9–5

PRETORIA ZOO

www.fotz.co.za

Now known officially as the National Zoological Gardens, this is South Africa's largest and best designed zoo. It is surprisingly spacious, with animal enclosures, an aquarium and a reptile park. There's a cableway that stretches right over the zoo, plus electric self-drive buggies to help you get around. The grounds are criss-crossed with 6km (4 miles) of trails with pleasant picnic sites.

✉ Corner of Paul Kruger and Boom streets
☎ 012-3283265 🕐 Daily 8–5.30 💰 Adult R55, child (2–15) R35

SUPERSPORT STADIUM

www.titans.co.za

Supersport Stadium, formerly Centurion Park, the ground where international cricket matches for Pretoria are played, is 23km (14 miles) from the centre of town. Home to the Nashua Titans cricket team, the Park is a modern, circular stadium dominated by a huge single grandstand. The rest of the boundary is made up of grass banks which are great places for spectators to have

FESTIVALS AND EVENTS

JANUARY

JOHANNESBURG INTERNATIONAL MOZART FESTIVAL

www.join-mozart-festival.org

Johannesburg's International Mozart Festival, held over two weeks, offers a range of concerts, featuring symphony and chamber orchestras as well as soloists. There are also talks, lectures and outdoor events.

✉ Linder Auditorium, 27 St Andrews Road, Parktown, Johannesburg ☎ 011-4479264 🕐 Late January to early February

FEBRUARY/MARCH

FNB VITA DANCE UMBRELLA FESTIVAL

www.artslink.co.za/arts

This annual event showcases contemporary dance and choreography, and has become one of the most important dance festivals in South Africa.

✉ Various venues around Johannesburg
☎ 011-4922030 🕐 Mid-February to mid-March

EASTER

RAND EASTER SHOW

www.randshow.co.za

This festival is held for 17 days around Easter at the Expo Centre, Nasrec, and is a lively mixture of

exhibitions, events, stalls, food, concerts and funfairs.

✉ Johannesburg Kagiso Exhibitions, 100 Northern Parkway Road, Johannesburg 2091
☎ 011-4767031

AUGUST/SEPTEMBER

STANDARD BANK JOY OF JAZZ INTERNATIONAL FESTIVAL

www.standardbankarts.com/Jazz

This three-day festival is one of the country's foremost jazz platforms, uniting the finest South African musicians with international jazz stars. It attracts more than 20,000 music fans to the Cultural Precinct every year.

✉ Newtown Cultural Precinct, Johannesburg ☎ 011-7888725

SEPTEMBER

ARTS ALIVE

www.artsalive.co.za

Johannesburg's Arts Alive International Festival promotes itself as a cultural celebration of spring. The festival showcases a mixture of activities: concerts, dance, cabaret, art and theatre. Many of the events take place around the Newtown Cultural Precinct (▷ 227).

✉ Locations around Johannesburg
☎ 083-9158000

picnics and *braais* (barbecues).

☎ 012-6631005 🕐 Cricket season: Nov–Mar 💰 From R40 for domestic matches, R180 for international matches 🚗 Off the R21, between Pretoria and Johannesburg

TINGS & TIMES

Recently moved to bigger premises, this bar is popular for live music and can get very crowded, so be sure to arrive mid-evening to guarantee a table. It serves great cocktails, and Middle Eastern and vegetarian bites are dished out for late-night snacks.

✉ 1065 Arcadia Street, Hatfield 0083
☎ 012-4303176 🕐 Mon–Sat noon–late
✋ Free

PRICES AND SYMBOLS

The restaurants are listed alphabetically (excluding The) by town or area, then by name. The prices given are the average for a two-course lunch (L) and a three-course dinner (D) for one person, without drinks. The wine price is for the least expensive bottle.

For a key to the symbols, ▷ 2.

BLOEMFONTEIN

AVANTI
www.avantirestaurant.co.za
No-nonsense Italian food—pizzas, pasta, saltimbocca—as well as a good range of fish and seafood are on offer here. Leave room for the creamy tiramisu for dessert. It's a good option for families too, with a short but adequate children's menu.
✉ Loch Logan Waterfront ☎ 051-4474198 🕐 Mon–Sat 8.30am–10pm, Sun 9–3 🖐 L R70, D R 120, Wine R65

DE OUDE KRAAL
www.deoudekraal.com
Despite its remote location, reservations are essential at De Oude Kraal, famous for its *boerekos*—typical Afrikaner farmhouse food. You can have a traditional sheep pit barbecue around the *lapa* (thatched outdoor eating area), or for more

formal dinners there are six-course set menus served in the main farmhouse, while the wine cellar is a romantic setting for candlelit dinners. Various events are held throughout the year, including a venison festival and wine-tasting evenings with a formal dinner.
☎ 051-5640733 🕐 Daily 12.30–3, 6.30–late; dinner starts at 8.30 🖐 L R225, D R265, Wine R60 🚗 35km (22 miles) out of town, off the N1 to Cape Town

JOHANNESBURG

BENKEI
The décor of this Japanese restaurant is airy and modern, with white-tiled floors and cherrywood and granite furnishings. Sushi with all the trimmings is on the menu, but so are seafood fusion (consisting of raw tuna or salmon, cooked prawns, and avocado with mayonnaise dressing) or minced salmon or tuna with caviar, capers and onion. For those who don't fancy raw fish there is a good range of other choices, as well as vegetarian dishes. And if you don't drink saki, you can choose from the restaurant's wine list.
✉ Illovo Square, 3 Rivonia Road, Sandton 2196 ☎ 011-2686622 🕐 Daily 12–late 🖐 L R135, D R160, Wine R70

Above *De Oude Kraal restaurant near Bloemfontein has a lovely setting*

THE BUTCHER SHOP & GRILL
www.thebutchershop.co.za
This award-winning steak house is famous for its aged steaks, and although there are a few outlets around the country, this is the original. The menu focuses on succulent steaks and other grills; when available there is a specially aged T-bone that is cut to order. There's also a wide selection of seafood, starters and desserts, but only salads and one hot daily special for vegetarians. You can also buy vacuum-packed meat to take away.
✉ Nelson Mandela Square, Corner of West and Maude roads ☎ 011-7848676/7 🕐 Mon–Sat 12–10.45, Sun 12–9.45 🖐 L R120, D R220, Wine R150

CARNIVORE
www.carnivore.co.za
This has become something of an institution and is hugely popular with visitors, who come here for the ultimate 'African' dining experience. The rustic interior is adorned with zebra-skin chairs and a large central fire pit. Meals are all-the-meat-you-can-eat, with game carved with

spears and served on cast-iron plates. There's a choice of at least 10 different types of meat every day, including ostrich, crocodile, warthog and zebra as well as more conventional meats such as beef and pork, served with a selection of salads and sauces. Despite the restaurant's name, vegetarians also have a good choice, including *aviyal*, a mix of vegetables cooked in spicy coconut sauce.

✉ 69 Drift Boulevard, Muldersdrift 1747 ☎ 011-9506000 🕐 Daily 12–4.30, 6–12 🖐 L R165, D R200, Wine R85 🚗 30-min drive (approx 30km/ 18 miles) from central Johannesburg on the N14

FOURNO'S BAKERY
www.fournos.co.za
Fourno's bakers arrive at midnight to prepare delicious pastries, cakes, croissants, quiches and pies. Locals come here for big breakfasts, good coffees or just to hang out. Other branches are dotted around the city, including the domestic terminal at the airport.

✉ Dunkeld West Centre, Jan Smuts Avenue ☎ 011-3252110 🕐 Mon–Fri 7–6, Sat 7–4, Sun 7–2 🖐 L R45, Wine BYO

GRAMADOELAS
www.gramadoelas.co.za
One of the best places to get an overview of southern African dishes is at this long-standing and popular venue. Starters include fried mopani worms in chilli sauce, followed by *sosaties* (spicy kebabs) or *bobotie* (sweet and spicy ground beef pie). A delicious dessert is the sticky *malva* (sponge) pudding, or *kneffa* (filo pastry with almonds and cinnamon). This is also the place to try home-brewed sorghum beer or *mageu* (fermented milk). The interior is in appealing Cape Dutch style.

✉ Market Theatre Complex, Bree Steet, Newtown 2001 ☎ 011-8386960 🕐 Tue–Sat noon–3pm, Mon–Sat 6pm–11.30pm 🖐 L R140, D R185, Wine R85

THE GRILLHOUSE
www.thegrill.co.za
South Africa is famous for its quality steaks and this restaurant is hugely

popular for its melt-in-the-mouth fillets and succulent sauces. Exposed brick, green leather furnishings, white linen, excellent service and a lively atmosphere add to the experience. Opposite is Katzy's late-night piano bar and cigar lounge, under the same ownership, which has live music most nights and is fast making its way on to Jo'burg's nightlife circuit.

✉ The Firs, Oxford Road, Rosebank 2196 ☎ 011-8803945 🕐 Sun–Fri 12–2.30, 6.30–11; Sat 6.30–11pm 🖐 L R180, D R250, Wine R114

WOMBLES
www.wombles.co.za
A relative new comer, Wombles has fast gained an excellent reputation for its matured steaks. The setting is attractive colonial style, with dark wood tables, high-backed chairs and white linen tablecloths. It has a simple menu, with traditional starters like grilled mushrooms or chicken liver salad followed by a selection of steaks and sauces. There's also a choice of poultry, fish and a couple of vegetarian dishes.

✉ 17 3rd Avenue, Parktown North 2193 ☎ 011-8802470 🕐 Mon–Fri noon–11pm, Sat 6pm–11pm 🖐 L R200, D R250, Wine R145

PRETORIA
CAFÉ RICHE
www.caferiche.co.za
The superb Café Riche is the oldest café in the city. The restored art deco building has a real European feel to it, and is perfect for sipping a cappuccino and watching the comings and goings on the square. The large breakfasts are hugely popular, and there is also a light lunch and late-night dinner menu. Don't miss the Sunday brunches, but be prepared for slow service.

✉ Church Square, City Centre 8881 ☎ 012-3283173 🕐 7am–midnight 🖐 L R50, D R100, Wine R65

CYNTHIA'S
www.cynthias.co.za
The décor at this popular establishment, set in the southern suburbs off the N1, has a modern

feel despite the Victorian touches and fine art on the walls. Dishes are a mix of traditional and modern, with starters such as salmon carpaccio leading on to tender chateaubriand steak. Ask about daily specials— these are often the best choice, especially if they include the Matupo prawns. There's an extensive, good value wine list, and service is swift and friendly.

✉ Maroelana Centre, near Pretoria Country Club, Maroelana 0081 ☎ 012-4603220 🕐 Mon–Fri 12–3, 6–10, Sat 6–9.30, Sun 12–2.30 🖐 L R130, D R170, Wine R65

LA MADELEINE
www.lamadeleine.co.za
This French restaurant is regarded as one of the top restaurants in South Africa. The emphasis is on superbly prepared French cuisine, with a changing daily menu dependent on what the markets have to offer. There are no printed menus—instead, the daily offerings are explained by the Belgian chef-proprietor. Expect classic starters such as oysters or foie gras, followed by langoustines or slow roasted lamb. The wine list is exceptional, and the Sunday lunch superb. Reservations are essential.

✉ 122 Priory Road, Lynnwood 0081 ☎ 021-3613667 🕐 Tue–Sat 7pm–late, Fri, Sun lunch 🖐 L R180, D R225, Wine R60

DIE WERF
www.diewerf.co.za
The cuisine and the cultural museum building in which this restaurant is housed are both traditionally South African. You can dine outdoors here in summer amid beautiful surroundings, under the shade of indigenous trees, or indoors before a log fire in winter. House specialties include *snoek* (a mackerel-like fish) with grape jam, curried mutton tripe, and neck of lamb with tomato sauce. The fixed-menu three-course meal served on Sundays represents excellent value.

✉ Olympus Drive, Faerie Glen 0081 (15km/9 miles east of central Pretoria) ☎ 012-9911809 🕐 Tue–Sat 8–3, 7–10, Sun 8–3 🖐 L R110, D R135, Wine R65

PRICES AND SYMBOLS

The hotels below are listed alphabetically (excluding The) by town or area, then by name. Prices are the average for a double room for one night, including breakfast. All the hotels listed accept credit cards unless otherwise stated.

For a key to the symbols, ▷ 2.

BLOEMFONTEIN
HOBBIT HOUSE

www.hobbit.co.za

Fans of author J. R. R. Tolkien, born in the town, will like this aptly named guesthouse, dating from 1925 and set in secluded gardens. The bedrooms are traditional, with a Victorian feel, with blue-and-white-patterned wallpaper and country-style furniture. Some rooms have fireplaces; all have large bathrooms. Breakfast and other meals are served in a rustic breakfast room.

✉ 19 President Steyn Avenue, Bloemfontein 9301 ☎ 051-4470663 ✋ R1,100 ⓘ 12 ≋

CLARENS
MALUTI MOUNTAIN LODGE

www.malutimountainlodge.co.za

This popular family weekend retreat has a fine setting with striking views of the mountains. Accommodation is a mix of double rooms with private bathrooms, three traditional *rondavels* (small, round thatched huts) and family suites. All have simple interiors, balconies where you can enjoy the sunset, and heating in winter. There are neat gardens, two restaurants, a pool and the popular Duck & Hound steak house.

✉ Steil Street, Clarens 9707 ☎ 058-2561422 ✋ R900 ⓘ 21 ≋

GOLDEN GATE HIGHLANDS NATIONAL PARK
GLEN REENEN CAMP

www.sanparks.org

Glen Reenen has two types of *rondavels* (thatched huts), each with a shower, fridge and cooking facilities. Some have a TV, two single beds and a double bed in the loft; others have three single beds in one room. Across the road is the campsite with a communal kitchen and shower blocks and electric points. It's a peaceful setting in a narrow, steep-sided valley, and several good walks start from here (pick up maps in the shop). It can be too cold for camping in the winter.

☎ 012-4289111 (reservations from SANParks); ☎ 058-2551000 (last-minute reservations) ✋ R155 (camping), R675 *(rondavel),* R1,100 (farmhouse) ≋ 🚗 On the main road through the park

JOHANNESBURG
BACKPACKERS RITZ

www.backpackers-ritz.co.za

One of Johannesburg's best established hostels, the Ritz has a garden and swimming pool and is set in a secure district. A mix of dorms and double rooms is available, and there's a pub and an internet 'corner', and breakfast and other meals are served. Knowledgeable staff offer tours in Soweto and around the city. Transfers can be arranged from the airport or bus/train station

✉ 1A North Road, Dunkeld West 2196 ☎ 011-3252520 ✋ R125 (dorm beds), R375 (double room) ⓘ 10 ≋

JOHANNESBURG SANDTON TOWERS

www.ichotelsgroup.com

This high-rise luxury hotel, part of the InterContinental chain, is popular with tour groups and businesspeople, as well as shoppers—it's next to the enormous Sandton City shopping mall. The rooms occupy 26 floors (those at the top have exceptional views), and are predictably comfortable with marble-effect bathrooms, air conditioning and satellite TV. There's a good range of facilities and two restaurants, one of which is the acclaimed Italian restaurant, The Vilamoura. Parking is also available.

✉ Corner of 5th and Maude streets, Sandton 2146 ☎ 011-7805555 🖤 R2,580 ⓘ 571 🔵 ♨ 📺

MERCURE JOHANNESBURG RANDBURG

www.mercure.com

Although the rooms here are quite narrow with small bathrooms, they are comfortable. The interiors nod toward ethnic-chic, and all rooms have satellite TV, minibar and modem connections. The public areas are fairly grand, with a mix of marble, African art and chunky furniture. Breakfast is the only meal offered, although the hotel has an arrangement with some of the restaurants in the adjacent Brightwater Commons mall whereby you can charge meals to your hotel account. Parking is available.

✉ Brightwater Commons, Randburg 2125 ☎ 011-3263300 🖤 R978, excluding breakfast ⓘ 104 🔵 📺

THE MICHELANGELO

www.michelangelo.co.za

This large, international hotel is a member of the Leading Luxury Hotels of the World. It is located in the upmarket suburb of Sandton, about 30 minutes' drive from the heart of Johannesburg. Fitted with plenty of marble in faux Renaissance style, it has everything you would expect of a quality hotel: executive suites, several restaurants, its own health spa, sporting facilities, pay-TV and WiFi in each room. On your doorstep are all the luxury theatres and restaurants in the adjoining Nelson Mandela Square.

✉ 135 West Street, Sandton, Johannesburg 2146 ☎ 011-2827000 🖤 R4,110, excluding breakfast ⓘ 242 🔵 ♨ 📺

SAXON

www.thesaxon.com

One of South Africa's leading hotels is this small boutique hotel in the suburb of Sandhurst. Nelson Mandela spent seven months here editing his book, *The Long Walk to Freedom*, and the presidential suite is named after him. The Saxon is set in 2.5ha (6 acres) of beautifully tended grounds with a huge heated swimming pool, gym and spa. The suites have large four-poster beds and a strong emphasis on African art, while the rooms have African textiles, bathrooms, polished wooden floors and large bay windows looking into the garden. All rooms have DVD and CD players.

✉ 36 Saxon Road, Sandhurst 2196 ☎ 011-2926000 🖤 R8,000 ⓘ 26 🔵 ♨ 📺

LADYBRAND
CRANBERRY COTTAGE

www.cranberry.co.za

This converted sandstone Victorian house has 18 rooms, varying in style from Victorian (with four-poster beds and antiques) to modern (neutral and stylish furniture), with private bathrooms. There are also garden suites with a more rustic theme, and the house is surrounded by English-style gardens with a swimming pool. Additional rooms are housed in the original ticket office and waiting rooms of Ladybrand Railway Station, and are decorated with railway memorabilia and antiques.

✉ 37 Beaton Street, Ladybrand 9745 ☎ 051-9242290 🖤 R900 ⓘ 25 ♨ 📺

PRETORIA
BATTISS GUEST HOUSE

www.battissguesthouse.co.za

The original home of the artist Walter Battiss is one of the more unusual guesthouses in South Africa. The house was renovated in the 1980s and Battiss's works remain on the walls and the floors. The bedrooms have high ceilings, shiny wood floors, large French windows opening on to a leafy courtyard, private bathrooms, TVs, fans and a daily serviced kitchenette. You will need your own

transport to get into town, but it is close to Menlyn Park shopping mall.

✉ 3 Fook Island, 92 20th Street, Menlo Park 0081 ☎ 012-3464145 🖤 R720 ⓘ 4

ILLYRIA HOUSE

www.illyria.co.za

This vast white mansion has a stunning setting and staying here comes at a high price, but for a special occasion (it's ideal for a honeymoon) it's worth it. Personalized butler service ensures that all your needs are met 24 hours a day, and the rooms, decorated with antiques, are the epitome of stylish luxury. There's a spa too, just in case you need more pampering.

✉ 327 Bourke Street, Muckleneuk Hill 0002 ☎ 012-3446035 🖤 R5390 ⓘ 12 apartments 🔵 ♨

LA MAISON

www.lamaison.co.za

This comfortable and quirky guesthouse is close to a good choice of restaurants and shops. It's a grand white Victorian mansion, with six individually decorated rooms with attractive antiques, brass beds and private balconies with views of the lush gardens and swimming pool. The restaurant serves excellent cuisine, and has interesting murals on the walls. Breakfast is served here or on the roof terrace.

✉ 235 Hilda Street, Hatfield 0083 ☎ 012-4304341 🖤 R900 ⓘ 6 ♨

WHISTLETREE LODGE

www.whistletreelodge.com

The smart Whistletree Lodge is on a hillside in Queenswood, close to the Union Buildings. The rooms are elegantly and traditionally decorated with warm tones, sturdy antiques and silk bedspreads and cushions; all have private bathrooms and balconies. The airy lounge opens out to the landscaped garden with its heart-shaped pool. There are also floodlit tennis courts, a sauna and a cocktail bar; meals are available on request. Parking is available.

✉ 1267 Whistletree Drive, Queenswood 0186 ☎ 012-3339915/6 🖤 R1,400 ⓘ 12 🔵 ♨ ❓ No children under 12

NORTHERN CAPE AND NORTH WEST PROVINCE

The Northern Cape is where the rock-strewn semi-desert of Namakwa merges with the red dunes of the Kalahari. It has a stark beauty with endless shimmering plains, hazy saltpans and a real sense of isolation. Although difficult to get to and relatively undeveloped, the remote Kgalagadi Transfrontier Park has excellent game viewing and is best known for its black-maned lions. Augrabies Falls National Park is not as well known for its game but does have some impressive waterfalls, while Namakwa, along with parts of the northern Western Cape, explode in colour in spring when the normally barren landscape is covered with wild flowers. The regional capital Kimberley has an interesting history built on the discovery of diamonds that is best explored at the World of Diamonds, which sits alongside the historical mine known as the Big Hole.

The sparsely populated North West Province is largely flat and featureless and is made up of undulating Kalahari grasslands and isolated farming communities. By contrast and built out of the dry bushveld, its best-known attraction, Sun City, is an amazingly extravagant man-made resort with numerous leisure facilities. Next to it and also artificially made, Pilanesberg Game Reserve lies in the caldera of an extinct volcano and is home to a good variety of animals including the Big Five. The province's best-kept secret is the Madikwe Game Reserve, which again is home to many species of animals and birds and offers some superb accommodation in well-designed lodges and tented camps. Closer to Gauteng, the low-lying Magaliesberg Mountains and Hartbeespoort Dam are pretty country weekend escapes for people living in Johannesburg and Pretoria.

AUGRABIES FALLS NATIONAL PARK
▷ 246.

COLESBERG
www.colesberginfo.co.za
Colesberg lies at the base of a distinctive landmark, Cole's Kop, visible from 40km (25 miles) away. This rounded rock outcrop is 1,700m (5,570ft) high and was an important landmark for early settlers, who moved inland across a largely featureless region. In its early days, Colesberg was a classic frontier town that conducted illicit trade in a wide range of commodities, especially gunpowder and liquor. During the Anglo-Boer War it was close to the front. The surrounding hills are named after the British regiments that held them: Suffolk, New Zealand, Worcester and Gibraltar.

Today Colesberg is the focus for two successful activities: horse breeding and sheep farming. Most visitors just stop off for a night as they pass through along the busy Cape road (N1). The town springs to life in the early evening as people arrive to perform errands, and then Colesberg reverts to a peaceful farming town for the rest of the day.
✚ 328 H8 🚹 Tourist Information Centre, Colesberg Kemper Museum, Private Bag X6, Colesberg 9795 ☎ 051-7530678 (after hours 051-7530390) 🕐 Mon–Fri 9–5

HARTBEESPOORT DAM
The proximity of Johannesburg and of Pretoria has made this dam in the Magaliesberg Mountains (▷ 247) a popular watersports resort and weekend retreat for city dwellers. Around the shoreline are smart marinas and large private homes overlooking the lake. This is a popular site for a variety of sports including hang-gliding and paragliding, as well as watersports on the lake. The dam waters and some of the surrounding land form a designated nature reserve; birds are the main feature of the Oberon section, and there's game to see in the Kommandonek portion. There's also a snake park, a zoo and an aquarium.
✚ 324 K4 🚹 Hartbeespoort Dam Information Shop, Damdoryn Crossroad, Hartbeespoort 0216 ☎ 083-9608606 🕐 Daily 8–5

KAKAMAS
The second most important agricultural town after Upington along this stretch of the Gariep (Orange) River is Kakamas. The meaning of the town's name is 'vicious, charging ox'. Legend has it that the quality of the pasture was so poor in this region that cattle often attacked their herders. The town, strung out along the main road parallel to the southern canal, has a pleasantly relaxed, rural atmosphere. Driving along Voortrekker Road, in the middle of town, look out for the set of giant waterwheels, part of an old irrigation system. The main industry in the town today is raisins, which are exported around the world. There are a number of wine cellars and dried fruit co-operatives that you can visit for tours and tastings, including Orange River Wine Cellars Co-Op, off the N14 (tel 054-3378800; www.orangeriverwines.com).
✚ 321 D6

KAMFERS DAM
Kamfers Dam is a natural heritage site and an important area for greater and lesser flamingos. It lies 5km (3 miles) out of Kimberley (▷ 250–251) on the N12 heading for Johannesburg, partially hidden from the road by the raised rail line. Merely driving past the dam will give you views of the carpet of pink created by the resident flamingos, but to see them closer, look for a gravel track leading from the road under the railway line, where there is a small parking area. The waters are under threat from continual agricultural pollution, and it has been predicted that all the flamingos will one day disappear from here.
✚ 323 G6

KGALAGADI TRANSFRONTIER PARK
▷ 248–249.

KGASWANE MOUNTAIN RESERVE
This is a popular mountain reserve (previously called Rustenburg Nature Reserve) along the northern slopes of the Magaliesberg range. The reserve is regarded as an important recreational area and a valuable educational environment for visitors from Johannesburg and Pretoria, a little more than 100km (60 miles) away.

The reserve consists of a mix of grassland and a lush valley basin which acts as a natural catchment area. Some antelope live in the park, but most visitors come for the walking—there are currently three marked trails, two of which are open to day visitors (overnight trails must be reserved up to six months in advance).
✚ 324 J4 ☎ 014-5332050 🕐 Sep–Mar 5.30am–7pm; Apr–Aug 6am–6.30pm ✋ Adult R20, child (2–12) R10, plus R10 per vehicle 🚗 Clearly signposted from the middle of Rustenburg

Opposite *The Crocodile River below Hartbeespoort Dam*

Right *The Eye of Kuruman spring* (▷ 247)

INFORMATION

www.sanparks.org

☐ 321 D6 ☎ 054-4529200 ⏰ Gates: daily 7–6.30; office: 7–7 💳 Adult R100, child (2–12) R50 🍴 Restaurant with views of the falls 🏪 Large shop selling selection of groceries including meat and fresh vegetables, plus beer and wine ❓ Fuel available next to entrance; public telephones (cards only) next to reception desk. Reservations for Klipspringer Trail, ☎ 012-4289111 🚌 From Upington, take N14 and turn onto R359 at Alheit. From Springbok, there is a left turning before you reach Alheit. All clearly signposted

TIPS

» A good time of day to visit is around sunset, when the swallows flitting through the gorge are slowly replaced by bats.

» There are some dangerously slippery spots at the edge of the gorge. Although there are fences, take care.

» March through to October is the best time to visit, as temperatures are not too high and there is limited rainfall. However, nights can be extremely cold.

Above *The Gariep River plunges over the Augrabies Falls*

AUGRABIES FALLS NATIONAL PARK

The remote location of the Augrabies Falls park, not far from the Namibian border, has saved it from mass development, and it remains one of the highlights of the north. The falls are the main reason for coming here—but the landscape is equally striking, a bizarre moonscape of curious rock formations surrounded by shimmering semi-desert. The park was created in 1966 to protect the waterfall and the seemingly arid and barren ecosystem, which is actually rich in wild plants and has a growing population of small mammals. There is good hiking here, and the Gariep (Orange) River above and below the falls has some excellent white-water rafting (▷ 262).

THE WATERFALL

The focus of the park is the waterfall, the sixth largest in the world. Above the falls, the Gariep (Orange) River drops over a series of cataracts, descending about 100m (300ft). From this point, the main channel passes over a drop of 56m (184ft) into a narrow gorge of steep, smooth rock, the water churning below like melted milk chocolate. There are a number of viewpoints dotted along the southern side of the gorge. The name Augrabies is derived from the Khoi term *!oukurubes*, 'Place of Great Noise'. Following heavy rains, a number of smaller waterfalls drop into the main gorge along the sides of the main fall—a tremendous sight, but fairly rare.

FLORA AND FAUNA

Walking along the cliffs above the river, you pass a number of unusual plants that have adapted to the harsh desert environment. Some of the more notable trees are the quiver tree, camel thorn, tree fuchsia and wild olive; there are some informative displays about these next to reception. There is also a fair range of wildlife, including various antelope—klipspringer, eland, kudu, gemsbok—and springbok, although these all tend to be elusive. You are more likely to see ground squirrels foraging between the rocks.

There are several short game drives (map available from reception) around the Augrabies Falls National Park, as well as walks, including the popular two-day Klipspringer Trail.

KIMBERLEY
▷ 250–251.

KURUMAN
There are two reasons why this isolated town is on the visitor map: the Moffat Mission and a natural spring known as The Eye. A series of restored buildings just outside the town, the mission can be visited (Mon–Sat 8–5, Sun 3–5). It was set up by Robert Moffat (his daughter was to marry the missionary-explorer David Livingstone) in 1821.

The Eye, or *'die oog'* in Afrikaans, on Main Street, is an extraordinary spring which produces some 20 million litres (94 million gallons) of fresh water per day, with little variation between the wet and dry seasons—a miracle in this arid region. The giant koi carp gliding through the pond created by the spring are a lovely sight. The gardens around the pond (daily dawn–dusk) are a popular picnic spot.

Half a day should be more than enough to see Kuruman, although once you have made it this far north it is also worth exploring the surrounding countryside.

🞧 322 F5 🛈 Tourist Office, Main Street, in an old cottage next to The Eye, Kuruman 8460 ☎ 053-7121001 🕓 Mon–Fri 8–4.30

Below *The cemetery at Mafikeng has graves from the Anglo-Boer War*

MADIKWE GAME RESERVE
www.madikwe-game-reserve.co.za
Madikwe is the fourth largest game reserve in South Africa. Covering more than 75,000ha (185,250 acres), it has the country's second largest elephant population, yet few people have heard of it. Madikwe is not open to day visitors; you need to stay in one of its luxury lodges.

The reserve lies entirely within South Africa, but it is only 35km (22 miles) from the Botswana capital, Gaborone. The northern limits are marked by the international border, while the park's southern limits coincide with the Dwarsberg Mountains. One of the best aspects of the reserve is its diverse geology, which has resulted in a broad mix of habitats suitable for a wide range of animals. Thanks to Operation Phoenix, one of the largest game translocation operations in the world, the park is well stocked and is an excellent place to see the 'Big Five'. Visitors are taken on game drives and walks from their lodges, and thanks to the wide dispersal of the camps it is easy to feel as if you have the whole reserve to yourself.

🞧 324 J3 ☎ Park office: 018-3509931 🚍 Off N4, on R49 following signs to Gaborone; 100km (60 miles) from Zeerust, just before the border crossing, turn right on to a sand road for 12km (7.5 miles) to the Tau Gate. There are other gates at Derdepoort and Abjaterskop

MAFIKENG AND MMABATHO
www.tourismnorthwest.co.za
Before free elections were held in South Africa and the new political boundaries came into effect, Mafikeng was in the old Western Transvaal, while its satellite town of Mmabatho was the capital of the homeland known as Bophuthatswana. When the North West Province was created, it was decided to retain Mmabatho as the regional capital. However, there has been a gradual shift of power back to the principal town in the region, Rustenburg (▷ 255).

As a rather garish concrete town, Mmabatho is best bypassed for Mafikeng. At the turn of the 20th century this hot, dusty little town—then called Mafeking—captured the imagination of the British public. In 1899, shortly after the outbreak of the Second Anglo-Boer War, the British-held town was besieged by a Boer force. The siege of Mafeking lasted 217 days, until 17 May 1900, when a combined force of Rhodesian troops from the north and Imperial troops from the south relieved the town. The British public were intrigued, their interest in the incident having been fired by the press: The Anglo-Boer War was the first war to be reported in detail in newspapers. The Mafikeng Museum (Mon–Sat 8–5), on the corner of Martin and Robinson streets, has an excellent series of displays outlining the events of the siege.

🞧 323 H4 🛈 North West Parks and Tourism Board, just off Mandela Drive near the entrance to Cooke's Lake, Mafikeng ☎ 018-3971500 🕓 Mon–Fri 8–4.30

MAGALIESBERG
The Magaliesberg is a range of flat-topped quartzite mountains extending roughly from Pretoria to just beyond Rustenburg. In 1977, the area was declared a Natural Heritage Site and, along with the Hartbeespoort Dam (▷ 245), it is an important recreational area for the residents of Pretoria and Johannesburg. The region witnessed a number of bloody battles during the 19th century. The first major conflicts were between the Ndebele, who arrived in the area from modern day KwaZulu-Natal, led by their chief Mzilikazi, and the local peoples. At a later date the mountains were the scene of several important battles during the Anglo-Boer War, including the British defeat at the Battle of Nooitgedacht in 1900.

Today the slopes are dotted with holiday resorts and have become popular for hiking; there are numerous shops, farm stalls, tea rooms and activities in the region marketed under the Magaliesberg Meander tourism initiative.

🞧 324 J4

INFORMATION

www.sanparks.org

✚ 322 D4 ☎ Park office: 054-5612000
⏰ Twee Rivieren: Jan–Feb 6am–7.30pm;
Mar 6.30am–7pm; Apr 7am–6.30pm; May
7am–6pm; Jun–Jul 7.30am–6pm; Aug
7am–6.30pm; Sep 6.30am–6.30pm; Oct
6am–7pm; Nov–Dec 5.30am–7.30pm;
office hours: 7.30–sunset 🚹 Adult
R180, child (under 12) R90 for day visitors
🏕 The three main camps all have small
shops selling basic groceries, firewood
and field guides ❓ Reservations from
SANParks, tel 012-4289111. On the
Botswana side of the park there are 3
campsites (reservations must be made
through the Botswana parks authority, tel
09267-3180774) 🚗 From Upington, the
first 190km (120 miles) are on an excellent
tarred road followed by 61km (38 miles)
of gravel. Allow 3 to 4 hours to the park
gates

Above *Gemsbok with their characteristic
straight horns*

INTRODUCTION

The park is remote and relatively undeveloped and suffers uncomfortably high
summer temperatures, but few visitors complain about the hot dusty roads once
they've glimpsed their first lion.

The area was declared a national park in 1931 as part of an initiative to
tackle the problem of poaching. The first visitor camp was built in 1940 near
the confluence of the seasonal rivers, the Auob and Nossob. Known previously
as the Kalahari Gemsbok National Park, the area merged with the adjacent
Gemsbok National Park in Botswana in 1999.

The roads follow the scrubby valleys of two rivers and cut across red sand
dunes typical of the Kalahari. The park shares a border with Botswana, but Twee
Rivieren is the only entrance on the South African side. Visitors wishing to visit
the Botswana side do not need a passport as long as entry and exit is made
through the same gate. All routes on the Botswana side of the park are strictly
4WD and must be travelled in a convoy of at least two vehicles. As with many of
the parks and reserves, you can choose to visit for the day in your own vehicle
or stay at one of the camps, renting a 4WD when you are there. Do bear in mind
when driving that the distances in the park are huge and the time it takes to
cover them will be even longer with game viewing. For example, it takes around
2.5 hours to drive from Twee Rivieren to Mata Mata, one of the main camps, so
plan carefully.

The nearest town of any size is Upington, where you can buy supplies and
visit the Upington Tourist Office (Mutual Street, tel 051-3387000; www.upington.
co.za or www.greenkalahari.co.za; Mon–Fri 7.30–5, Sat 9–12). The office can
supply you with information on the park and on the Kalahari area (▷ 266 for
information about accommodation within the park).

WHAT TO SEE

WILDLIFE

The park is celebrated for its predators, particularly the dark-maned Kalahari lion, which can sometimes be spotted lazing in the shade of trees along the river beds. Other predators to look for include cheetah, wild dog, spotted hyena, bat-eared fox, black-backed jackal and honey badger. Leopards are (as always) elusive, but they are seen relatively regularly in the park. Kgalagadi's prize antelope is the gemsbok, which has a dark glossy coat, strong frame and characteristic long, straight horns. You should also see giraffe, red hartebeest, Burchell's zebra and huge herds of wildebeest and springbok. Try to spot meerkat, too. These energetic mongoose-like animals can be seen at dawn and dusk scurrying around their burrows in search of food. Look for the windmills that pump the boreholes—these waterholes are usually frequented by some form of wildlife. The birdlife, too, is remarkable. More than 200 species have been recorded in the park, and it is known for its birds of prey, including tawny eagle, martial eagle, white-backed vulture and eagle owl.

LANDSCAPE

The aridity of the region means that vegetation is sparse, which is why game viewing is so good here. Watch for the windmills that pump the boreholes, as these waterholes are usually frequented by some form of wildlife.

The two seasonal rivers of Auob and Nossob rarely flow these days, but the great width of their valleys in some parts proves that they were once great, thundering waterways. Between the rivers stretch mighty red dunes, aligned from north to south and covered in yellow grass following good rains. These are fossil dunes, and their red tint is produced by an iron oxide coating on the white grains of sand. Two roads cross the dunes; never venture off them or you will get stuck in sand.

TIPS

» Although the park authorities insist that 4WD vehicles are not necessary, saloon (sedan) cars can be uncomfortable on the gravel roads and are quite likely to get flat tyres.

» There is now direct access from Namibia through the Mata Mata border gate.

» The best time to visit is between February and May. In summer the heat is intense and you should carry at least 10 litres (20 pints) of drinking water in your vehicle.

» If you're camping in winter you'll need a warm sleeping bag as temperatures fall below 0°C (32°F).

» Always check accommodation availability in advance: This is the end of the road, and even space for tents gets fully reserved.

» A major advantage is that Kgalagadi is malaria free.

Left *Vegetation is sparse and dry in the Kalahari Desert*
Below *Ground squirrels are well camouflaged against the sandy ground*

REGIONS | NORTHERN CAPE AND NORTH WEST PROVINCE • SIGHTS

INFORMATION

www.northerncape.org.za

⊕ 323 G6 ℹ️ Diamond Fields Tourist Information Centre, corner of Bultfontein and Lyndhurst streets, Kimberley 8300, ☎ 053-8312789 ⏰ Mon–Fri 8–5, Sat 8–12

Above *Modern Kimberley owes much to its diamond wealth*

INTRODUCTION

Kimberley, the capital of the Northern Cape, is famous for its diamonds, and the flat land surrounding the town is pockmarked with mines. The first significant find was in 1866 on a farm called De Kalk, near modern-day Hopetown. News soon spread and interest began to grow. Prospectors arrived quickly and, in 1870, more diamonds were found near Dorstfontein farm. The area was immediately flooded with fortune-seekers; within just a few months 50,000 diggers had turned the hill into a hole—today's 'Big Hole'.

As the miners delved deeper, it became clear that individual claims would have to merge: At one point there were 1,600 separate claims in the Kimberley mine. In addition to this, the price of diamonds started falling because of overproduction. It was at this point that Cecil John Rhodes and his partner Charles Dunell Rudd entered the scene. Together they began buying up claims in the mine, and in 1880 they founded the De Beers Mining Company. The Big Hole stopped producing diamonds in 1914, but three mines remain productive in the area today: Dutoitspan, Bultfontein and Wesselton.

Kimberley is now a bustling commercial place. Most of the sights are in some way connected to the diamond industry, although the town itself displays little evidence of this wealth. The suburb of Belgravia is the only area of fine Victorian houses; central Kimberley is made up of modern shops and office blocks, dominated by the Telkom Tower and the De Beers headquarters. The town can be seen on foot, and there is a tram that runs from City Hall to the Mine Museum—the only working tram in South Africa.

WHAT TO SEE

KIMBERLEY DIAMOND RUSH, BIG HOLE AND WORLD OF DIAMONDS

www.thebighole.co.za

The Diamond Rush area is a collection of 40 original and model buildings dating from the late 19th century. They have been arranged to form a jumble of streets, with sound effects such as singing or snatches of conversation. The area includes a bar, restaurants, shops and a guesthouse. In the Mining Hall, there are early photographs of the diggings that show the Big Hole gradually starting to take shape and provide a vivid impression of life during that time. To see what it was all about, have a look at the diamonds in the De Beers Hall.

The whole complex lies alongside the Big Hole—well named as it measures 1.6km (1 mile) in circumference and covers more than 13ha (32 acres). An impressive 90m-long (295ft) viewing platform sticks out over the rim of the hole so you can look down and see the murky green lake at the bottom. It is an astounding sight, especially when you remember that the excavation goes down 800m (2,600ft) and that every piece of earth and rock was removed by hand.

World of Diamonds opened in 2006. Here visitors can experience what it was like to go down a mine in the early diamond-mining days—complete with simulated dynamite blasts and mine dust filtering through the air. They also get the opportunity to look at real diamonds, among them the original, yellow Eureka Diamond, a 616-carat perfect octahedron. The viewing takes place in a vault that admits 15 people at a time. A fully operational pulsator machine shows how diamonds are separated from their surrounding rock in modern mining operations. And an audiovisual theatre runs a 20-minute film about influential personalities in the history of diamond mining, such as Cecil John Rhodes and his rival, Barney Barnato.

✉ Tucker Street, Kimberley 8301 ☎ 053-8304417 🕐 Daily 8–5 💷 Adult R90, child (4–17) R60, family R160 ◀ 1-hour guided tours every half hour on the half hour, last tour 4.30 🖥 🏛 Shops sell curios, precious stones and diamond jewellery

WILLIAM HUMPHREYS ART GALLERY

www.whag.co.za

For a break from the diamond world, head to this excellent gallery, with fine examples of 16th- and 17th-century art by British, Flemish and Dutch Old Masters. Also of interest is the newer collection of contemporary South African art. There is the work of South African Impressionists, an excellent graphics and prints display and a few individual highlights such as portraits by the artist Irma Stern (1894–1966).

✉ Civic Centre, Cullinan Crescent, Kimberley 8300 ☎ 053-8311724 🕐 Mon–Fri 8–4.45, Sat 10–4.45, Sun 2–4.45 💷 Adult R5, child (under 16) R2

MORE TO SEE

GALESHEWE

Galeshewe township was second only to Soweto as a hub of political activism during apartheid. It was home to Robert Sobukwe, the leader of the Pan African Congress (PAC), who spent the last days of his life, following his imprisonment on Robben Island, under house arrest in Galeshewe. For township tours, contact the Diamond Fields Tourist Information Centre (▷ left).

MCGREGOR MUSEUM

www.museumsnc.co.za

The collection in this Kimberley house is a mix of objects depicting the history of Kimberley and standard displays of natural history. Downstairs are a couple of rooms devoted to the Siege of Kimberley (1899–1900), including two small rooms occupied by Cecil Rhodes during the siege.

✉ 2 Egerton Road, Kimberley 8300 ☎ 053-8392700 🕐 Mon–Sat 9–5, Sun 2–5 💷 Adult R12, child (2–12) R6

Above *Old wheel tower*
Below *You can try your hand at prospecting*

INFORMATION

www.northerncape.org.za

✚ 320 C8 ℹ Namakwa Tourism Information, Voortrekker Street, Springbok 8240 ☎ 027-7128035 ◷ Mon–Fri 7.30–4.15, and in flower season until 6pm, Sat–Sun 9–6

Above *Orange and purple flowers contrast with the rocky, barren koppies in the Goegap Nature Reserve*

INTRODUCTION

Namakwa ('land of the Nama people'), formerly called Namaqualand, is the arid northwest corner of the Northern Cape, starting in the south at the Doorn River bridge near Klawer, and extending north to the Namibian border. The region is best known for its flowers, which have become a major visitor attraction—during flower season the still valleys and sleepy towns are transformed into busy places crowded with tour buses. However, the interaction between light, temperature, and the timing and intensity of rainfall all affect the occurrence and distribution of the flowers. The very fact that the flowers appear in different locations from year to year means that the flower-viewing industry has remained relatively low key. The town of Springbok, capital of Namakwa, is the most viable base for exploring the area.

In the past, the fortunes of Namakwa were closely linked with the copper industry. In 1852 copper production started in Springbok; this was the first commercial mining operation of any type in South Africa. Despite several other discoveries farther north, Springbok was able to develop into an important regional hub because of its abundant supply of drinking water from a spring, a valuable commodity in the region before dams and pipelines were built.

Port Nolloth was established as a harbour and railway junction for the copper industry in 1854, but the waters proved too shallow for the bulk ore carriers, and the trade moved north to Alexander Bay, which today bases much of its industry on diamonds.

WHAT TO SEE

THE PLANTS

More than 4,000 species have been identifed in the area, the most common of which is the orange and black gousblom, a large daisy. These flowers look their best when they occupy a valley floor, forming a stunning carpet of orange. On the mountainsides or rocky hills you will see *mesembryanthemums*, commonly known as vygies or Livingstone daisies. Their blossoms can be pink, scarlet, blue or yellow. Closer to Springbok are quiver trees (*Aloe dichotoma*), from which the San people made their quivers. Another interesting plant to look out for is the halfmens (*Pachypodium namaquanum*), a strange looking succulent which has a long spine with a clump of leaves at the top—some specimens are thought to be several hundred years old.

SPRINGBOK

Springbok sits in a narrow valley surrounded by the Klein Koperberge (Small Copper Mountains) and hemmed in by *koppies* (small hills) littered with rough yellow-gold rocks. It is a modern town with little of interest within its confines, but from it you can explore the countryside north to the Namibian border, and west to the Atlantic coast.

✚ 320 B7 ℹ Namakwa Tourism Information, Voortrekker Street, Springbok 8240
☎ 027-7128035 🕓 Mon–Fri 7.30–4.15, and (flower season only) Sat–Sun 9–12

AI–AIS/RICHTERSVELD TRANSFRONTIER CONSERVATION PARK

www.sanparks.org

The park of Ai-Ais/Richtersveld covers some of the most remote and starkly beautiful scenery in Namakwa. The park is both isolated and inaccessible, but that is much of its appeal. This is rough country, most of which can be reached only in a 4WD vehicle. Ai-Ais/Richtersveld encompasses a mountainous desert, seemingly barren but full of sturdy succulents, many of them endemic. This makes the park particularly appealing to botany enthusiasts, but the surreal, rugged terrain is another great attraction. A 4WD is essential in the park, and it's worth renting one in Springbok to explore this fascinating wilderness area. After much negotiation, the Richtersveld became part of a trans-frontier park in 2003, joining it with Namibia's Ai-Ais Hot Springs and Fish River Canyon over the border. You can stay in the park, which is camping only.

✚ 320 A6 ☎ 027-8311506 🕓 Daily 7–6; office: 8–4 ✋ Adult R120, child (2–15) R60
❓ Reservations from SANParks: ☎ 012-4289111 🚗 North from Springbok on N7 towards Steinkopf; take Port Nolloth turning and follow R382 to the coast via Annienous Pass. In Port Nolloth take the coast road north towards Alexander Bay. The park is signposted from Alexander Bay

TIPS

» For up-to-date information about where the best flower displays are, call the Namakwa Tourism Information office, which opens for extended hours in flower season (August–September).
» Namakwa has a fierce desert climate, so always carry several litres of water per person with you when driving.
» From Springbok, it is only another 118km (73 miles) on the N7 to the Namibian border, a popular crossing between the two countries.
» See pages 260–261 for a drive through Namakwa.

Below *Springbok makes a handy base from which to explore the Namakwa countryside*

GOEGAP NATURE RESERVE

Named after the Nama word for waterhole, this popular little reserve is a mix of granite *koppies* (small hills) and dry valleys, with a good cross-section of typical Namakwa vegetation, including a well-known aloe collection. Although the area looks parched and barren, it supports a surprising number of plant species—581 have been recorded in the reserve. The area is classified as semi-desert, with rain usually falling in winter; in summer temperatures soar and it is unwise to move around on foot under these conditions. The Hester Malan Wild Flower Garden is a highlight in spring.

✚ 320 B7 ☎ 027-7189906 ⏱ Daily 7.30–4 ✋ Adult R20, child (6–16) R10 🏧 🚌 From Springbok, pass under N7 towards the airport and turn right. Just before the airport, take a left turn; from here it's 15km (9 miles) to the reserve gates

PORT NOLLOTH

Port Nolloth is a little town on the windswept West Coast, important for fishing, but more intriguingly an area renowned for attracting fortune-seekers who trade (often, it is said, illegally) in diamonds. The town was established as a harbour and railway junction for the copper industry; today it has developed into a small holiday resort—the only one along this stretch of the coast. The beaches have a wild, desolate beauty, although the long stretches of sun-bleached sand can appear rather bleak.

✚ 320 A7 ℹ Municipality, Main Road, Port Nolloth ☎ 027-851111 ⏱ Mon–Fri 8–12, 12.45–4.30

ALEXANDER BAY

www.diamondcoast.co.za

The diamond industry becomes apparent in Alexander Bay, in the far north of the region, near the Namibian border. Diamonds were first found here in 1925, and today the town is run by the mining company Alexkor Ltd. Alexander Bay was closed to visitors until a few years ago, but now you can take part in diamond mine tours (▷ 263). It also has easy access to the Ai-Ais/Richtersveld Transfrontier Conservation Park. The Gariep (Orange) River estuary, at the Bay, is an important wetland area for birds.

✚ 320 A6 🚍 Alexkor Ltd conducts 3-hour tours of the mine on any weekday at 8am on request, min 4 people, booking is essential ☎ 027-8311330 ✋ R90, no children under 16 or pregnant women

Above *The Ai-Ais/Richtersveld Transfrontier Conservation Park*
Below *Namakwa windmill*

MAGERSFONTEIN BATTLEFIELD

On 11 December 1899 one of the most famous battles of the Anglo-Boer War took place here. The British force, under the command of General Lord Methuen, was defeated by a Boer force under General Piet Cronje, while attempting to come to the aid of besieged Kimberley (▷ 250–251). This was the first appearance of trench warfare, and it the first major defeat suffered by the British in the war (in the initial encounter, 239 British were killed and 663 wounded). The Boer trenches can still be seen from the hilltop.

There are nine memorials commemorating the dead, including a Celtic cross in memory of the Highland Regiment, a granite memorial to the Scandinavians who fought with the Boers, and a marble cross in memory of the Guards Brigade. In 1971, the area was declared a national monument. There is a small museum with weapons, uniforms and photographs.

✚ 323 G6 ☎ 053-8337115 ⊙ Daily 8–5 ☷ ☐ 32km (20 miles) from Kimberley; from Kimberley take the new road to Bloemfontein, following the signs to Modder River

MOKALA NATIONAL PARK

www.sanparks.org
South Africa's newest national park was proclaimed in June 2007. The name means 'camel thorn' in Setswana and aptly describes the 19,611ha (48,460-acre) region of dry savannah dotted with acacia trees. Mokala was created as a home for animals relocated from the former Vaalbos National Park closer to Kimberley, which was de-proclaimed after a successful land claim made by local people. Some 863 animals were moved to Mokala, including five white rhinos and 141 buffalo. The park has two lodges, two units with kitchen and a campsite.

✚ 323 G7 ☎ 053-2040158 ⊙ Daily 7–7 ✋ Adult R80, child (under 12) R40 ☐ Turn off the N12 57km (36.5 miles) southwest of Kimberley, at the Hayfield/Heuningneskloof Crossing, then carry on 21km (13.5 miles) to the park gate on a gravel road

NAMAKWA

▷ 252.

PAUL KRUGER COUNTRY HOUSE MUSEUM

The farm where Paul Kruger lived before becoming president of the Transvaal Republic from 1883 until the end of the Anglo-Boer War is at Boekenhoutfontein. The Paul Kruger Country House is actually a hotel, but buildings have been preserved and restored as a museum dedicated to the life of Kruger and the earliest farmers in the Transvaal. The main homestead contains many of Kruger's possessions, along with period furniture from other homes. There is also a small collection of local historical items. Look for the statue of Paul Kruger by French sculptor Jean Archand, discovered in Paris in 1919 by generals Louis Botha and Jan Smuts. It depicts the president sitting grumpily in his armchair during his last days while in exile in France.

✚ 324 J4 ☎ 014-5733218 ⊙ Daily 10–4 ✋ Adult R25, child (2–12) R12.50 ☐ 18km (11 miles) northwest of Rustenburg, off R565, en route to Sun City

PILANESBERG GAME RESERVE

www.pilanesberg-game-reserve.co.za
This is the fourth largest national park in South Africa, spread around an extinct volcanic crater. Although you can see all South Africa's big game here, the park itself is artificial, having been stocked with game from around the country in the 1970s. It's best to take a guided safari, as the rangers are in constant radio contact and monitor the movements of the 'Big Five' (safaris can be arranged in Sun City). There are several camps within the park if you want to stay.

✚ 324 J3 ☎ 014-5551600 ⊙ Nov–Feb 5.30am–7pm; Mar–Apr 6am–6.30pm; May–Aug 6.30am–6pm; Sep–Oct 6am–6.30pm ✋ Adult R45, child (6–17) R20, R20 per vehicle ☐ Follow signs to Sun City, R510 north from Rustenburg

RUSTENBURG

www.tourismnorthwest.co.za
Rustenburg ('castle of rest') is one of the oldest towns in the region and was important under the Transvaal Republic. Today it is a busy administrative hub for the many mining companies here, and sees many weekenders from Johannesburg and Pretoria, who come to enjoy the nearby Magaliesberg Mountains (▷ 247). It is also a useful stop en route to Sun City and the camps of the Pilanesberg Game Reserve.

✚ 324 J4 ℹ Rustenburg Tourism Information and Development Centre, corner of Nelson Mandela Drive and Kloof Street, Rustenburg 0300 ☎ 014-5970904 ⊙ Mon–Fri 8–4.30, Sat 8–12

Below *Elephant in Pilanesberg Game Reserve, home to the 'Big Five'*

INFORMATION

www.suninternational.com

324 J3 Sun City, 0316 North West Province 014-5575110 Adult and child R70, R30 of which is redeemable inside Day visitors can join a tour of the Palace of the Lost City, R60 Numerous restaurants, fast food outlets and bars around the complex The Welcome Centre, in the middle of the complex, provides maps of Sun City. A 'Sky Train' runs throughout the whole vast complex

SUN CITY

Tucked away on the fringes of the Kalahari desert is Sun City, a neon-lit extravaganza of kitsch surrounded by bush. It is South Africa's third most visited attraction, along with nearby Pilanesberg Game Reserve, after Soweto and the Kruger National Park. While it may not appeal to everyone, if you're in the area it is worth a visit just to experience the sheer indulgence of the place.

Sun City opened its doors in 1979, with the focus on the Sun City Hotel and a golf course designed by the South African golfer Gary Player. Within months it had become a huge success. As in Las Vegas in the USA, much emphasis was placed on the gambling element, as the hotel was in the homeland of Bophuthatswana, where gambling was legal, unlike the rest of South Africa at the time. However, the resort has experienced a drop in visitors since the first free elections were held in 1994. Gaming is now legal throughout South Africa, so the initial appeal of Sun City has gone. The resort is working hard to attract overseas visitors, and by closing all but one of its casinos is changing its image from a 24-hour gamblers' paradise to an international leisure, entertainment and conference destination.

SIGHTS AND ACTIVITIES

Some people will recognize the Palace of the Lost City, a magnificent hotel completed in 1992, from the publicity it gained at the time. The vaguely Moorish construction is characterized by soaring dome-capped towers ringed by prancing statues of antelope, and decorated with animal sculptures, mosaics, frescoes and hand-painted ceilings. Surrounding the hotel is a remarkable man-made forest, all 25ha (62 acres) of it, made up of 1.6 million separate plants.

The Valley of the Waves is a sandy beach complete with palm trees and a wave machine—all set in the arid bush landscape. You can even go surfing on the waves. There is an extra fee to enter the Valley for day visitors (adult R100, child (4–12) R50).

You'll find all sorts of sports here, including golf, horseback riding, squash, tennis, mountain biking and ten-pin bowling. There's also a whole host of watersports available at Waterworld: jet-skiing, parasailing, canoeing, sailing, water-skiing and windsurfing to name a few. If these don't appeal, you can go shopping, see a film or a show, visit the slot machines or the crocodile farm with its 7,000 animals, the cultural village or Butterfly World, or ride the 2km-long (1.2-mile) Zipliner.

Above *Find yourself transported to a lush tropical beach in the Valley of the Waves*

UPINGTON

www.upington.co.za

Upington is a modern town with attractive surroundings along the banks of the Gariep (Orange) River. It has searing summer temperatures, but is the largest town in this part of the Northern Cape, making it a welcome stop if you have been off the beaten track for a while. All the major South African shops and chains stores are here, and it's an excellent place to restock your supplies. As a major entry point to the Kalahari, Upington is also a good spot to organize trips to the Kgalagadi Transfrontier Park (▷ 248–249) and Augrabies Falls National Park (▷ 246).

The origin of the town is rather more disreputable than one might expect. In the mid-19th century, the northern reaches of the Cape Colony were home to a variety of outlaws and rustlers—there were no settlements, making it impossible for the police to track people into the uncharted wilderness. By 1879, the Cape government had had enough and founded a small settlement on the Gariep (Orange) River to try to exercise some control over the area. In 1884, Sir Thomas Upington, the new Prime Minister of the colony, visited the settlement, which was renamed in his honour.

➕ 321 D6 ℹ️ Upington Tourist Office, Mutual Street, Upington 8801 ☎ 051-3387000 🕐 Mon–Fri 7.30–5, Sat 9–12

VAN ZYLSRUS

Van Zylsrus is a typical Kalahari town—one dusty street is lined with all of its shops. Although there is little of interest here, it is a sensible place to stop for the night if en route to Kgalagadi. The Oasis Café is famous for its 'fairy garden', a glorious patch of shady green that's a welcome spot in the heat of the day. If you decide not to stop overnight in the town, have a snack here and fill up with fuel before pushing on.

➕ 322 E5 ℹ️ 14 Federale, Mynbou Street, Kuruman 8460 ☎ 053-7121001 🕐 Mon–Fri 8–4.30

VRYBURG

No matter from which direction you approach the town, the size of Vryburg (also known as Naldi) comes as a surprise. After miles of flat dry savannah, you suddenly find yourself in busy urban surroundings. There are few attractions in town, but the Leon Taljaardt Nature Reserve (Ganesa Road; daily 7–6), 5km (3 miles) away, is a pleasant little reserve stocked with game. Access to the park is by car (walking is not permitted) and you may see white rhino, buffalo, wildebeest and zebra, among other wildlife.

➕ 323 G5 ℹ️ Municipality, 19a Market Street, Vryburg 8600 ☎ 053-9282200; Mon–Fri 7.30–4

WILDEBEEST KUIL ROCK ART CENTRE

www.wildebeestkuil.itgo.com

This is a community-based public rock art project, where more than 150 rock engravings are spread over a small sacred hill. The site, surrounded by land owned by the !Xun and Khwe San people, some of whom act as guides, has a visitors' centre, where there are interesting displays, and an auditorium with a 20-minute introductory film. The 800m (875-yard) walkway weaves over the hill past information boards, while visitors listen to an audio commentary.

➕ 323 G6 ☎ 053-8337069 🕐 Mon–Fri 9–4, Sat–Sun 10–4 ✋ Adult R20, child (under 16) R10 🅿️ 🏧 🚌 16km (10 miles) from Kimberley on the R31 towards Barkly West

WONDERWERK CAVE

www.museumsnc.co.za

The Wonderwerk Cave is an important archaeological site on a private farm, set back from the road in the Kuruman Hills. The vast cave contains a collection of rock paintings and evidence of early human habitation, including fire. The cave has been extensively examined by experts from the McGregor Museum in Kimberley (▷ 251), where most of the discoveries from the excavations are now displayed. It stretches back 139m (456ft) into the hillside, with a level path leading into it; the rock paintings are close to the entrance. The grandparents of the current owners actually lived in the cave when they first settled in the region and started farming.

➕ 323 F6 ☎ 053-7121036 ✋ Adult R7, child (4–10) R5 🅿️ ❓ Access is with a guide only; toot your horn at the gate 🚌 Signposted 42km (26 miles) before Kuruman on the Kimberley Road

Below *Bridge over the Gariep (Orange) River at Upington*

MAGALIESBERG MEANDER

The modest range of hills to the west of Johannesburg and Pretoria is valued by jaded city-dwellers for its tranquillity, the beauty of its landscapes, its secluded hideaways and the lakeside pleasures of a spacious dam. This drive circles the uplands; the main route is in excellent condition, but along the way are some rougher roads that probe their way into the heart of the Magaliesberg.

THE DRIVE

Distance: 240km (150 miles)
Allow: 1 day
Start/end at: Pretoria (Tshwane)

★ Set off from Pretoria, taking the N4 highway that leads along the northern side of the Magaliesberg to Rustenburg, a run of 105km (65 miles). Much of this highway has been upgraded and the first segment is a toll road, but it is possible to use the alternative R27 along some of the route. With the hills on your left, the scenery along this stretch is pleasing. If you feel like taking a break, you could stop at Buffelspoort Dam—look for the turn about two-thirds of the way along, or 25km (15 miles) before

the town of Rustenburg; the resort development, with boating, fishing and picnic areas, is on the reservoir's western shores.

❶ Rustenburg (▷ 255) is a medium-sized country town and the hub of a flourishing farming region that produces large crops of wheat, maize, cotton, tobacco, fruit, vegetables and cut flowers. With plenty of rain and an average nine hours of sunshine a day throughout the year, Rustenburg's streets are a blaze of flowering trees and shrubs, including jacaranda, hibiscus, poinciana and billows of purple bougainvillea. There's industrial wealth in the area too: Nearby are

two of the world's biggest platinum mines. Kgaswane Mountain Reserve (▷ 245), in the hills to the south of Rustenburg, has good hiking trails and overnight facilities.

Leave Rustenburg on the R24/30, which swings to the southwest around Olifantsnek Dam and then, as the R24, makes its way southeast. There are broad views from Olifantsnek Pass. The 3,000ha (7,400-acre) reservoir irrigates citrus and tobacco plantations, and the dam wall captures the rush of the Hex River as it races through the pass. Just before you reach the tiny village of Maanhaarrand, 30km (18.5 miles) farther along the R24, turn left,

Opposite *Hartbeespoort Dam is popular for watersports of all kinds*
Right *Tobacco fields near Rustenburg*

and follow the road to the Mountain Sanctuary Park.

❷ The Mountain Sanctuary Park, whose owners are strict conservationists, is a private reserve covering 960ha (2,370 acres). It has nice picnic spots and a simple rest camp, and from here some attractive walks lead through the hilly countryside. There's a small entrance fee for day visitors.

Return to the R24 for just over 8km (5 miles) and turn left onto the R560 (signposted Hekpoort). After another 7km (4 miles) you'll see, a short distance to your left, a feature named Nooitgedacht, which is the Magaliesberg's highest hill (1,851m/6,071ft above sea level).

❸ Nooitgedacht has its place in the history of the Second Anglo-Boer War. It was on the hill's lower slopes that, in December 1900, a large British force found itself trapped in a gorge by Boer commandos, and lost 637 of its men before managing to make its escape.

Follow the R560 along the valley of the Magalies River, passing the village of Skeerpoort on your right. Just beyond this point the road branches to become the R512.

Follow the signs to Hartbeespoort Dam (▷ 245), a major reservoir fed by the Crocodile and Magalies rivers.

❹ The Hartbeespoort Dam is a well-developed recreational area, popular for watersports and fishing. Although it can get crowded, it has some peaceful corners and there are pleasant views from the perimeter road. There's a cableway that runs for 1km (0.6 miles) above the dam, from where there are superb views of the surrounding countryside.

The R512 intersects with the R27 11.3km (6 miles) from Skeerpoort. Turn right (east) on the R27, passing through Schoemansville and Hartbeespoort (the area's focal points) to rejoin the N4 highway and head back to Pretoria.

WHEN TO GO

Spring (September and October) and autumn (February and March) are the best months for visiting. Days in the middle of summer can be uncomfortably hot, with afternoon thunderstorms. Avoid this trip on weekends, when the roads are especially busy.

WHERE TO EAT
SQUIRES ON THE DAM

This popular steak house with a broad menu and wooden deck on the main road is opposite the snake park and zoo just before the road crosses the Hartbeespoort Dam.

✉ 1 Scott Street, Schoemansville ☎ 012-2531001 🕐 Mon–Sat 11–10, Sun 10–9

PLACES TO VISIT
MOUNTAIN SANCTUARY PARK

www.mountain-sanctuary.co.za
✉ Rustenburg ☎ 014-5340114
🕐 5.30am–7.30pm, book in advance as visitor numbers are strictly controlled
✋ Day visitors: adult R30, child (2–12) R20, car R10

HARTBEESPOORT DAM INFORMATION SHOP

✉ Next to the curio market ☎ 083-9608606 🕐 Daily 8–5

NORTHERN NAMAKWA

The northern half of Namakwa (Namaqualand) is a region of heat-hazed and often bleak semi-desert. But in parts the rugged terrain is spectacular, with a harsh beauty, and in spring the landscape is transformed by great carpets of wild desert flowers. This circular drive starts and ends in Springbok (▷ 253; 🚩 320 B7).

THE DRIVE

Distance: 230km (143 miles)
Allow: 1 day
Start/end at: Springbok

★ Start the drive at Springbok, the biggest town and commercial focus for this sparsely populated region. The town sits astride the N7 highway, which leads north all the way from Cape Town to the Namibian border.

❶ Much of Springbok's history is linked to the copper industry. Copper was worked by the Nama folk well before the colonial era, and the first modern mine was sunk in 1852.

Drive east along Voortrekker Street; turn right at the sign for the airport,

then left just before the airport. Continue for another 6km (3.5 miles), following the signs for 'Goegap', to reach the Goegap Nature Reserve (the total distance from Springbok is 15km/9 miles).

❷ The Goegap Nature Reserve (▷ 254) is renowned for its floral wealth (it has almost 600 different plant species) and displays of wild flowers after the brief spring rains. The reserve is an expanse of rough and rugged terrain covering some 15,000ha (37,000 acres) and is distinguished by huge, dome-like granite boulders. Once within the reserve, you can explore the area via a convenient loop road running for 17km (10.5 miles).

From the nature reserve, return to Springbok the way you came and drive back down Voortrekker Street, passing under the N7 bridge. You are now on the R64, which takes you through a stretch of rugged countryside.

Just 4km (2.5 miles) along the road, over to your right, you'll see Van Der Stel's Koperberg ('Copper Mountain'). To get to it, however, you'll have to follow a bit of a diversion. Drive straight on for another 2km (1.2 miles) until you get to the crossroads (6km/4 miles from town); turn right here, continue for 500m (550 yards), and turn right again onto a gravel road and continue south past the old mining community of Carolusburg.

❼ Komaggas is something of an oasis. Founded by the London Missionary Society in 1829 for its work among the local Nama people, it is blessed by a strong-flowing spring and its environs are refreshingly green.

From Komaggas the road runs west, then sweeps south and east to the Messelpad.

❸ During the heyday of copper mining, Carolusburg was a lively village. About 1km (0.6 miles) beyond the village is a parking area, from where you can walk up a steep path leading to the old mineshaft, which has splendid views over the surrounding landscape.

Back in the car, go back to the R64 and cross straight over it, following the winding route to Okiep for nearly 10km (6 miles).

❹ Okiep (the name translates as 'big brackish place') was at one time the region's richest and most important copper mine, operated by skilled miners from the English county of Cornwall, a copper and tin mining region for millennia. Production of copper ceased in 1918. The old chimney stack is clearly visible next to the pump house, with the steam engine that used to pump water from the mine.

Follow the signs back to the N7; turn south after 2.3km (1.4 miles) and, after another 2.3km, branch off west for Nababeep, 10km (6 miles) from the road.

❺ Nababeep is another town of copper workings and slag heaps. Of particular interest here are the old locomotive and its rolling stock, which were pulled by mules until the water supply problems were overcome. These relics are parked in front of the museum.

Head back out of town, turn right at the sign that reads 'Kleinsee via Spektakel', and then right again onto the R355, the gravel road that leads west to the Atlantic seaboard. The distance from Nababeep to the R355 is 11.5km (7 miles).

The countryside on the next (longer, lonelier and untarred) segment of the circular route is classed, botanically, as Namakwa (Namaqualand) Broken Veld. This comprises low shrublands that embrace, among much else, hardy succulents (notably *euphorbias* and *mesembryanthemums*, often known as vygies or sour figs). The monotony of the vegetation cover is relieved by taller species such as evergreen resin trees (*ozoroa*) and Namaqua figs. During the few brief weeks of spring, the plains and hill-slopes of the area are transformed by their bright floral tapestries. You reach the beginning of the Spektakel Pass after 17.5km (11 miles).

❻ Spektakel Pass was given its unusual name—the story goes—in 1685 by the first Governor of the Cape Colony, Simon van der Stel, who took in the glorious spectacle of the vistas on either side of the pass as he and his men travelled through in 1685.

Pull off at the viewing site, 3.5km (2 miles) farther on, to soak up the desert views, and then, after another 10km (6 miles), turn left for Komaggas. The good gravel road takes you through the hills and then the mountains, their distinctive rocks and cliff faces tinged with lichens and copper salts.

❽ The Messelpad, or 'masonry road'—a reference to the drystone reinforcing walls that line its trickier stretches—is a tortuous route, corrugated in a few places but perfectly negotiable. It dates back to the 1860s, when it served as the route along which waggon loads of copper were transported on their way to the sea at Hondeklip Bay.

The driving distance between Komaggas and the road is 34km (21 miles). At the 26km (16 miles) mark you'll begin to negotiate the Wilderperdehoek ('wild horses pass'), from which there are grand views across a vastness of empty plains and low hills. The road is very narrow in places but in generally good condition. It winds through the uplands, eventually emerging into a kindlier countryside of farmlands.

Continue north and then northeast for 25km (15.5 miles) until you rejoin the N7 highway. From here, it's a straight run back to Springbok.

WHEN TO GO

The flowers bloom for three or perhaps four weeks in the short spring period (August to September). Their appearance and lifespan, and the places where the best displays are to be seen, depend on the volume and distribution of the winter rains, and on whether or not the hot desert breezes (or 'berg winds') blow, and are therefore unpredictable. A late frost or intense sandstorm can ruin the flower season.

WHAT TO DO

Above *African Craft Market, Magaliesberg*

AUGRABIES FALLS
KALAHARI OUTVENTURE CENTRE
www.kalahari.co.za
An excellent way to experience the gorge is by rafting its rapids. The most popular stretch is known as the Augrabies Rush, an 8km (5-mile) section pulling out just 300m (985ft) above the falls. Longer two- and five-day trails involve rafting on some impressive rapids as well as calmer stretches of river.
☎ 082-4768213 ✋ Half-day rafting from R310 🚗 From Kakamas, turn right off the N14 towards Augrabies Falls. The lodge is 10km (6 miles) before the falls

HARTBEESPOORT DAM
ELEPHANT SANCTUARY
www.elephantsanctuary.co.za
Guests can interact with the six tame elephants, walk with them or ride them. Some of the tours include lunch or dinner, there's luxury accommodation and overnight guests can even 'brush down' the elephants first thing in the morning.
✉ Damdoryn Crossroad, Hartbeespoort 0216 ☎ 012-2580423 🕐 Daily, tours start at 8, 10 and 2 ✋ Adult from R425, child (3–14) from R215; elephant riding: adult R425, child (8–14) R250

HARTBEESPOORT SNAKE AND ANIMAL PARK
www.hartbeespoortsnakeanimalpark.co.za
In a pleasant location on the lakeshore, this zoo is old-fashioned but cares for its animals well and also breeds rare species, such as the two Bengal tigers, who are semi-tame and used for film shoots. Among the regular African animals are chimpanzees, panthers, jaguars, seals and a large collection of reptiles. Half-hour boat trips on the dam depart every hour, and there's a tea garden.
✉ Scott Street, Schoemansville, Hartbeespoort 0216 ☎ 012-2531162 🕐 Daily 8–5 ✋ Adult R50, child (under 16) R30

WELWITSCHIA COUNTRY MARKET
www.countrymarket.co.za
More than 40 shops in prefabricated sheds arranged in lanes sell crafts, clothes, snacks, furniture, toys and all manner of other things aimed at day trippers from the cities. There are also two open-air restaurants and a mini kids' fairground. There are many curios for sale down the side of the same road.
✉ Damdoryn Crossroad, Hartbeespoort 0216 ☎ 083-3028085 🕐 Tue–Sun 9–5

KIMBERLEY
DE BEERS DIAMOND OVAL
Occasional international cricket matches are played at Kimberley's De Beers Diamond Oval. Watching a game here makes a pleasant change from the large stadiums in the cities: The atmosphere here is very laid-back and you might even meet the players relaxing over a drink in the hotel bar after the game. During the domestic season, Kimberley is home to Griqualand West, one of the region's teams.
✉ Dickenson Avenue, Cassandra, Kimberley 8300 ☎ 053-8323775 (ticket enquiries) 🕐 Cricket season: Dec–Mar ✋ From R25

DIAMOND PAVILION
www.diamondpavilion.co.za
This is the Northern Cape's largest shopping mall, with a full range of South African chain stores and boutiques, many restaurants and cafés and various entertainments, including a games arcade and a multi-screen cinema.
✉ Corner of Oliver and McDougal streets, Kimberley 8300 ☎ 053-8329200 🕐 Mon–Thu 9–6, Fri 9–7, Sat 9–5, Sun 9–2

HALFWAY HOUSE

The historic Halfway House pub is famous for its bizarre drive-in section, which the owners claim was where Cecil Rhodes used to ride in on his horse to sip a quick beer. There's an enjoyable atmosphere here, with cold beer on tap and good, simple pub meals available, but it can get very busy at weekends.

✉ Du Toitspan Road, Kimberley 8300
☎ 053-8316324 ⏰ Mon–Sat 11am–2am
✋ Free

STAR OF THE WEST

Close to Kimberley's first diamond mine (▷ 250–251), the Star of the West claims to be the oldest pub in South Africa, dating from 1870. While it's a bit of a tourist trap these days it still retains a lot of character, with a long wooden bar and other original features. The tram to the mine museum stops across the road (on request).

✉ North Circular Road, Kimberley 8300
☎ 053-8326463 ⏰ Daily 10am–late
✋ Free

MAGALIESBERG

BILL HARROP'S ORIGINAL BALLOON SAFARIS

www.balloon.co.za

This company offers scenic one-hour early morning balloon flights over the Magaliesberg Mountains followed by a champagne breakfast. The direction the balloon takes cannot be guaranteed, as it is dependent on the wind, but usually there are good views of the Hartbeespoort Dam. The company can organize transfers from local lodges and hotels in Johannesburg and Sun City.

✉ Reservations: PO Box 67, Randburg 2125, Johannesburg ☎ 011-7053201
✋ R2,770 per person, min 2 people

THE CROCODILE RAMBLE

www.theramble.co.za

This is a successful tourism initiative that covers the region to the northwest of Johannesburg and includes Sterkfontein, Muldersdrift, Honeydew, Ruimsig, Lanseria, the Magaliesberg Mountains and Hartbeespoort Dam. The website and

a free leaflet available locally have detailed maps and lists of hotels, game farms and lodges, craft shops, restaurants and adventure activities in the region.

✉ PO Box 1320, Muldersdrift 1747
☎ 082-7894033

NAMAKWA

UMKULU

www.umkulu.co.za

Umkulu is one of many Cape Town companies to offer 60–80km (37- to 50-mile), four- to six-day fully catered canoe trips on the Gariep (Orange) River through the Ai-Ais/Richtersveld Transfrontier Park on the border with Namibia in two-man inflatable or fibreglass canoes. The trips pass amazing rock formations and each night is spent on the riverbank under the stars, with meals cooked over an open fire. Transport to and from Cape Town can be arranged.

✉ Cape Town ☎ 021-8537952 ✋ 4-day river trip: adult R2,850, child (under 12) R2,450

THE WORLD OF DIAMONDS MINE TOUR

Alexkor Ltd is a Namakwa diamond producer based at Alexander Bay, that runs tours on Thursday mornings. You need to reserve a week in advance as you need to supply copies of your passport. The tour starts at the town museum, which has exhibits on the history of the region's diamond industry and a video of the mine, and then goes into the mining region to visit the workshops and mining blocks, harbour area and an oyster farm and seal colony. No children under 16.

✉ Alexander Bay ☎ 027-8311330
⏰ Thu 8–12.30 ✋ Price depends on size of group

SUN CITY

SUN CITY

www.suninternational.com

This enormous resort has a vast range of entertainment facilities, including cinemas, and a theatre which has hosted a number of big-name stars such as Elton John, but the most popular is golf. The course

is internationally renowned, thanks to the Sun City Million Dollar Golf Challenge, founded in 1980 (now the Nedbank Golf Challenge), which has attracted most of the world's top golfers.

✉ North West Province ☎ 014-5575110
✋ Green fees R595 for residents, R695 for non-residents

UPINGTON

DESERT PALACE HOTEL & CASINO RESORT

www.desertpalace.co.za

The casino complex has six gaming tables, 158 gaming machines and an Italian-themed restaurant and bar serving standard pizza and pasta. There's also a hotel on the site, with an attractive swimming pool in terraced gardens.

✉ Upington Golf Course, 7km (4 miles) along the N14 towards Kuruman
☎ 054-3384100 ✋ Daily 10am–2am

KALAHARI TOURS & TRAVEL

www.kalahari-tours.co.za

Kalahari organizes a variety of tours in the region, including to the Kgalagadi Transfrontier Park, Augrabies and Namakwa. Particularly useful is their three-day, two-night trip up to Kgalagadi if you don't want to drive yourself.

✉ 12 Mazurkadraai, Upington 8800
☎ 054-3380375 ✋ 3-day trip R6,400 per person

WITSAND NATURE RESERVE

www.witsandkalahari.co.za

The highlight in this nature reserve is the collection of impressive white sand dunes set incongruously on the typical red sand of the Kalahari. The dunes are up to 60m (200ft) high and stretch for 9km (5.7 miles). Visitors can hike freely around the reserve but there is also a 4WD trail. Dune boarding is a new activity, and boards as well as bicycles can be hired from the information centre. Facilities include a comfortable resort with chalets and camping.

✉ 220km (141 miles) east of Upington towards Kuruman off the N14 ⏰ Day visitors daily 8–6 ✋ Adult R20, child (3–16) R10; dune board hire R90; bike hire R50

PRICES AND SYMBOLS

The restaurants are listed alphabetically (excluding The) by town or area, then by name. The prices given are the average for a two-course lunch (L) and a three-course dinner (D) for one person, without drinks. The wine price is for the least expensive bottle.

For a key to the symbols, ▷ 2.

AUGRABIES FALLS
VERGELEGEN GUESTHOUSE & RESTAURANT

www.augrabiesfalls.co.za
This is one of the best restaurants around the Augrabies Falls. Using seasonal ingredients, the chef produces dishes with a distinct regional flavour, such as biltong soup and Kalahari fillet schnitzels. For dessert be adventurous and try the chilli-flavoured ice cream or port-marinated prunes. The wine list is brief but well chosen.
✉ On N14 between Kakamas and Keimoes ☎ 054-4310976 ⏱ Mon–Fri 12–3, 7–11, Sat–Sun 12–3 🍴 L R75, D R100, Wine R45

HARTBEESPOORT DAM
CHAMELEON VILLAGE

www.chameleonvillage.co.za
Diners are spoilt for choice here, with restaurants spanning Indian, Chinese and Italian cuisines and two grill bars serving traditional steaks and burgers. After you've been fed and watered there are craft markets to browse and children's activities, including an adventure playground. One could easily while away an entire afternoon at the village.
✉ Broderstroom 0240, Hartbeespoort, junction of N4 and R560 ☎ 072 3267125 (or visit website for phone numbers of individual restaurants) ⏱ Daily 🍴 Vary

SQUIRES ON THE DAM

www.squiresonthedam.co.za
Not on the dam as such but across the road, this is a hugely popular family restaurant that gets packed out at weekends with day trippers from Johannesburg and Pretoria. The décor is chunky wooden furniture and bare brick walls, and there's an outside deck and large bar serving draft beer. There's a long menu of starters, salads, steaks, grills and seafood, including some with a German influence, and various gooey desserts. There is also an inexpensive children's menu.
✉ 1 Scott Street, Schoemansville, Hartbeespoort 0216 ☎ 012-2531001 ⏱ Mon–Sat 11–10, Sun 10–9 🍴 L R125, D R150, Wine R52

Above *Seafood pasta is always a hit*

KIMBERLEY
BUTLER'S

www.theestate.co.za
The Estate Private Hotel is in a house built in 1907 as a wedding present for diamond magnate Ernest Oppenhiemer's wife, Mary. The restaurant, Butler's, is a formal gourmet restaurant, very attractively done up with sweeping drapes, fine china and crystal glasses. The chef is very creative and the wine list is carefully chosen. Expect the likes of New Zealand mussels fried with sherry and biltong, followed by a game meat platter served with berry relish and rose petal ice cream with nuts.
✉ 7 Lodge Road, Belgravia, Kimberley 8300 ☎ 053-8322668 ⏱ Daily 6pm–10pm 🍴 D R160, Wine R90

GEORGE & DRAGON

The popular, English-style pub serves decent meals (don't miss their famous foot-long pies). This is part of a chain that is slightly more trendy than most bars, but retains a relaxed feel.
✉ Du Toitspan Road, Kimberley 8300 ☎ 053-8332075 ⏱ Daily 11am–1am

(kitchen closes at 11.30pm) 🖐 L R70, D R110, Wine R45

KALAHARI LODGE RESTAURANT
www.kalaharilodge.co.za
Enjoy a cocktail before relaxing in the comfort of this à la carte restaurant. Pub meals are served during the day, and on Sunday people come for the carvery-style lunch. Or come for breakfast, which is served from 7am.
✉ Corner N12 and Landbou Road, Kimberley 8300 ☎ 053-8315085
🕐 Mon–Sat 7am–10pm, Sun 7am–3pm
🖐 L R80, D R120, Wine R50

TIFFANY'S
www.don.co.za
Located in the Don Savoy Hotel in Kimberley, this is an elegant option for a romantic dinner with candlelight and white tablecloths. It specializes in South African cuisine, with the best use of local and seasonal produce. Barbecues are regularly held during the summer.
✉ 19 Old De Beers Road, Kimberley 8301
☎ 053-8326211 🕐 Daily 6.30pm–10pm
🖐 D R120, Wine R60

KGALAGADI TRANSFRONTIER PARK
MOLOPO KALAHRAI LODGE
www.molopolodge.co.za
The Molopo Lodge is on the way to the Kgalagadi Park and makes a welcome place to stop for lunch in the parched landscape. The cosy restaurant has outside wooden tables with safari canvas chairs and offers snack baskets, steaks, venison, ostrich, seafood, pastas and pizza. It's well known for its pepper steak, Kalahari lamb chops and home-made springbok pie.
✉ 15km (9 miles) from Askham on the R360, 50km (31 miles) from Kgalagadi Transfrontier Park gate ☎ 054-5110008
🕐 Daily 7am–10pm 🖐 L R125, D R155, Wine R65

NAMAKWA
ANITA'S TAVERN
This simple seafood restaurant at the bottom end of town near the pier has been a Port Nolloth staple for many years. Marine paraphernalia hangs

from the walls and there's a good range of inexpensive seafood on the menu, such as creamy mussels or stuffed calamari, while for dessert there's home-made malva pudding (similar to a sticky toffee pudding) and custard.
✉ Coastal road, next to First National Bank, Port Nolloth ☎ 084-7267090 🕐 Mon–Sat 12–2, 6–10 🖐 L R60, D R85, Wine R45

RUSTENBURG
KEDAR COUNTRY HOTEL
http://kedarcountry.warwickhotels.com
This is next to the historic farm of President Kruger, which is now a museum (▷ 255), in a lovely country location with zebras and ostriches wandering around the lawns. It's a good spot to stop for lunch en route for Sun City. The Armoury Restaurant specializes in South African dishes, and as the name suggests, is decorated with armoury memorabilia and portraits from the Anglo-Boer war period, while the Metswedi Bar offers inexpensive pub lunches and has tables outside with view over the indigenous gardens.
✉ On the R565, 20km (12.5 miles) from Rustenburg towards Sun City ☎ 014-5733218 🕐 Daily 12–2, 6–10 🖐 L R45, D R110, Wine R75

SUN CITY
SANTORINI
www.santorini-restaurants.co.za
Named after the Greek island, this restaurant pays tribute to Greek cuisine with a huge range of mezze, kebabs and specialities such as souvlaki and lamb cutlets. The fish and seafood are particularly tasty—try the fresh grilled sardines or the kingclip thermidor. Good for vegetarians too.
✉ Cascades Hotel, Sun City 0316
☎ 014-5575850 🕐 Daily 12–10
🖐 L R70, D R110, Wine R55

SUN CITY HOTEL
www.suninternational.com
The hotel overlooks Sun City's lovely man-made rain forest and the acclaimed Gary Player golf course, and offers various dining options for non-residents. Restaurants include

the Orchid, which serves pan-Asian cuisine like duck pancakes in sweet chilli sauce or Thai ice cream, while the Calabash offers a buffet of South African dishes such as *bobotie* (a local take on shepherd's pie with savoury custard on top instead of mashed potato) as well as some good curries, a carvery with steamed vegetables, and a choice of tempting desserts including traditional trifles and tipsy tarts.
✉ Sun City Hotel, Sun City 0316
☎ 014-5575110 🕐 Daily 12–3, 6–11
🖐 L R65, D buffet from R130, Wine R95

UPINGTON
DROS
Part of South Africa's good value steak house/pub chain, this branch has a long wooden bar and outside tables under umbrellas and enthusiastic young wait staff; it's a popular meeting point for local people. There's a very long menu filled with everything from simple baked potatoes, salads and pizzas to grilled meats such as half a barbecued chicken, rump with avocado and biltong or lamb shanks cooked in red wine. Finish off with a 'dom pedro'—an ice cream shake with a tot of alcohol.
✉ Shop 40, Kalahari Pick 'n' Pay Centre, corner Hill and Le Roux streets, Upington 8801 ☎ 054-3313331
🕐 Daily 11.30am–late 🖐 L R50, D R100, Wine R55

LE MUST
By far the best restaurant in town, and probably one of the best in the Northern Cape, Le Must is a smart set-up in a restored Upington town house. It serves well-prepared fusion dishes accompanied by an interesting local wine list. Intriguing items on the menu include biltong *bobotie* spring rolls with sultana compote and tender springbok shank with prune sauce. The décor is an interesting combination of retro style and antiques.
✉ 11 Schröder Street, Upington 8801
☎ 054-3326700 🕐 Mon–Fri 12–3, 6–10, Sat 6–10, Sun 11–3, 6–10 🖐 L R105, D R150, Wine R60

Above *Relaxing at the Mount Grace Spa complex in the Magaliesberg*

PRICES AND SYMBOLS

The hotels below are listed alphabetically (excluding The) by town or area, then by name. Prices are the average for a double room for one night, including breakfast. All the hotels listed accept credit cards unless otherwise stated.

For a key to the symbols, ▷ 2.

AUGRABIES FALLS
AUGRABIES FALLS NATIONAL PARK

www.sanparks.org

The park's camp is located right on the rim of the falls themselves, and there are excellent views from the glass-fronted restaurant. The cottages and campsite are well spaced out and private, and there are three small swimming pools, which are ideal for hot summer days. The two- to four-bed cottages are self-catering, but many guests choose to eat in the restaurant in the evening. At the campsite, which is a little dusty, not all of the 40 pitches have electricity, but the kitchen block has electric hot plates, laundry and an ironing room. The best shady spots get occupied quickly.

✉ Augrabies 8874 ☎ Reservations: 012-4289111; camp: 054-4529200 💷 RR165 (camping), R700 (chalet), R1,365 (cottage) ❶ 59 ⬛

KGALAGADI TRANSFRONTIER PARK
MATA MATA

www.sanparks.org

There are five camps in the park, but Mata Mata is one of the most pleasant, lying at the end of a beautiful road. Accommodation is in chalets which sleep up to six people and have a bathroom, kitchen and barbecue area. Huts are also available, with three beds in one room and a communal kitchen and shower block; the campsite has sandy plots in front of the chalets. There's little shade but the setting is fantastic, very close to a viewpoint. The camp has a shop selling basic groceries and firewood. Electricity is generated from 5am for two hours, and again from 5pm to 11pm.

☎ 012-4289111 (reservations) 💷 R180 (camping), R630–R1,710 (chalets) ❶ 5 🚌 118km (73 miles) from entrance gate; allow at least 2.5 hours to get there. Maps are available from the entrance gate

KIMBERLEY
CECIL JOHN RHODES GUEST HOUSE

www.ceciljohnrhodes.co.za

This luxurious, old-fashioned guesthouse is set in a converted Victorian house, now a national monument. The bedrooms are individually decorated with antiques and pale fabrics, and white linen on the four-poster beds. The floors are pale wood, and some rooms have original features such as fireplaces. All have small private bathrooms, air conditioning and TVs. The tea room has tables under the arms of a mulberry tree outside, and serves breakfast, light snacks and tea and cakes throughout the day.

✉ 138 Du Toitspan Road, Kimberley 8301 ☎ 053-8302500 💷 R740 ❶ 8 ⬛

MILNER HOUSE

www.milnerhouse.co.za

You will find this friendly, family-run guesthouse in the attractive Victorian district of Belgravia. The house has been converted into five rooms, each decorated with handmade pine furniture and bright white linen and floral curtains, with private bathroom, TV, air conditioning and heaters. There is an open-plan kitchen, lounge and dining room, with log fires in the winter, and breakfast is served on the outdoor patio when the weather is fine.

✉ 31 Milner Street, Kimberley 8301 ☎ 053-8316405 💰 R700 🛏 10 🔶 🏊

MADIKWE GAME RESERVE
JACI'S LODGES
www.madikwe.com

There are several luxury lodges to choose from within the Madikwe reserve; this one is split into the Safari Lodge and the Tree Lodge. The Safari Lodge takes just 16 guests in individual thatched suites with canvas walls, beautiful handmade furniture, handcrafted stone baths and an outside 'bush' shower, plus a private viewing deck. Prices include a personal safari guide for all game drives and walks. The Tree Lodge comprises eight tree houses built on stilts in the arms of giant leadwood or tambotie trees. The tree houses are linked by raised boardwalks, and meals are served in a central area. Rates include all meals, two game drives per day and drinks.

☎ 014-7789900/1 💰 R7,990 🛏 16 🏊 🍽

MAGALIESBERG
MOUNTAIN SANCTUARY PARK
www.mountain-sanctuary.co.za

The number of visitors to this mountain farm is controlled and there are strict regulations to preserve and maintain the wilderness, so reserve as early as possible. The accommodation consists of fully equipped, log cabins and chalets with kitchens (visitors must bring bedding, towels and food). A stunning pool has been built from natural stone on the lip of the valley offering fantastic views. This is an excellent place from which to explore the mountains, and guests have access to more than 1,000ha (2,470 acres) of hiking country.

☎ 014-5340114 💰 R80 (camping), R400 (chalets per person), R450 (log cabins per person) 🏊 🚗 35km (22 miles) from Rustenburg, off the R560

MOUNT GRACE COUNTRY HOUSE AND SPA
www.mountgrace.co.za

Guests at this elegant country house and spa can choose to stay in one of four 'villages': Mountain, Grace, Thatchstone or Treetop Village. Each has its own atmosphere and theme, offering guests something different. Natural stone has been used for the buildings, and the sound of constantly running water lulls and relaxes the visitor. Facilities at the spa include hydrotherapy, an Elixir Liquid Sound Flotation Pool, mudpacks and steam rooms. The Spa Café has a detoxifying course (on request), as well as salads, soups and sandwiches.

✉ Old Rustenburg Road ☎ 014-5775600 💰 R1,400–R2,200 🛏 121 🔶 🏊 🚗 Take the R24, approaching Magaliesberg village from Johannesburg

ORION SAFARI LODGE
www.oriongroup.co.za

In the foothills of the Magaliesberg range, very near Rustenburg Kloof nature reserve, this lodge is ideal for outdoor enthusiasts. It offers a wide range of activities including squash, swimming, volleyball and trampolining on the premises; with hiking, ballooning, golf, mountain biking, fishing and abseiling (rappelling) nearby. Game viewing at the Pilanesberg Game Reserve or gambling at Sun City are a short drive away. In 2007 the rooms had a refit and now have a contemporary feel, with added extras like plasma TVs and DVD players.

☎ 014-5979000 💰 R1,398 🛏 131 🔶 🏊 🍽 🚗 Just outside Rustenburg on the R27, going towards Mafikeng

PILANESBERG GAME RESERVE
IVORY TREE GAME LODGE
www.ivorytreegamelodge.com

This luxury game lodge lies in the northeast of the reserve. The thatched rooms and suites arranged in chalets in the bush are tastefully decorated in earthy tones, and have minibars, outside showers and covered patios. Each group of guests is assigned a personal safari guide who'll take them on game drives (no young children). Facilities include a swimming pool, beauty spa, curio shop, multi-tiered restaurant, several lounge areas and guests may be lucky enough to spot animals drinking at the waterhole.

✉ Just inside the Bakgatla Gate ☎ 011-7811661 💰 R2,550 🛏 60 🔶 🏊

SPRINGBOK
SPRINGBOK LODGE
www.springboklodge.com

The Springbok Lodge, run by Jopie Kotze, occupies a number of houses that have been converted into a series of double rooms and apartments with kitchens. Although the rooms are nothing special, they are good value and have a prime central location. The reception area of the main building also acts as an information desk, newsagent and curio shop, with an interesting semi-precious stone display and some old photographs of historic Springbok. There is a very popular restaurant and bar, which gets busy with visitors who come to hear Kotze's yarns about the town.

✉ 37 Voortrekker Street, Springbok 8240 ☎ 027-7121321 💰 R375 (R425 with air conditioning) 🛏 70

SUN CITY
CASCADES HOTEL
www.suninternational.com

One of four upscale hotels in Sun City, all of which are large and impersonal, this is ideally located to enjoy the resort's facilities. Cascades is set in tropical gardens complete with waterfalls and tranquil pools, and the rooms are in a commanding block with elevators that zip up the outside. The rooms have all mod cons and the suites also have spa baths. There are two restaurants, bars and a vast swimming pool surrounded by palm trees.

✉ Sun City 0316 ☎ 014-5575840 💰 R3,595 🛏 60 🔶 🏊

LESOTHO AND SWAZILAND

Completely surrounded by South Africa and with an elevation that is over 1,000m (3,300ft), with some peaks in excess of 3,000m (10,000ft), Lesotho is often referred to as the Kingdom in the Sky. Dramatic mountains, topped by snow in winter, cover three-quarters of the country where herd boys swaddled in blankets roam with their flocks, and farmers trot across the hillsides on their sure-footed ponies. There's just a small 'lowland' strip to the west where most of the population lives. Maseru, the capital, is located here. Lesotho has greatly benefited in recent years from the development of the Lesotho Highlands Water Project—a massive scheme largely funded by South Africa to provide electricity to the whole of Lesotho and water to thirsty industries in South Africa's Gauteng province. It will only be fully operational in the 2020s but already new dams linked by transit tunnels are pumping water and what were once perilously dangerous mountain tracks have been upgraded to smooth tar. This has opened up the mountain region, not to mention improved the local infrastructure.

Presided over by a king and the last absolute monarchy in Africa, the tiny kingdom of Swaziland shares its borders with South Africa and Mozambique and has a reputation for friendly people and craft-making. Its landscape features typical southern African scrubby bush and some low-lying mountains, and there is a handful of well-stocked wildlife reserves. The Ezulwini Valley has the country's best attractions, including the royal palace at Lobamba, the Mantenga Nature Reserve and the excellent Mlilwane Wildlife Sanctuary, which is a beautiful and peaceful place to go walking, cycling or horseback riding.

LESOTHO

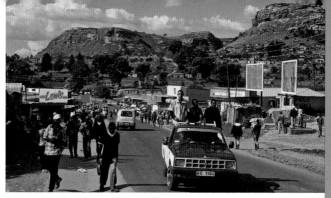

BOKONG NATURE RESERVE AND TS'EHLANYANE NATIONAL PARK

The establishment of this new national park and reserve, both north of the Katse Dam, is part of the Lesotho Highlands Water Project (▷ below). Bokong Nature Reserve covers 1,970ha (4,870 acres) and straddles the main road from Hlotse to Katse Dam at the Mafika-Lisiu Pass, at 3,090m (10,135ft). It claims to be one of the highest nature reserves in Africa and has outstanding views across the highlands. There is an exciting information centre (daily 8–5) perched on the edge of a cliff, with exhibits about the local ecology and information on the three-day 39km (25-mile) hiking trail to Ts'ehlanyane National Park and the network of shorter trails. Given the reserve's alpine altitude, there are few animals other than large colonies of ice rats, found only above 2,000m (6,500ft). Nevertheless, it is the scenery that makes a visit worthwhile.

Ts'ehlanyane National Park covers some 5,600ha (13,800 acres) and lies where the Ts'ehlanyane and Holomo rivers join, on the western range of the Maluti Mountains. The park has extensive tracts of woodlands and is full of rivers and streams bordered by bamboo. Again there are few animals but it's a haven for butterflies and birds.

✚ 330 K7 ☎ Lesotho Highlands: 266-22460723 ◷ Daily 8–5 🖾 Bokong: adult M5, child (under 12) M3; Ts'ehlanyane: adult M15, child (under 12) M5, car M5

BUTHA-BUTHE

Butha-Buthe is the most northerly town in the lowlands. It's a busy place with a number of stores where people from the highlands come every few weeks to stock up with provisions. You may notice the large suburb known as Likileng, which was built to provide accommodation for the workforce engaged on the Lesotho Highlands

Water Project. Butha-Buthe gets its name from the mountain that towers above the town; the name means 'place of lying down' or 'place of security', and it was here that Moshoeshoe (the early 19th-century chief of the Koena clan of the Sotho people) had his first mountain stronghold. The walk to the top of the mountain is fairly strenuous, but it's worth it for the fine views across the surrounding countryside.

✚ 330 K6 ❶ Information Centre, corner of Kingsway and Mpilo streets, Maseru, ☎ 266-22312427 ◷ Mon–Fri 8–5, Sat 8.30–1

HLOTSE

This town, known as both Hlotse and Leribe, is the administrative hub of Leribe district. Founded in 1876, it was also an administrative town for the British—you can still see the remains of a British fort and a statue of a kneeling British soldier. The Anglican Church dates from 1877 and is the oldest building in town. If you go some 8km (5 miles) north on the old Butha-Buthe road, and look in the Subeng stream about 400m (1,300ft) downstream from the bridge, you can see three- and five-toed dinosaur tracks estimated to be 108 to 200 million years old. Ask for directions in the village.

✚ 330 K6

KATSE DAM

Katse Dam in the Central Mountains (the most accessible highland region in Lesotho) is part of the massive

Lesotho Highlands Water Project, one of the biggest such schemes in the world. It will not be finished until the 2020s, but when it is, it should provide the whole of Lesotho with electricity. South Africa has been the main financier and it maintains a large degree of control over the project's administration (much of the water is pumped to Gauteng).

The new 121km (78-mile) road from Hlotse to the Katse Dam is an impressive feat of engineering and takes about three to four hours to drive—allow more time for stops at the tops of the mountain passes to take in the views. What used to be the roughest track in the country is now smooth tar, though there are some very steep ascents and sheer drops to the side of the road. The highest point is the Mafika-Lisiu Pass (3,090m/10,135ft), where there is a viewpoint and the visitor centre for the Bokong Nature Reserve (▷ above). The dam can hold over 2 billion litres (440 million gallons) of water, the dam wall is 185m (606ft) high and 60m (196ft) thick and is the second largest dam in Africa after Lake Volta Akosombo Dam in Ghana. Tours of the dam wall leave at 9 and 4 from the Lesotho Highlands Water Project's visitor centre (tel 266-22913206; daily 8–12, 1–4; M10 per person). Nearby are the Katse Alpine Botanical Gardens, which were created to replant some of the indigenous flora that was disrupted in the construction of the dam.

✚ 330 K7

Opposite The bridge going over the massive Katse Dam
Above Busy street in Butha-Buthe

MASERU

www.ltdc.org.ls

Maseru must be one of the world's sleepiest capital cities, although in comparison to the rest of the country, life here seems almost frantic. The heart of the city is along the Caledon River, and most shops, offices, hotels and restaurants are situated on the one long central street called Kingsway. This main road is choked with minibus taxis and busy with people milling in and out of the shops and offices.

Maseru was founded in 1869 when Lesotho's second colonial leader, Commandant J. H. Bowker, sited his headquarters here. The city grew slowly and it was not until the 1960s that the town began to expand into a city. It is a good place for a wander, and the Basotho people are outstandingly friendly; it's not uncommon for people to approach foreigners in the street to ask them how they are and where they come from. Unlike many South African downtown areas, where safety is in question, Maseru is safe to walk around and a great place to appreciate the vibrant atmosphere of an African city.

✚ 330 J7 ℹ️ Information Centre, Basotho Shield Building, Kingsway, Maseru ☎ 266-22312427 ⏰ Mon–Fri 8–5, Sat 8.30–1

MOHALE DAM

Completed in 2002 and again part of the Lesotho Highlands Water Project, this dam is connected to the Katse Dam by a tunnel. The irregular lake made by the dam is stunning and the drive is beautiful. From Maseru, the road dips through a series of valleys dotted with homesteads and rises over passes until eventually you catch your first glimpse of the impressive dam and the lake mirroring the peaks around it.

At the village of Likalaneng there's a visitor centre where you can organize a tour of the 165m-high (540ft) dam wall. From here, the road turns to gravel and continues over the mountains to Thaba-Tseka.

✚ 330 K7 ℹ️ Likalaneng ☎ 266-22936217 ⏰ Daily 8–5

MORIJA

Morija is the site of Lesotho's oldest church and the country's only museum. The French Protestant missionaries who established the church named the town after Mount Moriah in Palestine. Lesotho's first printing press was established here and the village is still important for culture, theology and printing. Books in more than 50 languages have been printed here for export to other African countries.

The museum (Mon–Fri 8–5, Sun 2–5) has a number of important historic and prehistoric exhibits, and an archive of personal and church papers. There is a large fossil collection and a good display about the dinosaur relics found throughout the country. The annual Morija Arts and Cultural Festival takes place in the first week of April, with concerts, traditional dance, choirs, horse racing and craft fairs (▷ 281).

✚ 330 J7

MOUNT MOOROSI

About 40km (25 miles) beyond Moyeni (Quthing), towards Qacha's Nek in the Southern Mountains, is Mount Moorosi along with the village of the same name, which has an important—if grim—history. In the mid-19th century it was the home of Chief Moorosi of the Baphuthi clan, who carried out raids against white settlers in nearby areas. After the British made Moyeni the district capital in 1877, they tried to subdue Moorosi by taking his son captive, but the chief resisted and managed to free his son. The British then spent more than two years trying to eliminate the threat posed by the Baphuthi chief, eventually capturing his mountain stronghold and massacring him and around 500 of his followers.

Nearby is Letsa-la-letsie (better known as Letsie) Lake, a reed-filled wetlands area which attracts water birds. A wildlife conservation project has been set up here involving the local people in the protection of the bearded vulture.

✚ 329 K8

MOYENI

Moyeni (meaning 'place of the wind') is the administrative hub of Quthing district; the town itself is often also called Quthing (Qu means river in the San language). On the northern outskirts there are some sets of dinosaur footprints along the riverbank, and some farther up the Qomoqomong valley, although these are difficult to find without a guide. The valley is also home to some of the best-preserved San cave paintings in Lesotho; follow the small road east out of Moyeni towards the village of Qomoqomong, where the road ends. The caves are in the hills to the southwest.

✚ 329 J8

NORTHERN MOUNTAINS

Commonly referred to as The Roof of Africa, the Northern Mountains are the highest in southern Africa. The high summits, unpopulated except for the occasional youth following his family herds in summer, have a harsh beauty. In winter the peaks are frequently under snow. There is one main road that runs across the area, from Butha-Buthe (▷ 271) to the Sani Pass, the highest road in all Africa. The 200km (125-mile) stretch between Butha-Buthe and Mokhotlong has now been tarred.

About 25km (16 miles) from Butha-Buthe is the small Muela Dam, and a short road leads up to a lookout point and visitor's centre on the right. This is another component of the Lesotho Highlands

Below *Street vendors selling corn on the cob in Maseru*

Above *The dramatic beauty of the Northern Mountains*

Water Project, and although you can't see it, the newly opened underground Muela hydroelectric power station now provides most of Lesotho with power.

About 30km (20 miles) from Butha-Buthe is the new Liphofung Cave Cultural and Historical Site (Mon–Fri 9–4.30), an initiative of the Lesotho Highlands Water Project to promote tourism in the region. There are some San rock paintings to see under and around a large overhang of rock that was once used as a hideout by Moshoeshoe (▷ Thaba Bosiu, below), the 19th-century Basotho chief who fled to the Northern Mountains in the 1820s. A new walkway, a small visitor centre, a shop and a rock art museum have been added to the site, and guides are available to explain the paintings and to tell you something about Moshoeshoe's history.

The scenic Moteng Pass lies between Butha-Buthe and Oxbow (68km/42 miles). This tightly twisting road goes northeast—for much of the way at an altitude of more than 2,500m (8,200ft)—climbing up gradients of more than 35 per cent to the summit, where there are excellent views of the Basotho homesteads in the valley below. This is the original route of the 'Roof of Africa' motor rally, which takes place annually at the start of summer. Oxbow is the centre of the tiny Lesotho ski industry, consisting of one operator (▷ 280), one 1km (0.6-mile) slope and a beginner's area, one T-bar lift and smaller rope lift, and a snow-making machine.
✚ 330 L7

QACHA'S NEK

This border town in the southeastern corner of Lesotho is on the only road pass from the southern mountain area into South Africa's Eastern Cape. This means it has residents from a number of southern African ethnic groups and you are as likely to hear Xhosa being spoken as Sesotho. Right up to 1970, Qacha's Nek had no direct road communication with the rest of Lesotho, and depended on the town of Matatiele in the Eastern Cape for supplies.

Qacha, meaning 'hideaway', was the name of a local 19th-century chief who was apparently able to disappear into the mountains for months at a time. The British established an administrative settlement here in 1888 in an attempt to maintain control of the region. Today, this is one of the few areas in Lesotho that is heavily forested—look for the giant California redwood trees, which are up to 25m (80ft).
✚ 330 K8

SANI PASS

This steep, tortuously corkscrewing road is the only road from the Northern Mountains into South Africa and is passable only in a 4WD vehicle (the KwaZulu-Natal government has begun upgrading the lowest section around Himeville). The pass, originally a bridleway for packhorses, was opened to vehicular transport in the 1950s. The views across the mountains of KwaZulu-Natal (▷ 179) from here are awe-inspiring. About 12km (7.5 miles) from the pass is Thabana-Ntlenyana, the highest mountain in southern Africa at 3,482m (11,424ft). The name means 'pretty little mountain', hardly fitting for what is the second tallest mountain in Africa after Kilimanjaro. There are some magnificent hikes in this rugged area (▷ 179), but most people prefer to stop off for a meal in the Sani Top Chalet (▷ 280).
✚ 330 L7

SEHLABATHEBE NATIONAL PARK

Lesotho's only fully established national park is isolated, inaccessible and rugged, but therein lies much of its appeal. In the far east of Lesotho on the border with South Africa, it is covered in subalpine grasslands at an average height of 2,400m (7,900ft). There is little large game, except for the occasional hardy eland or baboon, but plenty of birdlife, including the rare bearded vulture and black eagle. The park has excellent trout fishing, and is home to the Sehlabathebe water lily and the tiny Maluti minnow—a flower and a fish believed for many years to be extinct.
✚ 330 L7 ❓ Access is by 4WD vehicle only. There are two routes, one via Sehlabathebe village and one across the border from South Africa (by foot or horseback only)

THABA BOSIU

This mountain, 20km (12 miles) outside Maseru, was the stronghold of the founder of the Basotho nation, Chief Moshoeshoe. It is an isolated and steep-sided mountain with a large, flat plateau at the top. From this secure defensive position Moshoeshoe launched raids against his neighbours before retreating to safety. He and many other important Basotho are buried at the mountain's summit. There are remnants of Moshoeshoe's village and his restored two-roomed house, which has earned UNESCO World Heritage status for its importance to the Lesotho people.

Tour guides, who gather at the car park and small visitors' centre (tel 266-58883504; daily 8–5) at the base of the mountain will accompany visitors on the two-hour round walk to the top of Thaba Bosiu.
✚ 330 K7

SWAZILAND

EZULWINI VALLEY

The Ezulwini Valley ('Valley of Heaven'), clearly signposted from Mbabane, is the hub of most visitor activity in Swaziland. The area is also known as the Royal Valley as it is home to the Royal Village of Lobamba (see below). The valley itself has no real focus, but dotted along the road are craft shops, markets, hotels and restaurants; on weekends everyone in Swaziland seems to come here to play. The valley runs east for 30km (18.5 miles), ending at Lobamba. Here you'll see a service station, and just past it is the entrance to Mlilwane Wildlife Sanctuary (▷ 276).
✚ 325 M4

HLANE ROYAL NATIONAL PARK

www.biggameparks.org
Formerly a royal hunting ground, Hlane was declared a protected area in 1967 by King Sobhuza II. Following heavy poaching in the 1960s, the park has been restocked with wildlife and at 30,000ha (74,000 acres) is the kingdom's largest wildlife area. A number of predators have been reintroduced and lion, cheetah and leopard are already evident, as well as elephant, zebra, giraffe, impala, hyena, white rhino and herds of wildebeest. Sadly the rhinos have had to have their horns removed to protect them from poachers. Hlane supports the densest population of raptors in Swaziland; the nesting density for the white-backed vulture is the highest in the whole of Africa, and the most southerly nesting colony of the marabou stork is found here.

The western area of the park has a network of roads that visitors can drive along to view the animals. The area around the Black Mbuluzi River attracts animals during the dry winter season. Close to Ndlovu camp is an Endangered Species Area, where elephant and rhino have been concentrated for security reasons. The Mahlindza waterhole, with its hippo, crocodile and water bird population, is one of the most peaceful picnic sites in the country.
✚ 325 N4 ☎ Office: 268-5283943
🕐 Daily dawn–dusk 🖐 Adult E25, child (under 13) E12.50; 2-hour game drive costs E225 per person; guided walks cost E135 for 2.5 hours (child under 13 half price)
🚌 67km (42 miles) from Manzini along the road to Simunye. Turn left into the Ngongoni Gate, where all arrivals need to report

LOBAMBA

The royal village of Lobamba, at the eastern end of the Ezulwini Valley, is set amid open bush countryside. This is where the present king, Mswati III lives, and from where he rules Swaziland with the Queen Mother, whose title is Ndlovukazi (meaning 'she-elephant'). Every August the king adds to his growing harem of wives at the Umhlanga (Reed) Dance (▷ 281). All the royal buildings are closed to the public, and it is strictly forbidden to take photographs. However, the National Museum in the village (Mon–Fri 8–1, 2–3.45, Sat–Sun 10–1, 2–3.45) has excellent displays relating to Swazi life throughout history, with old photographs, traditional dress and Stone Age implements.

Opposite the museum is a memorial to King Sobhuza II and a small museum depicting his life. His statue stands under a domed cover with open arches and a white tiled floor.
✚ 325 M4

MALKERNS VALLEY

About 5km (3 miles) beyond Lobamba is a right turn for the Malkerns Valley, which is less geared to tourism than the Ezulwini Valley. But this does mean you get more of a feel for a typical Swazi lifestyle. There are restaurants and shops along the M13, including the well-known shop Swazi Candles (▷ 281). Items here are not all that cheap, but if you are on a budget, there are lower-price seconds with barely visible flaws.

South from Malkerns, the road continues towards Bhunya, which is 26km (16 miles) away. As the road climbs up into the highlands the forest closes in and it feels cool out of the sunlight. For part of this route the road follows the Great Usutu River, passing through rolling farmland.
✚ 331 M5

Above *Craft stalls selling locally made items are a main draw in the Ezulwini Valley; this one is at Tintsab*

MALOLOTJA NATURE RESERVE

www.sntc.org.sz

Malolotja is a wild region of mountains and forest along Swaziland's northwestern border with South Africa. This reserve has been designed as a wilderness area, with most of the park accessible only on foot. There's a network of gravel roads, covering 25km (15.5 miles), for self-guided game drives, but the best way to see the park is on foot along one of the hiking trails.

Mgwayiza, Ngwenya and Silotfwane are three of Swaziland's highest peaks, and the hikes around these ranges cross deep, forested ravines, high plateaux and grasslands. Archaeological remains show that this region has been inhabited for thousands of years. The site of the world's oldest mine, thought to be 43,000 years old, is within the park; the diggings were used to excavate red and black earth, possibly for use as pigments.

➕ 325 M4 ☎ Swaziland National Trust Commission: 268-4424241 ✋ Adult E28, child (4–12) E14 🎟️ 🚗 From MR3 turn, at Motjane, on to MR1; turn off after 7km (4 miles) and continue for another 18km (11 miles) to the reserve

MANTENGA NATURE RESERVE

www.sntc.org.sz

This area of outstanding beauty and patches of indigenous forest between the main road and the Mantenga Falls (a walk of 2km/1.2 miles) is best known for the Swazi Cultural Village. This 'show' village is based upon traditional building methods and sells itself as a living cultural museum: This is exactly how a medium-sized Swazi homestead would have looked 100 years ago. There are 16 beehive-shaped huts built from local materials. As the guides show you around, the complex comes to life, with people performing traditional dances and songs. You will also see food being prepared and clothes and household objects being made. The set-up is both informative and informal—you can turn up at any time.

➕ 331 M5 ☎ 268-4161151 🕐 Daily dawn–dusk ✋ E20; Swazi Cultural Village: adult E150, child (7–12) E60 🍴 🚗 Just past Lobamba in the Ezulwini Valley

MANZINI

This industrial town has a good market, held on the corner of Mhlakuvane Street and Mancishane Road on Friday and Saturday mornings, and is worth a browse. It's one of the busiest local markets in Swaziland, bringing people from the local farming communities into town to sell fresh fruit and vegetables, clothes, a good selection of curios and freshly cooked snacks.

The Bhunu Mall on Ngwane Street and The Hub on Mhlakuzane Street are Manzini's newest shopping malls. Tiger-City (daily 8.30–6) on Villiers Street is a small complex where you'll find the cinema and a couple of restaurants.

The first trading station was opened here in 1885 and was originally run from a tent. The plot was later sold on to Alfred Bremer, who built a hotel and a shop. Manzini was originally known as Bremersdorp after Alfred Bremer, but was renamed Manzini after the Boers burnt the settlement to the ground during the Anglo–Boer War. The administrative focus then moved to Mbabane. While Swaziland was being administered by a provisional government composed of representatives of the Transvaal, the British government and the king during 1894, the headquarters were in the local hotel.

➕ 331 N5

MBABANE

Mbabane, the capital of Swaziland, is a small modern town built on the site of a trading station on the busy route between Mozambique and the Transvaal. After the Boer War, the British established their administrative headquarters here and the town grew up around it. Over the last few decades, the town hasn't developed well; there's a snarled traffic system, and just a handful of shopping malls and hotels. But do have a look at the Swazi market, which is near the central roundabout (traffic circle). It has an excellent display of fresh produce and you can engage in some good-natured bartering with the stallholders. The town also has useful amenities before you move onto the attractive Ezulwini Valley to the south (▷ 274).

➕ 325 M4 ℹ️ Swaziland Information Office, Swazi Plaza ☎ 268-4042531 🕐 Mon–Fri 8–5, Sat 8.30–12.30

Left *Dusty gravel road leading into the wilderness that is the Malolotja Nature Reserve*

INFORMATION

www.biggameparks.org

➕ 325 M4 ☎ 268-5283943 🕐 Gates: daily 24 hours 💰 Adult E25, child (under 13) E12.50 🚶 Guided walks: E60 per hour; guided mountain biking: E105 per hour; 90-min game drives day or night E175; 90-min sunset drives with drinks: E225; village visits: E65 🍴 Restaurant in main camp overlooking a hippo pool ❓ Displays about conservation and poaching at Sangweni Gate 🚗 The reserve is signposted from Lobamba in the Ezulwini Valley

TIPS

» There are nightly performances of traditional Swazi dancing in the main camp; try to catch one, even if you're staying elsewhere.

» The reserve arranges visits to local villages which offer a valuable insight into local life.

MLILWANE WILDLIFE SANCTUARY

Mlilwane, stretching along a section of the Ezulwini Valley, is one of the most popular of Swaziland's nature reserves and covers a varied landscape of highveld and lowveld along a section of the Ezulwini Valley. The land, originally a ruined area of abandoned tin mines, scarred with ravines and slag heaps, is now filled with a variety of game including hippo, giraffe, crocodile, eland, zebra, kudu and the purple-crested lourie, the brilliantly plumaged national bird of Swaziland. There are more than 100km (60 miles) of dirt roads criss-crossing the reserve; some are for 4WDs only. There are several choices of accommodation, but places on all guided walks and rides can be reserved from the main camp.

ACTIVITIES IN THE RESERVE

As there are no big cats or rhino in Mlilwane, you can explore the reserve on horseback, by mountain bike or on foot, peaceful ways of experiencing the glorious landscape. The animals in the reserve are pretty docile, allowing close viewings; horseback riding among herds of zebra is an unforgettable experience. There is an extensive system of self-guided walking trails including the Hippo, Macobane, Sondzela and Mhlambanyatsi trails, each looping around the reserve and taking in a variety of environments. The Macobane Trail, which runs for 8km (5 miles), has an easy gradient and provides particularly spectacular views of the Ezulwini Valley as it winds its way along the contours of an old aqueduct on the Nyonyane Mountain (1,136m/3,726ft). For all activities, a minimum of two people is necessary.

MKHAYA GAME RESERVE

www.biggameparks.orgl

This small reserve, Swaziland's most exclusive, is now one of the best places in southern Africa to see black rhino. It is in an area of acacia lowveld southeast of Manzini. In 1995, the park received six black rhino from South Africa, a project funded, rather oddly, by the Taiwanese Government. During 1997, the first two baby elephants to be born in Swaziland in 100 years were born at Mkhaya. At present the only large cat you might see is the leopard. This is a private reserve and staying guests must arrange to arrive at either 10am or 4pm when the rangers will pick you up from the (locked) main gates. Day visits are allowed between these hours.

✚ 331 N5 ☎ 268-5283943 🕐 Daily 10–4 by pre-arranged tour only 🖐 Day visit and lunch E520 per person (no children under 6) 🚗 From Manzini, follow signs to Siteki for 8km (5 miles) and take a right turn and continue towards Big Bend (MR8); the reserve is signposted to the left after about 44km (27 miles)

MLAWULA NATURE RESERVE

www.sntc.org.sz

Mlawula is part of the new greater Lubombo Conservancy. The Siphiso Valley and the Mbuluzi Gorge are good areas for game viewing on hiking trails or game drives. The main appeal of Mlawula is the variety of landscapes, from forests to dry thorn savannah. More than 1,000

Left *Antelope preparing to dash across the road at Mlilwane*

Below *A selection of soapstone carvings on the road to Piggs Peak from Mbabane*

species of plant have been identified here and the region is famed for its birdlife—350 species have been recorded, including crested guinea fowl and yellow spotted nicator. The good facilities include a vulture feeding area and a birdwatching hide. Early traces of man dating back 100,000 years have been found in the riverbeds of the Mbuluzi and Mlawula rivers, which are also good places to spot crocodiles. The interesting plantlife includes the rare Lebombo ironwood and the *Encephalartos umeluziensis*, a cycad that grows only in the deep mountain valleys of the reserve.

Visitors are encouraged to hike on the network of trails, which pass through beautiful gorges, pools, waterfalls and rapids with views over Mozambique from the top of the escarpment. A leaflet on the trails and the reserve is available from the camp shop where you can also organize a guide to go with you.

✚ 325 N4 ☎ Swaziland National Trust Commission: 268-3838885 🖐 Adult E25, child (under 13) E12 🚌 🚗 67km (42 miles) from Manzini along the road to Simunye, signposted after Simunye

PHOPHONYANE NATURE RESERVE

www.phophonyane.co.sz

Close to the mountain community of Piggs Peak is this small reserve in an extensive tract of natural vegetation. It lies on an escarpment, where the environment changes dramatically over a relatively small area. The dense riverine forest is home to small mammals such as duiker, bushbuck and the clawless otter, and there are more than 200

species of bird. The Phophonyane Falls, the best known in Swaziland, are here, and an artifiical swimming pool has been created in the rocks at the bottom. You can explore the forest and mountains on foot or by 4WD vehicle. There's a comfortable lodge here for overnight guests.

✚ 325 N4 ☎ 268-4371429 🕐 Daily 7.30–5 🖐 Adult E45, child (under 12) E30 🚗 Signposted 14km (8.5 miles) north of Piggs Peak

PIGGS PEAK

This small town was named after William Pigg, a French gold prospector who came here in 1884. There was a working gold mine here until 1954, although no great fortunes were ever made. Today the town consists of little more than a string of shops along the main road. The principal industry here now is logging (as well as the huge Havelock asbestos mine). If you are going to and from South Africa through Jeppe's Reef border post, you are bound to pass through.

✚ 325 M4

SHEWULA NATURE RESERVE

www.shewulacamp.com

The community-owned Shewula Nature Reserve is just north of Mlawula. It is also part of the Lebombo Conservancy, straddling the Lebombo Mountains on the border with Mozambique and covering an escarpment of ancient ironwood mountain forest. The views from the Shewula Mountain Camp, perched on top of a mountain, are incredible. On a clear day the ocean and Maputo can be seen to the east, and there is an uninterrupted view of 100km (62 miles) across Swaziland. Apart from during heavy rains (December to February), the camp is accessible by ordinary cars. When the road is too muddy, you can leave your vehicle at the chief's office in the village and be transported in a 4WD.

✚ 325 N4 ☎ 268-6051160 🚗 10km (6 miles) south of the Lomahasha/Namaacha border with Mozambique; the camp is a further 30 minutes' drive

SWAZILAND: THE VALLEY OF HEAVEN

This circular drive takes you from Swaziland's capital, Mbabane, through the popular Ezulwini Valley, where the scenery is undulating savannah. Leaving behind the bustle of Swaziland's tourism hub, the drive continues into a region of farmland and forest and up into the relative cool of the highlands.

THE DRIVE

Distance: 120km (75 miles)
Allow: 1 day
Start/end at: Mbabane

★ Make your way from central Mbabane (▷ 275) southwest on the route designated 'Western Distributor Road' and then on the MR3, following the signs to the Ezulwini Valley.

This first steep, short and scenically dramatic stretch was once judged (by the *Guinness Book of Records*) as the world's most dangerous road, but don't worry— its two lanes make it safe enough today. From the crest of the hill, about 2km (1.2 miles) out of town, you can look down over the valley. At the bottom take the old main road (the MR103, signposted Ezulwini and Malkerns).

❶ The Ezulwini Valley (the Valley of Heaven) is the focus of tourism for Swaziland. Hotels, casinos, restaurants and craft shops line the old Ezulwini road. On your right (12km/7.5 miles from Mbabane), signposted off the road, you can get a taste of local culture at the all-singing, all-dancing Swazi Cultural Village (▷ 275) in the Mantenga Nature Reserve, and at the Mantenga Craft Centre, where carvings, fabrics, pottery and jewellery are all for sale.

A striking natural feature of the valley's skyline is the Lugogo massif, also known as Sheba's Breasts, which dominates the area.

A little farther along you'll see the signposted road that leads to the Mlilwane Wildlife Sanctuary.

❷ The Mlilwane Wildlife Sanctuary (▷ 276) consists of 4,500ha (11,000 acres) of once despoiled land that has been admirably restored and restocked with animals. Mlilwane began as a private enterprise but was donated to the nation in the 1960s. Its cause was enthusiastically taken up by King Sobhuza after a group of his hunters returned from a four-day foray into the game-rich countryside to the northeast bearing just two impala carcasses. If you have the time, Mlilwane makes for an excellent overnight stay.

Continue to the end of the valley, where you'll pass the National Museum (with exhibits illustrating Swazi life and culture), the country's Parliament, and the King Sobhuza II Memorial, all three of them on your left and set back a little from the road. A short distance beyond and to your right is Lobamba.

❸ Lobamba is the royal village, residence of the king and venue of the annual Incwala, an all-male ceremony in which young men bring special offerings to the king. The Swazi king does not inherit the throne from his father, but is always a member of the royal clan, chosen as a young unmarried man with no children. After he is crowned, he may take as many wives as he likes.

★ **Mbabane**

Mantenga Nature Reserve

① Ezulwini Valley

MR3

Mhlambanyatsi

Mlilwane Wildlife Sanctuary

Lobamba

⑤ MR19

② ③ MR103

④ Malkerns

Bhunya

MR18

0   10 km
0   5 miles

Malkerns

Follow the valley road for a further 5km (3 miles) and turn right on the MR18 to nearby Malkerns.

④ Malkerns is a standard Swazi country town largely sustained by the surrounding pineapple plantations. There are a number of craft shops en route worth a look, including the well-known Swazi Candles (▷ 281).

The road from Malkerns continues south and then west, passing through farmland and along the reaches of the Great Usutu River. This road then leads into the town of Bhunya, the focus of the region's forestry and timber industries. There is a giant pulp mill here that has provided much-needed income for local people. Pass through the town and take the MR19 north towards Mhlambanyatsi and Mbabane.

⑤ The village of Mhlambanyatsi ('the place of swimming buffalos') is in a delightful part of the country, full of scenic variety and graced by handsome pine plantations. The village itself is nothing special, but there are some rewarding destinations in the wider area, among

them the Forester's Arms (▷ 284). This inn, about 12km (7 miles) from Bhunya, stands among the trees in the cool highlands and is renowned for its sociability (signposted from the MR19).

From here, it's a straight run on the MR19 back to Mbabane, 34km (22 miles) from Bhunya.

WHEN TO GO

Summer days in the Ezulwini Valley can be stifling, and afternoon thunderstorms may spoil your drive, but this is the time that the countryside is at its lush best. It's

cooler on the higher ground north of Malkerns. Winter nights and early mornings are often chilly.

WHERE TO EAT

MALANDELA'S
www.malandelas.com
Good meals and snacks, including excellent chicken and mushroom pancakes.
☎ 268-5283115 ⏰ Daily 11–3, 6–late
🚗 On the Malkerns road (MR18), next to the market

CALABASH
German and Austrian dishes served in one of the best restaurants in the country.
☎ 268-4161187 ⏰ Daily 12–3, 6–11
🚗 Close to Timbali Lodge, MR103, Ezulwini Valley

PLACES TO VISIT

MANTENGA CRAFT CENTRE
⏰ Daily 8–5 🚗 Just off Ezulwini Valley (signposted)

SWAZI CANDLES
www.swazicandles.com
☎ 268-5283219 ⏰ Mon–Fri 10–4, Sat 10–3 🚗 1km (0.6 miles) from intersection between M19 and Ezulwini Valley, towards Malkerns

THE SWAZI SPA HEALTH & BEAUTY STUDIO
☎ 268-4064000 🚗 400m (436 yards) from turning for Royal Swazi Hotel, MR103, Ezulwini Valley

Opposite *Mlilwane Wildlife Sanctuary*
Below *Swazi Cultural Village*

Above Bright African-themed candles for sale at Swazi Candles, Malkerns

LESOTHO

MALEALEA
MALEALEA LODGE
www.malealea.com

This is the finest place in Lesotho for pony trekking around the local area, with treks lasting from one hour to six days. An average of seven hours are spent in the saddle each day, although the sure-footed ponies make it easy riding. Only local Basotho guides are used, and the owners are deeply involved with local sustainable tourism initiatives.

☎ 051-4366766 (reservations in South Africa)/082-5524215 (mobile phone)
✋ From M150 for 2- to 3-hour ride
🚌 10km (6 miles) south of Morija the B40 turns off from the Main South Road to the left, and follows through to Malealea 32km (20 miles) away

MASERU
BASOTHO HAT
This craft shop, with its unmissable conical roof shaped like a Basotho hat, has a good selection of local crafts—and hats, but prices are higher than in smaller towns.
✉ Central Kingsway, next to the tourist office ☎ 266-22322523 🕐 Mon–Sat 8–5

NORTHERN MOUNTAINS
AFRI-SKI
www.afriski.net

This is an Alpine-style lodge that offers skiing on a short slope. The ski season is generally from June through August, though the lodge is open all year and offers other activities, such as hiking.
☎ 086-1754669 ✋ 1-day ski pass: adult E350, child (under 6) M100 🚌 11km (7 miles) from the New Oxbow Lodge before the Mahlasela Pass

NEW OXBOW LODGE
www.oxbow.co.za

One of the best trout-fishing locations is on the Malibamatso River near the New Oxbow Lodge. The lodge arranges guided fishing trips to the river; these are very popular so reserve ahead
☎ 051-9332247 (reservations from South Africa) ✋ Free 🚌 Access from the lodge, just over the Moteng Pass. From Butha-Buthe, turn left at the T-junction in town and continue until you see the signs for the lodge

SANI PASS
SANI TOP CHALET
www.sanitopchalet.co.za

Intrepid visitors who make it to the top of the Sani Pass from South Africa stop here for a celebratory drink. The lodge and pub claim to be the highest in Africa and the views down the valley to KwaZulu-Natal are incredible. Also organizes hiking, horseback riding and visits to a Bosotho home.
☎ 033-7021069 (South Africa)/084-5851131 🕐 Daily 11am–midnight

TEYA-TAYANENG
HELANG BASALI HANDICRAFTS
This craft centre is run by a local mission and sells a good range of reasonably priced and well-made rugs, blankets, tapestries and other handicrafts.
✉ Main North Road 🕐 Mon–Sat 10–5 🚌 Just south of the town

SETSHOTO WEAVERS
Visitors can watch the weavers at work, then buy the finished product. There's the usual array of Basotho rugs and blankets on sale, for reasonable prices.
✉ Main North Road ☎ 266-58086312 🕐 Mon–Sat 10–5 🚌 Opposite Blue Mountain Inn, signposted off Main North Road

SWAZILAND

EZULWINI VALLEY
MANTENGA CRAFT CENTRE
One of the principal attractions along the Ezulwini Valley road is its array of craft stalls, and Mantenga, part of a self-sufficiency project, stocks an excellent range of crafts, including jewellery, screen prints, leather goods, ceramics, rugs and carvings.

✉ Mantenga Valley ☎ 268-4161136
🕐 Daily 8–5 🚌 1km (0.6 miles) after turn-off from Ezulwini Valley

ROYAL SWAZI SPA VALLEY
www.suninternational.com
This smart hotel complex has the country's top 18-hole golf course, which can be used by day visitors if they call in advance.

✉ Ezulwini Valley ☎ 268-4064000
🖐 Green fees E440 for guests, E520 for day visitors 🚌 Signposted from the MR3, Ezulwini Valley

THE SWAZI SPA HEALTH & BEAUTY STUDIO
This popular spa is set around Cuddle Puddle, a swimming pool fed by a hot natural mineral spring. Housed in buildings modelled on a Swazi village, it has two large saunas, two indoor hot mineral pools, plunge pools, an aromatherapy steam-tube and the outdoor Cuddle Puddle. The cost of the treatments are a fraction of what you'd pay in northern Europe or the US.

✉ Ezulwini Valley ☎ 268-4064000
🖐 Full day's use of saunas and mineral pools E75 🚌 400m (440 yards) from the turn-off for Royal Swazi Hotel, MR103, Ezulwini Valley

SWAZI TRAILS
www.swazitrails.co.sz
Swazi Trails is the leading adventure operator in Swaziland. Its white-water rafting trips take place year-round on the Great Usutu River. Two-man rafts are used, led by guides paddling in kayaks. With a new stretch of river opened in the remote Bulunga Gorge,

FESTIVALS AND EVENTS

APRIL
MORIJA ARTS AND CULTURAL FESTIVAL
www.morijafest.com
The annual Morija Arts and Cultural Festival takes place here in the first week of April, with concerts, traditional dance, choirs, horse racing, and food and craft fairs. This is Lesotho's only event of its kind so it's worth making an effort to see it.

✉ Morija, Lesotho ☎ 266-22360308

AUGUST/SEPTEMBER
UMHLANGA REED DANCE
If you're in Swaziland at the end of August into September, don't

a couple of adrenaline-pumping rapids have been added to the list. All the guides are Swazis with superb local knowledge. Swazi Trails can also arrange guided walking and hiking trails, including a two-hour Rhino Walk in the Hlane Royal National Park.

✉ Mantenga Centre, Mantenga Valley ☎ 268-4162180 🖐 Day rafting from E850 🚌 1km (0.6 miles) after turn-off from Ezulwini Valley

WHY NOT DISCO AND IF NOT GO-GO BAR
Don't be too put off by the peculiar name—this disco and bar has become an institution in Swaziland, and on weekends many top bands and performers come here to put on a show.

✉ Happy Valley Hotel, MR103, Ezulwini Valley ☎ 268-4161061 🕐 Bar, 24hrs; disco Mon–Sat 10pm–late 🖐 E30

MALKERNS
MALANDELA'S
www.malandelas.com
There's a lively party scene at this restaurant-cum-pub that serves good African and European food and beer on tap and has a big-screen TV for sports matches. It's a good place to meet the locals.

miss the spectacular Umhlanga Reed Dance. A huge number of Swaziland's girls and young women of marriageable age congregate at the Queen Mother's home to pay homage and repair her roof with reeds. This is followed by a mass display of bare-breasted dancing in the open-air National Stadium, where the King gets to pick out his next wife—an honour she cannot refuse. Visitors are welcome to join the crowds of Swazi spectators.

✉ Somhlolo National Stadium, Lobamba, Ezulwini Valley, Swaziland ☎ 268-4044556

☎ 268-5283115 🕐 Daily 11–3, 6–late 🖐 Free 🚌 1km (0.6 miles) from junction between M19 and Ezulwini Valley, towards Malkerns

SWAZI CANDLES
www.swazicandles.com
Swazi Candles is well known in the region for its beautiful handmade candles in a variety of designs and colours, many with a safari theme. In the same complex is Baobab Batik (www.baobab-batik.com) and Gone Rural (www.goneruralswazi.com), both shops selling stylish woven goods in bright colours.

☎ 268-5283219 🕐 Mon–Fri 10–4, Sat 10–3 🚌 1km (0.6 miles) from junction between M19 and Ezulwini Valley, towards Malkerns

MBABANE
AFRICAN FANTASY
If you'd rather not haggle for your souvenirs, head for this shop, which stocks a good selection of arts and crafts from around the country at fixed prices. Look out for the candles from the famous Swazi Candles shop. There's another branch in the Mantenga Craft centre in the Ezulwini Valley.

✉ The Mall, Mbabane ☎ 268-4040205
🕐 Mon–Fri 8–5, Sat 8–4, Sun 9–1

PRICES AND SYMBOLS

The restaurants are listed alphabetically (excluding The) by town or area, then by name. The prices given are the average for a two-course lunch (L) and a three-course dinner (D) for one person, without drinks. The wine price is for the least expensive bottle.

For a key to the symbols, ▷ 2.

LESOTHO

MASERU

LEHAHA GRILL

One of the country's smarter (and better) restaurants is in the Lesotho Sun Hotel. At lunchtime there are good-value buffets serving a wide choice, from vegetable stir-fries to pasta and roasts. There is also a snack menu, and in the evenings an à la carte menu. Reservations are necessary on weekends and public holidays.

✉ Lesotho Sun Hotel, Nightingale Road, behind the Queen Elizabeth Hospital, Maseru ☎ 266-22312960 🕐 Daily 7am–10pm ♿ L M120 (buffet), D M150, Wine M70

MOHOKARE RESTAURANT

There is a similar set-up to the Lehaha Grill in this Sun International

sister hotel, named after the Mohokare River which it overlooks. Again there are buffets including good Mongolian stir-fries, which you assemble yourself and the chef cooks in front of you, and an à la carte menu in the evenings. The comfortable lounge has views of the eastern Free State's farmland on a clear day and light meals are served by the pool in summer.

✉ Maseru Sun Hotel, 12 Orpen Road, Maseru ☎ 288-22312434 🕐 Daily 7am–10pm ♿ L M120 (buffet), D M150, Wine M70

STREET VENDORS

A good place to pick up a very cheap, filling local meal is one of the many street vendors lining Kingsway in central Maseru, around the taxi station. Be sure to select a vendor who is busy with locals, and where you can see the food is freshly prepared and served piping hot. You can usually choose from deep-fried samosas and the staple dish of stiff maize porridge served with a meat stew. A filling meal will rarely cost more than M10. A good on-the-go snack is roasted maize, blackened over coals.

✉ Kingsway, Maseru

Above *Looking out over the watering hole at the Hippo Haunt, Mlilwane*

SWAZILAND

EZULWINI VALLEY

BELLA VISTA PIZZERIA

Bella Vista is well placed for an evening meal before heading to the Why Not club (▷ 281) in the same complex. It serves large portions of Italian fare, including a good vegetarian pizza, pasta dishes and several meat choices. Also here is the Sir Loin restaurant, serving steaks and grills.

✉ Happy Valley Hotel, MR103, Ezulwini Valley ☎ 268-4161061 🕐 Mon–Sat noon–2am ♿ L E65, D E100, Wine E45

CALABASH

www.restaurant-calabash.com

The Calabash is widely rated as Swaziland's leading à la carte restaurant, and is consistently popular—expect to wait for a table at lunchtime, and be sure to book in the evenings. The menu has a northern European bias, with plenty of German and Austrian dishes. Meals are hearty and meat-heavy (stews and schnitzels are popular choices), but there are also fish and seafood dishes, and several French-style offerings. German beer is available on draught.

✉ Close to Timbali Lodge, MR103, Ezulwini Valley ☎ 268-4161187 ⏰ Daily 12–3, 6–11 ✋ L E105, D E140, Wine E60

MALANDELA'S
www.malandelas.com
This is an excellent restaurant in a stylish setting, surrounded by gardens, with a shady deck under impressive thatched roofs. The menu is chalked up on giant boards and offers fusion food, mixing African and European dishes using home-grown vegetables. There are also home-made cakes and bread. Monday is curry night and Tuesday is prawn night. The lively pub has draught beer on tap and giant TV screens for watching important sports matches or music videos.

✉ Malkerns road, 1km (0.6 miles) off the main Ezulwini Valley road ☎ 268-5283115 ⏰ Daily 11–3, 6–late ✋ L E55, D E90, Wine E60

ROYAL SWAZI SPA
www.suninternational.com
There are several top-class places to eat at this luxury hotel, where non-guests can also use the casino and spa facilities. There's the Terrace Restaurant, with its lovely white décor that serves buffets for breakfast, lunch and dinner, the Planters Restaurant, which has an à la carte menu and specializes in curries, grills and seafood, and the Sportsman Bar, which offers pub lunches in front of TVs showing sports. The hotel also holds a relaxed Sunday buffet next to the swimming pool.

✉ Old Manzini/Mbabane Main Road (MR103), Ezulwini Valley ☎ 268-4165550 ⏰ Times vary ✋ L from E60, set dinners from E155, Wine E80

MANTENGA NATURE RESERVE
SWAZI RIVER CAFÉ
www.swaziplace.com/swazirivercafe
Open all day for breakfast, lunch and dinner, plus teas and coffees,

this café offers different specials during the week such as fresh fish on Tuesday, buckets of giant prawns on Wednesday, a game menu of ostrich, impala and crocodile on Thursday, and a good-value all-you-can-eat buffet for Sunday lunch. Also look for the tasty monster crab claws imported from Maputo in Mozambique. This is a great place to come for a sundowner on the wooden deck, and the bar stays open late.

✉ Mantenga Nature Reserve, Ezulwini Valley ☎ 268-6022183 ⏰ Tue–Sat 7.30am–late, Sun 7.30am–5pm ✋ L E40, D E90, Wine E55

MANZINI
TUM'S GEORGE HOTEL
www.tgh.sz
This modern hotel and conference centre offers set menus in the main dining room, which has smartly dressed tables with white linen, an à la carte menu in the cosy St. George's Pub & Lounge, and a generous Sunday lunch around the swimming pool with its poolside cocktail bar. The food is a mix of African dishes and British-style pub grub. There's also a coffee shop that sells snacks.

✉ Corner of Ngwane and Du Toit streets, Manzini ☎ 268-5058991 ⏰ Daily 7am–10pm ✋ L E45, D E70, Wine E45

MBABANE
FRIAR TUCK
www.mountaininn.sz
The smart Mountain Inn on the road out of town also has the area's best restaurant, Friar Tuck. The interior is rather dark, with exposed brick walls, vaulted ceilings and wooden tables. The outside tables overlook the garden and pool, with beautiful views of the Ezulwini Valley. Reliable buffet lunches are served here, and in the evenings there's an à la carte menu with standard grills, chicken dishes and local specials.

✉ Mountain Inn, Mbabane ☎ 268-4042781 ⏰ Daily 12–2.30, 6.30–10 ✋ L E80, D E110, Wine E50 🚗 4km (2.5 miles) from central Mbabane, on Ezulwini Valley road; look for signs on the left

INDINGILIZI ART GALLERY
This quiet art gallery has a small restaurant in the back garden—a peaceful sanctuary from the noisy city streets outside. You can get wholesome light lunches, some with an African bias, as well as soups, sandwiches and salads. Snacks and cakes are also served throughout the day.

✉ 112 Dzeliwe Street, Mbabane ☎ 268-4046213 ⏰ Mon–Fri 9–5, Sat 9–1 ✋ L E40

MLILWANE WILDLIFE SANCTUARY
HIPPO HAUNT
Besides a snug indoor restaurant with fireplace, the Hippo Haunt comprises two outside wooden deck areas from which you can view hippos, crocodiles and terrapins comfortably at close quarters while enjoying meals and drinks from the bar. The food on offer is basic but wholesome, with lots of meat on the menu, including venison. The restaurant serves a wide range of wines, beers and spirits to accompany your meal.

✉ Mlilwane Wildlife Sanctuary, Ezulwini Valley, between Mbabane and Manzini ☎ 268-4161591 ⏰ Daily 12–2, 6–9 ✋ L E90, D E120, Wine E65

SIMUNYE
SIMUNYE CLUB RESTAURANT
www.simunyeclub.com
This is an old-style country club with a good choice of sporting facilities, including a nine-hole golf course and a pool, which visitors can use for a small fee. There's a popular family restaurant with an à la carte menu and carvery lunches on weekdays, and pizzas and braais (barbecues) every Friday evening. The setting is attractive, with seating on a pleasant terrace in the tropical gardens, with many different species of bird flitting around in the trees, including weavers and the rare brown-headed African parrot.

✉ Simunye, 22km (14 miles) south of the Lomhasha border with Mozambique ☎ 268-3134792 ⏰ Daily 8.30am–10.30pm ✋ L E55, D E75, Wine E45

PRICES AND SYMBOLS

The hotels below are listed alphabetically (excluding The) by town or area, then by name. Prices are the average for a double room for one night, including breakfast. All the hotels listed accept credit cards unless otherwise stated.

For a key to the symbols, ▷ 2.

LESOTHO

SEMONKONG
MALEALEA LODGE

www.malealea.co.ls

Owners Mike and Di Jones, both born in Lesotho, are passionate about the country and have done much to direct money from tourism back into local communities. Their lodge is a collection of rooms with private bathrooms, huts with kitchens and dorms in an old farmhouse, close to a charming Basotho village. There are three communal kitchens, and home-cooked meals are also available, plus there is an honesty bar, tennis court and general store. This is a great place to meet and learn more about the Basotho people, in beautiful surroundings.

☎ 082-5524215 (will return call) 🖐 M140 (camping), M280 (huts), M500 (rondavels)

SEMONKONG LODGE

www.placeofsmoke.co.ls

The Semonkong Lodge makes an excellent base for exploring the Lesotho countryside. There's a mix of rooms in attractive Basotho-style thatched huts, with private bathrooms. There is a restaurant and bar, as well as a communal kitchen and fire pits for cooking.

☎ 266-27006037 🖐 M70 (camping), M110 (dorm bed), M560 (hut) 🛏 12

🚌 Turn right at the end of the main road in Semonkong, past the soccer pitch, then right at the bar with a satellite dish on the roof

SWAZILAND

BHUNYA
FORESTER'S ARMS

www.forestersarms.co.za

Forester's Arms is surrounded by forests dotted with waterfalls and the hotel can organize activities in the region. Bedrooms are bright, with yellow walls, blue carpets and pale pine furniture. All guest rooms have private bathrooms and TVs, and some open out onto the garden. There is a good restaurant offering set menus, with an attractive outdoor terrace where lunch is served. The Sunday buffet is popular.

Above Beehive huts, Mlilwane

The pub has a blazing log fire, and there are occasional Swazi dancing performances in the evenings.

☎ 268-4674377 🖐 E1,040, including breakfast and dinner 🛏 30 🍴 🚌 12km (7.5 miles) north of Bhunya; on the MR19 between Bhunya and Mbabane

MLILWANE WILDLIFE SANCTUARY
MAIN CAMP

www.biggameparks.org

The Mlilwane Wildlife Sanctuary is a delightful place to stay. There is a range of accommodation to suit all budgets, from the backpacker lodge to the top-end guest lodge, but the most enjoyable is the original main camp, which has a mix of traditional Swazi beehive grass huts and wood-and-thatch huts (both with private bathrooms). The camp is unfenced, so don't be surprised to see impala, warthog and ostriches wandering around the place—beware of hippos at night. There is a communal seating area around a large log fire in the centre of the camp, a bar with a deck overlooking a hippo pool, and an open-sided restaurant, which also has views of the hippos.

☎ 268-5283944/3 🖐 R620 🛏 16

PRACTICALITIES

Practicalities gives you all the important practical information you will need during your visit, from money matters to emergency phone numbers.

SOUTH AFRICA

PRACTICALITIES

Above *On the beach at Muizenburg*

WEATHER

CLIMATE AND WHEN TO GO

» South Africa has a great variety of climates, ranging from the harsh dryness of the Kalahari desert to the lush tropical heat of KwaZulu-Natal.

» **Winter** is from June to the end of September. It is often sunny and mild during the day, although temperatures can drop below freezing at night in the Cape and the Karoo, and snow falls on higher mountain peaks.

» **Summer** is from November to the end of March. It tends to be hot and often humid, depending on where you are in the country. Temperatures can reach upwards of 30°C (86°F), although the Western and Eastern Capes are rarely hotter than 30°C. Gauteng and KwaZulu-Natal become very humid.

» Expect rainfall along the Garden Route all year round. As a general rule it becomes progressively wetter the farther east you travel. Most of the rain falls in summer, although the Cape can remain dry for most of the summer. In the interior, the summers are hot and dusty, with intermittent heavy rainfall; winters are cool with sunny days.

» Northern Cape summers have temperatures in the region of 45°C (113°F)—too hot, and unsafe, for hiking. Winter is the best time to visit the northern desert areas around Upington and the Kalahari, although temperatures at night can drop below freezing.

» The best time of year for game viewing is June to September, when vegetation is low and a lack of water forces animals to congregate around waterholes. Winter is also the best time for hiking, avoiding the high temperatures and frequent thunderstorms of summer.

WEATHER REPORTS

» The best sources of weather information are the international

SOUTH AFRICAN EMBASSIES AND CONSULATES ABROAD		
COUNTRY	**ADDRESS AND TELEPHONE NUMBERS**	**WEBSITE**
Australia	Corner Rhodes Place and State Circle, Canberra, tel 02-6272 7300	www.sahc.org.au
Canada	15 Sussex Drive, Ottawa K1M 1M8, tel 613-7440330	www.southafrica-canada.ca
Republic of Ireland	Alexandra House, Earlsfort Centre, Earlsfort Terrace, Dublin 2, tel 1-6615553	
UK	South Africa House, Trafalgar Square, London, WC2N 5DP, tel 020-7451 7299	
US	3051 Massachusetts Avenue NW, Washington, DC 20008, tel 202/232 4400	www.saembassy.org
	(Also consulates in Los Angeles and New York)	

news websites, such as www.bbc.co.uk or www.cnn.com.
» Alternatively, visit one of the specialist websites such as www.weather.com, or the South African Weather Service website at www.weathersa.co.za.

WILDLIFE
» The export of wildlife souvenirs from rare and endangered species may either be illegal or require a special permit. Before you make any purchase, check customs regulations in South Africa and your home country.

DOCUMENTS
PASSPORTS AND VISAS
» All visitors must carry a valid passport. All passports must have two clean facing pages, otherwise you'll be denied entry. Passports must be valid for six months after your date of arrival.
» EU nationals and citizens from the US, Canada, Australia and New Zealand do not need visas to enter South Africa, but it's best to confirm the situation before you travel.
» On arrival, you will be granted a temporary visitor's permit, lasting up to 90 days.

CAPE TOWN
TEMPERATURE

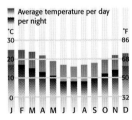

RAINFALL

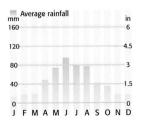

» You must have a valid return (round-trip) ticket to get a permit.
» It is possible to apply for an extension to the permit at one of the Home Affairs offices in the major cities (see below). This can take up to three weeks and costs around R400. Going to Lesotho or Swaziland and returning to South Africa is not a way to extend your holiday visa: when you re-enter, South African immigration will scan your original South African entry stamp, on which the given date of departure is still valid.
» Home Affairs offices include:
Cape Town: tel 021-4691635
Durban: tel 031-7539500

PRETORIA
TEMPERATURE

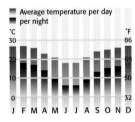

RAINFALL

TIME ZONES
South Africa is 2 hours ahead of Greenwich Mean Time (GMT). There is no daylight saving time. Compared to noon in Johannesburg, the time differences in other major cities are as follows:

CITY	TIME DIFFERENCE	NOON IN JO'BURG
Amsterdam	-1	11am
Auckland	+11	11pm
Berlin	-1	11am
Brussels	-1	11am
Chicago	-8	4am
Dublin	-2	10am
London	-2	10am
Madrid	-1	11am
New York	-7	5am
Paris	-1	11am
Perth	+6	6pm
Rome	-1	11am
San Francisco	-10	2am
Sydney	+9	9pm
Tokyo	+7	7pm

Johannesburg: tel 011-2429001
Port Elizabeth: tel 043-6422178
Pretoria: tel 012-8106421
» For more information visit the Department of Home Affairs at www.dha.gov.za.

TRAVEL INSURANCE
» It is vital to take out full travel insurance before departure, including cover for medical evacuation by air ambulance to your own country. At the very least, make sure you have medical insurance and cover for personal possessions.
» Check that your policy covers all activities that you may do, such as trekking or diving.
» Report stolen goods to the police to obtain a signed, dated and stamped statement for your insurer.

PLAN AHEAD
» Before you set off, have a dental inspection and get some spare glasses (also make sure you have the prescription).
» If you have a longstanding medical condition, arrange a check-up with your doctor.
» For more health information, see pages 290–291.

MONEY

BEFORE YOU GO

» How you carry your money largely comes down to personal preference — traveller's cheques and US dollars, euros and sterling cash are easily exchangeable. Credit cards are accepted almost everywhere and ATMs are prolific even in the smallest towns. Check what fee your bank will charge for using your credit card in South African ATMs.

LOCAL CURRENCY

» The South African currency is the Rand (R), which is divided into 100 cents (c). Notes available are: R10, R20, R50, R100 and R200. Coins available are: 5c, 10c, 20c, 50c, R1, R2 and R5. The R1 and R2 coins are a silver colour. The R5 coins are either plain silver or silver with a yellow band around them.
» Visitors are restricted to bringing in or taking out R5,000 cash in person.

NEARBY COUNTRIES

» The currency of Lesotho is the Maloti (M) and in Swaziland it is the Emalangeni (E). They are dependent on the rand and the exchange rate is identical. The currencies are interchangeable within each country, but this is not the case in South Africa. You will need to change your Maloti or Emalangeni into rand.
» Most currencies can be purchased only from within South Africa and not before you leave home. However, rand can easily be exchanged in neighbouring countries on arrival.
» Rand is also used interchangeably alongside the local currency in Namibia and is accepted as an alternative to the local currency in southern Mozambique.

BANKS AND BUREAUX DE CHANGE

» Normal banking hours are Monday to Friday 9–3.30; Saturday 9–10.30 or 11.
» All main banks provide foreign exchange services for a fee.
» You can also change money at branches of Rennies Travel (www.renniestravel.co.za), which acts as an agent for Thomas Cook. You will find branches in all regional and visitor hubs and in nearly all of the country's shopping malls.

» American Express Foreign Exchange Service has offices in the larger cities and offers a *poste restante* service to card holders. Visit their website at www.americanexpressforex.co.za for branch locations..
» Larger hotels will generally change money for you but often charge high fees.

EXCHANGE RATES

» The exchange rate is subject to daily fluctuation. At press time, exchange rates were approximately:
$1 = R7
€ = R9
£1 = R11
For up-to-the-minute exchange rates, go to www.xe.com.

ATMS

» Using an ATM (Automatic Teller Machine) is the most convenient and cheapest way of obtaining funds.
» ATMs are widely available and use the Plus and/or the Cirrus systems. Visa, MasterCard, American Express and Diners Club are also accepted.
» The amount you can withdraw varies between systems and cards,

CREDIT CARDS

Visa
www.visa.com

American Express
www.americanexpress.com

MasterCard
www.mastercard.com

Diners Club
www.dinersclubinternational.com

PRICES OF EVERYDAY ITEMS

50cl bottle of water	R7
Sandwich for eating out	R25
Cup of tea/coffee	R15
Bottle of beer	R18
Glass of wine	R20–R25
Daily newspaper	R7–R10
20 cigarettes	R20
Ice cream	R12
Litre of petrol	R9.5

TIPPING

Restaurants	10–15 per cent (service is included)
Bar service	loose change
Tour guides	optional, but can be up to 10 per cent of total cost of tour
Hairdressers	5–10 per cent
Taxis	5–10 per cent
Chambermaids	R10 per day
Porters	R3–R5
Petrol (gas) station attendants	R2–R5

but you should be able to take out up to R2,000 per day.

» Be aware of the risks of theft during or immediately after a withdrawal. Never accept a stranger's help with an ATM. Take note of your surroundings and use ATMs in banks or shopping malls, where guards are often on duty.

CREDIT CARDS

» Credit cards are a convenient way of covering major expenses, and also offer competitive exchange rates when withdrawing cash from ATMs (though this usually incurs a fee).

» Cards are particularly useful when renting a car: Many companies will rent out a car to foreign visitors only if they have a credit card.

» Credit cards are not accepted as payment for fuel, though many petrol (gas) stations, particularly in urban areas, have ATMs.

TRAVELLER'S CHEQUES

» These can be exchanged at banks in most main towns.

Opposite *Bank in Koffiefontein*

» There is an efficient system of replacement if cheques are lost or stolen.

» Make sure you keep a full record of the numbers and value of your cheques, and always keep the receipts separate from the cheques.

» The disadvantages of traveller's cheques are the time it takes to cash them, and the commission charged by banks, which can be high.

» The most widely recognized traveller's cheques are American Express, Thomas Cook and Visa.

» Traveller's cheques in US dollars, British sterling and euros can be exchanged at banks anywhere.

» American Express issues South African rand traveller's cheques, which are sometimes accepted as payment in shops and hotels in the main cities.

VAT REFUNDS

» Value Added Tax (VAT) of 14 per cent is levied on goods and services, but foreign visitors can get a refund on goods costing more than R250. You can do this at the airport before checking in when departing, or at the Victoria & Alfred Waterfront in Cape Town.

» To claim a VAT refund on goods, present a full receipt, a non-South African passport and the items that you have purchased.

» The procedure is simple at the airport but allow plenty of time, especially if your flight is at night.

» At border crossings such as Beitbridge (Zimbabwe) or Ramotswa (Botswana) the procedure is painfully slow, as there are few customs officials to check goods. Expect a lengthy wait. Visit www.taxrefunds.co.za for more information.

TIPPING

» Tipping is common but not compulsory. If you don't feel you've had good service, you don't have to leave anything, though as a visitor you are likely to be able to spare the tip. See the Tipping box above for a guide to amounts to leave.

Below *ATMs are widespread*

HEALTH

HEALTH SERVICES

» South Africa has a well-developed health service, but it suffers from being overused and underfunded.

» In the cities, hospitals tend to be fairly well maintained. However, you may prefer to follow the example of wealthy South Africans and opt for private medi-clinics, which are numerous in the cities and where standards rival those of Europe and the US.

BEFORE YOU GO

» See your doctor or travel clinic at least six weeks before your departure in case you need any anti-malaria tablets or vaccinations. Your doctor can also give advice on travel risks.

» Make sure you have full travel insurance (▷ 287).

» Have a dental check, especially if you are going to be away for more than a month.

» Obtain a spare set of glasses, and take a prescription with you in case you break your glasses.

» Make sure you know your blood group.

» If you suffer from a long-term condition, make sure that you have a Medic Alert bracelet/necklace with this information on it. See your doctor for a check-up before you leave.

HEALTH HAZARDS

» The most common hazards facing visitors are diarrhoea, sunstroke and sunburn.

» The main parasitic disease is malaria, and the key viral disease is dengue fever; both are transmitted by mosquitoes (malaria is transmitted at night and dengue fever in the day, so insect repellent should be worn at all times).

» The symptoms of dengue fever are fever and often intense joint pain, and some people develop a rash. It can take weeks to recover fully; rest, plenty of fluids and paracetamol (not aspirin) is the recommended treatment. Malaria often starts off feeling like an attack of flu so it is advisable to treat even vague symptoms seriously.

» Bacterial diseases include tuberculosis (TB).

» Bilharzia is an unpleasant water-borne parasite found in some areas: Don't swim or paddle in natural water without checking that the water is not infected. There's also a risk that hippos and crocodiles may be lurking in the water.

» Rabies is a risk in rural areas; dogs and monkeys are particularly common carriers.

» HIV/AIDS is a huge problem in South Africa, but remember that you're likely to be infected only through unprotected sex or intravenous drug use.

» Check with a doctor if you are bitten by a snake, spider or scorpion or an animal that might be carrying rabies, or if you stand on any creature in the ocean.

» Treat even minor grazes with caution, as there are parasites and poisonous plants to which you will have no immunity.

WHAT TO TAKE

Anti-malarials

» Most of South Africa is malaria-free, but if you visit some areas (see below), you must take anti-malaria pills as a precaution.

» Malaria occurs in northern and eastern Mpumalanga, eastern Limpopo province, northern KwaZulu-Natal and Swaziland, particularly in the Lowveld region in and around the Kruger National Park.

» You should consult your doctor six weeks before departure for full advice.

» The start times for anti-malarials vary. If you have never taken Lariam (Mefloquine) before, it is advised to start it at least two to three weeks before entering the malarial zone. Doxycycline and Malarone should be started only one to two days before entry to a malarial area.

» You should always check with your doctor, but general guidelines are that all except Malarone should be continued for four weeks after leaving the malarial area.

» Malarone needs to be continued for only seven days afterwards (but if a tablet is missed or vomited you should seek specialist advice).

Diarrhoea treatments

» Ciproxin (Ciprofloxacin) is a useful antibiotic for some forms of diarrhoea. Over-the-counter treatments are a great standby for awkward times (such as before a long bus/train journey or on a trek), although it is not a cure for any underlying causes.

Mosquito repellents

» DEET (Diethyltoluamide) is about the best you can buy. Apply the repellent every four to six hours, but more often if you are sweating heavily. If you want to use natural repellents like citronella remember that it must be applied very frequently (ideally hourly) to be effective.

WATER AND FOOD SAFETY

» Tap water is safe to drink, but check before drinking in bush camps.

» During treks, avoid drinking from streams; the best rule to follow is to boil water for 10 minutes before drinking it. Do not drink from rivers or lakes.

» Food safety is not usually a problem in South Africa, although it's always a good idea to stick to restaurants and food stands that are busy.

SUMMER HAZARDS

» Do not underestimate the strength of the African sun.

» Wear loose-fitting, lightweight clothing, cover your head with a wide-brimmed hat and wear a good pair of sunglasses.

» The absolute minimum sun screen protection factor you should use is 15, but higher factors are recommended.

» Stay out of the sun between 11am and 3pm.

» Drink at least 2 litres (4 pints) of water per day.

CAUTION BILHARZIA INFECTED RIVER

GUIDE TO VACCINATIONS

All vaccinations should be organized six weeks before departure	
BCG (anti-TB)	Required, if staying for more than 1 month
Hepatitis A	Required; the disease can be caught easily from food/water
Polio	Required, if last vaccination was at least 10 years ago
Rabies	Advisable for rural areas
Tetanus	Required, if last vaccination was at least 10 years ago (but after 5 doses you've had enough for life)
Typhoid	Required, if last vaccination was at least 3 years ago
Yellow fever	South Africa is not regarded as a risk area for this disease but other African countries, to the north, are. Visitors who have travelled through yellow fever zones are required to show their yellow fever vaccination card on arrival. If you don't have one, you will be given the jab at the airport before being permitted entry.

CASUALTY DEPARTMENTS

Netcare private hospitals	tel 082-911 for emergencies; www.netcare.co.za
Medi-Clinic private hospitals	tel 021-8096500; www.mediclinic.co.za
MAJOR STATE HOSPITALS	
Cape Town	Groote Schuur, Main Road, Observatory, tel 021-4049111
Johannesburg	Johannesburg General Hospital, Jubilee Road, Parktown, tel 011-4884911
Pretoria	Academic Medical Hospital, corner of Voortrekkers Road and Malan Street, Capital Park, tel 012-3541000

EMERGENCIES

» Dial 10177 for an ambulance in the case of an emergency. Otherwise, drive to the casualty department (ER) of the nearest hospital. Note that you will have to pay for medical treatment (and claim the cost back later from your insurer).

FINDING A HOSPITAL, DOCTOR OR DENTIST

» The best source for finding these is the Yellow Pages, listed under 'Medical Practitioners'.
» Local pharmacies have a list of doctors and dentists. It's also worth asking at your hotel.
» There are two leading private hospital companies in South Africa. The largest is Netcare (tel 011-3010000 or 082-911 for emergencies; www.netcare.co.za). The other company is Medi-Clinic (tel 021-8096500; www.mediclinic.co.za).
» www.travelclinic.co.za lists travel clinics around the country.

PHARMACIES

» Pharmacies can be found in all towns and cities in South Africa, usually providing excellent over-the-counter advice.
» The drugs that they stock often have different brand names from those you may be used to. Make sure you know the chemical name of the drug you require.
» Some drugs that require a prescription in Europe or the US can be bought without one in South Africa.
» Towns and cities always have at least one pharmacy open for 24 hours. Check with local tourist offices.

HEALTHY FLYING

» Visitors to South Africa from as far as the UK or US may be concerned about the effect of long-haul flights on their health. The most widely publicized concern is deep vein thrombosis, or DVT. Misleadingly called 'economy class syndrome', DVT is the forming of a blood clot in the body's deep veins, particularly in the legs. The clot can move around the bloodstream and could be fatal.
» Those most at risk include the elderly, pregnant women and those using the contraceptive pill, smokers and the overweight. If you are at increased risk of DVT see your doctor before departing. Flying increases the likelihood of DVT because passengers are often seated in a cramped position for long periods of time and may become dehydrated.

To minimize risk:
Drink water (not alcohol)
Don't stay immobile for hours at a time
Stretch and exercise your legs periodically
Do wear elastic flight socks, which support veins and reduce the chances of a clot forming

Exercises

1. Ankle Rotations	2. Calf Stretches	3. Knee Lifts
Lift feet off the floor. Draw a circle with the toes, moving one foot clockwise and the other counterclockwise	Start with heel on the floor and point foot upward as high as you can. Then lift heels high, keeping balls of feet on the floor	Lift leg with knee bent while contracting your thigh muscle. Then straighten leg, pressing foot flat to the floor

Other health hazards for flyers are airborne diseases and bugs spread by the plane's air-conditioning system. These are largely unavoidable but if you have a serious medical condition seek advice from a doctor before flying.

BASICS

CLOTHING

» During the day, the general attitude towards clothes is a relaxed one (▷ What to Take, below). However, in the evening, a smarter style is appreciated (such as long trousers or skirts), particularly if you are going to a club, bar or restaurant. Women may want to be more covered up in conservative rural or Muslim areas.

ELECTRICITY

» Current is 220/240 volts at 50 cycles per second.

» Plugs have three round pins. US visitors should bring a transformer. Adaptors are widely available in South Africa.

» Bring a torch (flashlight) for more rural areas.

WHAT TO TAKE

» Items such as medicines, contact lens solution, insect repellent and sunscreen are widely available from pharmacies, usually at lower prices than you'll pay at home.

» Summers are hot, so bring loose-fitting clothes, a wide-brimmed hat, sunglasses and sunscreen.

» South Africans are casual, so shorts and T-shirts are fine during the day. Men may need long trousers (pants) and a shirt, and women a skirt, for evenings.

» If you plan to go on safari, bring lightweight clothes in beiges and browns (anything bright might disturb the animals) and a good pair of binoculars.

» Footwear should be as airy as possible in the hot weather. Bring boots for longer hikes—lightweight water-repelling synthetic fabrics are best in summer, leather in winter.

» Mosquito nets are useful in wilderness areas, depending on the season.

» In winter, from June to the end of September, bring a sweater and jacket (note that most guesthouses do not have any heating).

» Bring photocopies of all important documents (passport, travel tickets, driver's licence) and keep these separate from the originals.

Above *South Africa is a family-friendly destination, with substantial discounts for children at attractions and museums*

LAUNDRY

» Towns and cities have self-service launderettes, with coin-operated washers and dryers. Most also have a service where you can drop off laundry and have it cleaned by staff.

» Almost all hotels, guesthouses, bed-and-breakfasts and hostels have laundry services.

» The larger camps in the national parks have launderettes for their guests to use; all camps have large sinks where you can hand wash items.

MEASUREMENTS

» South Africa uses the metric system.

» Distances are measured in kilometres, petrol (gas) is priced by the litre, and food is sold in grams and kilograms.

» Temperatures are given in degrees Celsius (centigrade).

PUBLIC TOILETS

» There are few public toilets in towns and cities, although all the main visitor sights, museums and galleries have them, as do department stores and shopping malls.

» The busier public beaches in the Western Cape and KwaZulu-Natal have toilets and shower facilities.

» National parks and reserves have toilets near main parking areas (maps provided on entry will mark these).

SMOKING

Most restaurants have designated non-smoking areas, although this is less common in rural areas. Smoking is prohibited in many public areas, such as shopping malls, and public transport—keep a look out for signs. Bars and nightclubs allow smoking, although the bar areas are sometimes smoke free.

GAY AND LESBIAN VISITORS

The South African constitution is one of the most progressive in the world—and Cape Town is the self proclaimed 'Gay Capital' of Africa. The city has a number of big festivals and events aimed at the gay population, such as the annual Mother City Queer Project (▷ 89). However, the picture is not the same across the entire country, and away from the cities South Africa is a conservative place, so be prepared for at least some disapproval.

» For listings of gay-friendly accommodation, restaurants, nightlife, gyms etc in Cape Town, visit www.gaycapetown.co.za.

» If you want advice on a range of issues, as well as listings, visit www.gaynetcapetown.co.za.

» Exit (www.exit.co.za) is a leading gay and lesbian online newspaper. www.q.co.za is South Africa's main gay and lesbian lifestyle website with travel and entertainment news.

VISITING WITH CHILDREN

» As an outdoors destination, South Africa is a great place for children. South African families like to holiday in their own country, generally in high season—from December to February—so you'll find plenty of family-friendly hotels, guesthouses and restaurants. Family rooms, with four to six beds, are common.

» Most sights, museums, galleries, aquariums and theme parks have substantial discounts for children (defined as 'learners', meaning under-18s). Children's entry fees mentioned in this book apply to under-18s unless otherwise stated.

» Local tourist offices often have lists of attractions for children. The larger offices have booklets outlining things for families to do.

» Babylite (www.babylite.co.za) rents out baby equipment such as strollers, car seats, travel cots and baby monitors to visitors, and there are now branches in the major cities; delivery/collection can be arranged at the airports.

VISITORS WITH A DISABILITY

» Although the situation regarding people with disabilities was for many years neglected, things have markedly improved in recent years.

» Large hotels in the main cities usually have wheelchair access and rooms adapted for guests with disabilities. The better-known museums, galleries and sights are also often wheelchair-friendly, although the farther you are from the cities, the less likely you are to find disabled access.

» National parks are improving their facilities for guests with disabilities, with more accessible accommodation, and the introduction of amenities such as Braille or wheelchair trails.

» Transport is variable. The national train system has trains with wide doors and aisles, and ramps are available. Domestic flights can usually accommodate wheelchair users, although the airline needs prior warning. The larger car rental firms rent out automatic cars with hand controls. Most major sights and shopping malls have disabled parking right by the entrance. See page 58 for more information on getting around with a disability.

CONVERSION CHART		
From	To	Multiply by
Inches	Centimetres	2.54
Centimetres	Inches	0.3937
Feet	Metres	0.3048
Metres	Feet	3.2810
Yards	Metres	0.9144
Metres	Yards	1.0940
Miles	Kilometres	1.6090
Kilometres	Miles	0.6214
Acres	Hectares	0.4047
Hectares	Acres	2.4710
Gallons	Litres	4.5460
Litres	Gallons	0.2200
Ounces	Grams	28.35
Grams	Ounces	0.0353
Pounds	Grams	453.6
Grams	Pounds	0.0022
Pounds	Kilograms	0.4536
Kilograms	Pounds	2.205
Tons	Tonnes	1.0160
Tonnes	Tons	0.9842

» Proudly Accessible (www.disabledtravel.co.za) is a useful website that lists wheelchair-friendly accommodation and tour operators specializing in tours in South Africa for travellers with a disability.

» The National Council for Persons with Physical Disabilities in South Africa (tel 011-7268040; www.ncppdsa.org.za) has advice on renting wheelchairs and other services for people with disabilities.

» Disabled People South Africa, (tel 021-4220357; www.dpsa.org.za), a national body representing people with disabilities, can provide contact details for finding out about transport and accessibility.

PLACES OF WORSHIP

» The majority of South Africa's population is Christian, but this congregation is by no means homogeneous. There are three main Christian denominations: indigenous African churches; Dutch Reformed Church; and Church of England.

» There are also significant Muslim and Hindu populations, and a small Jewish community.

» Local tourist offices will provide you with details of local places of worship and service times.

FINDING HELP/SAFETY

There are many stories and rumours about the crime rate in South Africa, but while some areas certainly have a high incidence of violent crime, visitors are rarely affected. As for visits to any country, safety is mostly an issue of common sense. If you take sensible precautions, it is highly unlikely that you'll become a victim.

PERSONAL SECURITY

» Never carry more cash than you need, and place valuables in your hotel safe.
» Avoid looking like a tourist, so do not sling your camera around your neck.
» Expensive jewellery should be left at home and keep all valuables out of sight.
» Carry a bag that can be hung diagonally across the body (rather than a shoulder bag or rucksack).
» Keep belongings close to you in public areas. If you're sitting in a crowded restaurant or bar, it's good practice to loop a strap of your bag around your leg, or use bag clips when available.
» Follow local advice on where it is safe to walk. In general, walk around towns and cities in daylight only; take a taxi at night. Some areas

Below *Police officer taking a break on his motorbike in Mbabane*

should be avoided altogether (such as Hillbrow in Johannesburg).
» Even in a safe area like the Victoria & Alfred Waterfront in Cape Town, it is still advisable to stick to well-lit, busy areas at night.
» You should not visit townships without a guide or on an organized tour.
» Avoid beaches at night.
» Plan your route before you leave your hotel—standing at a street corner peering at a map will only attract attention.
» If you feel unsafe or threatened in any situation, don't hang around: Make as swift an exit as possible.
» Be cautious of anyone invading your personal space, and watch for ploys to distract your attention, particularly at ATMs.
» Take your mobile (cell) phone with you, or rent one at the airport. It can be useful in an emergency, but keep it out of sight.
» Don't give spare change, sweets (candy) or pens to begging children. Instead, consider making a donation to a local charity.
» Beware of tricksters, such as people in the street with clipboards asking for sponsorship for their studies.
» If you are unfortunate enough to be a victim of a mugging or bag snatching, do not resist. There is a high incidence of gun crime in

South Africa and assailants may use weapons if they feel threatened.
» See page 57 for car and driving safety advice.

FEMALE VISITORS

If you observe the advice on personal security, then there is no reason for you to be at greater risk than male visitors. However, make sure you don't travel alone at night and never hitchhike. You might also want to consider dressing more conservatively in quieter, rural areas. This will help protect you against any unwanted attention.

LOST PROPERTY
If you lose your passport

» Always keep a separate note of your passport number and a photocopy of the page that carries your photo, and visitor's permit. Keep the copy separate from your passport, and leave another copy with someone reliable at home. Alternatively, scan the relevant pages and email them to yourself at a web-based email address you can access anywhere (such as www.hotmail.com or www.yahoo.com).
» Report the loss or theft of a passport as soon as possible to the police, and then contact your embassy or consulate (see box on page 295 for contact details).
» The Tourist Assistance Unit of the South African police will help you with processing reports as quickly as possible, but cutting through bureaucratic red tape may still take some time.
» For more information call the Tourism Information and Safety Call Line (tel 083-1232345).

If you lose money or other valuables

» Inform your travel insurance company as soon as possible.
» In the case of theft, inform the police and make sure you get a copy of your written, signed, dated and stamped statement for your insurance claim.
» If you have lost your traveller's cheques, or they've been stolen,

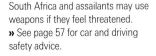

notify the issuing company. Always keep a record of the numbers and denominations of your cheques, and keep receipts separate from cheques (if receipts are also lost, the issuing company may not replace the cheques).

» Given the amount of time it takes to process a complaint, it is usually not worth the trouble for inexpensive items.

POLICE

» In an emergency, you should call 10111. If necessary, a flying squad car can be deployed to assist you.

» To report a minor crime or theft, visit the local police station (for their address, look in the Yellow Pages or ask at the local tourist office or at your hotel).

» All towns have local police stations, and cities have several.

» The South African government has given high priority to protecting visitors: Recent initiatives include the deployment of tourist police in some large towns.

» There is a nationwide Tourist Assistance Unit to help visitors process reports and complaints more swiftly.

» If you are arrested, remain calm and contact your embassy or consular service as soon as you can.

GAME VIEWING

It is not just in urban areas that you need to be aware of your surroundings. Game viewing here has become an increasingly independent activity and you have the opportunity to drive on an extensive network of roads—and there are times when you will find yourself on your own. There are also rules and regulations to protect the wildlife and the landscape.

» It is strictly forbidden to feed the animals.

» Never get out of your car unless it is a designated area. You will be liable to be prosecuted—and you may well be seriously injured or even killed.

» Don't leave your car in search of help if it breaks down while in a

Above Make sure that you heed all warnings posted in game parks—they are for your own protection

game park or reserve. Stay inside the car until a park ranger comes to help you.

» Pass a message to other visitors in their own vehicles for them to relay to the park authorities.

» If night falls, remember that there will be a record of your car entering the park, but not leaving. This will alert the park rangers and they will organize a search party.

» Keep your litter inside the car and dispose of it when you reach a camp.

» There are speed limits around the parks, which need to be adhered to. If you don't, you could be fined, and you are also likely to miss the wildlife.

» If you decide to go bush walking, make sure you let someone know where you are going and at what time you plan to return.

» Shake your sleeping bag out before settling down for the night and hang shoes upside down.

» Make sure you have enough supplies for the day, and in particular enough water, whether you are driving or hiking.

» For more information contact South African National Parks (www.sanparks.org) or KZN Wildlife (www.kznwildlife.com). Between them they run the majority of parks you are likely to visit.

EMERGENCY NUMBERS	
Police and Fire	10111
Ambulance	10177
From mobile phone	112

EMBASSIES/CONSULATES	
Australian Embassy	292 Orient Street, Arcadia, Pretoria 0083, tel 012-4236000
Canada	1103 Arcadia Street, Pretoria 0083, tel 012-4223000
Irish Embassy	1st Floor, Southern Life Plaza, 1059 Schoeman Street, Arcadia, Pretoria 0083, tel 012-3425062
New Zealand Embassy	125 Middle Street, New Muckleneuk, Pretoria 0083, tel 012-4359000
UK Embassy	255 Hill Street, Arcadia, Pretoria 0083, tel 012-4217500
US Embassy	877 Pretorius Street, Arcadia, Pretoria 0083, tel 012-4314000

OPENING TIMES AND TICKETS

BANKS

Banks are usually open Mon–Fri 9–3.30, Sat 8.30–11. At the airport banks are open to meet all flights.

BARS

Bars open mid-morning and close around 11pm, but much later in the big cities.

CAFÉS

Most cafés open at around 7am and close in the late afternoon (5–6). Cities and main towns always have a few 24-hour cafés.

DOCTORS AND PHARMACIES

These function under normal business hours (usually 8.30–5 or 6), but most towns have 24-hour doctors and pharmacies providing a service in rotation. Ask at the local tourist office.

GOVERNMENT OFFICES

These are open only on weekdays and usually close for lunch (8.30–1, 2–4.30).

MUSEUMS AND GALLERIES

Opening times vary around the country. In the cities, most are open from around 9 or 10 until 5. Some museums close on Sundays or Mondays. Rural museums often close for lunch. See individual entries in The Sights section for details.

OFFICES

Businesses are usually open Mon–Fri 8.30–5, Sat 8.30–2.

PLACES OF WORSHIP

Many places of worship are kept locked and can be visited only during services. Times are usually posted at entrances, or check with the local tourist office.

POST OFFICES

Post offices in towns and cities are open Mon–Fri 8.30–5, Sat 8–12. These times are shorter in more rural areas.

RESTAURANTS

Lunch is usually served between 12 and 3. Many kitchens close until 6, then stay open until 10 or 11. Some, like those in hotels, also open for breakfast from about 7.30 to 9.30.

SHOPS

Opening times vary widely depending on where the shop is. As a general guide, shops are open Mon–Fri 8–6, Sat 8 or 9–2 or 3, Sun 9–1. Malls in cities are often open until 9pm, but note that even in Jo'burg or Cape Town, shops usually close on Saturday afternoons. Larger supermarkets usually stay open until around 8pm. In rural areas, shops are closed on Sundays.

DISCOUNTS AND CONCESSIONS

» Children under the age of 18 can sometimes get discounts of up to 50 per cent on entry to museums, galleries and other attractions.
» Children under 5 often get in free.
» Seniors receive discounts on most admission charges, but may need to present ID.
» International Student Identity Card (ISIC) carriers will receive discounts on admission to some museums and attractions. The cards are issued by student travel agencies across the world, and give special rates on some forms of transportation, including the (Baz Bus ▷ 52),and mainline coach companies, as well as other discounts and services.
» Youth Hostel Association (YHA) card carriers are eligible for discounts. The cards themselves can be bought from some South African backpackers' hostels for considerably less than in other countries. Card holders get 10 per cent off at YHA affiliated backpackers' hostels and 5 per cent off Baz Bus tickets (▷ 52).
» Resident South Africans sometimes qualify for a discount on entry to national parks, but need to prove their identity.

NATIONAL HOLIDAYS	
1 Jan	New Year's Day
21 Mar	Human Rights Day
Friday before Easter Sunday	Good Friday
Monday after Easter Sunday	Family Day
27 Apr	Freedom Day
1 May	Workers' Day
16 Jun	Youth Day
9 Aug	National Women's Day
24 Sep	Heritage Day
16 Dec	Day of Reconciliation
25 Dec	Christmas Day
26 Dec	Day of Goodwill

TOURIST OFFICES

South Africa has an excellent infrastructure of tourist offices, and even the smallest town has some sort of visitor information bureau. The cities have particularly good services: Expect a wealth of free information and advice on what to do, special events, where to eat and stay, what's available for families, access to sights for people with disabilities and nightlife. Some also offer internet access and have gift shops.

If you're touring the country, it's a good idea to visit the main tourist office whenever you arrive in a city or the main town of a region, to pick up vital information on activities, and to stock up on maps.

Most offices have regional information, and leaflets about national parks and game reserves. You can usually expect to find an accommodation reservation service (either by phone or in person; some offices have online reservations as well), for which you pay a small fee (this is usually in the form of slightly higher room rates). In addition to the tourist offices, you will find a great deal of visitor information available on the internet.

TOURIST OFFICES

City Tourist Offices

Bloemfontein Tourist Centre, 60 Park Road, Bloemfontein 9301, tel 051-4124000, www.bloemfontein.co.za

Cape Town Tourism, The Pinnacle, corner of Burg and Castle streets, tel 021-4054500, www.tourismcapetown.co.za

Ceres Tourism, in the town library on Owen Street, Ceres 6835, tel 023-3161287, www.ceres.org.za

Citrusdal Tourist Office, 39 Voortrekker Street, Citrusdal 7340, tel 022-9213210, www.citrusdal.info

Durban Tourist Junction, Station Building, 160 Pine Street, Durban 4001, tel 031-3667500, www.durban.kzn.org.za

Graskop, Tourist Information, Louis Trichardt Street, Graskop 1270, tel 013-7671886, www.graskop.co.za

Greater Hermanus Tourism Bureau, Old Station Building, Mitchell Street, Hermanus 7200, tel 028-3122629, www.hermanus.co.za

Jeffreys Bay Tourism, Shell Museum Complex, Jeffreys Bay 6330, tel 042-2932923, www.jeffreysbaytourism.org

Johannesburg Tourism Company, 195 Jan Smuts Avenue, Johannesburg 2001, tel 011-2140700, www.joburgtourism.com

Kimberley, Diamond Fields Tourist Information Centre, corner of Bultfontein and Lyndhurst streets, Kimberley 8300, tel 053-8327298, www.kimberley.co.za

Knysna Tourism, 40 Main Street, Knysna 6571, tel 044-3825510, www.visitknysna.co.za

Makana (Grahamstown) Tourism, 63 High Street, Grahamstown 6139, tel 046-6223241, www.grahamstown.co.za

Mbombela (Nelspruit), Explore Mpumalanga, Hall's Gateway, N4, Mbombela, tel 013-7595300, www.mpumalanga.com

Oudtshoorn Tourist Bureau, Baron van Reede Street, Oudtshoorn 6625, tel 044-2792532, www.oudtshoorn.com

Pietermaritzburg Tourism, Publicity House, 177 Chief Albert Luthuli (Commercial) Road, Pietermaritzburg 3201, tel 033-3451348, www.pmbtourism.co.za

Pilgrim's Rest Tourist Information Centre, Main Street, Upper Town, tel 013-7681060, www.pilgrims-rest.co.za

Plettenberg Bay Tourism, Melville's Corner Mall, Main Street, Plettenberg Bay 6600, tel 044-5334065, www.plettenbergbay.co.za

Port Elizabeth, Nelson Mandela Bay Tourism, Donkin Lighthouse Bldg, Belmont Terrace, Port Elizabeth 6001, tel 041-5822575, www.nmbt.co.za

Pretoria (Tshwane) Tourism Information Bureau, Old Netherlands Bank Building, Church Square, City Centre 0002, tel 012-3581430, www.tshwanetourism.co.za

Springbok, Namakwa Tourism Information, Voortrekker Street, Springbok 8240, tel 027-7128035, www.namakwa-dm.gov.za

Stellenbosch Tourist Office, 36 Market St, tel 021-8833584, www.stellenboschtourism.co.za

Upington Tourist Office, in the Kalahari Oranje Museum, Schröder Street, Upington 8801, tel 054-3326064, www.upington.com

Regional Tourist Offices

Eastern Cape Tourism, tel 043-7019600, www.ectourism.co.za

Gauteng Tourism Authority, tel 011-6391600, www.gauteng.net

Lesotho Tourist Board Office, central Kingsway, Maseru, tel 22312238, www.ltdc.org.ls

Limpopo Province Tourism Board, tel 015-2933600, www.golimpopo.com

Mpumalanga Tourism Authority, tel 013-7595300, www.mpumalanga.com

Northern Cape Tourism Authority, tel 053-8322657, www.northerncape.org.za

North West Province, tel 018-3971500, www.tourismnorthwest.co.za

Swaziland Information Office, Swazi Plaza, Mbabane, tel 404-9693, www.welcometoswaziland.com

Tourism KwaZulu-Natal, tel 031-3667500, www.kzn.org.za

Western Cape Tourism, tel 021-4054500, www.tourismcapetown.co.za

USEFUL WEBSITES

BACKPACKERS

www.hihostels.com
Advice and information from Hostelling International.

www.coastingafrica.com
Useful hostel reviews from Coast to Coast, which publishes a free annual backpackers' guide to hostels across the country.

www.btsa.co.za
Hostel information from BTSA (Backpacking Tourism South Africa).

DOCUMENTATION

www.fco.gov.uk
Comprehensive travel advice from the UK Foreign and Commonwealth office.

www.travel.state.gov
US Department of State travel advice.

DRIVING

www.aa.co.za
The Automobile Association of South Africa, with road safety advice and emergency breakdown information.

www.nra.co.za
Road and traffic information from the South African National Road Agency (SANRAL).

HEALTH

www.cdc.gov
Website of the US government's Centers for Disease Control and Prevention, with excellent advice on travel health.

www.dh.gov.uk
Useful UK department of health website with advice on vaccinations.

www.tmb.ie
Irish-based website with a good collection of tropical travel health information.

www.who.int
Website of the World Health Organization, with lists of diseases and vaccines.

MUSEUMS

www.museumsonline.co.za
Museums Online South Africa provides a number of links to museums around the country.

MUSIC

www.putumayo.com
Lively website with interesting articles on world music, including the music scene in South Africa.

NATIONAL PARKS AND GAME RESERVES

www.sanparks.org
Comprehensive details of all the country's national parks, including prices, news and online reservations.

www.capenature.org.za
Official data on the game reserves in the Western Cape.

www.kznwildlife.com
Outline of all the game reserves in KwaZulu-Natal.

www.exploresouthafrica.net
A general overview of the main tourist attractions.

NEWS

www.iol.co.za
Nationwide website for the main daily and weekly newspapers.

www.sabc.co.za
Daily news from the state broadcaster, SABC.

www.mg.co.za
In-depth news articles from the *Mail & Guardian,* the leading weekly paper.

RESPONSIBLE TRAVEL

www.fairtourismsa.org.za
Information on fair trade in tourism in South Africa.

www.responsibletravel.com
UK-based portal for alternative, responsible holidays.

www.tourismconcern.org.uk
Details of this UK charity's work in promoting community tourism — tourism that benefits local people and businesses.

TOURIST INFORMATION

www.southafrica.net
Comprehensive country information from SATOUR, the national tourism board.

www.overberginfo.com
Wide-ranging information on the Overberg region of the Western Cape.

www.gardenroute.co.za
Useful travel tips covering one of the most popular regions in South Africa.

www.go2africa.com
Full accommodation and holiday reservation service for Southern Africa, with useful practical information and links to overland companies.

For websites of city and regional tourist offices, see page 297.

WINE ROUTES

www.wine.co.za
Details of all the wine routes available in South Africa, plus articles on South African wines.

COMMUNICATION

South Africa has a good telephone system, an easy-to-use (if slow) mail service, and a large number of internet cafés, all making it easy for you to stay in touch with home during your visit.

TELEPHONES

The telephone service is very efficient, although numbers tend to change every couple of years.

» When telephoning within South Africa, you need to dial the full area code for every number, even if you are calling from within that area.

» When dialling a number in South Africa from abroad, drop the first 0 in the area code.

» Card and coin phones are widespread and work well; even in remote national parks there are usually card phones from which you can direct dial to anywhere in the world.

» Blue public phone booths are coin-operated, but these are becoming rare as green card phones take over.

» Phonecards are sold for R10, R20, R50 and R100. They are available from larger supermarkets, newspaper stores, some pharmacies and Telkom

USEFUL NUMBERS	
International operator	10903
International enquiries	10900
Directory enquiries	1023
Police	10111
Ambulance	10177
Emergency number from mobile phone	112

vending machines. A R50 card is sufficient to make an international call to Europe or the US for at least 10 minutes.

» Hotels often double the normal rates, and even a short international call can become very expensive.

» There are a number of private companies that offer fax and mail services, but these tend to charge about double the usual rate for making calls.

» In Lesotho, the local telephone system is reasonable in the lowlands but there is poor or no coverage in the mountain areas.

MOBILE PHONES (CELL PHONES)

» South Africa uses the GSM system for mobile phones. You should be able to use your mobile, as long as

you have arranged to do so with your service provider before you left your home country.

» Mobile phone numbers in South Africa start with 072, 073, 082, 083 or 084.

» It's a good idea to replace your SIM card with a South African one on arrival. These can be rented at the international airports (▷ 44–45), as can complete phones, at a cost of about R20 per day, and R2.50 for a minute-long local call. You can also buy a pay-as-you-go SIM card for around R200 or hire one for about R10 per day.

» If you are not bringing your own mobile phone and you are driving yourself, it is essential to rent one for emergencies. Many of the car hire companies now rent out phones with their vehicles.

» Mobile phone reception is improving steadily in Lesotho and you can pick up reception in some remote places—largely owing to the number of mobile phone towers that have been put in place in outlying areas during the Lesotho Highlands Water Project.

ROADSIDE PHONES

There are telephones at regular intervals along all major roads. They are directly linked to the emergency services, so should only be used in a genuine emergency. However, it's still best to carry your own mobile phone.

Left *Card phones are green and coin-operated phones are blue*
Below *Public phone in Butha-Buthe, Lesotho*

ESSENTIAL INFORMATION

PRACTICALITIES

MAIL

The internal mail service is notoriously slow, but the international service is generally reliable if you use airmail.

» Letters to Europe and the United States should generally take no more than a week, although over the busy Christmas season it can take up to a month.

» Stamps can be bought at post offices and at stationers.

» Mailboxes are usually just outside post offices and are bright red.

» Opening times for post offices are Mon–Fri 8.30–5, Sat 8–12. A branch locator can be found at www.sapo.co.za.

» Parcels have been known to disappear en route, so it's a good idea to send valuable items as registered mail.

» Postnet (www.postnet.co.za) is a private mail company with outlets all over South Africa, providing mail services, fax, telephone service and internet access, as well as a *poste restante* service. Although their charges are slightly higher, they are generally regarded as more reliable than the national mail system.

LAPTOPS

If you intend to bring your own laptop to South Africa, remember to bring a power converter to recharge it and a plug socket adaptor. A surge protector is also a good idea. To connect to the internet you will need to bring an adaptor for the phone socket.

If you use an international internet service provider, such as AOL or Compuserve, it's cheaper to dial up a local node rather than the number you use at home. Dial-tone frequencies vary from country to country, so set your modem to ignore dial tones.

INTERNET

South Africa is well served by the internet, and most companies, tourist offices, hotels and guesthouses have email addresses and websites. There are plenty of internet cafés in all major towns and cities (usually costing around R5 for 10 minutes). Many hotels, guesthouses and backpacker hostels offer email access as a service, although rates are higher than in internet cafés. You can also check emails at Vodacom and Postnet shops, and the Post Office has started introducing internet access. In the more remote regions, you are unlikely to see internet cafés unless the town is served by a university or college.

WiFi hotspots are now found in a number of public places, including the larger airports and hotel lobbies, and some of the café/coffee shop chains.

COUNTRY CODES FROM SOUTH AFRICA	
International access code	00 +
Australia	61
Belgium	32
Canada	1
France	33
Germany	49
Greece	30
Ireland	353
Netherlands	31
New Zealand	64
Spain	34
Sweden	46
UK	44
USA	1

To call home from South Africa, dial 00, then the country's access code. To call South Africa from home, the country code is 27.

AREA CODES	
Cape Town	021
Bloemfontein	051
Durban	031
East London	043
Kimberley	053
Johannesburg	011
Mafikeng/Mmabatho	018
Pietersburg/Polokwane	015
Port Elizabeth	041
Pretoria	012

POSTAGE RATES	
Domestic stamps:	R22.40 for book of 10 stamps
Postcard sent by airmail to anywhere in the world:	R4.90
Letter (maximum weight 50g) sent by airmail to anywhere in the world:	R5.75

Left *Internet cafés, like this one in Cape Town, are a handy way to stay in touch on your travels*

MEDIA

NEWSPAPERS

The *Sunday Times* and *Sunday Independent* are weekly English-language papers. They have national coverage, although several editions are produced for different areas. The excellent weekly *Mail & Guardian* provides the most objective reporting on South African issues, and has in-depth coverage of international news.

Daily English-language newspapers include: *The Star* and *The Citizen* (Johannesburg); *The Daily News* and *The Natal Mercury* (Durban); the *Cape Argus* and *The Cape Times* (Cape Town). *The Sowetan* provides a less white-orientated view of South African news and has the best coverage of international soccer.

MAGAZINES

There are a number of South African publications that visitors will find useful. The yearly *Eat Out* magazine lists reviews of the best restaurants in the country, but it tends to concentrate on rather smart and expensive eateries. *Time Out Cape Town* is another useful annual magazine with good nightlife and culture listings. The monthly *Getaway* is aimed at the South African love of the outdoors, but has excellent travel features and ideas, as well as reviews of different accommodation and activities throughout the whole of southern Africa. *Africa Geographical* is a glossy monthly with high-quality photographs, which publishes regular articles on southern Africa's parks, reserves and wildlife.

RADIO

Radio is the most popular medium in the country, and even the most remote corners are reached by broadcasters. The South African Broadcasting Corporation (SABC) has numerous national stations catering to speakers of the country's 11 official languages. The corporation has an agreement with the UK's BBC, which means that listeners can hear BBC news and other broadcasts at certain times of day. 5FM is the SABC national pop music station, while Metro FM offers R 'n' B, hip hop and kwaito (▷ 21). There are also many local commercial and community radio stations.

TELEVISION

The SABC—the state broadcaster—has restructured its service in the last decade to accommodate all official languages. Most of its output is in English, followed by Afrikaans, Zulu and Xhosa.

There are now four free channels available: SABC 1, 2 and 3, and the newer e channel. The last is the most popular and tends to have better news and entertainment.

The paying channel M-Net is available in most hotels, and shows a range of sports, sitcoms and movies. It is free from 5pm to 7pm ('open time').

BOOKS, MAPS AND FILMS

BOOKS

The following books provide valuable insights into the history and culture of South Africa.

Fiction

» *Disgrace* by J. M. Coetzee, about a Cape Town academic's fall from grace.
» *July's People* by Nadine Gordimer, the story of a white family rescued from revolution by their gardener.
» *Dry White Season* by André Brink, the moving tale of a teacher's attempt to uncover politically motivated murders in the 1980s.
» *Indecent Exposure* by Tom Sharpe, a riotous South African-based tale.
» *Cry the Beloved Country*, Alan Paton's poignant view of black urban migrants in 1940s South Africa.
» *The Story of an African Farm* by Olive Schreiner, about two women living on a Karoo farm.

Autobiography and Non-Fiction

» *Long Walk to Freedom* by Nelson Mandela, the most important autobiography to come out of South Africa.
» *No Future Without Forgiveness*, former Archbishop and Nobel prize winner Desmond Tutu's account of his experience of the Truth and Reconciliation Committee.
» *The Lost World of the Kalahari*, Laurens van der Post's famous 1958 travelogue is an entertaining read.
» *A Field Guide to the Larger Mammals of Africa*, Jean Dorst and Pierre Dandelot.
» *Birds of South Africa*, Gordon Maclean Roberts.

MAPS

The Map Studio (tel 0860-105050; www.mapstudio.co.za) produces a wide range of maps covering much of southern Africa.

FILMS

South Africa's film industry is small but growing, and South Africa is booming as a film location thanks to its terrific landscapes. Leon Schuster is South Africa's best-known director and actor, and his slapstick films are hugely popular with South Africans.
» *District 9* (2009), a science fiction take on the apartheid era and the clearances of Cape Town's District Six (▷ 69), directed by Neill Blomkamp, became an international hit and was nominated for four Academy Awards.
» *Invictus* (2009), directed by Clint Eastwood, deals with a more positive period in South African history post-apartheid with the story of Nelson Mandela's successful attempt to get the country's black population to unite behind the white Springboks rugby team in the 1995 Rugby World Cup.

SHOPPING

Johannesburg, Durban and Cape Town have the country's largest shopping malls—slick complexes with a mix of local and international chain stores and exclusive boutiques. At the other end of the scale there are the street vendors and African markets, great trawling grounds for attractive gifts, well-made crafts and souvenirs. But wherever you shop in South Africa, prices should be lower than in Europe and the US. Although the rand is no longer as weak as it was a few years ago, prices are still very reasonable and it's always possible to find a bargain.

SHOPPING MALLS

South Africans love shopping malls, and in Johannesburg affluent locals won't shop anywhere else. Many of the country's smarter malls are like self-contained towns, complete with alfresco restaurants, bars and cinemas all within one complex. Most cater to a mix of locals and visitors, with popular clothing, household and book shops interspersed with smart African curio shops. The Victoria & Alfred Waterfront in Cape Town is one of the most popular, while Johannesburg's enormous malls are some of the best places to seek out designer bargains. They are also good for slightly less expensive versions of international chains such as Guess or Quiksilver. The Gateway Shopping Mall, just outside Durban, claims to be the largest mall in the southern hemisphere— 'Shoppertainment' is beginning to feature in the South African vocabulary.

MARKETS

Craft and curio markets can be an excellent introduction to African souvenirs, as they are often manned by people from across the continent who import a range of crafts—from soapstone carvings from Zimbabwe to masks from Mali. Prices here tend to be slightly lower than in shops, and you can generally bring prices down further with a bit of friendly bartering, although you need to know your stuff if you're looking for genuine antiques or works of art. Bear in mind that local crafts and curios are significantly cheaper in neighbouring countries such as Lesotho and Swaziland.

OPENING TIMES

» Large malls tend to stay open all day, seven days a week, usually until around 9pm.
» Smaller shops usually open around 9am and close at 5pm, although on Saturdays they will open later and close earlier (often as early as 1pm).
» Even in the big cities, most shops close on Sundays, and in rural areas you won't find anything open.

METHODS OF PAYMENT

South African services and shops have very similar methods of payment to those in Europe and the US. Credit and debit cards are widely accepted in shops, restaurants and hotels (notable exceptions are petrol/ gas stations, where you need to pay in cash). In more remote locations, cash may be the only accepted form of payment.

VAT REFUNDS

Value Added Tax (VAT) of 14 per cent is levied on goods and services, but foreign visitors can get a refund on goods over R250. You can do this at the airport before checking in when departing, or at some of the bigger shopping malls. To get the refund, present a full receipt (which acts as a tax invoice), a non-South African passport and the goods purchased. The procedure is simple enough at the airport, but allow plenty of time, especially if your flight is at night. At the border crossings, such as Beitbridge (Zimbabwe) or Ramotswa (Botswana), the procedure is very slow, as there are few officials to check goods against receipts. For more information about the procedure visit www.taxrefunds.co.za.

WHAT TO BUY

Animal products

Animal products made from ivory and reptile skins are on sale in some areas, but if you take them back home you could well fall foul of the Convention on International Trade in Endangered Species of Wild Fauna and Flora (CITES) regulations. A more popular, and acceptable, animal product is an ostrich egg (painted, carved or plain, but empty), which you can find in most curio shops.

Basketwork

The majority of baskets in craft markets and gift shops are made by the Zulus. They have traditional functions, and most are decorated with distinctive triangular patterns (denoting femininity), or diamonds or zig-zags (masculinity or warfare).

The baskets are usually crafted from ilala palm fronds and grass, and dyed with natural tones—muted browns, beiges and greys—but you'll also see unusual baskets made out of telephone wire.

Beadwork

Zulu beadwork was always far more than the decorative art of weaving small glass beads into attractive patterns. Instead, the designs were a form of communication, with different colours representing different emotions—known popularly as Zulu 'love letters'. Today, most beadwork is decorative, and you'll see plenty of examples of *umgexo*—small rectangular shapes attached to a safety pin — as well as necklaces, ankle bracelets and head adornments.

Clothes and jewellery

Clothes and jewellery are often good buys, with a number of South African designers making it big both at home and abroad. Traditional African jewellery can be bought in most curio shops; the bigger shops in the malls stock interesting pieces from across Africa. There are also some high-end shops selling South African diamonds.

Pottery

South Africa's best-known potters are the VhaVenda from Limpopo province, and their pots are sold throughout the country. All traditional clay pots are made by women and fired in grass-filled holes in the ground. The pots, which vary in size, have specific functions, such as storing traditional beer or maize flour, and their characteristic rough-

hewed surfaces are glazed with silvery-grey graphite stripes or patterns.

Township crafts

Some of the most interesting contemporary purchases are arts and crafts produced in the townships. These include wire sculptures—anything from toy cars and key rings to candlesticks—paper lampshades and sculptures made from recycled cans. In the major cities, these are often sold at busy intersections and in most markets.

Wine

Individual wine estates are the best places to buy wine and most will be able to ship abroad as part of their service. Transport and taxes can be expensive (expect to pay from R1,700 for the transport of a case of 12 bottles to Europe), although the good value for money of the actual wines still makes it quite a tempting prospect. Larger supermarkets and bottle stores also stock most good South African wines. See page 311 for more details on what to buy.

Wood carvings

VhaVenda men, from the Venda region in Limpopo province, are traditionally known as carvers, although women, too, have more recently taken up the craft. Venda carving has gained in popularity, with a range of interesting figures being produced by craftsmen, as well as practical items such as walking sticks or bowls. Craftsmen use traditional carving methods and work with local woods such as the strong *muhiri* (leadwood).

CHAIN STORES			
NAME	DESCRIPTION OF GOODS	CONTACT NUMBER	WEBSITE
Clicks	Cosmetics, photographic equipment, household goods	0860-254257	www.clicks.co.za
CNA	Books, magazines	0860-692274	www.cna.co.za
Edgars	Department store	0860-203925	www.edgars.co.za
Exclusive Books	Coffee-table books, paperbacks, travel guides	011-7980111	www.exclusivebooks.com
Musica	CDs, DVDs	0860-687422	www.musica.co.za
Pick 'n' Pay	Food, household goods	0800-112288	www.picknpay.co.za
Woolworths	Fashion, household goods, food	0860-100987	www.woolworths.co.za

South Africa's cultural scene has flourished in recent years, and the cities in particular offer a wide choice of theatre, musical performances and nightlife, from full-on dance clubs to venues for stand-up comedy. Nightlife is at its best in the cities. Johannesburg is renowned for its cutting-edge bars and slick clubs, while Pretoria, Port Elizabeth and Cape Town have more laid-back, studenty scenes. Although Saturday nights are the main event, Wednesdays are also popular for going out. Opening hours are fairly flexible. Bars tend to fill up from around 6pm, clubs are virtually deserted before midnight, and some stay open until well into the next morning. Away from the biggest cities, things are considerably more sedate: Don't expect much more than a local pub in small towns. In major tourist areas, however, lively nightlife scenes have developed. In the resorts on the Garden Route, for example, bars get busy most nights in high season, while popular backpacker areas such as the Wild Coast or KwaZulu-Natal have busy bars that attract a lively surfer crowd.

BARS

Nightlife in big cities usually focuses on particular areas, making bar-hopping popular. Away from the larger cities, though, sophisticated bars are rare. Instead, small towns have traditional pubs, often with a 'ladies bar'—in some places women still avoid the 'saloon' section.

CINEMA

Multi-screen modern cinema complexes are prolific across South Africa and are usually found in the shopping malls. For many years there was little in the way of local South African cinema. The only exception to this had been the films by Leon Schuster, South Africa's best-known slapstick comic director and actor, responsible for the country's highest-earning films.

However, this is all beginning to change. A South African film, *Tsotsi,* won an Academy Award for Best Foreign Language Film in 2006 and South Africa has become a major film location. A major new film studio opened in Cape Town in 2010 and a number of independent films have made an impact.

There is a popular annual gay and lesbian film festival held in Cape Town and Johannesburg, with smaller satellite events in other cities, known as Out in Africa. The annual South African International Documentary Festival, also known as Encounters, is held at cinemas in Johannesburg and Cape Town during the summer (the month varies from year to year).

CLASSICAL MUSIC, OPERA AND DANCE

The main cities have well-established classical music, opera and dance companies. Classical music and opera are becoming increasingly accessible, thanks in part to the success of outdoor festivals such as the summer concerts held at the Kirstenbosch Botanical Gardens in Cape Peninsula (▷ 74).

Ballet is no longer the prominent dance form, but you will find examples of interesting modern dance, especially when it incorporates aspects of African dance. Traditional tribal dance performances are very popular with visitors, but these vary widely in authenticity.

CONTEMPORARY MUSIC

Music is the cultural focal point of South Africa's arts scene, with live music—particularly jazz—remaining hugely popular. In and around Cape Town, you'll hear Cape Jazz, while Johannesburg offers

Left *Spier Music Festival, in the Western Cape*

new and traditional sounds in its many jazz bars. There are several jazz festivals around the country; the most popular is the Cape Town International Jazz Festival (▷ 89).

Live pop and rock concerts have boomed since the end of the apartheid era, when the cultural boycott was lifted and international artists began to tour here.

CLUBS

Music is central to a night out. You'll mostly hear mainstream house, but hip hop and techno are popular, as are drum 'n' bass, Latin and home-grown rock. You should also listen to some kwaito (▷ 21), a relaxed form of house with booming bass—it is the sound of a young, confident and black Johannesburg. There are a number of large-scale dance events held around the country. Popular nights include Vortex and Alien Safari, both of which are all-night techno parties held at outdoor venues around the country.

Clubs usually charge you an entry fee—from about R25 up to R70.

THEATRE

South Africa's theatre scene has rediscovered its feet following a tricky few years of freezes on government funding. Political theatre, once a pivotal genre during apartheid, is proving popular once again. Cutting-edge productions are also on the up and there remains a good selection of arts theatres around the country.

Large-scale musicals are also very popular. The annual National Festival of the Arts in Grahamstown, which, in its 27 years has showcased the cream of the country's emerging talent in both the performing and graphic arts, has spawned a variety of smaller festivals across the rest of the country.

GAY AND LESBIAN

The government legalized same-sex marriages in 2006, the fifth country in the world to do so, and the South African constitution is one of the most gay-friendly and progressive in the world. Cape Town is the self-proclaimed 'Gay Capital' of Africa and it proudly promotes itself as such. The city has a good range of bars, clubs and events aimed specifically at a gay crowd. The area around Green Point, known as De Waterkant Village, is the gay and lesbian hotspot, and all the main bars and clubs are found along Somerset and Main Road. This is the location of the Cape Town Pride march (www.capetownpride.co.za, ▷ 89) held every February, but the main gay event is the Mother City Queer Project (www.mcqp.co.za, ▷ 89), a fantastically extravagant costume party and rave—not to be missed if you're in town in December, since it's one of the highlights of the city's social calendar.

Up the coast from Cape Town, the Pink Loerie Mardi Gras is held in Knysna in May (www.pinkloerie. com). For more information on the event, pick up the free Pink Map, available at tourist offices.

However, away from the main cities, South Africa remains deeply conservative and overtly affectionate behaviour between gay and lesbian couples may elicit a disapproving response—from both black and white communities.

INFORMATION AND TICKETING

Tourist offices will have the latest information on which companies and performers are coming to the local area. Drop in, or visit their websites (▷ 297). Computicket (tel 083-9158000; www. computicket. com) sells tickets for theatre, concerts and sports events across the country. Although this is the best source for tickets, it only accepts South Africa-issued credit cards for phone and internet bookings, so foreign visitors have to go to a Computicket outlet to purchase tickets in cash. You will be able to find these in major shopping malls in the big cities.

Another good source of entertainment listings is www.tonight.co.za.

HOW TO FIND OUT MORE

The best source of information on nightlife is the local newspapers, which have daily, up-to-the-minute listings on clubs, bars and also one-off events such as stand-up comedy nights. Tourist offices, particularly in the cities, are also good sources of information. For venue information in Johannesburg, Pretoria, Cape Town and the East Coast, visit www.topclubs.co.za.

Cape Town
» The Cape Times and Cape Argus have excellent listings sections, as does Cape Etc. magazine. The tourist office hands out the free Pink Map, with gay and lesbian listings, and also the Cape Gay Guide, an annual booklet with information on nightlife and gay-friendly accommodation in Cape Town.

Johannesburg and Pretoria
» Listings are published in the local papers The Star and The Citizen, as well as in the national Mail and Guardian and the bi-monthly magazine, SA City Life.

Durban
» Check listings in The Daily News and The Natal Mercury.

Below The Boardwalk Bar in Port Elizabeth

SPORTS AND ACTIVITIES

All South Africans love watching sport. Racial divisions used to play a role in who watches what—cricket and rugby were largely the preserve of white South Africans, while soccer was hugely popular among the black population—but today audiences are much more mixed. South Africa hosted the highly successful 2010 FIFA World Cup, the first African nation to hold the event. This not only saw the completion of new state-of-the-art stadiums in Cape Town, Durban, Port Elizabeth, Polokwane and Mbombela (Nelspruit), but was a source of much national pride and renewed international interest in the country. The country promotes an outdoors, get-fit lifestyle, and hiking, jogging and surfing are all popular activities. But the real attraction in South Africa is adventure sports, such as bungee jumping, white-water rafting or kitesurfing, and surfing and scuba diving are big business along the Garden Route and in KwaZulu-Natal. Hiking, however, is the most popular activity overall and every national park and game reserve is criss-crossed with trails.

BIRDWATCHING

With more than 700 species of bird recorded, birdwatching has grown into a popular activity in South Africa and there are now organized birdwatching tours. The country has such diverse landscapes that many of the breeds are rare and specific to South Africa. For details contact Southern African Birding (tel 031-2665948, www.sabirding.co.za).

BUNGEE JUMPING

The most popular place in the country for bungee also claims to be the highest commercial bungee jump in the world. The drop at the Bloukrans River Bridge (▷ 130) between Plettenberg Bay and Tsitsikamma is approximately 200m (655ft). The first rebound is higher than the full descent at the famous drop in Victoria Falls.

CRICKET

South Africa hosted the 2003 Cricket World Cup, with more than 54 matches being played, and its international team, the Proteas, is well respected and has great successes in both test and one-day cricket. Cricketing facilities are therefore excellent. The domestic season runs from October to April.

For more information about venues and how to obtain tickets visit www.cricket.co.za.

FISHING

Deep-sea fishing is big business, as is shore-fishing. Some of the most common catches are mako shark, long fin tuna and yellowtail, but there are strict rules governing all types of fishing. The simplest way of dealing with permits and regulations is to make a reservation through a charter company. Fly-fishing for trout is also popular, particularly in the Drakensberg and around the Western Cape.

GOLF

South Africa has some wonderful golf courses, such as the championship course at Milnerton in Cape Town, the Fancourt Country Club in George or Houghton in Johannesburg, venue for the South African Open. The most famous South African golfer is probably Gary Player, although Ernie Els is one of the most successful today.

HIKING

There is an enormous number of well-developed hiking trails across the country, many of which go through spectacular areas of natural beauty. These range from pleasant afternoon strolls through nature reserves to challenging hikes in wilderness regions. Hiking in South Africa involves some forward planning and permits, but the rewards and the choice of trails are well worth the effort. Opportunities begin in Cape Town on Table Mountain and the coastal trails around Cape Point, with a number of longer trails along the Garden Route. Inland, the Cederberg is an excellent and isolated hiking area, but the most popular and best-known region is the uKhahlamba-Drakensberg National Park, bordering Lesotho. The park, nearly 300km (186 miles) long, with a network of trails (some climbing to more than 3,000m/9,845ft) offers hikers a vast mountain region with undiscovered hiking possibilities comparable to regions of the Himalayas.

Day hikes are very popular, and well-signposted trails can be found in most nature reserves—ask at the park or reserve office. Longer trails involve at least one night in the wild, and you will need to bring a sleeping bag, tent, water, food and cooking equipment.

Some reserves and national parks have overnight huts, or if not, there will be campsites. Wilderness trekking, available in the Cederberg

and the Drakensberg, involves hiking away from designated footpaths. There is usually no specific overnight accommodation—you sleep in rock shelters or pitch a tent wherever possible. Hikers should have a good experience of map-reading and dealing with extreme weather conditions. Some national parks have guided wilderness trails which concentrate on game viewing and are accompanied by rangers.

HORSEBACK RIDING

Horseback riding is a popular activity among farming communities and in the mountains, particularly in the kingdom of Lesotho. The Drakensberg is a good place, and hotels can organize anything from a short morning trot to a six-day mountain safari. Longer treks are available in Lesotho, where ponies are the main form of transport in rural areas. On the Garden Route you can ride in the forests close to Knysna, and on the beaches in the Western Cape.

KLOOFING

Kloofing (also known as canyoning) is a popular adrenaline activity, especially with backpackers. It involves hiking, boulder-hopping (literally, jumping from boulder to boulder) and swimming along mountain rivers. It is available around Table Mountain in Cape Town, along the Garden Route and in the Drakensberg.

MOUNTAIN BIKING

Many nature reserves and wilderness areas have increased their accessibility for mountain bikes, and many routes have been planned to suit all levels of fitness. Some of the best organized regions include: De Hoop Nature Reserve, in the Overberg; Tulbagh Valley; Kamiesberg, close to Garies in Namakwa; Goegap Nature Reserve, outside Springbok; and the mountains around Citrusdal.

There are a number of cycling events in South Africa that are open to foreign cyclists. The largest and

best-known is the Cape Argus Pick 'n' Pay Cycle Tour (▷ 89).

PARAGLIDING

South Africa has several world-renowned paragliding locations. Leaping from Lion's Head in Cape Town, or wafting above the Kalahari are two of the most exhilarating options. Most of the action is around Kuruman in the Northern Cape and Barberton in Mpumalanga. Climatic conditions in South Africa are ideal—good thermal activity allows paragliders to climb between 6m and 8m (20ft and 26ft) per second and the cloud base is usually at 5,000m (16,400ft). The best season for gliding is between November and February.

RUGBY

South Africa's rugby team, nicknamed the Springboks, hosted and won the Rugby World Cup in 1995 and then-president Nelson Mandela memorably awarded the trophy in a Springbok jersey. Formerly rugby was a sport watched and played by whites, so when Mandela embraced Francois Pienaar, the white team captain, it was seen as a gesture to the world that the country was embracing racial reconciliation. The Springboks won the World Cup again in 2007 and are a force to be reckoned with on an international level.

SCUBA DIVING

The South African coastline has particularly rich and diverse marine flora and fauna. The Agulhas current continually sweeps warm water down from the subtropical Indian Ocean and meets the cold nutrient-rich waters of the Atlantic. This mixing of water temperatures has created an incredible selection of marine ecosystems, from the tropical coral reefs of KwaZulu-Natal through to the temperate kelp forests around Cape Point. The diving community in South Africa is widespread and the facilities are generally excellent—but see Responsible Tourism on page 308.

SOCCER

Soccer is the country's most popular sport; the Premier Soccer League is the most important league, but there are a number of knock-out competitions. The season runs from August to May. The national team is known as Bafana Bafana (roughly meaning 'our boys'), and the best-known local teams include Kaizer Chiefs and Orlando Pirates, both from Johannesburg. A cause of much excitement was the 2010 World Cup, the first time that the championship had come to an African nation.

SURFING

South Africa has established itself as a major surfing hotspot, and has some of the best waves in the world. Jeffreys Bay on the south coast of the Eastern Cape is undoubtedly South Africa's surfing captial, known for its consistently good surf, and host to the annual Billabong surf championships in July. This is also a good place to learn to surf, with a number of courses available and areas of reliable, small breaks, perfect for learning. The whole southern coast is dotted with good breaks, particularly around Port Elizabeth and East London. Cape Town,

too, has some excellent, reliable breaks on the Atlantic and False Bay beaches. The Golden Mile on Durban's beachfront has good surf, well protected by lifeguards and equipped with shark nets.

SWIMMING

Given South Africa's extensive coastline and beautiful beaches, swimming is often a top priority for visitors. The beaches of KwaZulu-Natal and the Garden Route have well-established swimming beaches catering to the domestic family market, which means patrolling lifeguards, changing facilities, toilets, picnic areas and kiosks selling cool drinks. In KwaZulu-Natal, the biggest beaches also have shark nets to protect swimmers. Less tourist-orientated areas are obviously much less developed, and bathers must take extreme care. The seas around South Africa are renowned for their strong rips and swimmers should never venture out farther than they can stand. Although shark attacks are rare, it is worth bearing in mind that South Africa's waters are home to a variety of the creatures. Note, too, that the sea around Cape Town and the west coast is very cold and only really

warms up towards the Garden Route (as the waters here come from the Indian Ocean, not the Atlantic).

WHALE WATCHING

The Whale Coast in the southwestern Cape is one of the best places in the world to see whales. Between July and November, southern right and humpback whales mass to calve. You can also whale watch in the sheltered bays on the west coast and from boats on the KwaZulu-Natal coast, especially between June and October.

WHITE-WATER RAFTING

Rafting is popular for visitors and is generally very well organized, with a high degree of safety. There are several excellent rapids: the Umzimvubu Falls in Transkei; along the Umzimkulu River in KwaZulu-Natal; on the Gariep River by the Augrabies Falls or near Kimberley; on the Great Usutu River in Swaziland; and on the Sabie, Olifants and Blyde rivers in Mpumalanga.

WINE TASTING

Wine tasting is big business. The Winelands in the Western Cape has several routes that take you through beautiful valleys and hundreds of estates. Look out for more unusual routes, such as along the Gariep River. But be sensible if you are driving—one of you should stay off the alcohol.

RESPONSIBLE TOURISM

If you take part in any of these activities, especially scuba diving, you will come into close contact with South African ecosystems. Some, such as the coral reefs, are particularly sensitive. Be sure to follow the instructions given to you by your instructor or guide; these will help protect the landscape for future visitors. Staff in local tourist offices will be able to recommend responsible operators.

Left *South Africa offers great surfing for all levels of ability*

HEALTH AND BEAUTY

The spa and wellness industry has grown dramatically in South Africa over the last decade—today just about every upmarket hotel has a spa, often in sublime locations such as mountain hideaways, beach retreats and remote game reserves. Indeed, these days most guests of private safari lodges expect to be able to have a massage after bouncing around the bush on a game drive. Some treatments use indigenous plants or techniques that have been used for centuries by Africans to calm and cure. You can expect standards, and the range of treatments on offer, to be very similar to those found in Europe and the US. However, prices are considerably lower and you are likely to pay about half of what you would pay at home. Many establishments offer accommodation and treatment packages.

FOR CHILDREN

South Africa is a great place to bring the kids, with plenty of sights that interest adults while at the same time keeping children busy. Outdoors activities such as game walks, safaris or simply spending a day at the beach are very much part of a holiday in South Africa, with excellent facilities, particularly along the Western Cape and KwaZulu-Natal coasts. These areas have long been popular for domestic family holidays, so overseas visitors will find family-friendly hotels and restaurants, kids' clubs and plenty of child-orientated entertainment.

In the cities, museums and more traditional sights are starting to catch on to the importance of the family market, with some introducing fun interactive displays and special exhibits aimed at children. There are a handful of theme parks around the country, including Ratanga Junction in Cape Town, Gold Reef City in Johannesburg and the new uShaka Marine World water park in Durban.

TAKING YOUR KIDS
» Most hotels and restaurants are family-orientated, so extra beds in rooms are rarely a problem, and smaller family-run bed-and-breakfasts will let you use the kitchen to prepare baby food.
» Only the larger hotels have babysitting services; you'll find most South African families bring their children out to restaurants with them.
» Restaurants in tourist areas and big cities often have children's menus and baby chairs.
» Central heating is a rarity in much of South Africa; bear this in mind if you're visiting in winter.
» Most attractions will offer some form of discount for children, with free entrance for the very young.

» The sun is extremely strong, so be sure to cover up children and use high-factor sun protection. Avoid the sun between 11 and 3.
» Bear in mind that some wildlife safaris involve a lot of driving; smaller private reserves or animal sanctuaries may be more entertaining for small children.

FESTIVALS AND EVENTS

Festivals and events are a relatively new concept in South Africa, but they are catching on fast, even in smaller towns. There is a wide range held throughout the year, from traditional carnivals and sports events to sophisticated arts festivals and music concerts. Perhaps the most important festival is the Grahamstown Arts Festival, where the country's actors, playwrights, musicians and comedians congregate to present the newest in South African arts. Other major festivals include Karnaval in Cape Town, the Cape Town Jazz Festival, the Splashy Fen music festival near Underberg, and the Umhlanga Reed Dance held in Swaziland. Many small festivals celebrate the harvesting of local produce, from fruit to oysters, Afrikaner culture and traditions, and the wildlife of South Africa, such as the whales off the coast of Hermanus.

Sports events are always popular, with several large-scale races and timed events taking place in Cape Town every year. These include the Cape Argus Pick 'n' Pay Cycle Tour and the Two Oceans Marathon, both of which race around the scenic Cape peninsula and attract international participants.

Christmas is also well observed—a time when there is plenty going on all over the country. Cape Town's Victoria & Alfred Waterfront is particularly beautiful, decked out in Christmas lights. The area is also a hive of activity and partying during New Year's celebrations.

South Africa has an abundance of fresh produce, from the fantastic variety of fish along the coast to the exotic fruit plantations of the northeast. The country—particularly the cities—has undergone something of a culinary revolution in recent years and South Africa is emerging as a gastronomic hotspot.

WHAT TO EAT AND WHERE

» Cape Malay cooking is found in Cape Town and is the regional cuisine originating from the Cape Malay community, with an interesting blend of spicy curries softened with fruit. Desserts include *malva* pudding, a sticky sponge made with jam. Although there are surprisingly few Cape Malay restaurants, some of the more popular dishes such as *bobotie,* a sweet-spicy dish of minced beef, are hugely popular and served in a number of mainstream restaurants.

» The Indian influence in KwaZulu-Natal means that the best curries are found in Durban. One of the most popular take-out meals is *bunny chow,* a half-loaf of bread with the middle scooped out and filled with curry—the scooped out bread is used as a 'spoon' to soak up the sauce.

» You'll find good seafood along all of South Africa's coasts, and game fish such as yellowtail, snoek and tuna are becoming more popular

everywhere. South Africans have a national passion for prawns imported from Mozambique cooked in peri-peri (hot) spices.

» Afrikaner cooking is much in the mainstream of South African cuisine. Staples throughout the country include biltong (dried, salted strips of meat) and *boerewors* (a strong, spicy sausage) usually grilled on a *braai* (barbecue).

» Restaurants vary wildly in quality and service, depending largely on where you are. In most small towns, your choice will be limited to branches of one of the South African steak-house chains, such as Spur or Saddles. Don't be put off, however, as these offer good standards of steak and grills.

CAFÉS

Many of the places that are called cafés are not the equivalent of a café in Europe or north America. A café in South Africa tends to refer to a small store selling soft drinks, magazines and a selection of food items.

BRAAIS

Braais (barbecues) are the most ubiquitous Afrikaner influence you'll find, and are incredibly popular throughout South Africa. Every picnic spot, camping site or rest area has at least one permanent grate, and cooking on a *braai* is seen as something of an art form.

MEAT AND VEGETABLES

» South Africans are big meat-eaters. Meat is almost always of a high standard wherever you are, and you'll be hard pressed to find a menu that doesn't feature steak. Lamb, especially Karoo lamb, is delicious.

» Don't miss trying some of South Africa's game. Ostrich is the most widespread, tasting much like steak (and served similarly), but with a lower fat content. Other game you're likely to come across is springbok, kudu, crocodile and warthog. Big cities have restaurants specializing in exotic game.

» Vegetarians will find their choice greatly limited. South Africa is a

meat-loving country and menus rarely include anything but the most basic dishes for vegetarians. Away from the major cities, you'll have to make do with salads, pasta and chips (fries). Cape Town, Pretoria and Johannesburg have a better range for vegetarians, with some trendy meat-free restaurants. Catering for yourself is often an easier option.

ALCOHOLIC DRINKS

» South Africa has made its mark on the international wine scene, and produces a wide range of excellent wines. The Winelands (▷ 115–119) in the Western Cape have the best-known labels, but there are a number of other wine routes dotted around the country.

» The *John Platter Wine Guide,* South Africa's best-known annual wine critic book (from www.cybercellar. com), awards 21 wines each year with a grade of five stars from about 6–7,000 entrants.

» The prestigious Veritas double gold awards were given in 2010 to Simonsig's Méthode Cap Classique, and in 2007 to Nederburg Edelkeur Private Bin Chenin Blanc 2005, Nederburg Private Bin R163 Cabernet Sauvignon 2004, Spier Private Collection Chardonnay 2006, Spier Sejana Merlot 2005, Bon Courage Hillside White Colombar/Chardonnay

2007, Bon Courage Pinotage 2006, and Nuy White Muscadel 2003.

» Most South African wines aren't labelled by region, but rather by grape variety and style. The grape itself, and the reputation of the winery that made the wine, are the two things to watch for—region is of lesser value.

» There is a good range of locally produced beers, as well as imports. Major labels include Black Label, Castle and Windhoek. *Maheu,* home-brewed beer made from sorghum or maize, is widely drunk by the African population. It has a thick head, is very potent and is not very palatable to the uninitiated. Bitter is harder to come by, although a good local variety is brewed at Mitchell's Brewery in Knysna and Cape Town, and found at good outlets along the Garden Route (▷ 103).

» No liquor may be sold on Sundays except in restaurants licensed to serve alcohol with meals. Liquor stores or off-licences are known as bottle stores. These are usually open Monday to Friday 8–6 and Saturday 8.30–2. Supermarkets do not sell beer or spirits; they stop selling wine at 8pm, and don't sell alcohol on Sundays.

NON-ALCOHOLIC DRINKS

» Tap water is chemically treated and safe to drink. Bottled mineral water is available at all restaurants, snack bars and supermarkets, as are international soft drinks such as coke or Fanta.

» There is also a good range of fruit juices available at most outlets—the Ceres and Liquifruit brands are the best varieties.

» Another popular non-alcoholic drink is *rooibos* tea, literally red bush tea. This is a caffeine-free tea with a smoky taste, usually served with sugar or honey.

SUPERMARKETS

If you are planning to camp or go self-catering, then you will be able to get most of your supplies at supermarkets. They have a similar selection to those in Europe—meat is often cheaper, but fresh fruit and vegetables can be expensive. South Africa is, however, a great source of fresh fruit, and local produce such as apples in Ceres or pineapples along the Wild Coast should be good. Main supermarkets include Pick 'n' Pick, OK Bazaars and Shoprite Checkers.

PRICES AND TIMES

» Eating out continues to be very good value. A three-course meal in a mid-price range restaurant will rarely cost you more than R250 per person, including the wine.

» Service isn't usually included in a bill. If you find the service is good, the standard amount to tip is 10–15 per cent.

» Outside the major tourist places, people eat early and many kitchens close around 9pm, although this is later at the weekend. Some restaurants are often closed on Sunday evenings, when hotel dining rooms or fast-food outlets may well be the only choices for eating out. In cities, restaurants are open throughout the day and kitchens shut around 10–11pm.

MORE INFORMATION

A good starting point for choosing a restaurant is buying the latest edition of *Eat Out,* which features South Africa's best choice of restaurants. The magazine costs around R40 and is available in newsagents and tourist offices.

atjar mango relish served with Cape Malay curries

biltong air-dried, cured meat, usually made from beef or venison

biryanis rice-based curry

bobotie spiced, minced beef cooked with dried fruit and a savoury custard topping

boerekos Afrikaner country cooking

boerewors spicy beef sausage

braai barbecue

bredie meat and vegetable stew

bunny chow Durban curry served in a hollowed-out loaf of bread

cool drink soft (non-alcoholic) drink

dop drink (alcoholic)

frikkadels meat balls or patties

koeksisters deep-fried plaited doughnuts, soaked in syrup

konfyt candied fruit

malva pudding a sticky sponge made with jam

melktert custard flan dessert

mielie maize

monkey gland sauce piquant sauce of onion, tomato, fruit chutney and Worcestershire sauce, designed for meat (no monkey)

pap (or mieliepap) stiff, savoury maize porridge

peri-peri Portuguese chilli flavouring

potjiekos stew cooked in a cast-iron cauldron over hot coals

rusks dried pieces of bread

sambal spicy relish served with Cape Malay curries

samp mashed maize, usually served with beans

snoek local fish, often served as pâté

sosaties skewered meat; kebab

umqombothi African beer made from maize

waterblommetjie bredie mutton stew made with indigenous water-flowers

South Africa has an excellent range of accommodation options, covering everything from inexpensive backpacker hostels to super-luxurious safari camps. On the whole, rooms are good value, and although prices are rising as the rand gets stronger, you'll be surprised at the degree of comfort your money will buy.

CAMPING AND CARAVAN PARKS

Camping is the least expensive and most flexible way of staying in South Africa. Every town has a municipal campsite, many with simple chalets with kitchens. As camping is very popular with South Africans, sites tend to have excellent facilities, including electric points and lighting, shower blocks and sometimes kitchen blocks. At the most-frequented visitor spots, campsites are more like holiday resorts with shops, swimming pools and a restaurant. They can get very busy and often have to be reserved months in advance, especially in the most popular reserves and national parks during the school holidays. For most of the year the weather is ideal for camping, but be prepared for frosts at night in some parts.

Camping fees are either per tent or per person, and on average should

Above Spacious bathroom in the Bush Lodge, Sabi Sabi, Kruger
Left Seafood is widely available on the coast

be no more than R70 per tent and R80 per person.

If you prefer not to camp, the least expensive alternative to a backpacker hostel is staying in a chalet with kitchen, often offered by municipal and national park sites. These vary in quality and facilities, from basic *rondavels* (small, round huts with thatched roofs) with bunks to chalets with a couple of bedrooms and fully equipped kitchens. They are often the only budget accommodation available in a town or park.

BACKPACKER HOSTELS

Backpacker hostels are among the cheapest form of accommodation in South Africa. A bed in a dormitory will cost between R80 and R120 a night, while a double room costs between R180 and R300. Standards vary, but stiff competition means that most are clean and with good facilities. You can usually expect a kitchen, hot showers, a TV/video room and internet access. Many hostels also have bars and offer meals or nightly *braais* (barbecues), plus gardens and plunge pools. Most

hostels are a good source of travel information and many act as booking agents for bus companies, budget safari tours and car rental.

The Baz Bus (▷ 52) caters to backpackers and links most backpacker hostels along the coast between Cape Town and Durban, and Durban and Johannesburg and Pretoria, via either Swaziland or the Drakensberg, and includes Swaziland. More than 140 hostels are visited on the route.

Visitors who have a rental car should note that most backpacker hostels and cheaper guesthouses do not have secure off-street parking.
» Hostelworld.com has details of international hostels, including a good selection in South Africa.
» Coast to Coast, www. coastingafrica.com, is a free backpackers' guide to hostels across the country.

BED-AND-BREAKFAST

Bed-and-breakfast accommodation is hugely popular in South Africa, and even the smallest town will usually have one private home that rents out rooms. Local tourist offices are the best source of information. Standards vary, but increasingly establishments are providing TVs and air conditioning or fans, and have separate entrances for those who want more privacy.

The generous breakfasts that come with the deal are almost always good. They are usually full English breakfasts (eggs, bacon, sausages and toast), but it is now common to have a choice of continental breakfast or even South African dishes, such as mince on toast and mealie porridge.

Prices vary according to the facilities, and a bed-and-breakfast in a Victorian house filled with antique furniture will be more expensive than a converted spare room. Prices start at around R180 per person sharing and can go up to as much as R500. At the top end of the market the luxury bed-and-breakfasts in spectacular locations such as the Winelands (▷ 115–119) can charge as much as R750.
» Bed and Breakfast Association of South Africa, tel 082-2392111, www.babasa.co.za.

GUESTHOUSES
Guesthouses can offer some of the most unusual accommodation in South Africa, with more and more interesting places springing up in cities and small towns all the time. Many are in historic homes, and offering impeccable service; in fact most luxurious rooms outside the major cities tend to be in guesthouses, not hotels. Standards vary enormously; much of what you'll get has to do with the character of the owners and the location of the homes.

Expect to pay from R250 per person for the simplest room, with prices increasing rapidly with quality. Making reservations by phone in advance is always a good idea.
» Guest House Association of Southern Africa, tel 021-7620880, www.ghasa.co.za.
» The Portfolio Collection, tel 021-6894020, www.portfoliocollection.com.

HOTELS
Traditional hotels have generally become a less attractive option as the number of boutique hotels and guesthouses increases. Many are either large-scale chain hotels or 1970s hangovers, lacking the character and service that are found in newer establishments and that visitors have come to expect. Nevertheless, in the main cities, hotels often remain a practical option. Cape Town and Johannesburg suffer from a shortage of hotel beds, so it is always advisable to reserve well in advance.

Generally, rooms reserved through agents in Europe and the US will be more expensive than if you contact the hotel direct, due to agent booking fees. Many chain hotels have an online reservation service via their websites.

LUXURY GAME LODGES
The most famous luxury game lodges are on private game reserves adjoining Kruger National Park, although there are others dotted around the country. Their attraction is a combination of exclusive game viewing in South Africa's prime wilderness areas, top-class accommodation and gourmet meals, and a spectacular natural setting.

The cost of staying in a luxury game lodge varies from around R2,500 to over R7,000 per person each night. This includes all meals, drinks and game-viewing trips. In order to get the most from their stay, guests tend to spend at least two nights in a lodge. The lodges are often isolated and not easily accessible by road, so many reserves have their own airstrips where light aircraft can land.

NATIONAL PARKS AND GAME RESERVES
Parks offer a range of accommodation, from basic campsites to functional chalets. If you plan on staying overnight, be sure to reserve ahead through the central reservations office of the relevant authority. All reservations

can be made over the telephone, by email or on the website. Most international credit cards are accepted. In high season, it's wise to make reservations a month or two in advance.

National parks across the country are under the jurisdiction of South African National Parks, tel 012-4289111, www.sanparks.org. In the Western Cape, the game reserves are managed by Cape Nature Conservation, tel 227-3628873, www.capenature.org.za, and in KwaZulu Natal, KZN Wildlife, tel 033-8451000, www.kznwildlife.com.

SELF-CATERING APARTMENTS
Self-catering apartments are particularly popular with resident South African holidaymakers and there is an enormous choice, especially along the coast. Prices vary with the seasons: Unsurprisingly, Christmas is the most expensive time of year, but off-season (May to the end of September) many resorts are virtually empty and discounts can often be negotiated.

If you are in a group, an apartment could cost as little as R70 a day per person. Local tourist offices are the best source of information on self-catering accommodation.

PRICES IN THIS BOOK
The prices given in the listings are the average cost of a double room based on two people sharing in high season, including 14 per cent VAT and breakfast. Prices do not include the one per cent tourist levy charge, unless otherwise stated.

Below *Comfortable bedroom in Fugitives Drift Lodge, on the Battlefields Route*

LANGUAGE GUIDE

South Africa has 11 official languages, and scores of other, 'unofficial' African languages are spoken. Most people understand and speak English, which tends to dominate much of the cultural and political scene.

However, English is actually the mother tongue of a relative minority —just 9 per cent of the population. isiZulu, the language of the Zulus, is the largest, at around 28 per cent of the population and Afrikaans is the mother tongue of over 14 per cent. Most Afrikaans-speakers are not white, but 'coloured' (▷ 7). The other official languages in South Africa are:
» Sesotho sa Leboa
» Sesotho
» Setswana
» SiSwati
» Tshivenda
» Xitsonga
» isiNdebele
» isiXhosa.

With such a wide variety of languages, you will hardly have time to learn more than a smattering of even one or two. However, you'll find that learning a few phrases of whichever language dominates the area you are in will be appreciated by the people living there.

It's worth noting that the English spoken in South Africa uses British English rather than American terms. For example, South Africans refer to the 'boot' of a car (not the trunk) and 'petrol' (instead of gas). The influence of American television and films is being felt, however. You will often hear 'cell phone' and 'movie', for example, rather than 'mobile phone' and 'film'.

ENGLISH

South African English has a large vocabulary, borrowing a wide range of terms, phrases and words from Afrikaans and various African languages. See page 316 for a list of common colloquialisms.

AFRIKAANS

Afrikaans is the language of around 60 per cent of the white population, and 90 per cent of 'coloured' people. It is probably the language, aside from English, which you will come across most often as a visitor. Many Afrikaans words are used in South African English (see South African/English Colloquialisms box). It is widely spoken in the Western and Northern capes, where it is the first language of much of the population. Derived from Dutch, it also incorporates words from English, East Africa, Indonesia and from the indigenous Khoi and San languages. While most Afrikaans-speakers understand English, many do not, so it's worth learning a few phrases.

THE NGUNI LANGUAGES

isiZulu, isiXhosa, SiSwati and isiNdebele are collectively referred to as the Nguni languages, and have a lot of similarities in syntax and grammar. isiZulu is the most widely spoken. It is the first language of much of KwaZulu-Natal's population, and is spoken by many in Gauteng, Free State and Mpumalanga.

SiSwati, spoken in Swaziland, is very similar to isiZulu, as is isiNdebele, which is spoken in North West Province and part of Gauteng. isiXhosa is the language of the Eastern Cape (and Nelson Mandela's mother tongue), as well as in the townships of Cape Town.

THE SOTHO LANGUAGES

This group of languages includes Setswana, Sesotho sa Leboa and Sesotho, and all three are again very similar. Sesotho is the language of the Lesotho people, and is also spoken in Free State. Sesotho sa Leboa (also known as Northern Sotho) is concentrated in the northeast of South Africa. Setswana is the main African language of Botswana, and is also spoken south of the border, in parts of the Northern Cape and North West Province.

EMERGING LANGUAGES

A lingua franca of the urban townships is Tsotsi taal, widely spoken by young males. This is a hybrid of Afrikaans, English and African languages, which evolved as a result of linguistically diverse populations living side by side. It is a dynamic language, with new words and phrases regularly being created.

SOUTH AFRICAN/ENGLISH COLLOQUIALISMS

Most of these are derived from Afrikaans, but are widely used in South African English.

Ag .... pronounced like the German 'ach'. Used at the beginning of a sentence, often to indicate irritation
Babelas .... hangover
Bakkie .... small pick-up van
Bergie .... homeless person/tramp
Biltong .... dried, cured meat
Bob .... money
Boet .... brother/guy/dude
Braai .... barbecue
Bru .... brother/guy (affectionate term between men)
Cooldrink ..soft (non-alcoholic) drink
Dingus .... thing (used when the speaker does not know the word for something, as in 'thingy' or 'whatchamacallit')
Doff .... stupid/idiot
Dop .... drink (alcoholic)
Frikkadel .... meatball
Gatvol .... fed up
Hap .... bite (as in 'bite to eat')
Howzit .... hello/how are you?
Izzit ......used widely in conversation, meaning 'really?', or 'is that so?'
Jawelnofine .... how about that?
Jol .... party
Just now .... soon (this implies someone will do something in the near future, but not immediately)

Koppie .... small hill
Kos .... food
Larny .... well-dressed, smart
Lekker .... good/nice/tasty/fun
Madiba .... Nelson Mandela's clan name, used widely as a term of endearment (including in the press), also meaning 'grandfather'
Nooit .... no/never
Now now ... in a little while (as in 'I'll be with you now now')
Oke .... guy/man
Padkos .... food for the road
Platteland .... flatlands, rural areas
Robot .... traffic lights
Shame ..... used to denote sympathy
Skrik .... fright
Slip-slops ..... flip-flop or thong shoes
Stoep .... veranda
Tackies .... sports shoes/sneakers
Yebo .... hello/yes

USEFUL WORDS IN AFRIKAANS

For translations of Afrikaans road signs, ▷ 56.
Airplane .... Vliegtuig
Airport .... Lughawe
Arrival .... Aankoms
Bank .... Bank
Barbecue .... Braai
Bed and breakfast ..... Bed en ontbyt
Beach .... Strand
Bill .... Rekening
Border .... Grens
Borough .... Burg

Breakfast .... Ontbyt
Cheap .... Goedkoop
Cheque .... Tjek
Church .... Kerk
City .... Stad
Credit card .... Kredietkaart
Departure .... Vertrek
Dinner .... Aandete
Expensive .... Duur
Exit .... Uitgang
Field .... Veld
Good/nice .... Lekker
Information .... Inligting
Left .... Links
Low-lying lake or swamp .... Vlei
Lunch .... Middagete
Market .... Mark
Mountain .... Berg
Petrol .... Brandstoff
Pharmacy .... Apteek
Police .... Polisie
Post Office .... Poskantoor
Pub/bar .... Kroeg
Right .... Regs
Station .... Stasie
Ticket .... Kaartjie
Town centre .... Middestad
Traveller's cheque .... Reisigerstjek
Village .... Dorp
Wine .... Wyn

USEFUL WORDS AND PHRASES

ENGLISH	AFRIKAANS	ISIZULU	ISIXHOSA	SETSWANA	SESOTHO	SISWATI
Hello	Hallo	Sawubona	Molo (good morning) Rhoananai (good evening)	Dumela	Dumela	Sawubona
Goodbye	Totsiens	Sala kahle	Sala sentle	Sala sentle	Sala Hantle	Salakahle
How are you?	Hoe gaan dit?	Ninjani?	Kunjani?	O tsogile jang?	O kae?	Ninjani?
Fine, thank you	Goed, dankie	Ngisaphila	Ndiphilile, enkosi	Ke tsogile sentle	Ke phela hantle	Kulungile
Please	Asseblief	Uxolo	Nceda	Tsweetswee	(Ka kopo) hle	Ngicela
Thank you	Dankie	Ngiyabonga	Enkosi	Ke a leboga	Ke a leboha	Ngiyabonga
Yes	Ja	Yebo	Ewe	Ee	E	Yebo
No	Nee	Cha	Hayi	Nnyaa	The	Cha
Excuse me	Verskooon my	Uxolo	Uxolo	Intshwarele	Ntshwaerele	

GLOSSARY FOR US VISITORS

anticlockwise .... counterclockwise
aubergine .... eggplant
bank holiday .... public holiday
bill .... check (at restaurant)
biscuit .... cookie
bonnet .... hood (car)
boot .... trunk (car)
busker .... street musician
caravan .... house trailer or RV
car park .... parking lot
carriage .... car (on a train)
casualty .... emergency room
(hospital department)
chemist .... pharmacy
chips .... french fries
coach .... long-distance bus
concessions .... reduced fees for
tickets, often available
to students, children
and elderly people
courgette .... zucchini
crèche .... day care
crisps .... potato chips
directory enquiries .... directory
assistance
dual carriageway .two-lane highway
en suite .... a bedroom with its
own private bathroom;
may also just refer
to the bathroom

football .... soccer
full board .... a hotel tariff that
includes all meals
garage .... gas station
garden .... yard (residential)
GP .... doctor
half board .... hotel tariff that
includes breakfast and
either lunch or dinner
handbag .... purse
high street .... main street
hire .... rent
jelly .... Jello™
jumper, jersey .... sweater
junction .... intersection
layby .... rest stop, pull-off
level crossing .... grade crossing
lorry .... truck
licensed .... a café or restaurant
that has a license to
serve alcohol (beer and
wine only unless it's
'fully' licensed)
lift .... elevator
nappy .... diaper
note .... paper money
off-licence .... liquor store
pants .... underpants
pavement .... sidewalk
petrol .... gas

plaster .... Band-Aid or bandage
post .... mail
public school .... private school
pudding .... dessert
purse .... change purse
pushchair .... stroller
return ticket .... roundtrip ticket
rocket .... arugula
roundabout ..... traffic circle or rotary
self-catering .... accommodation
including a kitchen
single ticket .... one-way ticket
stalls ...... orchestra seats (in theater)
surgery .... doctor's office
traffic jam .... tailback
takeaway .... takeout
taxi rank .... taxi stand
ten-pin bowling .... bowling
tights .... panty-hose
T-junction .... an intersection
where one road meets
another at right angles
(making a T shape)
toilets .... restrooms
torch .... flashlight
trolley .... cart
trousers .... pants
underpass .... subway
way out .... exit
windscreen .... windshield (car)

SIGNIFICANT DATES

40,000BC	Country inhabited by the San people
26,000BC	Earliest recorded San rock art
1488	Bartholomeu Dias, the Portuguese navigator, rounds the Cape of Good Hope
1580	Sir Francis Drake rounds the Cape
1652	The Dutch establish a supply station under the command of Jan van Riebeeck
1795	The British occupy the Cape
1835–54	Afrikaner Voortrekkers leave the Cape to establish their own rule in other regions
1838	Boer-Zulu War
1866	Diamonds are discovered near the Vaal River
1886	Gold is discovered in present-day Johannesburg
1879	Anglo-Zulu War
1880–81	First Anglo-Boer War
1899–1902	Second Anglo-Boer War
1912	The South African Native National Congress is founded, later becoming the ANC
1948	The implementation of apartheid begins
1990	President F. W. de Klerk lifts the ban of the ANC
1994	ANC wins the first democratic elections with Nelson Mandela becoming president
2010	South Africa is the first African nation to host the FIFA World Cup

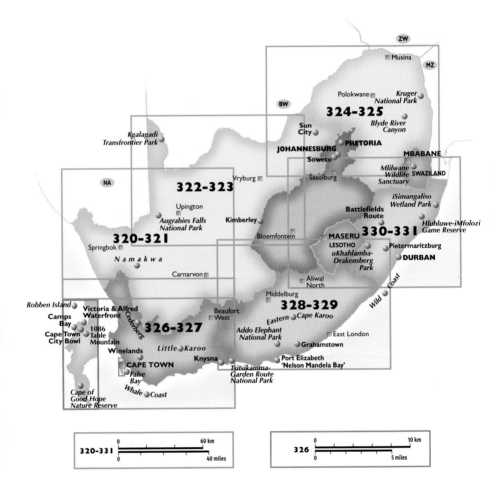

ZW

Musina

MZ

Polokwane

Kruger
National Park

BW

324-325

Blyde River
Canyon

Sun
City

PRETORIA

Kgalagadi
Transfrontier Park

JOHANNESBURG

Soweto

MBABANE

Mlilwane
Wildlife SWAZILAND
Sanctuary

NA

322-323

Vryburg

Sasolburg

iSimangaliso
Wetland Park

Upington

Kimberley

Battlefields
Route

Hluhluwe-iMfolozi
Game Reserve

Augrabies Falls
National Park

Bloemfontein

320-321

MASERU

330-331

Springbok

LESOTHO

Pietermaritzburg

Namakwa

uKhahlamba-
Drakensberg
Park

DURBAN

Carnarvon

Aliwal
North

Middelburg

Wild Coast

Robben Island

Victoria & Alfred
Waterfront

Beaufort
West

328-329

Camps
Bay

1086
Table
Mountain

326-327

Eastern

Cape Karoo

Cape Town
City Bowl

Addo Elephant
National Park

East London

Winelands

Little Karoo

Knysna

Grahamstown

CAPE TOWN

False
Bay

Tsitsikamma-
Garden Route
National Park

Port Elizabeth
'Nelson Mandela Bay'

Cape of
Good Hope
Nature Reserve

Whale Coast

| **320-331** | 0 ————————— 60 km |
| | 0 ————————— 40 miles |

| **326** | 0 ————————— 10 km |
| | 0 ————————— 5 miles |

═══ Motorway (Expressway)

⬤ Featured place of interest

━━━ National road

■ Town / Village

━━━ Regional road

▨ Built-up area

━━━ Local road

▨ National park / Nature reserve / Game reserve

━━━ Minor road

✕ Kruger entry gate

──── Railway

✗ Battlefield

▥▥▥ International boundary

✈ Airport

- - - Provincial boundary

621
▲ Height in metres

─ ─ Tropic of Capricorn

━○━ Border crossing

═══ Mountain pass

MAPS

Map references for the sights refer to the atlas pages within this section or
to the individual town plans within the regions. For example, Durban has the
reference ✚ 331 M7, indicating the page on which the map is found (331)
and the grid square in which Durban sits (M7).

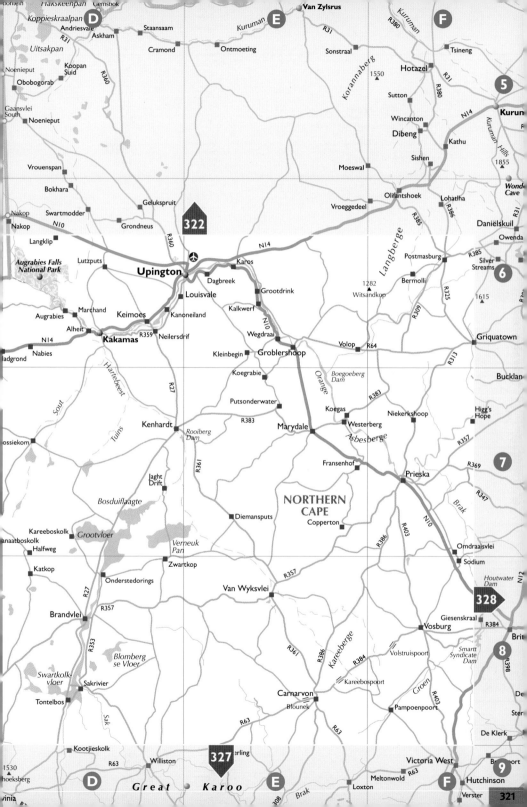

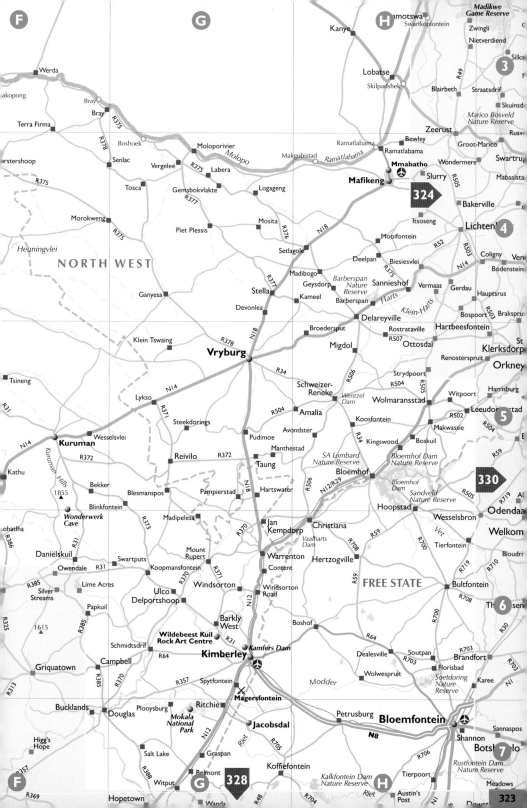

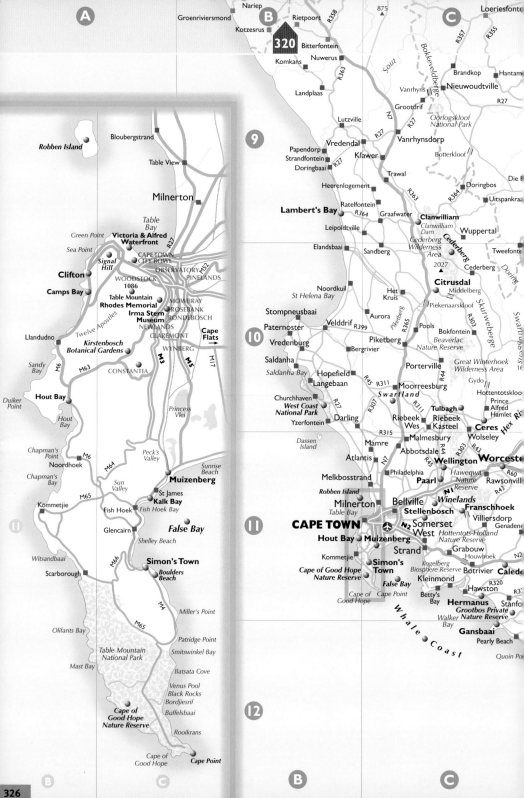

A B C

Nariep
Groenriviersmond
Kotzesrus
Rietpoort R358
875
Loeriesfonte

320
Bitterfontein
Komkans
Nuwerus
Landplaas
R363
Brandkop
Hantam
Nieuwoudtville
R27
Lutzville
N7
Grootdrif
Vanrhyns
Botterkloof
R357
R355

Bokkeveldberge
Vanrhynsdorp
Oorlogskloof
National Park
Doringbos
Die
Uitspankra

9

Papendorp
Strandfontein
Doringbaai
Vredendal
Klawer
R27
R363
R364

Heerenlogement
Trawal
Ratelfontein
Graafwater
Clanwilliam
Wuppertal
Clanwilliam
Dam
Cederberg
Wilderness
Area

Lambert's Bay
R364
Leipoldtville
Elandsbaai
Sandberg
Citrusdal
Middelberg
Cederberg
2027
Cederberg
Tweefonte

Stompneusbaai
Noordkuil
St Helena Bay
Het
Kruis
Piekenaarskloof
Beaverlac
Nature
Reserve
Skurweberge
Swartrugg-vis 1

10
Paternoster
Velddrif R399
Aurora
Piketberg
Pools
Bokfontein
Great Winterhoek
Wilderness
Area
Gydo
Vredenburg
Bergrivier
Porterville
Hottentotskloo
Prince
Alfred
Hamlet
Saldanha
Saldanha Bay
Hopefield
Langebaan
R45 R311
Moorreesburg
Swartland
Tulbagh
Ceres
Hex Ri

Churchhaven
**West Coast
National Park**
Yzerfontein
R27
Darling
R307
R315
Riebeek
Wes
Riebeek
Kasteel
Wolseley
Dassen
Island
Mamre
Malmesbury
R43
Abbotsdale
R303
Wellington
Worcest

Atlantis
N7
Philadelphia
Haweqwa
Nature
Reserve
R60
Rawsonvill
Melkbosstrand
Paarl
R43

11
Robben Island
Table Bay
Winelands
Villiersdorp
Genade

CAPE TOWN
Milnerton
Bellville
Stellenbosch
Franschhoek

Hout Bay **Muizenberg**
N2
Somerset
WEST
Hottentots-Holland
Nature Reserve
Grabouw
Houwhoek
N2

Kommetjie
Strand
**Simon's
Town**
Kogelberg
Biosphere Reserve
Botrivier
Caled
R320

Cape of Good Hope
Nature Reserve
False Bay Cape Point
Kleinmond
Betty's
Bay
Hawston
Stanfo
R3

Cape of
Good Hope
Hermanus
Grootbos Private
Nature Reserve
Walker
Bay
Gansbaai
Pearly Beach
Quoin Po

Whale Coast

12

B C

B (left inset)

Blouberegstrand
Robben Island
Table View
Milnerton

Table
Bay
**Victoria & Alfred
Waterfront**
Green Point
Sea Point
CAPE TOWN
CITY BOWL
OBSERVATORY
Clifton
Signal
Hill
WOODSTOCK
PINELANDS

Camps Bay
1086
Table Mountain
MOWBRAY
ROSEBANK
RONDEBOSCH
Rhodes Memorial
**Irma Stern
Museum**
NEWLANDS

Llandudno
Twelve Apostles
**Kirstenbosch
Botanical Gardens**
CLAREMONT
WYNBERG
**Cape
Flats**

Sandy
Bay
Duiker
Point
CONSTANTIA

Hout Bay
Hout
Bay
Princess
Vlei

Chapman's
Point
Noordhoek
Peck's
Valley
Sunrise
Beach

Chapman's
Bay
Sun
Valley
Muizenberg
St James
Kalk Bay
Fish Hoek Bay
Kommetjie

Fish Hoek
False Bay
Glencairn
Shelley Beach

Witsandbaai
Scarborough
Simon's Town
**Boulders
Beach**

Olifants Bay
Miller's Point
Table Mountain
National Park
Patridge Point
Smitswinkel Bay
Batsata Cove

Mast Bay
Venus Pool
Black Rocks
Bordjiesrif
Buffelsbaai

**Cape of
Good Hope
Nature Reserve**
Rooikrans

Cape of
Good Hope
Cape Point

A B C

This is a map of the Western Cape region of South Africa, showing the Great Karoo, Little Karoo, and Garden Route areas. Key place names visible include:

Tontelbos, Carnarvon, Blouнек, Pampoenpoo, De Klerk, Ster

Kootjieskolk, Sterling, Williston, R63, Victoria West, Brakpoort

Great Karoo, Meltonwold, R63, Hutchinson, Verster, N1

1530, hoeksberg, R63, Loxton, Biesiespoort, 9

vinia, R354, Fish, Quaggasfontein Poort, R308, Brak, R356, Saaifontein, R381, Wagenaarskraal, Three Sisters

Bonekraal, Sneeukraal, Nelspoort

Middelpos, Snyderspoort, Bastersberge, Renoster, Riet, Fraserburg, Rosedene, Renosterkop, Kariega

Roggeveldberge, 1735, R354, Hondefontein, Teekloof, 1913, Karoo National Park, Beaufort West

kwa-Karoo, ional, k, Rooipoort, R356, Sutherland, Droërivier

Bo-Wadrif, Verlatekloof, Rooikloof, 1721, Leeugamka Dam, N1, Letjiesbos, R306, Wiegnaarspoort, 328

Komsberge, Merweville, Luttig, Sout, Rietbron, SO

Koringplaas, Leeu-Gamka, N12, Seekoegat, Witteberge, Beervlei Dam, Volstruisleegte, 10

WESTERN CAPE, Hillandale, Kruidfontein, Kommandokraal, 1414, Perdepo

Buffels, Prince Albert Road, R409, Buyspoort, Willd

Laingsburg, Koup, Gamka, Prince Albert, 2152, R407, Klaarstroom, R407, Meiringspoort, Ghwarriepoor

Pieter Meintjies, Vleifontein, Groot Swartberge, Swartberg Pass, Cango Caves, Swartberg Nature Reserve, Olifants

Touws River, Matjiesfontein, Witberge, Rouxpos, Matjiesrivr, De Rust, Zaaimansda

Matroosbe, 1382, Anysberg Nature Reserve, R323, Klein-swartberge, Kraaldorings, Schoemanspoort, Oudtshoorn, Dysselsdorp, R341, Koug

Doorns, Avondrust, Ladismith, Calitzdorp, De Hoop, N12, Uniondale, Haarlem

ex River, Anysberg, R62, Rooiberg, Van Wyksdorp, Gamka Mountain Nature Reserve, R328, Kammanassie Nature Reserve, Tsitsikamma Garden Rou National Pa

R318, Boerboonfontein, Plathuis, Groot, Daskop, Prince Alfred's

Kogmanskloof, Lemoenshoek, Little Karoo, Langberg, Robinson, Outeniqua, N9, Noll, Knysna National Lake Area, R340, Garden Ro

Montagu, Barrydale, Brandrivier, Cloetes, Blanco, George, Wilderness, Knysna

bertson, Ashton, Langeberg, Garcia, Herbertsdale, Outeniqua Mountains, Pacaltsdorp, Wilderness-Garden Route National Park, Plettenberg Bay, 11

R317, Bonnievale, Marloth Nature Reserve, R62, Boosmansbos Wilderness Area, Riversdale, Du Plessis, Brandwag, Groot-Brakrivier, N2

Swellendam, R322, Heidelberg, Askraal, N2, Mossel Bay

Gregor, Bontebok National Park, Stormsvlei, Vermaaklikheid, Albertinia, Vleesbaai, Vleesbaai

R406, Riviersonderend, Breede River Valley, Malgas, R324, R322, St Sebastian Bay, Still Bay, Gouritsmond

Rietpoel, R317, R319, Ouplaas, Witsand, Cape Barracouta

Fairfield, Overberg, De Hoop Nature Reserve, Cape Infanta

Napier, Bredasdorp, R316, Skipskop

Elim, Arniston

Agulhas, ional Park, Struisbaai, L'Agulhas, Cape Agulhas

321, 328

Place	Page	Grid
Dabenoris	320	C7
Dagbreek	321	E6
Dalton	331	M7
Daniëlskuil	323	F6
Danielsrus	330	K6
Dannhauser	331	L6
Darling	326	B10
Darnall	331	M7
Daskop	327	F11
Dasville	330	K5
Davel	325	L4
De Aar	328	G8
Dealesville	323	H6
De Doorns	327	C11
Deelfontein	328	G8
Deelpan	323	H4
De Hoop	327	E11
De Klerk	328	F8
Delareyville	323	H4
Delmas	324	K4
Delportshoop	323	G6
Deneysville	330	K5
Dennilton	325	L3
Derby	324	J4
Derdepoort	324	J3
De Rust	327	F10
Despatch	328	H11
Devon	325	K4
Devonlea	323	G4
Dewetsdorp	330	J7
Dibeng	322	F5
Die Bos	326	C9
Diemansputs	321	E7
Dieput	328	G8
Dirkiesdorp	331	M5
Dlolwana	331	M6
Donkerpoort	328	H8
Donnybrook	330	L7
Dordrecht	329	J9
Doringbaai	326	B9
Doringbos	326	C9
Douglas	323	F7
Dover	330	K5
Driefontein	330	L6
Droërivier	327	F10
Dullstroom	325	M4
Dundee	331	M6
Dupleston	328	H8
Durban	331	M7
Dutywa	329	K9
Dwaal	328	G8
Dysselsdorp	327	E11
East London	329	K10
Eastpoort	328	H10
Edenburg	328	H7
Edendale	331	L7
Edenville	330	K5
Eksteenfontein	320	A7
Elandsbaai	326	B10
Elandsdrift	328	H9
Elandskraal	331	M6
Elim	327	D11
Elim Hospital	325	M2
Elliot	329	K9
Elliotdale	329	K9
Elmeston	324	K2
eMalahleni (Witbank)	325	L4
eMangusi	331	N5
eMpangeni	331	N7
eNtumeni	331	M7
Erasmia	324	K4
Ermelo	325	L4
eShowe	331	M7
Estcourt	331	L7
Evander	325	L4
Evangelina	325	L1
Evaton	324	K4
Excelsior	330	J7
Fairfield	327	D11
Fauresmith	328	H7
Felixton	331	N7
Ficksburg	330	K6
Fish Hoek	326	C11
Flagstaff	329	L8
Florisbad	323	H6
Fochville	324	J4
Fort Beaufort	328	J10
Fort Brown	328	J10
Fort Hare	329	J10
Fort Mistake	331	L6
Fort Mtombeni	331	M7
Fouriesburg	330	K6
Frankfort	330	K5
Franklin	329	L8
Franschhoek	326	C11
Fransenhof	321	E7
Fraserburg	327	E9
Ga-Mankoeng	325	L2
Gamoep	320	B7
Gansbaai	326	C12
Ganskuil	324	J3
Ganyesa	323	G4
Ga-Rankuwa	324	K4
Garies	320	B8
Garryowen	329	J9
Gege	331	M5
Geluksburg	330	L6
Gelukspruit	322	D6
Gemsbokvlakte	323	G4
Genadendal	326	C11
Geneva	330	J6
George	327	E11
Gerdau	323	H4
Germiston	324	K4
Geysdorp	323	H4
Giesenskraal	328	F8
Gilead	325	L2
Gingindlovu	331	N7
Giyani	325	M2
Gladdeklipkop	325	L2
Glencairn	326	C11
Glencoe	331	L6
Glenconnor	328	G10
Glenrock	330	J7
Gloria	325	L4
Goedemoed	328	J8
Gompies	325	L3
Gonubie	329	K10
Goodhouse	320	B7
Gouritsmond	327	E11
Graaff-Reinet	328	G9
Graafwater	326	C9
Grabouw	326	C11
Grahamstown	328	J10
Granaatboskolk	321	C7
Graskop	325	M3
Graspan	323	G7
Gravelotte	325	M2
Gregory	325	L1
Greylingstad	330	K5
Greystone	328	G10
Greytown	331	M7
Griquatown	323	F6
Groblersdal	325	L3
Groblershoop	321	E6
Groenriviersmond	320	B8
Groenvlei	331	M5
Groesbeek	324	K2
Grondneus	322	D6
Groot-Brakrivier	327	E11
Grootdrif	326	C9
Grootdrink	321	E6
Groot-Marico	324	J4
Grootmis	320	A7
Grootpan	324	J4
Grootspruit	331	M5
Grootvlei	330	K5
Gumtree	330	K6
Haakdoring	325	L3
Haarlem	328	F11
Haenertsburg	325	M2
Haga-Haga	329	K10
Halcyon Drift	329	K8
Halfweg	321	D7
Ha-Magoro	325	M2
Hamburg	329	J10
Hankey	328	G11
Hanover	328	G8
Hanover Road	328	G8
Hantam	326	C9
Harding	329	L8
Harrisburg	330	J5
Harrismith	330	L6
Hartbeesfontein	330	J5
Hartbeespoort	324	K4
Hartswater	323	G5
Hattingspruit	331	L6
Hauptrus	324	J4
Hawston	326	C11
Hazyview	325	M3
Hectorspruit	325	N4
Heerenlogement	326	C9
Heidelberg	324	K4
Heidelberg	327	D11
Heilbron	330	K5
Helpmekaar	331	M6
Helvetia	330	J7
Hendriksdal	325	M3
Hendrina	325	L4
Hennenman	330	J6
Herbertsdale	327	E11
Hermanus	326	C11
Hermanusdorings	324	K2
Herschel	329	J8
Hertzogville	323	H6
Het Kruis	326	C10
Heuningspruit	330	J5
Heydon	328	G9
Hibberdene	331	M8
Higg's Hope	323	F7
Highflats	329	L8
Hildreth Ridge	325	M2
Hillandale	327	D10
Himeville	330	L7
Hlabisa	331	N6
Hlobane	331	M6
Hlotse	330	K6
Hluhluwe	331	N6
Hobhouse	330	J7
Hoedspruit	325	M3
Hofmeyr	328	H9
Hogsback	329	J10
Holbank	325	M4
Holme Park	324	K3
Holmedene	330	L5
Holy Cross	329	L9
Hondefontein	327	E9
Hondeklipbaai	320	B8
Hoopstad	323	H5
Hopefield	326	B10
Hopetown	328	G7
Hotazel	322	F5
Hottent-otskloof	326	C10

Name	Page	Grid	Name	Page	Grid	Name	Page	Grid	Name	Page	Grid
Hout Bay	326	B11	Kendal	325	L4	Kriel	325	L4	Logageng	323	G4
Houtkraal	328	G8	Kendrew	328	G10	Kromdraai	325	L4	Lohatlha	323	F6
Howick	331	L7	Kenhardt	321	D7	Kroonstad	330	J5	Loskop	330	L7
Humansdorp	328	G11	Kenton on Sea	328	J11	Krugers	328	H7	Lothair	325	M4
Hutchinson	328	F9	Kestell	330	K6	Krugersdorp	324	K4	Louis Trichardt	325	M1
			Kidd's Beach	329	J10	Kruidfontein	327	E10	Louisvale	321	D6
iMpendle	330	L7	Kimberley	323	G6	Kruisfontein	328	G11	Louwsburg	331	M5
iNanda	331	M7	Kingsburgh	331	M8	Kuboes	320	A6	Loxton	327	E9
Indwe	329	J9	Kingscote	330	L8	Ku-Mayima	329	K9	Luckhoff	328	G7
Ingogo	331	L5	Kingsley	331	M6	Kuruman	323	F5	Lundin's Nek	329	J8
iNgwavuma	331	N5	Kingswood	323	H5	KwaDukuza			Luneberg	331	M5
iSipingo	331	M8	King William's			(Stanger)	331	M7	Lusikisiki	329	L9
Iswepe	331	M5	Town	329	J10	Kwaggaskop	325	L4	Luttig	327	E10
Itsoseng	324	H4	Kinirapoort	329	K8	KwaMashu	331	M7	Lutzputs	321	D6
iXopo	331	L8	Kinross	325	L4	KwaMbonambi	331	N6	Lutzville	326	B9
			Kirkwood	328	H10	Kwamhlanga	325	K3	Lykso	323	G5
Jacobsdal	323	G7	Klaarstroom	327	F10						
Jagersfontein	328	H7	Klawer	326	C9	Labera	323	G4	Maartenshoop	325	M3
Jaght Drift	321	D7	Kleinbegin	321	E6	Ladismith	327	E11	Maasstroom	324	K1
Jambila	325	M4	Kleinmond	326	C11	Lady Frere	329	J9	Mabaalstad	324	J3
Jamestown	329	J8	Kleinpoort	328	G10	Lady Grey	329	J8	Mabaalstad	324	J4
Jammerdrif	330	J7	Kleinsee	320	A7	Ladybrand	330	J7	Mabeskraal	324	J3
Jan Kempdorp	323	G6	Klein Tswaing	323	G5	Ladysmith	331	L6	Mabopane	324	K4
Jansenville	328	G10	Klerksdorp	330	J5	L'Agulhas	327	D12	Mabula	324	K3
Janseput	324	K2	Klerkskraal	324	J4	Lahlangubo	329	K8	Machadodorp	325	M4
Jeffreys Bay	328	G11	Klipfontein	328	H10	Laingsburg	327	D10	Macleantown	329	J10
Jeppe's Reef	325	N4	Klipplaat	328	G10	Lambert's Bay	326	B9	Maclear	329	K8
Joel's Drift	330	K6	Kliprand	320	C8	Lammerkop	325	L4	Madadeni	331	L6
Johannesburg	324	K4	Klipspruit	325	M3	Landplaas	326	B9	Madibogo	323	H4
Joubertina	328	G11	Knapdaar	328	H8	Langberg	327	E11	Madipelesa	323	G6
Jozini	331	N5	Knysna	327	F11	Langebaan	326	B10	Mafeteng	330	J7
			Koegas	321	E7	Langklip	321	D6	Mafikeng	323	H4
Kaapmuiden	325	N4	Koegrabie	321	E7	Lavumisa	331	N5	Mafube	330	K8
Kaapsehoop	325	M4	Koffiefontein	323	G7	Leandra	325	L4	Mafutseni	325	N4
Kakamas	321	D6	Koingnaas	320	B8	Lebowa Kgomo	325	L2	Magaliesburg	324	J4
Kalk Bay	326	C11	Kokstad	329	L8	Leeudoringstad	323	H5	Magudu	331	N5
Kalkbank	325	L2	Komaggas	320	B7	Leeu-Gamka	327	E10	Magusheni	329	L8
Kalkwerf	321	E6	Komatipoort	325	N4	Leeuport	324	K3	Mahlangasi	331	N6
Kamberg	330	L7	Komga	329	K10	Lehlohonolo	330	K8	Mahwelereng	325	L2
Kameel	323	H4	Komkans	326	B9	Leipoldtville	326	B9	Maizefield	330	L5
Kamiesberg	320	B8	Kommandokraal	327	F10	Lekfontein	329	J10	Makwassie	323	H5
Kamieskroon	320	B8	Kommetjie	326	B11	Lekkersing	320	A7	Malaita	325	L3
Kammiebos	328	G11	Koopan Suid	322	D5	Lemoenshoek	327	D11	Maleoskop	325	L3
Kanoneiland	321	D6	Koopmansfontein	323	G6	Lephalale	324	K2	Malgas	327	D11
Karee	330	J6	Koosfontein	323	H5	Letjiesbos	327	E10	Malmesbury	326	C11
Kareeboskolk	321	D7	Kootjieskolk	327	D9	Letsitele	325	M2	Maloma	331	N5
Kareedouw	328	G11	Koperspruit	324	K1	Libertas	330	K6	Mamaila	325	M2
Karkams	320	B8	Koppies	330	J5	Libode	329	K9	Mamre	326	C11
Karos	321	E6	Koringplaas	327	D10	Lichtenburg	324	H4	Mandini	331	M7
Kathu	323	F5	Koster	324	J4	Limburg	325	L2	Manthestad	323	G5
Katkop	321	D8	Kotzesrus	320	B8	Lime Acres	323	F6	Mantsonyane	330	K7
Keate's Drift	331	M7	Koukraal	328	J8	Lindley	330	K6	Manzini	331	N5
Kei Mouth	329	K10	Koup	327	E10	Lindley	328	J8	Mapumulo	331	M7
Kei Road	329	J10	Kraaldorings	327	E10	Llandudno	326	B11	Marakabei	330	K7
Keimoes	321	D6	Kraankuil	328	G7	Lobamba	325	M4	Marble Hall	325	L3
Keiskamma-hoek	329	J10	Kransfontein	330	K6	Lochiel	325	M4	Marchand	321	D6
Kempton Park	324	K4	Kranskop	331	M7	Lofter	328	H8	Margate	329	L8

Place	Map	Grid	Place	Map	Grid	Place	Map	Grid	Place	Map	Grid
Maricosdraai	324	J3	Modjadjiskloof	325	M2	Nariep	320	B8	Olifantshoek	322	F6
Marite	325	M3	Moeswal	322	E5	Ndumo	331	N5	Olyfberg	325	M2
Marke	324	K2	Mogalakwe	325	K2	Neilersdrif	321	D6	Omdraaisvlei	321	F7
Marnitz	324	K1	Mogwadi	325	L2	Nelson Mandela			Onderstedorings	321	D8
Maropeng	324	K4	Mohales Hoek	330	J8	Bay	328	H11	Ons Hoop	324	K2
Marquard	330	J6	Mokamole	324	K2	Nelspoort	327	F9	Onseepkans	320	C6
Marydale	321	E7	Mokhotlong	330	L7	New England	329	J8	Ontmoeting	322	E5
Maseru	330	J7	Mokopane	325	L2	New Hanover	331	M7	Oorwinning	325	M1
Mashashane	325	L2	Moloporivier	323	G4	New Machavie	330	J5	Oostermoed	324	J3
Mashishing/			Molteno	328	H9	Newcastle	331	L6	Orania	328	G7
Lydenburg	325	M3	Monk's Cowl	330	L7	Ngcobo	329	K9	Oranjefontein	324	K2
Masisi	325	M1	Montagu	327	D11	Ngobeni	331	M6	Oranjerivier	328	G7
Matatiele	329	K8	Mooi River	331	L7	Ngome	331	M6	Oranjevill	330	K5
Matavhelo	325	M1	Mooifontein	323	H4	Ngqamakhwe	329	K9	Orkney	330	J5
Matjiesfontein	327	D10	Mooketsi	325	M2	Ngqeleni	329	K9	oSizweni	331	M6
Matjiesriv	327	E10	Mookgophong	325	K3	Ngqungu	329	K9	Ottosdal	323	H5
Matlabas	324	K2	Moorreesburg	326	C10	Nhlangano	331	M5	Oudtshoorn	327	E11
Matlala	325	L2	Morebeng	325	M2	Niekerkshoop	321	F7	Ouplaas	327	D11
Matroosbe	327	D10	Morgenzon	330	L5	Nietverdiend	324	H3	Oviston	328	H8
Mavamba	325	M1	Morija	330	J7	Nieu-Bethesda	328	G9	Owendale	323	F6
Mazeppa Bay	329	K10	Morokweng	323	F4	Nieuwoudtville	326	C9	Oxbow	330	K6
Mbabane	325	M4	Morristown	329	J9	Nigel	324	K4	Oyster Bay	328	G11
Mbazwana	331	N5	Moshesh's Ford	329	K8	Nigramoep	320	B7			
Mbombela/			Mosita	323	G4	Nkambak	325	M2	Paarl	326	C11
Nelspruit	325	M4	Mossel Bay	327	E11	Nkau	330	K7	Pacaltsdorp	327	E11
Mbotyi	329	L9	Mossiesdal	325	L3	Nkomo	325	M2	Paddock	329	L8
McGregor	327	D11	Motetema	325	L3	Nkwalini	331	N6	Pafuri	325	N1
Mdantsane	329	J10	Mount Ayliff	329	L8	Nobhokwe	329	K9	Palala	324	K2
Meadows	330	J7	Mount Fletcher	329	K8	Noenieput	322	D5	Palmerton	329	L9
Melkbosstrand	326	C11	Mount Frere	329	K8	Noll	327	F11	Palmietfontein	329	J8
Melmoth	331	M6	Mount Rupert	323	G6	Nondweni	331	M6	Pampierstad	323	G5
Meltonwold	327	F9	Mount Stewart	328	G10	Nongoma	331	N6	Pampoenpoort	321	F8
Memel	330	L5	Moyeni	329	J8	Noordhoek	326	B11	Panbult	331	M5
Merindol	324	J4	Mpemvana	331	M5	Noordkuil	326	B10	Papendorp	326	B9
Merriman	328	F8	Mphaki	330	K8	Normandien	331	L6	Papkuil	323	F6
Merweville	327	E10	Mpolweni	331	M7	Northam	324	J3	Park Rynie	331	M8
Mesa	324	J4	Mpumalanga	331	M7	Nottingham Road	331	L7	Parys	330	J5
Mesklip	320	B7	Mt Moorosi	330	K8	Noupoort	328	G8	Patensie	328	G11
Meyerton	324	K4	Mthatha	329	K9	Nqabarha	329	K10	Paternoster	326	B10
Mgwali	329	J10	Mtkonjeneni	331	M6	Nqutu	331	M6	Paterson	328	H10
Mhlosheni	331	M5	Mtubatuba	331	N6	Nsoko	331	N5	Paul Roux	330	K6
Mica	325	M2	Mtwalume	331	M8	Ntabankulu	329	L8	Paulpietersburg	331	M5
Middelburg	325	L4	Muden	331	M7	Ntseshe	329	K9	Pearly Beach	326	C12
Middelburg	328	G9	Muizenberg	326	C11	Ntshilini	329	L9	Pearston	328	H10
Middelfontein	324	K3	Munster	329	L8	Ntywenke	329	K8	Peddie	329	J10
Middelpos	327	D9	Munyu	329	K9	Nutfield	325	L3	Peka	330	K7
Middelwit	324	J3	Murchison	325	M2	Nuwerus	326	B9	Pella	320	C7
Middleton	328	H10	Murraysburg	328	F9	Nyokana	329	K10	Penge	325	M3
Migdol	323	H5	Musina	325	M1				Perdekop	330	L5
Miller	328	G10	Mynfontein	328	G8	Oatlands	328	G10	Petersburg	328	G9
Millvale	324	J4				Obobogorab	322	D5	Petrus Steyn	330	K5
Milnerton	326	C11	Nababeep	320	B7	Odendaalsrus	330	J6	Petrusburg	323	H7
Mirage	330	J5	Nabies	321	D6	Ofcolaco	325	M2	Petrusville	328	G7
Mkambati	329	L9	Nakop	322	D6	Ogies	325	L4	Phalaborwa	325	M2
Mkuze	331	N6	Namakgale	325	M2	Okiep	320	B7	Philadelphia	326	C11
Mmabatho	323	H4	Namies	320	C7	Old Bunting	329	L9	Philippolis	328	H8
Modimolle	324	K3	Napier	327	D11	Old Morley	329	K9	Philippolis Road	328	H8

Place	Page	Grid
Sun City	324	J3
Sunland	328	H11
Sutherland	327	D10
Sutton	322	F5
Swaershoek	328	H10
Swartberg	329	L8
Swartkops	328	H11
Swartmodder	322	D6
Swartplaas	324	J4
Swartputs	323	G6
Swartruggens	324	J4
Swartwater	324	K1
Swellendam	327	D11
Swempoort	329	J8
Swinburne	330	L6
Syfergat	328	H9
Table View	326	C11
Tafelberg	328	H9
Taleni	329	K9
Tarkastad	328	H9
Taung	323	G5
Temba	324	K3
Tembisa	324	K4
Terra Firma	323	F3
Teviot	328	H9
Teyateyaneng	330	K7
Teza	331	N6
Thaba Bosiu	330	K7
Thaba Chitja	329	K8
Thaba Nchu	330	J7
Thaba Tseka	330	K7
Thabazimbi	324	J3
The Downs	325	M2
The Haven	329	K9
The Ranch	331	M7
Theron	330	J6
Theunissen	330	J6
Thoyoyandou	325	M1
Three Sisters	327	F9
Tierfontein	323	H6
Tierpoort	323	H7
Tlokoeng	330	K7
Tolwe	324	K1
Tom Burke	324	K1
Tompi Seleka	325	L3
Tongaat	331	M7
Tontelbos	321	D8
Tosca	323	G4
Touws Rivier	327	D10
Trawal	326	C9
Trichard	325	L4
Trichardtsdal	325	M2
Trompsburg	328	H7
Tshakhuma	325	M1
Tshaneni	325	N4
Tshani	329	L9
Tshipise	325	M1
Tsineng	323	F5
Tsoeli	330	K8
Tsolo	329	K9
Tsomo	329	J9
Tugela Ferry	331	M6
Tugela Mouth	331	M7
Tuinplaas	325	L3
Tulbagh	326	C10
Twee Rivieren	322	D4
Tweefontein	326	C10
Tweeling	330	K5
Tweesprui	330	J7
Tylden	329	J9
Tzaneen	325	M2
Ubombo	331	N5
Ugie	329	K9
Uitenhage	328	H11
Uitkyk	320	C7
Uitspankraal	326	C9
Ulco	323	G6
uLundi	331	M6
uMbogintwini	331	M8
uMkomaas	331	M8
uMlazi	331	M8
Umtentu	329	L9
uMtentweni	331	M8
Umzimkulu	329	L8
uMzinto	331	M8
Underberg	330	L7
Uniondale	327	F11
Upington	321	E6
Usutu	325	K1
Utrecht	331	M5
uVongo	329	L8
Vaalplaas	325	L4
Vaalwater	324	K2
Valsrivier	330	K6
Van Reenen	330	L6
Van Wyksdorp	327	E11
Van Wyksvlei	321	E8
Van Zylsrus	322	E5
Vanalphensvlei	325	K3
Vanderbijlpark	330	K5
Vanderkloof	328	G7
Vandyksdrif	325	L4
Vanrhynsdorp	326	C9
Vanstadensrus	330	J7
Vant's Drift	331	M6
Vegkop	330	K5
Velddrif	326	B10
Ventersburg	330	J6
Ventersdorp	324	J4
Venterstad	328	H8
Vereeniging	330	K5
Verena	325	L4
Vergeleë	323	G4
Verkeerdevlei	330	J6
Verkykerskop	330	L6
Vermaaklikheid	327	D11
Vermaas	323	H4
Verster	328	F9
Verulam	331	M7
Victoria West	327	F9
Viedgesville	329	K9
Vierfontein	330	J5
Viljoensdrif	330	K5
Viljoenskroon	330	J5
Villa Nora	324	K2
Villiers	330	K5
Villiersdorp	326	C11
Vineyard	329	J8
Virginia	330	J6
Visrivier	328	H9
Vivo	325	L1
Vleesbaai	327	E11
Vleifontein	327	D10
Volksrust	331	L5
Volop	321	E6
Volstruisleegte	328	F10
Vorstershoop	323	F4
Vosburg	321	F8
Vrede	330	L5
Vredefort	330	J5
Vredenburg	326	B10
Vredendal	326	B9
Vroeggedeel	322	F6
Vrouenspan	322	D5
Vryburg	323	G5
Vryheid	331	M6
Wagenaarskraal	327	F9
Wakkerstroom	331	M5
Wallekraal	320	B8
Wanda	328	G7
Warburton	325	M4
Warden	330	L6
Warrenton	323	G6
Wasbank	331	L6
Waterford	328	G10
Waterkloof	328	H8
Waterpoort	325	L1
Waterval-Boven	325	M4
Wavecrest	329	K10
Weenen	331	L7
Wegdraai	321	E6
Welgeleë	330	J6
Welkom	330	J6
Wellington	326	C11
Welverdiend	322	C4
Wepener	330	J7
Wesley	329	J10
Wesselsbron	330	J6
Wesselsvlei	323	F5
Westerberg	321	E7
Westleigh	330	J5
Westonaria	324	K4
White River	325	M3
Whites	330	J6
Whitmore	329	K9
Whittlesea	329	J9
Wiegnaarspoort	328	F10
Wilderness	327	F11
Williston	327	D9
Willowmore	328	F10
Willowvale	329	K9
Winburg	330	J6
Wincanton	322	F5
Windsorton	323	G6
Windsorton Road	323	G6
Winkelpos	330	J5
Witkop	328	J8
Witmos	328	H10
Witpoort	323	H5
Witput	323	G7
Witsand	327	D11
Witteklip	328	H11
Witwater	320	B8
Wolmaransstad	323	H5
Wolseley	326	C10
Wolwehoek	330	K5
Wolwespruit	323	H6
Wonderkop	330	J6
Wondermere	324	J4
Woodlands	328	G11
Worcester	326	C11
Wuppertal	326	C9
Xolobe	329	J9
Yzerfontein	326	B10
Zaaimansdal	328	F11
Zastron	330	J8
Zebediela	325	L3
Zeerust	324	H3
Zunckels	330	L7
Zwartkop	321	D8
Zwelitsha	329	J10
Zwingli	324	H3

PICTURES

The Automobile Association would like to thank the following photographers, companies and picture libraries for their assistance in the publication of this book.

Abbreviations for the picture credits are as follows: (t) top; (b) bottom; (c) centre; (l) left; (r) right; (AA) AA World Travel Library.

2 AA/C Sawyer;
3i South African Tourism;
3ii AA/C Sawyer;
3iii South African Tourism;
3iv AA/C Sawyer;
4 Fraser Hall/Robert Harding;
5 South African Tourism;
6 South African Tourism;
7bl South African Tourism;
7br AA/C Sawyer;
8 AA/S McBride;
9 AA/P Kenward;
11t South African Tourism;
11b AA/C Sawyer;
13(1) South African Tourism;
13(2) South African Tourism;
13(3) South African Tourism;
13(4) South African Tourism;
13(5) South African Tourism;
13(6) South African Tourism;
13(7) AA/S McBride;
13(8) South African Tourism;
13(9) South African Tourism;
14(10) South African Tourism;
14(11) South African Tourism;
14(12) South African Tourism;
14(13) South African Tourism;
14(14) South African Tourism;
14(15) South African Tourism;
14(16) South African Tourism;
14(17) South African Tourism;
14(18) South African Tourism;
15(19) South African Tourism;
15(20) South African Tourism;
15(21) South African Tourism;
15(22) South African Tourism;
15(23) South African Tourism;
15(24) South African Tourism;
15(25) South African Tourism;
15(26) South African Tourism;
15(27) South African Tourism;
16(28) South African Tourism;
16(29) South African Tourism;
16(30) South African Tourism;
16(31) South African Tourism;
16(32) South African Tourism;
16(33) AA/C Sawyer;
17 AA/P Kenward;

18 South African Tourism;
19bl AA/C Sawyer;
19br AA/S McBride;
20 AA/C Hampton;
21t AA/C Sawyer;
21b South African Tourism;
22 AA/S McBride;
23tl AA/C Hampton;
23tr Mala Mala Game Reserve;
24 © AfriPics.com/Alamy;
25bl AA/C Sawyer;
25br © Werner Dieterich/Alamy;
26 South African Airways;
27l South African Tourism;
27r © Sipa Press/Rex Features;
28l Penguin Group (USA);
28r AA/C Sawyer;
29 AA/C Sawyer;
30 © Stapleton Collection/Corbis;
31t South African Tourism;
31b Gallo Images/Corbis;
32 Mary Evans Picture Library;
33bl Sipa Press/Rex Features;
33br Mary Evans Picture Library;
34 The Art Archive/National Army Museum London;
35t © Bob Thomas/Popperfoto/Getty Images;
35b Spion Kop, 1900, chromolitho by Neuman/Africana Museum, Johannesburg, South Africa/Bridgeman Art Library;
36 AA/C Sawyer;
37t © Carlo Mydans/Time & Life Pictures/Getty Images;
37b Mary Evans Picture Library;
38 AA/C Sawyer;
39bl © William F. Campbell/Time & Life Pictures/Getty Images;
39br © Mark Peters/Getty Images;
40 Sipa Press/Rex Features;
41t © Per-Anders Pettersson/Getty Images;
41b ©William F. Campbell/Time & Life Pictures/Getty Images;
42l © Wirelmage/Getty Images;
42r Anna Zieminski/AFP/Getty Images;
43 AA/C Sawyer;
44 AA/C Sawyer;
45 Digital Vision;
46 AA/C Sawyer;
47 AA/C Sawyer;
48 AA/C Sawyer;
50 AA/C Sawyer;
53 Cape Town Station, owned and managed by the Passenger Rail Agency of South Africa (PRASA)
55 AA/S McBride;
57tl AA/C Sawyer;
57tr AA/C Sawyer;
58 AA/C Sawyer;

59 AA/C Sawyer;
60 AA/C Sawyer;
62 AA/C Sawyer;
63 AA/C Sawyer;
64 AA/C Sawyer;
65tl AA/C Sawyer;
65tr AA/C Sawyer;
66 AA/C Sawyer;
67 AA/C Sawyer;
69t AA/C Sawyer;
69b AA/C Sawyer;
70tl AA/C Sawyer;
70bl AA/C Sawyer;
71tr AA/C Sawyer;
71br AA/C Sawyer;
72 AA/C Sawyer;
73bl AA/C Sawyer;
73br AA/C Sawyer;
74 AA/C Sawyer;
75 AA/C Sawyer;
76 AA/C Sawyer;
77 AA/C Sawyer;
78 AA/C Sawyer;
79 AA/C Sawyer;
80 AA/C Sawyer;
81 South African Tourism;
82 AA/C Sawyer;
83 AA/C Sawyer;
84 AA/C Sawyer;
87 AA/C Sawyer;
88 AA/C Sawyer;
89 South African Tourism;
90 AA/C Sawyer;
93 AA/C Sawyer;
94 AA/C Sawyer;
97 AA/C Sawyer;
98 © Chris Bradley/Axiom Photographic Agency/Getty Images;
100 AA/C Sawyer;
101 AA/C Sawyer;
102 AA/C Sawyer;
103 South African Tourism;
104 AA/C Sawyer;
105 AA/C Sawyer;
106 AA/C Sawyer;
107 AA/C Sawyer;
108 AA/C Sawyer;
109t AA/C Sawyer;
109b AA/C Sawyer;
110 AA/C Sawyer;
111 South African Tourism;
112 AA/C Sawyer;
113 South African Tourism;
114 Simonsig Wine Estate;
116 AA/C Sawyer;
117 AA/C Sawyer;
118 AA/C Sawyer;
119 AA/C Sawyer;
120 AA/C Sawyer;
122 © Hein von Horsten/Gallo Images/Getty Images;

123 © Westend 61 GmbH/Alamy;
124 AA/C Sawyer;
126 AA/C Sawyer;
127 AA/C Sawyer;
128 AA/C Sawyer;
131 AA/C Sawyer;
132 AA/C Sawyer;
133 South African Tourism;
134 AA/C Sawyer;
136 AA/C Sawyer;
139 AA/C Sawyer;
140 AA/C Sawyer;
142 AA/C Sawyer;
143 AA/C Sawyer;
144 South African Tourism;
145 AA/C Sawyer;
146t AA/C Sawyer;
146bl AA/C Sawyer;
147 AA/C Sawyer;
148 AA/C Sawyer;
149 AA/C Sawyer;
150 AA/C Sawyer;
151 AA/C Sawyer;
152 AA/C Sawyer;
153 AA/C Sawyer;
154 South African Tourism;
156 Imagestate;
158 AA/C Sawyer;
160 AA/S McBride;
162 Ann and Steve Toon/ Robert Harding;
163 South African Tourism;
164 South African Tourism;
165t AA/C Sawyer;
165b AA/C Sawyer;
166 AA/S McBride;
167t AA/P Kenward;
167b AA/P Kenward;
168tl AA/S McBride;
168tr AA/S McBride;
169 South African Tourism;
170 South African Tourism;
171 AA/R Strange;
172 AA/S McBride;
173 South African Tourism;
174 AA/S McBride;
175 AA/S McBride;
176 AA/S McBride;
177t AA/S McBride;
177b AA/S McBride;
178 AA/S McBride;
179 AA/S McBride;
180 AA/S McBride;
181t © AfriPics.com/Alamy;
181b AA/S McBride;
182 AA/S McBride;
184 AA/S McBride;
186 Imagestate;
189 AA/S McBride;
191 AA/S McBride;

192 AA/C Hampton;
194 AA/S McBride;
195 AA/S McBride;
196 AA/C Sawyer;
197 AA/S McBride;
198 AA/S McBride;
199 South African Tourism;
201l South African Tourism;
201r AA/S McBride;
202l AA/C Sawyer;
202r AA/C Sawyer;
203 AA/S McBride;
204t South African Tourism;
204b AA/S McBride;
205l South African Tourism;
205r AA/S McBride;
206 AA/S McBride;
208 South African Tourism;
210 AA/S McBride;
211 AA/S McBride;
212 Photodisc;
214 Rissington Inn;
216 AA/S McBride;
218 AA/S McBride;
220 AA/S McBride;
221 AA/C Sawyer;
222 AA/C Sawyer;
223 AA/S McBride;
224 © José Fuste Raga/zefa/Corbis;
225l AA/S McBride;
225r AA/P Kenward;
226l AA/S McBride;
226r ©altrendo travel/Getty Images;
227 AA/S McBride;
228 South African Tourism;
229 AA/S McBride;
230 AA/S McBride;
231 AA/C Sawyer;
232 AA/S McBride;
233 AA/S McBride;
234 AA/S McBride;
236 AA/P Kenward;
238 De Oude Kraal;
240 AA/S McBride;
242 AA/S McBride;
244 AA/S McBride;
245 South African Tourism;
246 South African Tourism;
247 AA/S McBride;
248 AA/C Sawyer;
249l AA/C Sawyer;
249r AA/C Sawyer;
250 © Images of Africa Photobank/ Alamy'
251t AA/P Kenward;
251b AA/S McBride;
252 South African Tourism;
253 South African Tourism;
254t South African Tourism;
254b South African Tourism;

255 AA/S McBride;
256 AA/S McBride;
257 © Ariadne Van Zandbergen/Alamy;
258 South African Tourism;
259 South African Tourism;
260 South African Tourism;
261 Photolibrary Group;
262 AA/S McBride;
264 Photodisc;
266 AA/S McBride;
268 AA/S McBride;
270 © Frans Lemmens/The Image Bank/Getty Images;
271 AA/S McBride;
272 AA/S McBride;
273 AA/S McBride;
274 AA/S McBride;
275 AA/S McBride;
276 AA/S McBride;
277 AA/S McBride;
278 AA/S McBride;
279 AA/S McBride;
280 AA/S McBride;
282 AA/S McBride;
284 AA/S McBride;
285 AA/C Sawyer;
286 AA/C Sawyer;
288 AA/S McBride;
289 AA/C Sawyer;
291 AA/S McBride;
292 AA/C Sawyer;
294 AA/S McBride;
295 AA/S McBride;
296 AA/C Sawyer;
298 AA/S McBride;
299l AA/C Sawyer;
299r AA/S McBride;
300 AA/S McBride;
302 AA/C Sawyer;
304 Spiers Music Festival;
305 AA/C Sawyer;
306 AA/S McBride;
308 AA/C Sawyer;
309 AA/P Kenward;
310 Sabi Sabi;
311t AA/C Sawyer;
311b Sabi Sabi;
312 South African Tourism;
313 Sabi Sabi;
314 Outpost;
315 AA/C Sawyer;
319 AA/C Sawyer

Every effort has been made to trace the copyright holders, and we apologise in advance for any unintentional omissions or errors. We would be pleased to apply any corrections in a following edition of this publication

CREDITS

Series editor
Sheila Hawkins

Project editor
Dorothy Stannard

Design
Tracey Butler

Picture research
Liz Allen

Image retouching and repro
Jacqueline Street

Mapping
Maps produced by the Mapping Services
Department of AA Publishing

Main contributors
Lizzie Williams, Matthew Buckland, Peter Joyce, Francisca
Kellet, Richard Whitaker

Updater
Zoe Ross

Production
Lorraine Taylor

Published by AA Publishing, a trading name of AA Media Limited, whose registered office is
Fanum House, Basing View, Basingstoke, RG21 4EA. Registered number 06112600.
A CIP catalogue record for this book is available from the British Library.

ISBN 978-0-7495-6236-6

KeyGuide is a registered trademark in Australia and is used under licence.
Colour separation by Digital Department AA Publishing
Printed and bound by Leo Paper Products, China

We have tried to ensure accuracy in this guide, but things do change, so please let us know if you have any comments at
travelguides@theAA.com.

A04600
Maps in this title produced from map data © New Holland Publishing (South Africa) (PTY) Limited 2009
and © Footprint Handbooks Limited 2004
Transport maps © Communicarta Ltd, UK
Weather chart statistics supplied by Weatherbase © Copyright 2006 Canty and Associates, LLC.

Find out more about AA Publishing and the wide range of travel publications and services the AA provides by visiting our website at
theAA.com/shop

Thank you for buying this KeyGuide. Your comments and opinions are very important to us, so please help us to improve our travel guides by taking a few minutes to complete this questionnaire.

You do not need a stamp (unless posted outside the UK). If you do not want to cut this page from your guide, then photocopy it or write your answers on a plain sheet of paper.

Send to: **KeyGuide Editor, AA World Travel Guides**
FREEPOST SCE 4598, Basingstoke RG21 4GY
Email: **travelguides@theaa.com**

Find out more about AA Publishing and the wide range of travel publications the AA provides by visiting our website at www.theAA.com/shop

ABOUT THIS GUIDE

Which KeyGuide did you buy? ....

Where did you buy it? ....

When? .... month ....year

Why did you choose this AA KeyGuide?
☐ Price ☐ AA Publication
☐ Used this series before; title
☐ Cover ☐ Other (please state)

Please let us know how helpful the following features of the guide were to you by circling the appropriate category: very helpful (VH), helpful (H) or little help (LH)

Size	VH	H	LH
Layout	VH	H	LH
Photos	VH	H	LH
Excursions	VH	H	LH
Entertainment	VH	H	LH
Hotels	VH	H	LH
Maps	VH	H	LH
Practical info	VH	H	LH
Restaurants	VH	H	LH
Shopping	VH	H	LH
Walks	VH	H	LH
Sights	VH	H	LH
Transport info	VH	H	LH

What was your favourite sight, attraction or feature listed in the guide?

Page...................Please give your reason ....
....

Which features in the guide could be changed or improved? Or are there any other comments you would like to make?

....

ABOUT YOU

Name (Mr/Mrs/Ms)...

Address ....

....

....

....

Postcode.. Daytime tel nos ....

Email...
Please only give us your mobile phone number/email if you wish to hear from us about other products and services from the AA and partners by text or mms.

Which age group are you in?
Under 25 ☐   25–34 ☐   35–44 ☐   45–54 ☐   55+ ☐

How many trips do you make a year?
Less than 1 ☐   1 ☐   2 ☐   3 or more ☐

ABOUT YOUR TRIP

Are you an AA member?   Yes ☐ No ☐

When did you book? .... month .... year

When did you travel?...............month .... year

Reason for your trip?   Business ☐   Leisure ☐

How many nights did you stay? ....

How did you travel?   Individual ☐   Couple ☐   Family ☐   Group ☐

Did you buy any other travel guides for your trip? ....

If yes, which ones? ....

Thank you for taking the time to complete this questionnaire. Please send it to us as soon as possible, and remember, you do not need a stamp (unless posted outside the UK).

Titles in the KeyGuide series:
Argentina, Australia, Barcelona, Berlin, Brazil, Britain, Brittany, Canada, China, Costa Rica, Croatia, Florence and Tuscany, France, Germany, Ireland, Italy, London, Mallorca, Mexico, New York, New Zealand, Normandy, Paris, Portugal, Prague, Provence and the Côte d'Azur, Rome, Scotland, South Africa, Spain, Thailand, Venice, Vietnam, Western European Cities.

The information we hold about you will be used to provide the products and services requested and for identification, account administration, analysis, and fraud/loss prevention purposes. More details about how that information is used is in our privacy statement, which you'll find under the heading "Personal Information" in our terms and conditions and on our website: www.theAA.com. Copies are also available from us by post, by contacting the Data Protection Manager at AA, Fanum House, Basing View, Basingstoke, Hampshire RG21 4EA.

We may want to contact you about other products and services provided by us, or our partners (by mail, telephone, email) but please tick the box if you DO NOT wish to hear about such products and services from us. ☐

AA Travel Insurance call 0800 072 4168 or visit www.theaa.com